Purinton Pottery

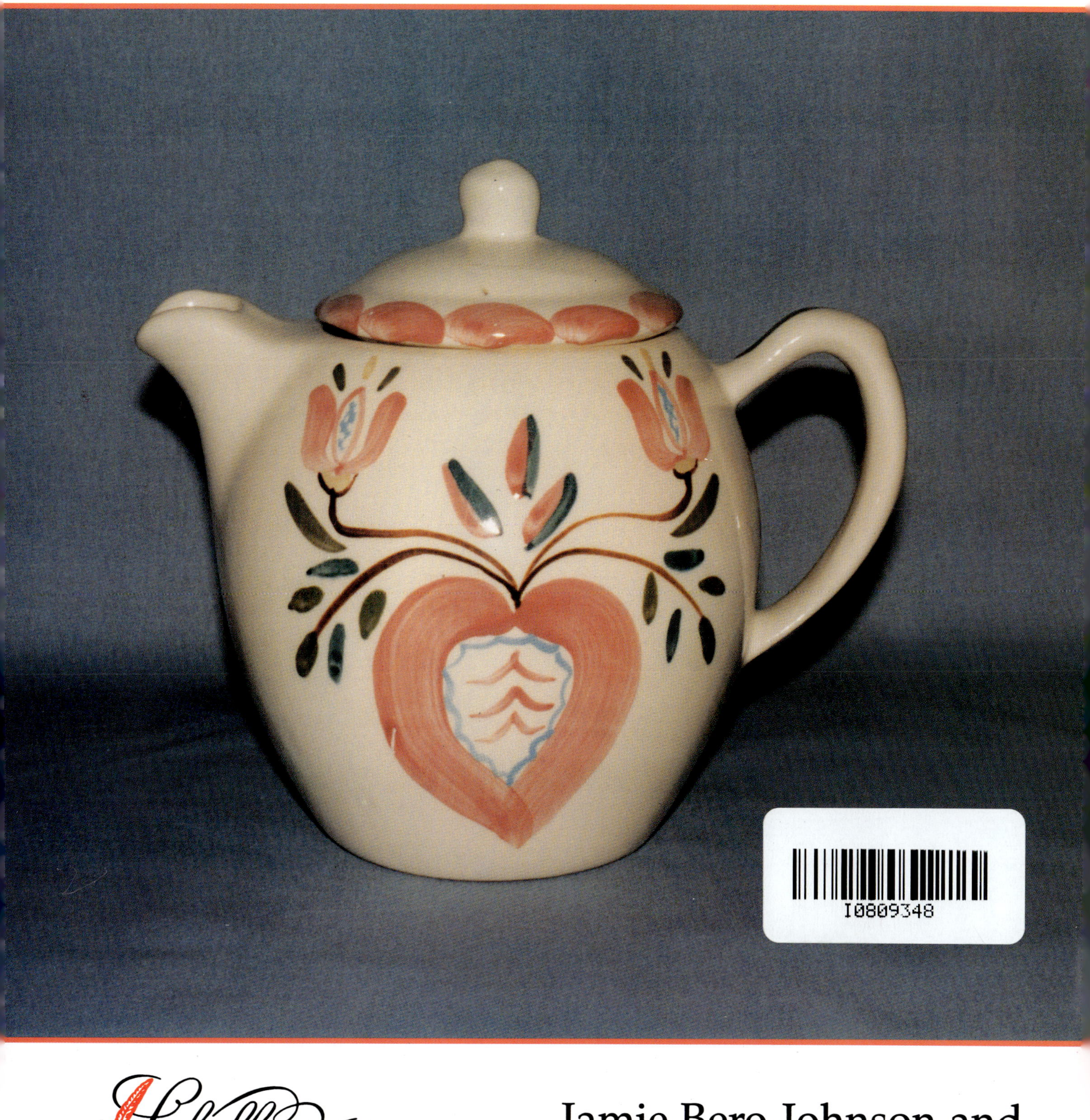

Schiffer Publishing Ltd
4880 Lower Valley Road, Atglen, PA 19310 USA

Jamie Bero-Johnson and
Jamie Johnson

Dedication

We would like to dedicate this book to our parents: Janet and David Bero and Mildred and Raphael Johnson. As parents and role models, you have taught and shown us what hard work, love, support, and perseverance can contribute to accomplishing goals. You have given us the opportunity to believe in ourselves. You have always been there for us, whatever our aspirations.

We would especially like to thank you for enlightening us as to the merits of collecting things.

Thank you.

Acknowledgements

The authors would like to thank the following people who graciously allowed us to photograph portions of their collections: Joanne and Ora Beary, Leroy and Janice Beary, Susan Lauer Birocco, Suzanne E. Blair, Sheila Cantor, Dick and Bernice Cochran, Sam and Patty Derugen, Bob and Nancy Fesemeyer, John Fisher, Ron and Carol Harris, Harriet S. Hearst, Lori Hinterleiter, Richard and Karen Hogue, Vada Marie Oakley Holter, Dan and Shirley King, Karen Leopold, Esther and Mark Lutz, Joseph McManus, Mark and Sheila Moore, Paul and Maxine Moore, Blair and Doris Purinton, Will and Maryann Rosena, William Rowe, Darlene Schelter, Catherine D. and John F. Schmader, Ken and Sandra Schmitt, Marian Schmitt, Jim Schulte, Joanne and Ron Steiner, Chuck and Bonnie Strandburg, Timothy J. Sweet, Peggy Thompson, 2 Hats Antiques and Ken Yurkewecz.

The authors would like to especially thank the following for their time and contributions to the book:

Lori Hinterleiter for the time she spent taking extra photographs, her publicity through the *Purinton Pastimes*, and her detailed information on William Blair.

Joanne and Ora Beary for allowing us to photograph, photograph, and photograph some more. You have the best collection of Purinton known.

Mark and Esther Lutz for allowing us access to their collection and time.

Blair and Doris Purinton for their information and insight into the Purinton family and the pottery. Both their hospitality and the opportunity they gave us to photograph their items were really appreciated.

Bill Bower for information and records on the pottery — a fine gentleman who is a joy to know.

Phil Hammer for his insightful conversations and information.

Finally, we wish to thank Julie Doel for all of her library research.

For more information on Purinton Pottery

For more information about Purinton Pottery please contact the authors. Jamie Bero-Johnson and Jamie Johnson, P.O. Box 241, Clarion, PA 16214-0241, 1-800-820-5087

Library of Congress Catalog Card Number: 97-66896

1 2 3 4

ISBN: 0-7643-0290-6
Printed in China

Designed by Bonnie M. Hensley

Published by Schiffer Publishing Ltd.
4880 Lower Valley Road
Atglen, PA 19310
Phone: (610) 593-1777; Fax: (610) 593-2002
E-mail:Schifferbk@aol.com
Please write for a free catalog.
This book may be purchased from the publisher.
Please include $3.95 for shipping.
Try your bookstore first.

We are interested in hearing from authors
with book ideas on related subjects.

Contents

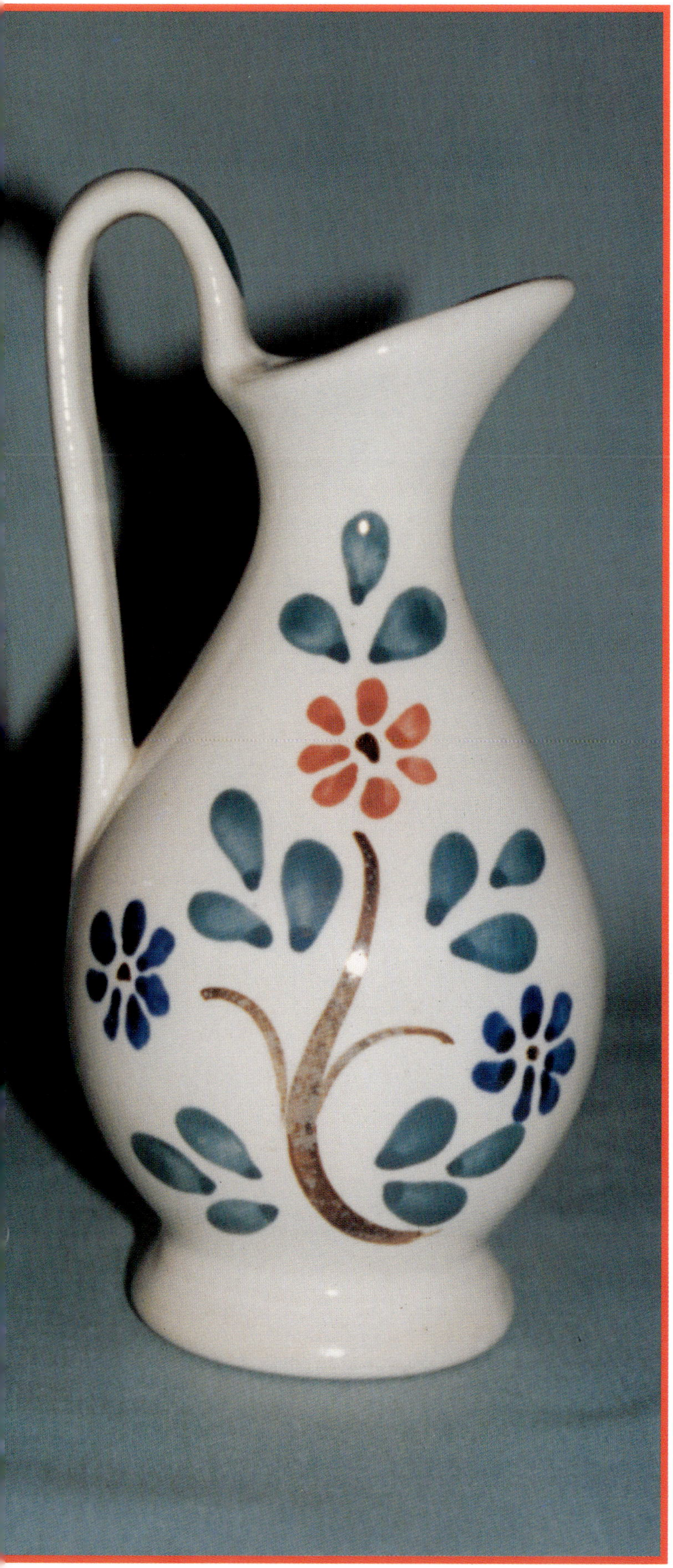

Introduction

Purinton Pottery began its 23-year history in the town of Wellsville, Ohio, when a man named Bernard Purinton acquired the East Liverpool Pottery Company. His dream was to make a more cost effective and efficient pottery casting method. While at Wellsville, he perfected his innovative casting method and obtained a patent for it. He then moved his operation from Wellsville to Shippenville, Pennsylvania, in the Northwestern part of the state. Bernard produced ceramics using his new method of casting and called the product slip ware. His Shippenville plant ironically started operation on December 7, 1941, when the Japanese bombed Pearl Harbor. World War II provided an opportunity for the American pottery industry to flourish, as the competitive import market decreased. Purinton did succeed during that time. The company's ware was in such demand another plant was built in nearby Tionesta, Pennsylvania. However, in 1959 the Purinton company could no longer compete with the import market and had to close its operations.

The Purinton Company is known for its hand painted slip wares. Each piece of Purinton was unique in that an item was decorated by hand and was not stenciled or decorated with decals. Dorothy Purinton (wife of Bernard) and William Blair (brother of Dorothy) were two individuals who designed and developed the Purinton patterns. From the primitive Peasant Ware in Wellsville to the famous Apple and the folk art Pennsylvania Dutch designs, Purinton offered over 20 different patterns on a variety of shapes from floral industry wares to dinnerware items.

Purinton made its own products and contracted out to other companies such as Rubel, NAPCO, Esmond, and Taylor Smith Taylor. They produced souvenirs for shops in tourist areas. Palm Tree was made for an outlet in Florida. Dorothy created special blessing plates for friends and for sale. Purinton offered a diverse line of dinnerware which was sold throughout the United States. Some patterns were made continually throughout the time Purinton was in business and could be purchased as open stock items. Other decorations were limited and had a short production span.

Purinton is usually identified by its decoration and off-white slip color. However, the Maywood pattern is the exception, it has a green slip. Purinton may also be identified by its shapes. Molds in Wellsville were unique to that time and limited to teapots and serving pieces. A few of their molds were used in the early years of the Shippenville plant. Many molds were from other companies with whom Purinton contracted work. Many common shapes seen were used as vases such as the rebecca jug, basket planter, kent jug and winged vase. Teapots were a specialty in the early years and many can still be found with a Fruit or Ivy decoration. In the late 1940s Purinton developed its dinnerware line. Accessory pieces were also made available for purchase until the plant's closing. Dinnerware was sold in starter sets of 4, 6, or 8 piece place settings and you could purchase accessory pieces to accompany your dinnerware.

Purinton's hand painted decoration is the beauty of a piece. In Wellsville, the "Peasant Ware" and "Fruit" and "Crescent" decorations were produced. These were the only decorative motifs produced in Wellsville. When the company moved to Shippenville, Fruit and Crescent followed. Fruit was used on decorated items for Esmond. Apple and Intaglio were the first of the Shippenville decorations and were the backbone of the company until 1959. During the late 1940s and throughout the 1950s, a variety of decorations developed by Dorothy Purinton were introduced.

Records for the pottery are almost nonexistent. Information has been gathered from Bill Bower (the company secretary/treasurer), Blair Purinton (son of Bernard), and Phil Hammer (son of John Hammer, Purinton's first sales manager). Local newspapers contain information about the opening of the Shippenville plant in 1941. Other information has been made available through employees recalling what occurred.

Purinton is collected and appreciated by people from all over the country. Pat Dole first brought attention to Purinton through her newsletter *The Glaze* and later through her two published books which identified a few pieces. Sue Morris brought more attention to Purinton with her more extensive guide. Since then, many more items and a little additional information have appeared, presenting this opportunity to further the identification and history of Purinton Pottery.

We have attempted to photograph as many items as possible for this book. Due to circumstances and time constraints, not every known Purinton item could be pictured. Thankfully, unique items are being discovered annually.

This book is designed to provide both a history and a guide to the value of Purinton Pottery. The chapters are laid out in chronological order to the best of our knowledge. Each chapter has a brief introduction explaining the decoration presented and its availability to collectors. At the end of the chapters concerning regular company production is a chapter titled "Miscellaneous." This includes a variety of items which were not decorated on many shapes. There are also chapters on Christmas, Children's, and Figural items. A detailed chapter shows the special pieces created by William Blair and Dorothy Purinton. Unusual or experimental items also have their own chapter.

In the back is a Table of Measurements. The table identifies the measurements of each piece pictured. If an item is unique and not in the table, the dimensions are given in the caption.

Price Guide

The pricing information presented in this book is only meant to be a guide and should be used in that fashion. Pricing is a sensitive matter, and there are several important factors that should be considered. The factors that we consider to be the most important are condition, rarity, and desirability.

Prices are for complete items in mint condition (with a lid or insert, if necessary), whether or not the item in the picture is in that condition.

Some prices are elaborated on within the captions under the pictures, specifying each item's rarity and desirability. Extremely rare and desirable items are designated with an open-ended price ($750+).

Prices are retail selling prices that could be expected to be paid to a dealer. Collectors frequently pay more than dealers. Prices were determined based on current market supply and demand, auctions, antique shops and shows, and collectors' input.

History

In 1936, Bernard S. Purinton incorporated the Purinton Pottery Company in Wellsville, Ohio. This was the first of twenty-three years that Purinton Pottery existed to produce hand decorated slip ware. Purinton Pottery created a product that used an innovative casting method and simple hand decorated motifs from 1936 to 1941 in Wellsville, Ohio, then from 1941 to 1959 in Shippenville, Pennsylvania, and also for a period from 1948 to 1953 in Tionesta, Pennsylvania. Purinton pottery was distributed throughout North America and was also exported to a few countries in Central America and Africa. During the Wellsville period, the pottery had few shapes and the company's limited range of designs were known collectively as "Peasant Ware". While in Pennsylvania, the designs and variety of items increased.

East Liverpool, Ohio, is known for its pottery industry. This is the town where the Purinton family of more than three generations resided. Bernard Purinton, son of John J. Purinton, went off to The Ohio State University to study ceramics. After a few years at the university, Bernard came back to East Liverpool and started his work in the pottery industry. Bernard became general manager of the East Liverpool Potteries Co., located in nearby Wellsville, Ohio. There he was in active charge of production. For approximately five years before 1936, Bernard worked on perfecting a new casting method. Finally, Bernard became owner of the plant and changed the name to Purinton Pottery in 1936.[1]

As owner of his own pottery company, Bernard could further perfect his casting method and produce a pottery distributed throughout the United States. In 1936, pottery sold in the United States was mostly imported. Bernard felt he could make cost effective pottery that could compete with foreign competitors. He also planned to improve upon his method and increase his production.

The Wellsville plant was a small building and Purinton Pottery shared it with what is believed to be Chic Pottery. A ledger book from the Wellsville operation was found and seems to support this.[2] The plant building was diminutive and did not have updated equipment, therefore, the pottery was only made on a limited basis at first. As time moved on, Bernard, with his own financial resources and time, improved and perfected his system. He produced wares sold and used throughout the country. Bernard gained patent rights to his casting process while at Wellsville. This made the method of producing the pottery more profitable.

The pottery made at Wellsville was marketed to women who wanted "to give a note of informal color to a room or table....either at parties or within the family circle".[3] Primitive designs were popular during the late 1930s. Bernard used his pottery designs and accessory pieces to capture a share of that market. The wares were simple. As stated before, they were made for informal events such as a picnics or a gatherings of friends for coffee, tea or snacks on the back porch. The line was limited to snack plates, cups, teapots, coffee carafes, pitchers, tumblers, and a few other simple items. The oasis jug may have been used for serving lemonade and the peasant lady candle holders as decoration. It seemed people had a fascination with native designs and Purinton capitalized on this interest. Therefore, "Peasant Ware" was produced. The items manufactured were of simple taste and design, using uncomplicated brush strokes to produce the decorations. This was meant to emulate wares used and decorated by peasant people.

Not much information is available about the pottery during the Wellsville years. We know of another important person during that time. William H. Blair was influential in the design of many Purinton patterns. Bill Blair was the brother of Dorothy Purinton, Bernard's wife. His innovation in the decoration of Purinton was not only seen in Wellsville, but also in Shippenville when Purinton expanded their decoration line. Bill Blair studied art formally and went to work with the pottery company when it opened in 1936. (A background of William H. Blair is detailed in Chapter 23.) He, along with about five decorators, produced the highly sought after Wellsville or Peasant Ware items. When the wares were sold, there was no formal name to each pattern. Patterns were sold by numbers which corresponded to a combination of the following colors: Brown, Rose, Blue, Burnt Orange, Yellow, and Turquoise.

Purinton Pottery continued to succeed while in Wellsville. The pottery was distributed to large department stores in cities such as New York, Boston, Cleveland, San Francisco, Dallas, and Washington DC.[4] As the war in Europe escalated during 1940, imports of pottery began to decrease. Bernard saw the opportunity for the company to expand and gain a bigger share of the pottery market as the demand for wares in the United States increased. Figures show in 1938 that 85% of the pottery sold in the United States was imported from Germany, Czechoslovakia, and Japan. By the time Purinton moved to Shippenville, the figure had decreased to less than 15%. He also wanted to use his casting method in a larger and more modern plant. At this point, John Hammer, Roy Underwood, and William Bower enter the picture.

In Clarion County, Pennsylvania, Roy R. Underwood, president of the Knox Glass Associates and a county civic and business leader, was completing the formation of the Clarion County Chamber of Commerce. With the direction of Mr. Underwood, the Chamber of Commerce was interested in attracting new business to the county. Mr. Underwood learned about Bernard Purinton's interest in relocating his facilities through John Hammer. Mr. Hammer, who later became the company sales manager for Purinton Pottery, had been the executive secretary of the Association of Glass and Pottery Manufacturers for 17 years and was also the manager of the Pittsburgh Glass and Pottery show. In addition, he was the editor of trade journals in the glass and pottery fields. Based on involvements with these organizations, Mr. Hammer knew Mr. Underwood through the Knox Glass Associates and made him aware of Purinton's intentions.

Mr. William J. Bower was the executive secretary of newly formed Chamber of Commerce and was instructed to travel to Wellsville and meet with Bernard Purinton. After securing his interest in Clarion County over sights in the state of Kentucky, Mr. Bower and Bernard traveled in October 1940 throughout Clarion County to find a location for the new plant. Bernard chose for its location a vast open pasture that bordered the Shippenville borough in proximity to a railroad siding with immediate access to a major highway, Route 322, the Lakes to Sea highway.

Through the Chamber of Commerce, a bond for $100,000 was secured to build the plant. Ground for the new 100 foot by 300 foot structure was staked out on April 9, 1941. During the construction, a 70-foot circular kiln was installed by workers from Ohio and a few equipment items were brought to Shippenville from the Wellsville plant. Two women and two men from Clarion County went to Wellsville to learn the job of casting and decoration. When the plant opened in Shippenville, Ollie Earl was the only pottery worker to come from Wellsville and he became the shop foreman. The rest of the work force came from the Clarion County area. The plant was projected to employee 75 to 100 people.[5]

Purinton Pottery was established as a corporation and stock was sold. Mr. Bower, Mr. Hammer, and Mr. Underwood were all instrumental in bringing Purinton Pottery to Clarion County. Their role with Purinton did not stop with the completion of the plant. Mr. Bower became secretary/treasurer of the new corporation. Mr. Hammer became sales manager and Mr. Underwood was made vice-president of the corporation.

Through his affiliation with the Pottery and Glass Association, Mr. Hammer secured an exhibit at the New York Glass and Pottery show in 1941. This led to the contract with the McCormick Tea Company from Baltimore, Maryland, for more than 50,000 individual teapots. Drinking tea was becoming more popular in the late 1930s and early 1940s and there was a large demand for individual teapots.

McCormick had a mail in offer of 25 cents with a coupon for a teapot. Purinton made approximately 7 cents on each one.[6]

With a large contract to make individual teapots and plans to continue making wares produced in Wellsville, Purinton Pottery was set to begin operations. After much fanfare with an open house in late November of 1941, the first teapots were molded on December 2, 1941. Bernard incised on the bottom of the first one hundred "12-2-41, BP". On December 7, 1941, they were gathered from the circular kiln as the first products in the Shippenville plant. The teapots were not hand decorated, they received a yellow glaze.

Purinton was now well prepared to start making pottery with Bernard's new casting methods. Since his method of casting used slip, he preferred the items to be called "slip ware" and not pottery.[7]

How was the slip ware produced? Bernard's method was more efficient and utilized machinery to replace workers, enabling more items to be cast at one time. Casting the handles with the body of the item, instead of as separate castings, ensured a stronger product. Previous methods placed the handles on separately. The lids and body of an item were cast together, again saving material and work time. Bernard had a patent on his one piece mold and slip method, which was the most revolutionary of its time. Molds could be dipped into a tank full of slip. Excess slip ran out the bottom and the air escaped from a hole in the top of the mold. Enough slip remained to form the item within the mold.

The process for casting the slip ware was as follows. Clay ingredients were carefully measured and placed in large mixing vats. This formed the liquid clay or slip. The slip then went through hoses to the mold trays. Two piece molds made of plaster were used and held together by narrow strips of rubber from inner tubes. Molds were carefully cleaned and rough edges taken off after each use prior to the molds being placed on trays and moved to a drying shed to dry before refilling. The air used to dry the molds came through a vent from the kiln.

Once the molds were prepared, they were placed on trays and moved to the slip tub area. Hydraulic lifts raised the tubs of slip up to the racks holding the molds. They then immersed the molds in the slip. It took approximately two hours for the slip in the mold to set up. Then the molds were turned upside down and the excess slip was drained from the mold. The slip that remained in the mold to form the item was the production piece.

Molds were opened and the wet slip ware was removed and placed on boards. Lids were separated from the items while they were still wet. They were then moved to the drying racks where they remained for another two hours to set. The wet ware was then taken to the finishing table. Rough edges, mold marks, and seams were scraped from each object. They were then sponged off with water to make a smoother surface.

The wares were then taken to the decorating department. If they were to be a solid color, pieces were dipped into a glaze. Most items were to be decorated. At this point the decorators, local women, hand painted the various decorations. All decorations were painted under the glaze. William Blair or Dorothy Purinton trained these decorators.

After the items were decorated, they moved to the glaze vat. The bottom of each item was covered with paraffin or wax so that the glaze would not cling to the base and stick the base to the saggers. (A sagger is a rough clay container in which decorated items are placed. Purinton's saggers kept the direct flame from the newly glazed items.) Some slip ware was not waxed but was placed on pins so as not to come into direct contact with the sagger.

Once prepared, slip wares were dipped into the glaze, which appeared to be an all white powder prior to firing. This powder became the hard, translucent glaze covering when fired in the kiln. Once covered in the powdered glaze, wares were placed into the saggers and taken to the kiln.

The kiln at Shippenville was circular and the one at Tionesta was straight. The saggers were placed on a cart on an electric-powered moving floor that went slowly through the kiln. The temperature of the kiln grew constantly hotter until it reached 1900 degrees and then slowly decreased so the slip ware would not break.

When wares had completed the kiln heating process, they were then moved to the selection table where each was checked for defects such as poor glazing, cracks, decoration errors, and out-of-shape wares. The bottoms of the wares were then smoothed off with a pumice stone. Seconds were sold either from the plant or at the Corner Cupboard, a local outlet shop. First quality items were boxed and stored for shipping.

The Purinton Company brought with it from the Wellsville plant many of its molds and a few of its decorations. Included in this transfer were the five and two pint dutch jug (iced lip pitcher), tumbler, teapots, fruit bowl, chop plate, oasis jug, tea and toast plate, kent jug, seahorse cocktail dish, tall oil and vinegar bottle, peasant lady candle holder, three part relish, and "old salt and wife pepper" shakers. The Peasant Ware decoration did not seem to follow the company to Shippenville. Fruit and Crescent were used at the Wellsville plant and may be the only patterns that the Shippenville plant used from Wellsville. Fruit was popular and would remain so throughout the life of the company. Crescent was made for a few years and then discontinued.

With the United States' involvement in World War II, resources for metals and glass became scarce. Clay, however, was not a rationed item, and the demand for pottery wares increased. Companies who sold metal and glass items were now looking for other items such a pottery to fill the void. Purinton was there to meet the demand. They continued to make slip ware in solid glazes. As their decorating force became more skilled, they branched out to other items. It is believed that Red and Yellow Ivy were introduced during the early to mid-1940s. The war also cut back on the supply of tea and McCormick did not continue their contract with Purinton. They did, however, utilize Purinton teapots again in the late 1940s when the Mountain Rose decoration was employed. With the decreased demand for teapots, Purinton needed to produce other utilitarian pieces and introduce some new decorations to their items.

William Blair left Purinton Pottery during its transition to Shippenville and returned for a short period after 1943. As he had at Wellsville, Bill Blair would use his artistic skills to again influence Purinton's future. Bill designed the famous open Apple pattern and it was brought to life in the company's first dinnerware line. Bill also originated the Brown Intaglio pattern, using it first in Wellsville with stylized animals and cherubs.

The Apple was called D-46 at the plant. Wares and decorations were never referred to by their shape or design, but by a pattern number assigned to them, as seen in the brochures and ordering forms. Later, in the 1950s, decorations were called by their names for marketing purposes.

With new patterns and the introduction of a dinnerware line, demand for Purinton's wares increased. In 1946 Phil Hammer, the first in-house salesman for the company (and son of John Hammer), stated that he could not fill orders quickly enough because of the demand for the pottery. Purinton was also in the process of doing contract work with NAPCO, the National Pottery Company from Cleveland. NAPCO dealt specifically with floral items, such as vases, planters, and floral bowls. NAPCO had their own molds and decorations. These included Ming Tree and Leaf, but most items used solid glaze decoration. In later years, Purinton Pottery took some NAPCO molds and designed its own wares from them.

With the demand of pottery high after the war, Roy Underwood came forward with a proposal to Bernard Purinton to build a sister plant in nearby Tionesta, in Forest County, about 25 miles north of Shippenville. With funds raised by the townspeople of Tionesta, another plant was constructed. It was similar to the Shippenville plant but with modifications, which included airbrushing equipment and a tunnel kiln instead of a circular one. Floyd Wills, who was in charge of installing the new kiln, was asked to be the plant manager. On October 14, 1948, an open house sponsored by the Tionesta Lions was held. To commemorate the opening, two cup teapots sporting both a red petal decoration and "Tionesta Lions 10/14/48" were given out. The plant not only made the speciality planters and items for other companies, it also manufactured the dinnerware line of Brown Intaglio and Apple as demand rose.

The Tionesta plant stayed in operation until 1953 when the demand for American-made pottery started to decline and the extra plant was no longer needed to fill orders. During its five years of operation, Tionesta served other contracts Purinton had acquired. Rubel out of

New York was a company who had a diversified gift ware line. The Tionesta plant supplied Rubel with pieces designed to stack and fit into metal racks. Most of these items were painted with a solid color or a drip glaze and were marked Rubel on the bottom. Purinton utilized some of Rubel's molds. This was only done on a limited basis and a Purinton decoration on a Rubel mold can be quite the find.

Another company that contracted with Purinton was Taylor Smith Taylor from West Virginia. The most famous molds TST supplied were the Howdy Doody cookies jar and bank. Utilizing the air brush modifications in the Tionesta plant, Purinton could easily decorate the cookies jars and banks. A coffee server, tureen, and gravy boat in a tulip and vine decoration were also molds of TST and that specific decoration is only seen on those body styles. Other products produced for TST were life-size cats and squirrels, and the decoration called Southwestern.

In the early 1950s, the import trade started to affect Purinton and the entire American pottery trade. Floyd Wills stated that NAPCO contracted with a company in Japan for certain planters that could be shipped to Cleveland cheaper than Purinton could make and deliver them from only four hours away.[8] The import market had an effect which could be labeled negative for Purinton at the time, but positive for collectors of today.

With the market of American pottery decreasing, the need to find new designs and wares which people would buy was important for the financial success of Purinton. During the mid-1940s, Bill Blair had left the company. In the late 1940s, Purinton had shifted their focus to more of a dinnerware line. Selling starter dinnerware sets and accessory pieces to accompany the sets was becoming increasingly popular. However, the market was demanding different decorations. Through the late 1940s, Apple would be the backbone of the decorating line. Daisy was used on a limited basis, but not in a dinnerware line. Fruit was used on teapots and canister sets and on a few other items but not with dinnerware.

Dorothy Purinton was the wife of Bernard and the sister of Bill Blair. (A more detailed background of Dorothy is given in Chapter 23). Although she had no formal art training and was not officially employed by the company, Dorothy was one of the most influential people in the company's history. Her inspiration and insight into new designs was a plus for both Purinton and for collecting history. Her first role was to help train the decorators after Bill Blair had left. She then started using the Apple design Bill Blair developed. She is credited with decorating the Intaglio with a flower. It is believed she can be credited with many Purinton decorations from 1948 onward. She is most noted for her personalized plates given to friends as gifts and which were made in a limited number for sale. Her simple, yet creative, folksy decorations on these plates are the most desirable Purinton items on the market today.

Dorothy designed the final decorations Purinton Pottery used on its wares, but she was probably inspired by the number of experimental items produced by employees. Purinton encouraged employees to utilize their talents in designing new patterns. In the plant was a long table full of experimental plates. These plates were created by Dorothy or other employees. Many employees designed their own items or made whimsy pieces. In Chapter 28, and throughout the book, you will see these creations and artistic talents.

Purinton was also approached by many people and companies with new wares that they thought might be put into production. Bill Bower remembers a representative from Old Spice meeting with him and Bernard to discuss making containers for their after shave. Purinton could not make the item cost effective because of the time and effort required to make the hole in the top fit the metal stopper. Local people would come with ideas and if they had the money, about $150 to make the sculpture and the mold, Purinton would try a casting.[9]

Some investors in Purinton Pottery and local business men opened an outlet, The Corner Cupboard. It was established in 1952 in the town of Marianne at the crossroads of Route 322 and Route 66 about two miles from Shippenville. From this shop a variety of items were sold, including gifts, glassware, and other pottery. Many irregular and first quality Purinton production pieces were sold there. With its location on both the Lakes to Sea Highway, the main route from Cleveland to Philadelphia, and Route 66, the gateway to Cook Forest State Park and Allegheny National Forest, many Purinton items were bought and taken back home throughout the United States.

During the late 1940s, Chartreuse and Mountain Rose were on the market. Some limited Pennsylvania Dutch designs had been tested. Items were being made and sent to the different shows to see if buyers wanted them. Some were successful, and some were not. In 1950, Apple and Brown Intaglio had been featured in the Home of the Century in Atlantic City, New Jersey. As Japanese imports increased, Purinton made other designs to stay ahead in the market. Saraband was a multicolored pattern like Intaglio but not incised. Other colors were used for Intaglios, most notably Turquoise, followed by Green, and Golden Brown (Caramel). In later years, Purinton Pottery used Coral, Light Blue, and Cobalt. Normandy and Heather Plaid patterns were also introduced, Heather as a sister pattern to Normandy.

Maywood was an innovative slip, having a green slip body and a white decorated dogwood flower. Ming Tree, a decoration NAPCO used for their planters, was put onto a dinnerware line. Peasant Garden was brought back from the Wellsville years when it was used to decorate the Peasant Lady candle holders. Petals was a contract through Sears and Roebuck which was made in the Tionesta plant. However, Sears changed buyers and the new buyer did not like the pattern, so production was limited.

Purinton's colors became more vibrant and colorful as the taste and lifestyle of America was changing in the 1950s. Pennsylvania Dutch, a favorite pattern of Dorothy's, had the country motif, but was more colorful in pink and blue. Seaform and Tea Rose also used brighter colors in their design. Provincial Fruit or, as some call it, "modern fruit" was more stylized than the old Fruit pattern.

With the introduction of these patterns through the 1950s production period, Apple, Brown Intaglio, Plaids, Pennsylvania Dutch, Saraband, Maywood, and Provincial Fruit seem to have been the most utilized. Late in the 1950s, only Apple, Brown Intaglio, and Pennsylvania Dutch were active patterns. Other patterns went out of production or were made on a special order basis. Patterns such as Sunny, Shooting Star, Half Blossom, and Blue Pansy were mainly used on floral items and were limited to those products. Red Ivy was reintroduced on jardinieres made for both NAPCO and Purinton.

A tally of orders from a log in October 1954 showed 58 orders for Intaglio, 47 for Apple, 21 for Normandy Plaid, 14 for Saraband, 8 for Pennsylvania Dutch, 6 for Heather Plaid, 3 for Maywood, 1 for Chartreuse, and 1 for Incised Palm. These orders were from stores throughout the country from Florida to Texas, from South Dakota to Massachusetts. The outlets for these items included jewelry, hardware, department, gift, grocery, paint, furniture, and drug stores. One order was for 1000 irregular dinner plates and 60 platters to be sent to a fairground for a carnival in Virginia.[10]

The shapes of the wares changed with the introduction of new items. The square apartment canister set was created from the NAPCO pillow vase. The roll tray was a floral bowl for NAPCO. The winged grease jar changed to a vase as contracts for floral items were met. Included in those floral items were the honey jug (which was used to hold honey as a premium), the rebecca jug, and the kent jug.

Purinton also made figural items for the market. Humpty Dumpty, chicken, and pig cookies jars were all Purinton products. Christmas items were produced, as were small pig, owl, and Uncle Sam banks. Some small animal figures were also made. The company also experimented with a variety of shapes.

Purinton contracted with a variety of places for souvenir items. Souvenir products with the name of the Cook Forest Park in northern Clarion County were among the most popular souvenir items. Products with the park's name and "Pennsylvania" on it were sold to shops throughout the tourist area. Purinton made souvenirs for places throughout Pennsylvania and some surrounding states. The best known, and hardest to find, Purinton speciality item is "Palm Tree". Made with hand decoration or incised on Intaglio, Palm Tree was made for an outlet in Ft. Myers, Florida. Bernard's son, John "Pete" Purinton, operated the shop with his wife Kay. She sold a jewelry line from the shop called "Kay Kraft" which was also made by Purinton. Most of the Palm Tree was sold through the Ft. Myers shop, the sales from 1954 show it being sold to another outlet in Florida under the name of Treasure Island.

Esmond was another big contract for Purinton during the late 1940s or early 1950s. Based in New York City, Esmond did not make its own pottery but contracted to a variety of companies including Watt and McCoy. Purinton made a variety of products for Esmond including lazy susans, revolving canisters, and covered casseroles on wire racks. All of these had a Fruit pattern decoration. The Esmond design is distinctive from the original Purinton Fruit. The most popular item made for Esmond was a four-section straight-sided revolving canister. This was Purinton's original design and they used their own decorations on some of these canisters. Although they are plentiful with the Esmond Fruit, to find a revolving canister with a design other than Fruit is much more difficult. It seems a limited number were given away as premiums at grocery stores.

As the 1950s were coming to an end, Purinton could not meet the cost of imports. The life of Purinton Pottery had run full circle. The import market, which at one time had driven the demand for the company's products to great heights when imported pottery was limited, had now driven Purinton to the brink of disaster. In 1958, Taylor Smith Taylor bought the majority stock in the Purinton Pottery Corporation and ran it for a year as a subsidiary. In the Fall of 1959, Purinton closed its doors forever. The plant in Shippenville was sold. The remaining stock filled outstanding orders and was also sold through the Corner Cupboard until 1962.

Endnotes

1. *Clarion Republican,* April 1941.
2. Purinton Pottery Records, 1940.
3. *New Yorker Magazine* advertisement, 1939.
4. Purinton Pottery Records, 1940.
5. *Clarion Republican,* April 1941.
6. Hammer, Phil, interview by authors, Knox, PA, August 1996.
7. Purinton, Blair, interview by authors, Clarion, PA, October 1996.
8. Hinterleiter, Lori and Schulte, Jim. *Purinton Pastimes* 2, no. 3 (October 1994).
9. Bower, Bill, interview by authors, Knox, PA, November 1996.
10. Purinton Pottery Sales Log Entry, October 1954.

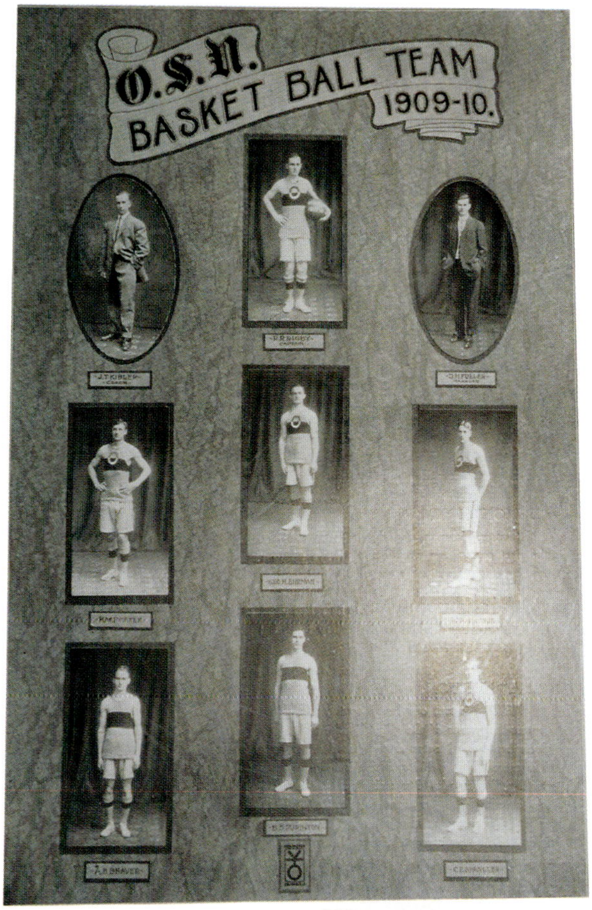

Bernard Purinton is in the middle of the bottom row.

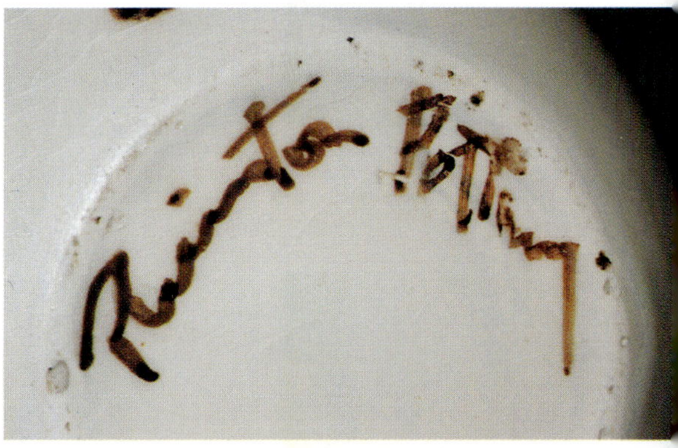

A Wellsville Purinton Pottery mark.

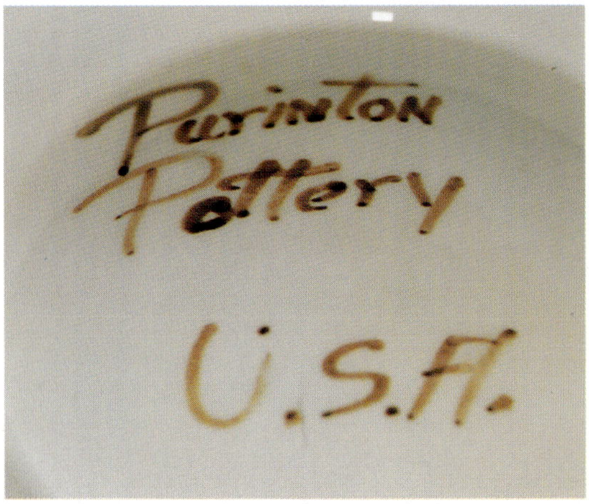

A Wellsville Purinton Pottery mark, probably made for export since it is marked U.S.A.

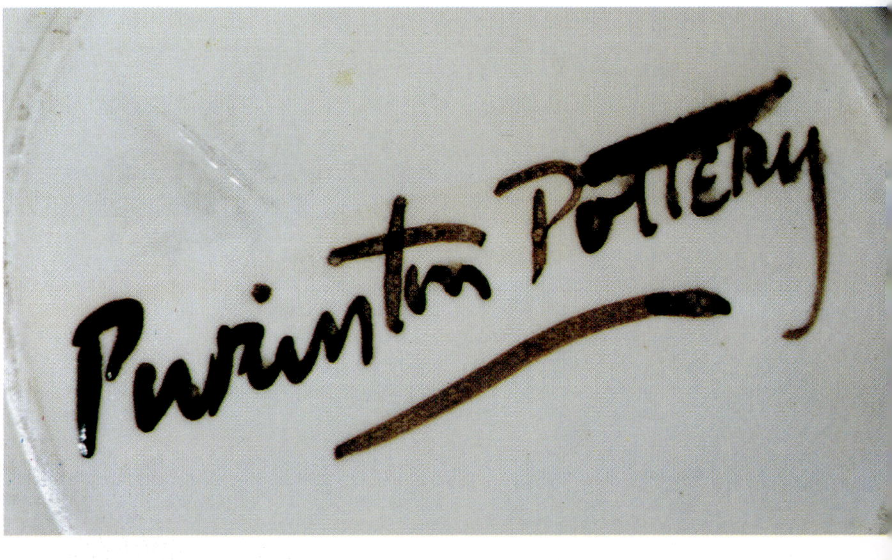

A Wellsville Purinton Pottery mark.

The first employees at the Shippenville plant. Front row (left to right): Park Schwab, Ed Reese, Biago Frisina, Everett Anderson, Jim Cousins, Dave Moore, Charles Passaver, and Steve Johnson. Back row: Bob Ellis, Herb McWilliams, Tim Vogus, Charles Blum, and Art Rowe.

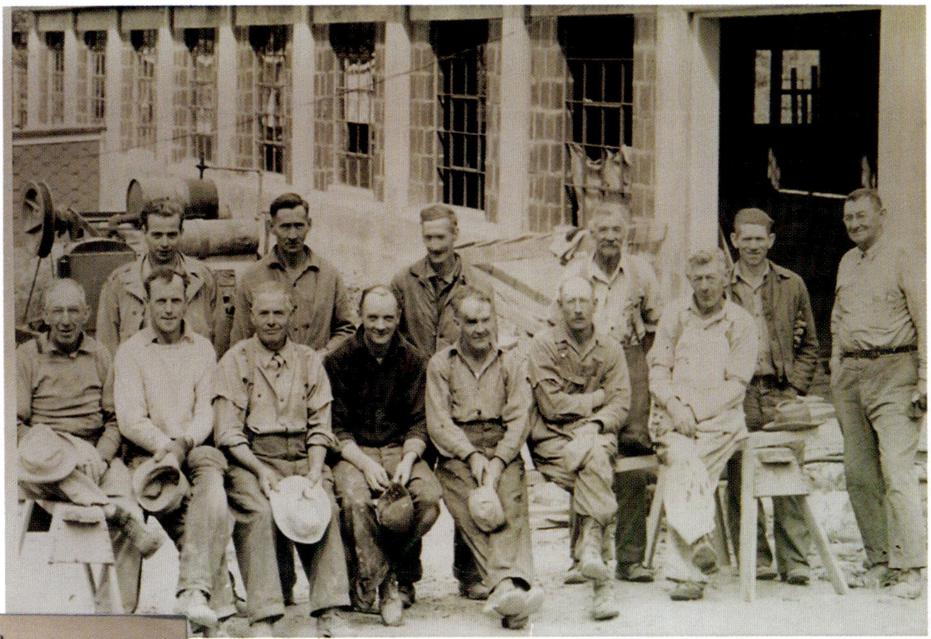

Purinton Pottery stock certificate.

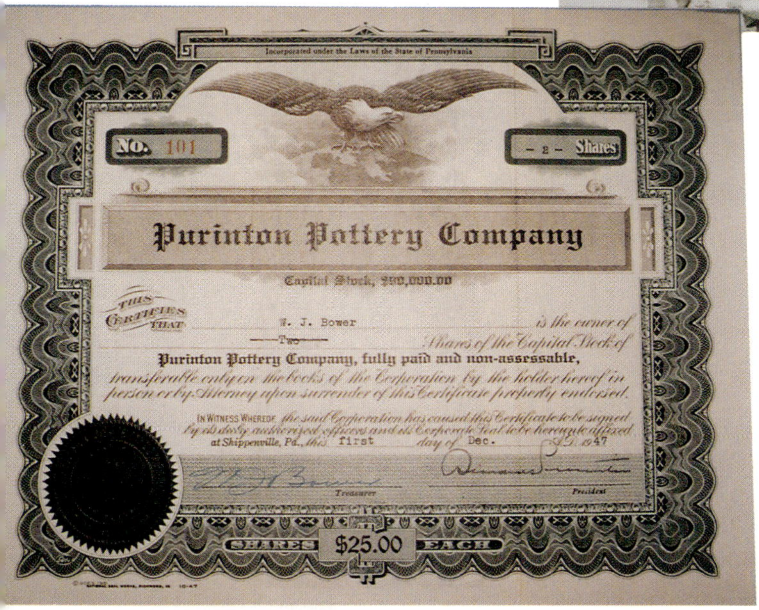

Incorporated under the Laws of the State of Pennsylvania

No. 101

- 2 - Shares

Purinton Pottery Company

Capital Stock, $[illegible]

This Certifies that W. J. Bower is the owner of —Two— Shares of the Capital Stock of Purinton Pottery Company, fully paid and non-assessable, transferable only on the books of the Corporation by the holder hereof in person or by Attorney upon surrender of this Certificate properly endorsed.

In Witness Whereof, the said Corporation has caused this Certificate to be signed by its duly authorized officers and its Corporate Seal to be hereunto affixed at Shippenville, Pa., this first day of Dec. A.D. 1947

Treasurer

President

Shares $25.00 Each

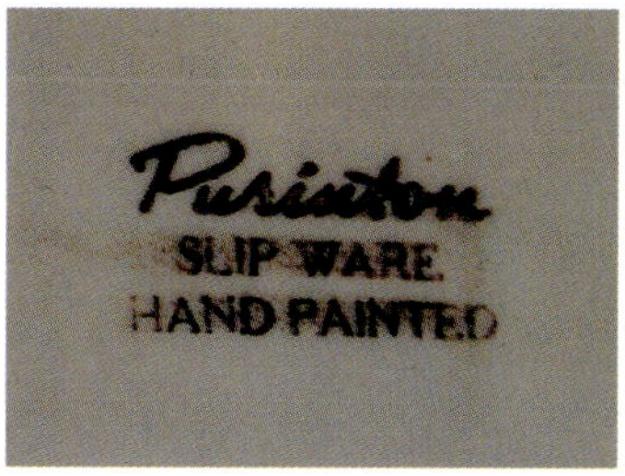

Shippenville slip ware mark. Only about 30% of the pottery was marked.

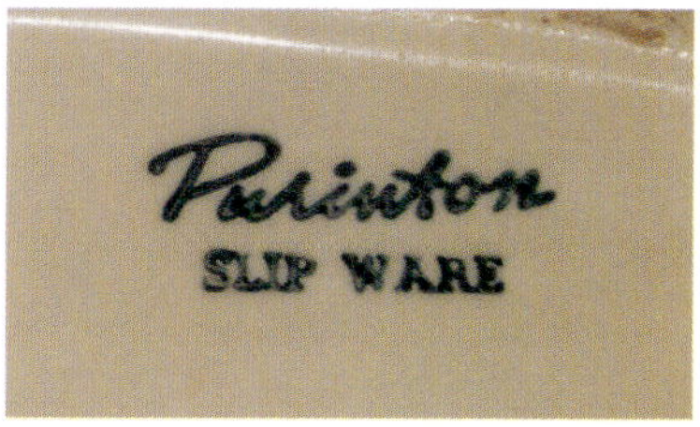

Shippenville slip ware mark, teal in color.

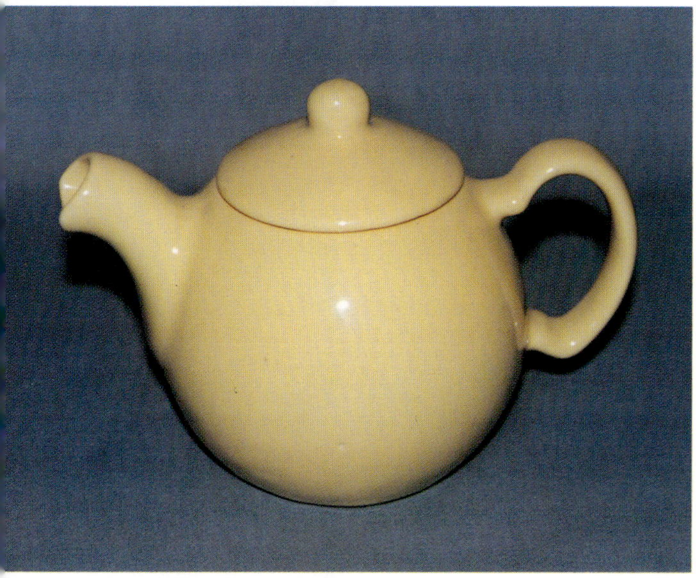

One of the first 100 two cup teapots produced at the Shippenville plant. $125.

The incised bottom on the first 100 two cup teapot reads 12-2-41, BP.

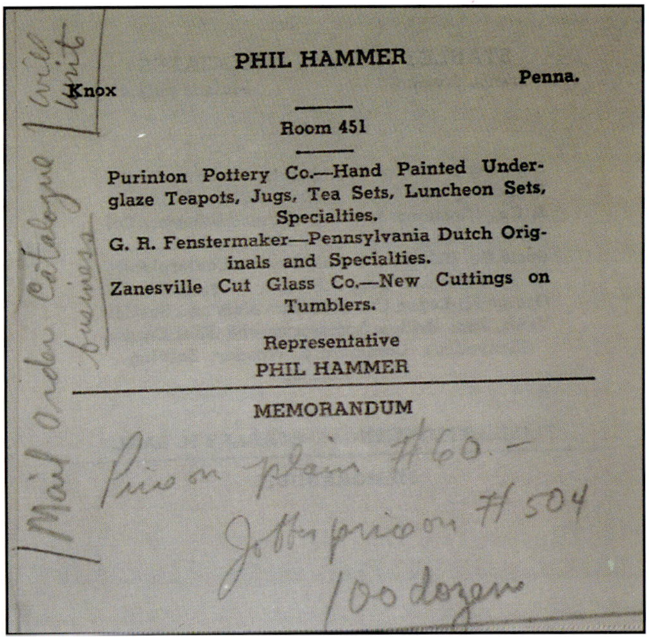

PHIL HAMMER

Knox Penna.

Room 451

Purinton Pottery Co.—Hand Painted Underglaze Teapots, Jugs, Tea Sets, Luncheon Sets, Specialties.

G. R. Fenstermaker—Pennsylvania Dutch Originals and Specialties.

Zanesville Cut Glass Co.—New Cuttings on Tumblers.

Representative
PHIL HAMMER

MEMORANDUM

A page from Phil Hammer's 1949 Pittsburgh Glass Show Directory.

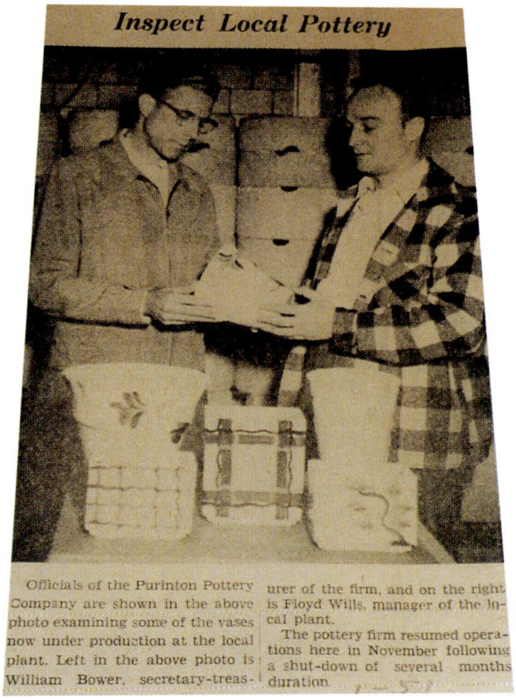

Inspect Local Pottery

Officials of the Purinton Pottery Company are shown in the above photo examining some of the vases now under production at the local plant. Left in the above photo is William Bower, secretary-treasurer of the firm, and on the right is Floyd Wills, manager of the local plant.

The pottery firm resumed operations here in November following a shut-down of several months duration.

Bill Bower and Floyd Wills, Tionesta Plant Manager, examining vases produced at the Tionesta plant.

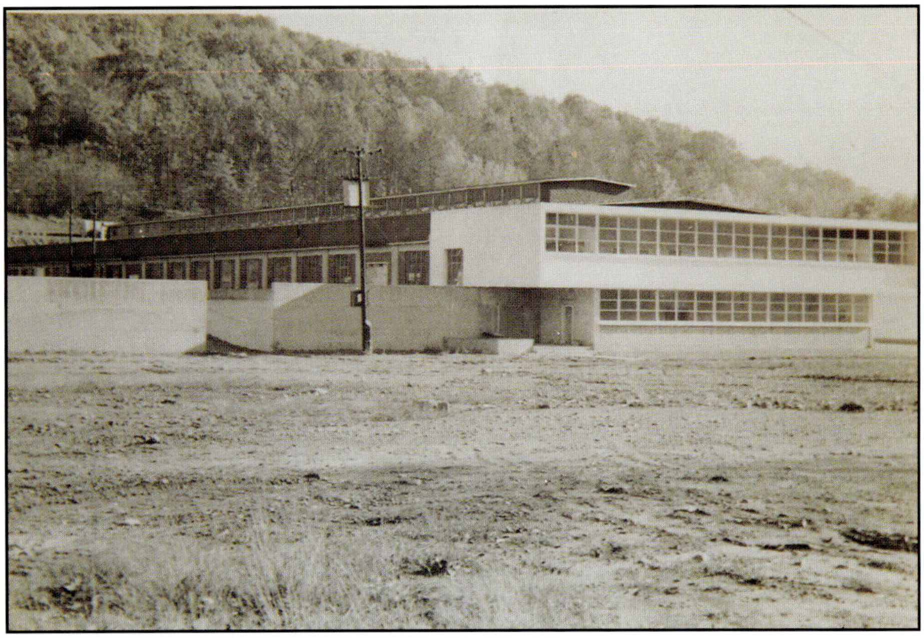

The Tionesta plant.

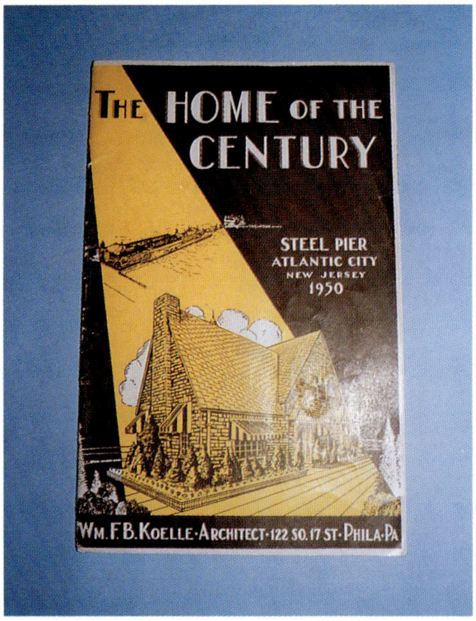

Purinton Pottery was the feature dinnerware in the 1950 Home of the Century in Atlantic City.

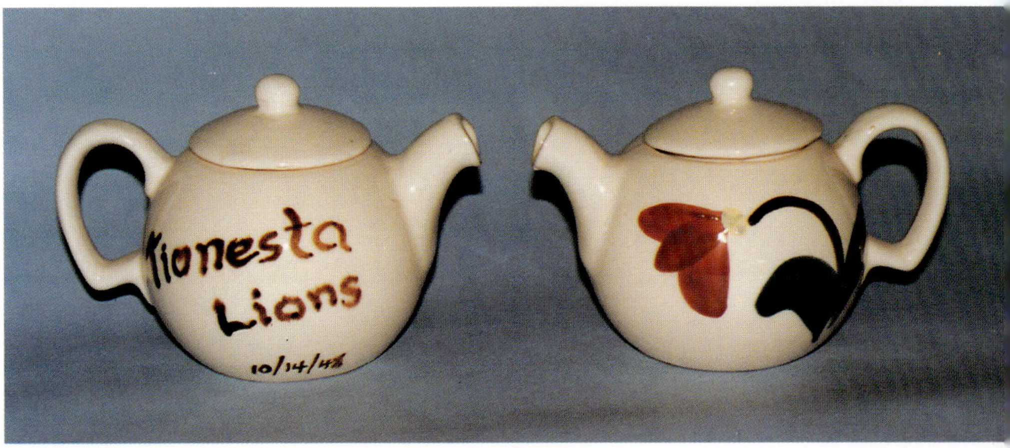

Front and back view of the two cup teapots given out at the open house for the Tionesta plant. $250 each.

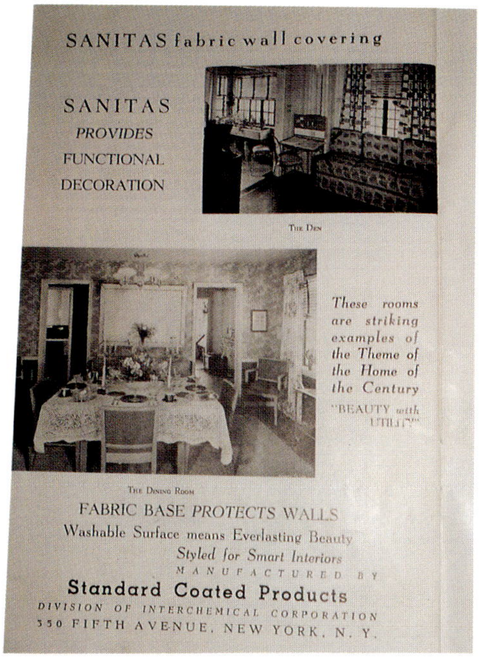

Brown Intaglio dinnerware is the place setting on the dining room table in the 1950 Home of the Century in Atlantic City.

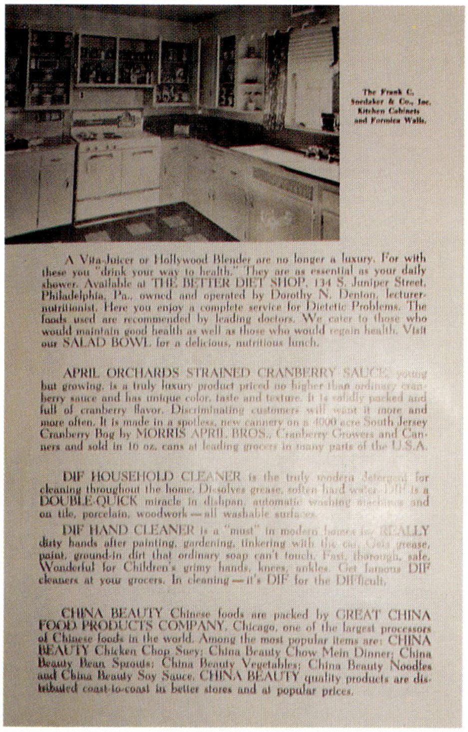

The Frank C. Sneidaker & Co., Inc. Kitchen Cabinets and Formica Walls.

A Vita-Juicer or Hollywood Blender are no longer a luxury. For with these you "drink your way to health." They are as essential as your daily shower. Available at THE BETTER DIET SHOP, 134 S. Juniper Street, Philadelphia, Pa., owned and operated by Dorothy N. Denton, lecturer-nutritionist. Here you enjoy a complete service for Dietetic Problems. The foods used are recommended by leading doctors. We cater to those who would maintain good health as well as those who would regain health. Visit our SALAD BOWL for a delicious, nutritious lunch.

APRIL ORCHARDS STRAINED CRANBERRY SAUCE, young but growing, is a truly luxury product priced no higher than ordinary cranberry sauce and has unique color, taste and texture. It is solidly packed and full of cranberry flavor. Discriminating customers will want it more and more often. It is made in a spotless, new cannery on a 4000 acre South Jersey Cranberry Bog by MORRIS APRIL BROS., Cranberry Growers and Canners and sold in 16 oz. cans at leading grocers in many parts of the U.S.A.

DIF HOUSEHOLD CLEANER is the truly modern detergent for cleaning throughout the home. Dissolves grease, soften hard water. DIF is a DOUBLE-QUICK miracle in dishpan, automatic washing machines and on tile, porcelain, woodwork—all washable surfaces.

DIF HAND CLEANER is a "must" in modern homes for REALLY dirty hands after painting, gardening, tinkering with the car. Gets grease, paint, ground-in dirt that ordinary soap can't touch. Fast, thorough, safe. Wonderful for Children's grimy hands, knees, ankles. Get famous DIF cleaners at your grocers. In cleaning—it's DIF for the DIFficult.

CHINA BEAUTY Chinese foods are packed by GREAT CHINA FOOD PRODUCTS COMPANY, Chicago, one of the largest processors of Chinese foods in the world. Among the most popular items are: CHINA BEAUTY Chicken Chop Suey; China Beauty Chow Mein Dinner; China Beauty Bean Sprouts; China Beauty Vegetables; China Beauty Noodles and China Beauty Soy Sauce. CHINA BEAUTY quality products are distributed coast-to-coast in better stores and at popular prices.

Apple canisters, tumblers, and an oil and vinegar set are utilized in the kitchen of the 1950 Home of the Century in Atlantic City.

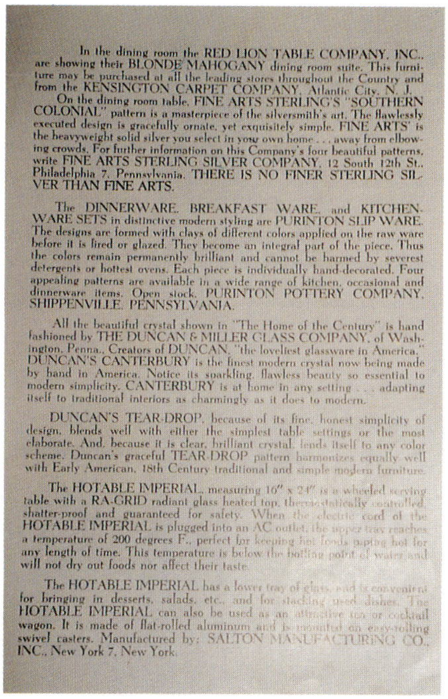

In the dining room the RED LION TABLE COMPANY, INC., are showing their BLONDE MAHOGANY dining room suite. This furniture may be purchased at all the leading stores throughout the Country and from the KENSINGTON CARPET COMPANY, Atlantic City, N. J.

On the dining room table, FINE ARTS STERLING'S "SOUTHERN COLONIAL" pattern is a masterpiece of the silversmith's art. The flawlessly executed design is gracefully ornate, yet exquisitely simple. FINE ARTS' is the heavyweight solid silver you select in your own home . . . away from elbowing crowds. For further information on this Company's four beautiful patterns, write FINE ARTS STERLING SILVER COMPANY, 12 South 12th St., Philadelphia 7, Pennsylvania. THERE IS NO FINER STERLING SILVER THAN FINE ARTS.

The DINNERWARE, BREAKFAST WARE, and KITCHENWARE SETS in distinctive modern styling are PURINTON SLIP WARE. The designs are formed with clays of different colors applied on the raw ware before it is fired or glazed. They become an integral part of the piece. Thus the colors remain permanently brilliant and cannot be harmed by severest detergents or hottest ovens. Each piece is individually hand-decorated. Four appealing patterns are available in a wide range of kitchen, occasional and dinnerware items. Open stock. PURINTON POTTERY COMPANY, SHIPPENVILLE, PENNSYLVANIA.

All the beautiful crystal shown in "The Home of the Century" is hand fashioned by THE DUNCAN & MILLER GLASS COMPANY, of Washington, Penna., Creators of DUNCAN, "the loveliest glassware in America." DUNCAN'S CANTERBURY is the finest modern crystal now being made by hand in America. Notice its sparkling, flawless beauty so essential to modern simplicity. CANTERBURY is at home in any setting . . . adapting itself to traditional interiors as charmingly as it does to modern.

DUNCAN'S TEAR-DROP, because of its fine, honest simplicity of design, blends well with either the simplest table settings or the most elaborate. And, because it is clear, brilliant crystal, lends itself to any color scheme. Duncan's graceful TEAR-DROP pattern harmonizes equally well with Early American, 18th Century traditional and simple modern furniture.

The HOTABLE IMPERIAL, measuring 16" x 24" is a wheeled serving table with a RA-GRID radiant glass heated top, thermostatically controlled, shatter-proof and guaranteed for safety. When the electric cord of the HOTABLE IMPERIAL is plugged into an AC outlet, the upper tray reaches a temperature of 200 degrees F., perfect for keeping hot foods piping hot for any length of time. This temperature is below the boiling point of water and will not dry out foods nor affect their taste.

The HOTABLE IMPERIAL has a lower tray of glass, and is convenient for bringing in desserts, salads, etc., and for stacking used dishes. The HOTABLE IMPERIAL can also be used as an attractive tea or cocktail wagon. It is made of flat-rolled aluminum and is mounted on easy-rolling swivel casters. Manufactured by: SALTON MANUFACTURING CO., INC., New York 7, New York.

Purinton Pottery is described in the 1950 Home of the Century brochure.

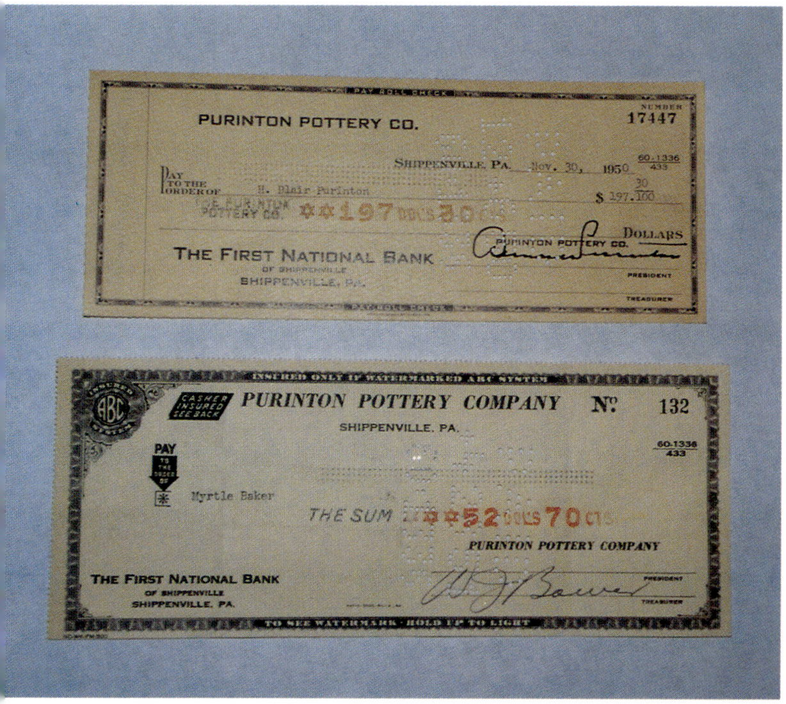

Checks issued by the Purinton Pottery Company.

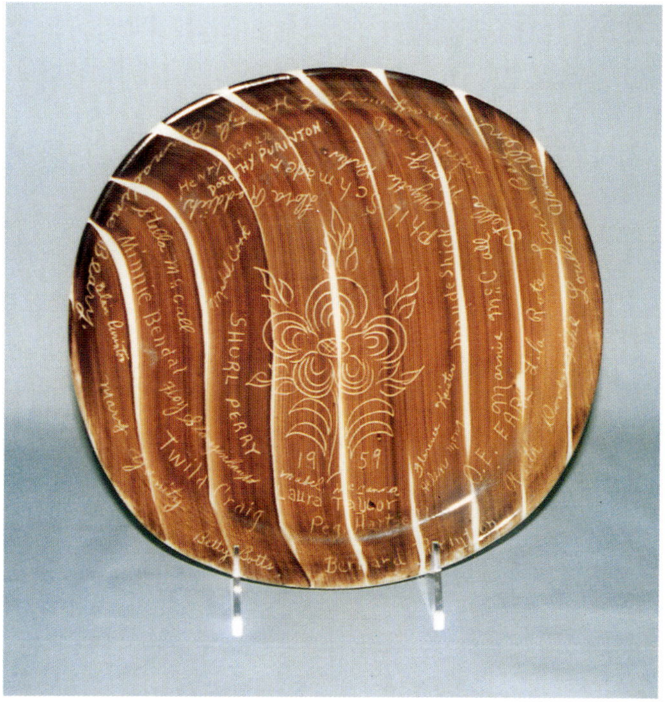

Brown Intaglio dinner plate inscribed by the employees at the close of the plant in 1959. Signatures include Dorothy, Bernard, and Blair Purinton.

Peasant Ware

From 1936 until 1941 Purinton Pottery developed its wares in Wellsville, Ohio. Located near East Liverpool, Ohio, Purinton faced competition from a variety of pottery companies. Known for its hand painted, underglaze wares, Purinton provided a product of simple, native decoration called "Peasant Ware." This primitive serving ware reflected society's demand. There was a demand for simpler, less formal place settings at informal gatherings.

Limited product lines were available which would be used to serve people on informal occasions. Teapots were sold in sets, each set containing a creamer, sugar, and tea tile. Pitchers, five pint dutch jugs with tumblers, and two pint dutch jugs with juice mugs were popular as were oasis jugs with tumblers. Salad sets included four plates and a bowl (what is now called a fruit bowl). Punch sets were offered in a Tom and Jerry pattern, among others. Coffee sets came with a creamer, sugar bowl, coffee carafe, cups, saucers, and a marmalade jar. Other products included ball salt and pepper shakers, peasant lady candle holders, a bird pitcher, tea and toast sets, "old salt and wife pepper" shakers, a two-part seahorse cocktail dish, and a few other items.

Each item was sold by a number/letter code which corresponded to a certain color combination. The 6A code stood for a combination of brown, yellow, and burnt orange — or as we collectors know it, Sunflower. Some items were decorated with people who appeared to be peasants. Other decorations in the Peasant Ware line included desert plants or scenes named Cactus, Cactus Flower, Ribbon Flower, and Sunflower. Some items were decorated with geometric lines representing designs from the Southwest and a few pieces were painted with buildings. The most notable pattern developed in Wellsville was Fruit. Fruit continued to be a popular decoration in Shippenville and was later transformed into the decoration for Esmond. Crescent was used on limited basis in the later years of the plant. Note: Peasant Garden was derived from the decoration on a peasant lady candle holders but was not considered a line of ware from Wellsville. It was developed at Shippenville and used on dinnerware.

William Blair receives the most credit for developing the Peasant Ware patterns. He utilized earthy color with bold, primitive designs. He also can be credited with the development of the out of round plate that Purinton continued to use throughout its history. He did not like the perfectly circular, flat plates produced by companies during that period.

Today Peasant Ware is in great demand and is one of the more sought after decorations. The supply is low and the demand is high. This is reflected in the values attributed to Peasant Ware. Any item with a peasant man or woman painted on it is the hardest to find, followed by those items with a desert plant. Fruit is the most commonly found decoration and the least desirable. Shapes are also important in desirability. Oasis jugs command the highest prices as they were limited in production because they were difficult to make, frequently collapsing after being taken out of the mold. Five pint and two pint dutch jugs and tumblers with desert scenes or plants are very difficult to find. The peasant lady candle holder demands a good price and you can add 20 percent to the price if the piece is signed by William Blair.

Purinton Pottery mark 6A.

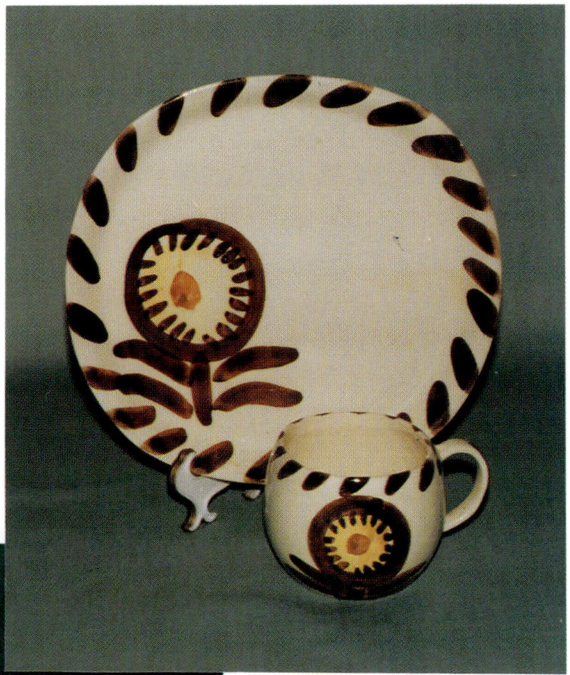

Sunflower breakfast plate. $125. Sunflower cup. $50.

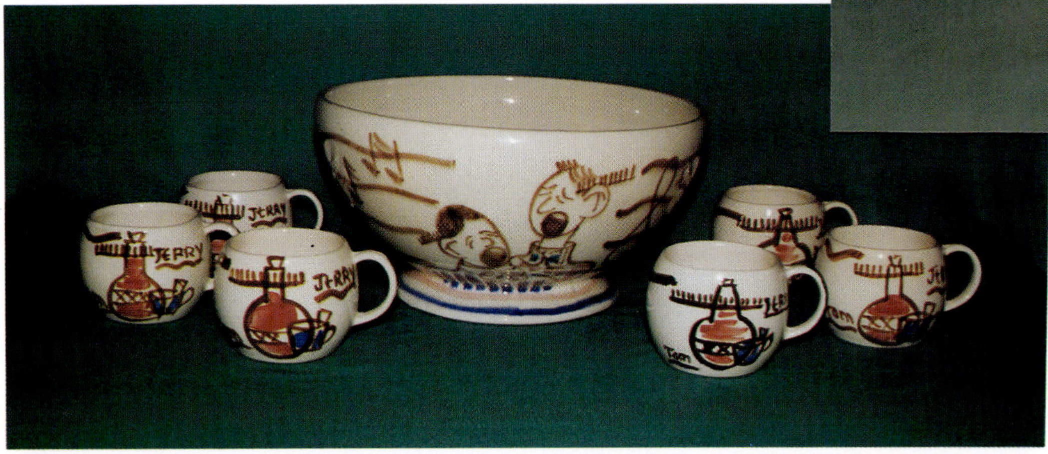

Tom and Jerry punch cup. $50. Tom and Jerry punch bowl. $300+.

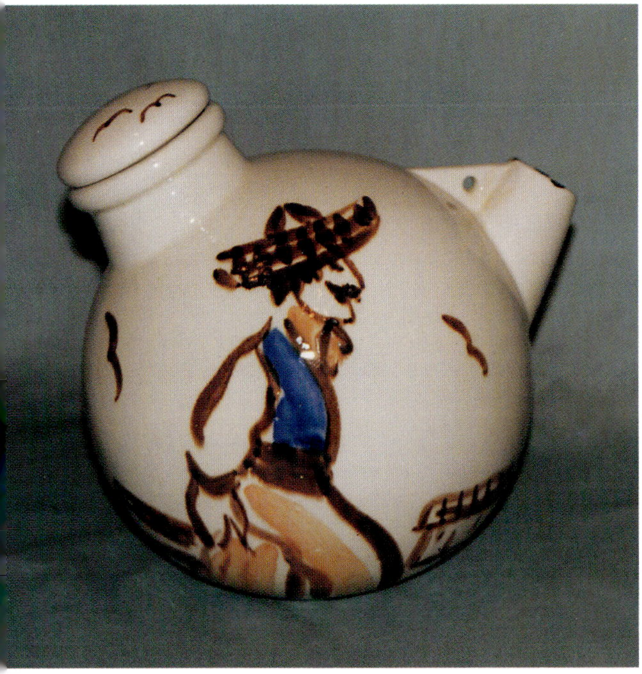

Oasis jug with a peasant man (rare). $1000+.

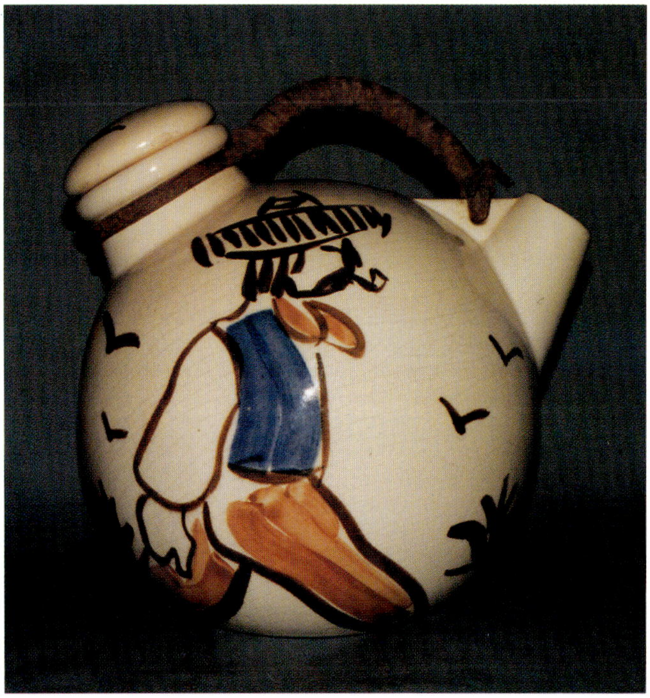

Oasis jug with peasant man and intact leather handle. $1000+.

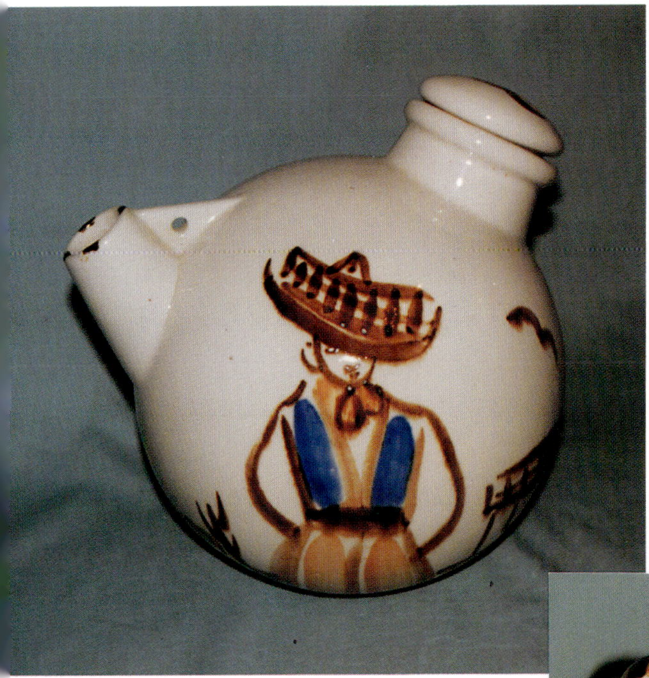

Reverse of the oasis jug with the peasant man.

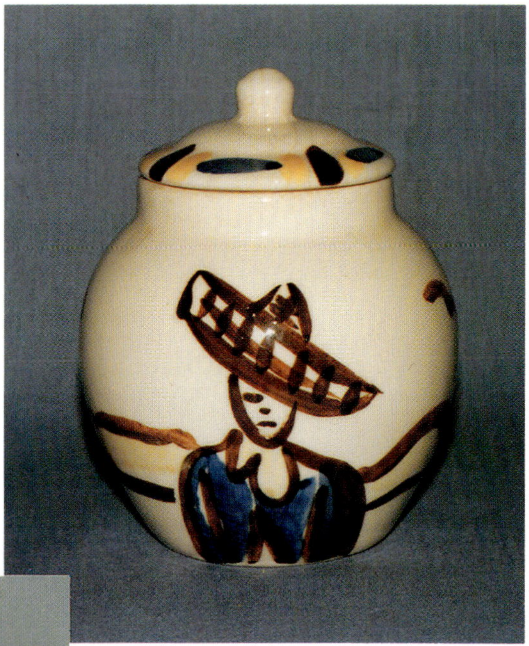

Marmalade with peasant man. $200+.

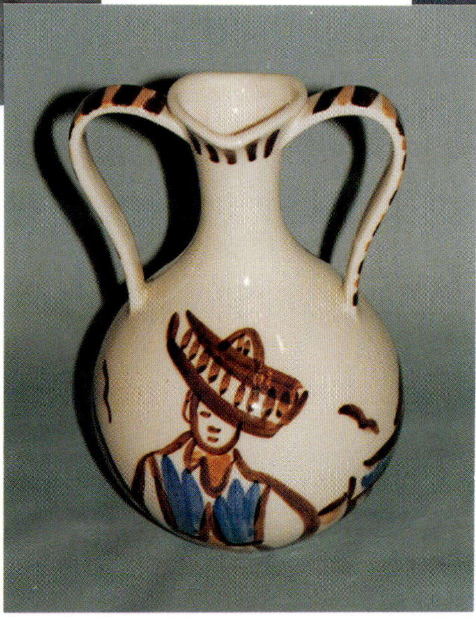

Coffee carafe with peasant man. $250+.

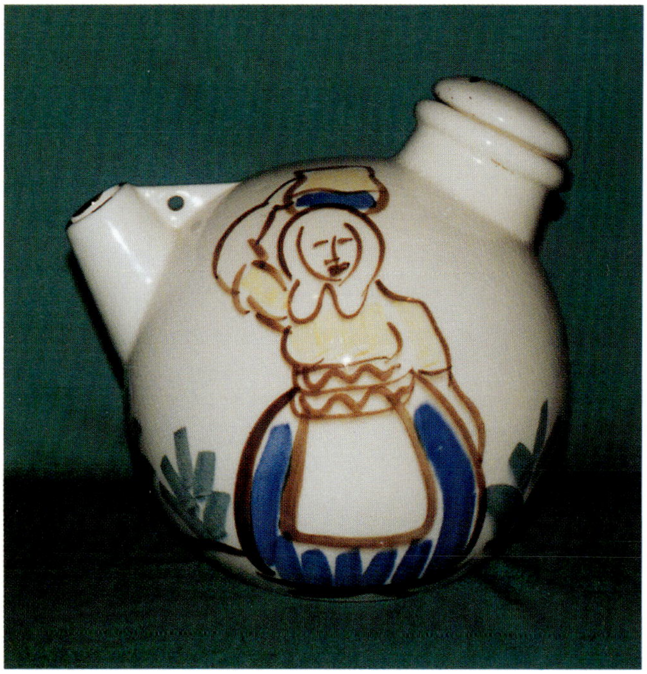

Oasis jug with peasant woman. $1000+.

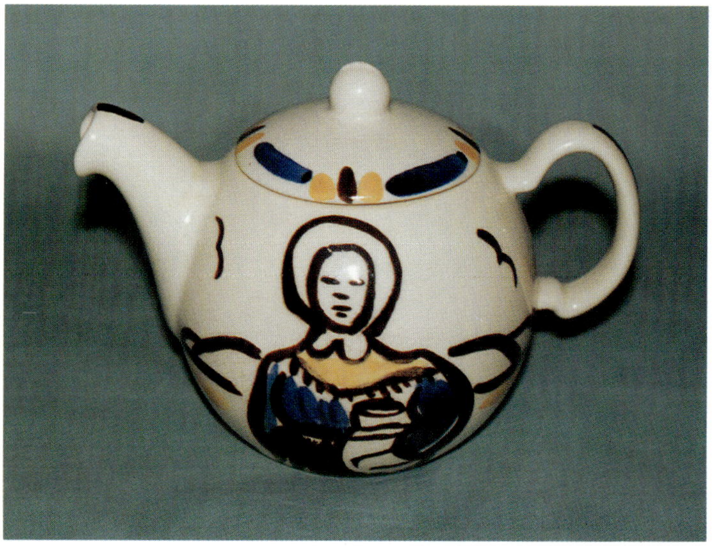

Two cup teapot with peasant woman holding a pot. $200+.

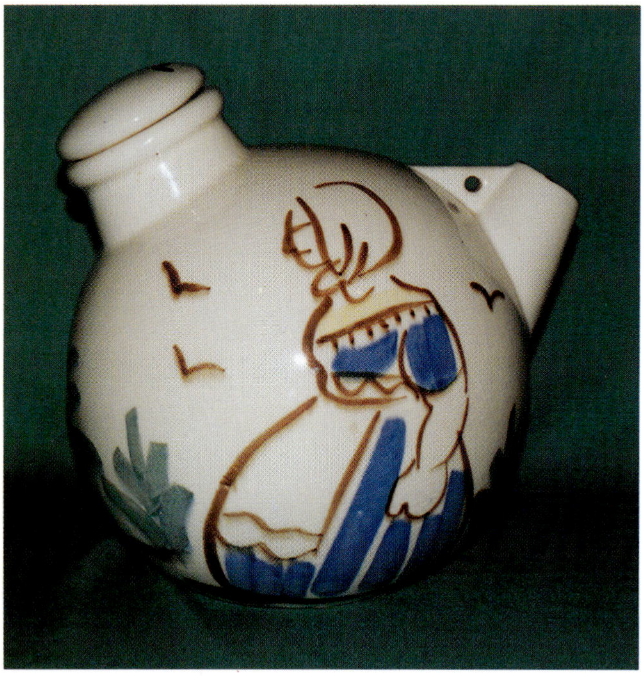

Reverse of oasis jug with peasant woman.

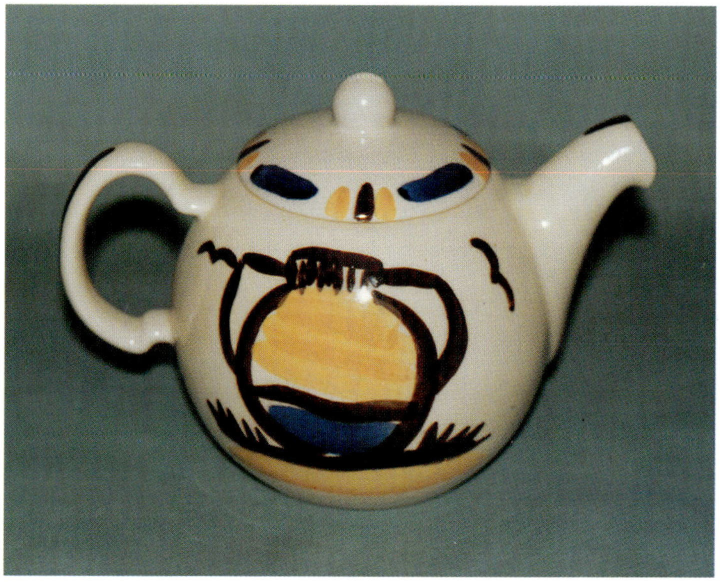

Reverse side of the two cup teapot.

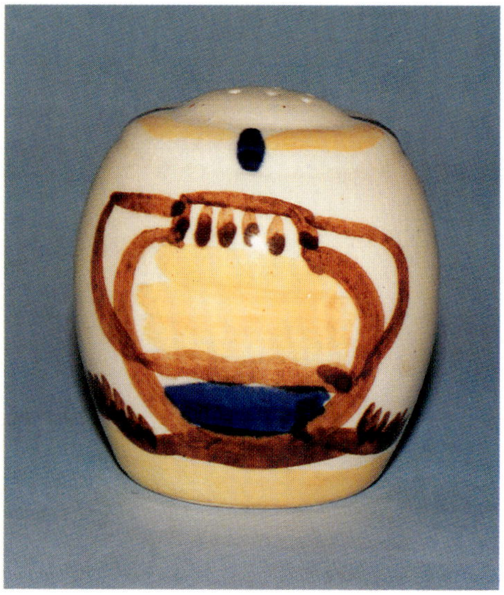

Ball salt shaker with pot decoration. $100.

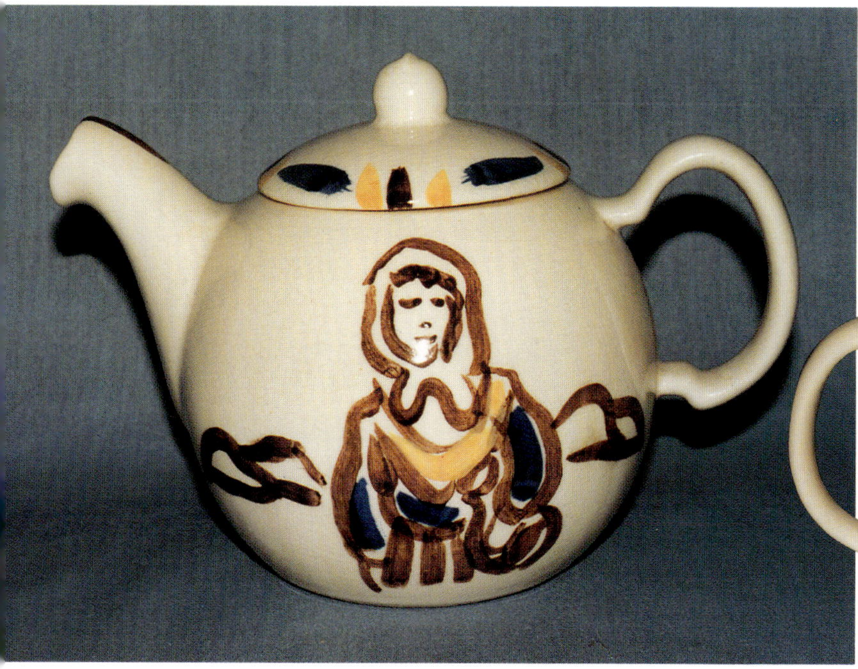

Reverse side of two cup teapot.

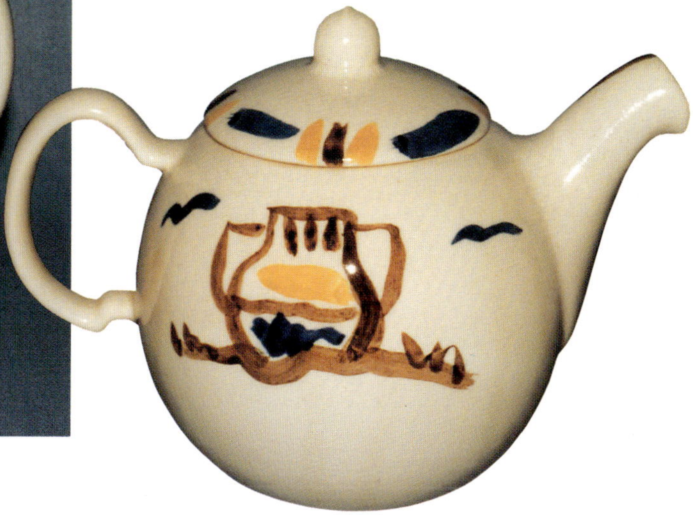

Two cup teapot with peasant woman holding a pot (decoration is more crude than previous teapot). $200+.

Two cup teapot with peasant woman. $200+.

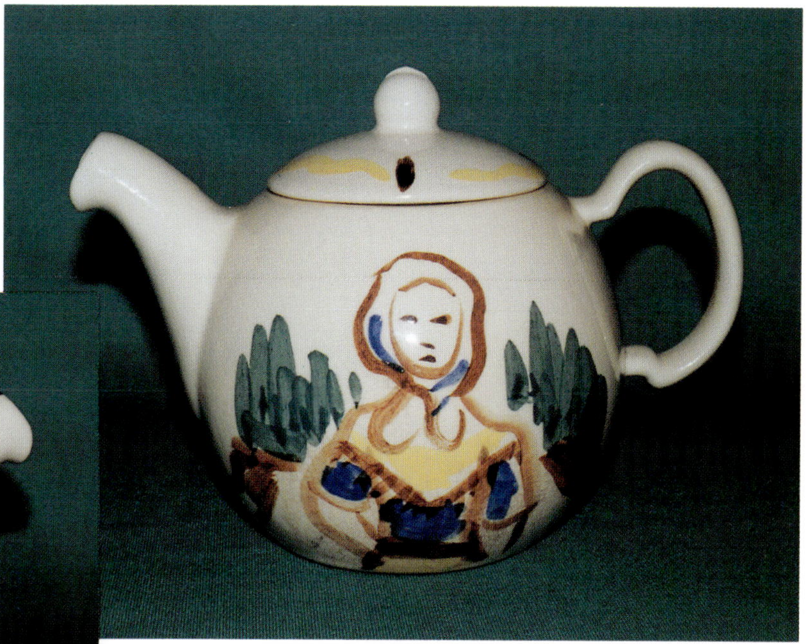

Reverse of two cup teapot with desert scene decoration.

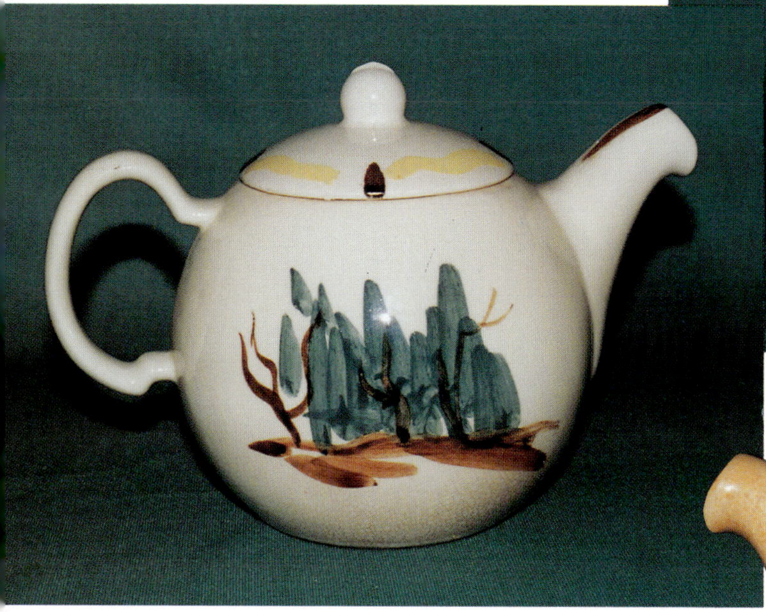

Four cup teapot with peasant woman decoration. $200+.

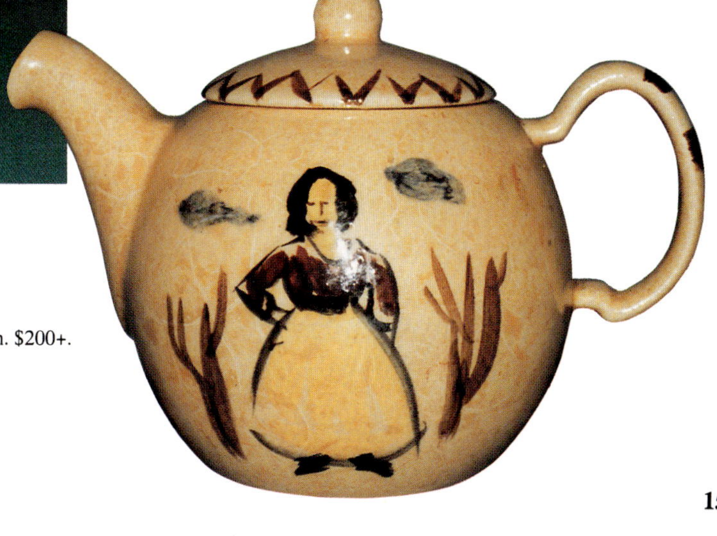

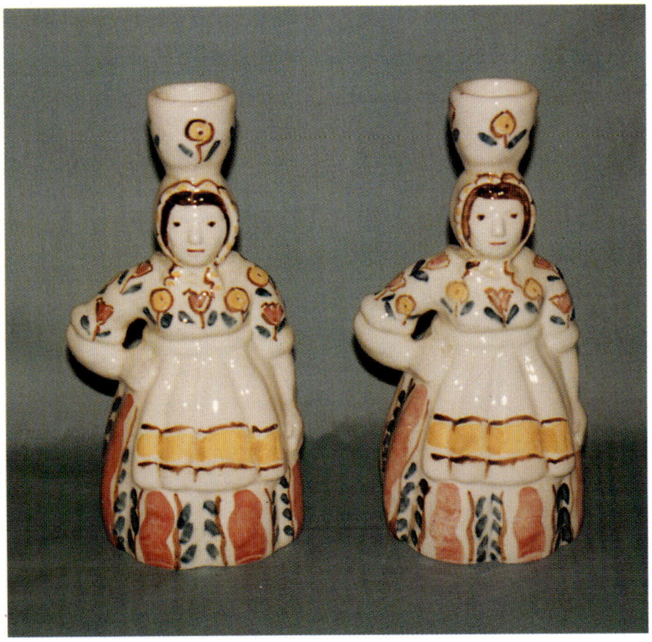

Peasant lady candle holders, production pieces. $400 each. If signed by William Blair, $475 each.

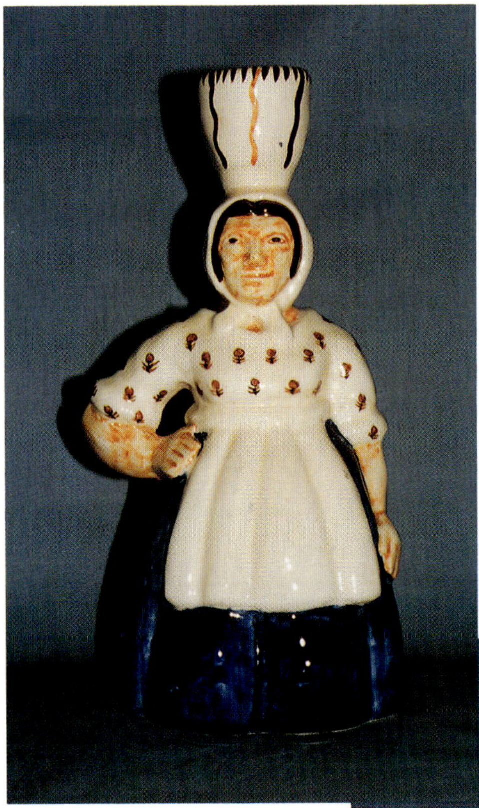

Peasant lady candle holder with variant decoration. $400.

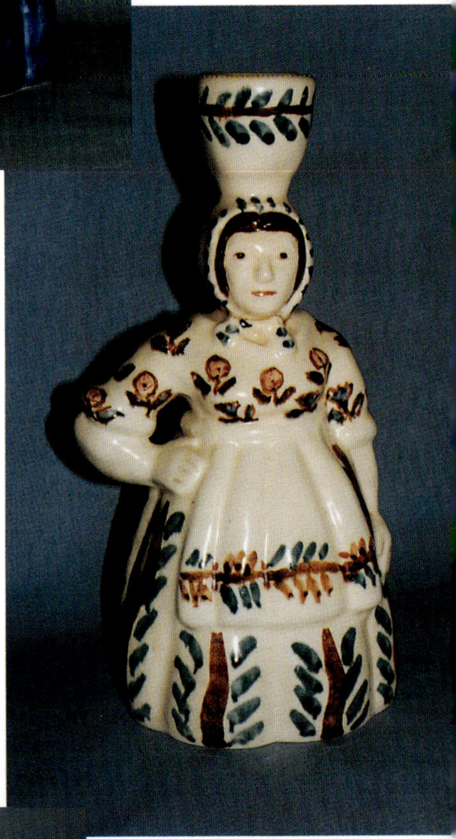

Peasant lady candle holder with variant decoration. Signed by William Blair. $475.

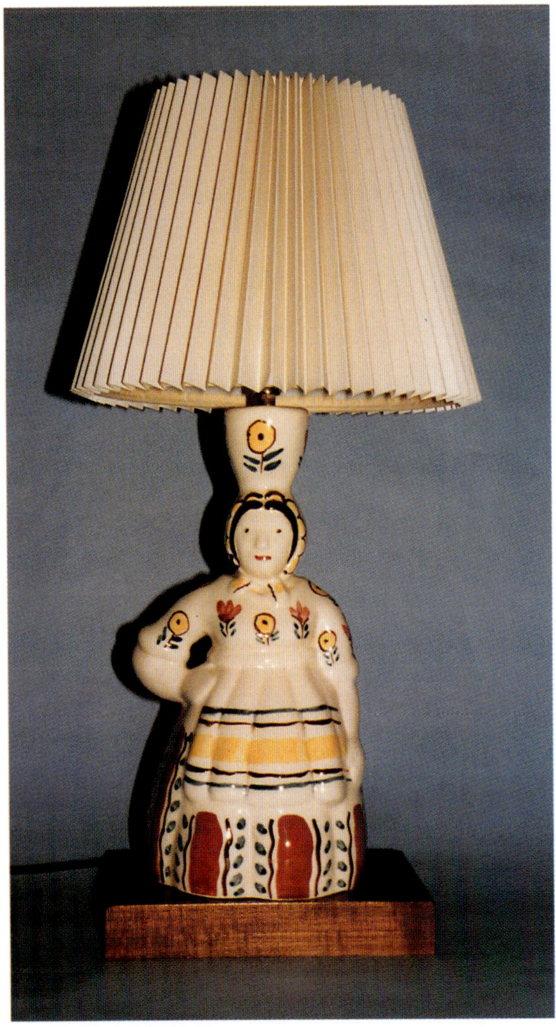

Peasant lady candle holder drilled as a lamp by Bill Bower, Jr. $400+.

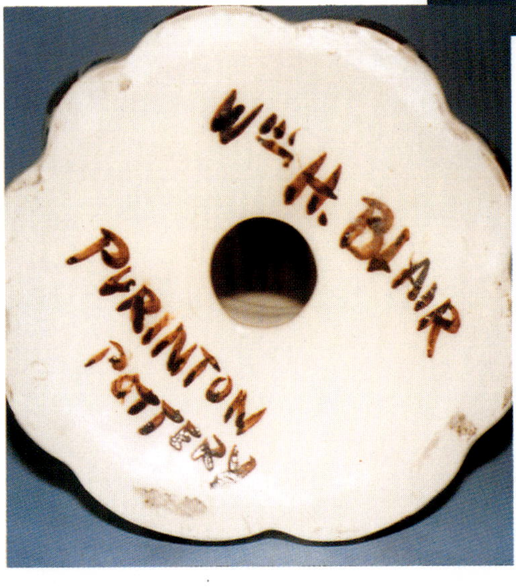

William Blair signature.

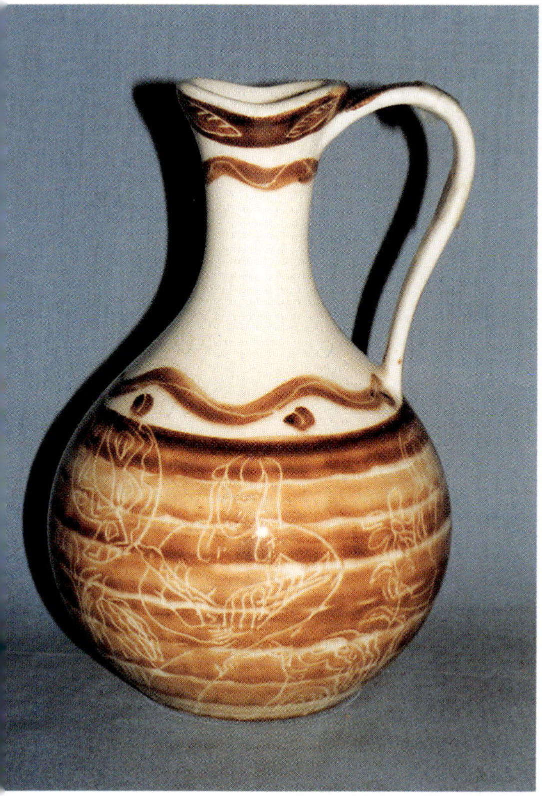

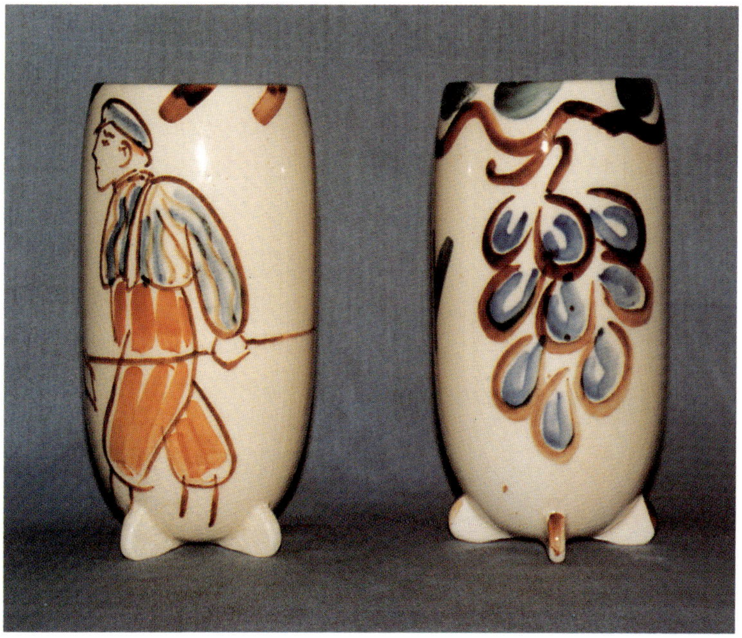

Footed tumbler with peasant man, not a production piece. $100. Footed tumbler with grapes, not a production piece. $100.

Water pitcher with Intaglio design and incised pictures of people. Attributed to William Blair. $300+.

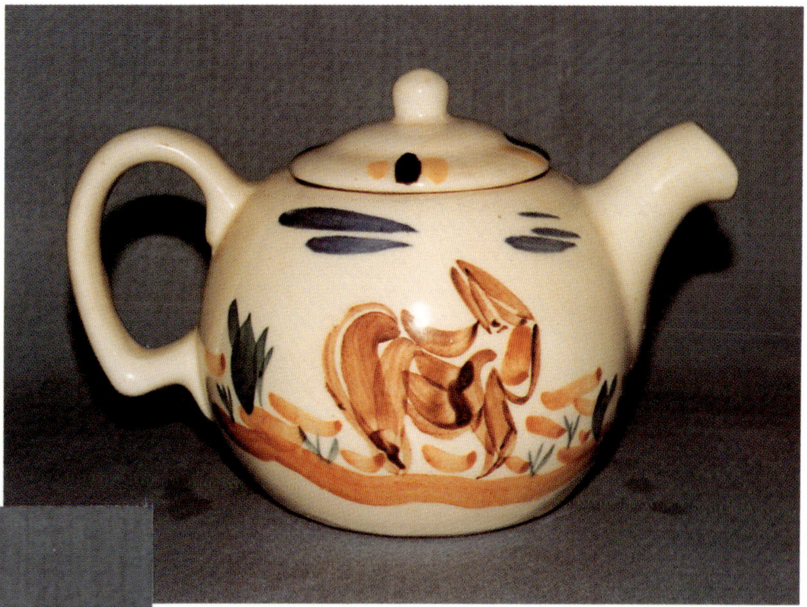

Reverse side of two cup teapot with crude donkey decoration.

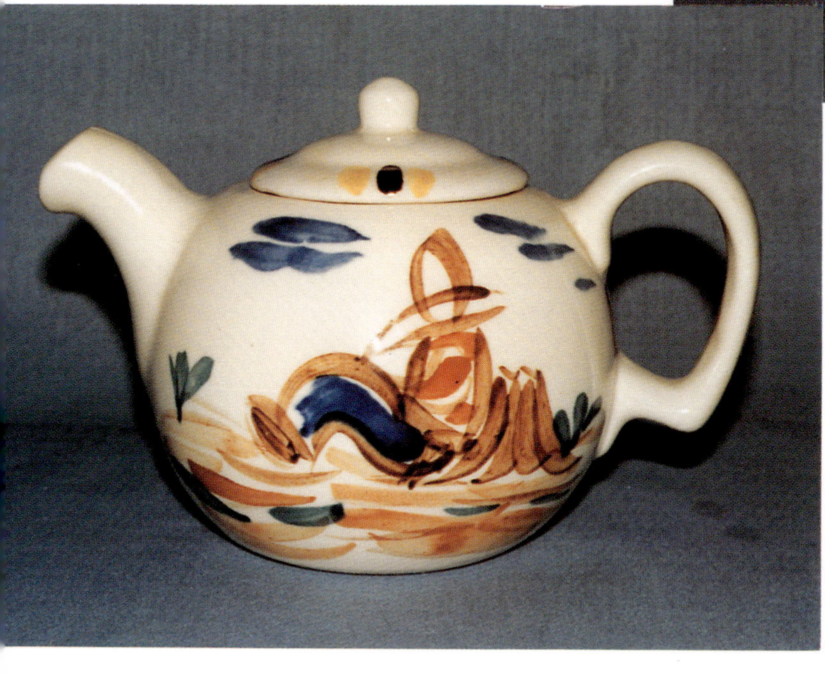

Two cup teapot with peasant man decoration. $200+.

Cactus

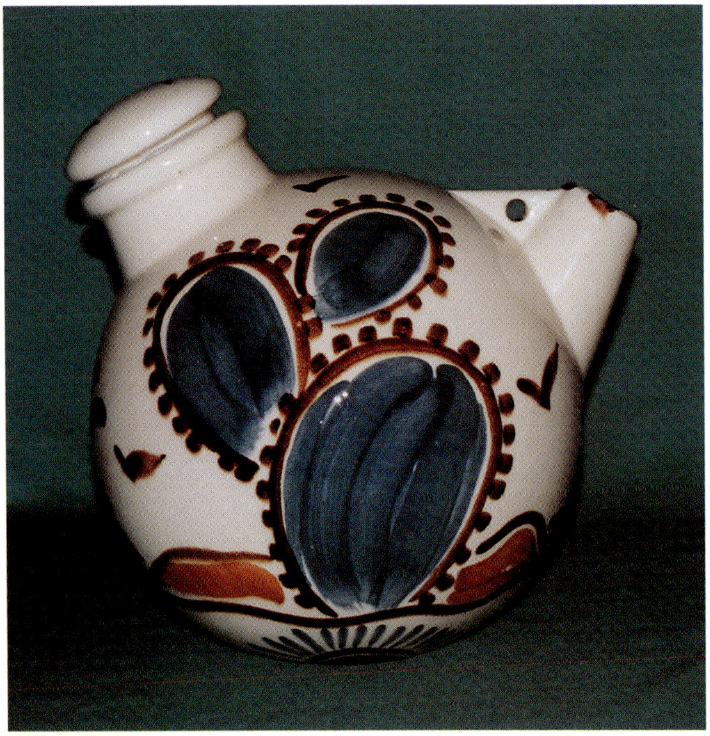

Oasis jug with prickly pear Cactus. $900+.

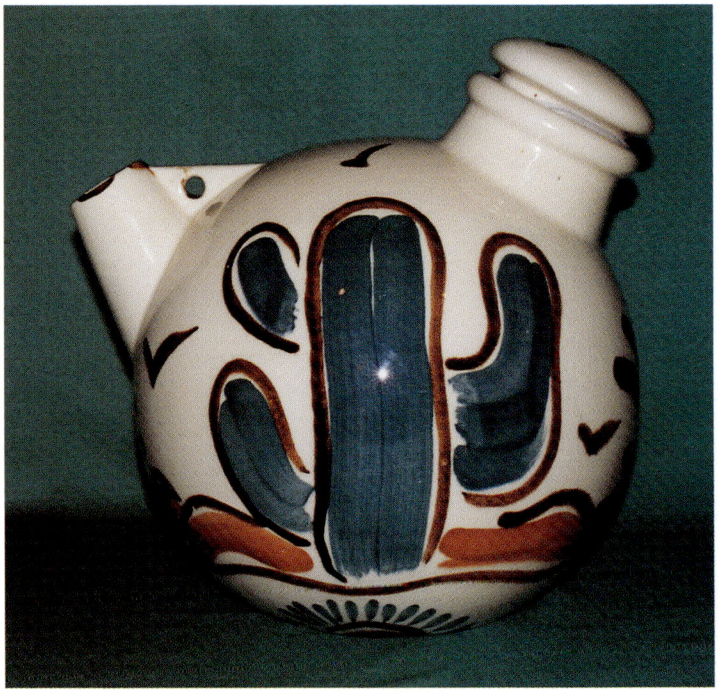

Reverse of Cactus oasis jug showing Snoopy style Cactus.

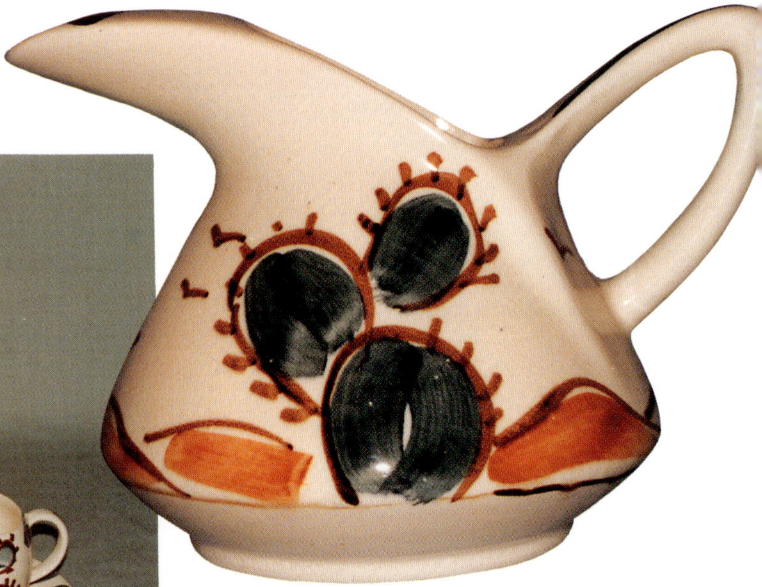

Cactus two pint dutch jug. $300.

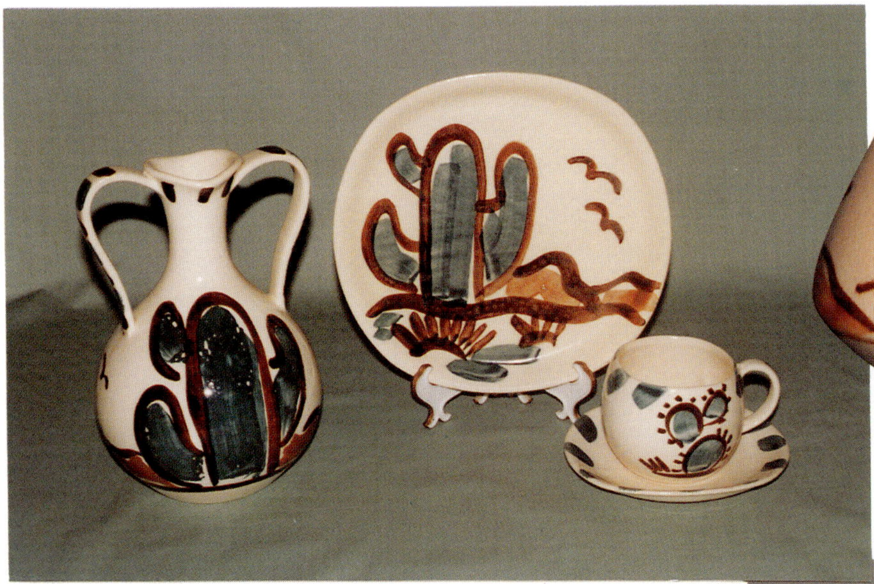

Cactus coffee carafe. $150+. Cactus breakfast plate. $125. Cactus cup. $50. Saucer. $20.

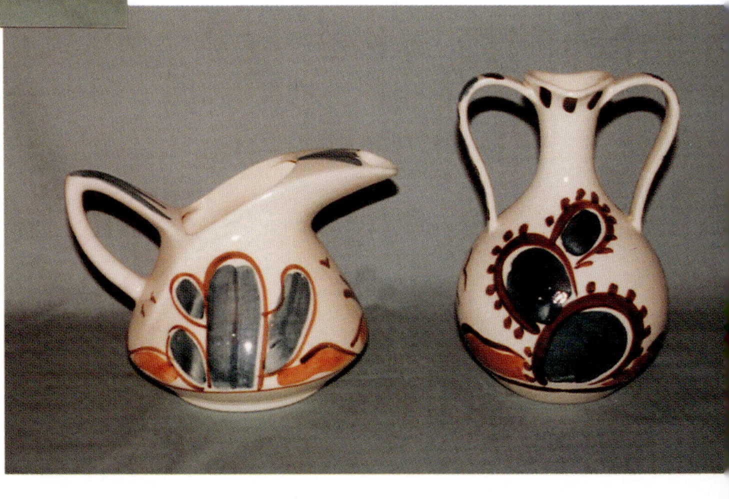

Reverse of Cactus two pint dutch jug and Cactus coffee carafe.

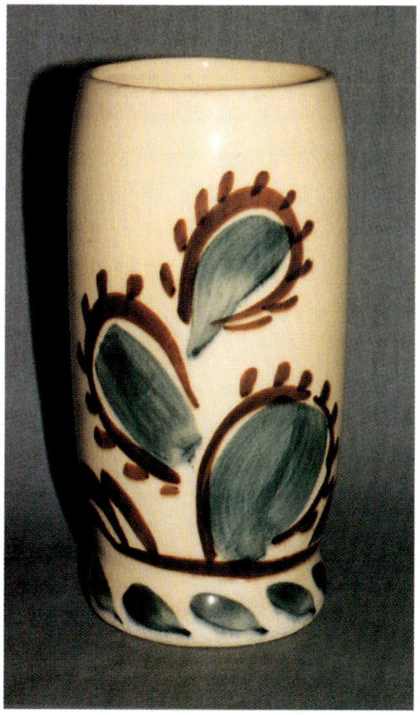

Cactus tumbler. $100.

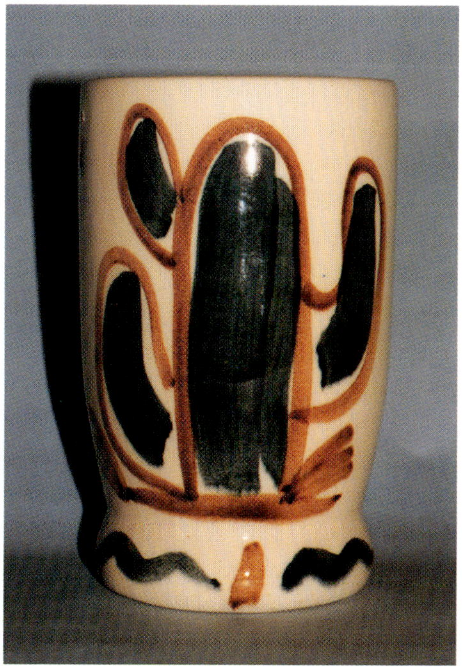

Cactus tumbler. $100.

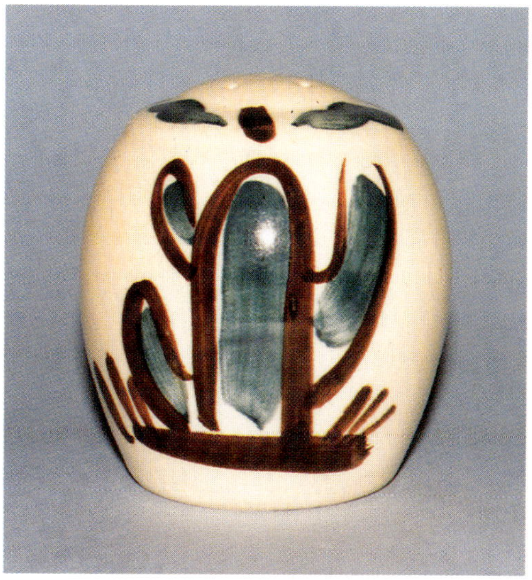

Ball salt shaker with Cactus decoration. $100.

Cactus Flower

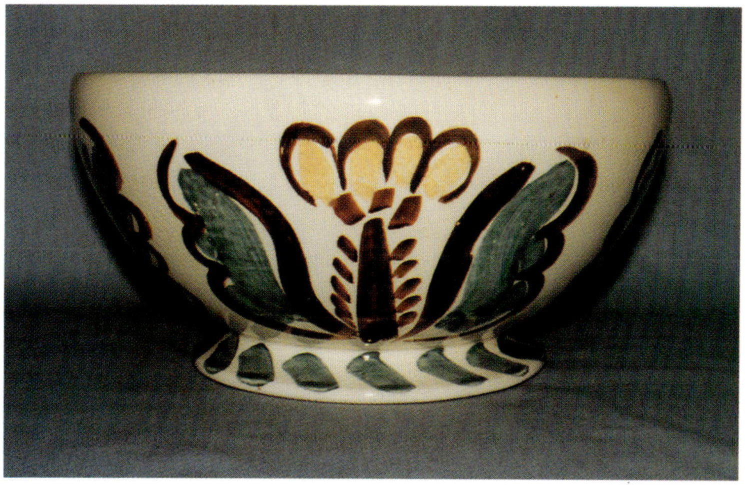

Cactus Flower punch bowl. $300+.

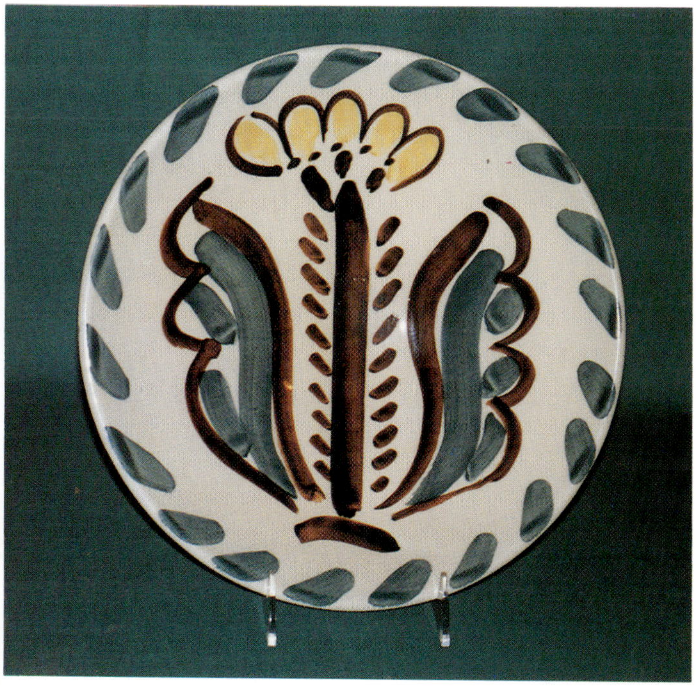

Cactus Flower fruit bowl. $300+.

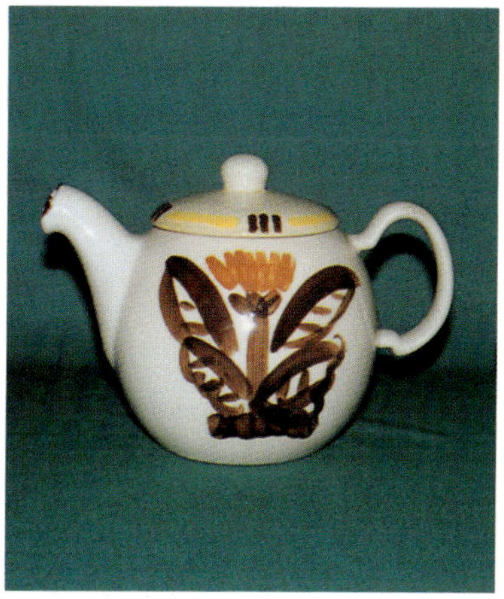

Cactus Flower variant four cup teapot. $150+.

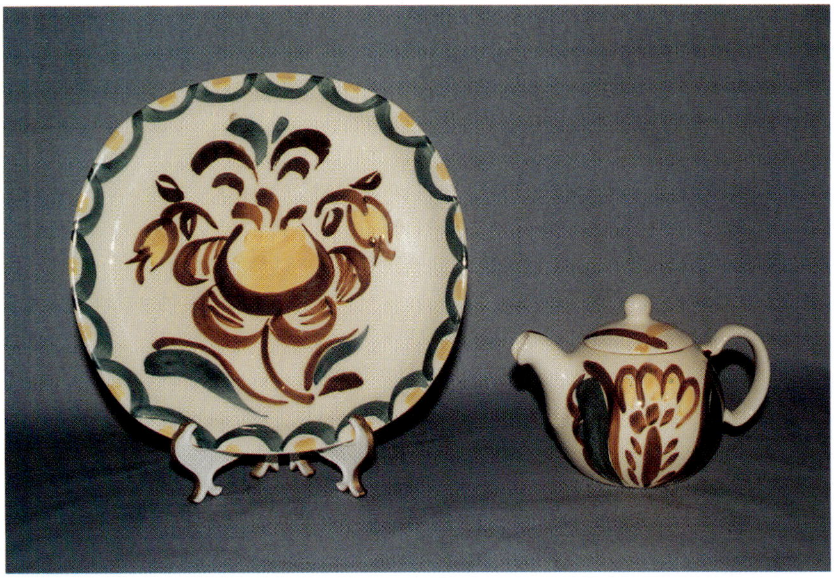

Cactus Flower variant dinner plate. $125. Cactus Flower two cup teapot. $150+.

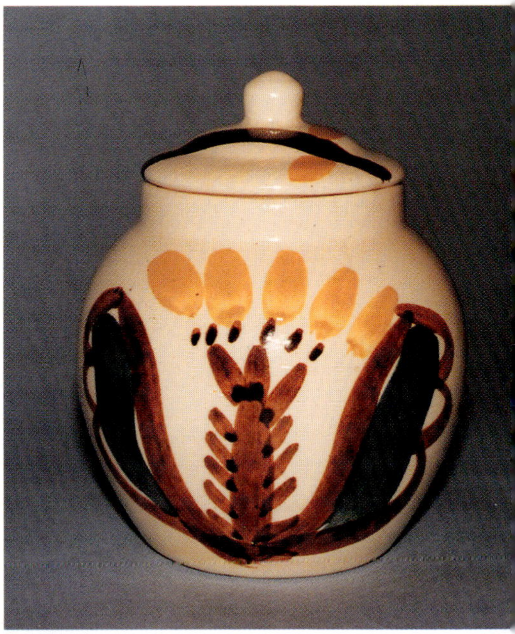

Cactus Flower marmalade. $150+.

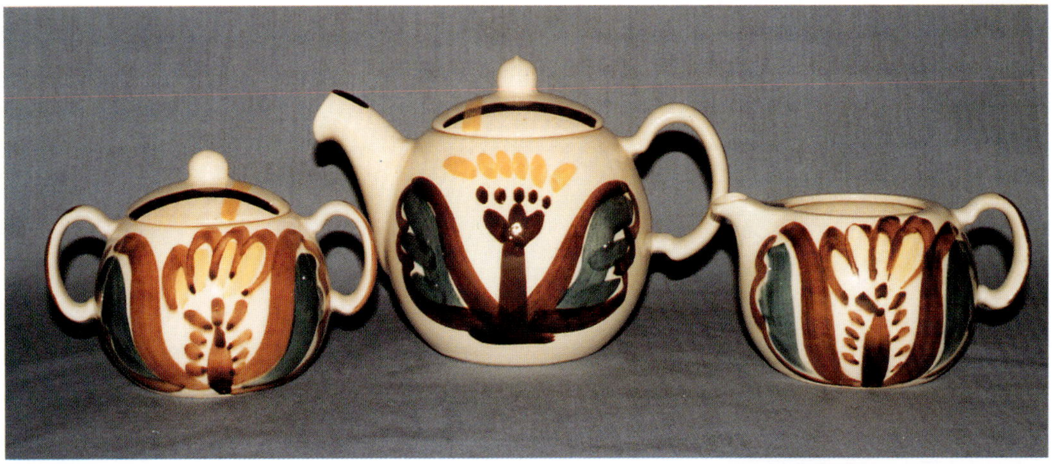

Cactus Flower covered sugar and creamer. $200+ set. Cactus Flower four cup teapot. $150+.

Cactus Flower variant fruit bowl attributed to William Blair. $300+.

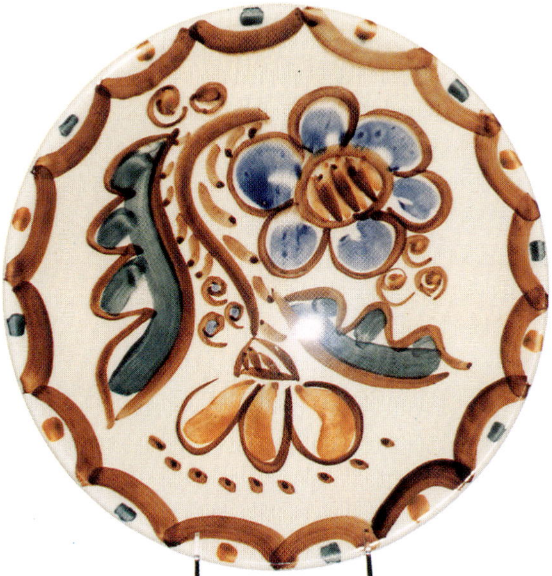

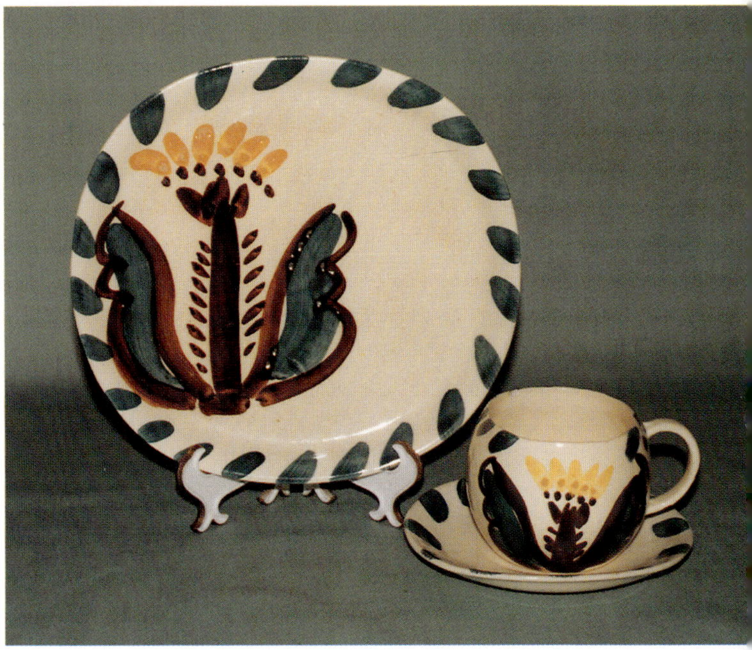

Cactus Flower breakfast plate. $125. Cactus Flower cup. $50. Cactus Flower Saucer. $20.

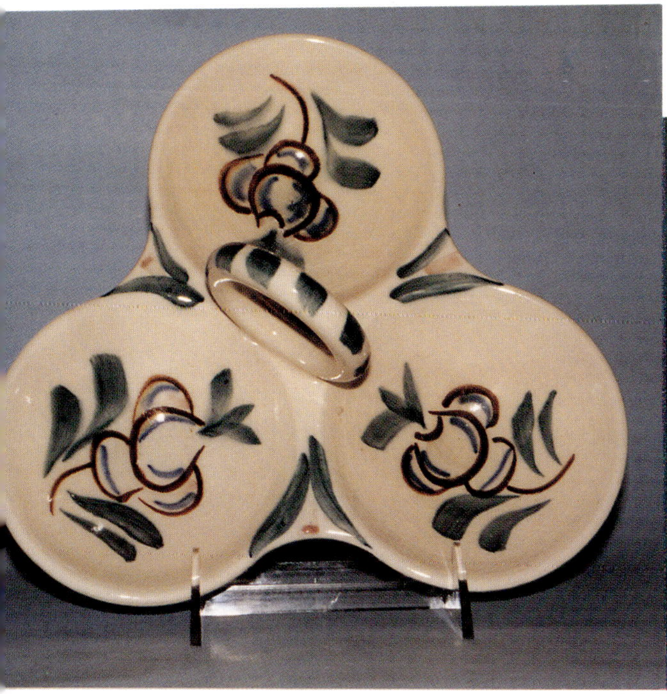

Three part relish with Cactus Flower variant decoration. $150+.

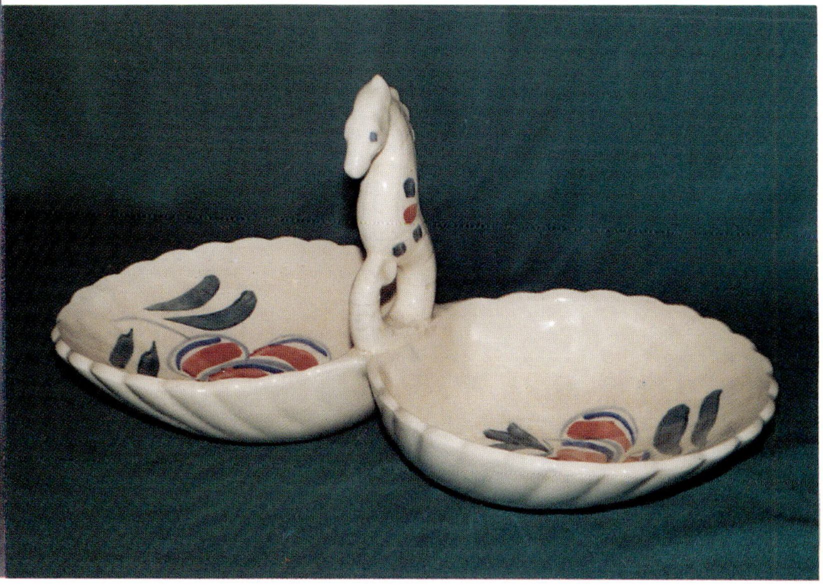

Seahorse cocktail with Cactus Flower variant decoration. $150+.

Ribbon Flower

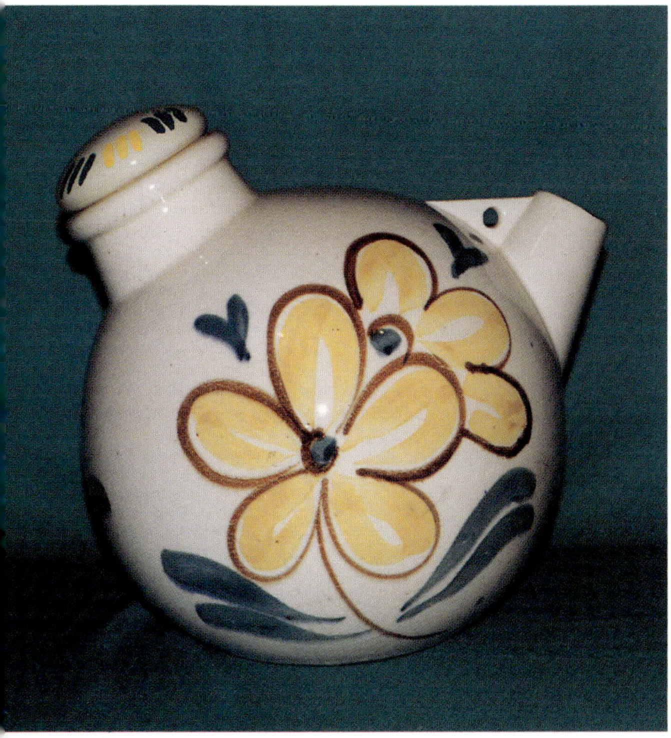

Ribbon Flower oasis jug. $900+.

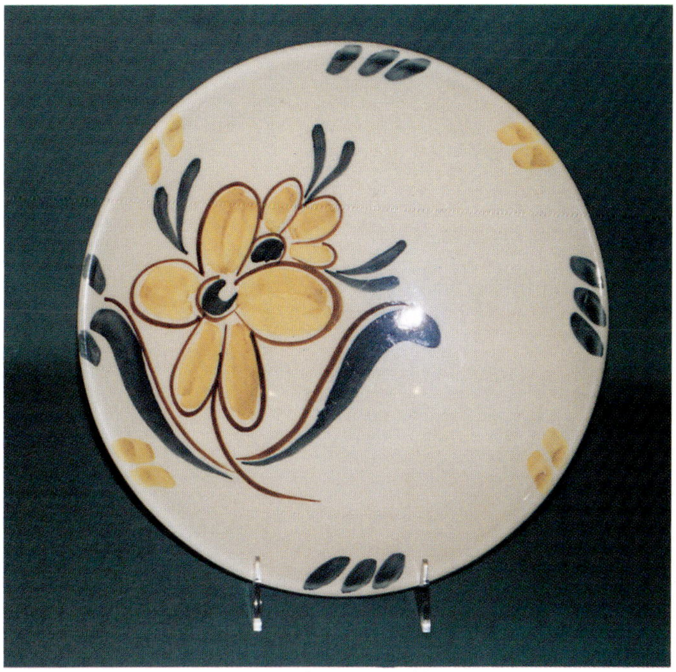

Ribbon Flower fruit bowl. $300+.

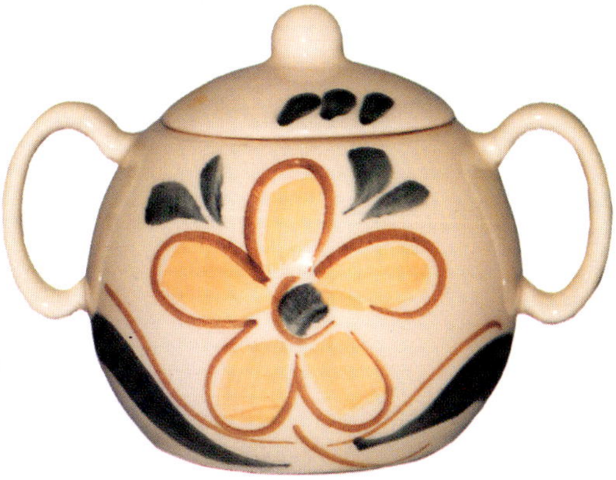

Ribbon Flower covered sugar, Wellsville mold. $100.

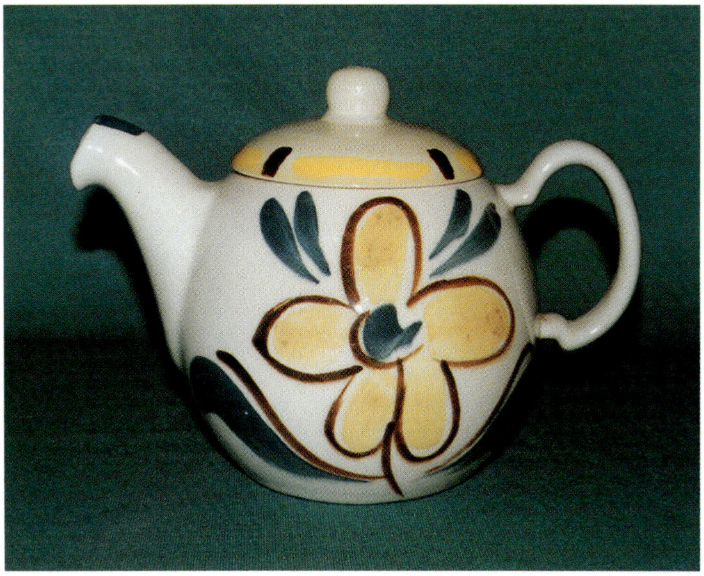

Ribbon Flower four cup teapot. $150+.

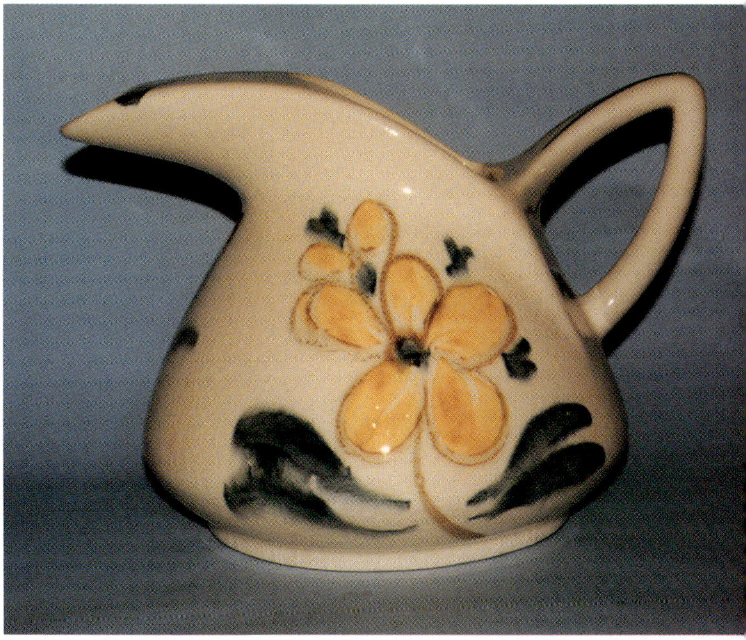

Ribbon Flower five pint dutch jug. $300+.

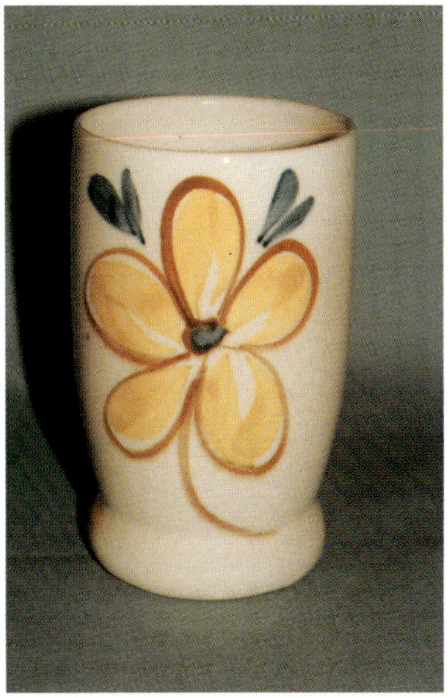

Ribbon Flower tumbler. $100.

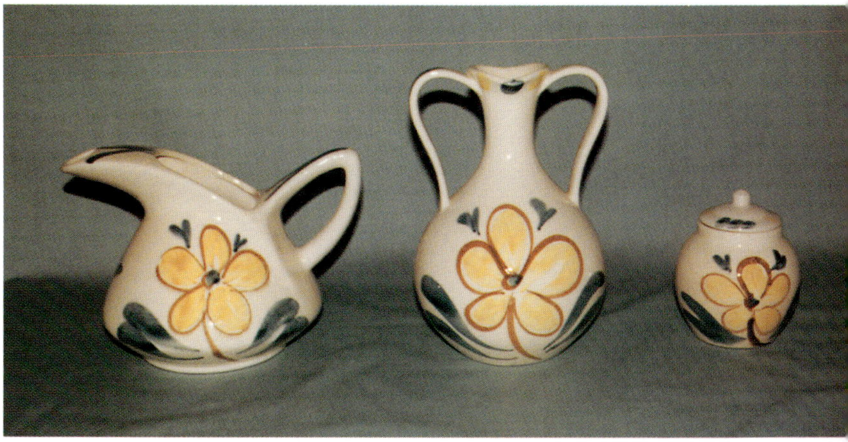

Ribbon Flower two pint dutch jug. $300+. Coffee carafe. $150+. Marmalade. $150+.

Sunflower

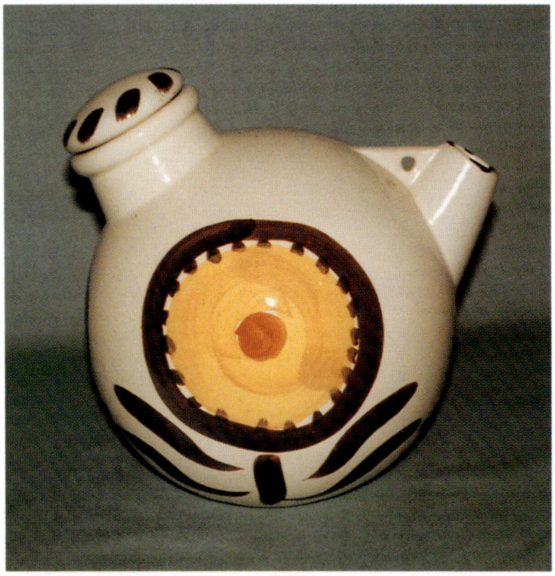

Sunflower oasis jug. $900+.

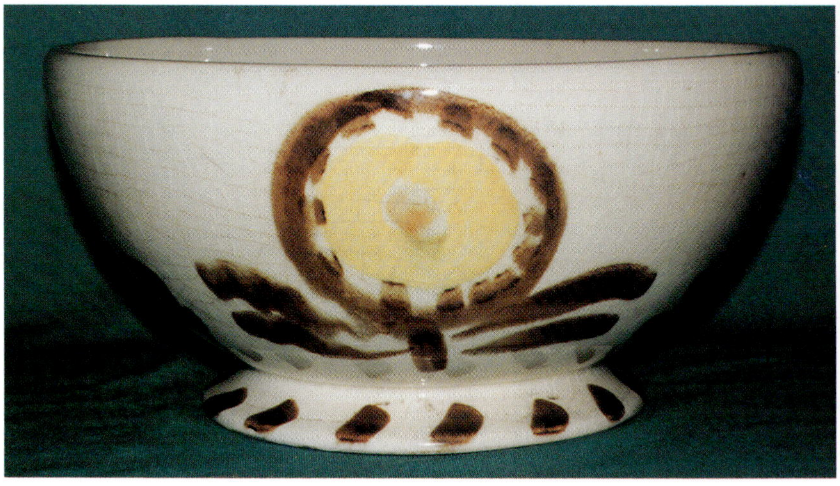

Sunflower punch bowl. $300+.

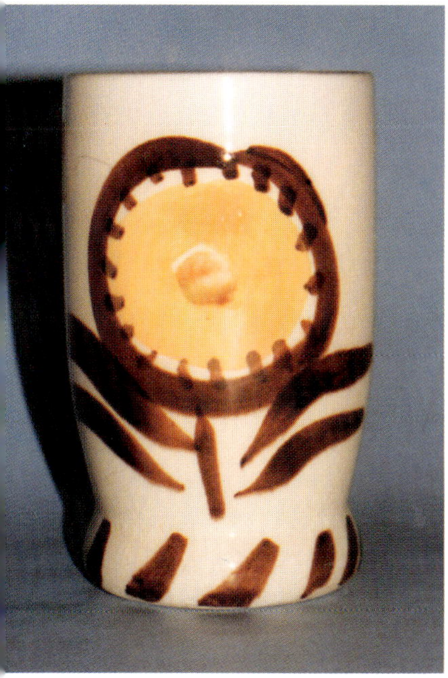

Sunflower tumbler. $100.

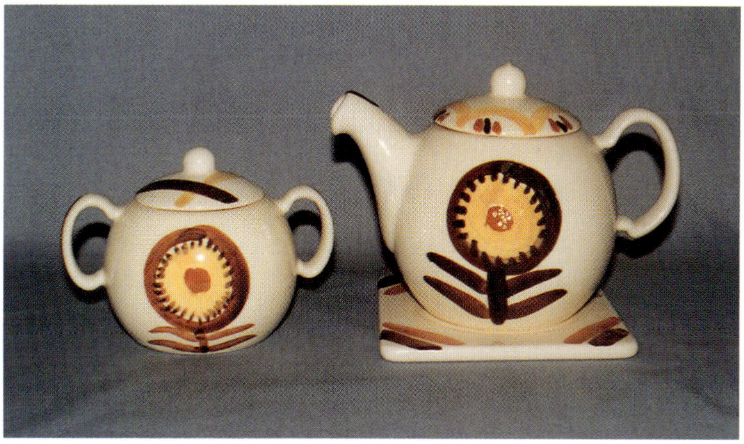

Sunflower covered sugar. $100. Six cup teapot. $150+. Tea tile under the teapot. $150.

Sunflower ball salt and pepper shakers. $175+ set.

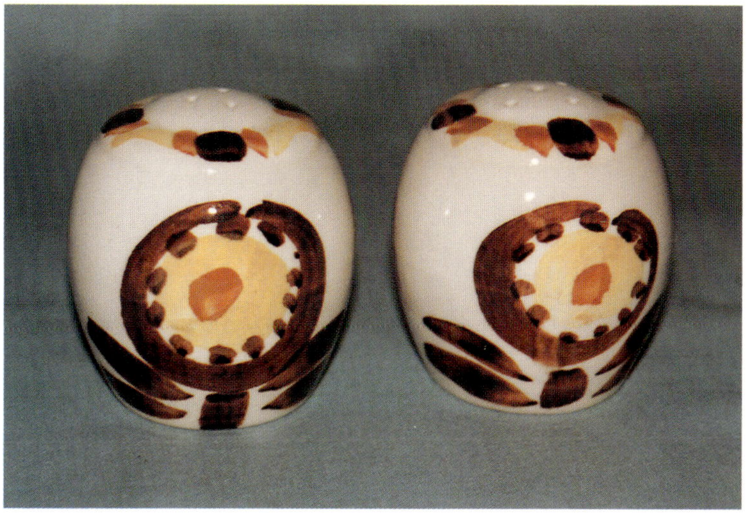

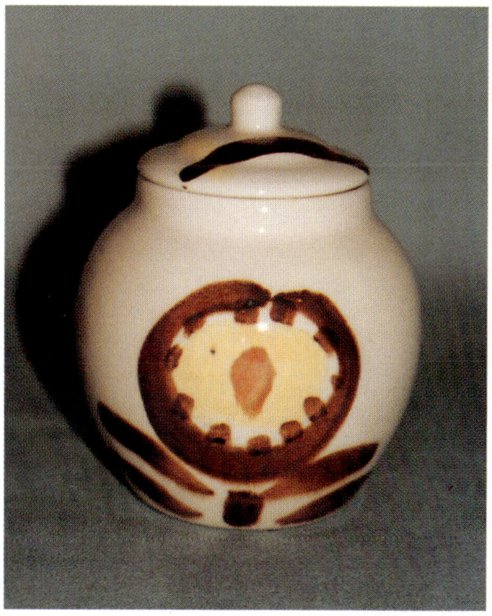

Sunflower marmalade. $150+.

Miscellaneous Peasant Ware

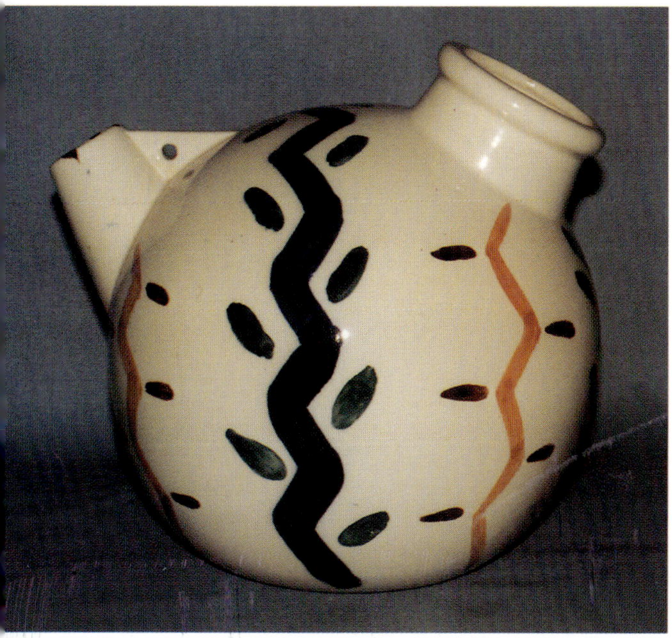

Oasis jug (missing lid in picture) with Nittany Line decoration. $750+.

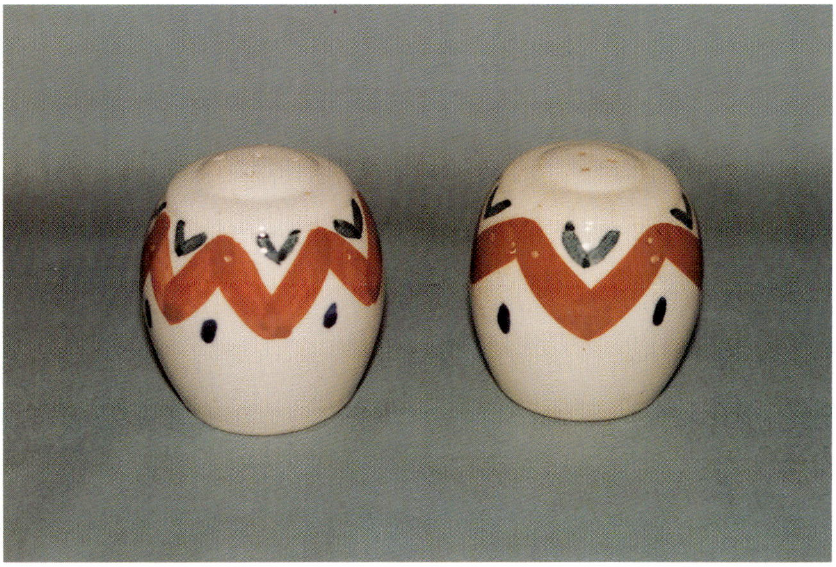

Ball shakers with Golden Crown decoration. $150+ set.

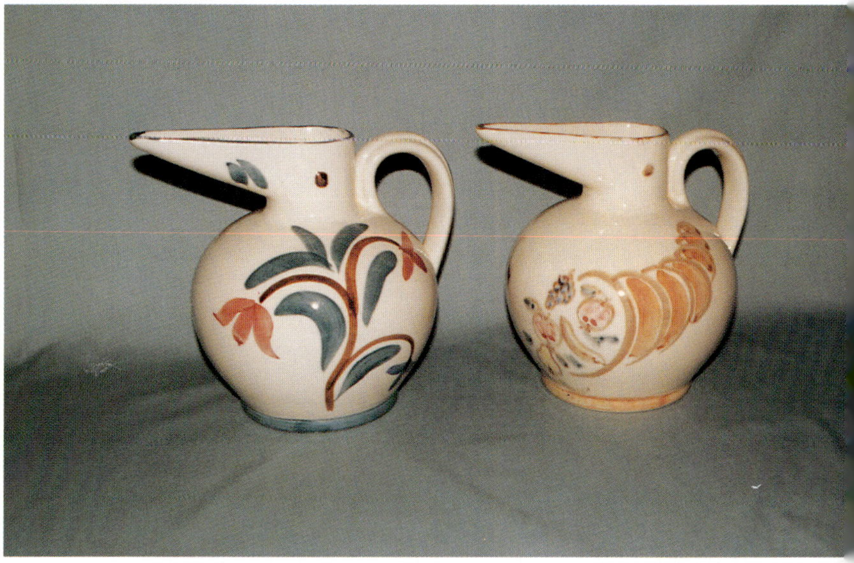

Bird pitcher Wind Flower decoration. $125. Bird pitcher, Cornucopia decoration. $200.

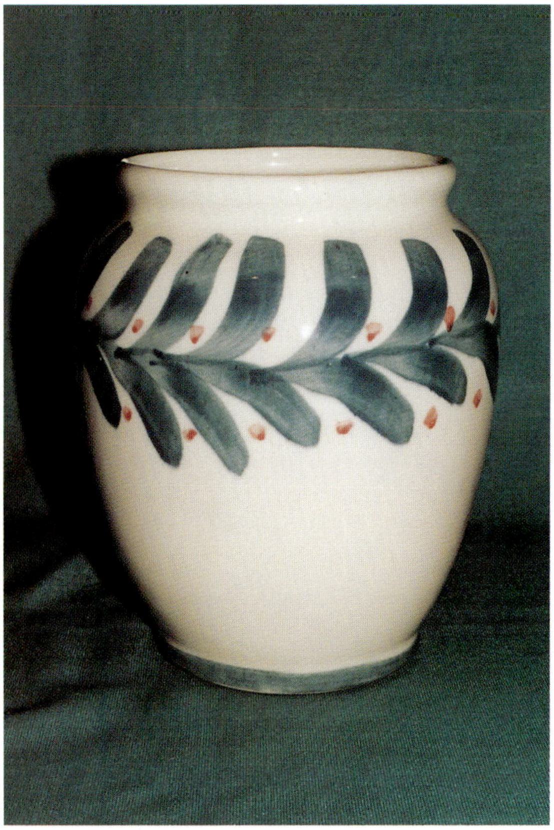

Wellsville style vase with green striped decoration. $150+.

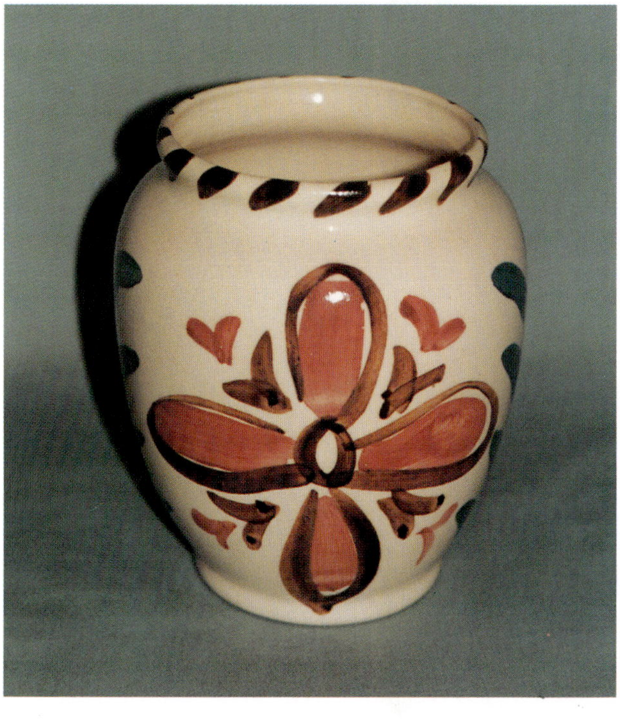

Wellsville style vase with large red flower decoration. $150+.

Crescent

Crescent decoration was used in a transition period from Wellsville to Shippenville. The pattern was given its name by Pat Dole, and we do not know if it went by any other name. With red, turquoise, and blue decoration, Crescent is one of those elusive patterns we do not know much about. We know Crescent was brought to Shippenville and used on dinner plates, individual creamers and sugars, jug style salt and pepper shakers, and teapots from a Shippenville mold. However, most of the objects to be collected will be found decorating items produced from Wellsville molds.

Most items seen with the Crescent decoration are teapots, creamers, and sugars in the Wellsville mold. Five and two pint dutch jugs are also more common with this decoration. Finding an oasis jug with the Crescent decoration would be rare, only two are currently known. Crescent dinner plates are also very difficult to find and only a few are known. Anything in dinnerware pieces would be rare. Crescent on chop plates or fruit bowls are not easily located and command a high price. Some later Purinton molds may have a slight variation of the decoration but these are not too desirable.

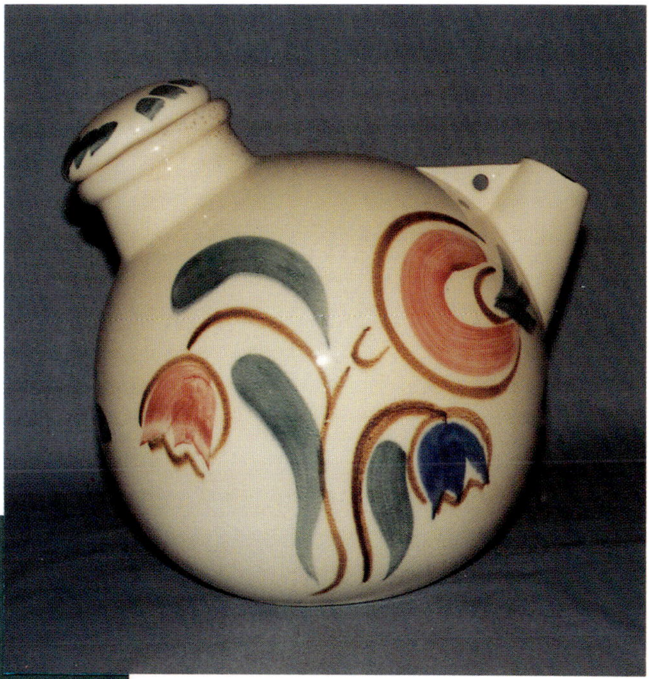

Crescent Oasis jug. $900+.

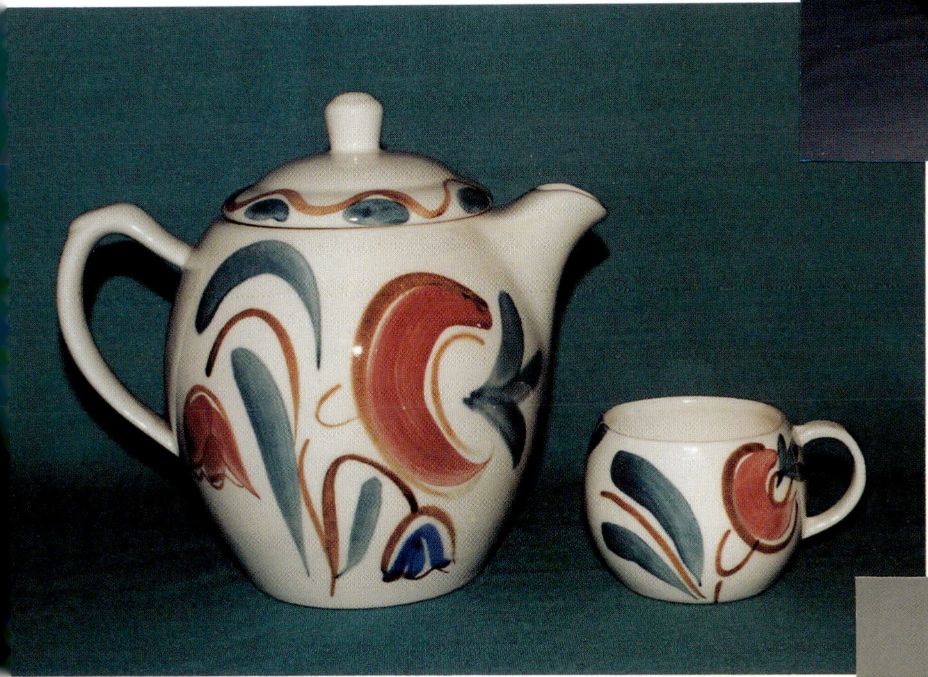

Eight cup coffee pot. $100. Cup. $30.

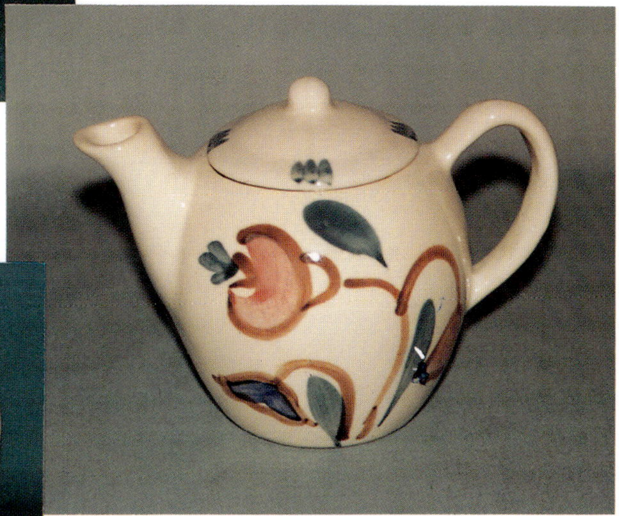

Two cup teapot, Shippenville mold. $75.

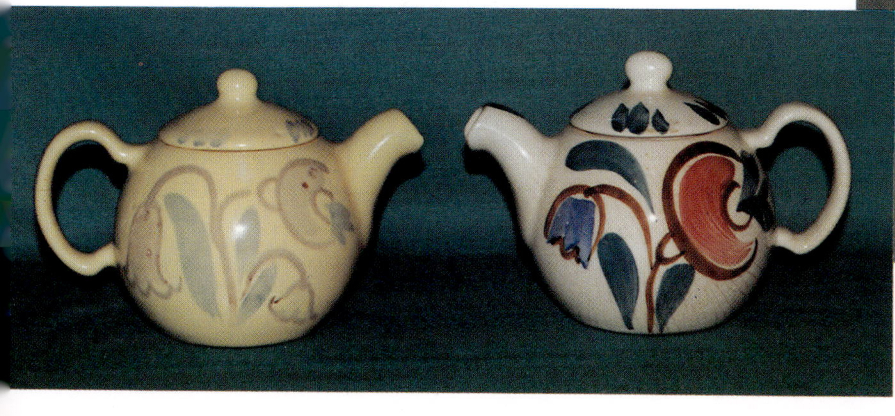

Two cup teapot, glazed with yellow glaze instead of the regular clear glaze, Wellsville mold. $50. Two cup teapot, Wellsville mold. $75.

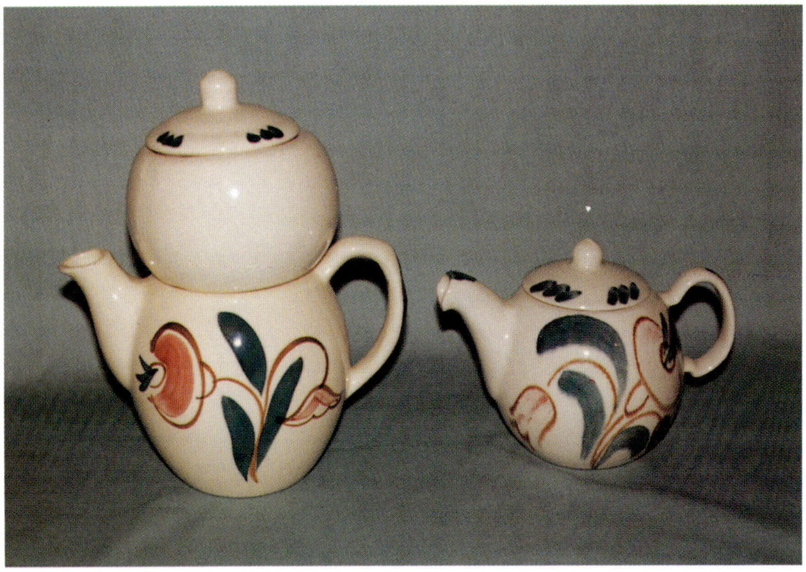

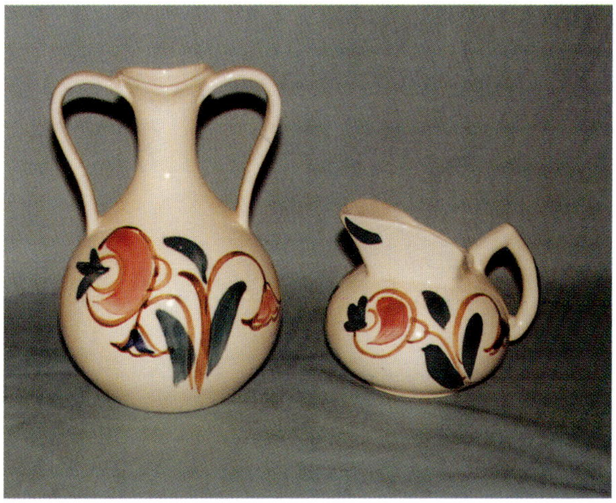

Coffee carafe. $150. Kent jug. $150.

Six cup teapot with drip filter, Shippenville mold. $150. Four cup teapot, Wellsville mold. $125.

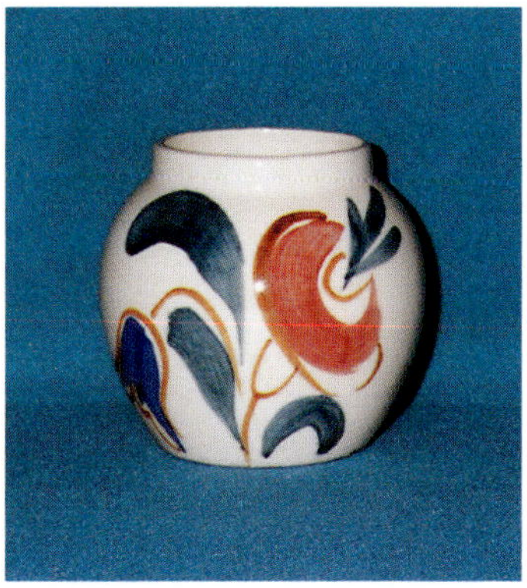

Marmalade without lid. $75. $100 with lid.

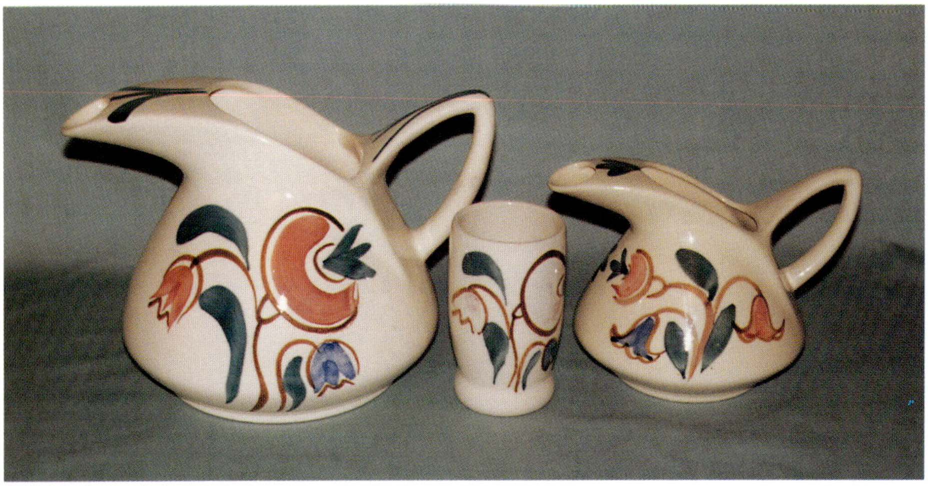

Five pint dutch jug. $200. Tumbler. $60. Two pint dutch jug. $80.

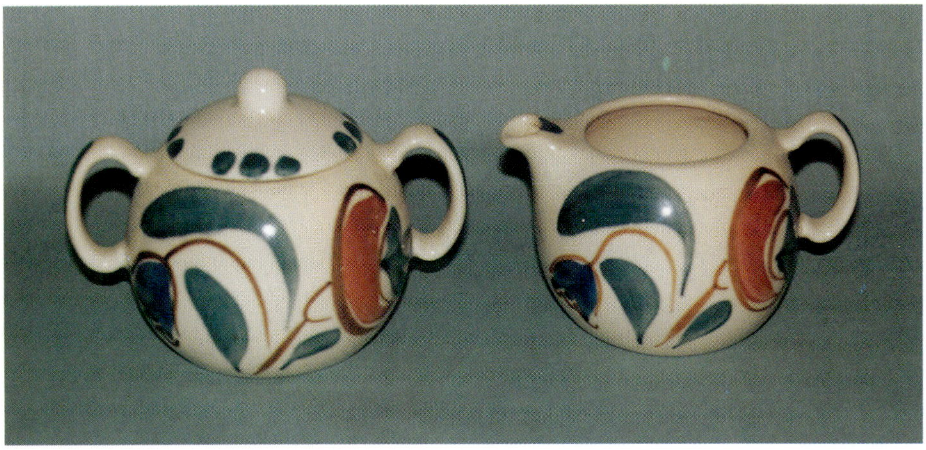

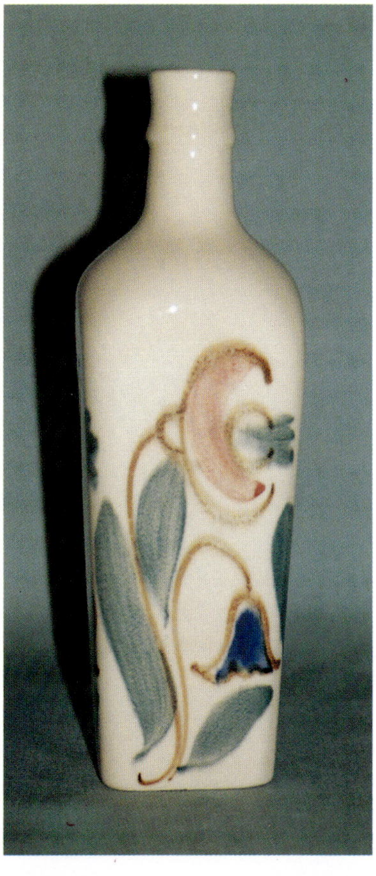

Crescent covered sugar and creamer, Wellsville style. $100 set.

Tall oil and vinegar style bottle. $100.

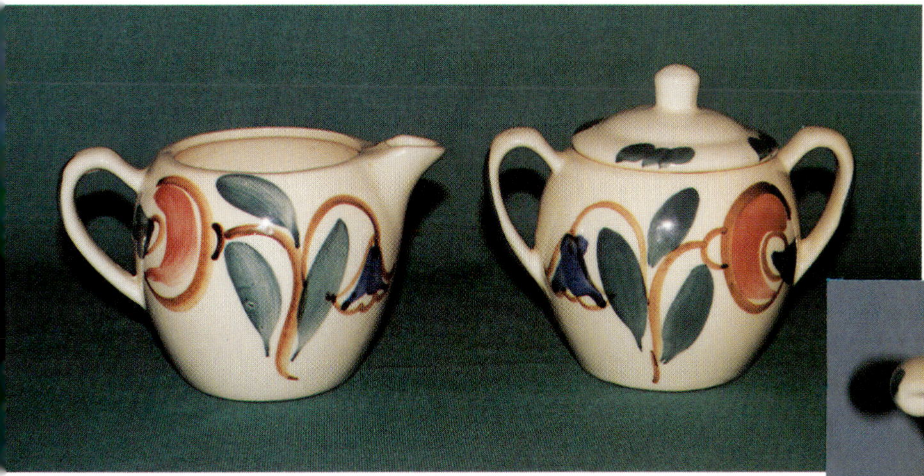

Creamer and covered sugar, the round style was most likely made in Shippenville. $75 set.

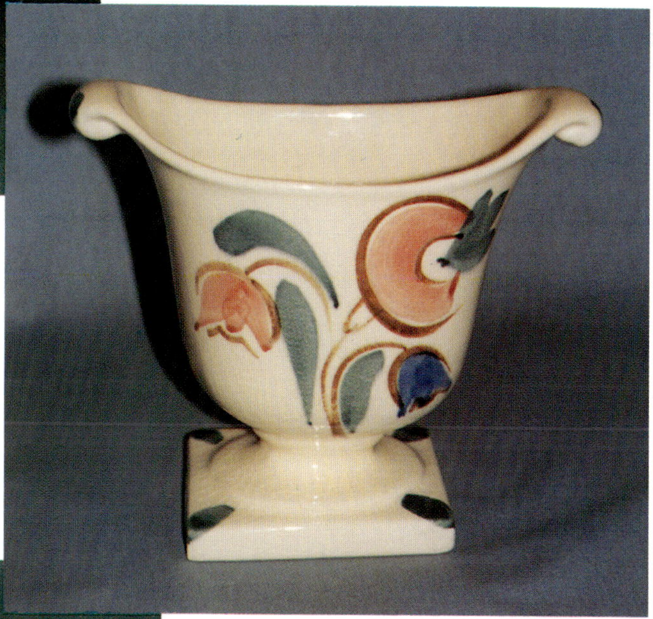

Scroll handled vase, 6" high, 7" wide. $150.

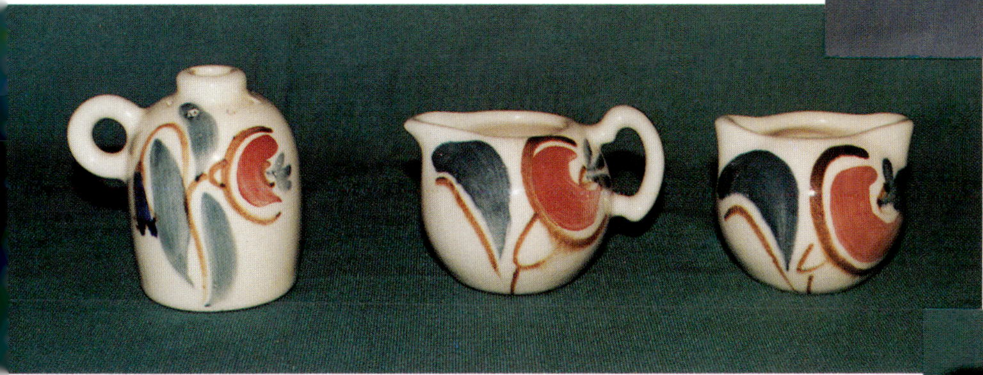

Jug style salt shaker. $40. Individual creamer and sugar. $80 set.

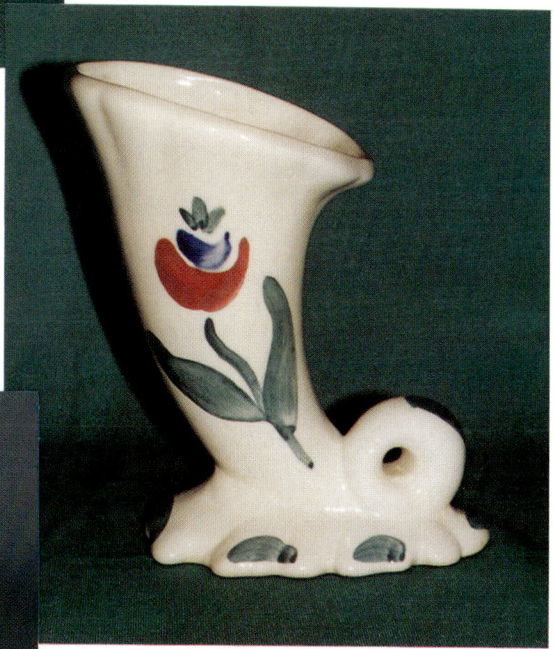

Cornucopia vase with Crescent variant decoration. $35.

Ball style salt and pepper shakers, Wellsville mold. $150 set. Coaster. $50.

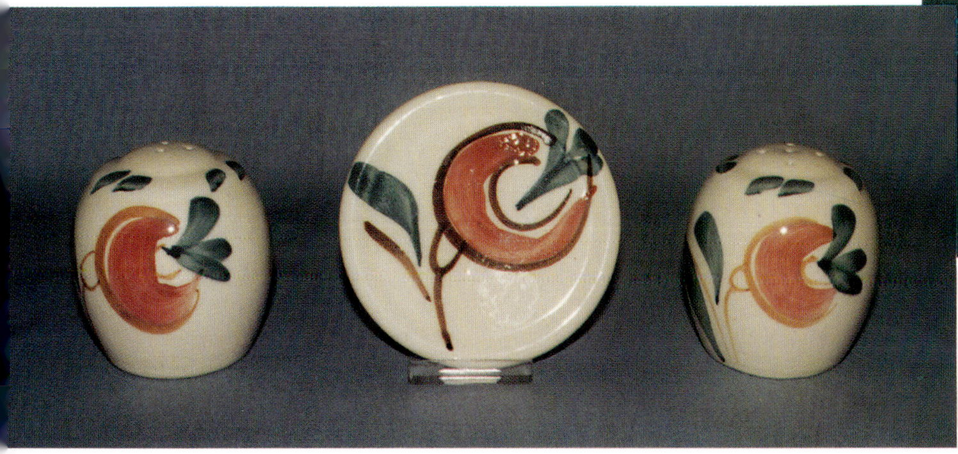

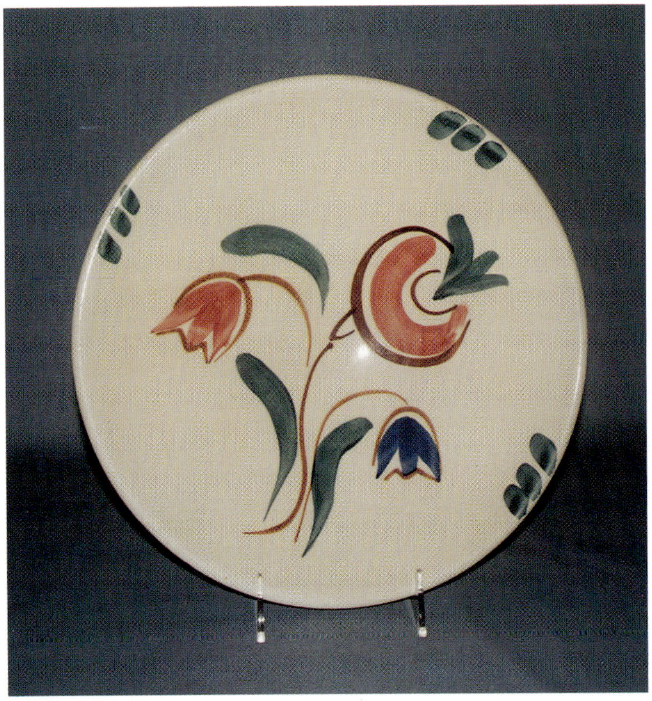

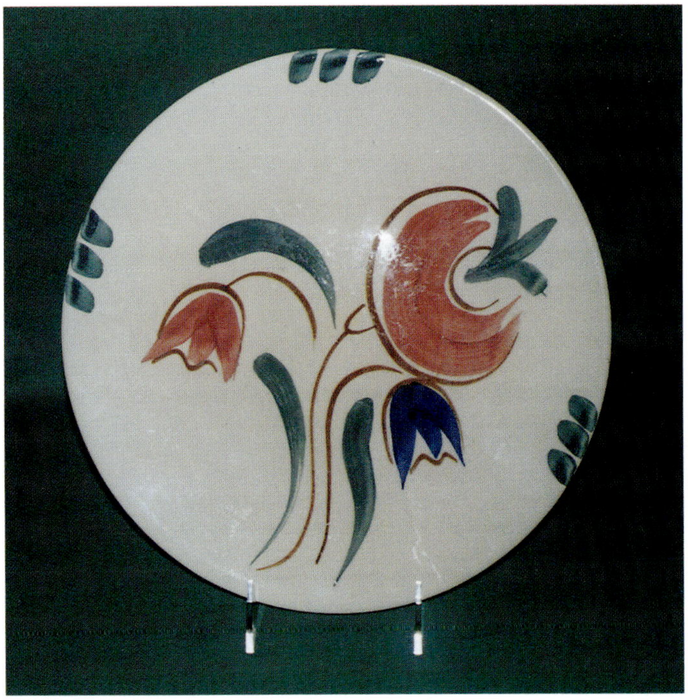

Fruit bowl. $250+.

Chop plate. $250+.

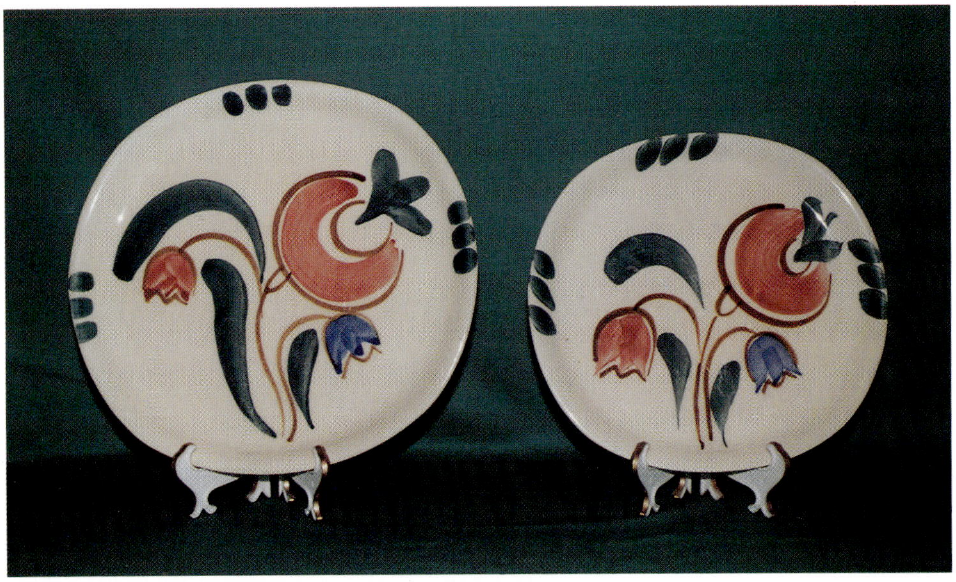

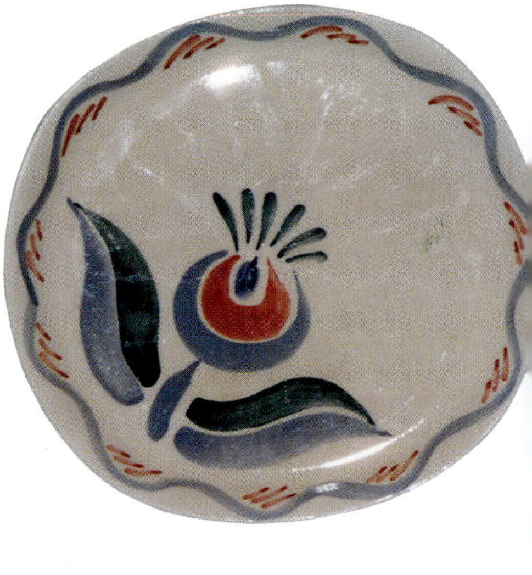

Breakfast plate, variant decoration. $80.

Dinner plate. $100. Breakfast plate. $60.

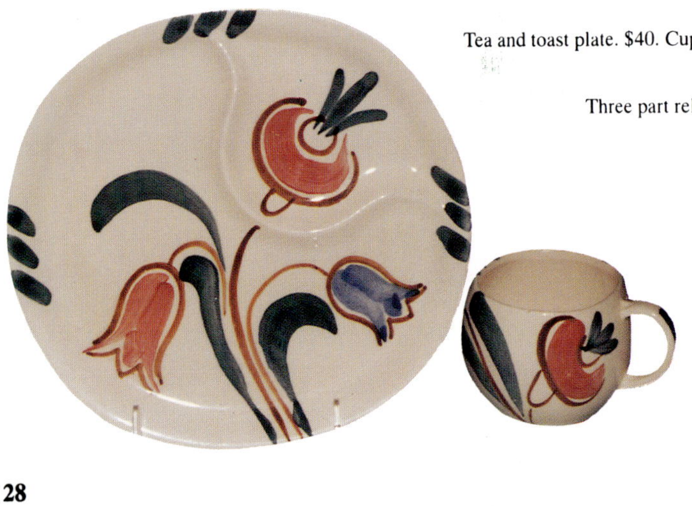

Tea and toast plate. $40. Cup. $30.

Three part relish with ceramic handle. $100.

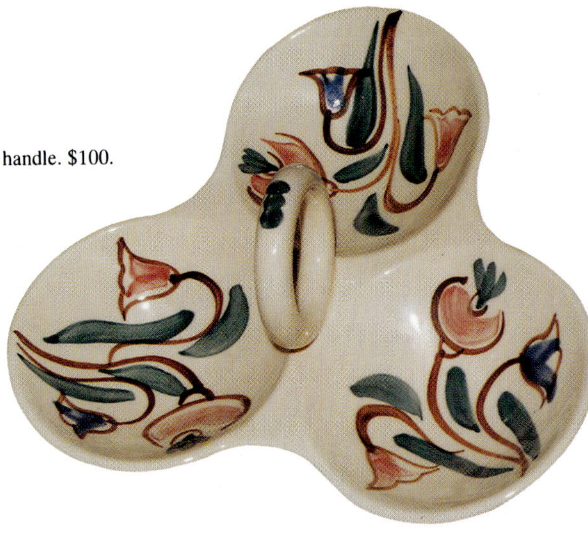

Fruit

Fruit can be considered Purinton's most versatile decoration. First developed in Wellsville and continued through the years at Shippenville, companies such as Esmond utilized a slight variation of Fruit on their contracted products. Fruit was known as D-14. In the 1950s, Provincial Fruit emerged from the old Fruit decoration and was even called "modern fruit" by the employees.

In this chapter we combine all the Fruit patterns produced at Wellsville, and Shippenville with those decorated for Esmond and Rubel (of which there are only a few Rubel examples). Most of the decoration is of the apple, pear, grapes, and pineapple variety. Cherries are also included in this chapter, but the only production piece known is on a seaform style salad plate made as a set with apple, pear, and grape decorations. We attempt to clarify and give information with each picture in this chapter to disseminate the diverse Fruit history.

Fruit is plentiful and the demand for it is not high. The Wellsville Fruit items command the highest price, with the oasis jug and oasis cookie jug being the rarest. Breakfast size plates are difficult to find. Tea and toast plates are more common. Wellsville style marmalades are difficult to find and should have a lid to bring the best price. Cups for the Fruit pattern are plain. They have a scalloped turquoise decoration outlined in brown around the edge of the cup. These cups are harder to find items. Teapots in the Wellsville mold command a higher price than those made in Shippenville.

Of all the Fruit items made, among the most difficult to find are the dinner plates. Fruit was not made into a dinnerware line. Some individual dinner plates do exist, but no other dinnerware pieces are known. As mentioned before, breakfast size plates were made in Wellsville for their salad set. You can tell these because of their more primitive decoration. Some experimental plates have surfaced with the Esmond fruit which is more stylized and defined in its painting.

In the Fruit pattern the beverage pitcher is not common and the oversized kent jug, a bulbous pitcher, is a rare item. Fruit was probably phased out of the product line in the late 1940s when the pattern was being used by the Esmond contract. Prices for Fruit made at Shippenville are not strong, but it may be a sleeper as more people are beginning to appreciate Fruit's country look.

A variety of items made for Esmond was painted in the Fruit motif. As a decorative motif, Esmond's Fruit is a little more stylistic and defined. The best known Esmond piece is probably the four-section revolving canister. Purinton made this item for Esmond, but it was Purinton's design mold. This product is probably the most common of Esmond items. Contrary to some stories, the miniature four-section revolving canister was not a salesman's sample. It was was sold as a production piece and was probably meant to contain spices. The miniature set commands one of the higher prices for Esmond pieces. Some Purinton items, such as the honey jug, are decorated with the Esmond Fruit and demand a higher price.

For the apple decoration clarification, the apple used in the Fruit decoration is painted solid and is sometimes called a closed apple. The Apple pattern is identified as an apple painted with a red border with yellow and brown highlights inside it and is sometimes called an open apple. In this chapter we included some patterns that have the "Apple" apple decoration combined with a pear or other fruit. Some of these items may have been experimental and not production pieces, but we try to clarify that in the captions.

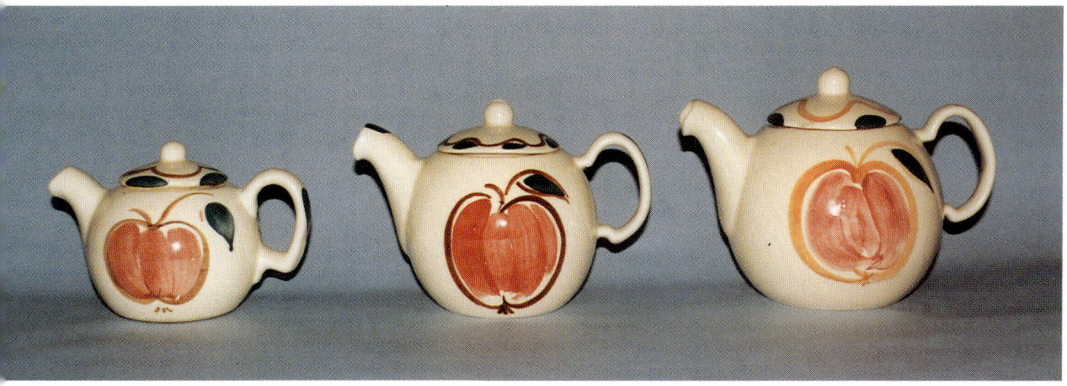

Wellsville style teapot, Fruit (apple) decoration: two cup teapot $25; four cup teapot $40; six cup teapot. $60. The pear side of these teapots is illustrated later in this chapter.

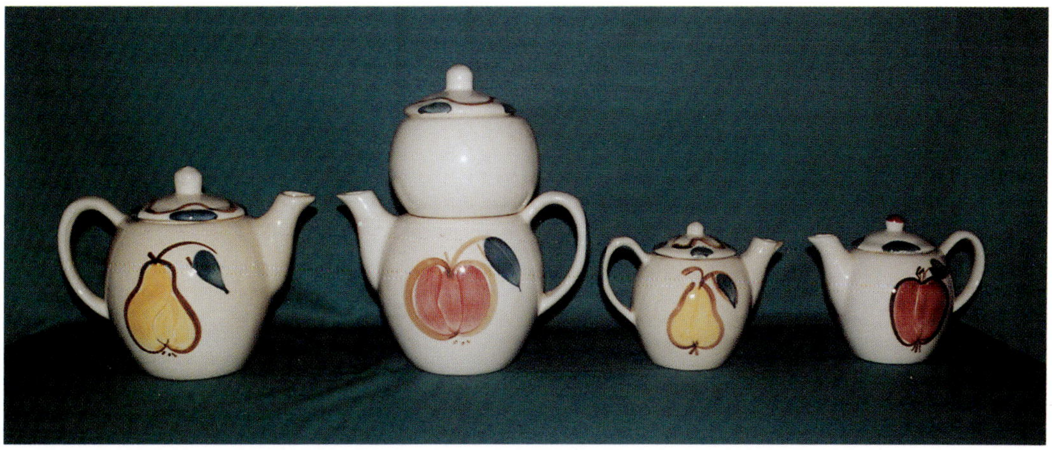

These are the teapot styles that were predominantly made at the Shippenville plant. In this text, these are simply referred to as teapots. Six cup teapot. $15. Six cup teapot with drip filter. $45. Two cup teapots. $15 each.

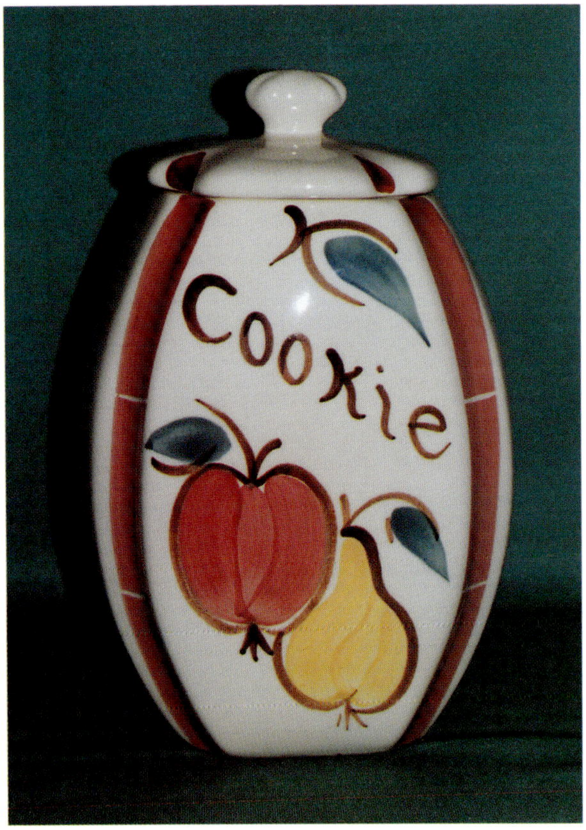

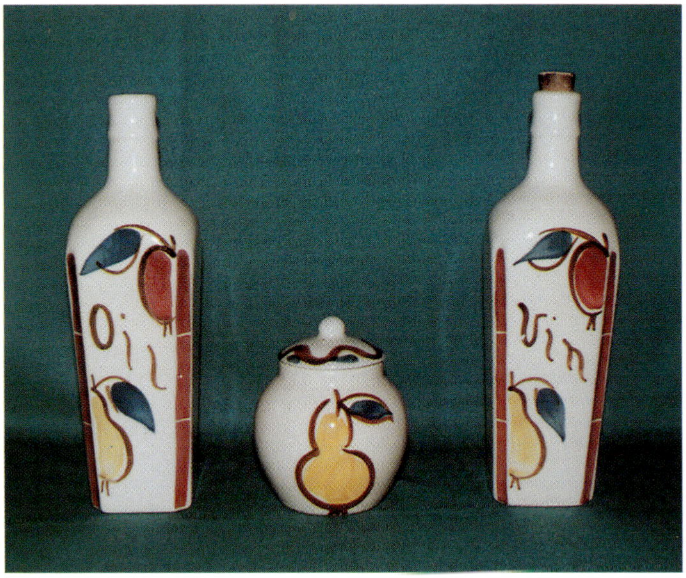

Tall oil and vinegar. $40 set. Marmalade, pear, Wellsville item. $100.

Tall oval cookie canister with red trim. $40.

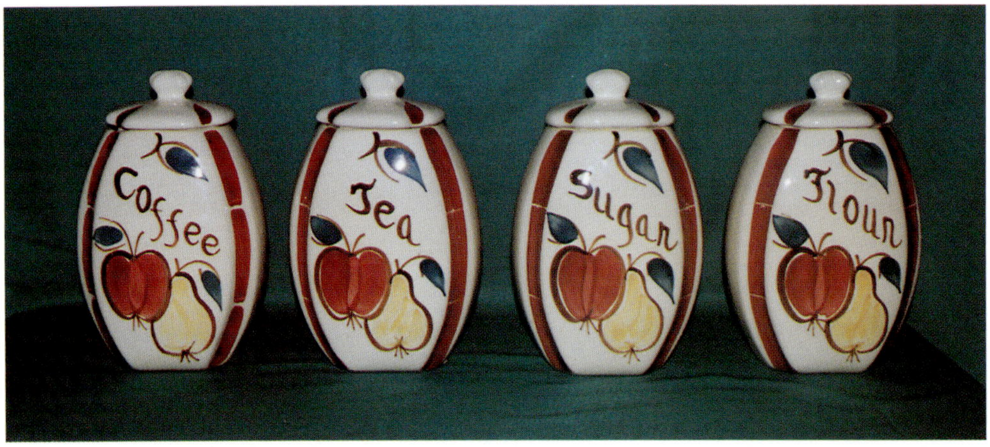

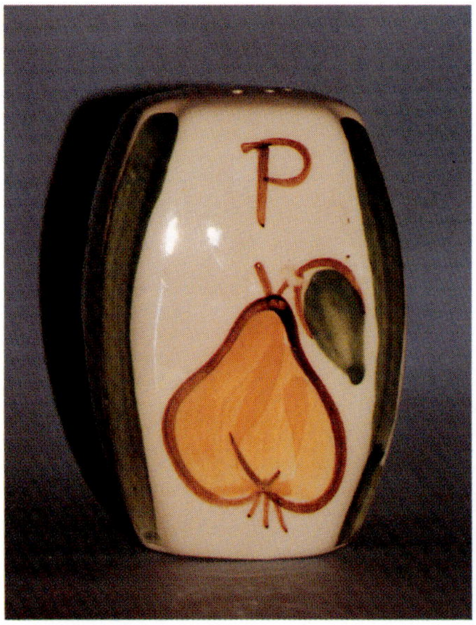

Tall oval four piece canister set with red trim. $25 each.

Range pepper with green trim. $50. This color of trim was NOT a production color.

Tall oval four piece canister set with cobalt trim. $25 each.

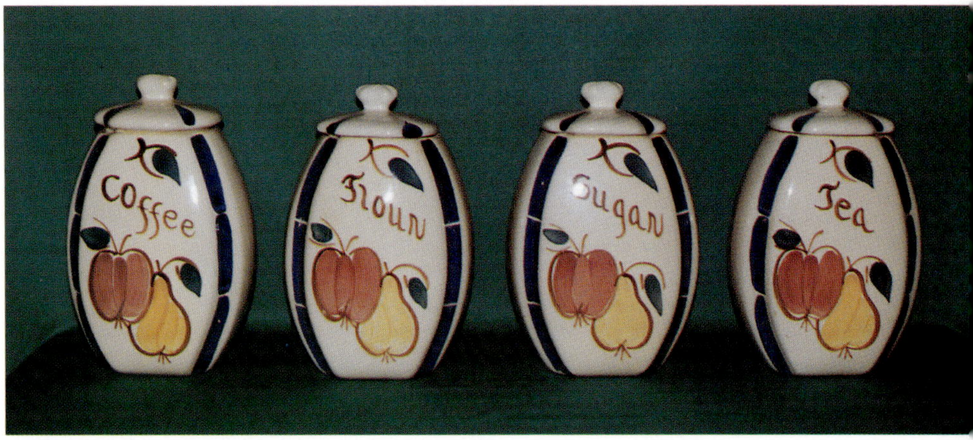

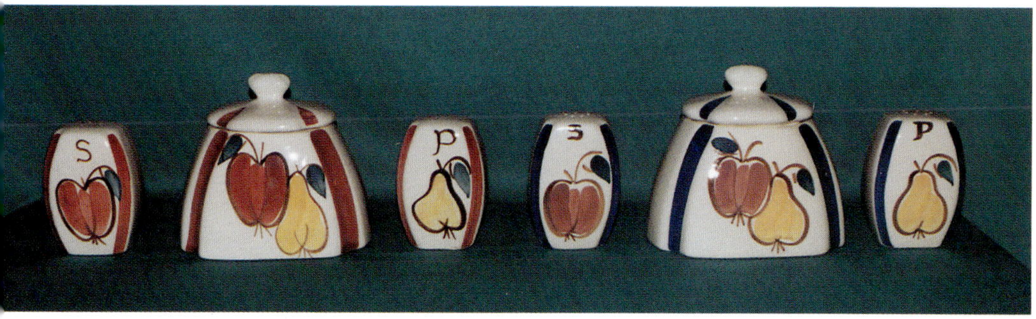

Range salt and pepper shakers with red trim. $30 set. Range grease jar with red trim. $25. Range salt and pepper shakers with cobalt trim. $30 set. Range grease jar with cobalt trim. $25.

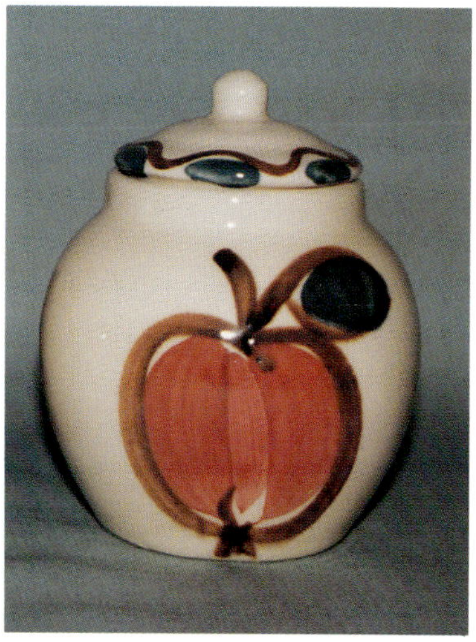

Marmalade, apple, Wellsville item. $100.

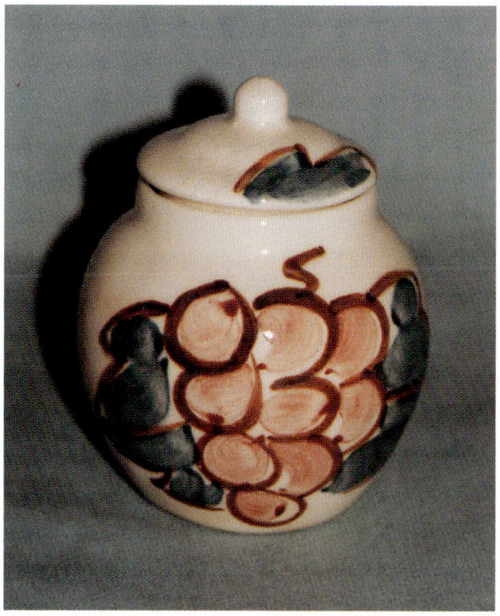

Marmalade, grapes, Wellsville item. $100.

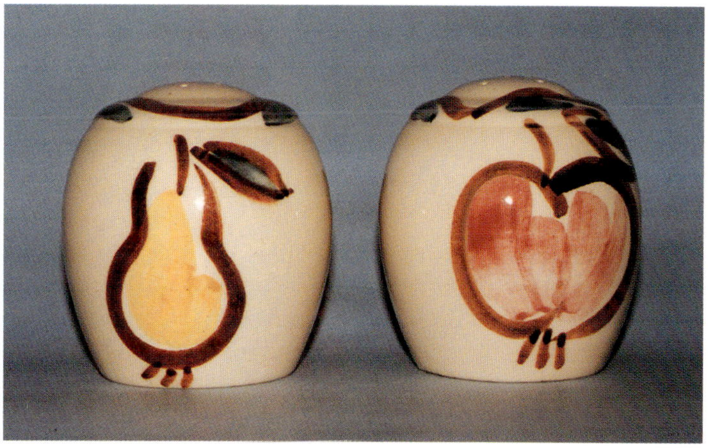

Salt and pepper shakers, ball style, Wellsville item. $150+.

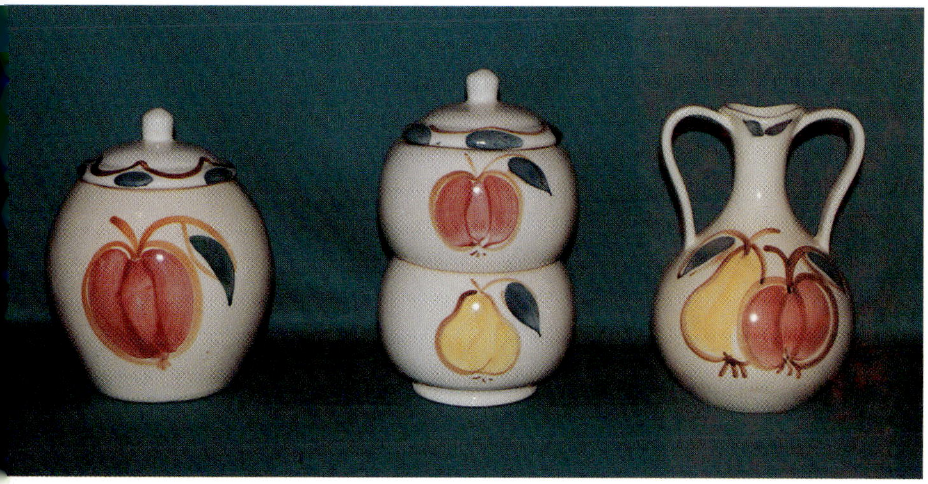

Biscuit jar. $45. Stacking storage jars. $30 set. Coffee carafe, Wellsville item. $100.

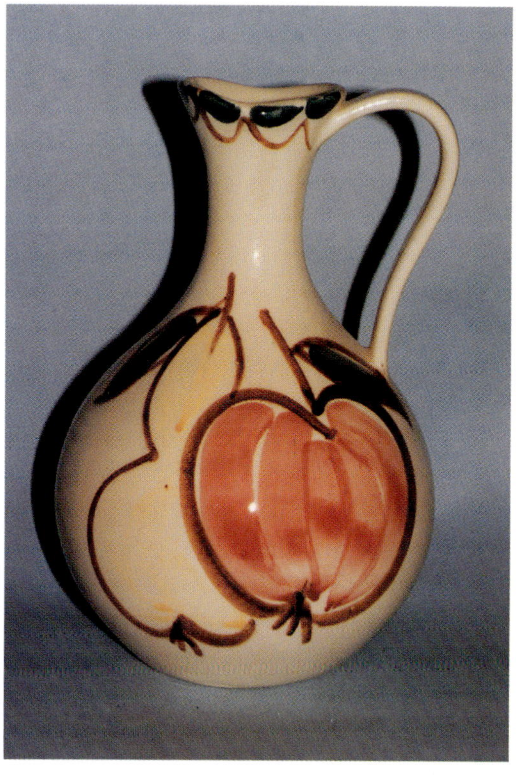

One-handled decanter, Wellsville item. $150. The one-handled decanter is harder to find than the two-handled decanter.

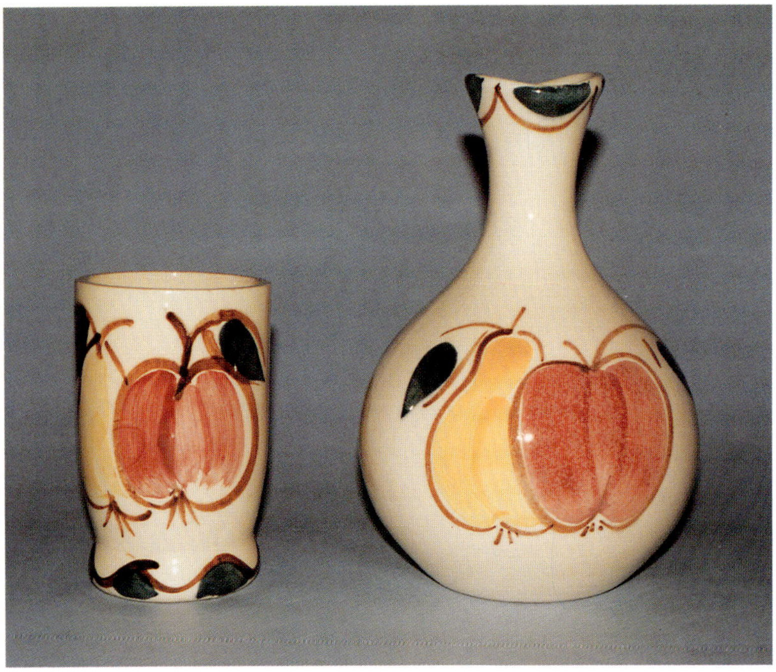

Tumbler. $10. Night bottle. $30.

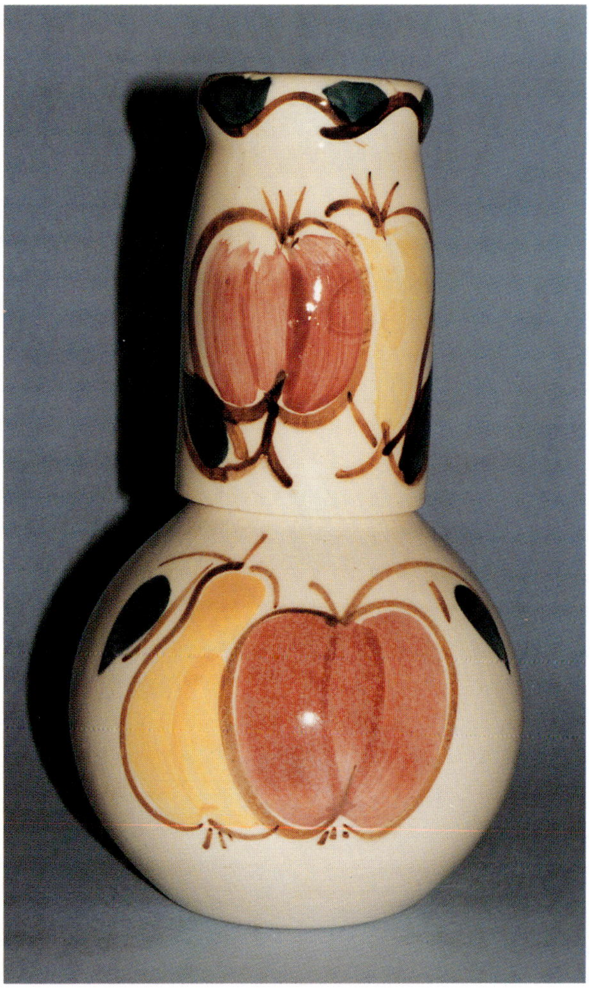

Night bottle with tumbler inverted on top.

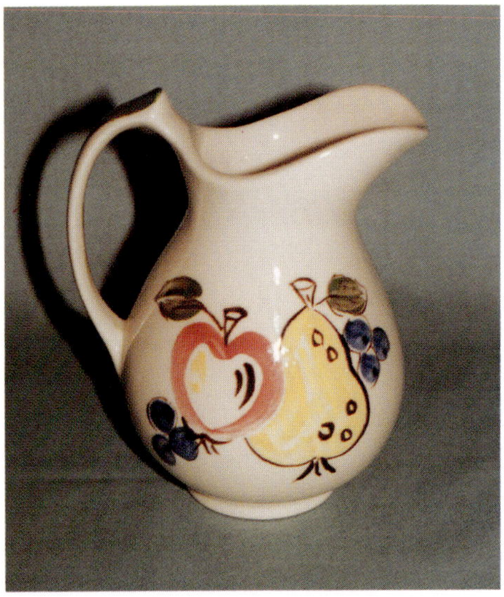

Pitcher, 5" high. Experimental. $75.

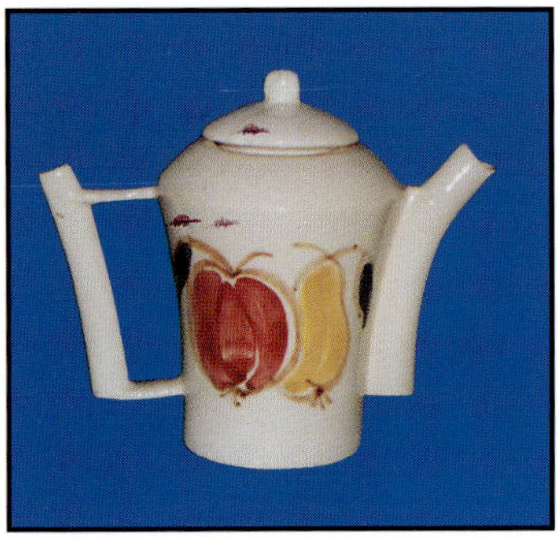

Two cup teapot, Taylor Smith Taylor mold, 5.75" high. $75.

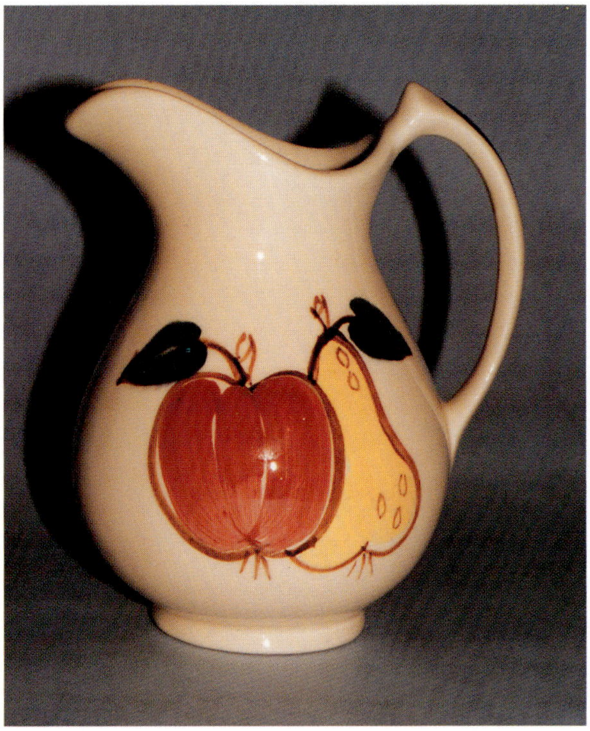

Pitcher, 5.5" high. $50.

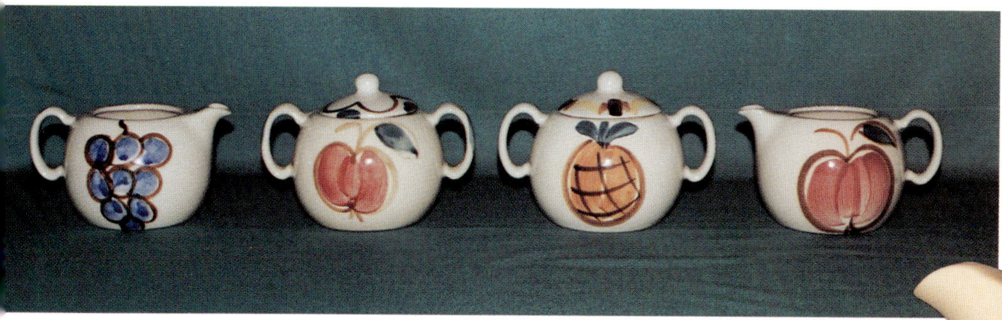

Creamer and covered sugar sets, Wellsville items. (Note: the pineapple sugar has the wrong lid. The correct lid is pictured on the other sugar in the photo.) $40 set.

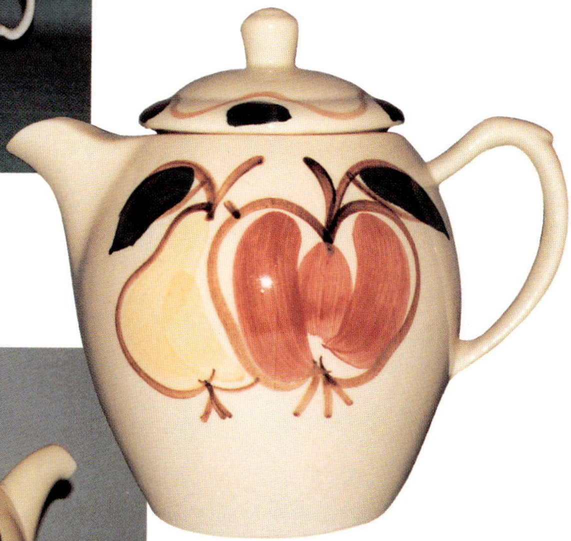

Eight cup coffee pot. Probably a Wellsville item with apple and pear decoration on both sides. $75.

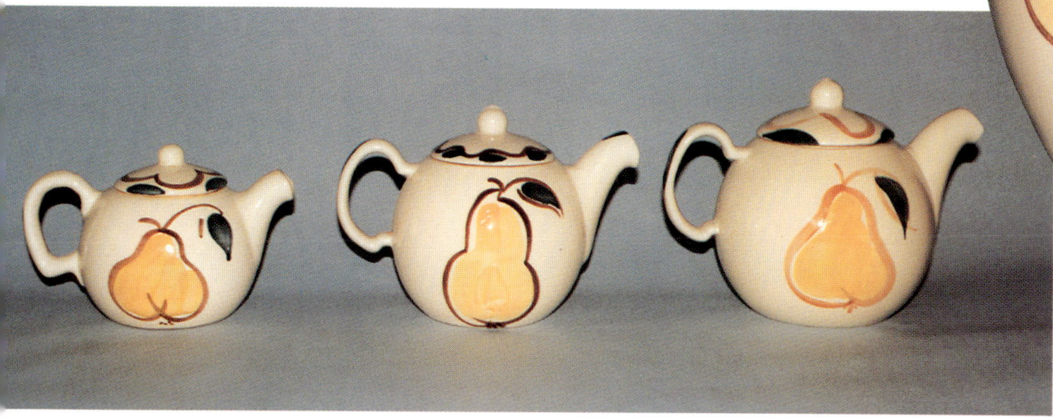

Pear decoration: two cup teapot, Wellsville style, $25; four cup teapot, Wellsville style, $40; six cup teapot, Wellsville style. $60. The apple side of these teapots is illustrated at the beginning of the Fruit chapter.

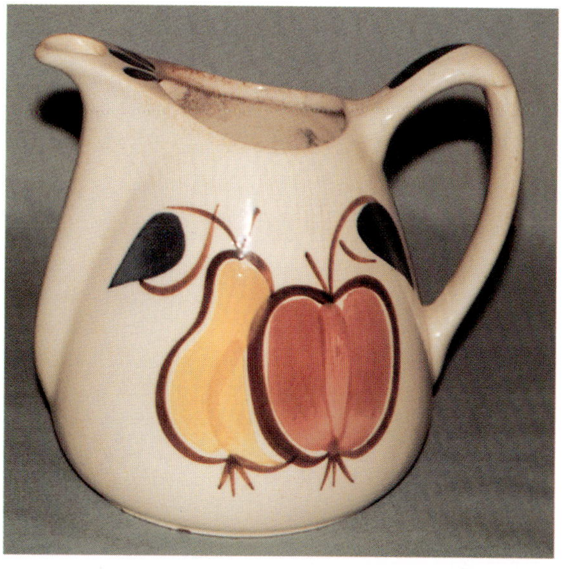

Beverage pitcher. $50.

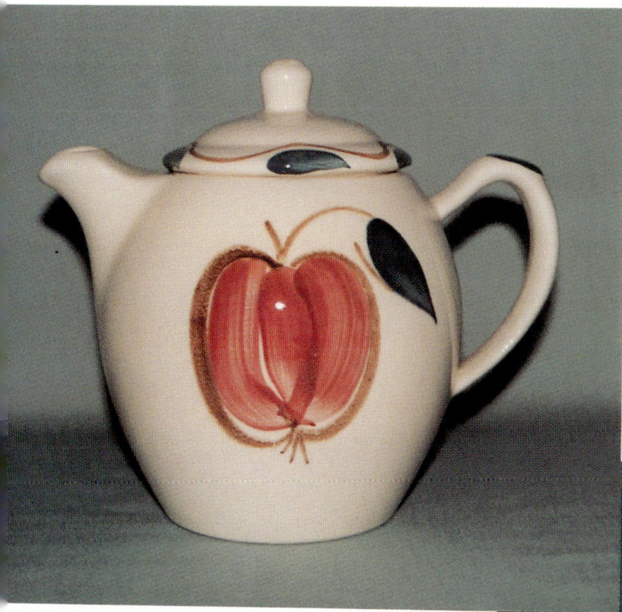

Eight cup coffee pot. $40.

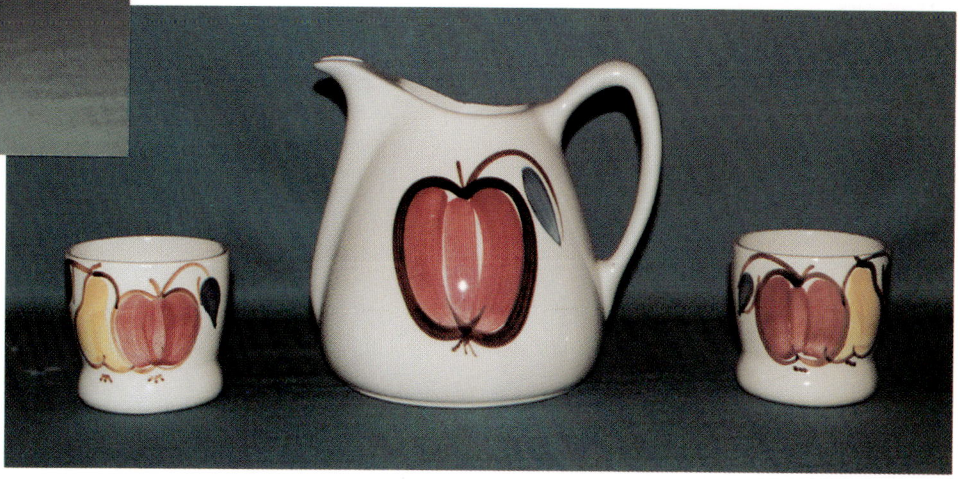

Juice mug. $10. Beverage pitcher. $50.

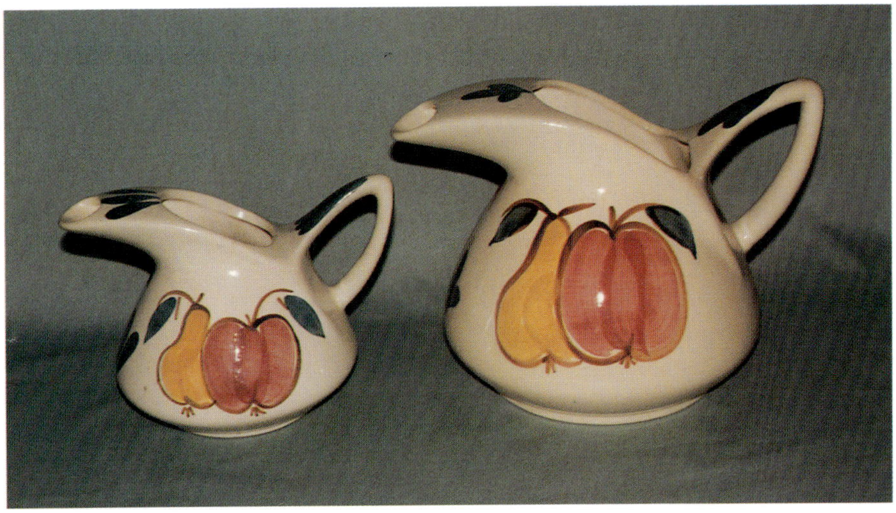

Two pint dutch jug. $25. Five pint dutch jug. $35.

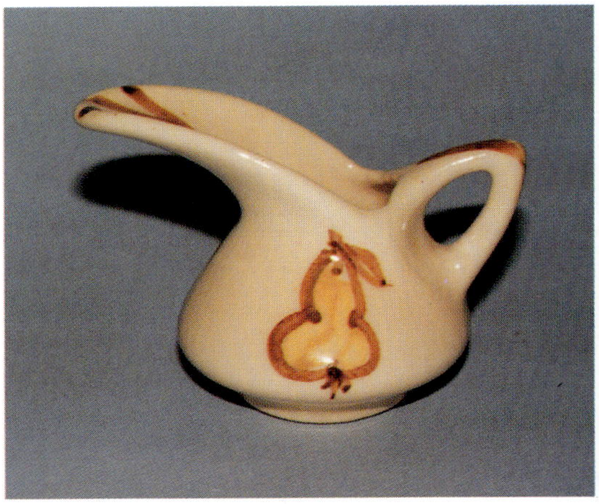

Jigger jug with pear decoration. $35.

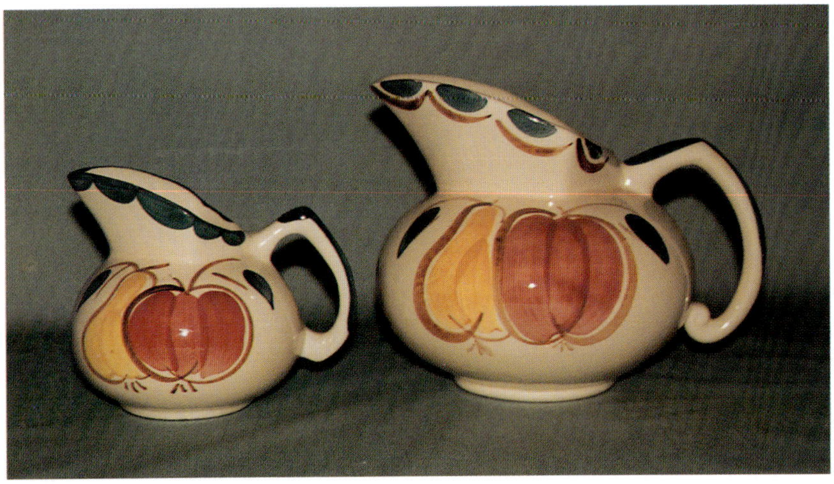

Kent jug, 4.5" high. $15. Oversized kent jug, 6.25" high, rare. $125.

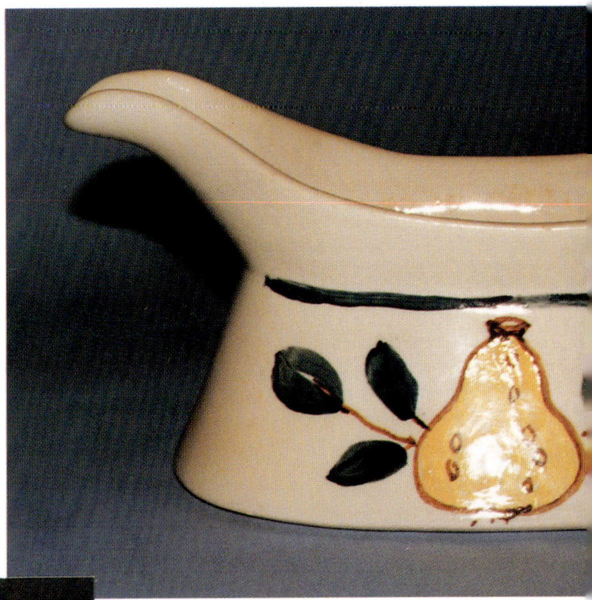

Gravy boat, reverse side with pear decoration.

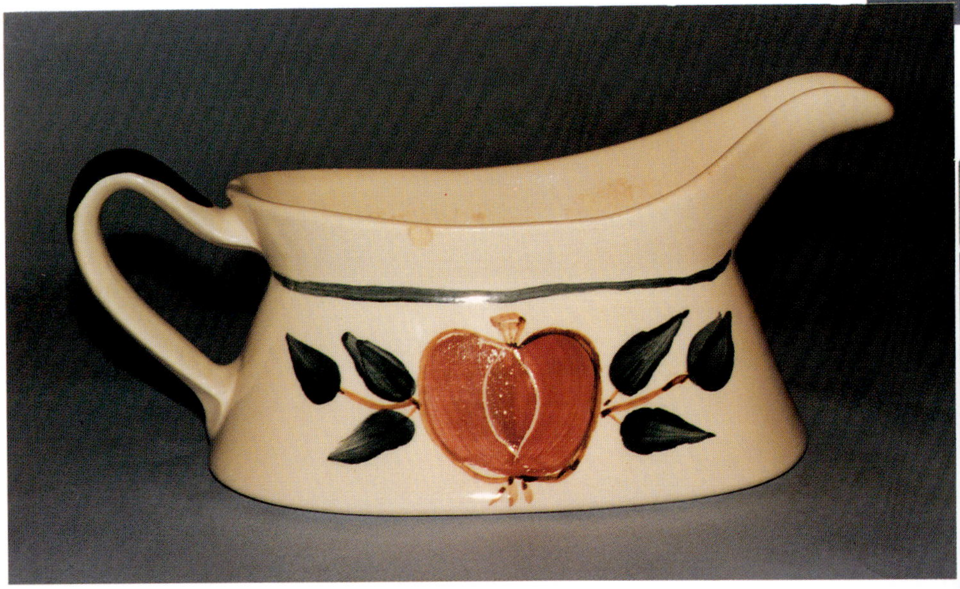

Gravy boat, Taylor Smith Taylor mold, apple decoration. $100+.

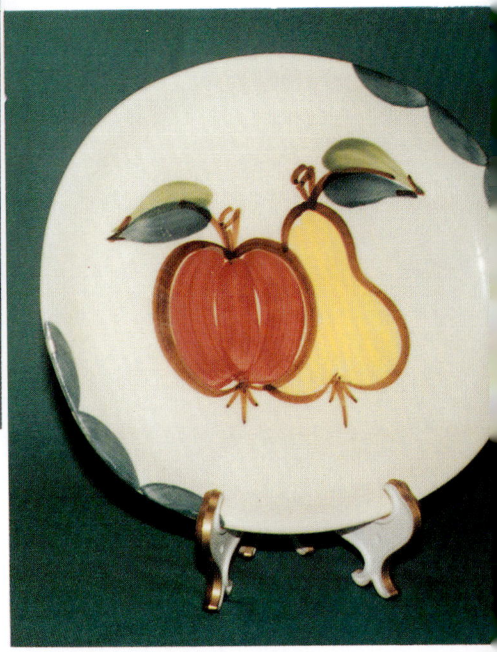

Salad plate, experimental. $75.

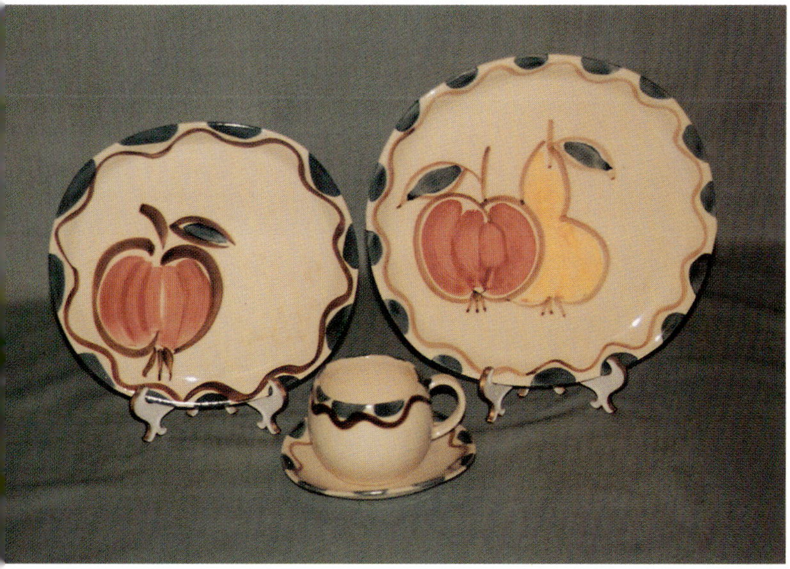

Breakfast plate, apple decoration, Wellsville item. $75. Cup. $25. Saucer. $10.
Dinner plate (rare). $100+.

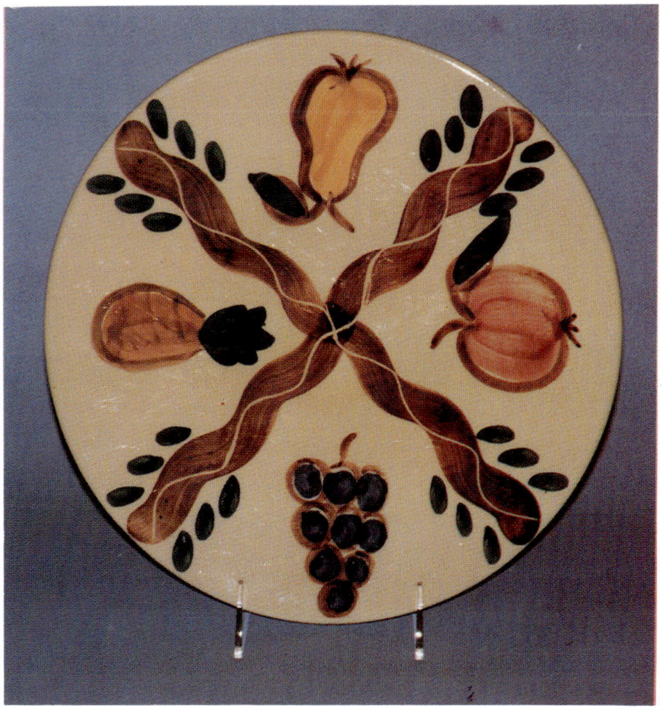

Chop plate. $30.

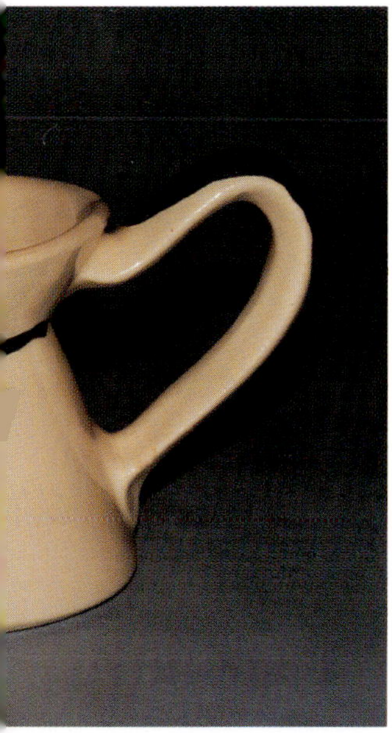

Coasters. $40 each.

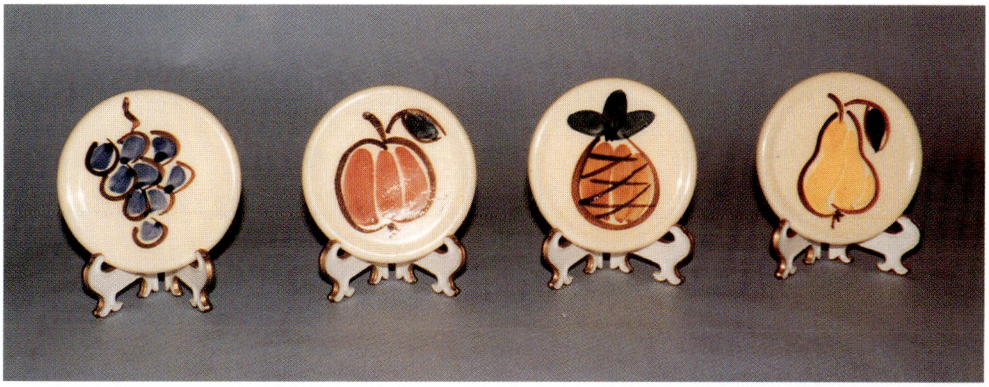

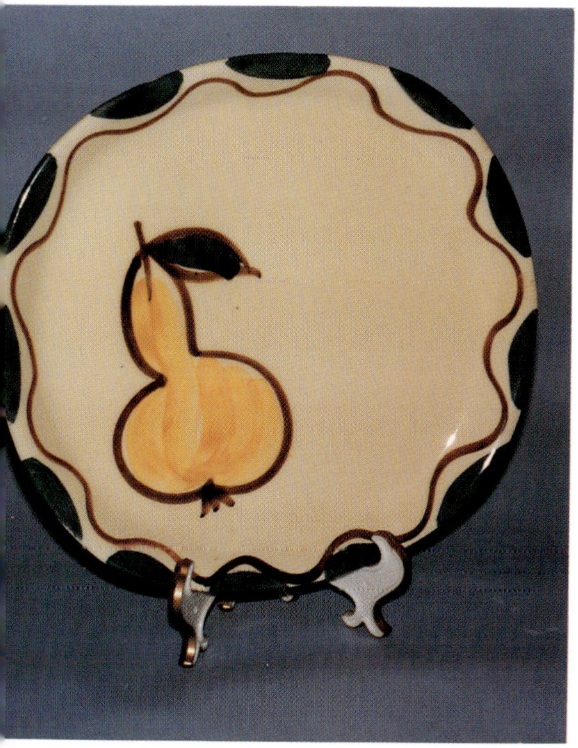

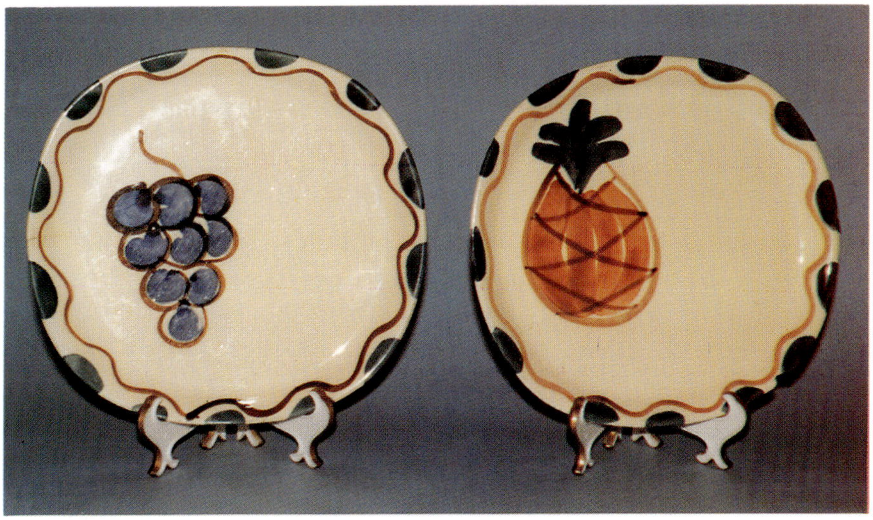

Breakfast plate, grapes decoration, Wellsville item. $75. Breakfast plate, pineapple decoration, Wellsville item. $75.

Breakfast plate, pear decoration, Wellsville item. $75.

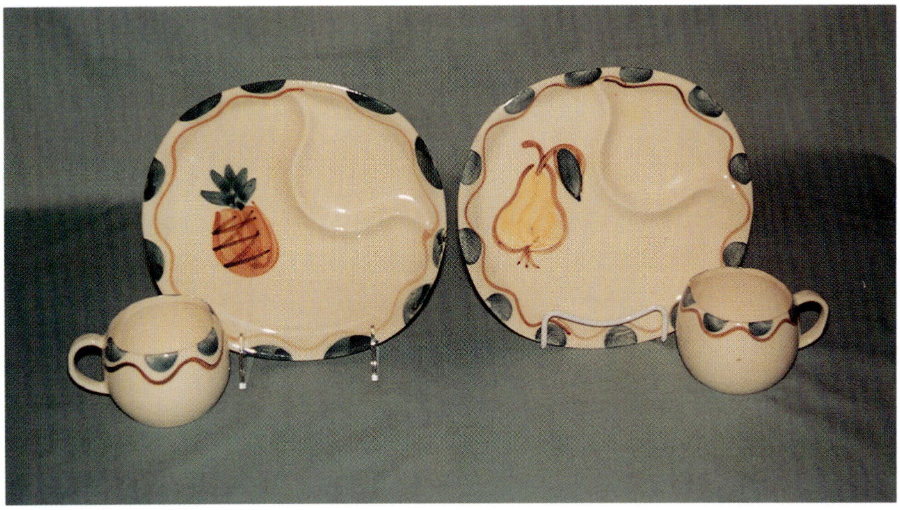

Tea and toast plates. $40 each. Cups. $25 each.

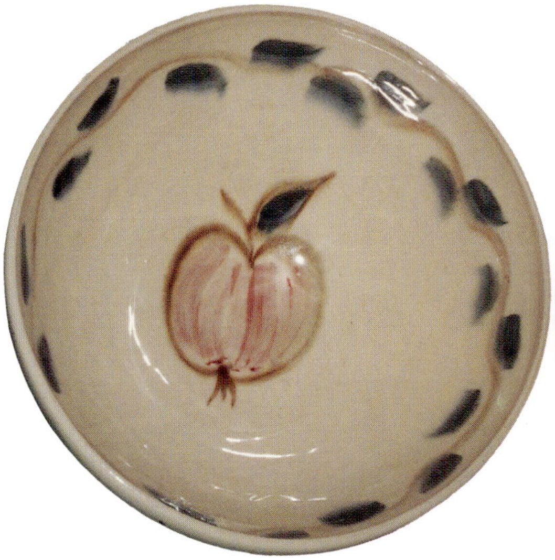

Punch bowl, Wellsville item. Top view.

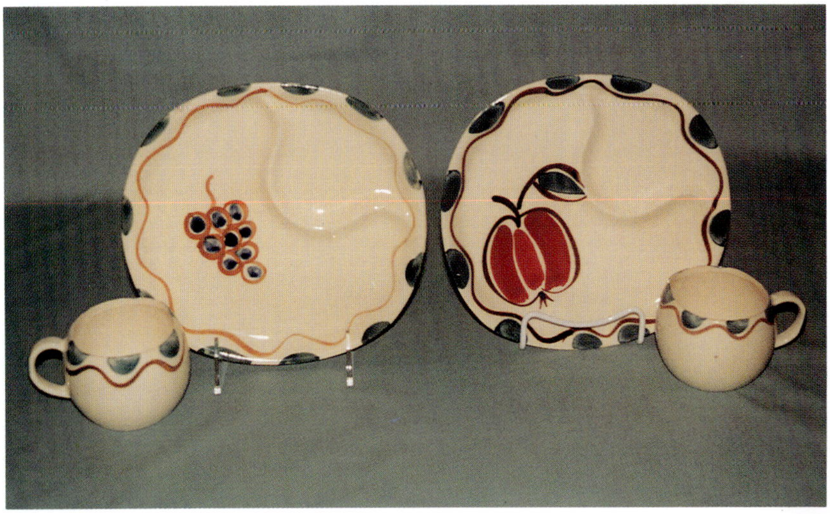

Tea and toast plates. $40 each. Cups. $25 each.

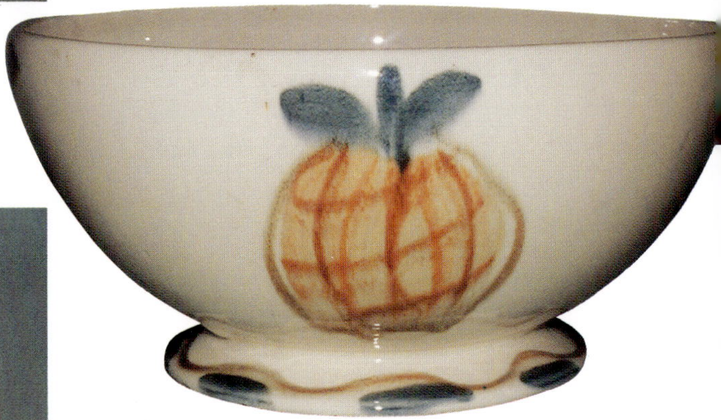

Punch bowl, Wellsville item. $150.

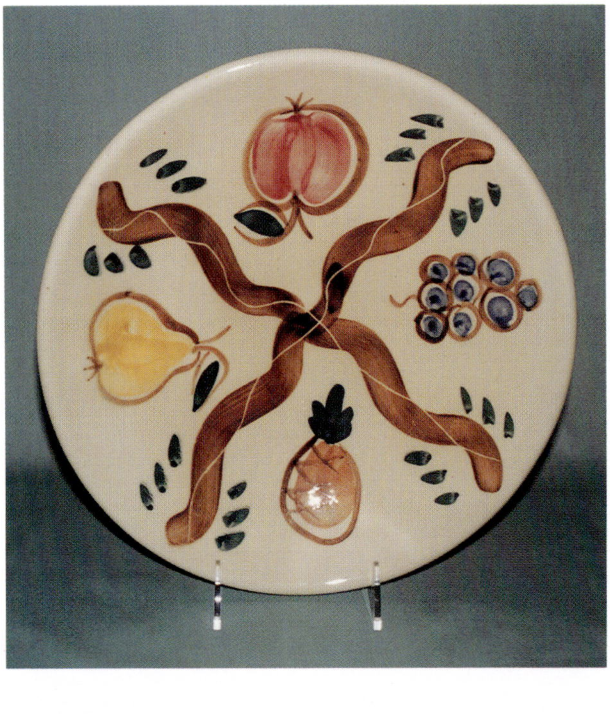

Fruit bowl. $30.

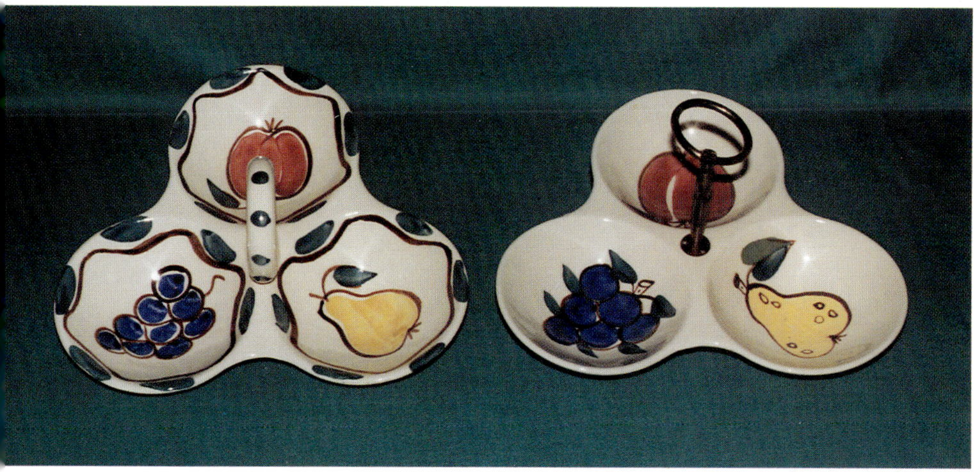

Three part relish with ceramic ring handle. $25. Three part relish with metal handle, Esmond. $25.

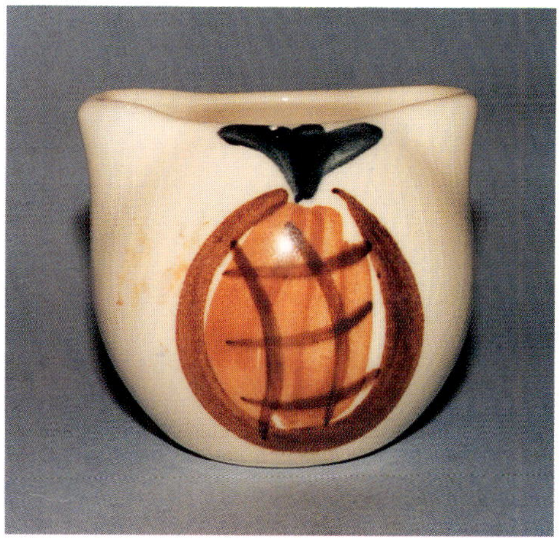

Individual sugar with uncommon pineapple decoration. $20.

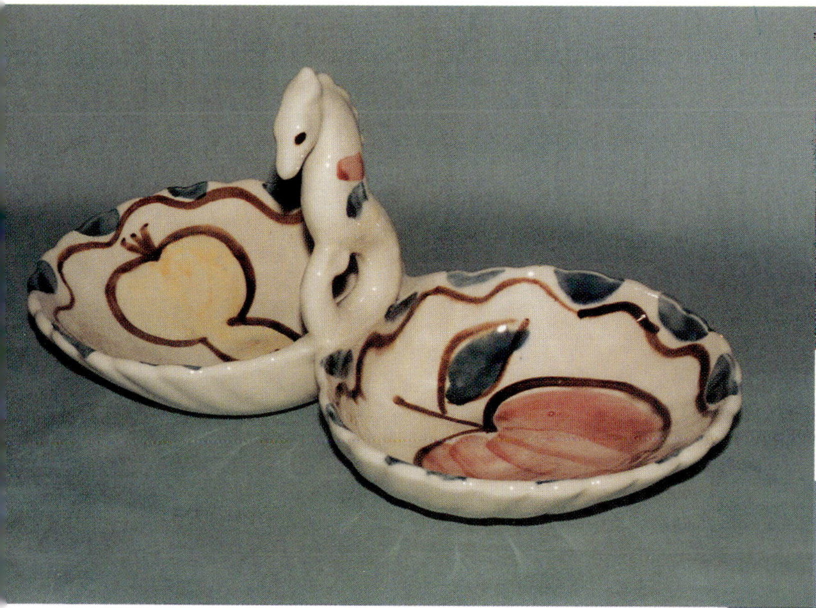

Seahorse cocktail dish, Wellsville item. $100.

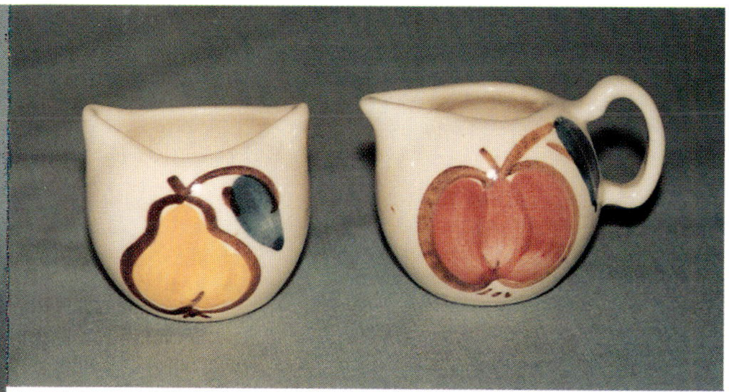

Individual sugar and creamer. $20 set.

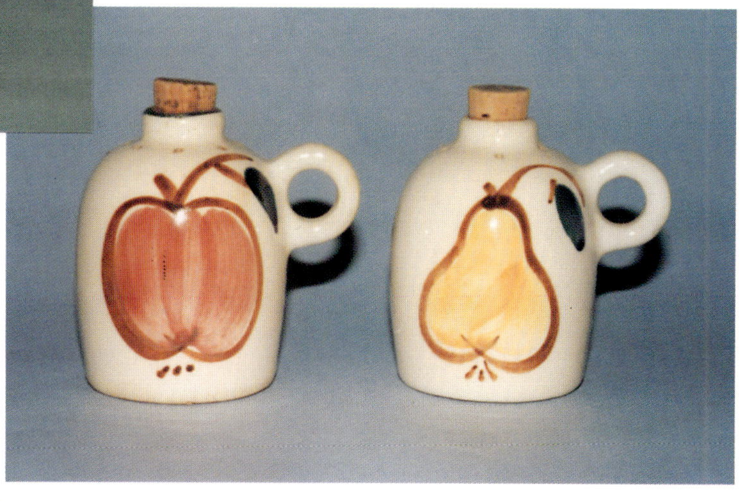

Jug style salt and pepper shakers. These shakers are not labeled salt or pepper; the difference between them is the green slip painted around the neck of the left shaker. $15 set.

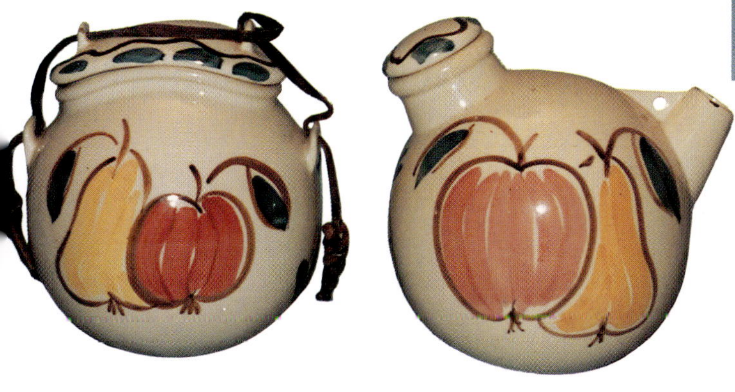

Oasis cookie jug, Wellsville item. $900+. Oasis jug. $750+.

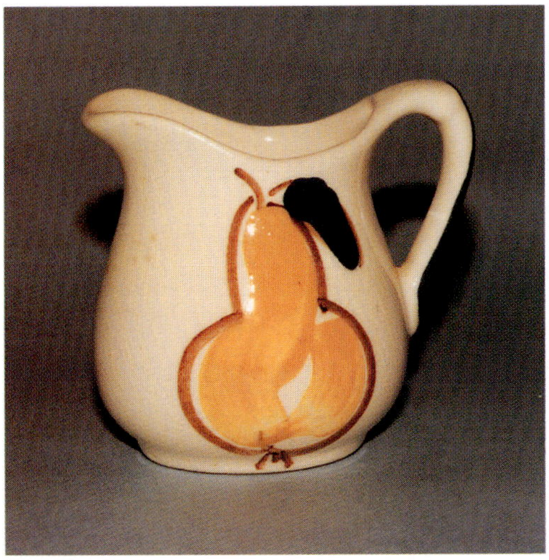

Miniature pitcher with pear decoration. $35.

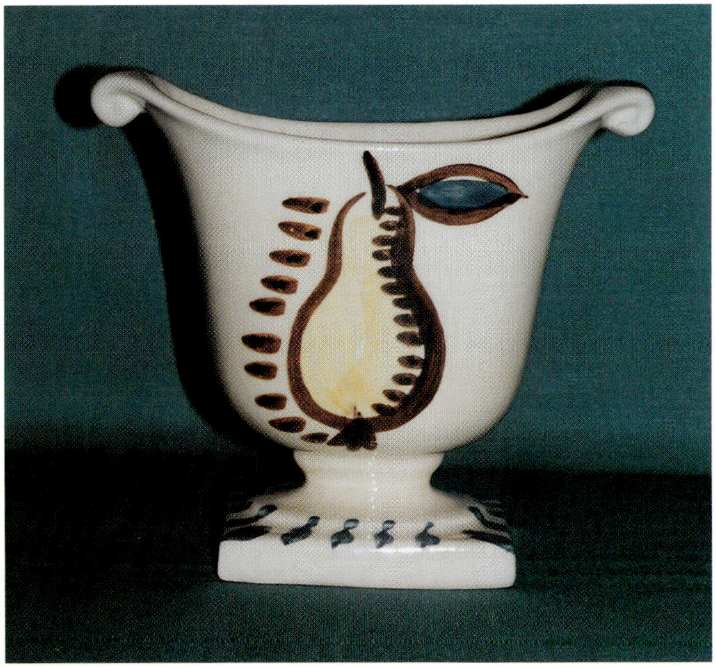

Scroll handled vase, 6" high, 7" wide, Wellsville item. $125+.

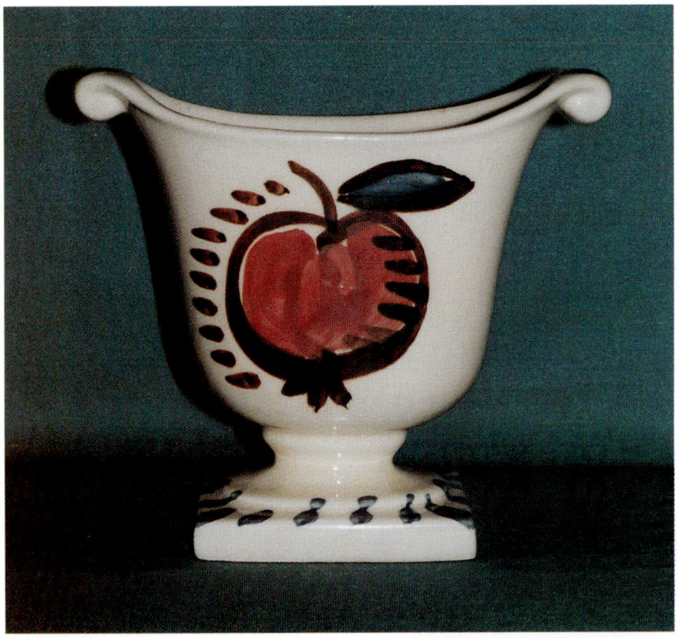

Reverse side of scroll handled vase.

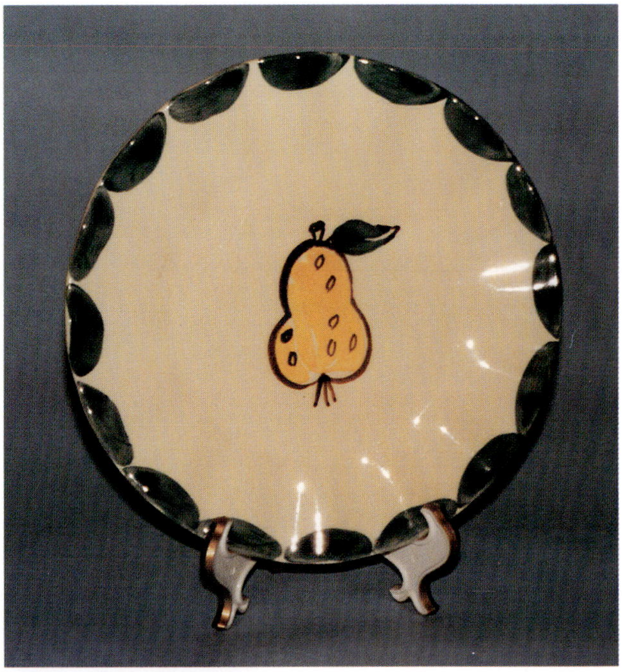

Salad plate, Seaform style, Esmond pear decoration. $90.

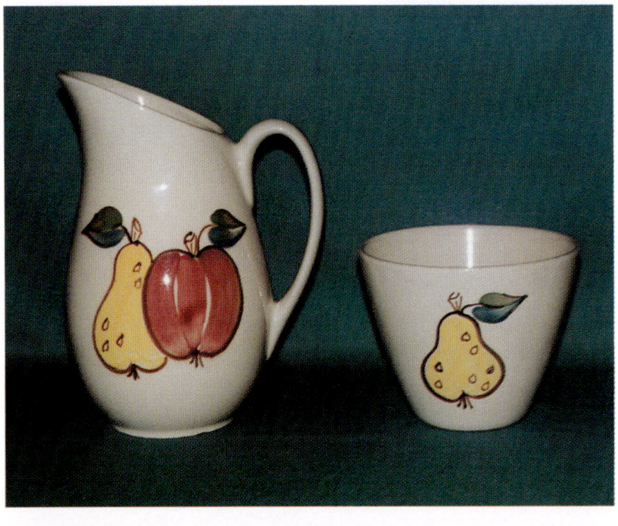

Milk pitcher, Esmond mold. $75. Bowl. $20.

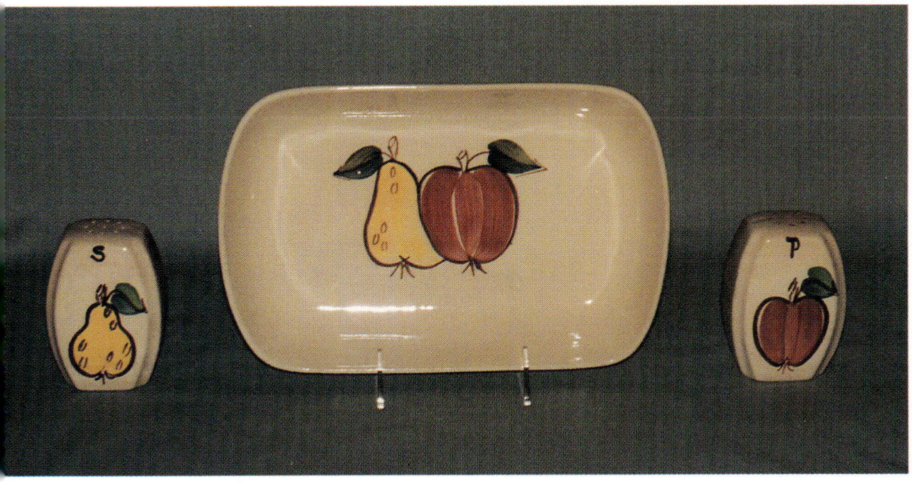

Range salt and pepper shakers. $30 set. Roll tray. $40. This set is decorated with the Esmond style of the Fruit decoration.

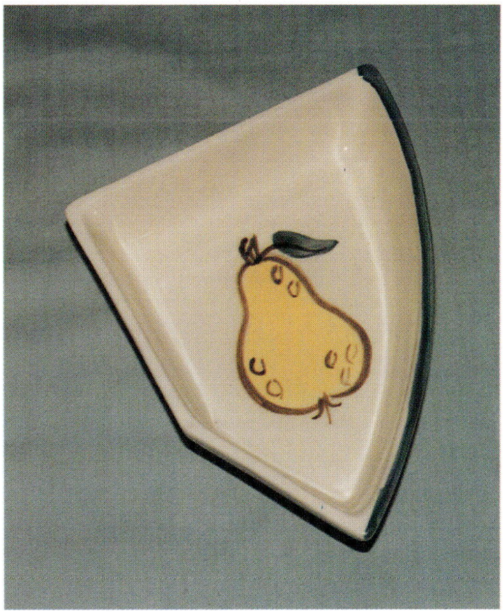

Relish section, may be part of a lazy susan set, possibly Rubel. $15.

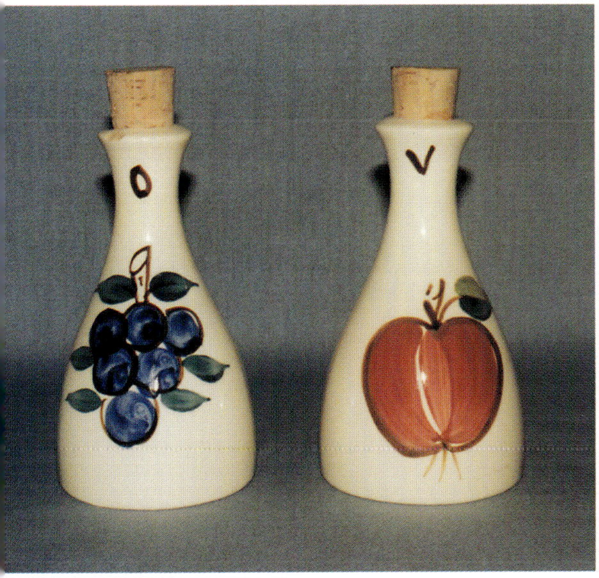

Oil and vinegar. $30 set.

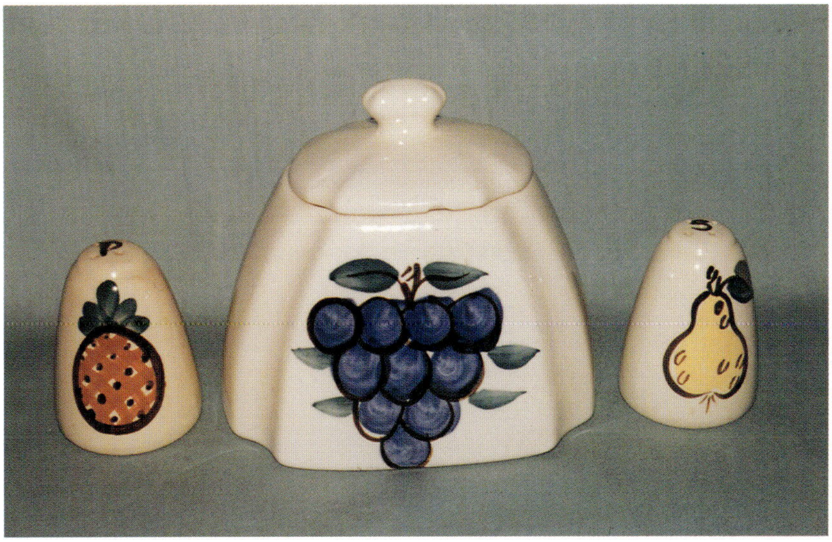

Cone salt and pepper shakers. $25 set. Range covered grease jar. $25.

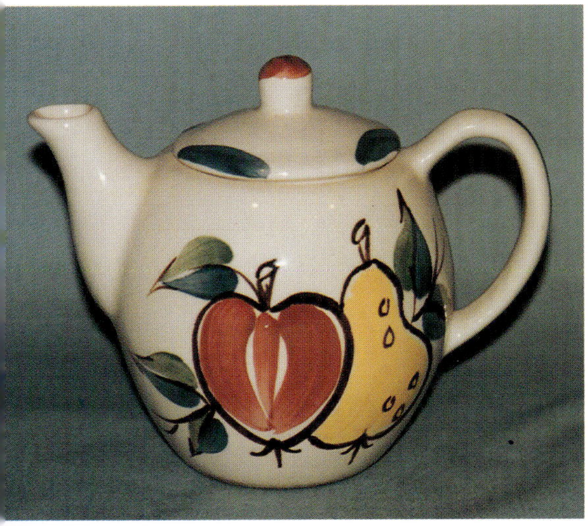

Six cup teapot, unusual design on this style. $60.

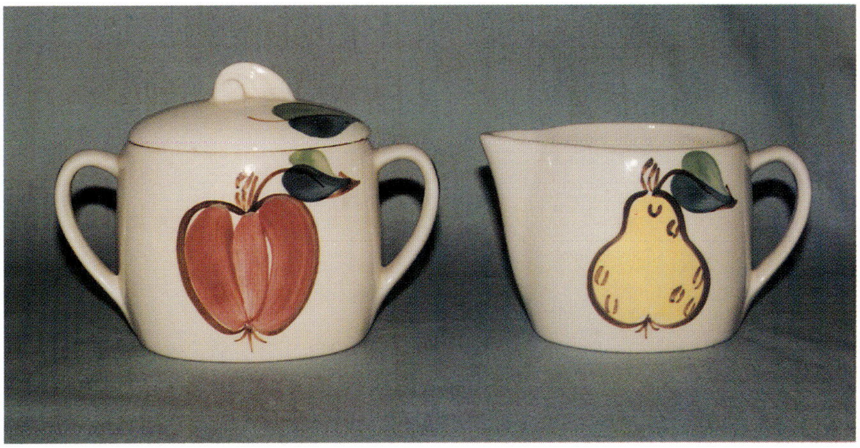

Covered sugar and creamer. $40 set.

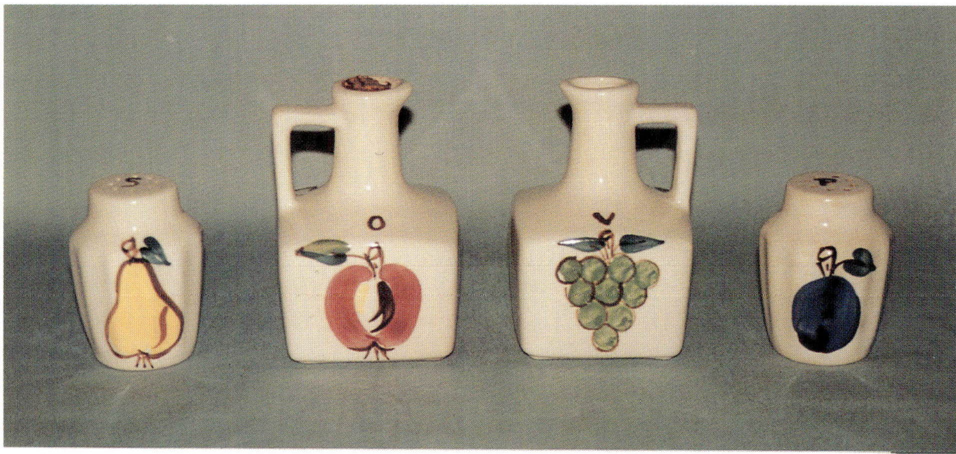

Seaform style salt and pepper shakers. $20 set. Square oil and vinegar. $30 set.

Honey jug, Esmond style pear, uncommon decoration on this mold. (The honey jug was a floral vase, flowers are a common decoration.) $150+.

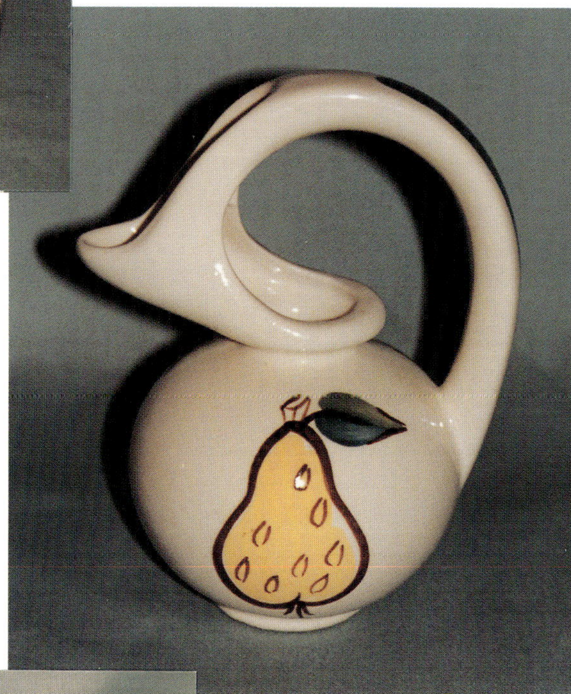

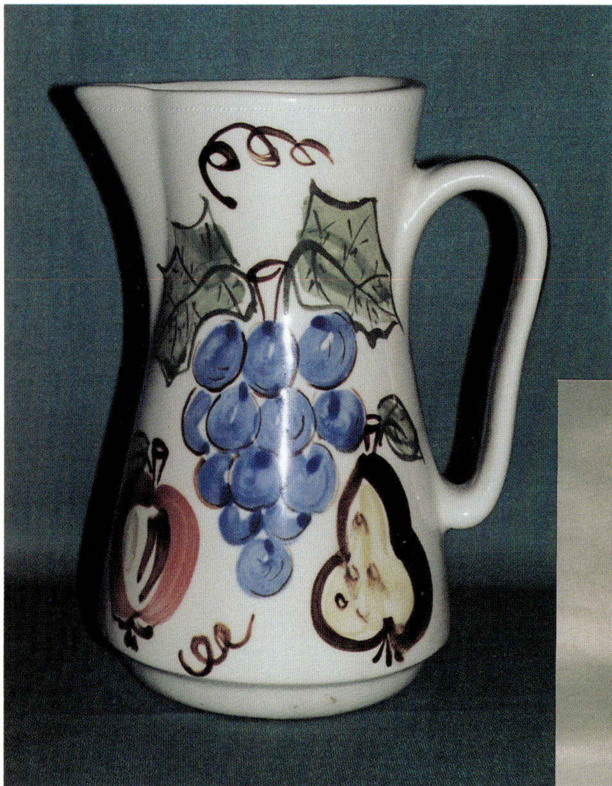

Rubel pitcher, 8.5" high. Signed by Dorothy Purinton. $400+.

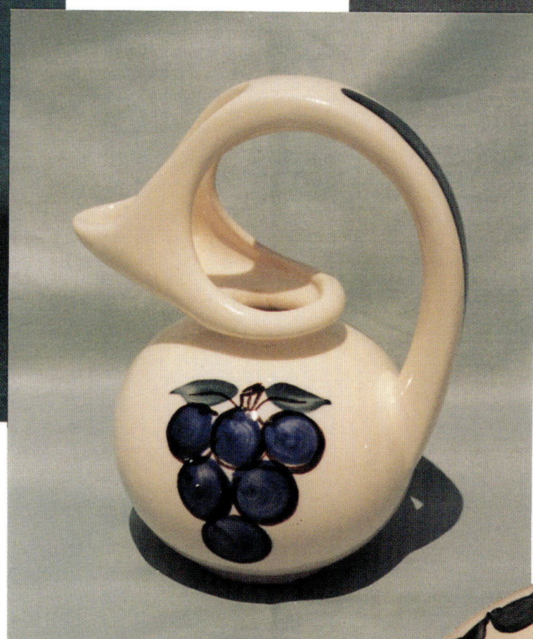

Honey jug, grapes decoration, uncommon decoration on this mold. $150+.

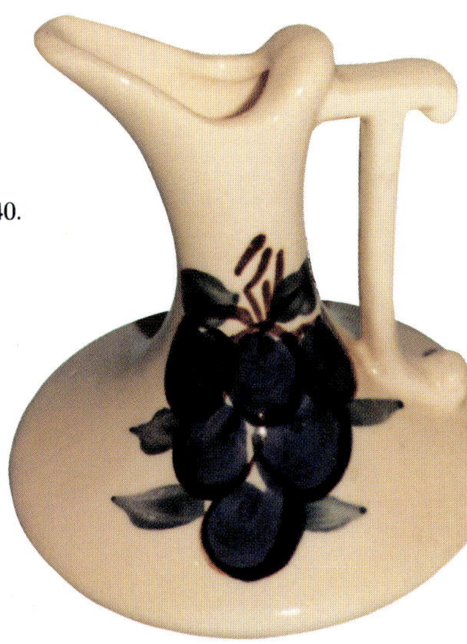

Ewer. $40.

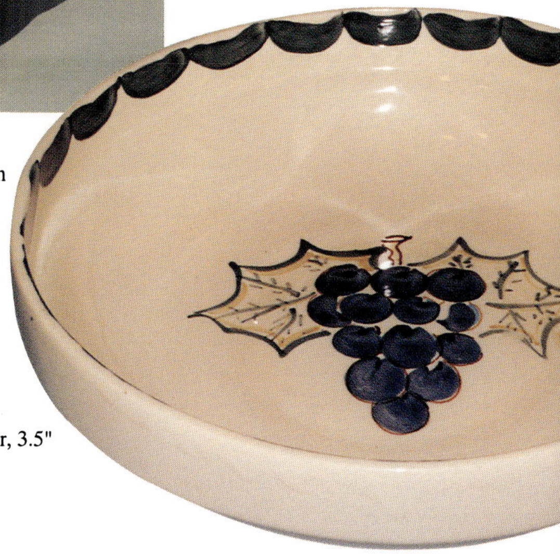

Grapes bowl, Rubel mold, 13.5" diameter, 3.5" high. $100+.

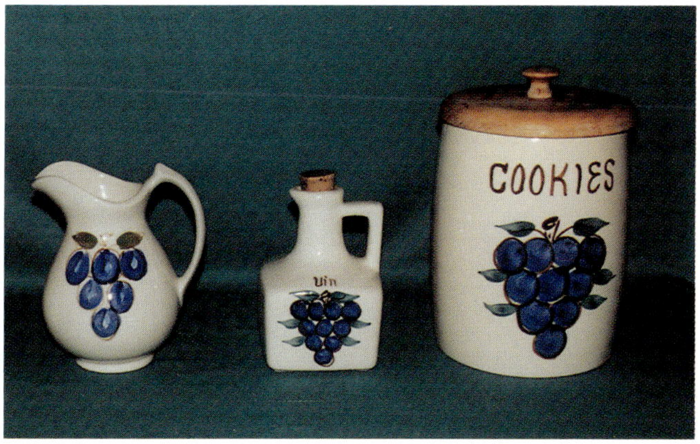

Pitcher, 5.5" high. $35. Square vinegar. $20. Round cookie canister, 8" high. $30.

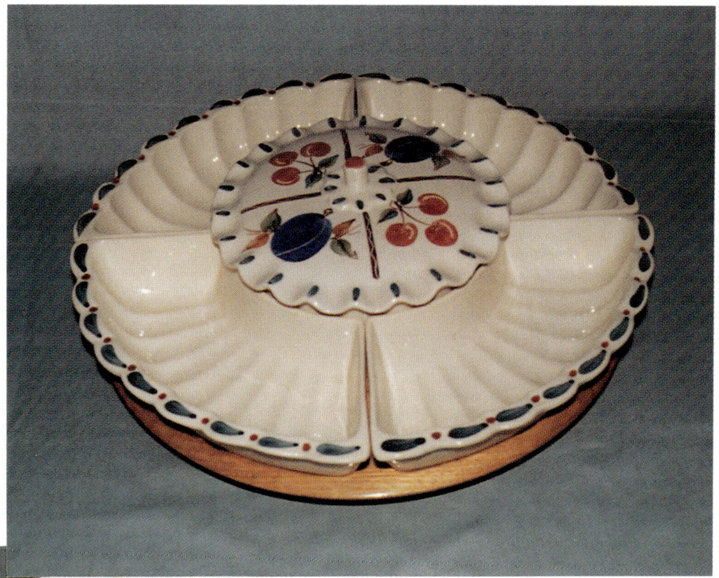

Lazy susan, Esmond. $75.

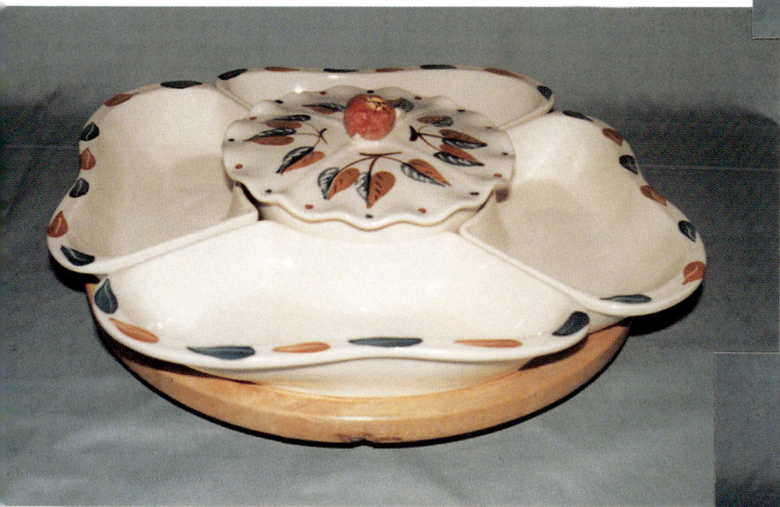

Lazy susan, Esmond. $75.

Lazy susan, Esmond. $75.

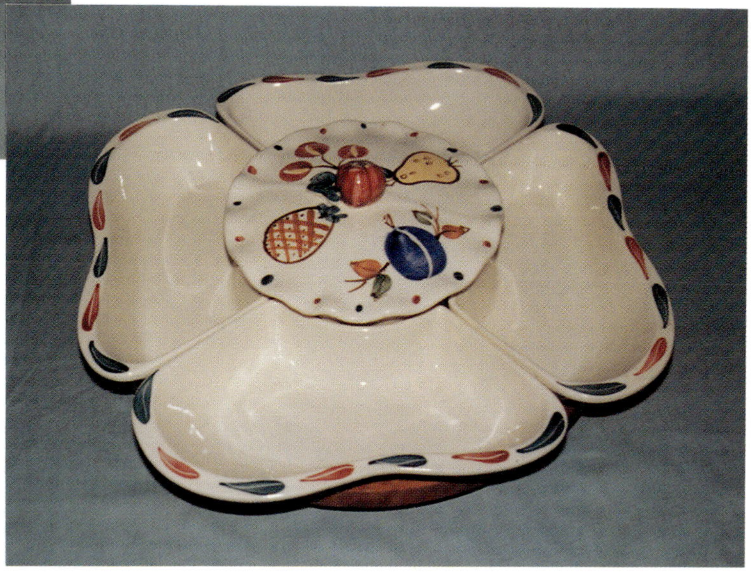

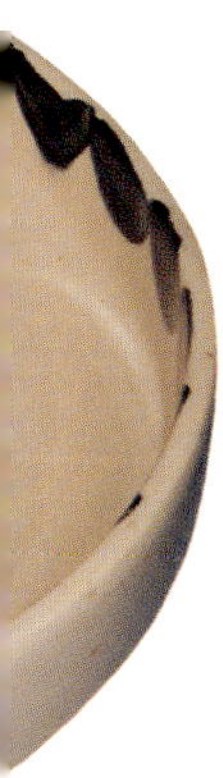

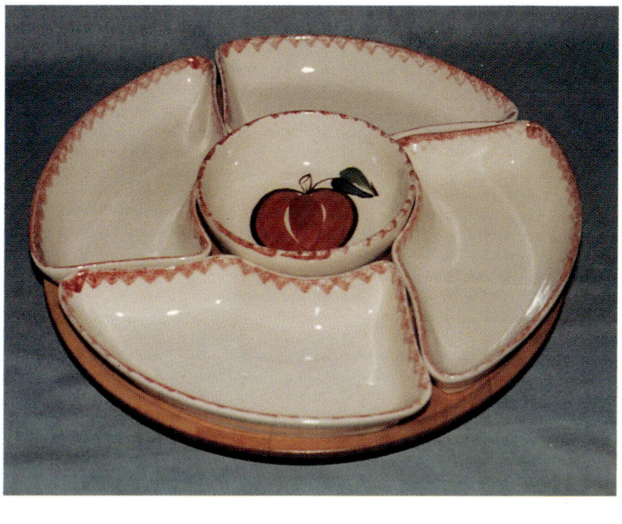

Lazy susan, Esmond. $50.

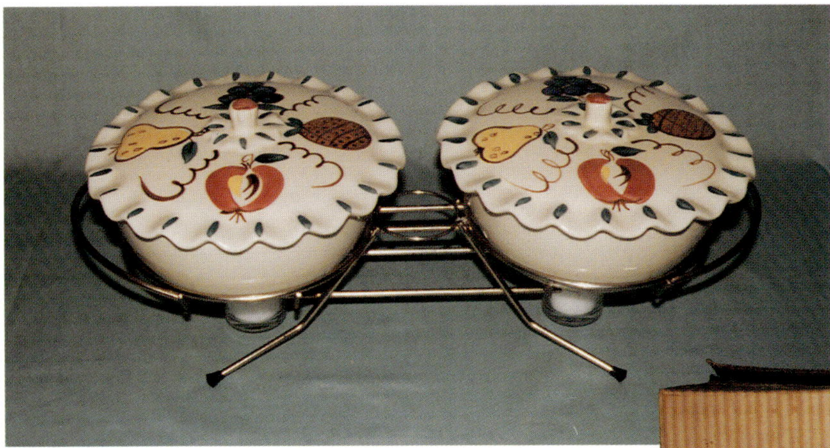

Twin casserole, Esmond. $75.

Esmond twin casserole box.

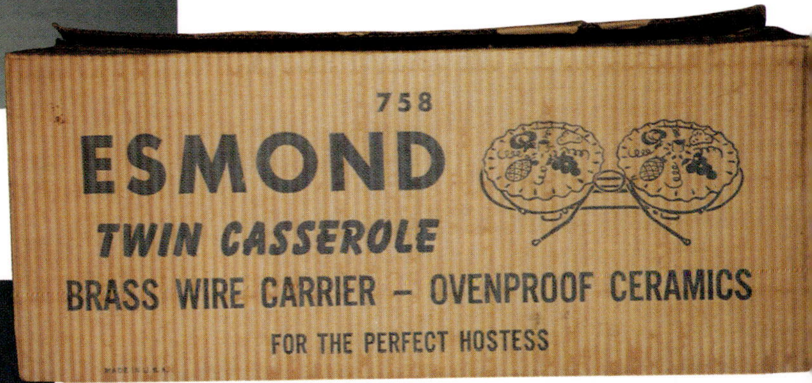

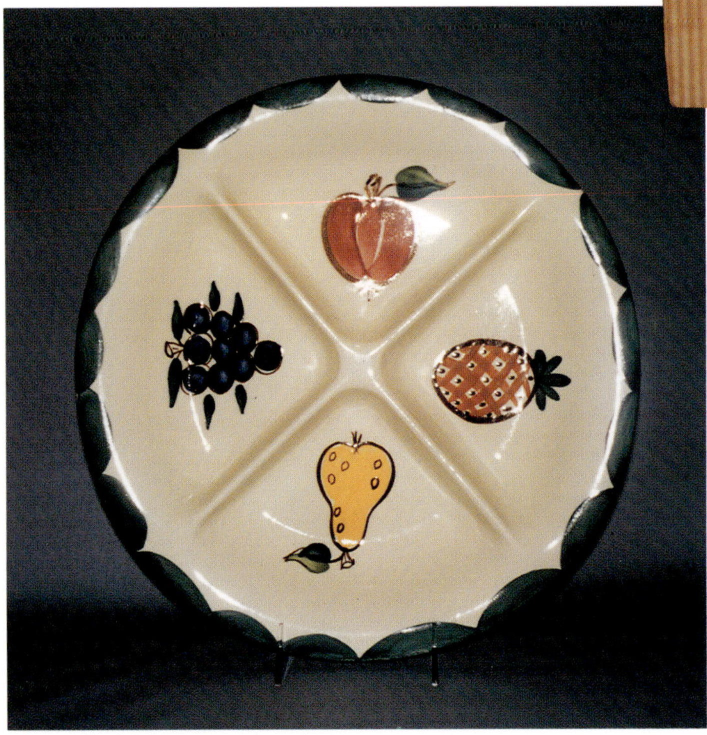

Sectional relish dish, 13.5" diameter, Rubel mold, rare. $125+.

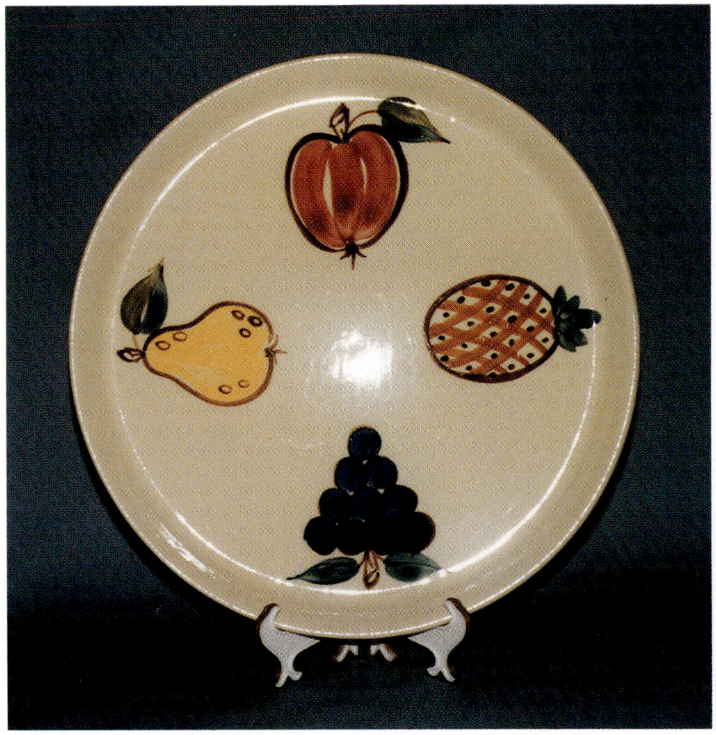

Chop plate, 13.5" diameter, Rubel mold, rare. $125+.

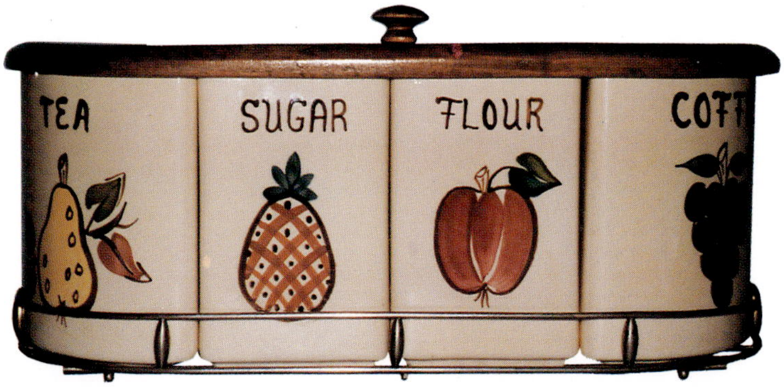

Long canister, four section, 19" diameter, Esmond. $100.

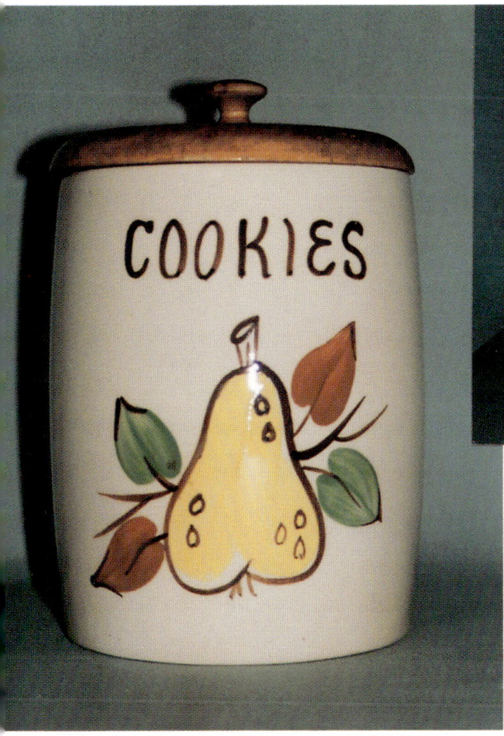

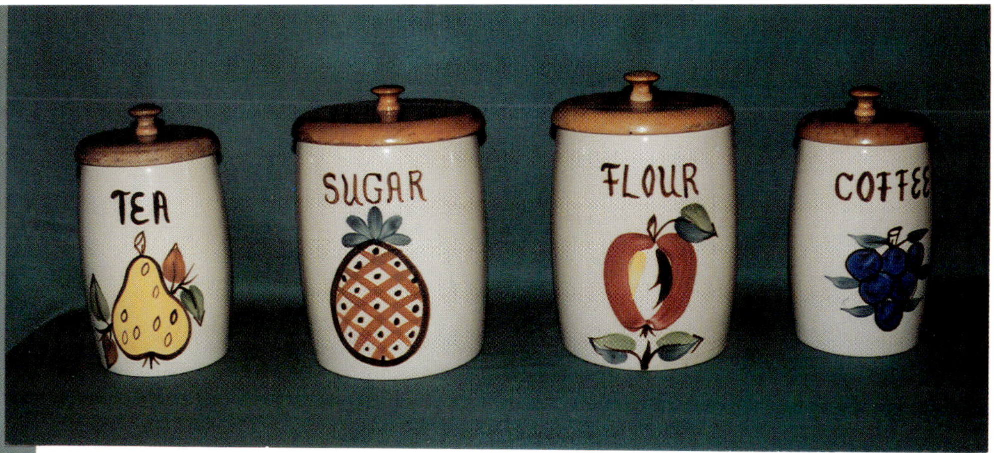

Round canister set, flour and sugar 8" high, tea and coffee, 7.5" high. $150 set.

Round cookie canister, 8" high. $30.

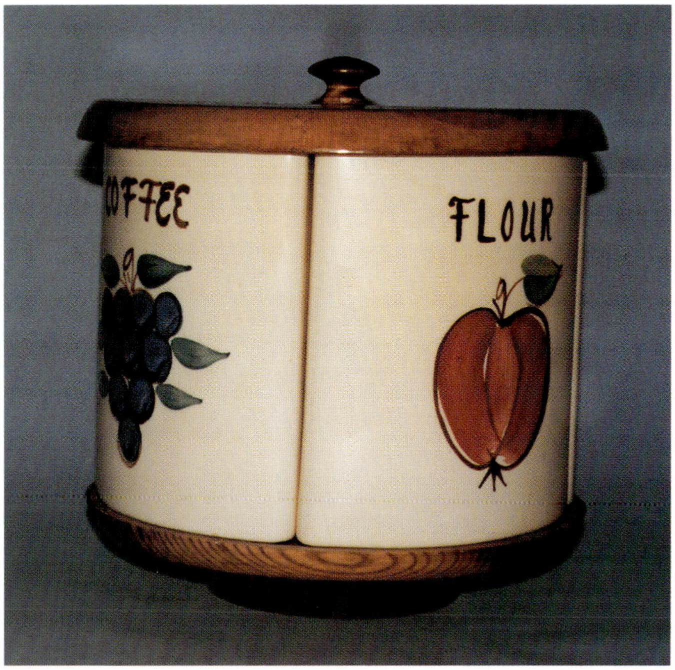

Four-piece canister set, Esmond. $35.

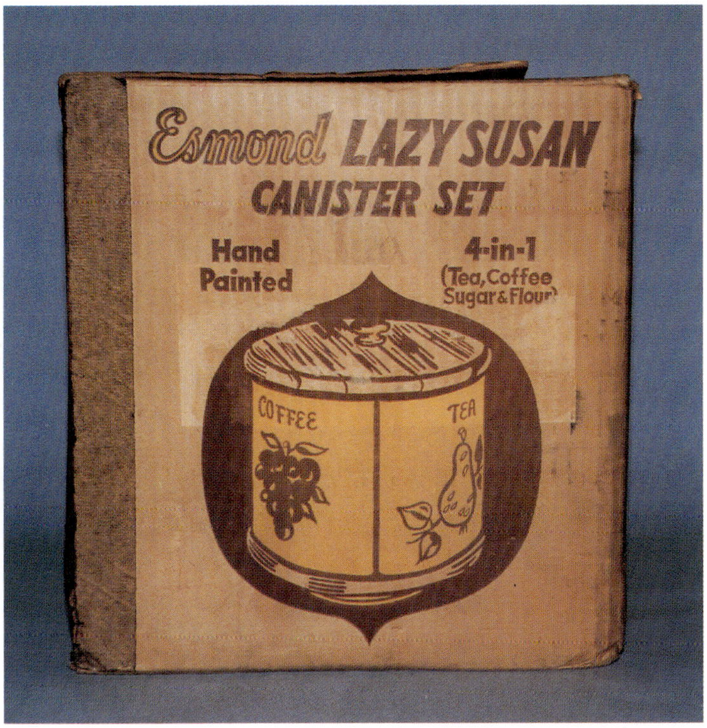

Photo showing all four pieces of the Esmond revolving canister set.

Box for Esmond canister set.

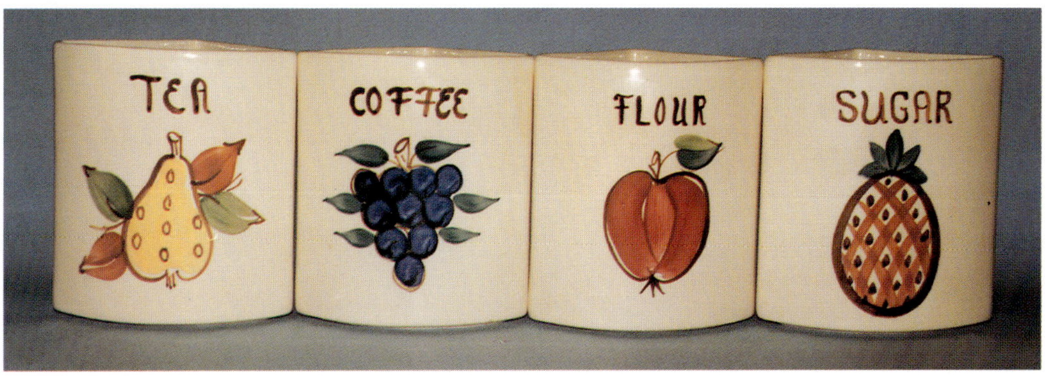

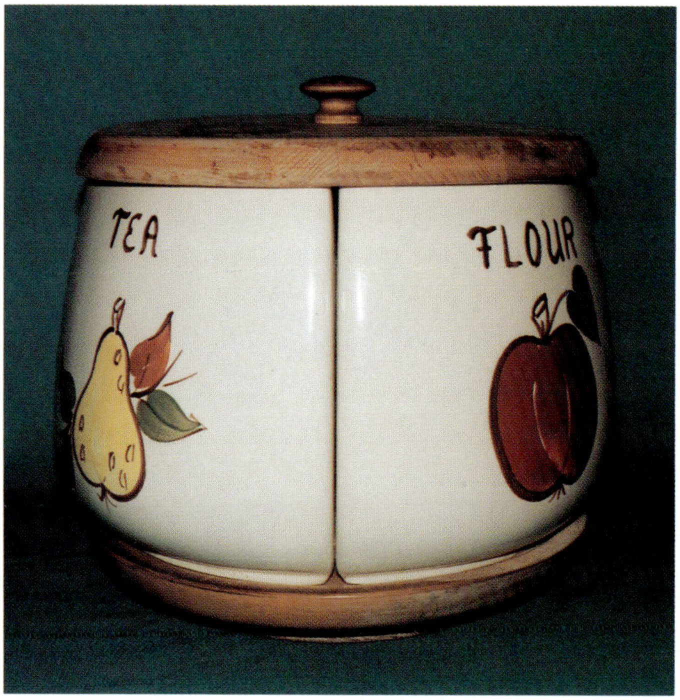

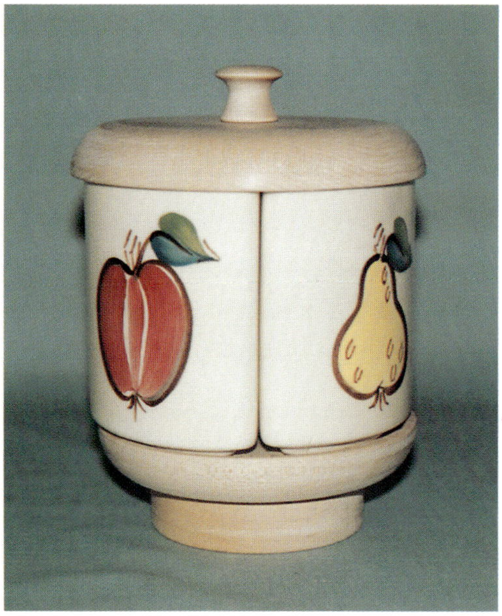

Miniature revolving canister set. $200. This piece was a production piece, not a salesman's sample.

Bulbous revolving canister set, Esmond. $50.

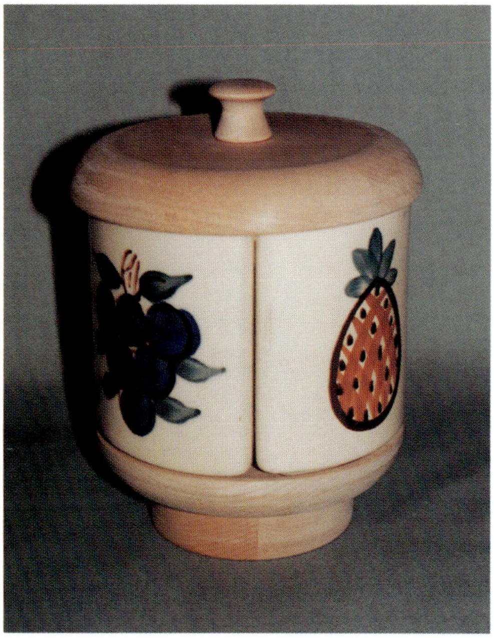

Reverse side of miniature revolving canister set.

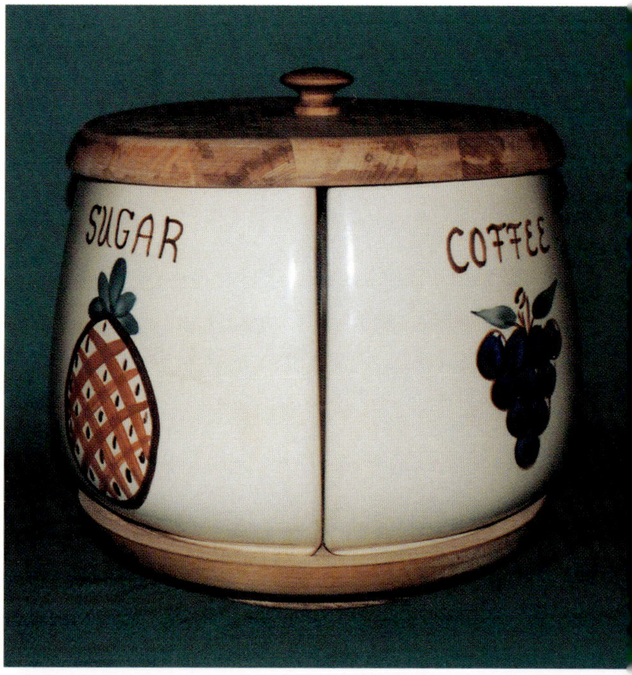

Reverse side of bulbous revolving canister set, Esmond.

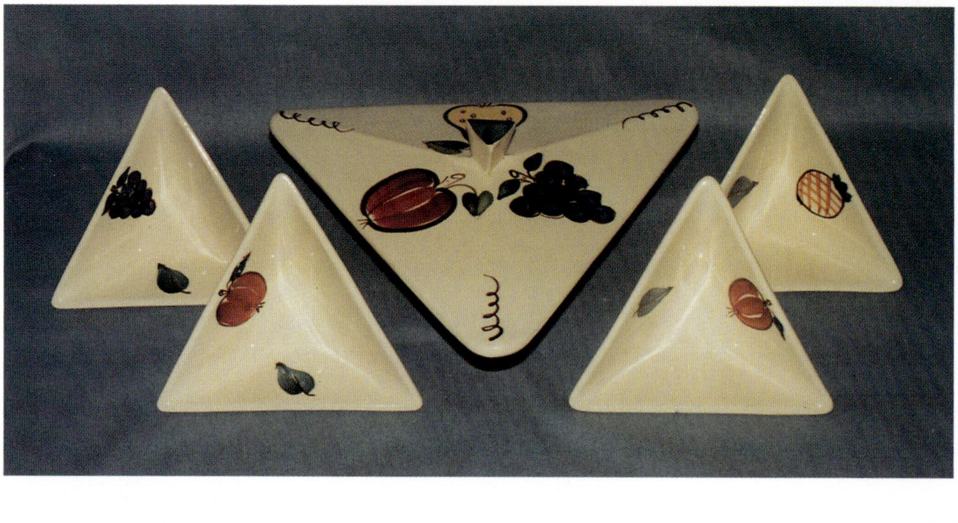

Triangular covered serving dish, 12" diameter, 3.5" diameter. $100. Individual triangular bowls. $30 each.

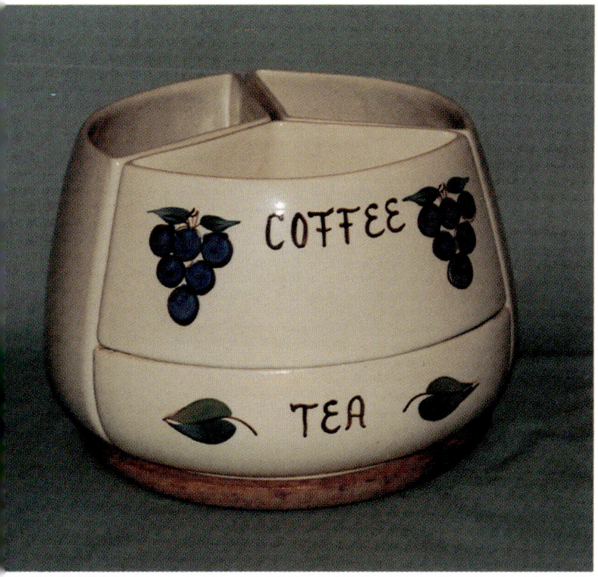

Stacking bulbous canister set, Esmond. $100.

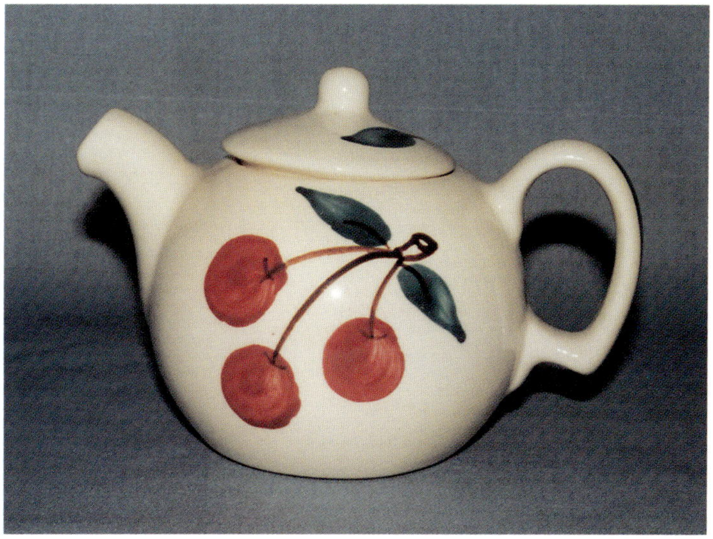

Cherries two cup teapot. $75.

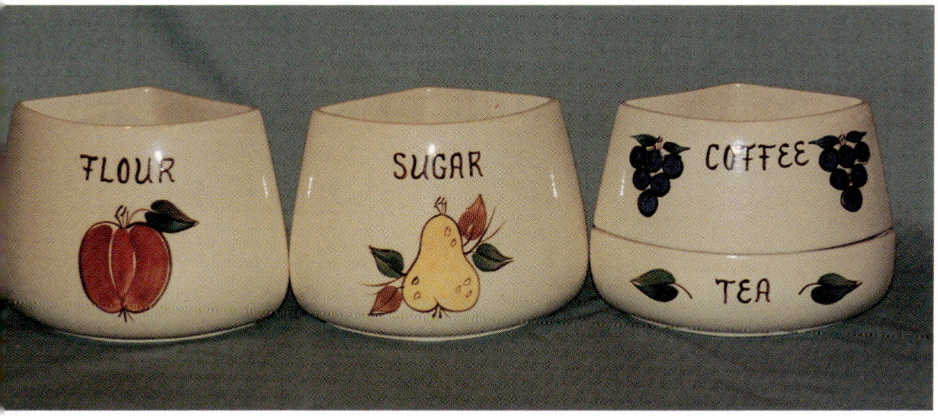

Stacking bulbous canister set, Esmond. This view shows the complete set.

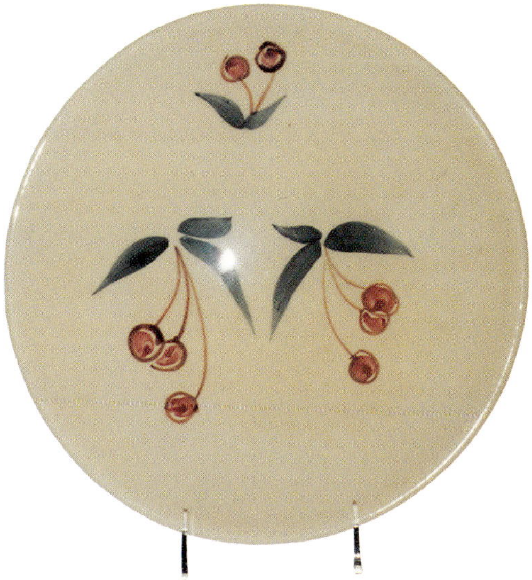

Cherries fruit bowl. $125.

Salad plate, Seaform style, cherries decoration. $90.

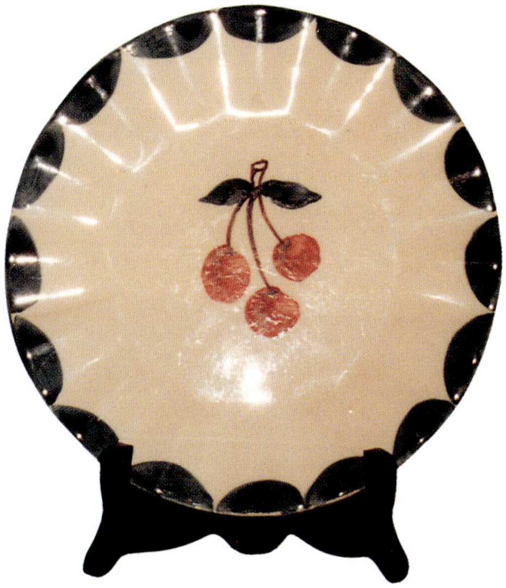

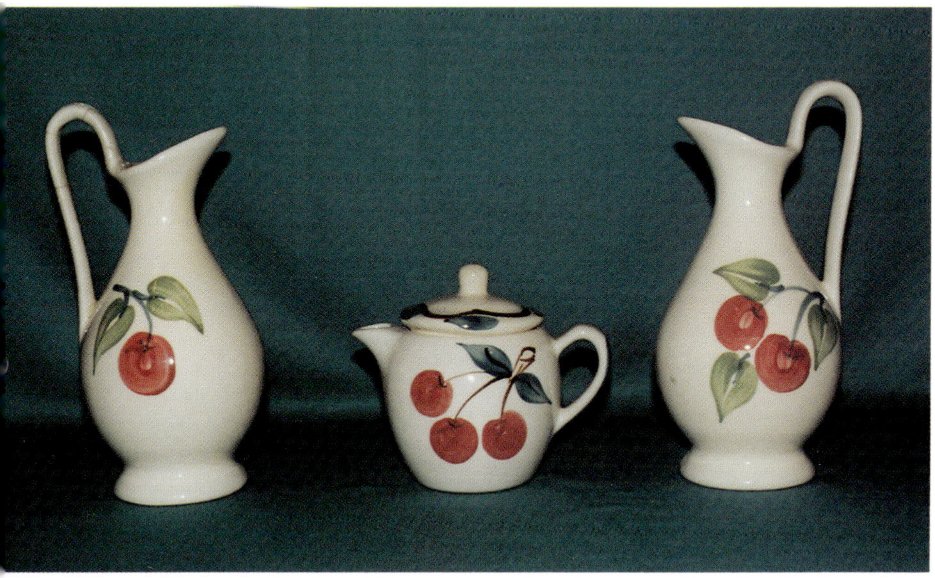

Cherries rebecca jugs. $50 each. Cherries covered creamer. $45.

Cherries angle handled teapot. $100.

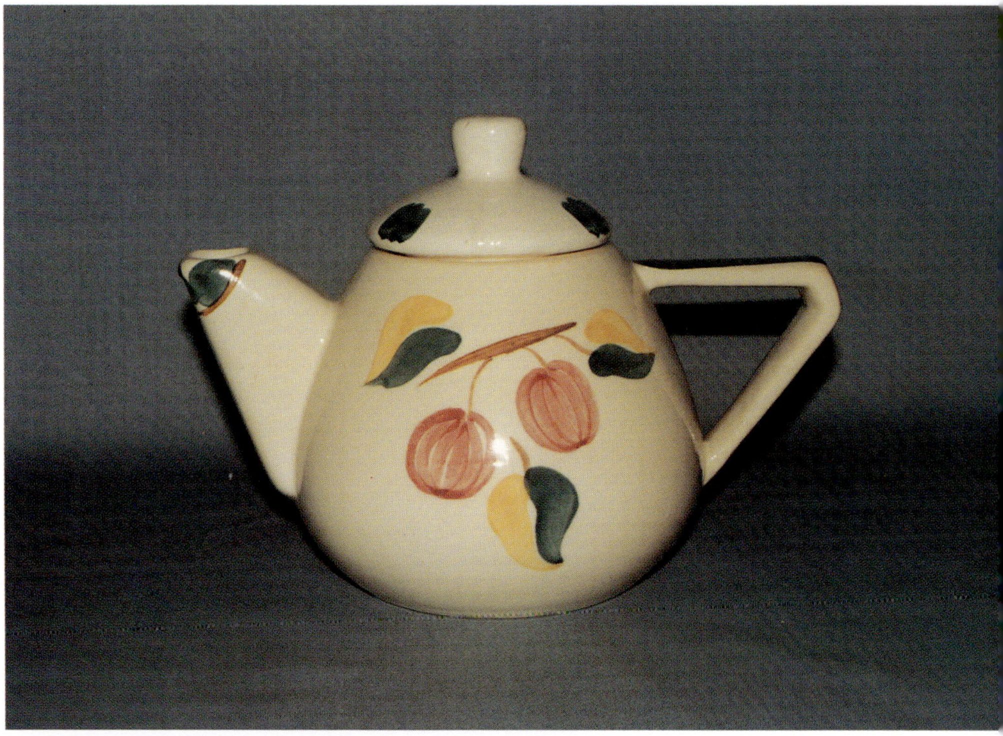

Salad plate, experimental: cherries. $90. Salad plate, experimental: apple and pear. $125.

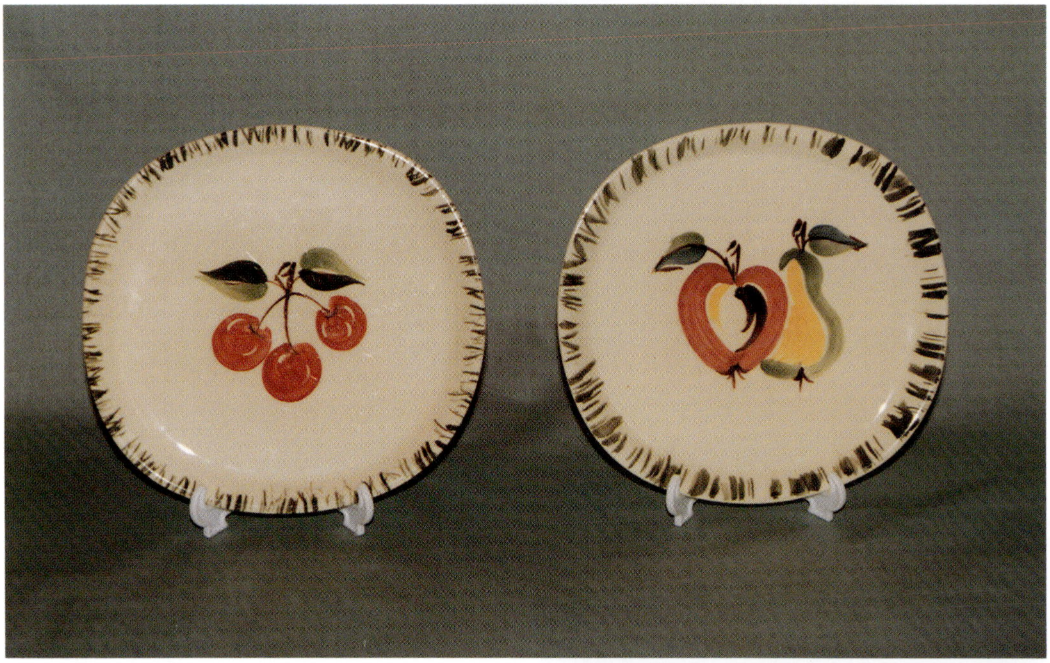

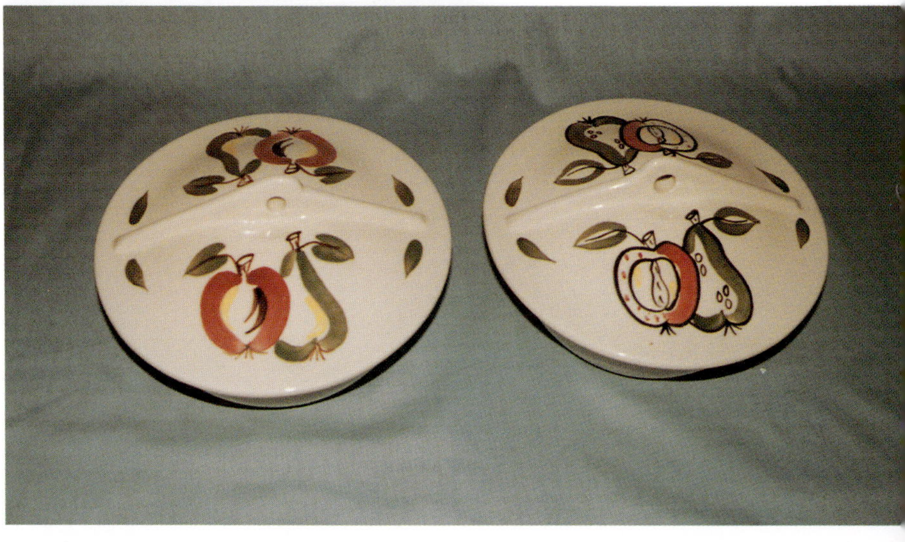

Covered casseroles. $100 each. Unusual apple-pear color combination.

Red and Yellow Ivy

Red and Yellow Ivy are two decorations used sparingly. D-504 is their decoration number. Red Ivy is the more familiar of the two patterns. NAPCO decorated their jardinieres with it. Not much is known about this pattern. No dinnerware items have been found and most of the products seen with Ivy are dated to the early and mid-1940s. Because of its simple design, allowing for easier painting by company employees, it was probably one of the first new patterns utilized by the pottery at Shippenville.

The demand for Ivy is low and prices for Red and Yellow are about the same. The harder to find items in Red are the five pint dutch jug, the nine inch jardiniere, and the three inch jardiniere. The production of five pint dutch jugs, although limited, indicates a few Red Ivy tumblers were produced. Finding one of those tumblers or any dinnerware line would be rare.

Yellow Ivy has an even more limited product base. A few teapots, honey jugs, and some other common items are decorated with the Yellow Ivy. The individual creamer and sugar set is probably the hardest to find of the items pictured. A five pint dutch jug, wide oval cookies jar, or any dinnerware line would be a good find.

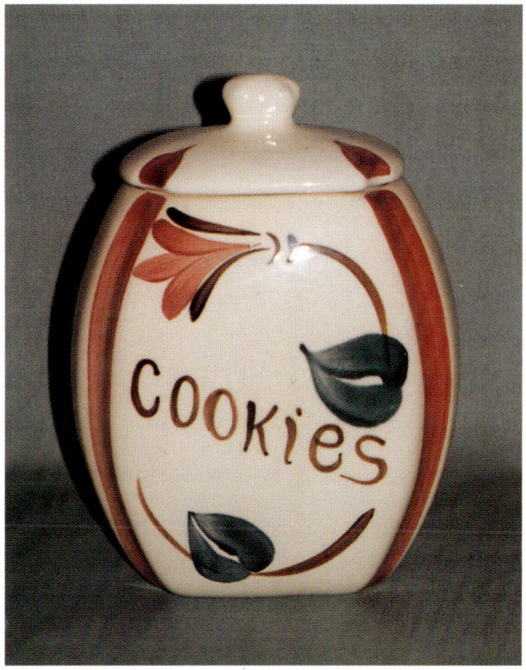

Red Ivy wide oval cookies jar. $60.

Red Ivy

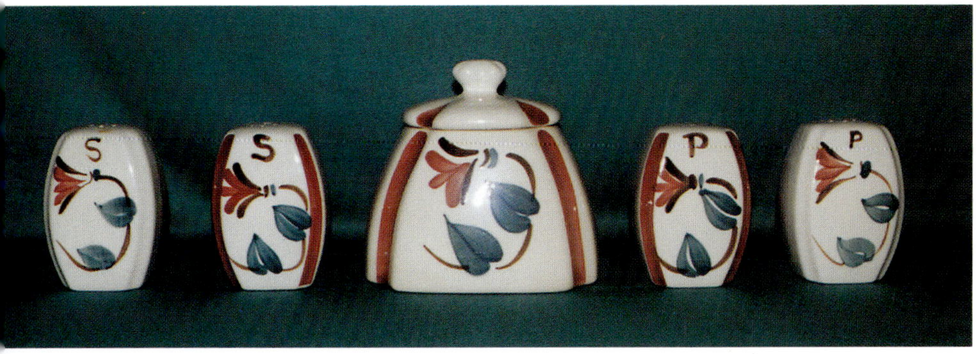

Range salt and pepper shakers with no red trim (uncommon). $50 set. Range salt and pepper shakers with red trim. $30 set. Range covered grease jar. $30.

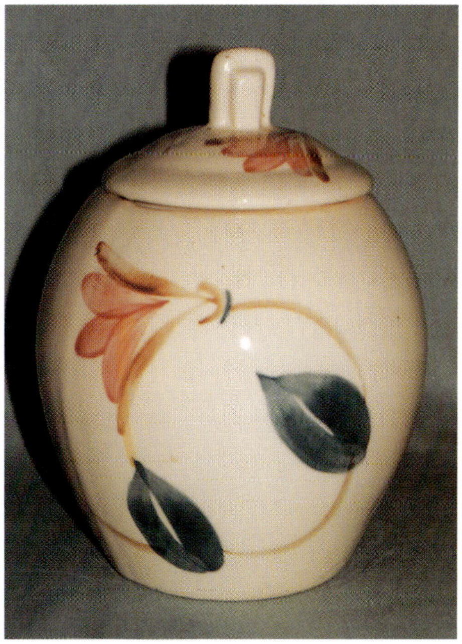

Biscuit jar. $30.

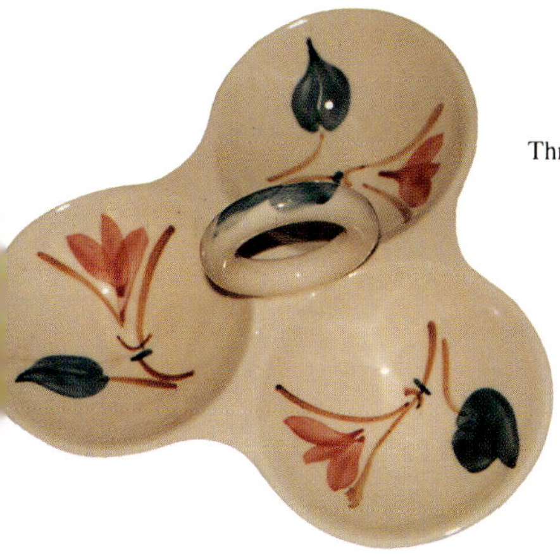

Three part relish with ceramic ring handle. $30.

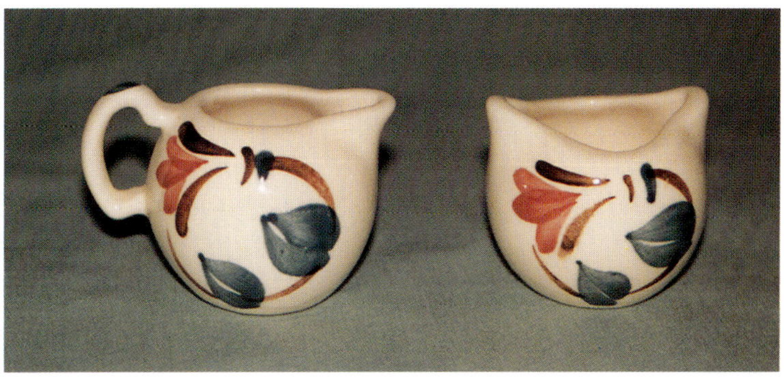

Individual creamer and sugar. $20 set.

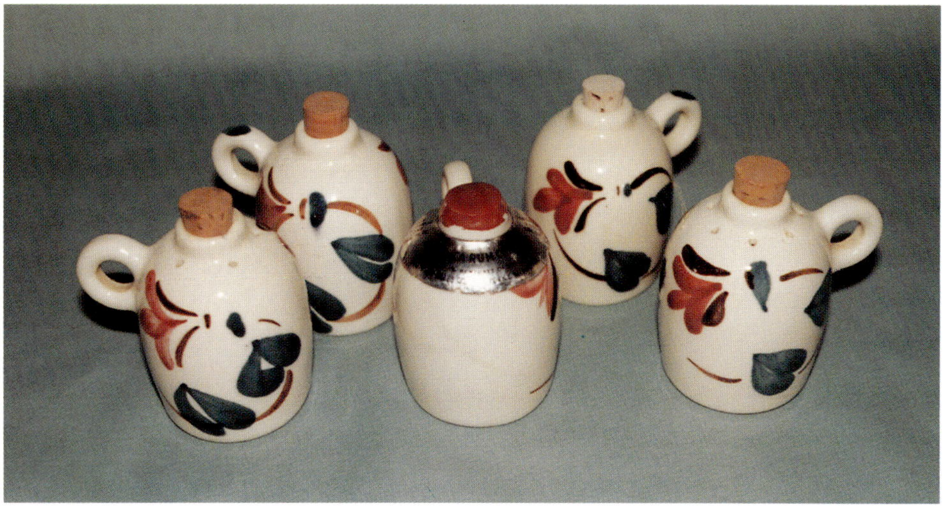

Items on each end are jug style salt and pepper shakers. $20 set. The three small jugs in the middle have no holes and were used as premiums, each containing cordials as seen on the middle example carrying the label from Jamaica Rum Cordials. $20 each.

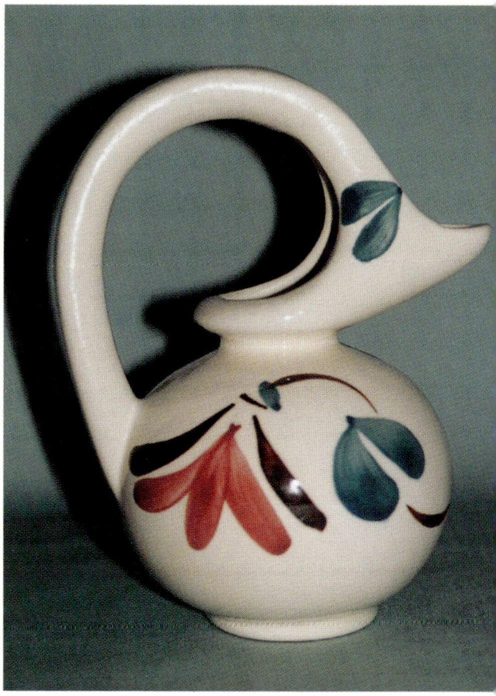

Honey jug. $15.

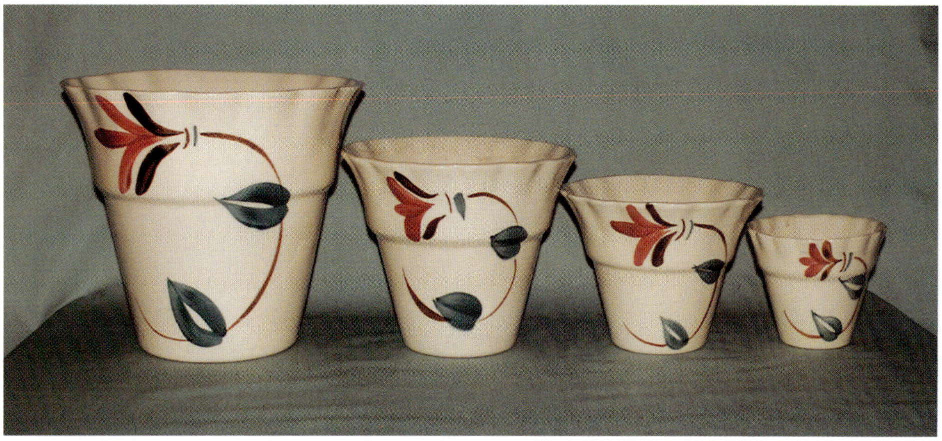

Jardiniere 9" high. $75. Jardiniere 7" high. $30. Jardiniere 5" high. $30. Jardiniere 3" high. $40.

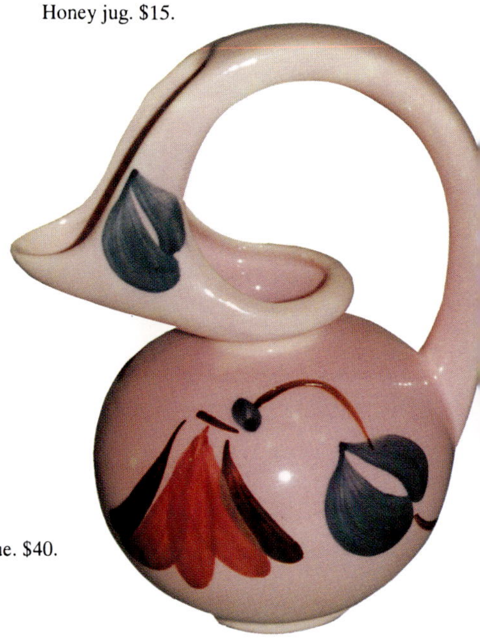

Honey jug with unusual pink hue. $40.

Juice mug. $10. Stacking storage container. $30 set.

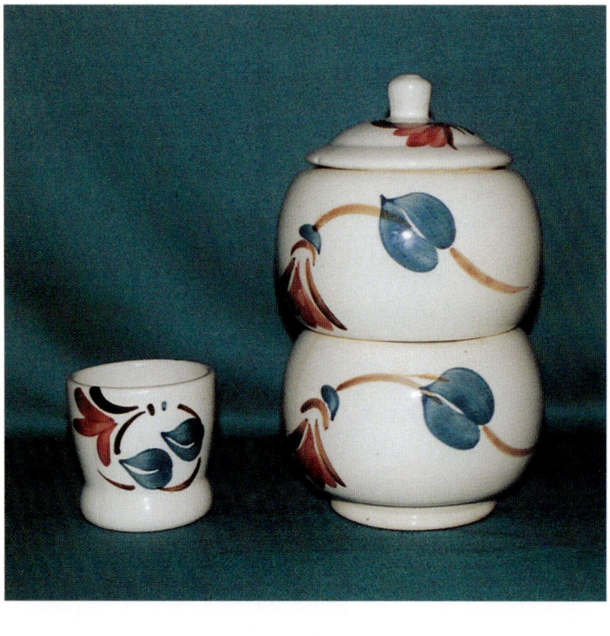

Two cup teapot. $20.

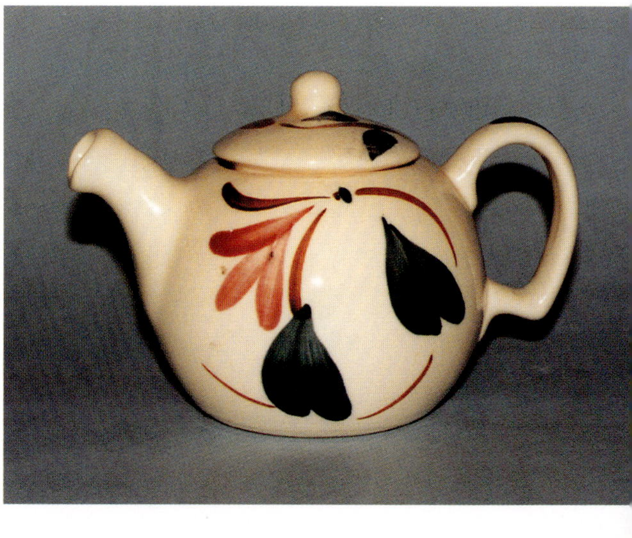

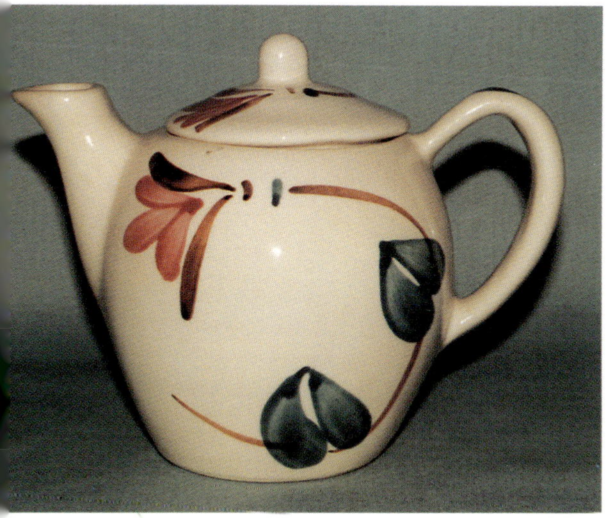

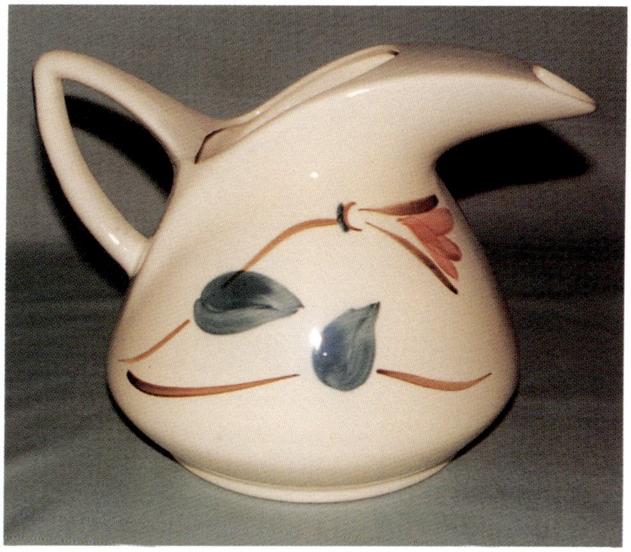

Five pint dutch jug. $60.

Four cup teapot. $15.

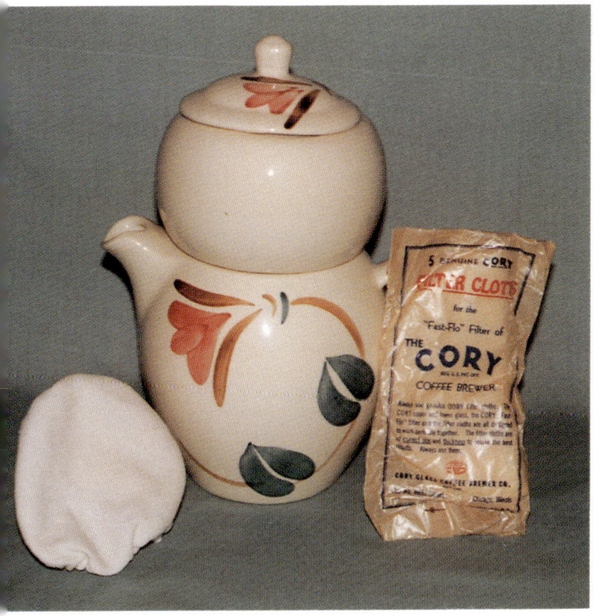

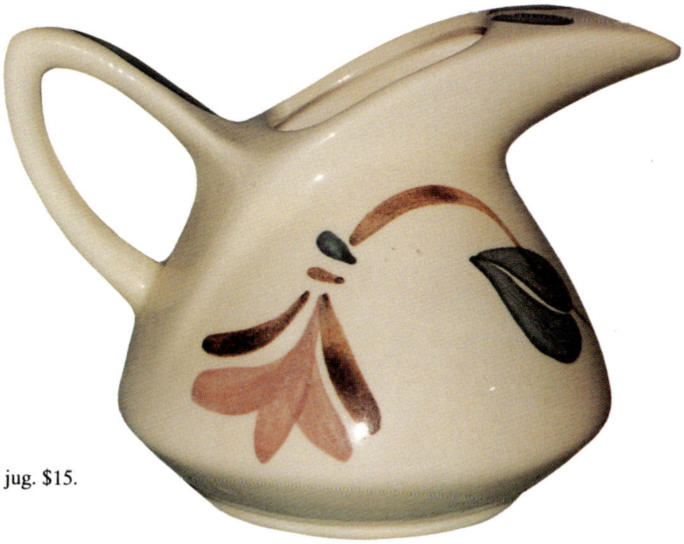

Two pint dutch jug. $15.

Eight cup coffee pot with original drip filters. $65.
Eight cup coffee pot alone. $30.

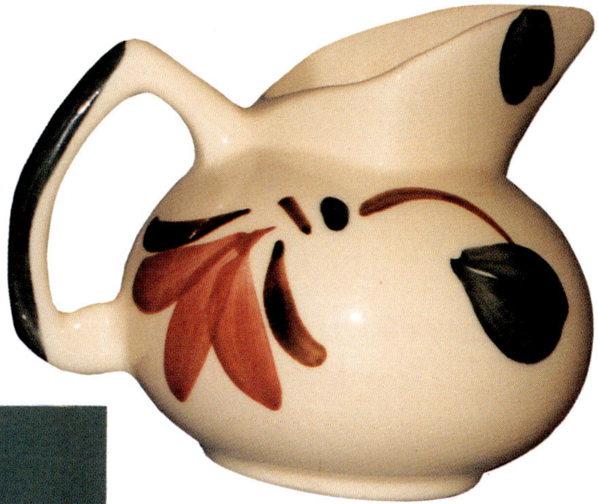

Round covered creamer and covered sugar. $15 set. Six cup teapot. $15.

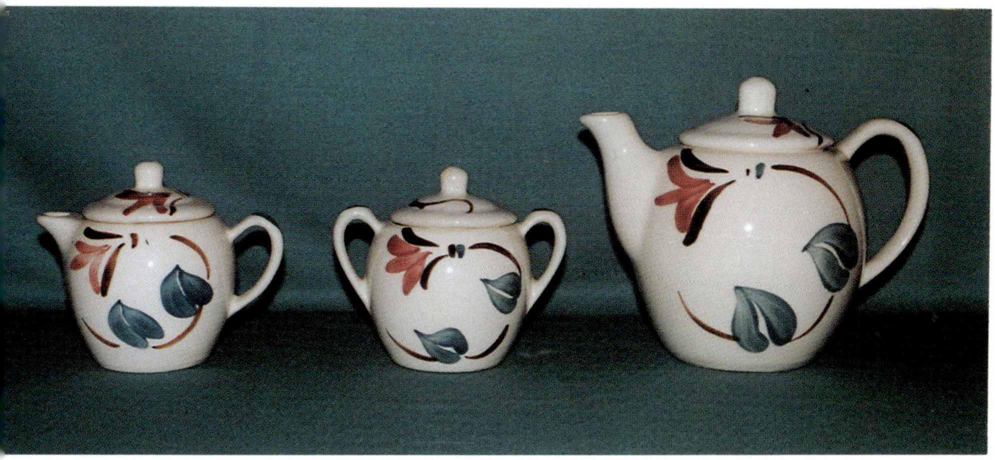

Kent jug. $15.

Yellow Ivy

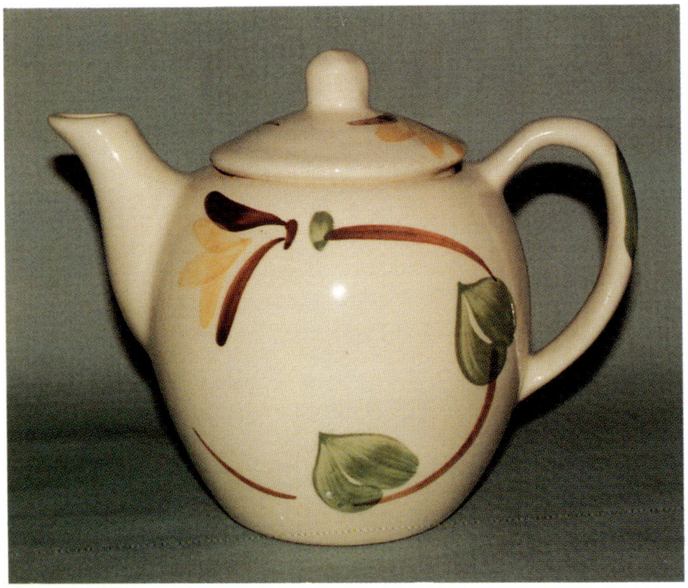

Six cup teapot. $15.

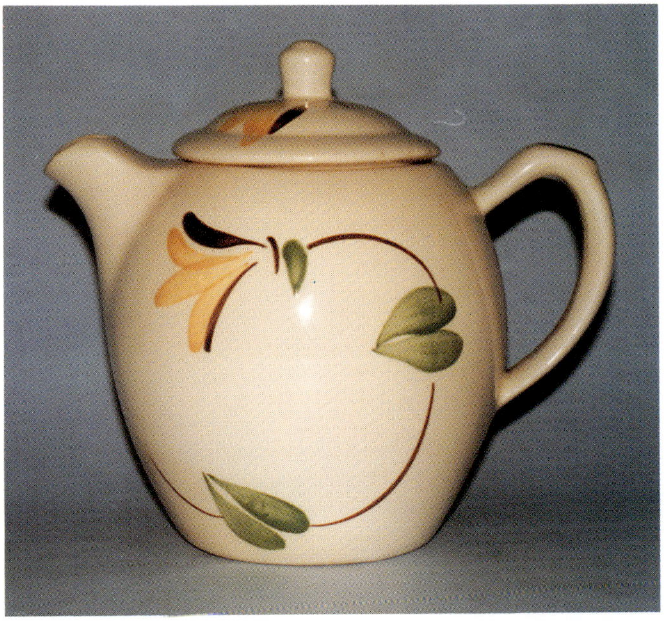

Eight cup coffee pot. $30.

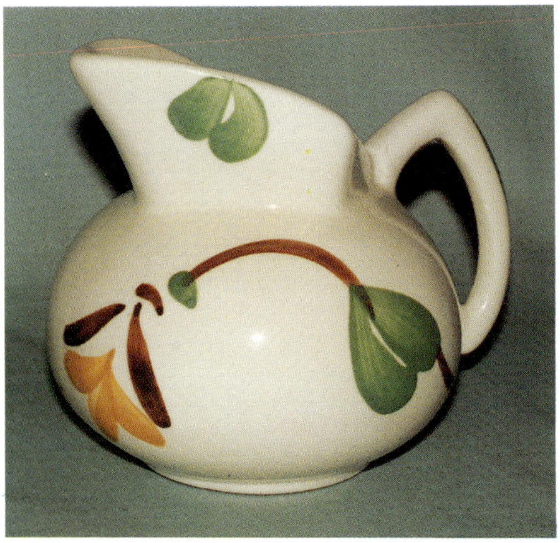

Kent jug. $15.

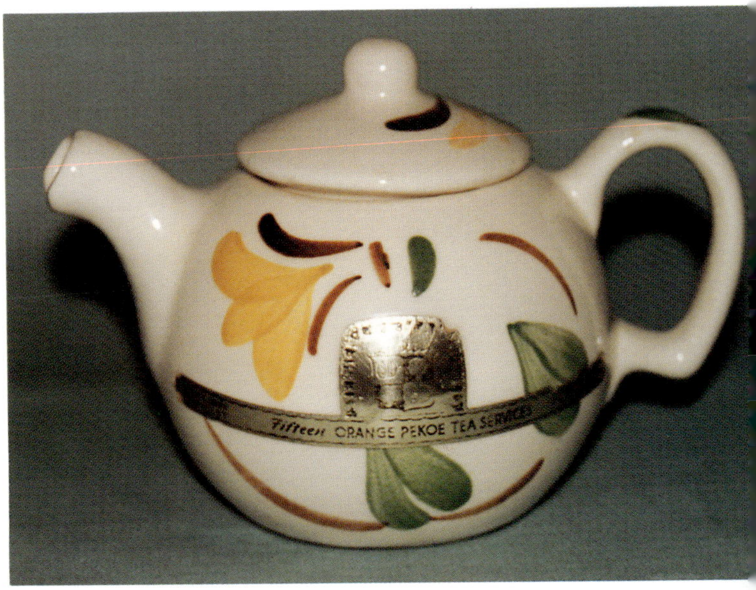

Two cup teapot with original paper label for the Orange Pekoe Tea Services. $30. Without original paper label. $20.

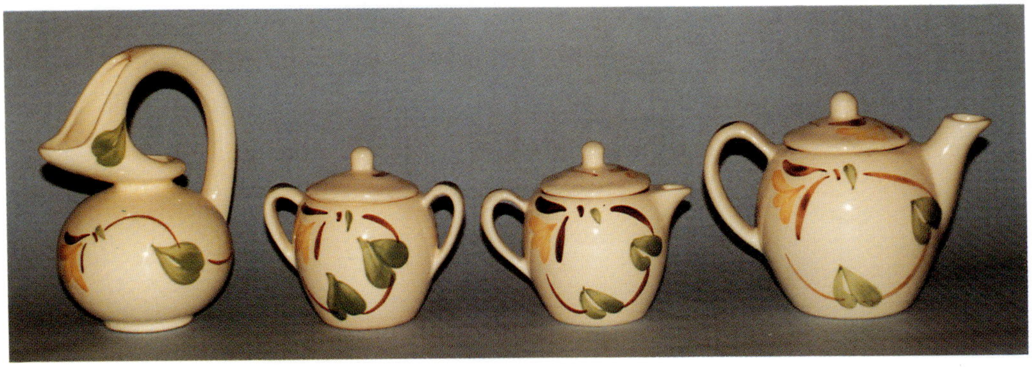

Honey jug. $15. Round covered sugar and covered creamer. $15 set. Four cup teapot. $15.

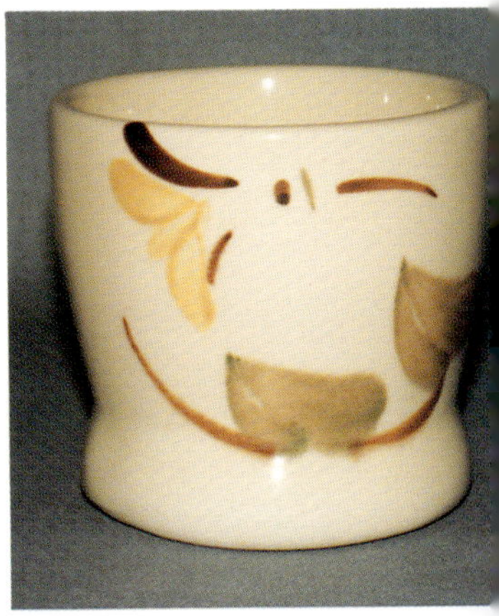

Juice mug. $10.

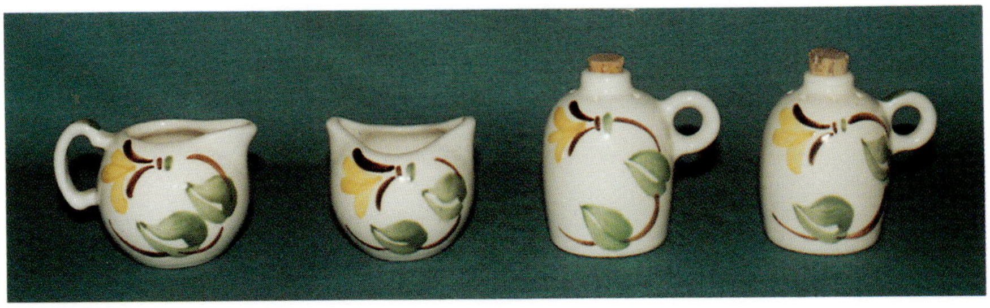

Individual creamer and sugar. $20 set. Jug style salt and pepper shakers. $15 set.

Apple

Apple is the best known and most widely collected pattern of Purinton Pottery. You may say it is the signature decoration. William Blair is credited with developing the open Apple. Dorothy Purinton was the first to use it on production pieces. Apple was the backbone of Purinton Pottery and was in continuous production from the 1940s to the closing of the plant.

Apple was given the code designation D-46 in the plant. Apple was probably first used in the mid-1940s and is known to have decorated Purinton's first dinnerware line. Do not confuse it with the apple used in the Fruit decoration. Apple in Fruit is painted a solid red color while the Apple pattern is outlined in red, with yellow and brown accents inside. Many people call it the open apple.

Apple has a country look that was so popular when introduced that buyers would take as many products decorated in that pattern as possible. Throughout the history of Purinton, Apple remained a consistent seller. Today, Apple continues to be in great demand as collectors cannot get enough of some products.

The price for Apple varies greatly. As people try to complete their collection, harder to find items command top dollar. Dinnerware and a few of the accessory pieces are not too difficult to find. Coffee and beer mugs are harder to find. Sometimes Apple will appear on items from Rubel or NAPCO. These items will demand higher prices as they were not part of the regular production. Harder to find items from the Purinton line are the honey jug, butter dish, star candle holders, spaghetti bowl, and oversized kent jug. Prices have been left open ended on some items as rare pieces have commanded prices not easily set. Dorothy Purinton painted a few specialty plates with the Apple decoration and these are rare items.

Apple will continue to be in strong demand and new collectors can find items at reasonable prices. Apple's bold red decoration and eye appealing country look will continue to be a favorite.

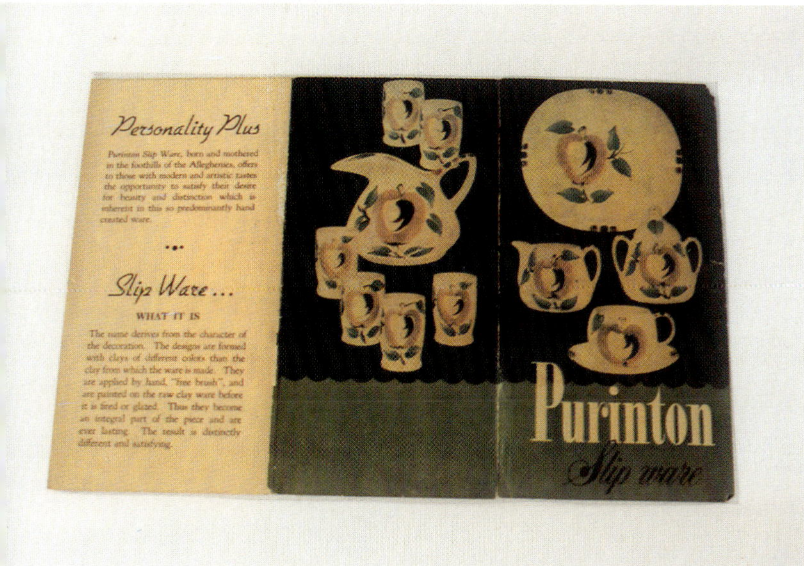

Purinton Pottery Apple pattern tri-fold brochure.

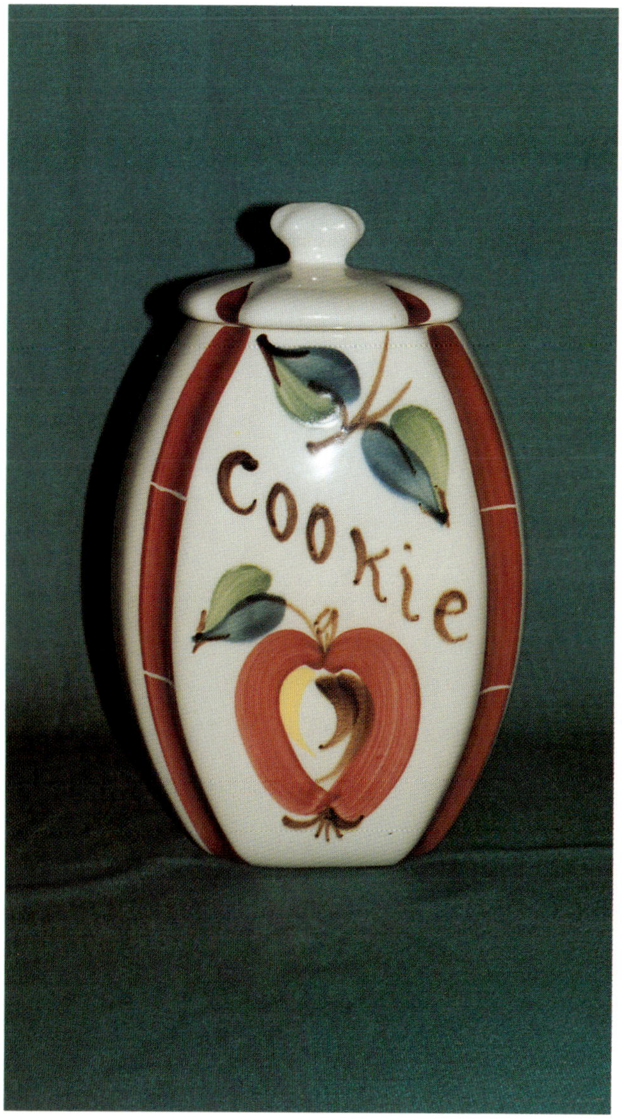

Tall oval cookies jar. $60.

Inside of Apple tri-fold brochure.

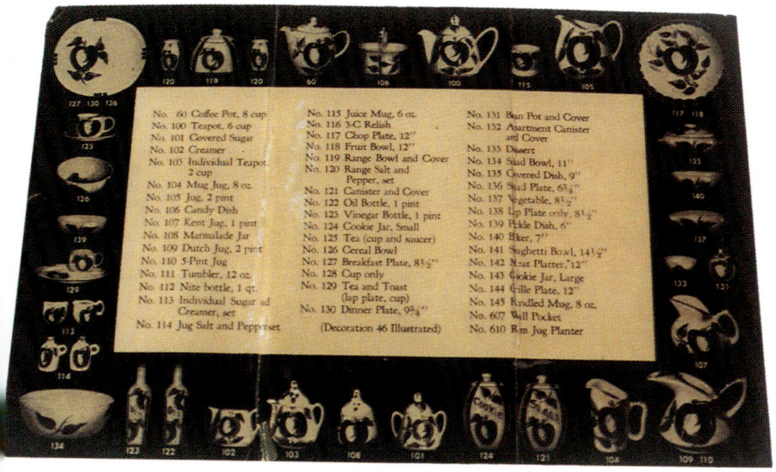
No. 60 Coffee Pot, 8 cup
No. 100 Teapot, 6 cup
No. 101 Covered Sugar
No. 102 Creamer
No. 103 Individual Teapot 2 cup
No. 104 Mug Jug, 8 oz.
No. 105 Jug, 2 pint
No. 106 Candy Dish
No. 107 Kent Jug, 1 pint
No. 108 Marmalade Jar
No. 109 Dutch Jug, 2 pint
No. 110 5-Pint Jug
No. 111 Tumbler, 12 oz.
No. 112 Nite bottle, 1 qt.
No. 113 Individual Sugar and Creamer, set
No. 114 Jug Salt and Pepper set
No. 115 Juice Mug, 6 oz.
No. 116 3-C Relish
No. 117 Chop Plate, 12"
No. 118 Fruit Bowl, 12"
No. 119 Range Bowl and Cover
No. 120 Range Salt and Pepper, set
No. 121 Canister and Cover
No. 122 Oil Bottle, 1 pint
No. 123 Vinegar Bottle, 1 pint
No. 124 Cookie Jar, Small
No. 125 Tea (cup and saucer)
No. 126 Cereal Bowl
No. 127 Breakfast Plate, 8½"
No. 128 Cup only
No. 129 Tea and Toast (lap plate, cup)
No. 130 Dinner Plate, 9¾"
(Decoration 46 Illustrated)
No. 131 Bean Pot and Cover
No. 132 Apartment Canister and Cover
No. 133 Dessert
No. 134 Salad Bowl, 11"
No. 135 Covered Dish, 9"
No. 136 Salad Plate, 6¾"
No. 137 Vegetable, 8½"
No. 138 Lap Plate only, 8½"
No. 139 Pickle Dish, 6"
No. 140 Baker, 7"
No. 141 Spaghetti Bowl, 14½"
No. 142 Meat Platter, 12"
No. 143 Cookie Jar, Large
No. 144 Grille Plate, 12"
No. 145 Handled Mug, 8 oz.
No. 607 Wall Pocket
No. 610 Rum Jug Planter

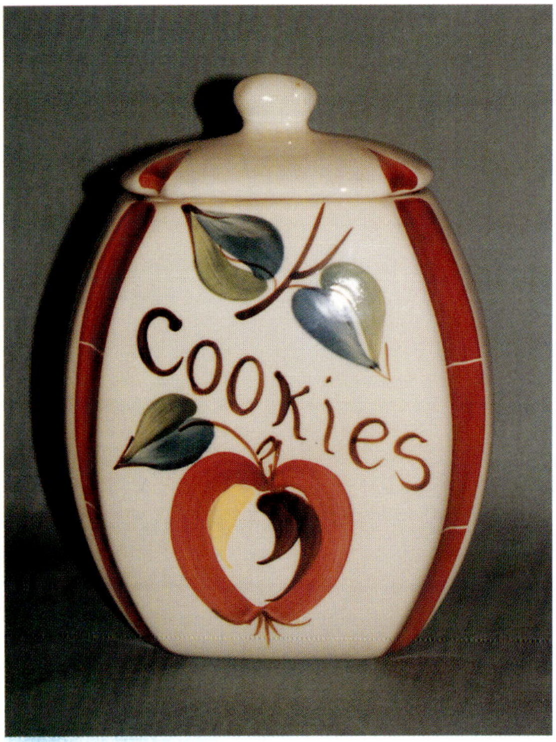

Wide oval cookies jar. $75.

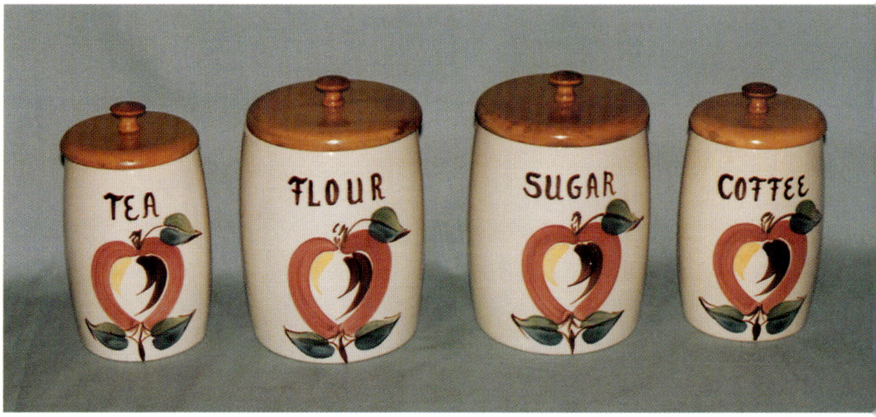

Round four piece canister set with wooden lids. Tea and coffee 7.5" high; flour and sugar 8" high. $125 each.

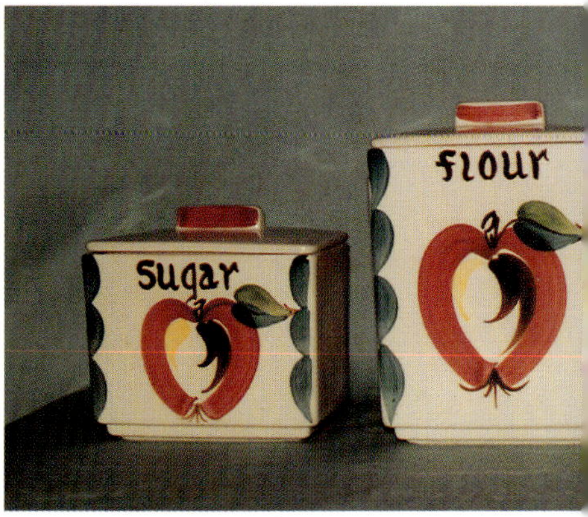

Four piece apartment canister set. $50 each.

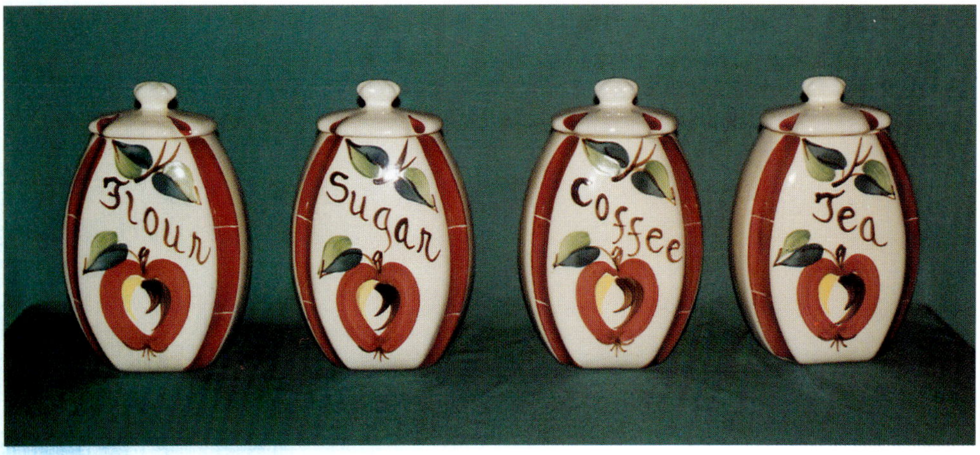

Tall oval four piece canister set. $50 each.

Four-piece revolving canister set. Left: snacks, chips, pretzels, nuts. Right: sugar, coffee, flour, tea. $150 each set.

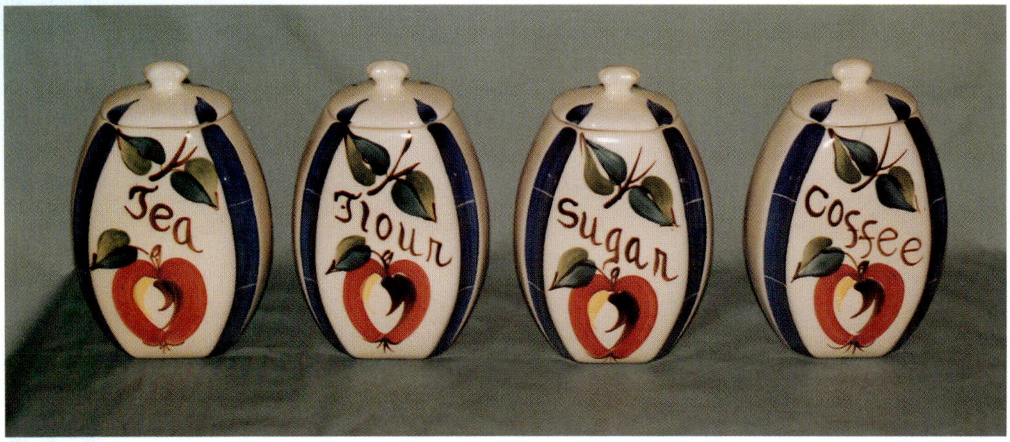

Tall oval four piece canister set with cobalt trim. $100 each.

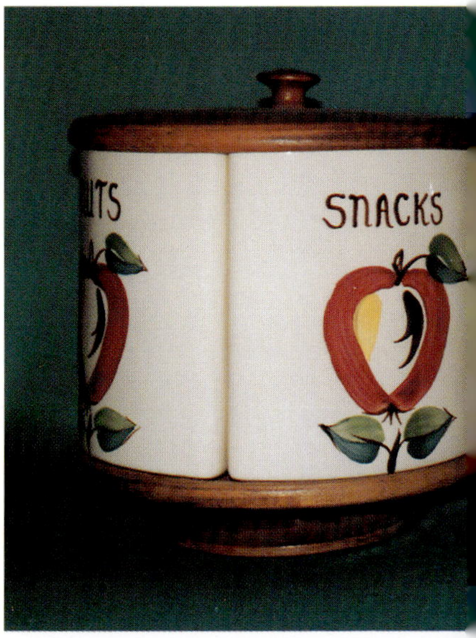

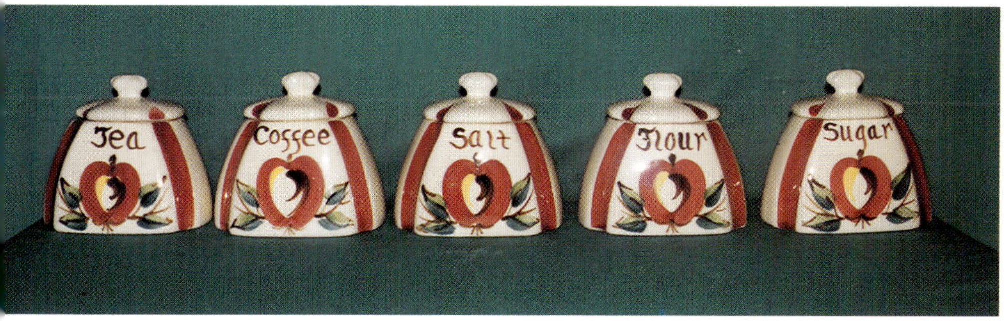

Half oval five piece canister set. $75 each.

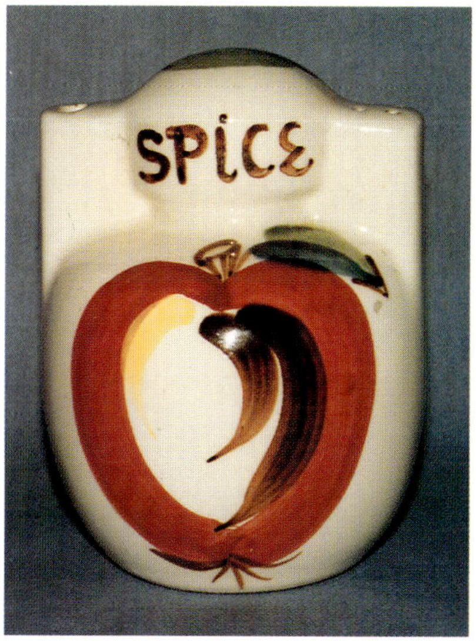

Pour and shake, spice (rare). $300.

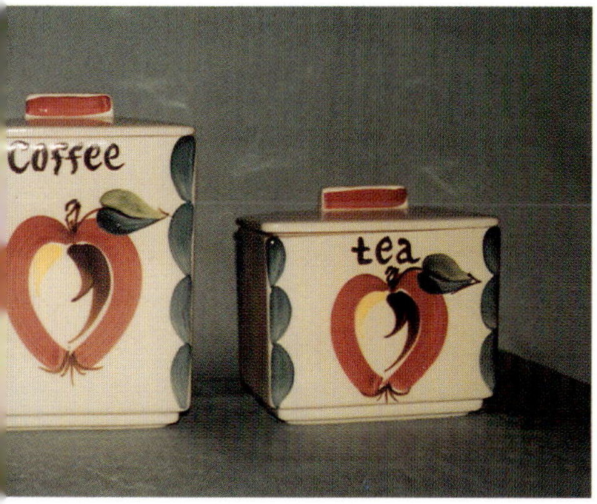

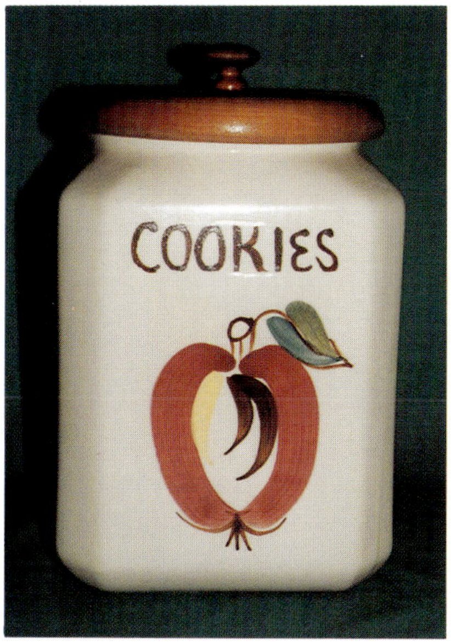

Square cookies jar with wooden lid. $80.

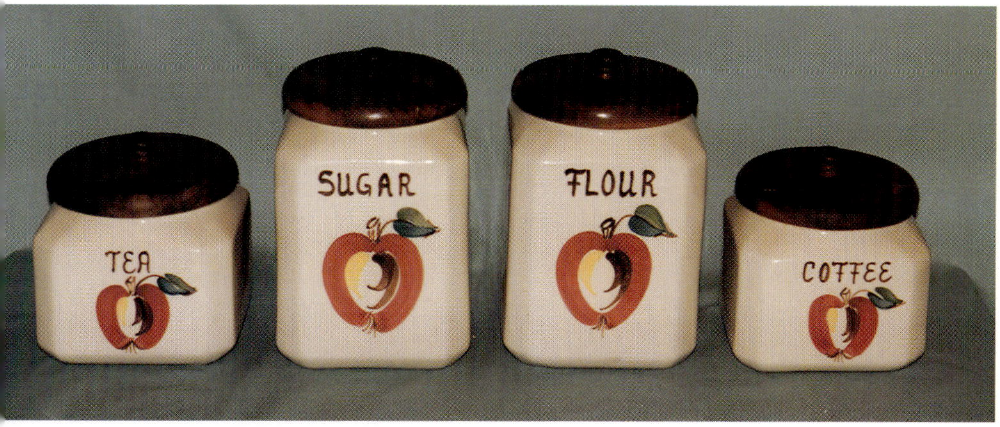

Four piece square canister set with wooden lids. $100 each.

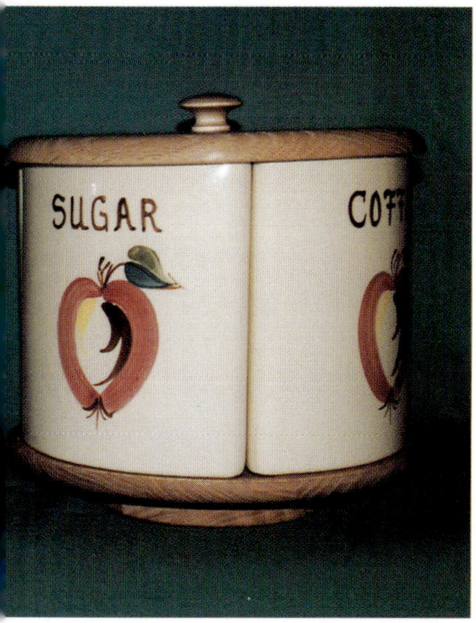

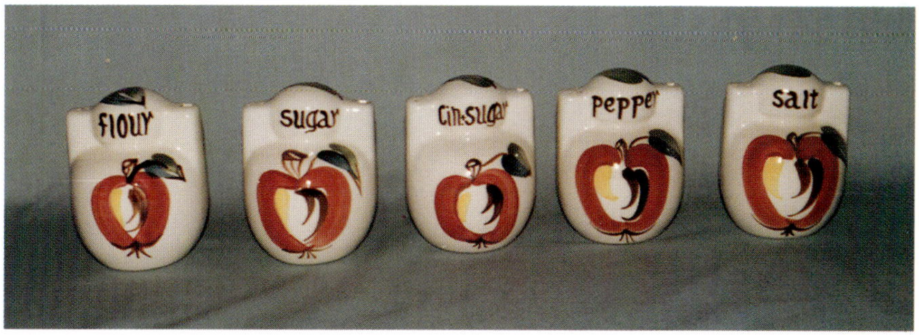

Five piece pour and shake set: flour $150, sugar $150, cin. + sugar $175, pepper $25, salt $25.

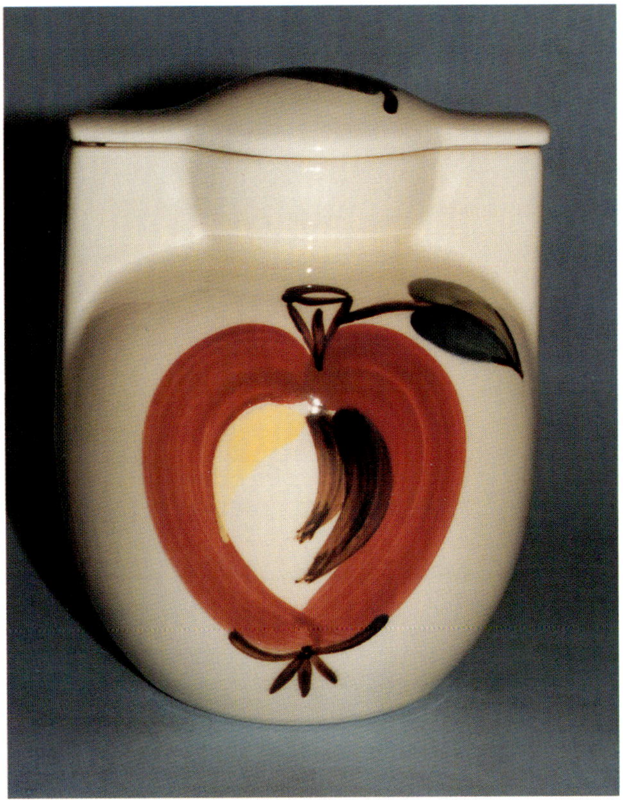

Winged covered grease jar. $80.

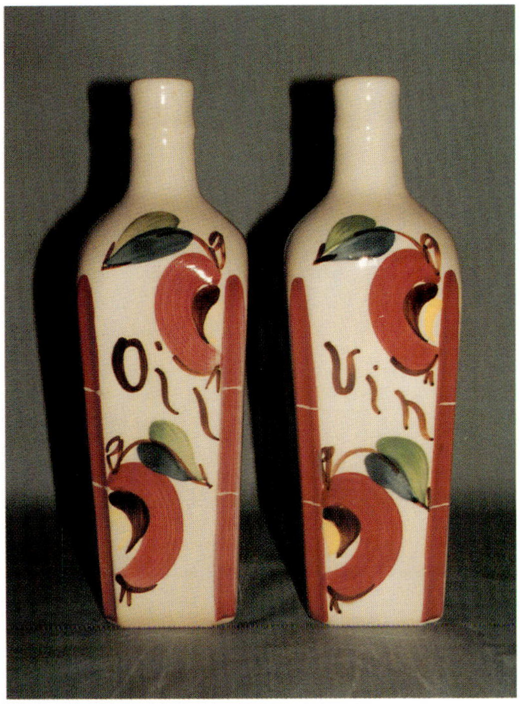

Tall oil and vinegar. $90 set.

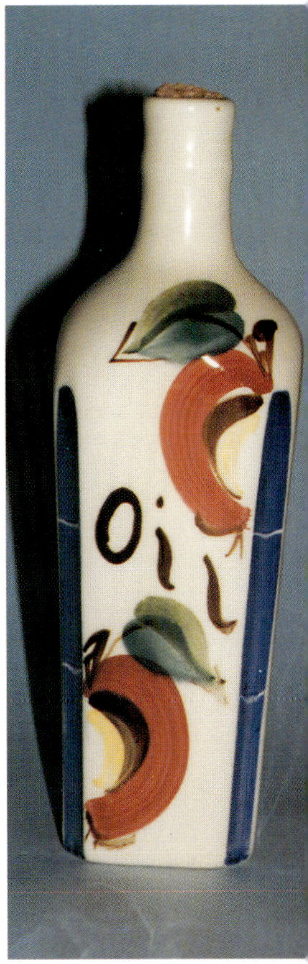

Tall oil and vinegar with cobalt trim. $150 set.

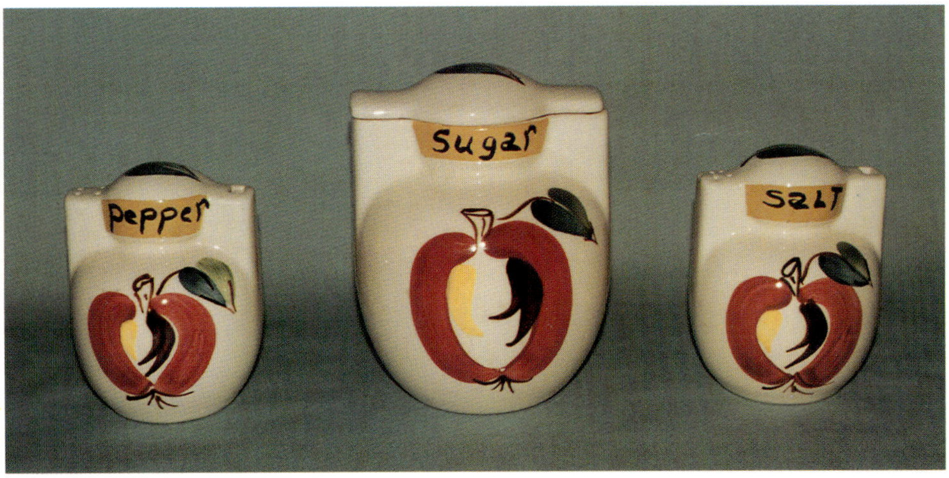

Winged table set with applied yellow banding, not a production set. $150 set.

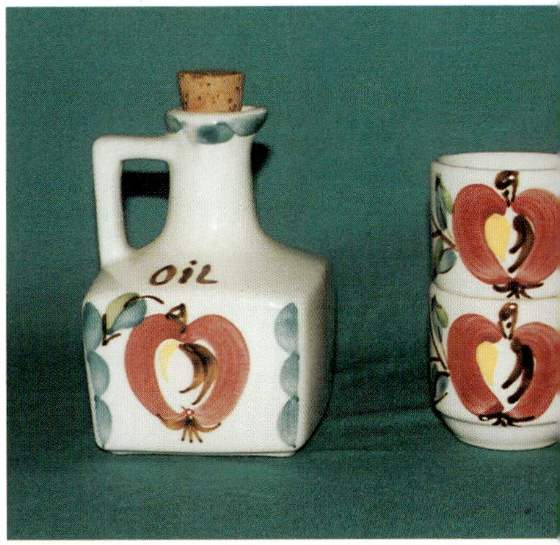

Square oil and vinegar. $50 set. Stacking salt and pepper shakers. $100 set.

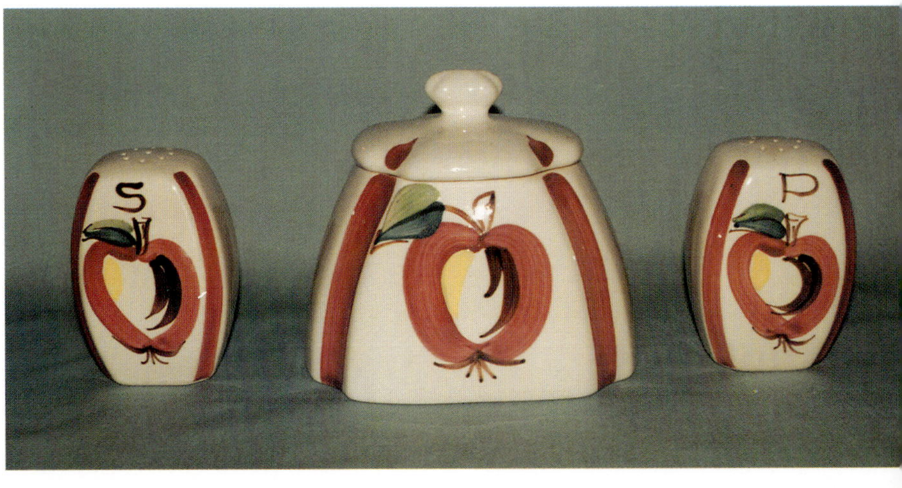

Range set: covered range grease jar, $50; range salt and pepper, $40 set.

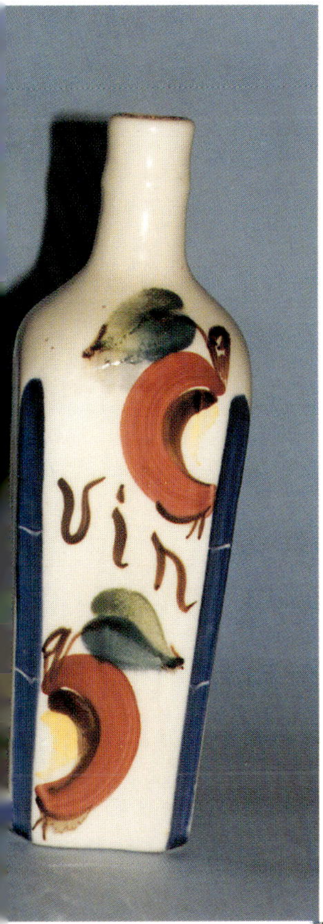

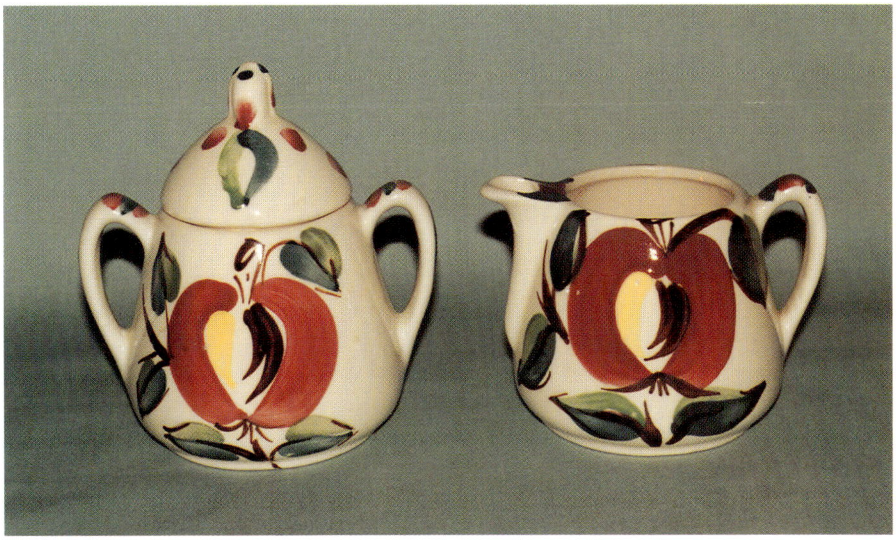

Covered sugar and creamer. $35 set.

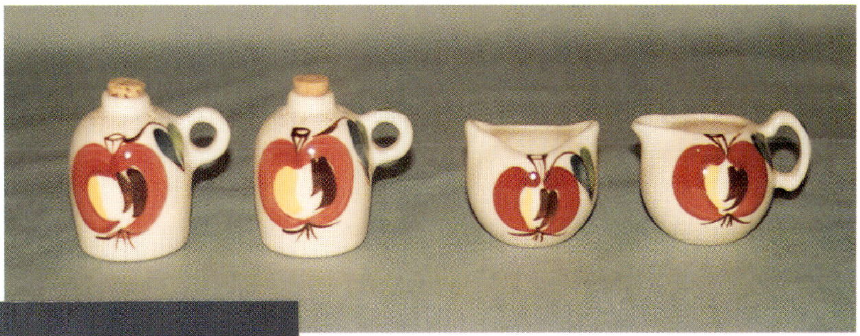

Jug salt and pepper. $20 set. Individual sugar and creamer. $20 set.

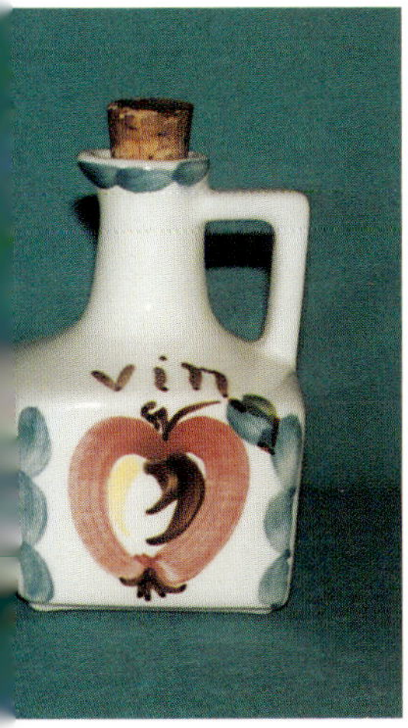

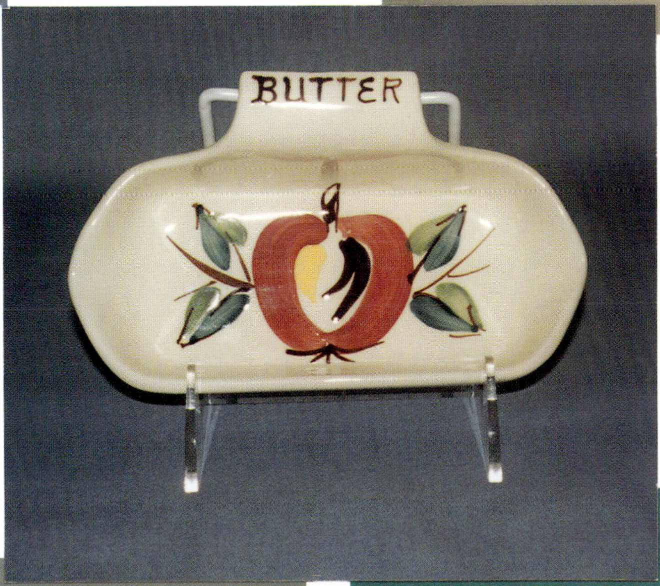

Butter dish. $200. If marked "spoon" instead of "butter," $300+.

Individual bean pot with cover. $75. Marmalade jar. $60.

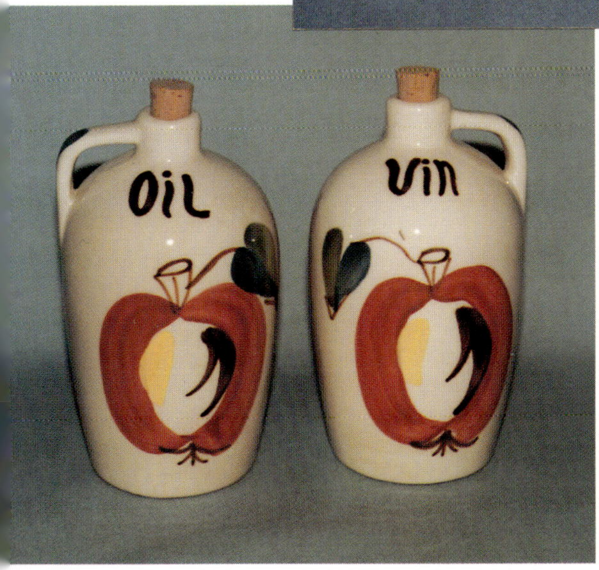

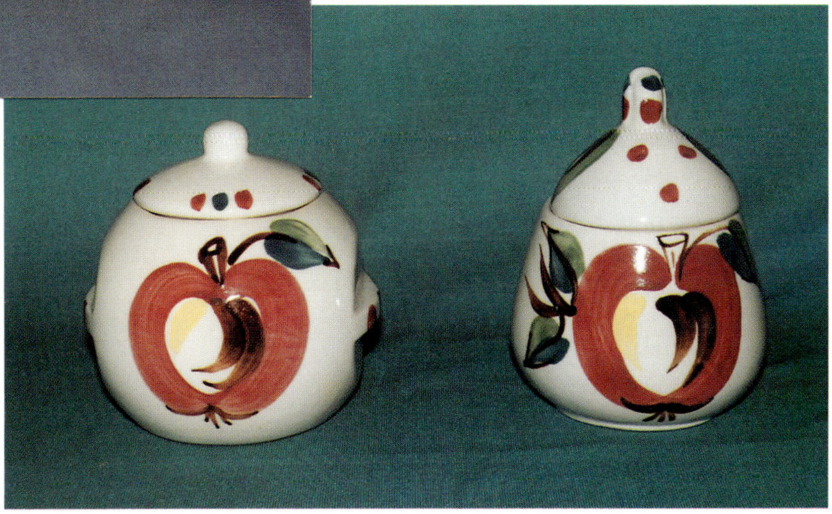

Jug style oil and vinegar set. $150.

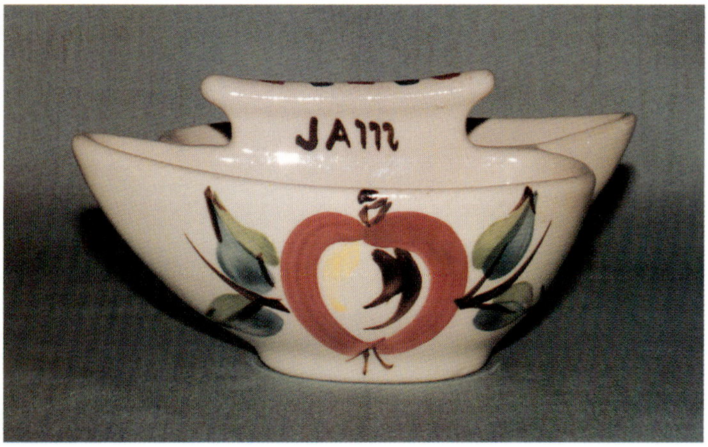

Jam and jelly. $50.

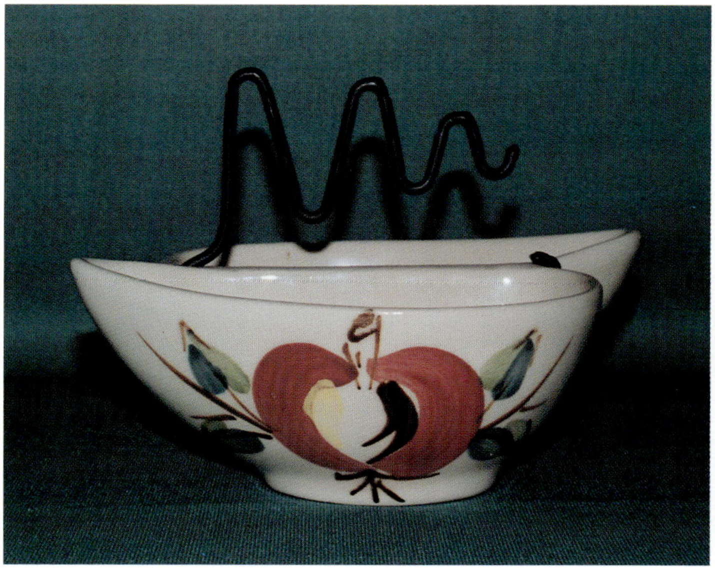

Ashtray. $35.

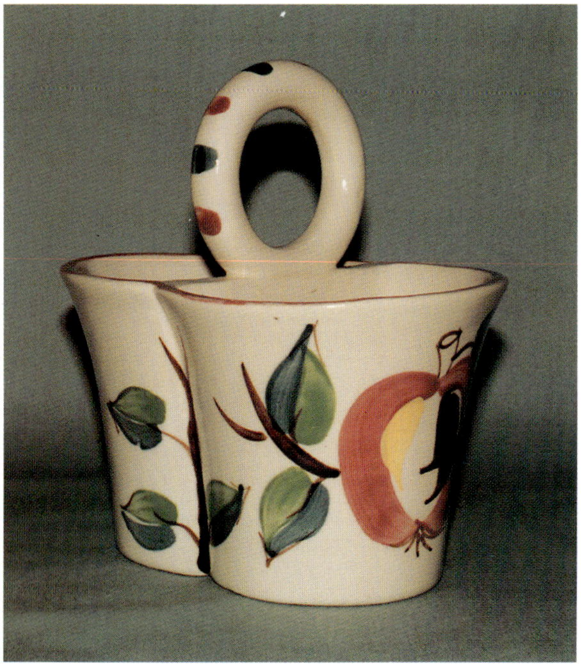

Candy dish. $80.

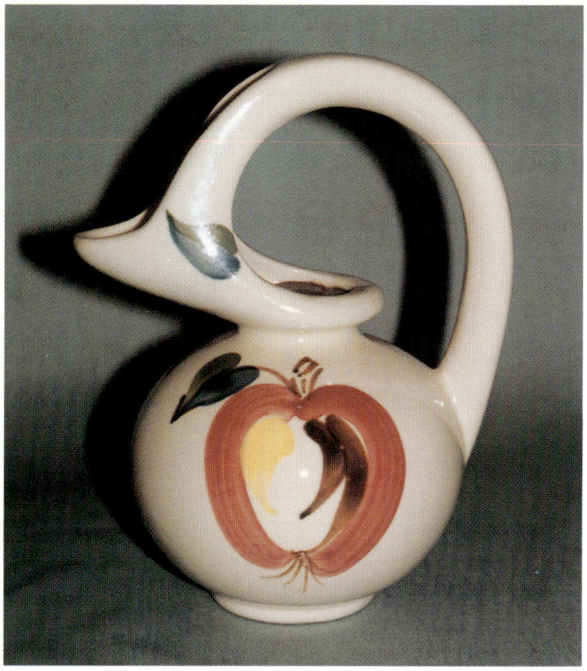

Honey jug. $250.

Rum jug planter without cutout. $100.

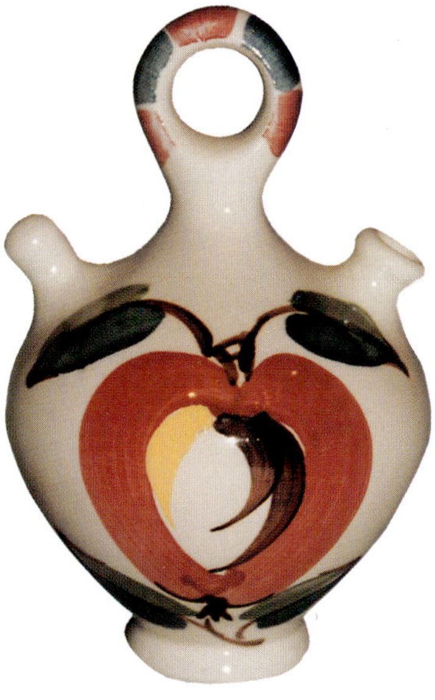

Star candle holders with inserts. $400 pair. Rum jug planter. $75.

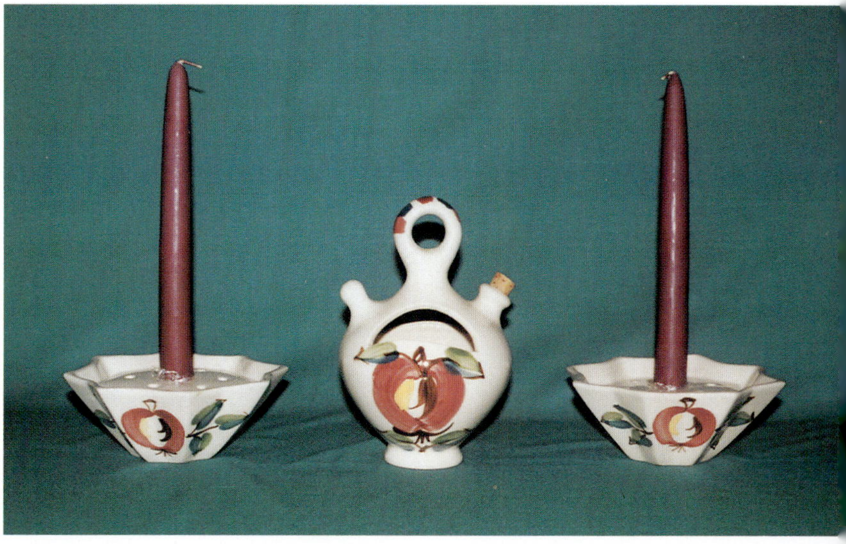

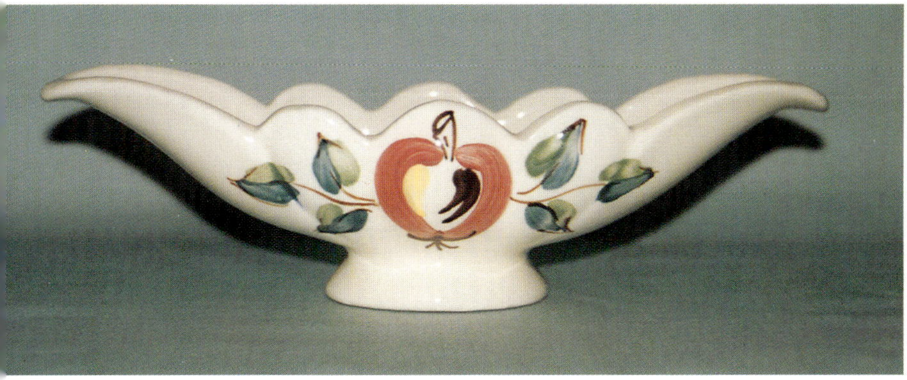

Console bowl, NAPCO mold. $250.

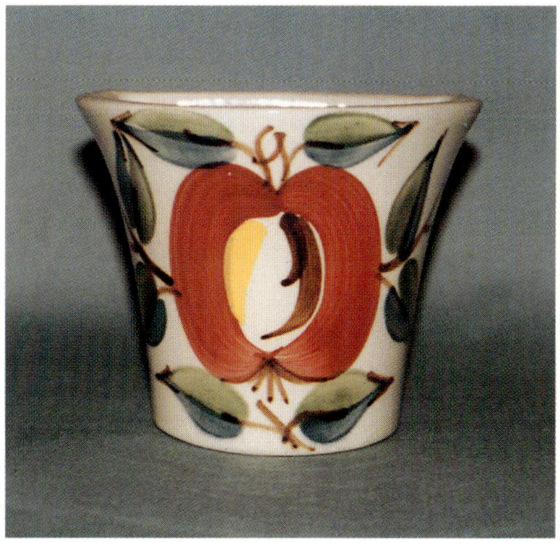

Wall pocket. $90.

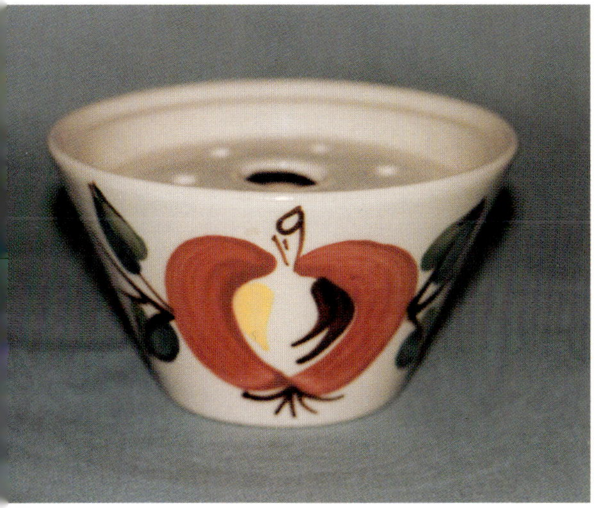

Round candle holder with insert. $250.

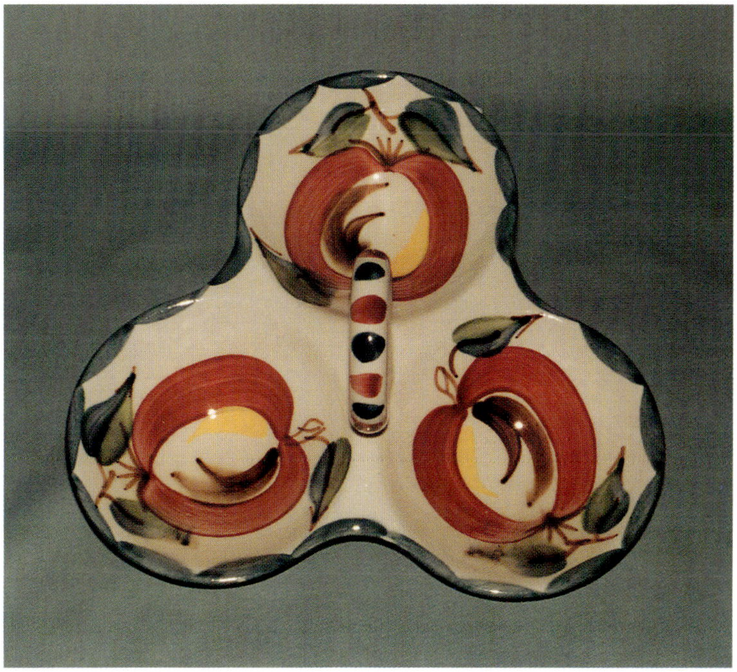

Three part relish with ceramic ring handle. $40.

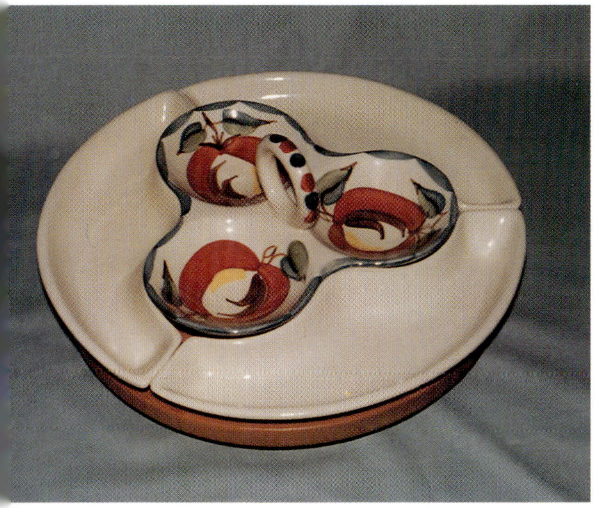

Three part relish lazy susan with wooden base. $90.

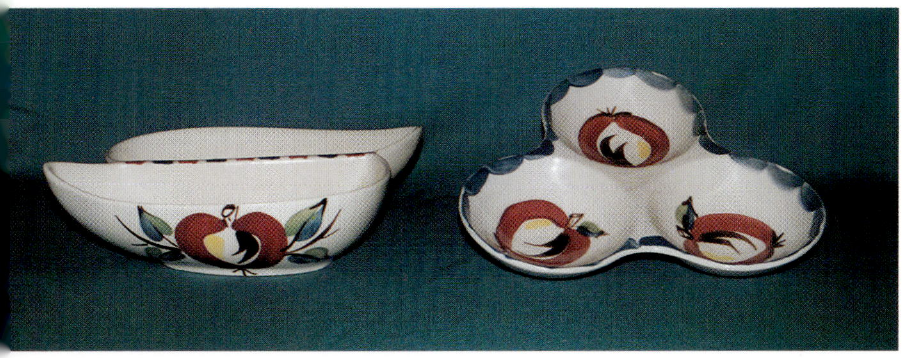

Divided vegetable. $25. Three part relish with no handle. $40.

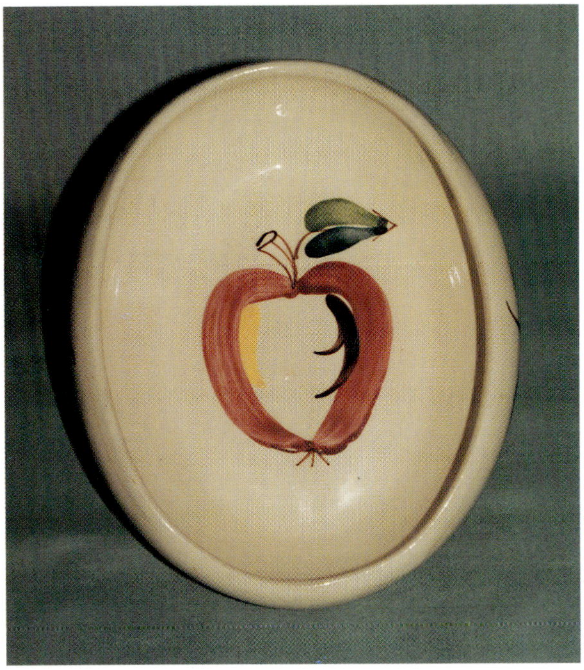

Salad bowl. $80.

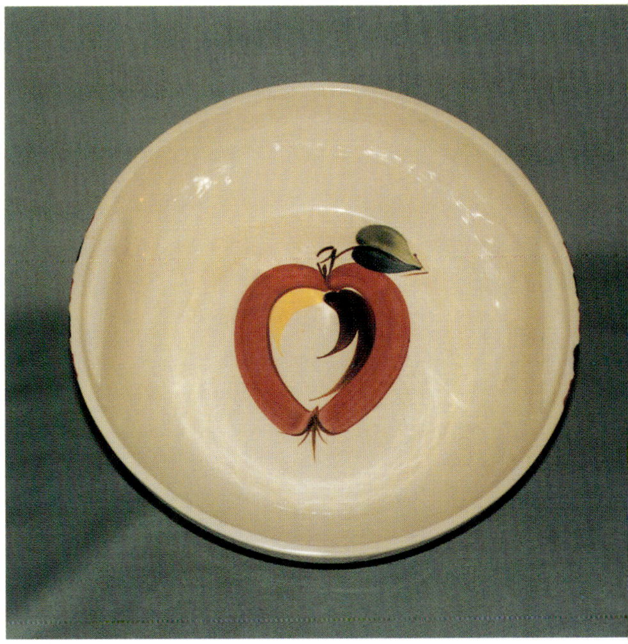

Open vegetable. $20.

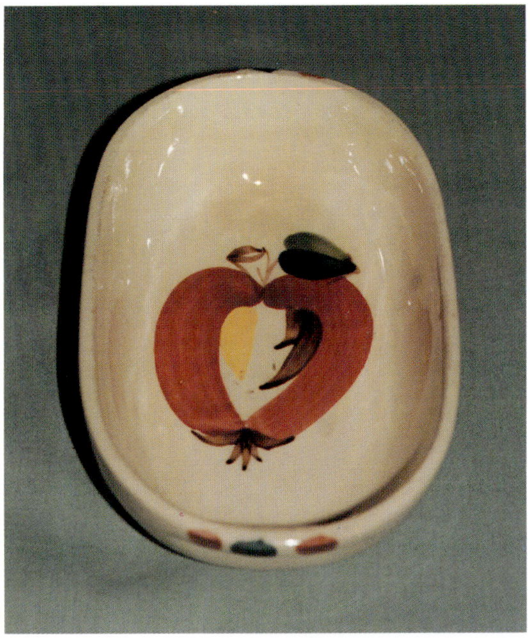

Pickle. $20.

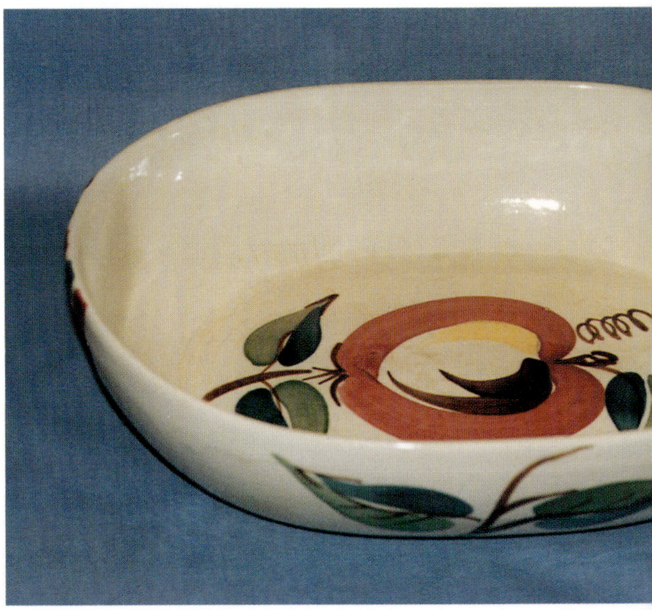

Spaghetti bowl. $150.

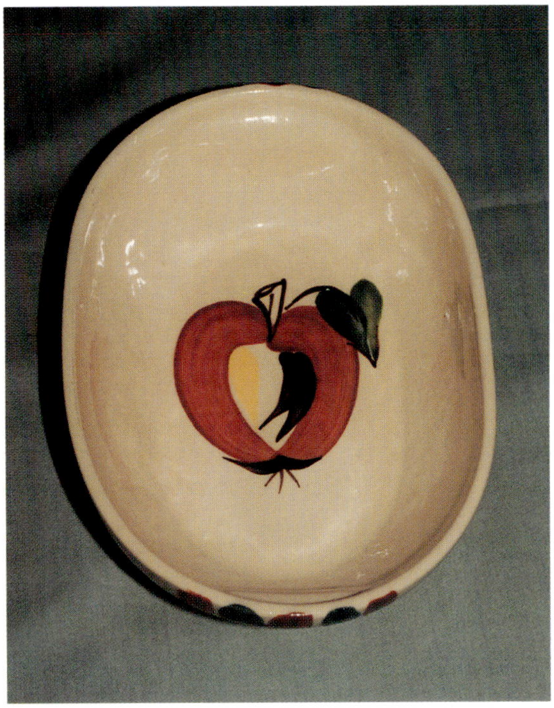

Baker. $25.

Oblong planter, NAPCO mold. $250.

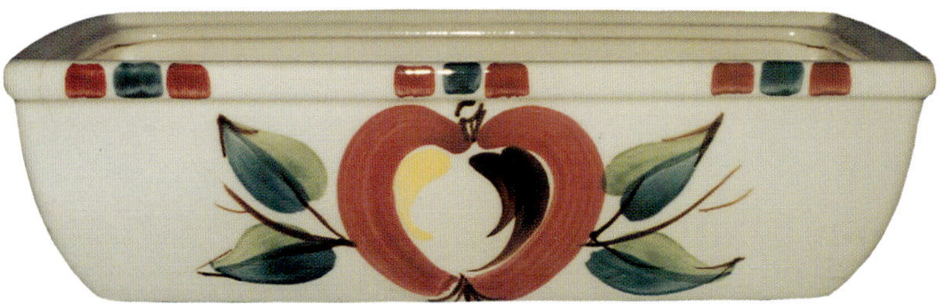

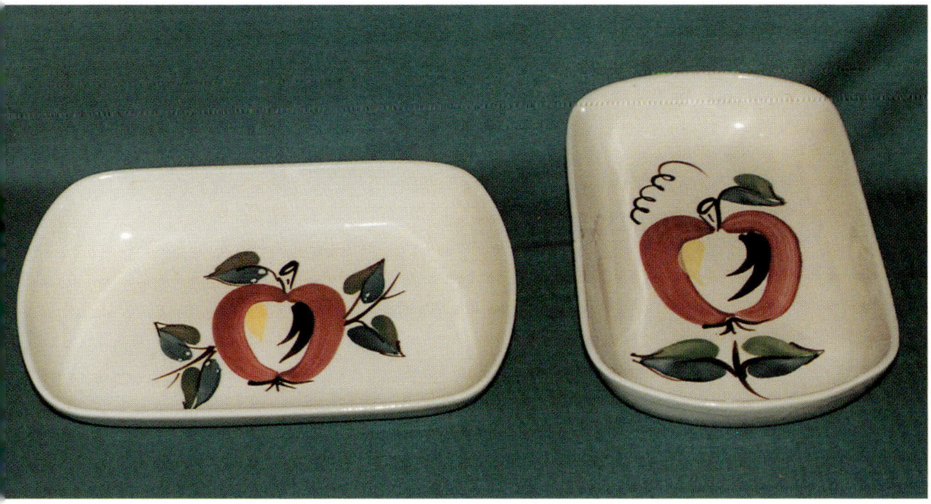

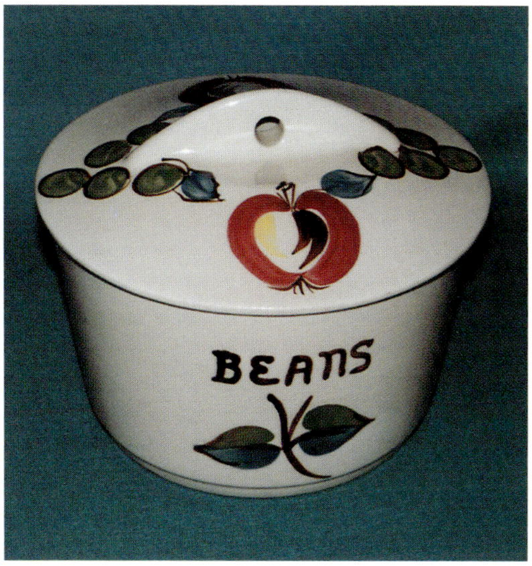

Roll trays. Left, common orientation. $30. Right, uncommon orientation. $50.

Beans pot with cover. $70.

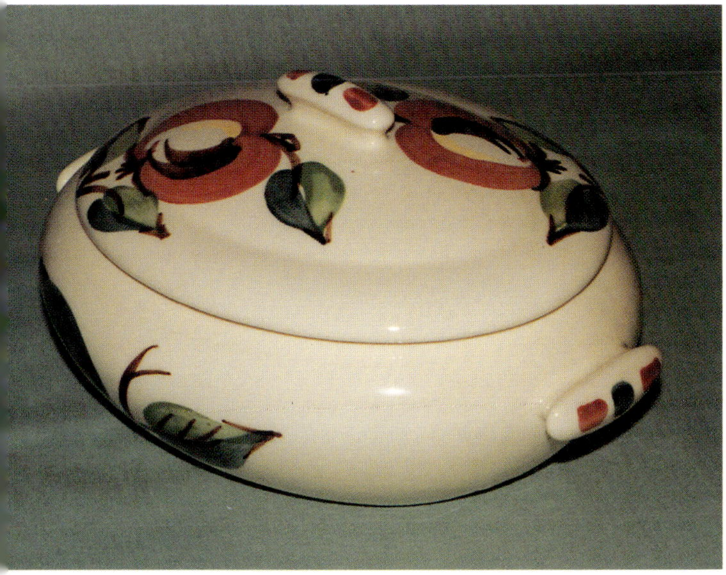

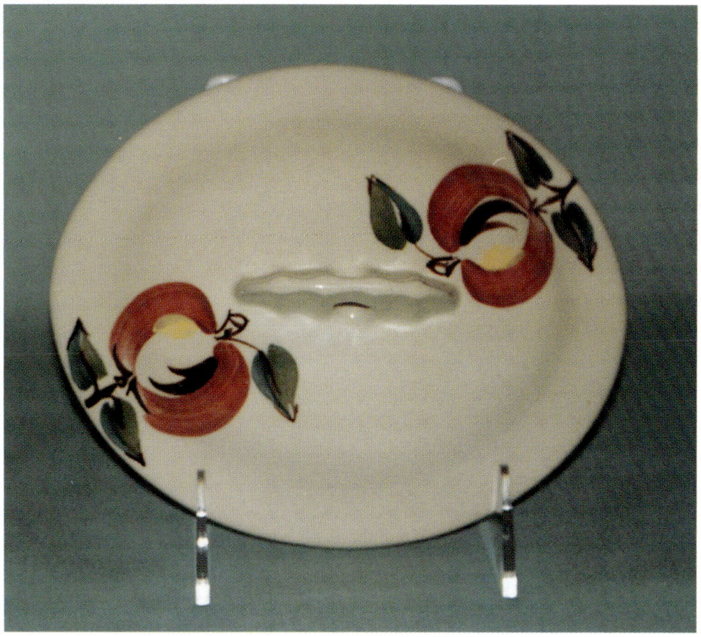

Covered vegetable. $60.

Covered vegetable lid, odd shaped handle. $30.

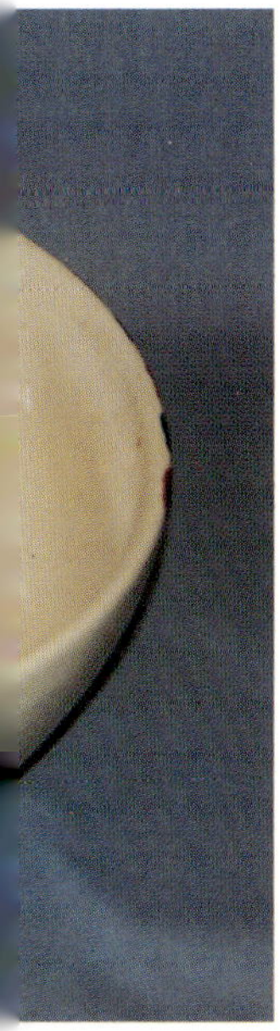

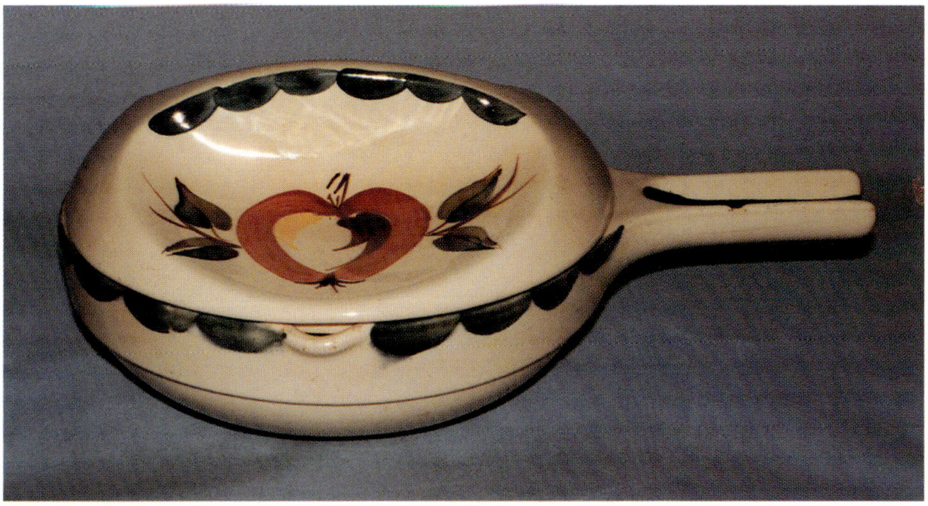

Two quart covered casserole, Rubel mold. Rare piece. $400+.

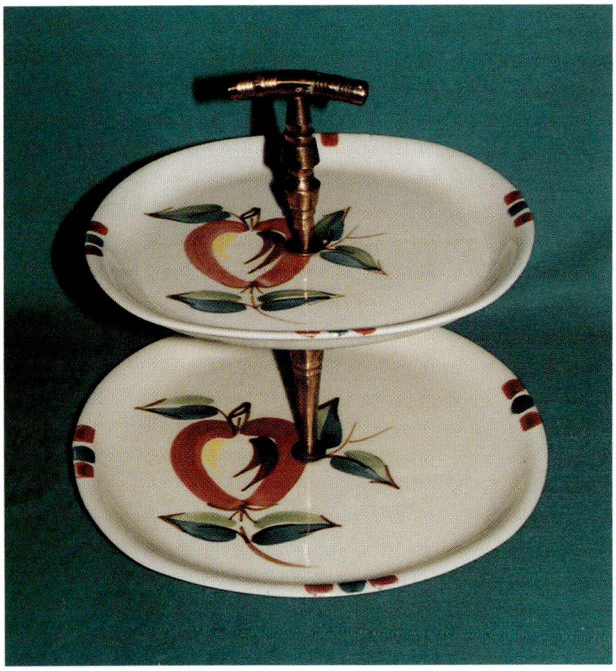

Two tiered tidbit tray, dinner and breakfast plates. $75.

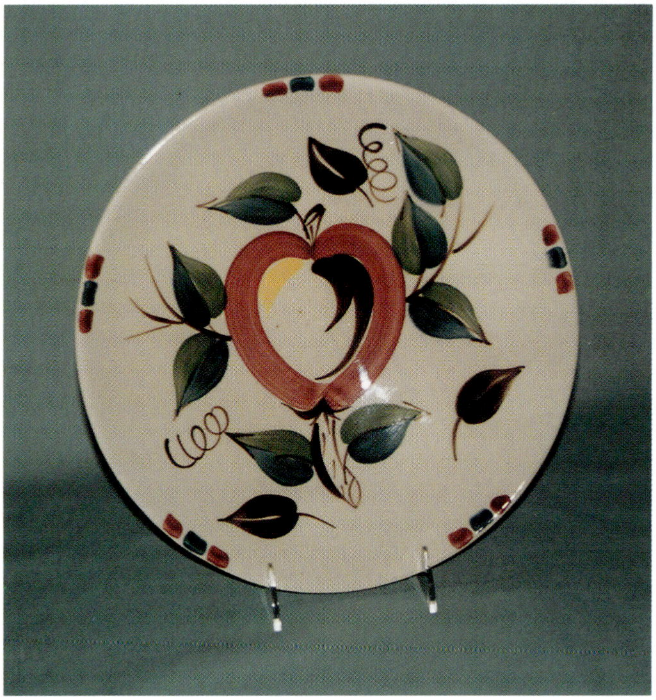

Fruit bowl, plain edge. $60.

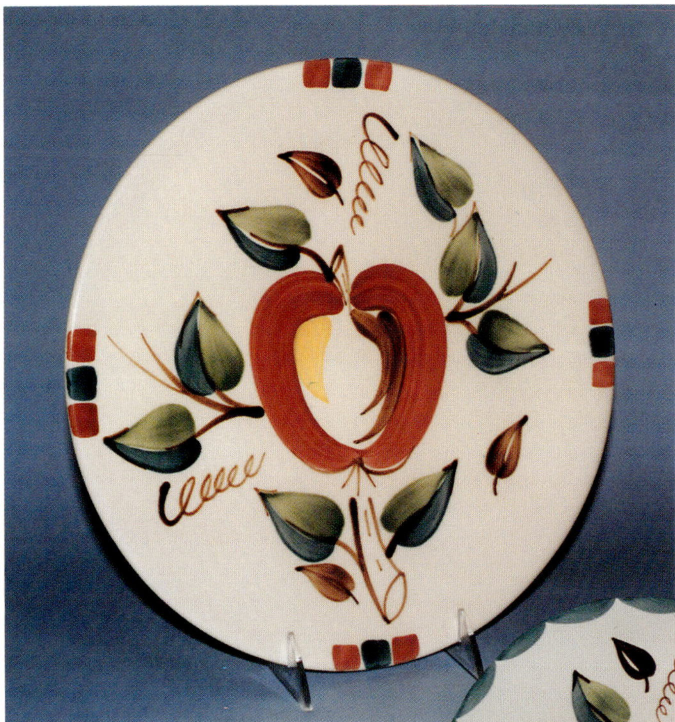

Chop plate, plain edge. $40.

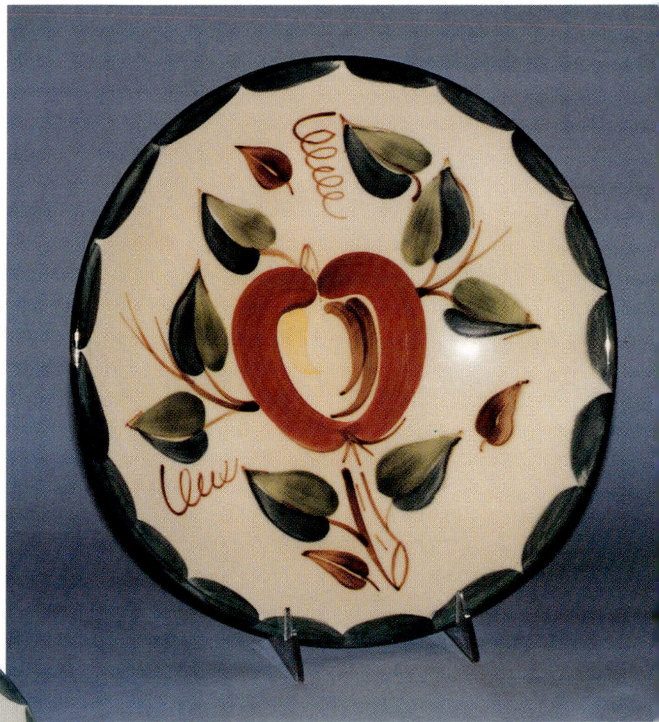

Fruit bowl, scalloped edge. $60.

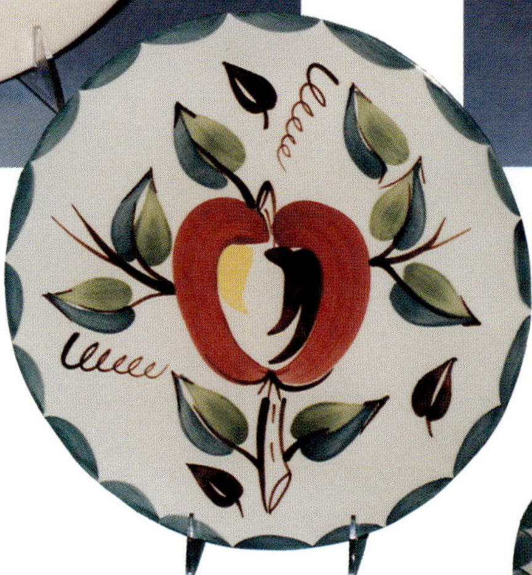

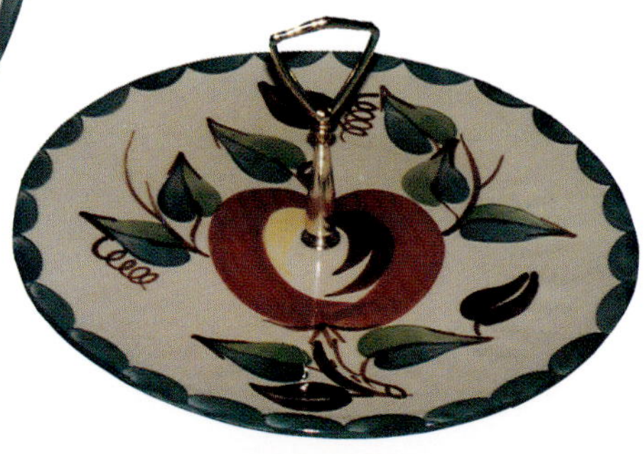

Chop plate, scalloped edge. $40. Sandwich plate. $50.

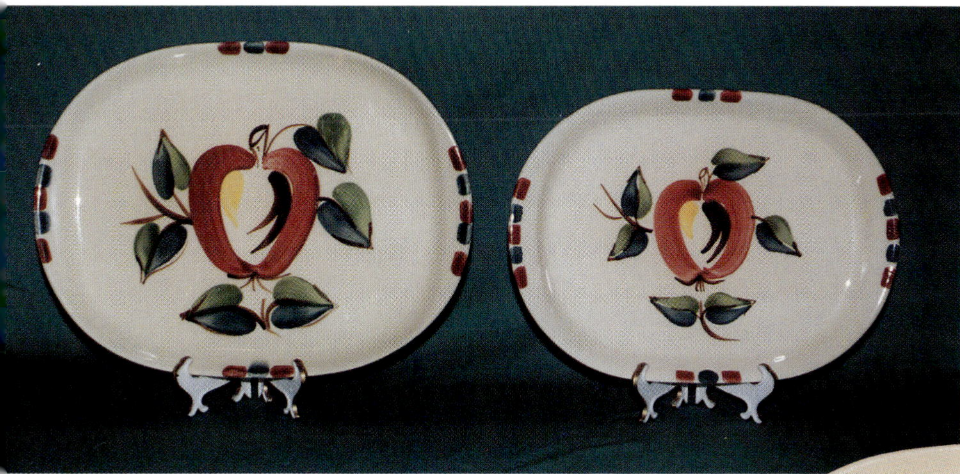

Large platter. $45. Small platter. $55.

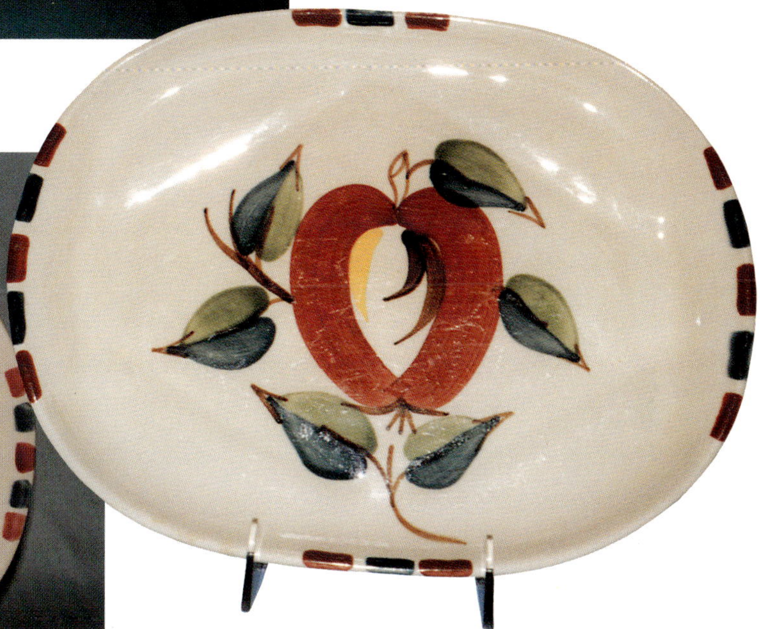

Diamond grill platter. $60

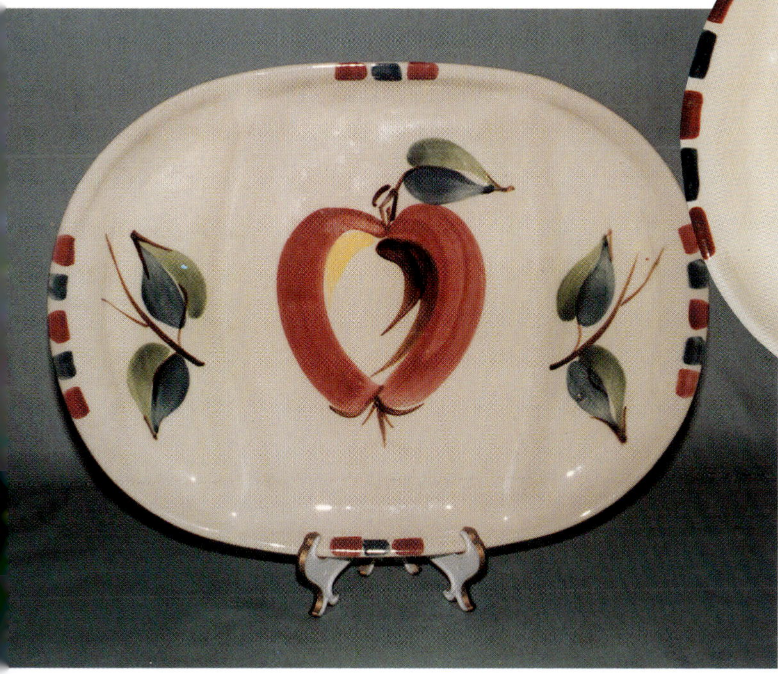

Three line grill platter. $80.

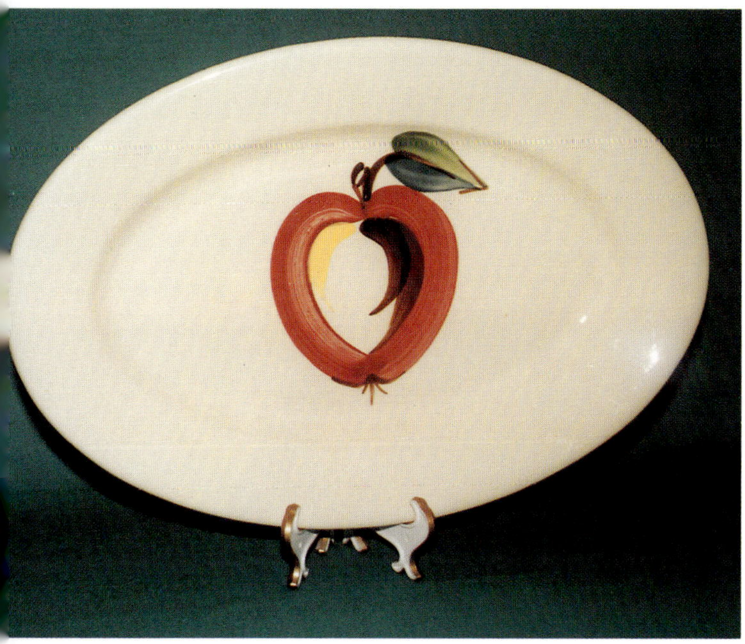

Oval platter, unknown mold. $200+.

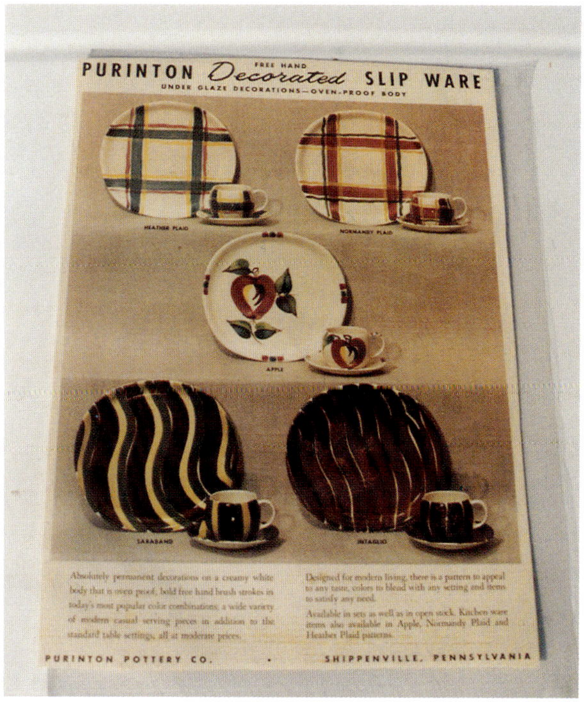

Purinton Free Hand Decorated Slip Ware brochure.

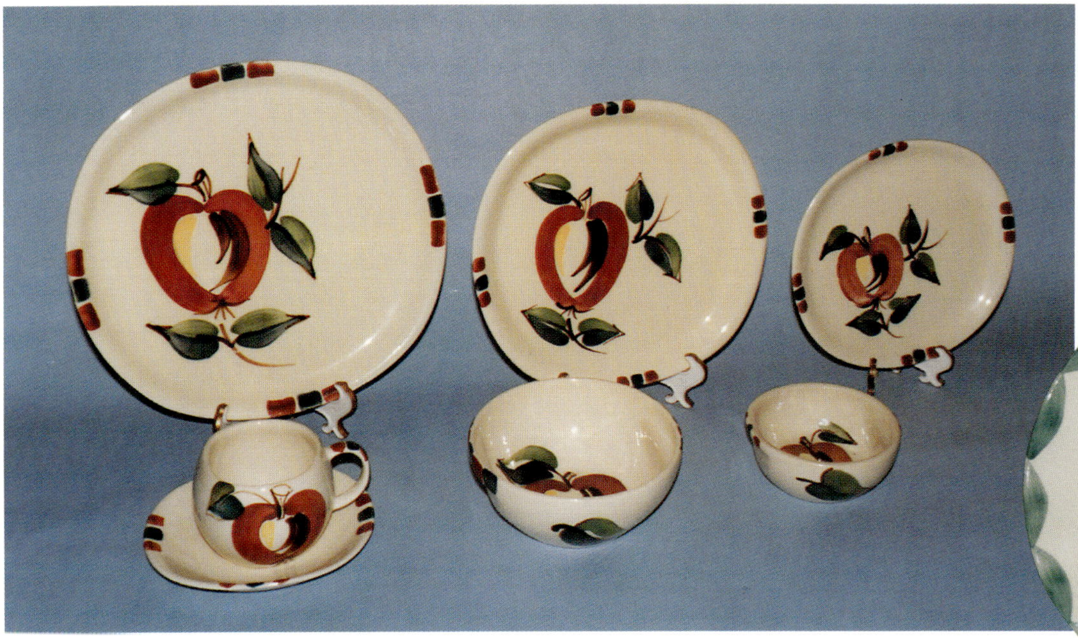

Salad plate, Seaform style. $150+.

Dinner plate. $20. Breakfast plate. $20. Salad plate. $20. Cup. $10. Saucer. $3. Cereal bowl. $15. Dessert bowl. $15.

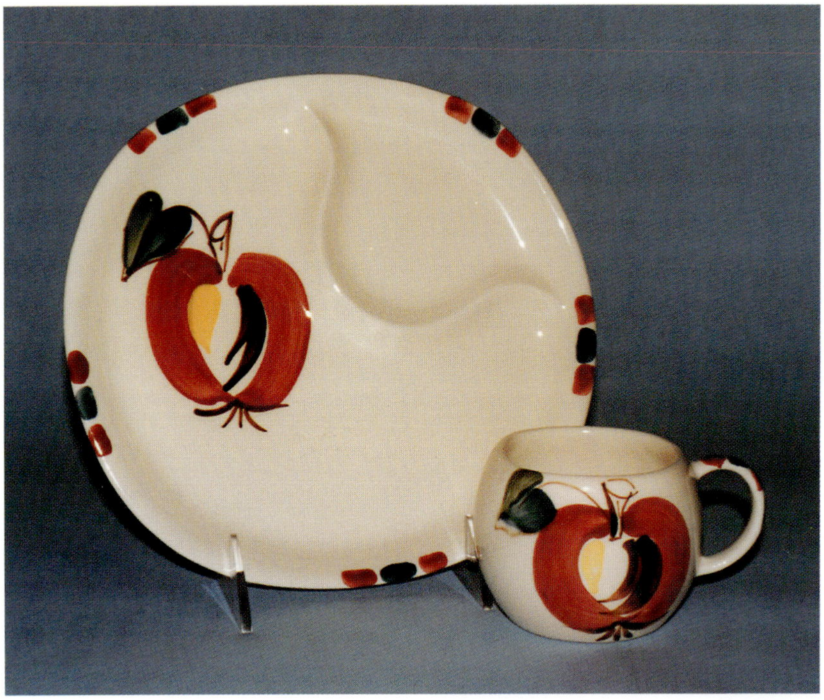

Tea and toast plate. $20. Cup. $10.

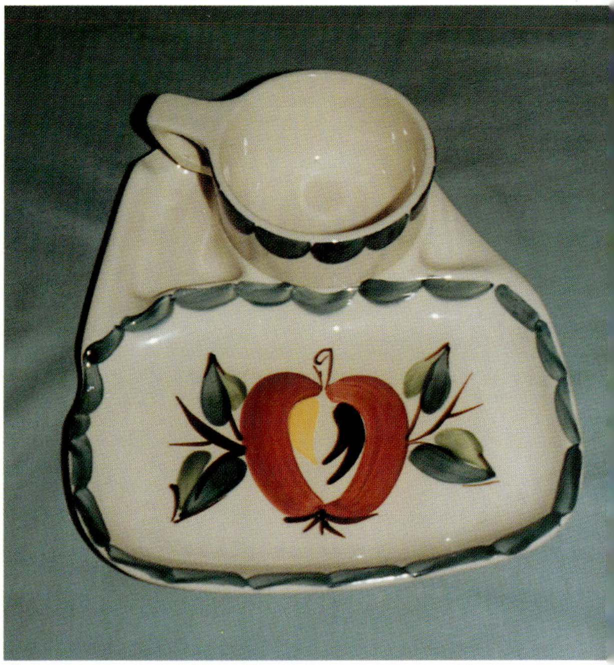

Soup and sandwich, Rubel mold. $200+.

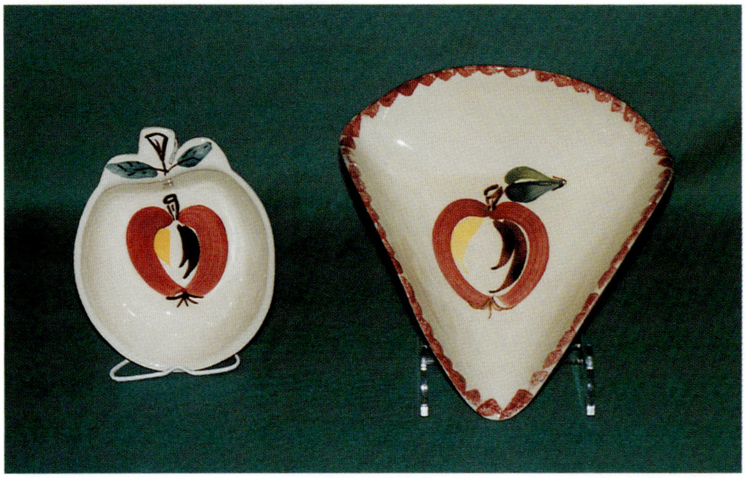

Apple shaped candy dish, unknown mold, 5.75" diameter. $150+. Experimental candy dish, 7.5" diameter. $125+.

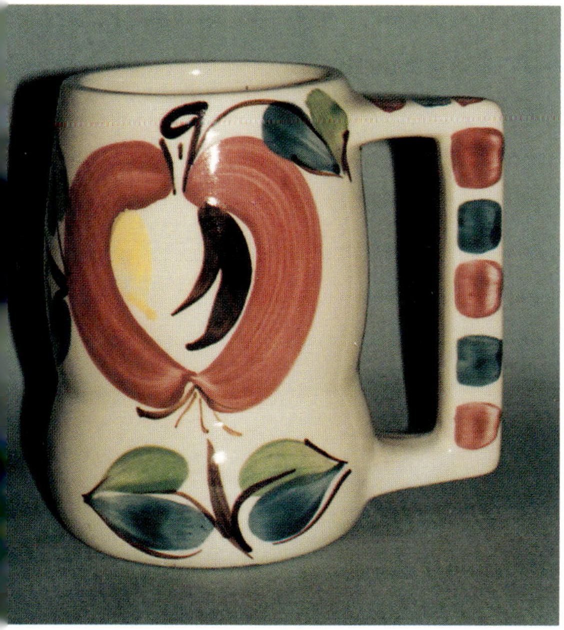

Beer mug. $75.

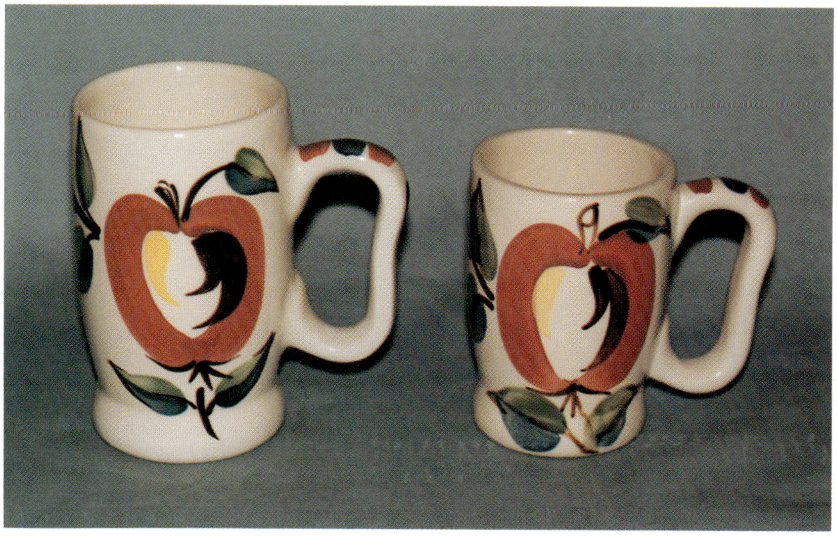

Hot chocolate mug, 4.75" high. $125. Coffee mug. $60.

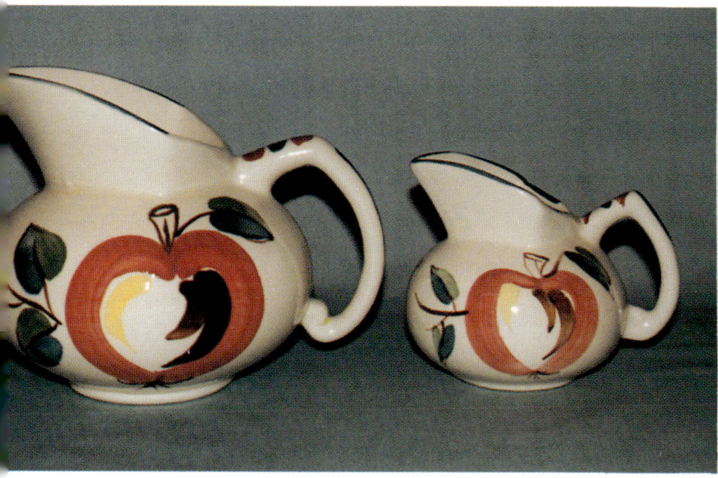

Oversized kent jug, 6.25" high (rare). $400+. Kent jug. $25.

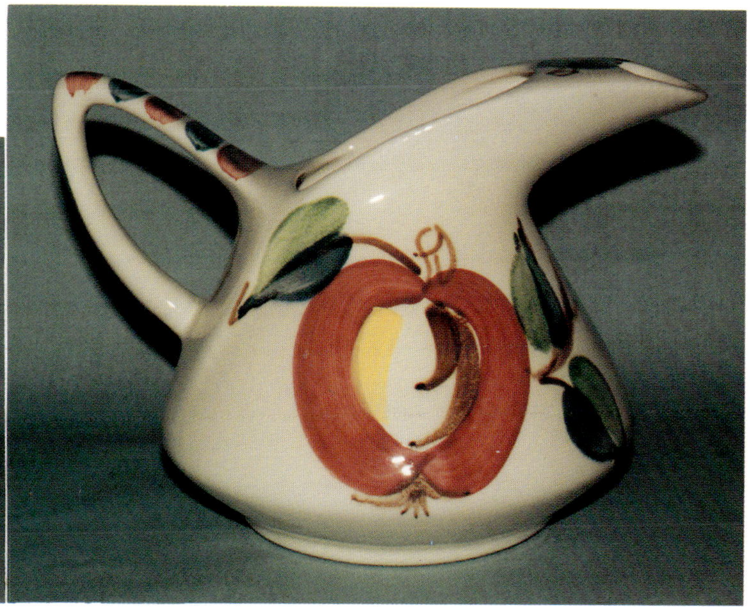

Two pint dutch jug. $35.

Tumbler. $25. Night bottle. $90. Five pint dutch jug. $50.

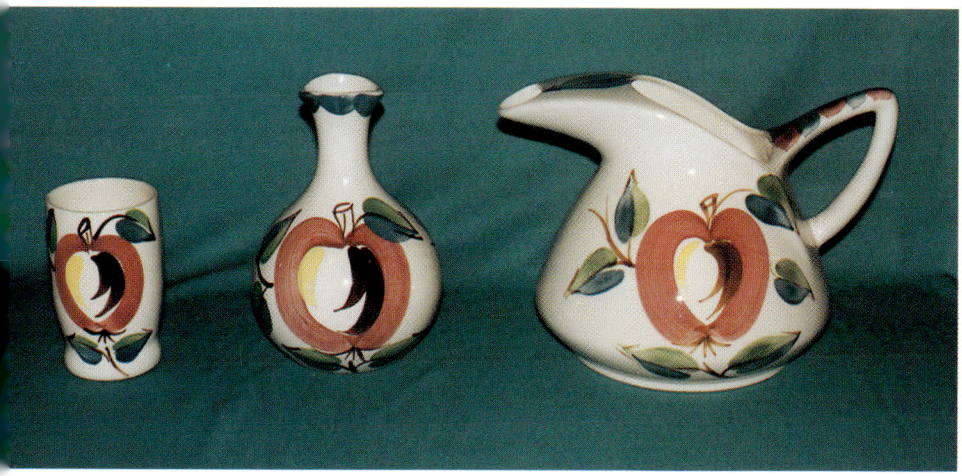

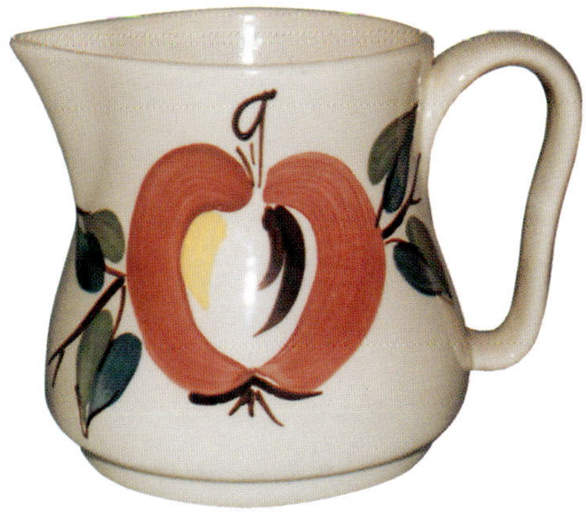

Pitcher, Rubel mold. $500+.

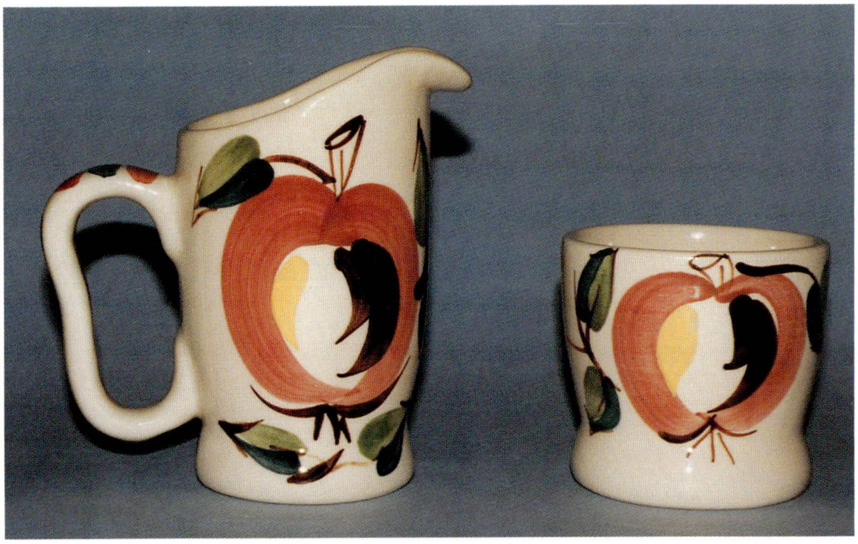

Mug jug. $50. Juice mug. $15.

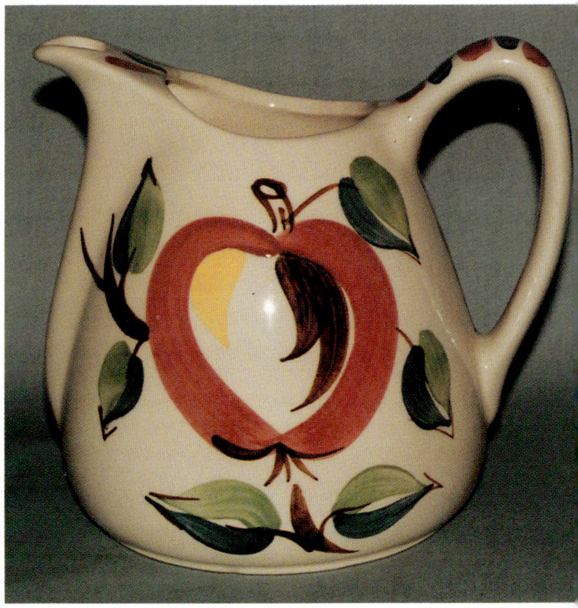

Beverage pitcher. $45.

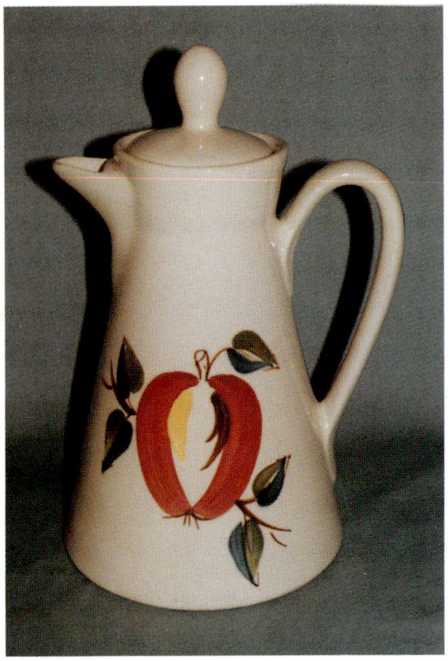

Coffee tureen, Taylor Smith Taylor mold. $400+.

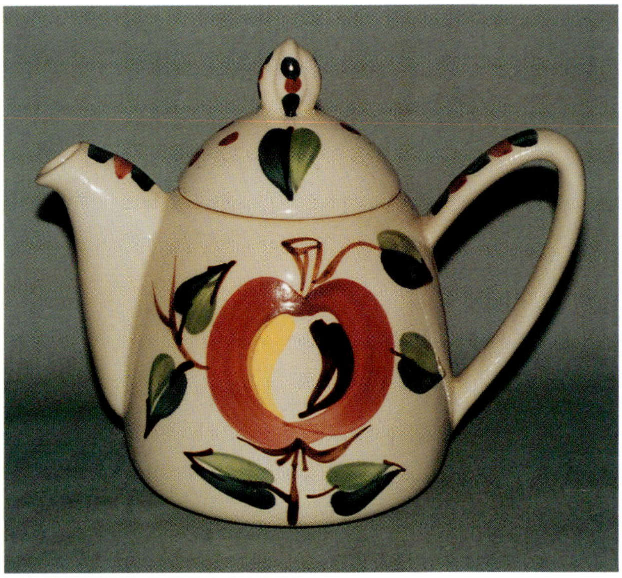

Six cup domed lid teapot. $50.

Eight cup coffee pot with drip filter. $125. Without drip filter. $90. Two cup teapot (rare). $250+.

Six cup teapot (rare). $150+.

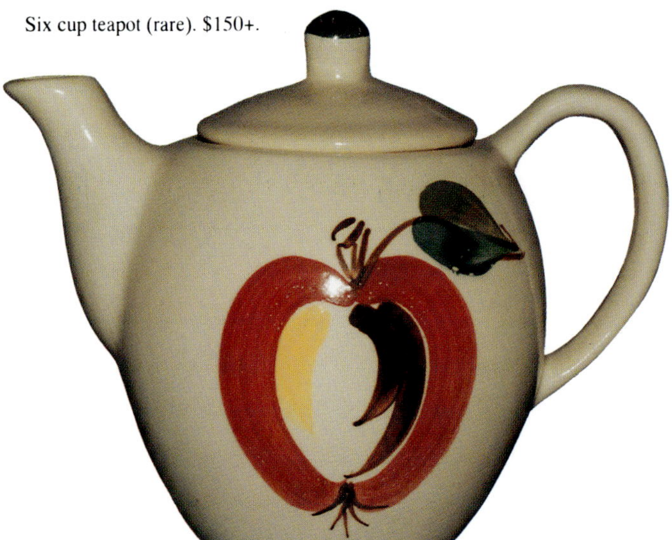

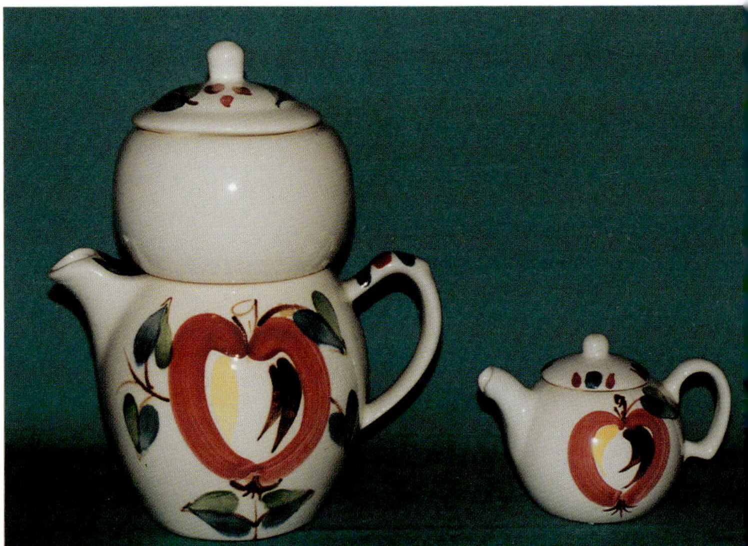

Intaglio

Intaglio was first developed by Bill Blair during the Wellsville years. Dorothy Purinton created the flower design seen on most of those intaglio pieces. Intaglio means incising. After the item is painted, the design is incised into the color, creating quite a bit of dust. The glaze is then applied and the item is fired in the kiln. The most desirable intaglio pieces are those created by Bill Blair and Dorothy Purinton; the Palm Tree etches and the souvenir pieces are also very desirable. In this chapter we feature the production items that Purinton made for sale.

Intaglio was introduced in 1950. Brown was the first color used, followed by Turquoise. Golden Brown (caramel) was listed as a color you could buy in open stock. Green and Coral saw limited production. Light Blue, Cobalt, and Purple are seen on a few items. One piece has been found in Black. In this chapter, each color is given a section.

Brown Intaglio was one of the best sellers for Purinton and rivaled Apple during its time. Supply is plentiful and the demand is low. Brown may not be as appealing to people now as it was in the 1950s. However, do not underestimate this woodsy-looking pattern. When pieces are placed together, Brown Intaglio is very attractive and satisfying to view. Most items are easy to find and are reasonably priced. The higher priced pieces are the ones the Purinton Company either did not use in their open stock line or which they may have made for another company. Some more difficult items to find are the wall pocket, individual cream and sugar, the basket planter, and the canister set. The two cup teapot is rare. A few pieces contracted for other companies have been found in Brown Intaglio and are desirable.

Turquoise Intaglio was an open stock item which was not as popular as Brown. The supply of Turquoise Intaglio is limited but the demand is not too high, keeping prices moderate. The harder to find accessory items command a higher price. Dinnerware is not common.

Golden Brown Intaglio has a caramel-colored appearance. An order form from the Corner Cupboard shows it was sold as an open stock item. The supply for this decoration is very limited, and finding any piece would be quite good.

Examples of Green and Coral Intaglio are seen on a few pieces. The evidence suggests that ceramics decorated with Green and Coral Intaglio were sold as single items and probably not as sets. You see their coloring on some items made for other companies. Green is pictured on some dinnerware. Supply is low and discovering a piece would be uncommon.

Light Blue, Cobalt, Black, and Purple (pictured with Palm Tree etch in Chapter 17) are very limited Intaglio colors. Items in these colors are uncommon. The Blues are very attractive.

When displaying a variety of Intaglios together, they do make for a colorful, contrasting appearance. Brown is going to be one of the sleeper patterns for Purinton. Low prices make this a decoration that is affordable. As people recognise its beauty, Brown Intaglio will become less plentiful. The other Intaglios fit any collection and will continue to be in short supply.

Brown Intaglio

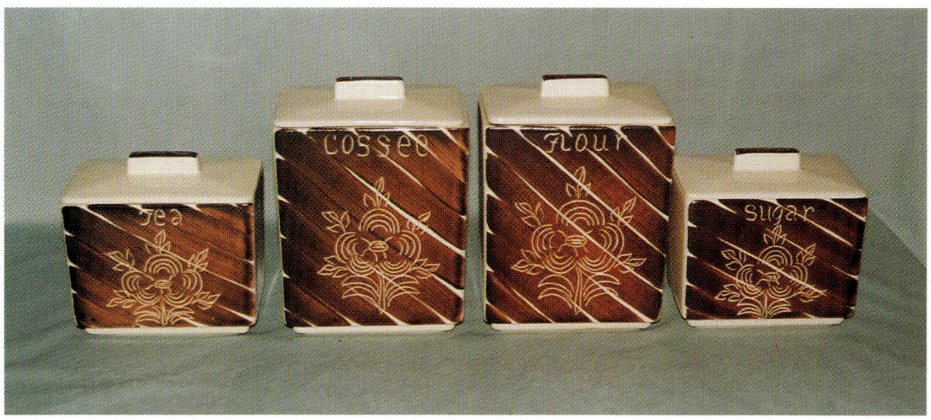

Brown Intaglio four piece apartment canister set.
$40 each.

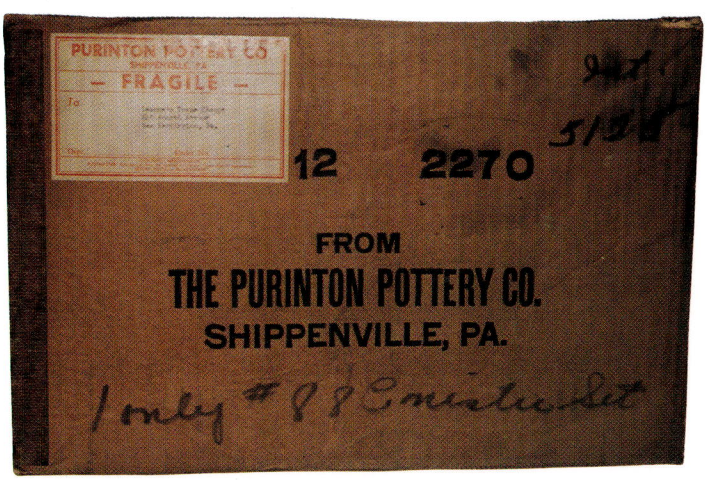

Box for the #88 apartment canister set.

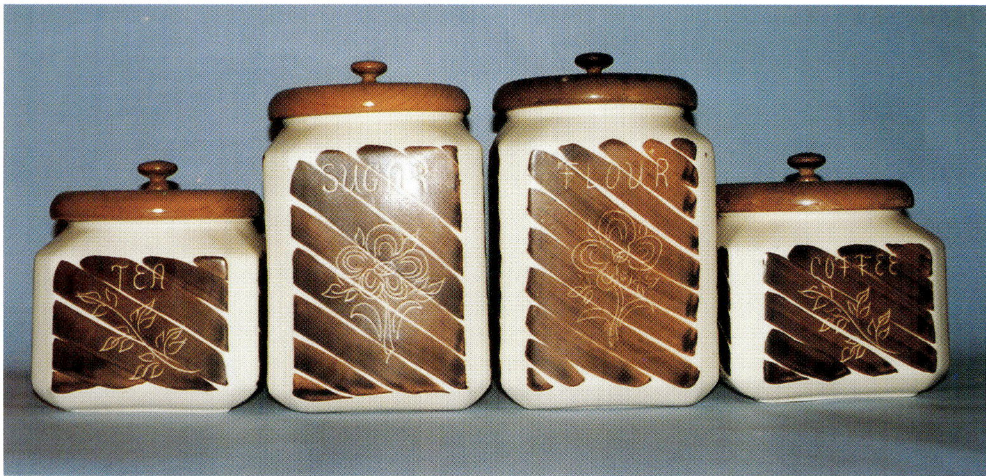

Four piece square canister set with wooden lids. $30 each.

Wide oval canister. $80.

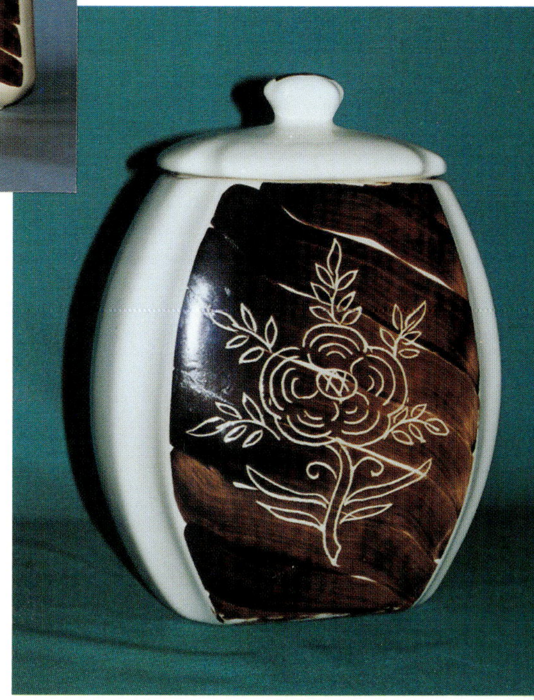

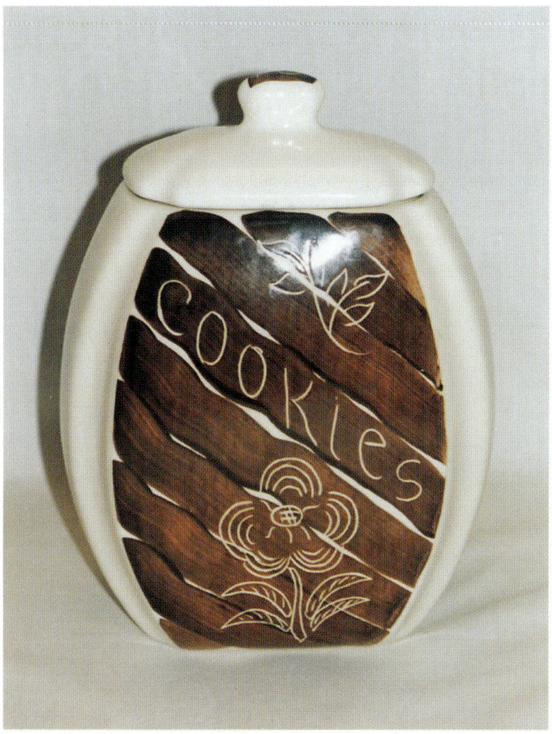

Wide oval cookies jar. $60.

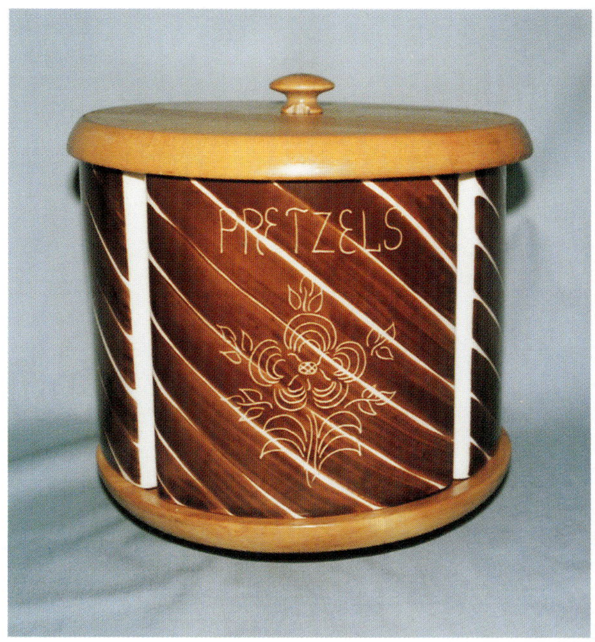

Revolving canister set with wooden base and lid. $200.

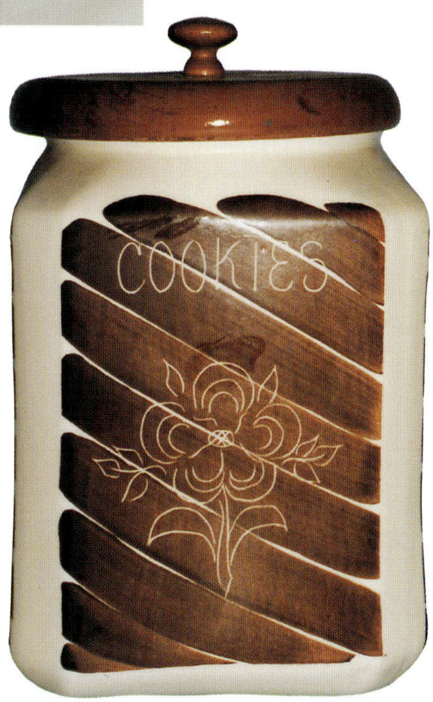

Square cookie canister with a wooden lid. $40.

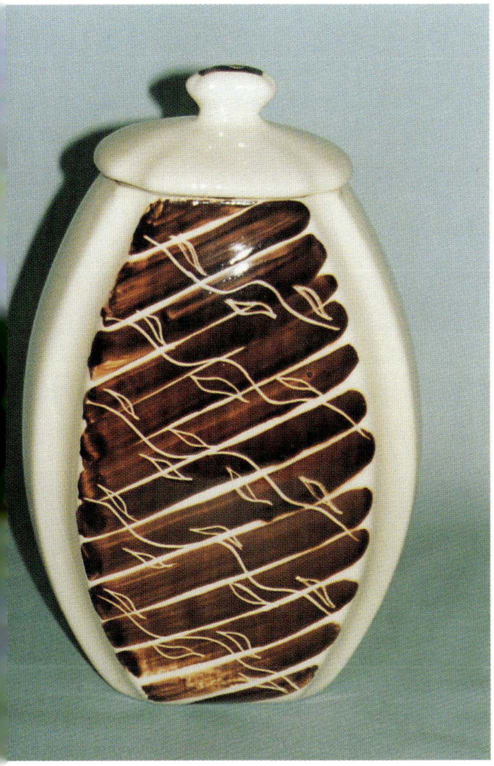

Tall oval canister with leaf design. $75.

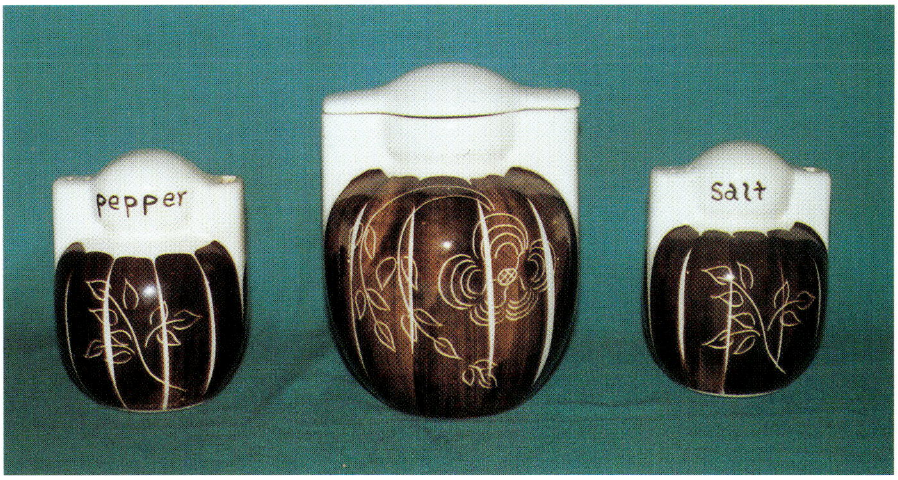

Pepper and salt pour and shake shakers. $35 set. Covered winged grease jar. $50.

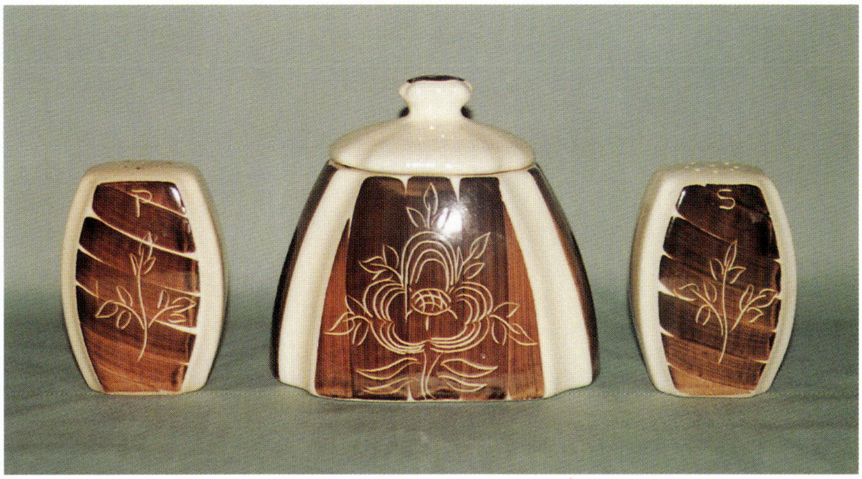

Range pepper and salt shakers. $40 set. Covered range grease jar. $40.

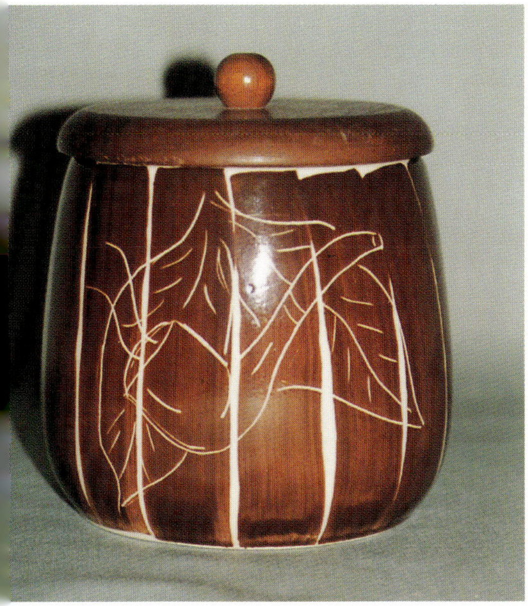

Tobacco humidor with pipe etching. $100.

Large jug style decanters. $50 set.

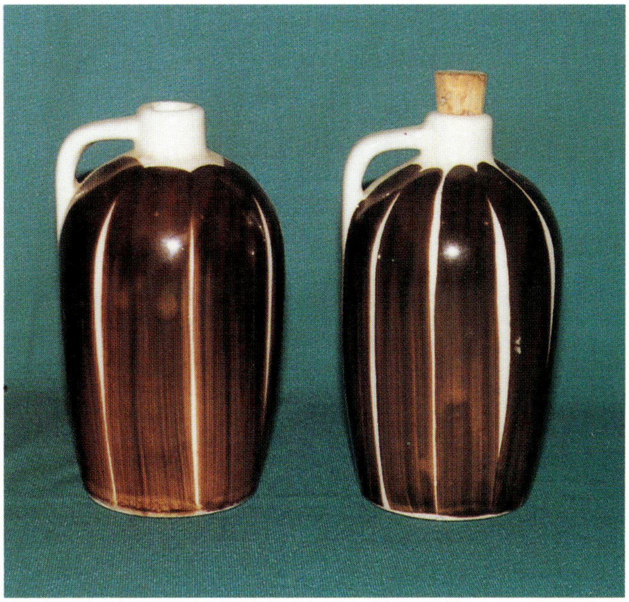

Individual sugar and creamer. Difficult set to find. $50 set.

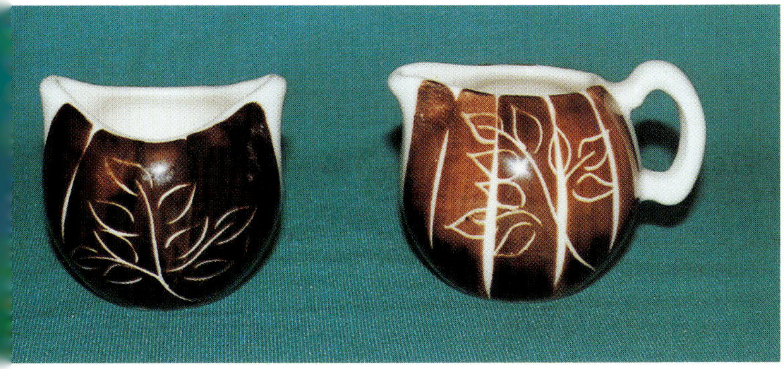

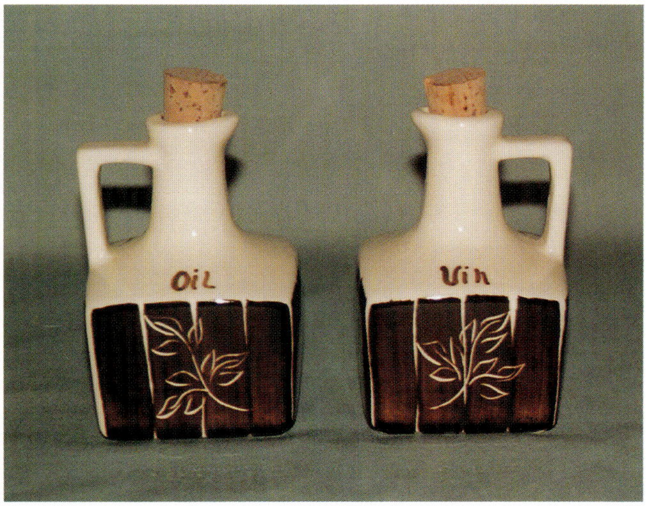

Square oil and vinegar. $20 set.

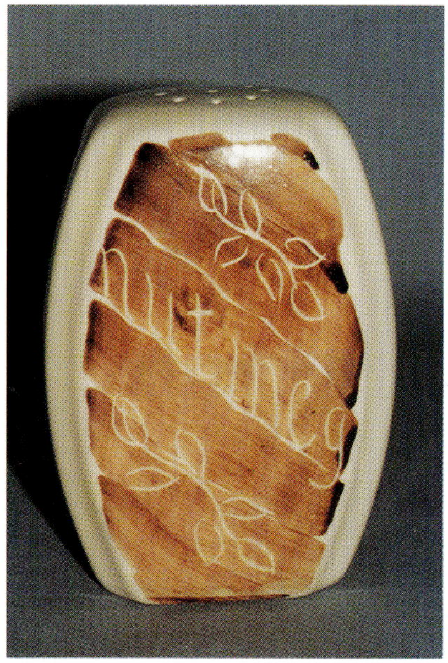

Range shaker, nutmeg. Rare spice to find incised on a shaker. $75.

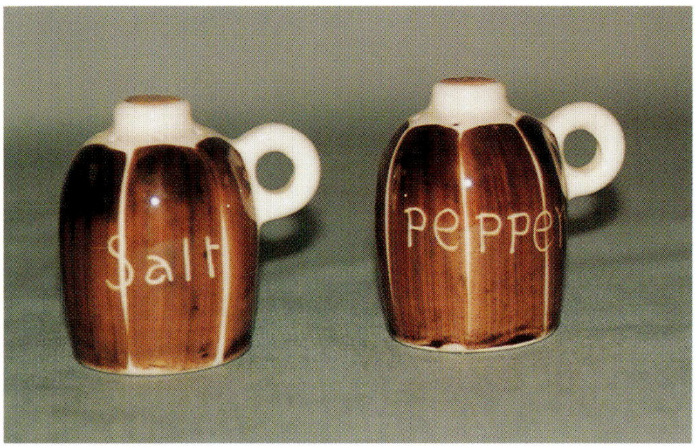

Jug salt and pepper shakers. $15 set.

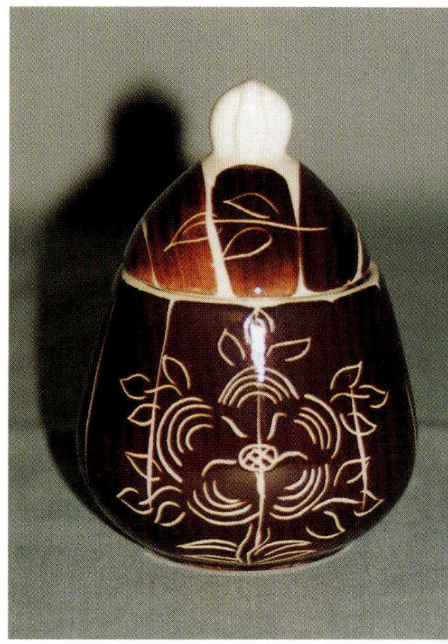

Marmalade jar. $30.

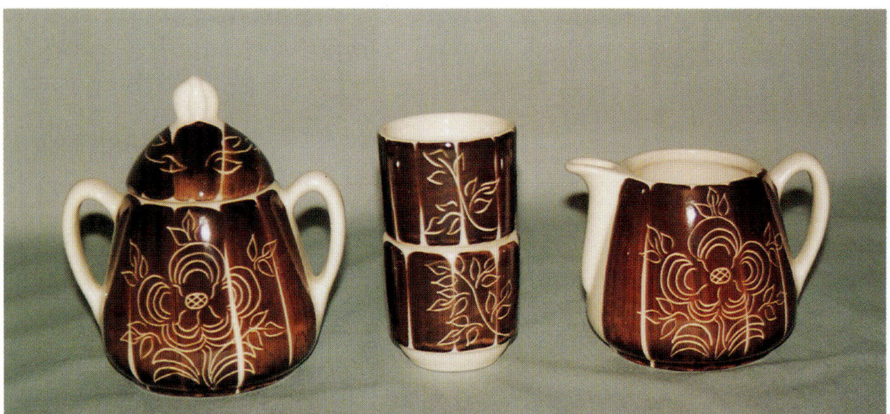

Covered sugar and creamer. $20 set. Stacking salt and pepper shakers. $35 set.

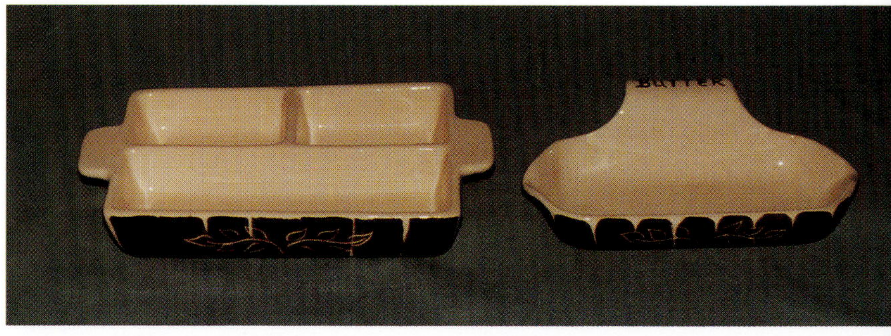

Relish, three part rectangular. $30. Butter dish. $50.

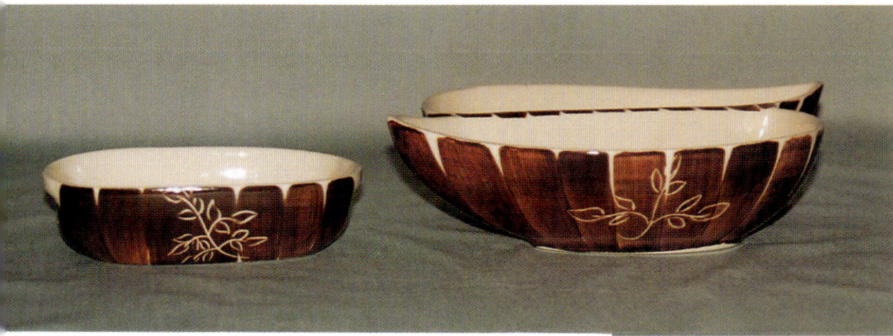

Pickle. $10. Divided vegetable. $10.

Open vegetable. $10.

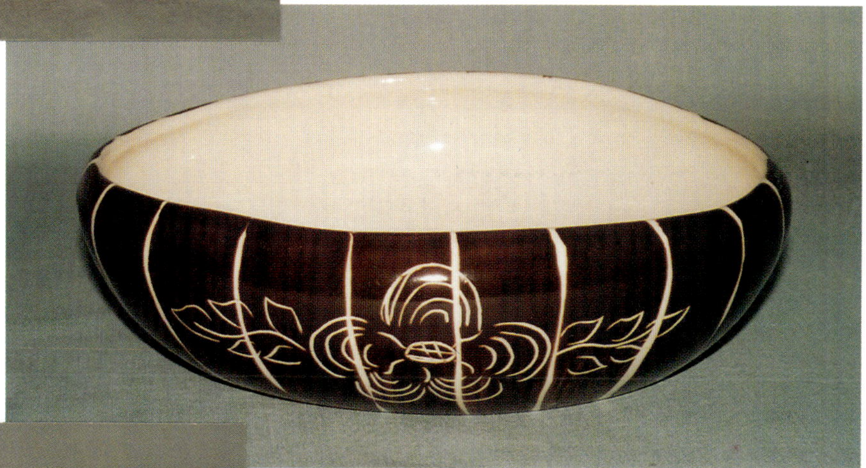

Roll tray. $10.

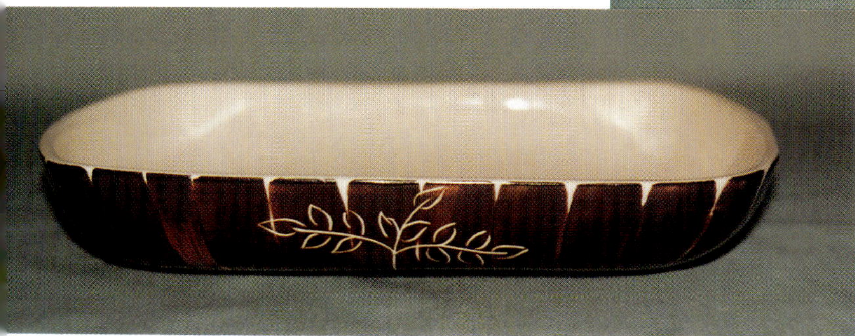

Jam and jelly. $20. Ashtray. $25.

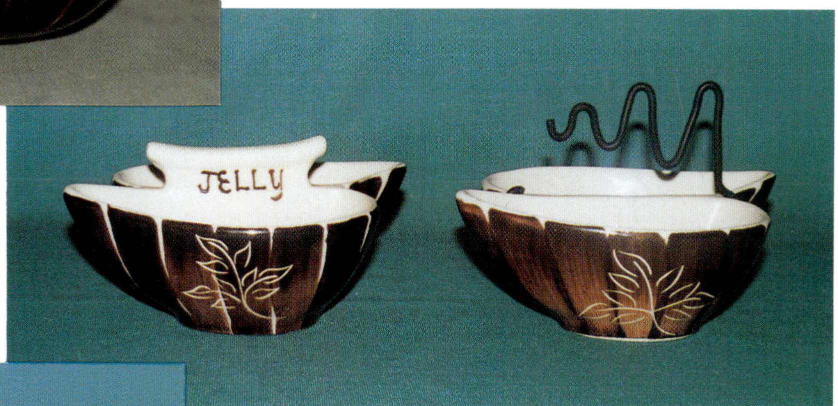

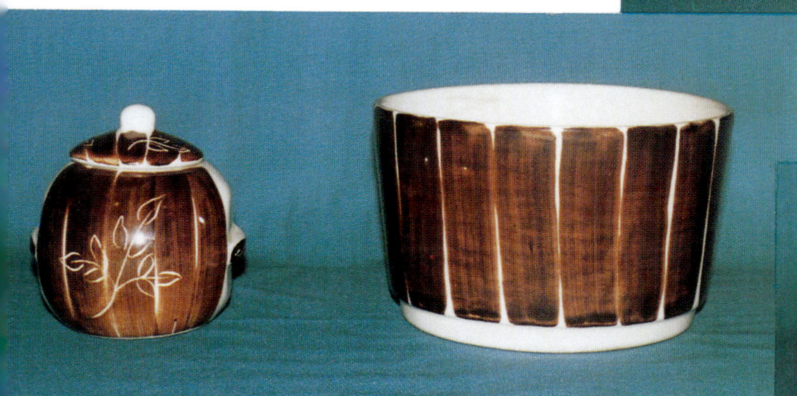

Individual bean pot. $25. Beans pot, no lid. $50.

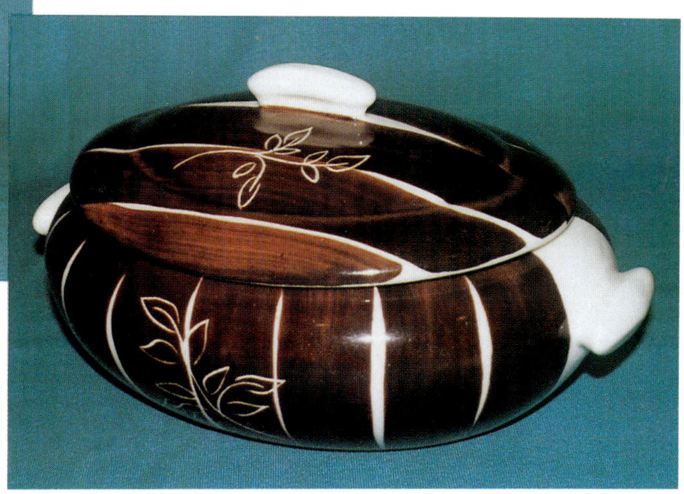

Covered vegetable. $35.

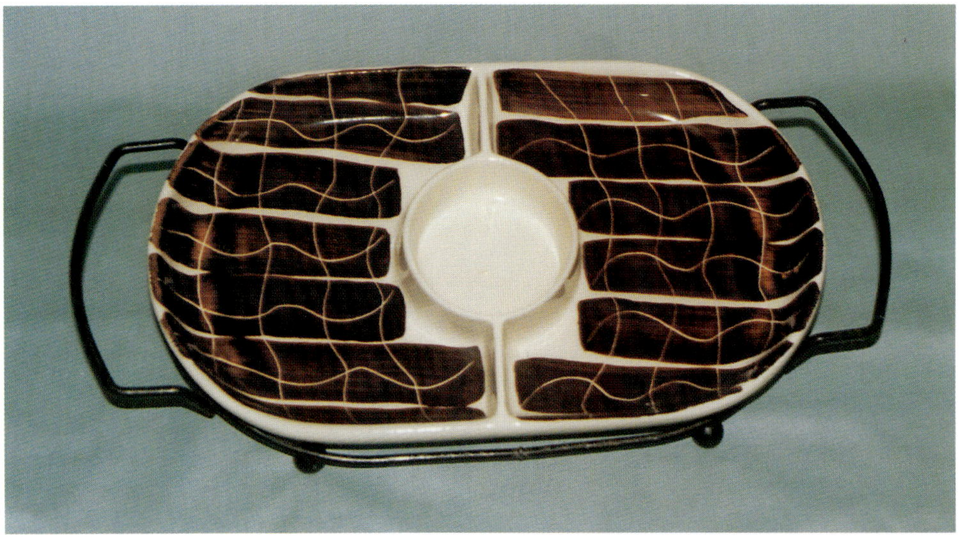

Plate, three part divided, unknown mold, on metal stand. $40.

Spaghetti bowl. $100.

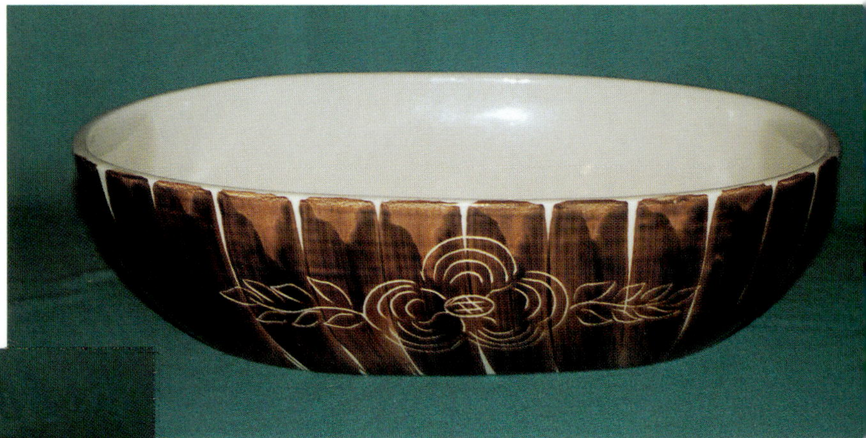

Baker. $15.

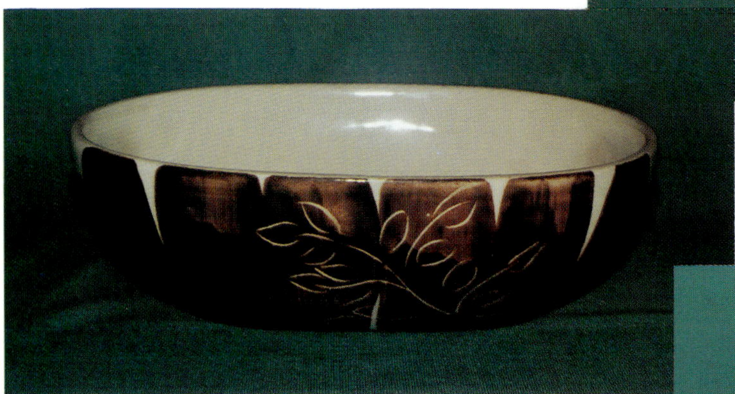

Salad bowl. $75.

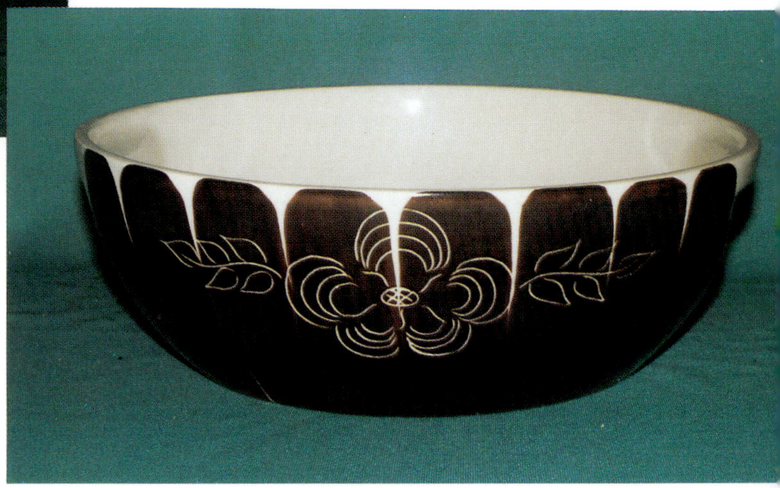

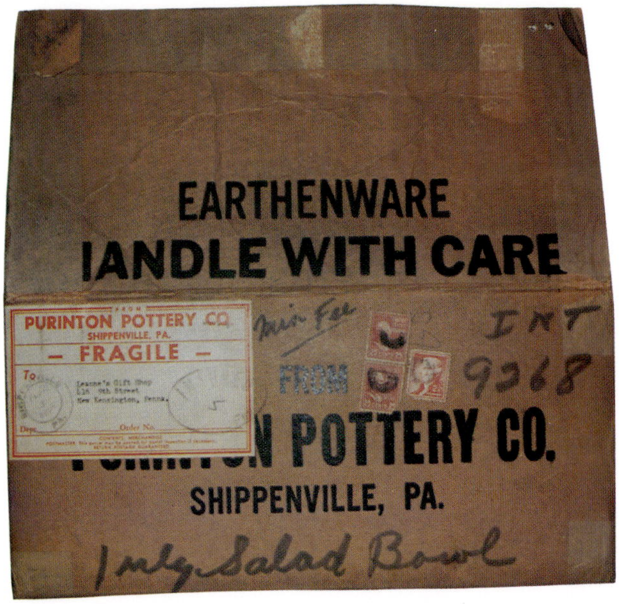

Original box in which the salad bowl was shipped.

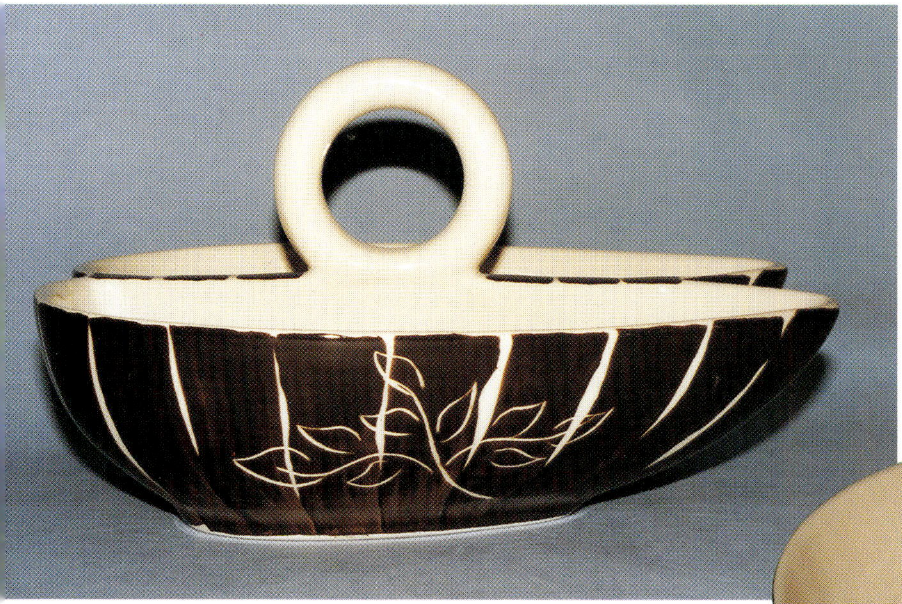

Top view of this unusual divided vegetable with its ceramic handle.

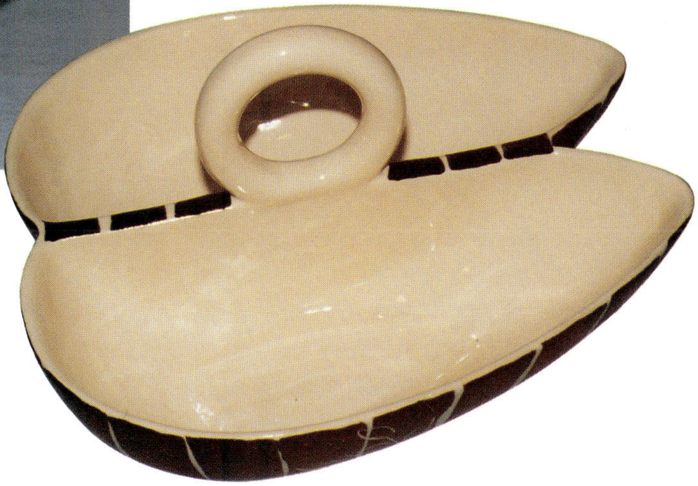

Unusual divided vegetable with ceramic handle, not a production piece. $50. Suggestions are being sought as to how this piece was produced.

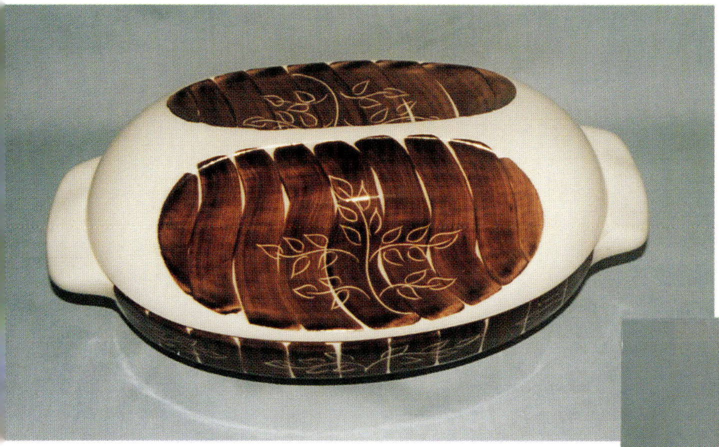

Side view of Rubel large covered casserole.

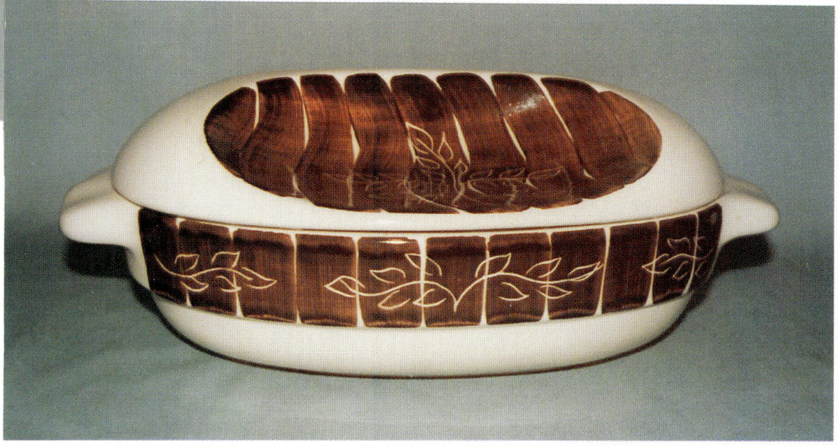

Rubel large covered casserole. $125.

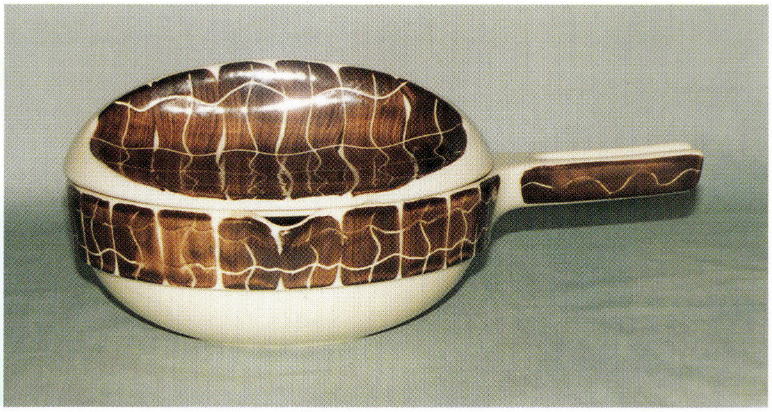

Rubel one quart handled casserole with lid. $50.

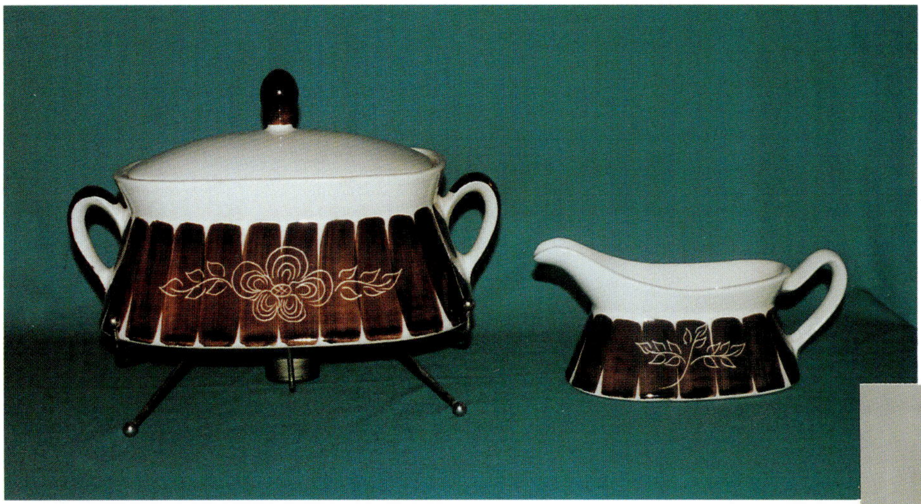

Tureen, Taylor Smith Taylor mold. $150. Gravy boat, Taylor Smith Taylor mold. $100.

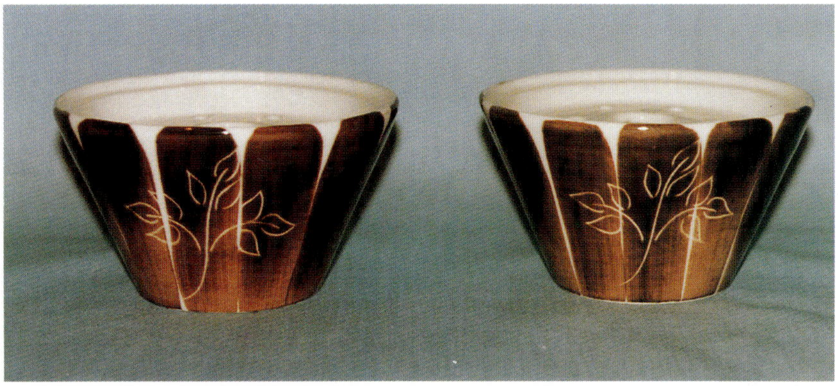

Round candle holders with inserts. $200 set.

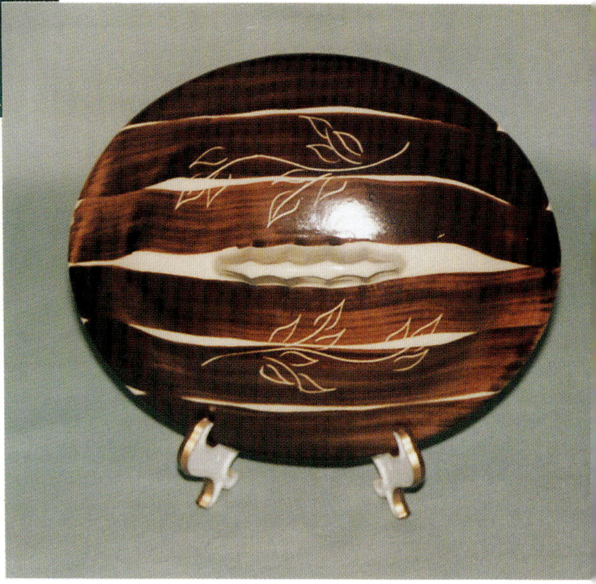

Odd handled covered vegetable lid. $25.

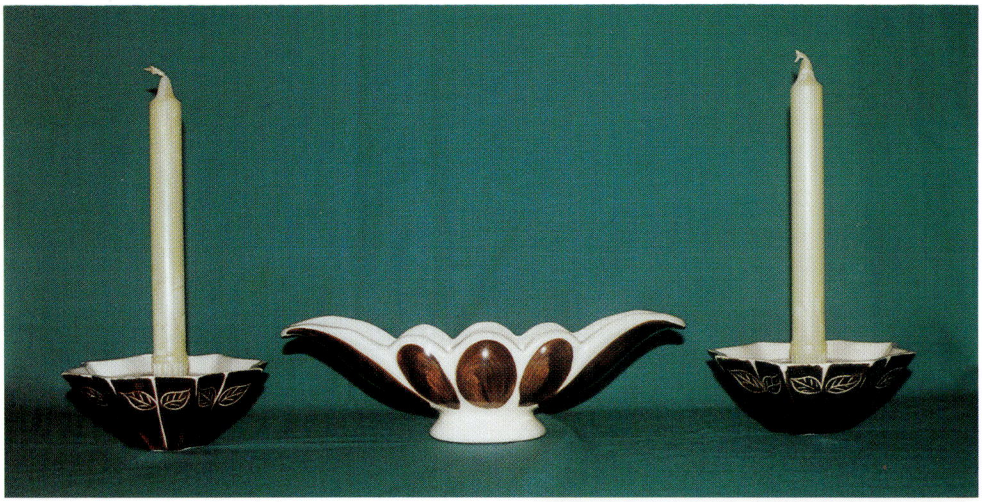

Star candle holders with inserts. $60 set. Console bowl, NAPCO mold, no decoration. $75.

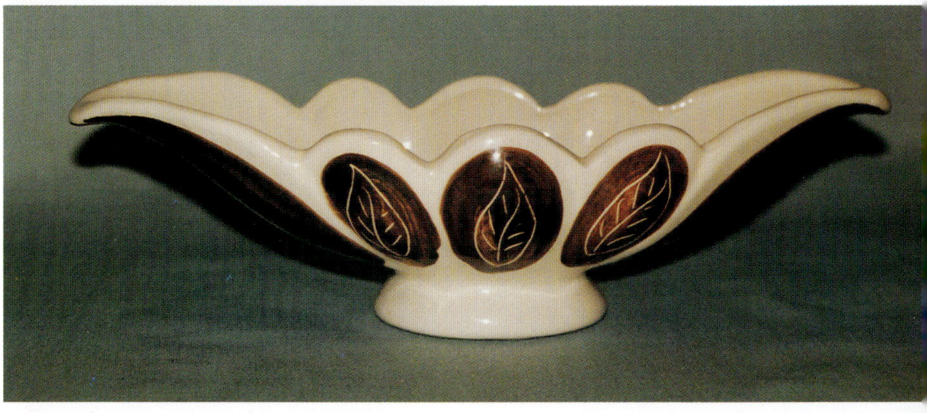

Console bowl, NAPCO mold. $75.

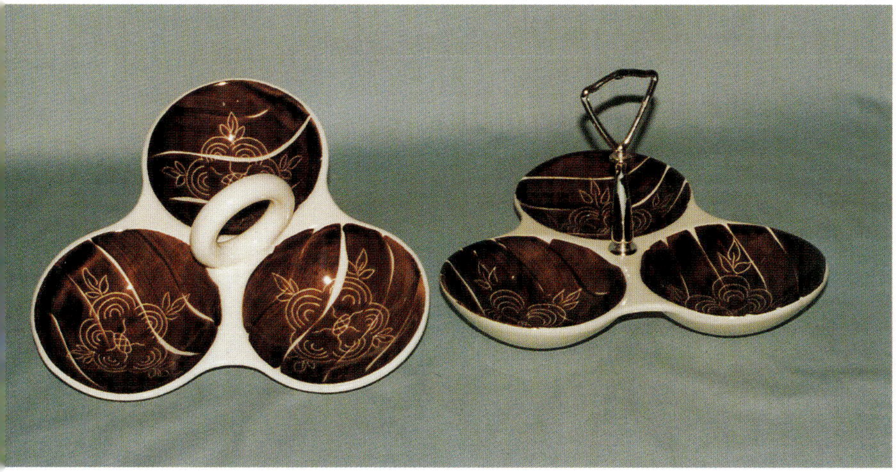

Three part relish with ceramic handle. $20. Three part relish with metal handle. $20.

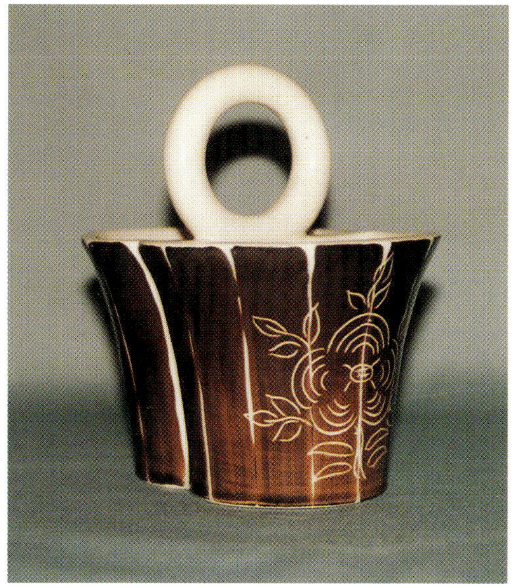

Candy dish. $40.

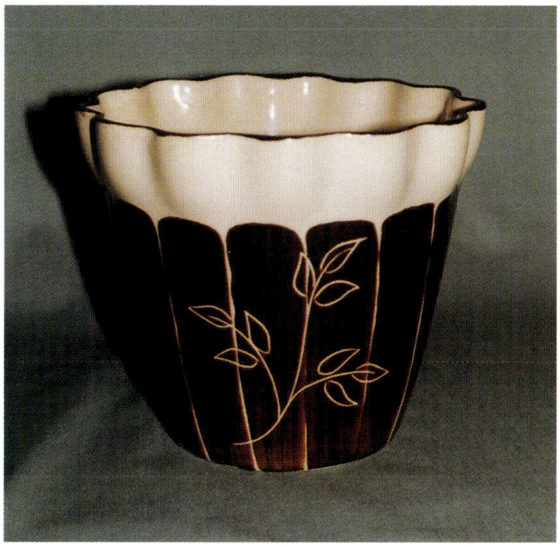

Jardiniere, 5" high. $50.

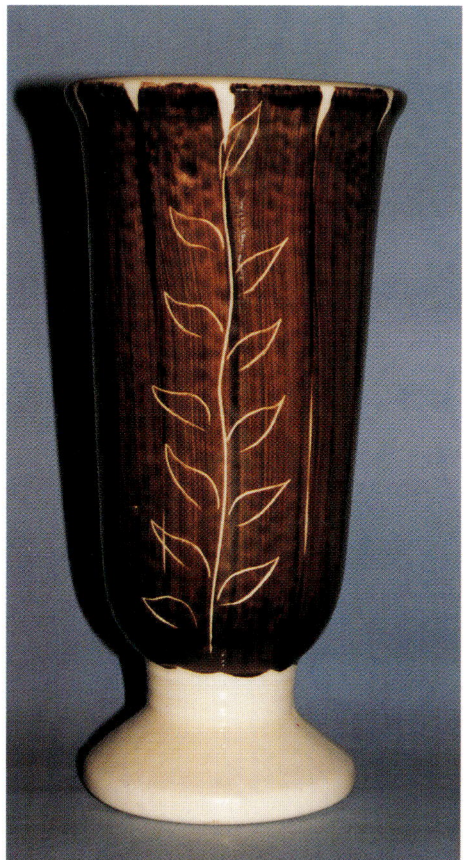

Tall vase. $75.

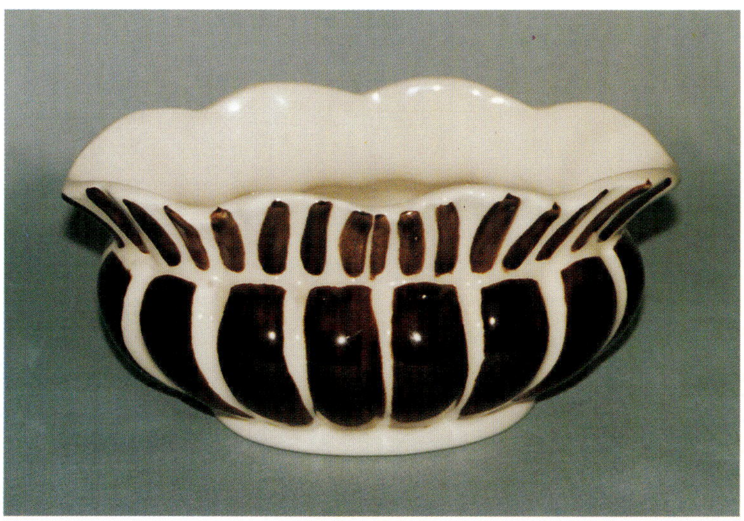

Planter with ruffled edge, unknown mold. $50.

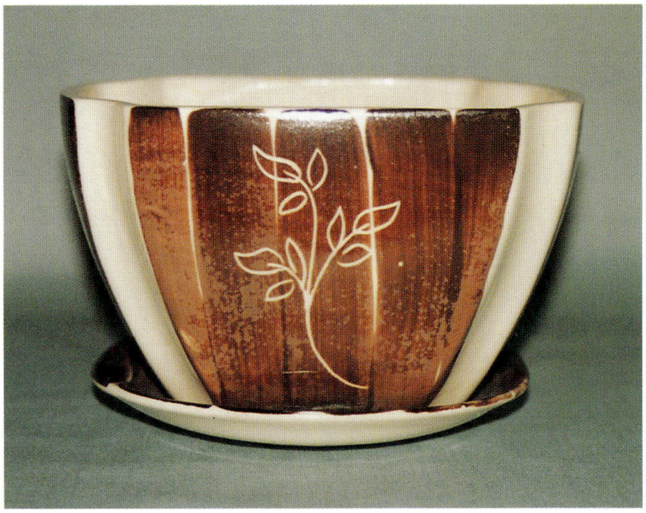

Planter. $40.

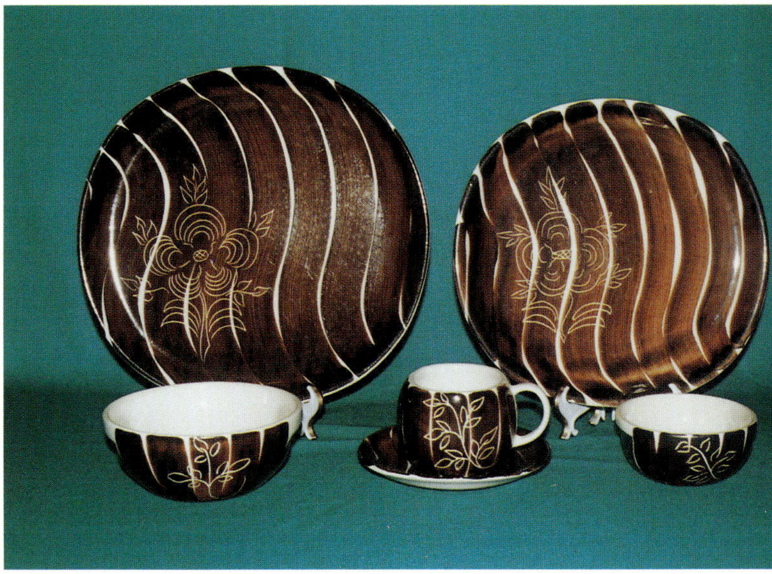

Oversized dinner plate. $25. Dinner plate. $7. Cereal bowl. $3. Cup. $2. Saucer. $1. Dessert bowl. $3.

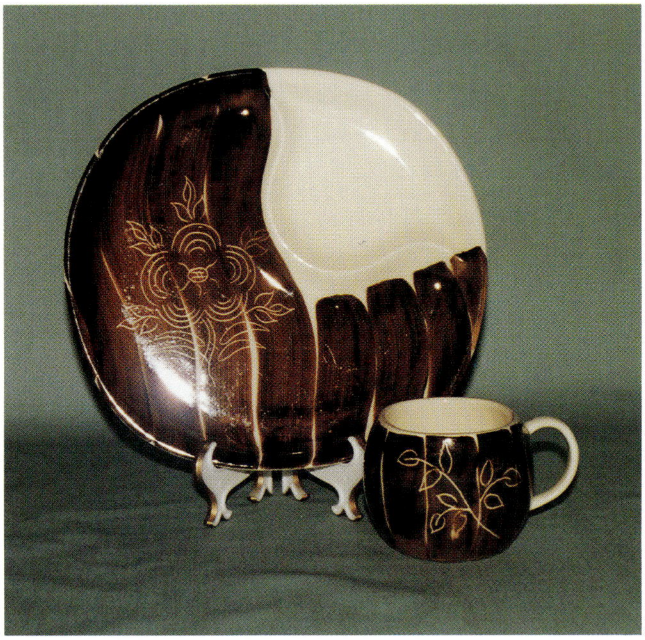

Tea and toast plate. $7. Cup. $2.

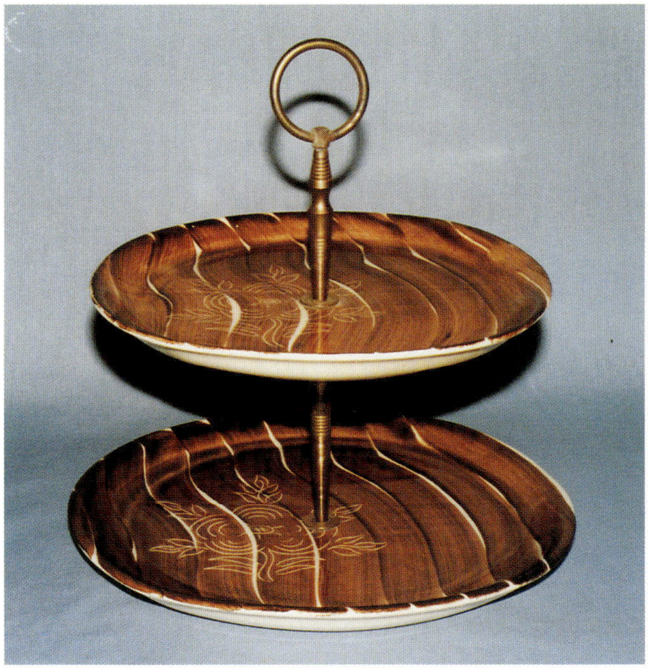

Tidbit tray with metal handle made from dinner plates. $25.

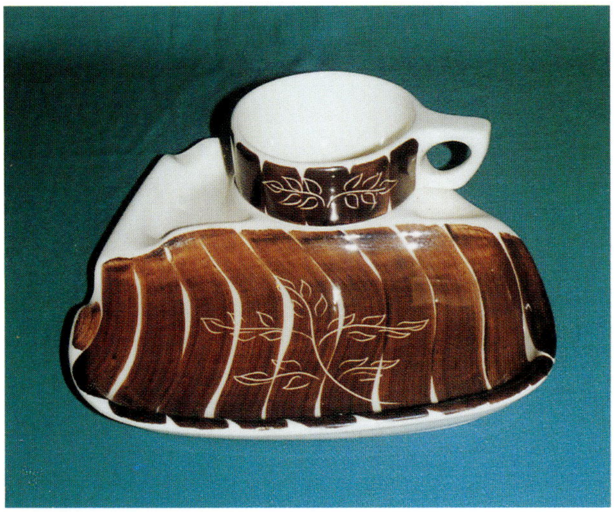

Soup and sandwich plate, Rubel mold. $30. Cup for soup and sandwich plate, Rubel mold. $15.

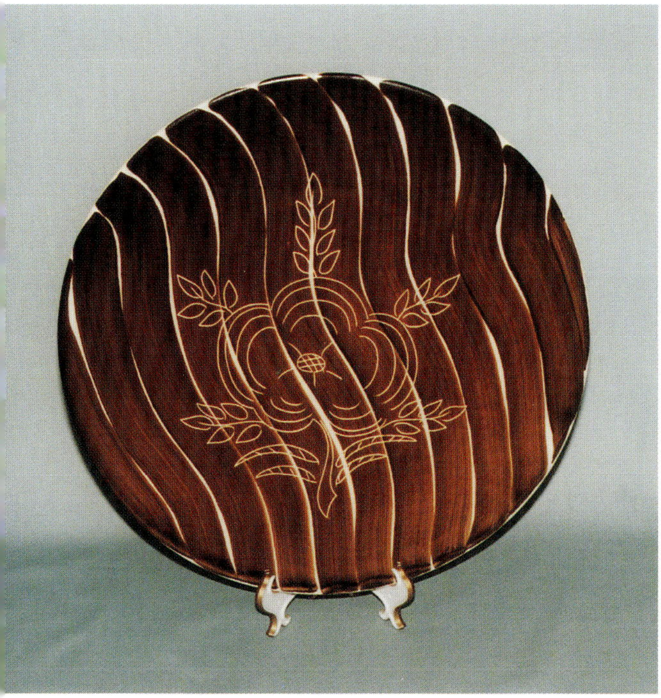

Chop plate. $20.

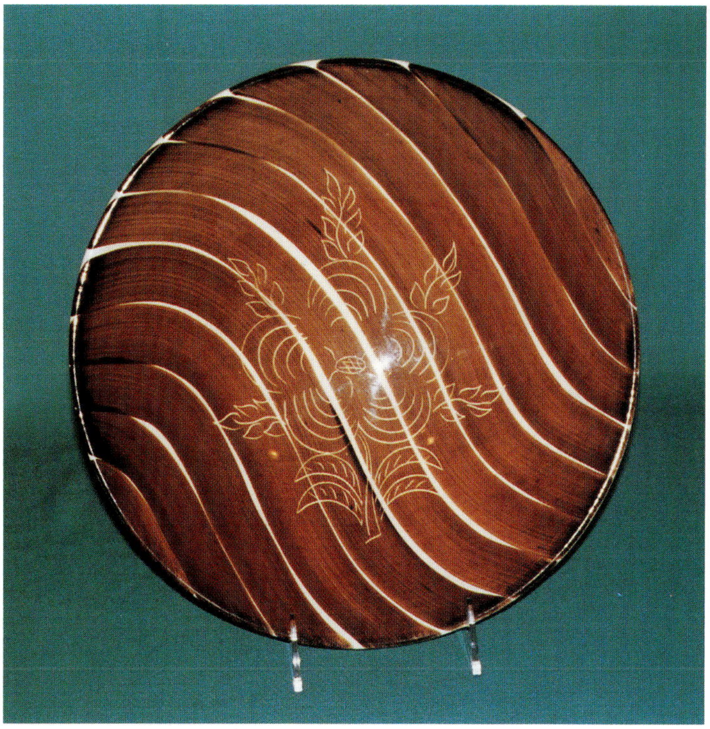

Fruit bowl. $25.

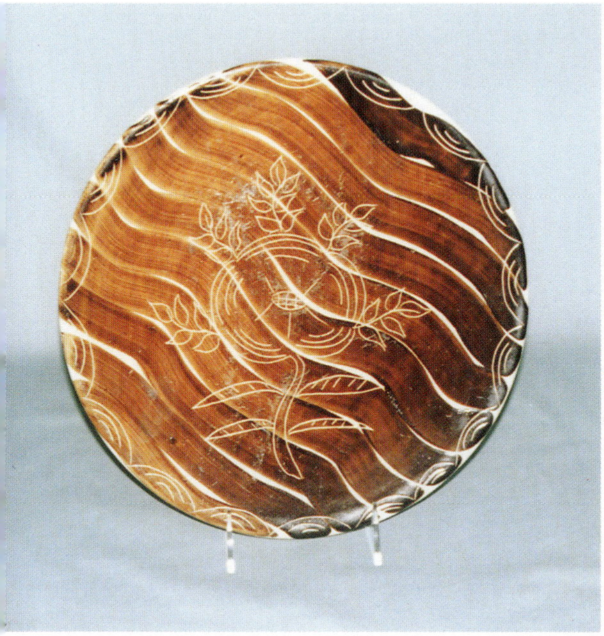

Chop plate with scalloped edges. $50.

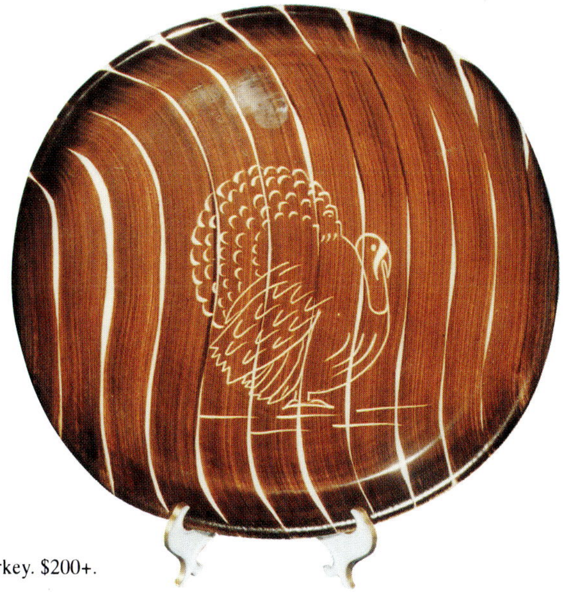

Dinner plate with incised turkey. $200+.

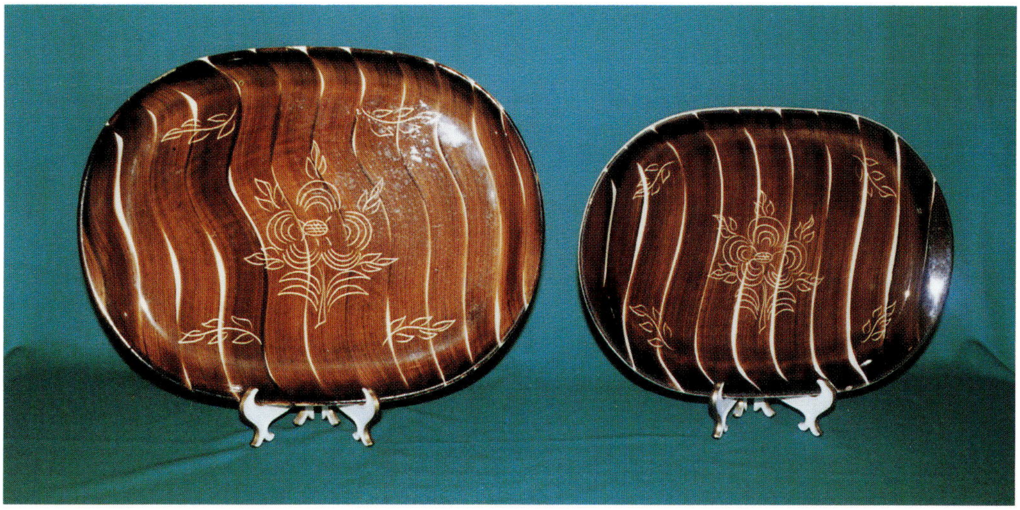

Large platter. $15. Small platter. $15.

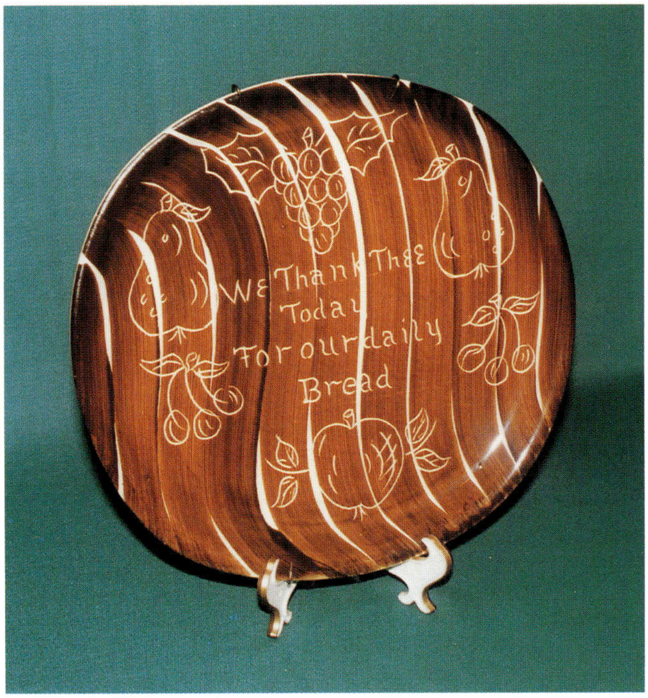

Dinner plate with "We thank thee today for our daily bread" blessing, incised Fruit decoration. $300+.

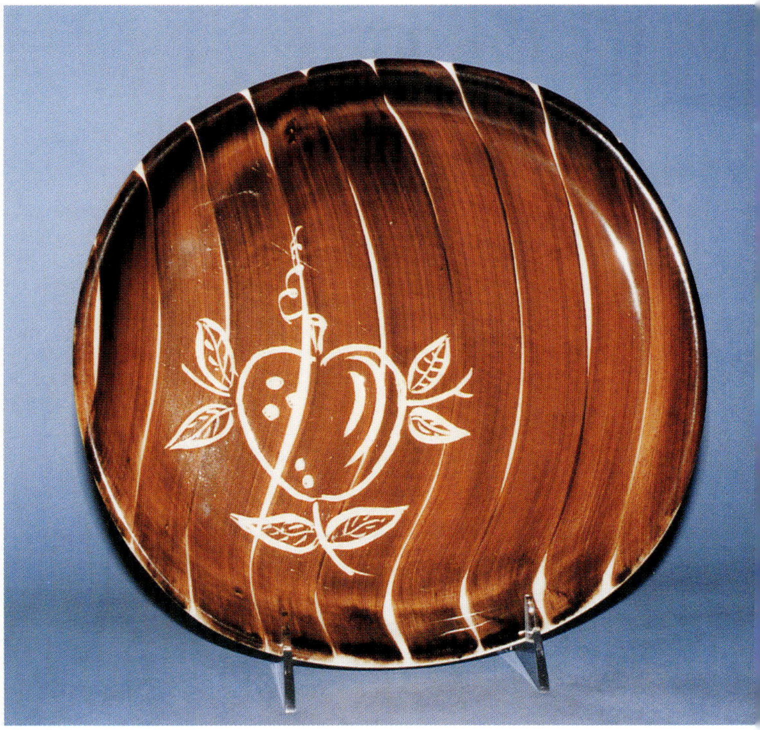

Dinner plate with incised apple. $75.

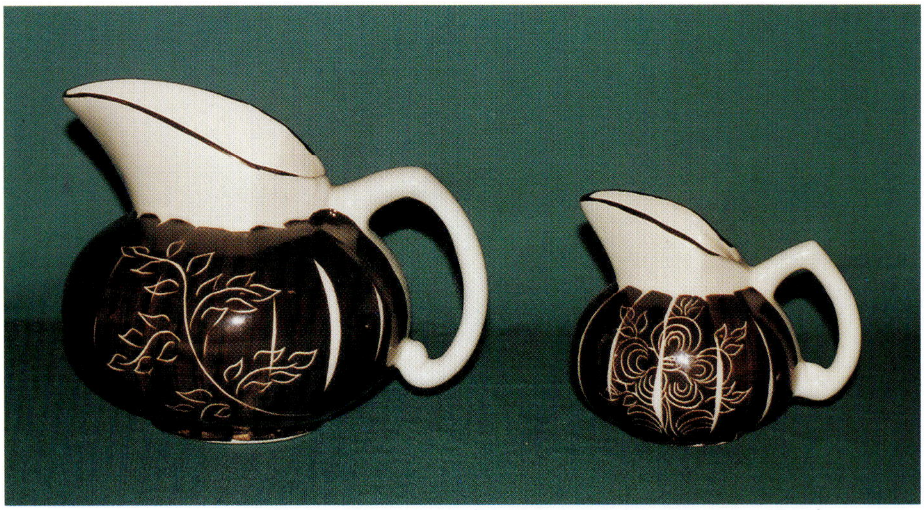

Oversized kent jug, 6.25" high (rare). $250+. Kent jug, 4.5" high. $15.

Kent jug with incised leaf. $30.

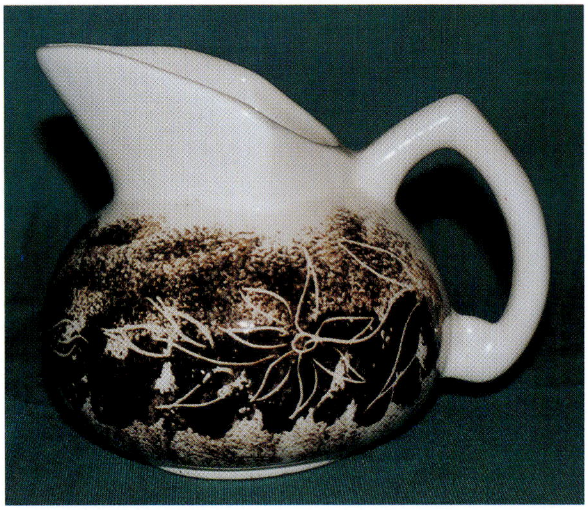

Kent jug with odd leaf decoration, experimental. $75.

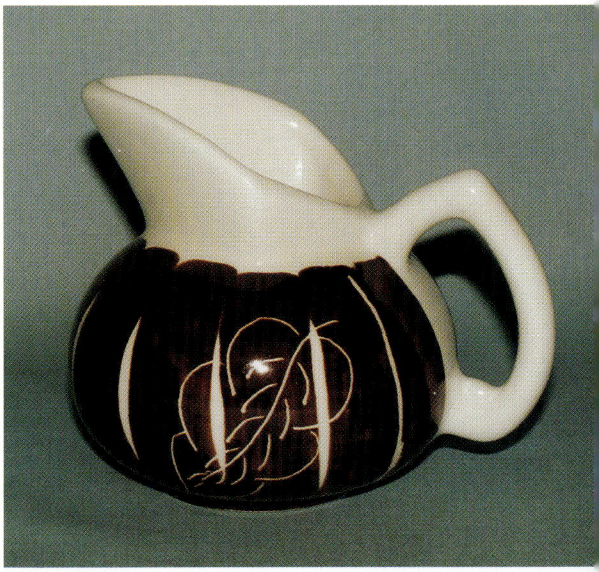

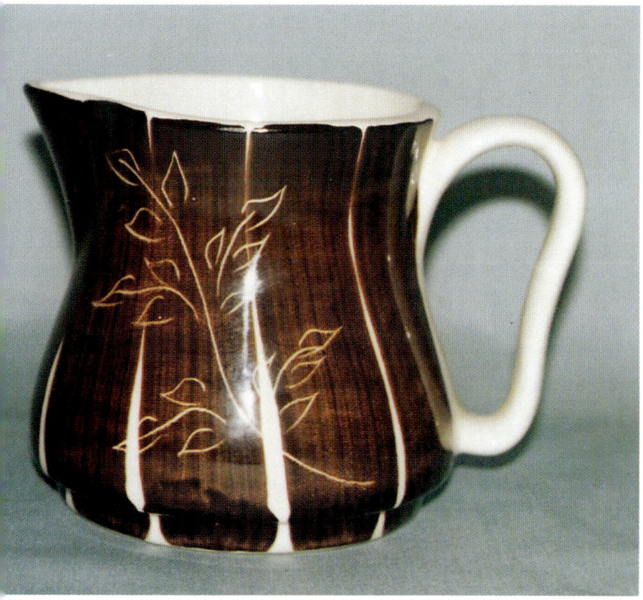

Pitcher, Rubel mold. $75.

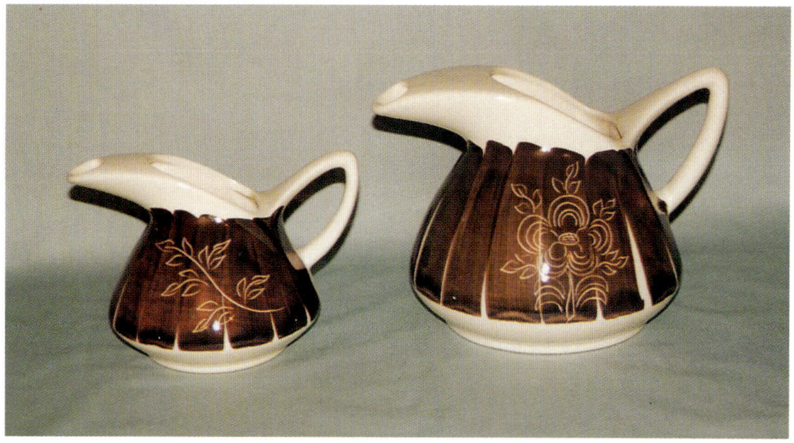

Two pint dutch jug. $40. Five pint dutch jug. $40.

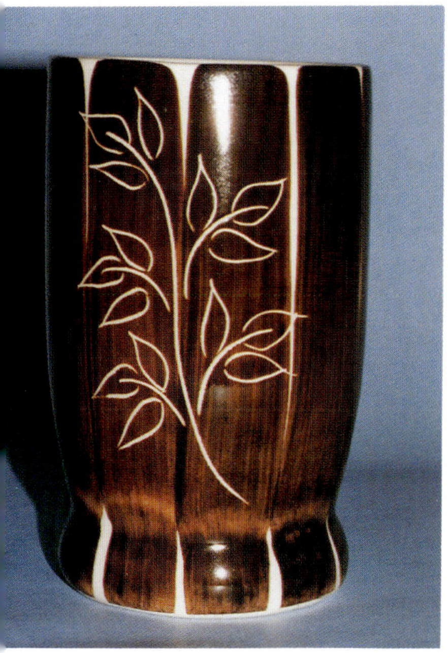

Tumbler. $30.

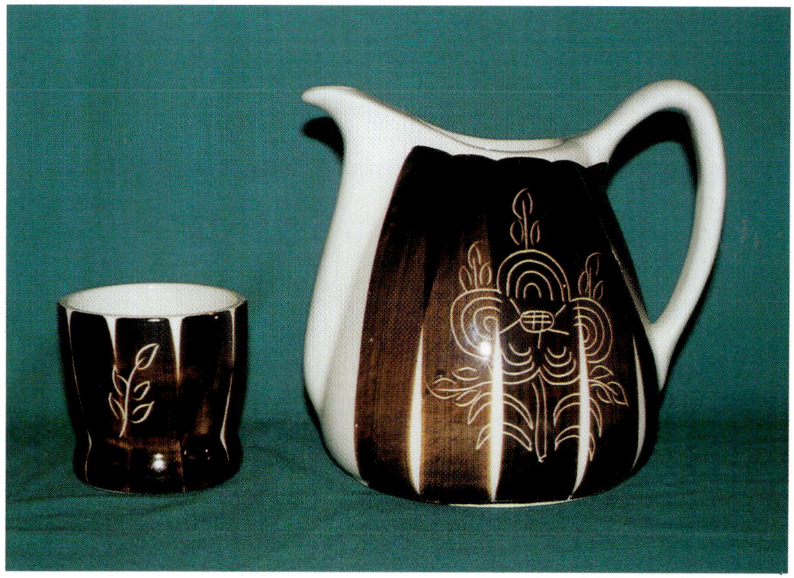

Juice mug. $10. Beverage pitcher. $50.

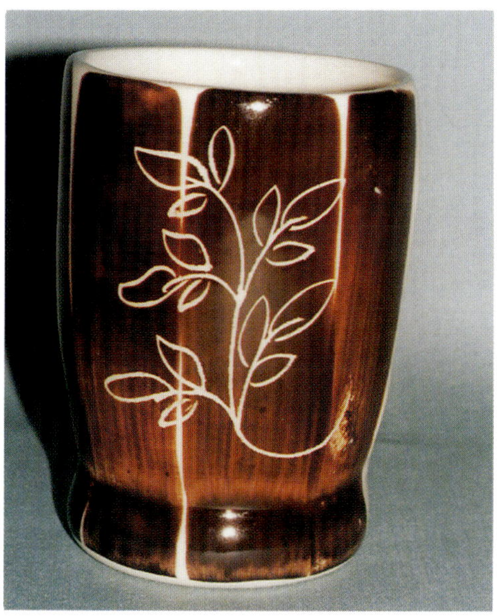

Coffee mug with no handle, whimsy made into a tumbler, 3.75" high. $25.

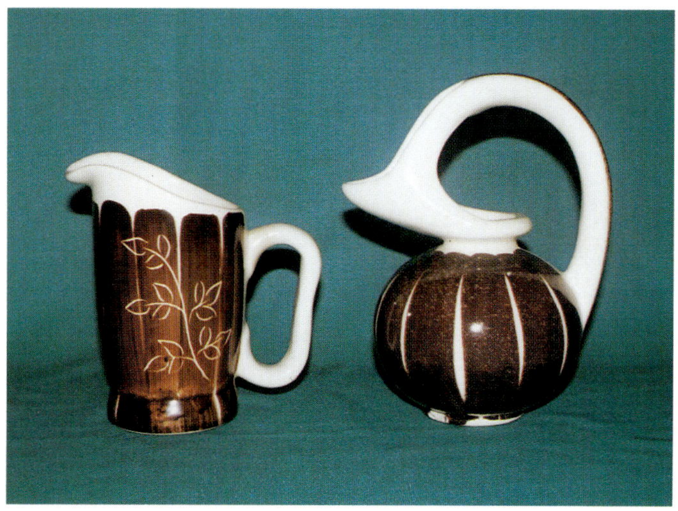

Mug jug. $40. Honey jug. $75.

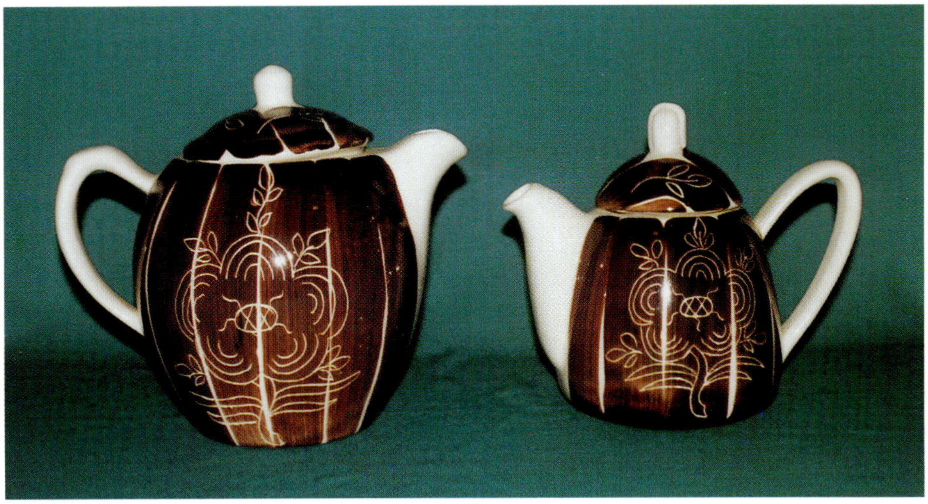

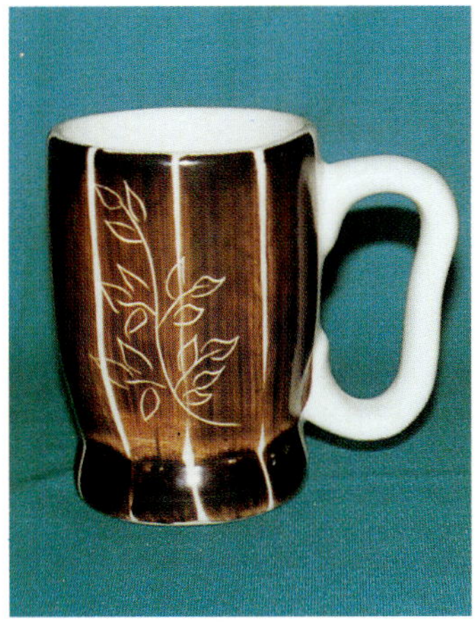

Eight cup coffee pot. $50. Six cup domed lid teapot. $40.

Coffee mug. $15.

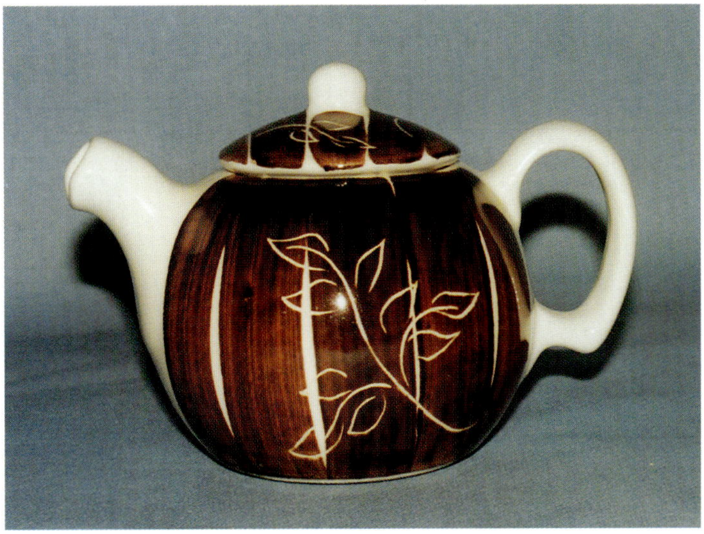

Two cup teapot (rare). $150+.

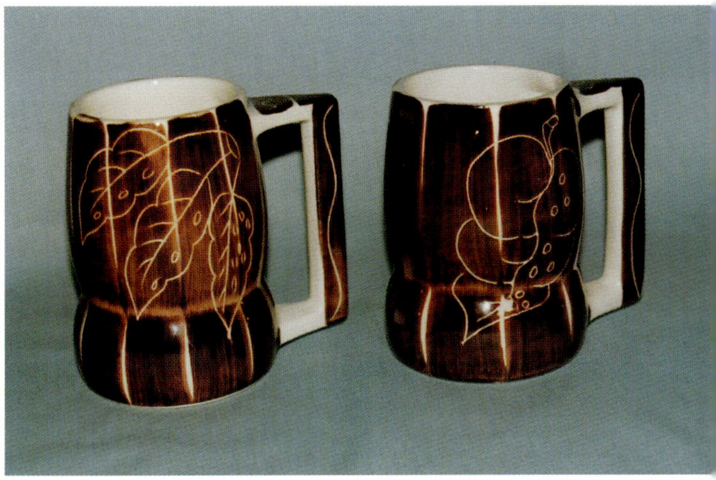

Beer mug. $20. Beer mug, odd leaf. $25.

Beer mug, personalized Father on handle. $75.

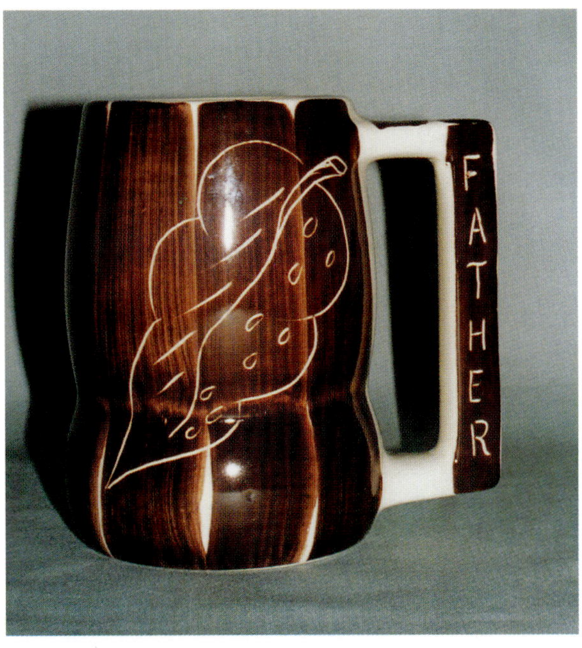

Beer mug, personalized Ann, Buss's Cafe. $100.

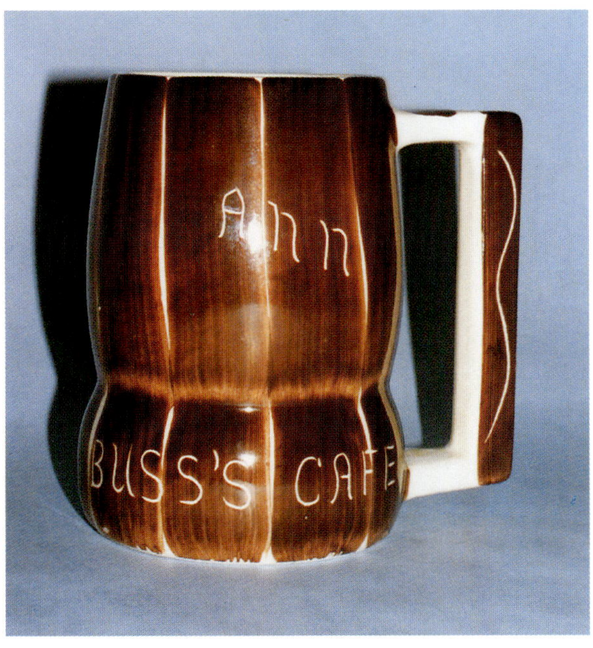

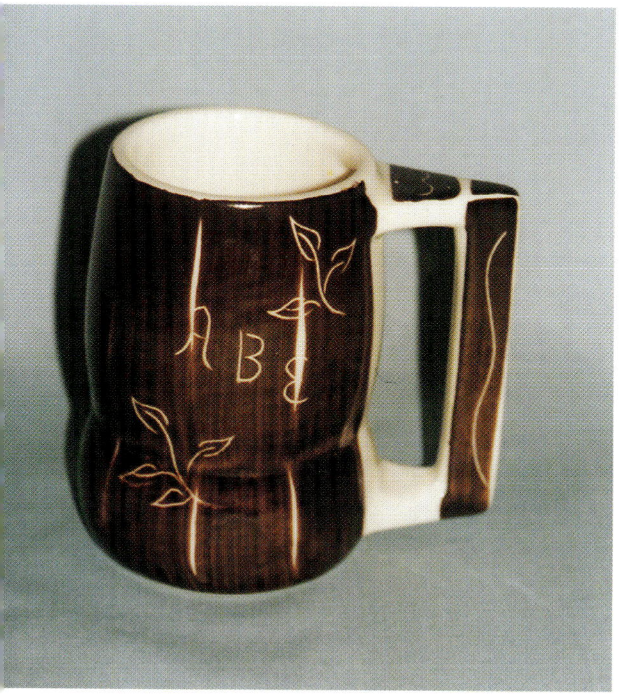

Beer mug, personalized Abe. $75.

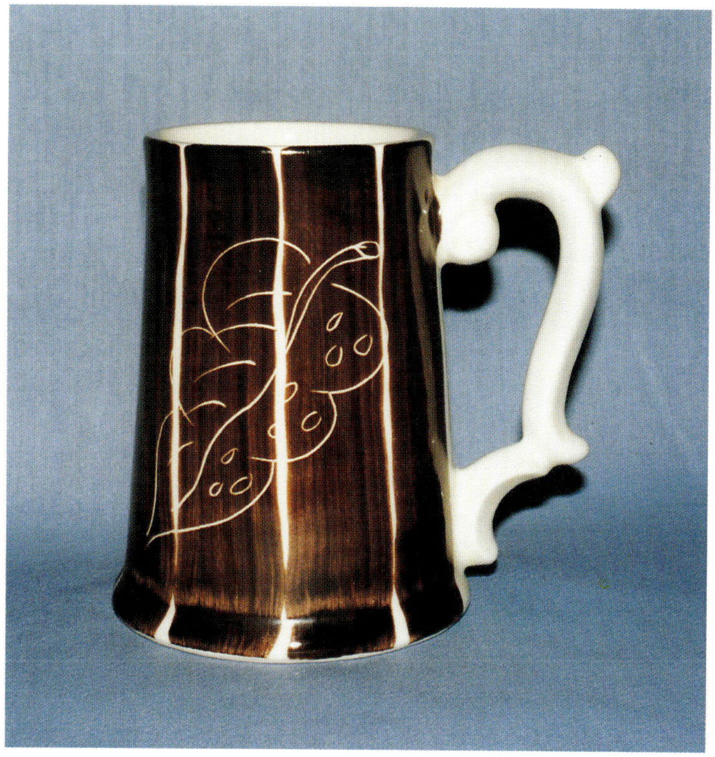

Beer mug, odd handle, experimental. $100.

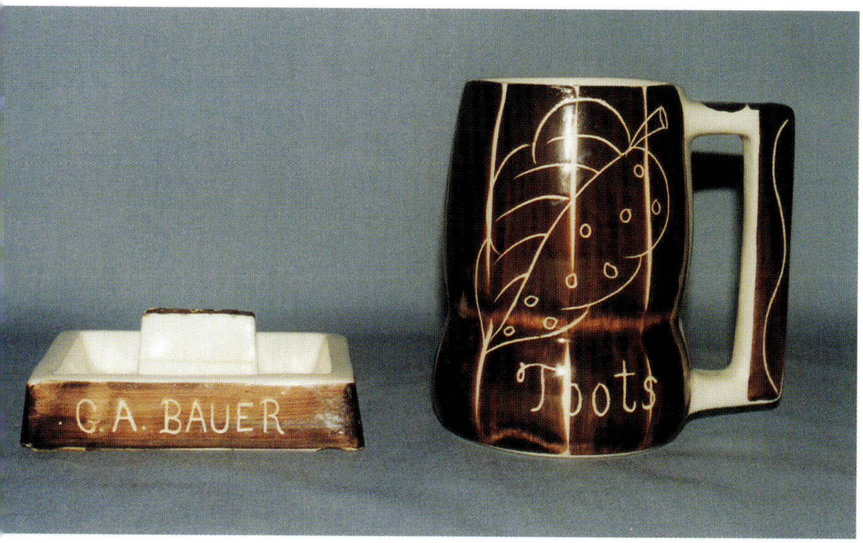

Blind man's ashtray personalized G.A. Bauer. The center is the key feature of this ashtray type. $40. Beer mug personalized Toots. $75.

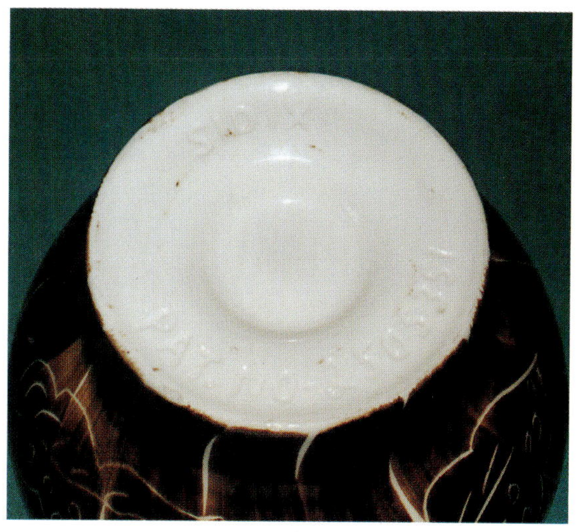

Bottom of ashtray, reads SIDIX, PAT. NO. 2505351.

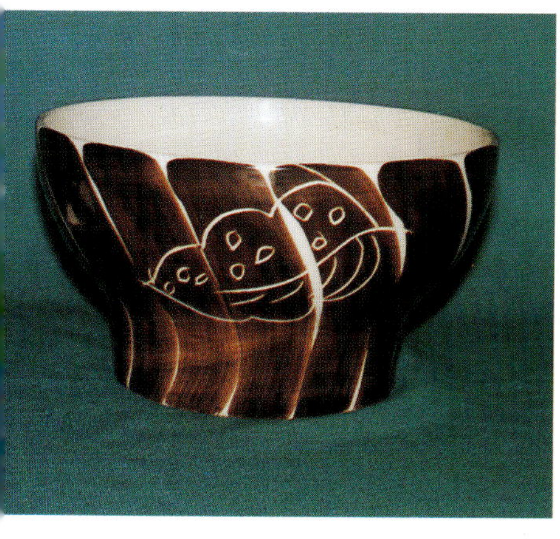

SIDIX ashtray. This was an experimental mold. $75.

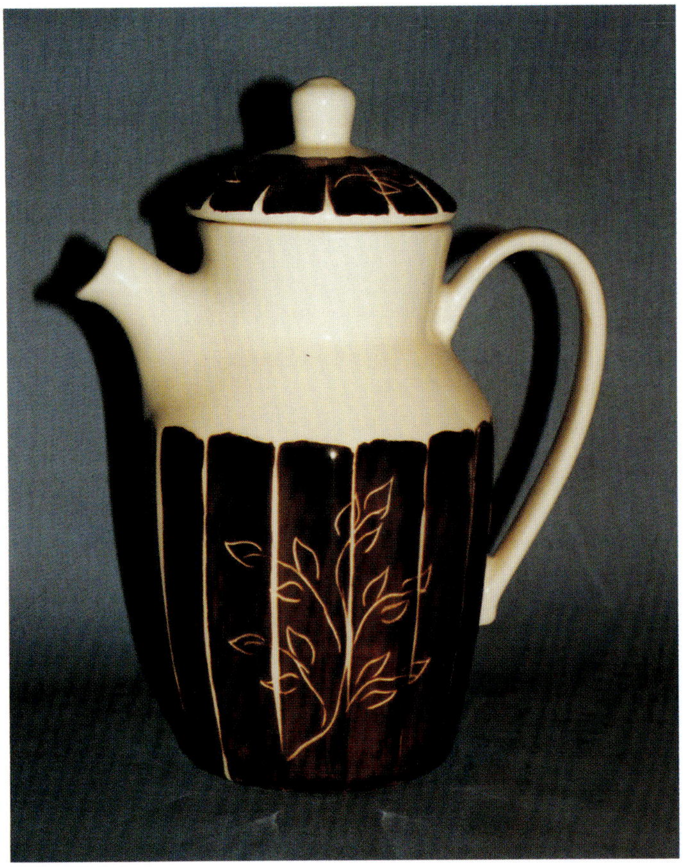

Coffee server, Seaform style, rare in this decoration. $250+.

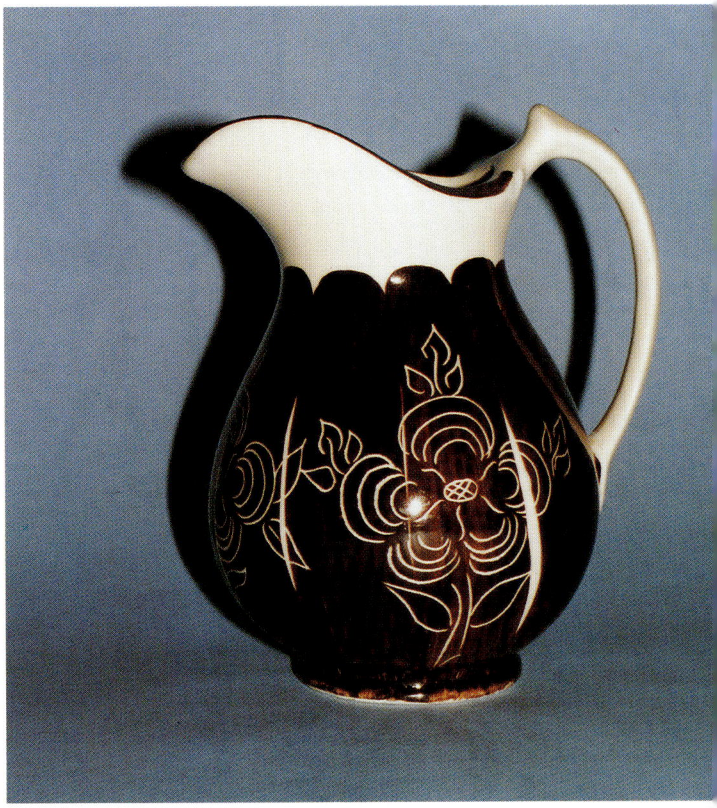

Pitcher, 6" high. $75.

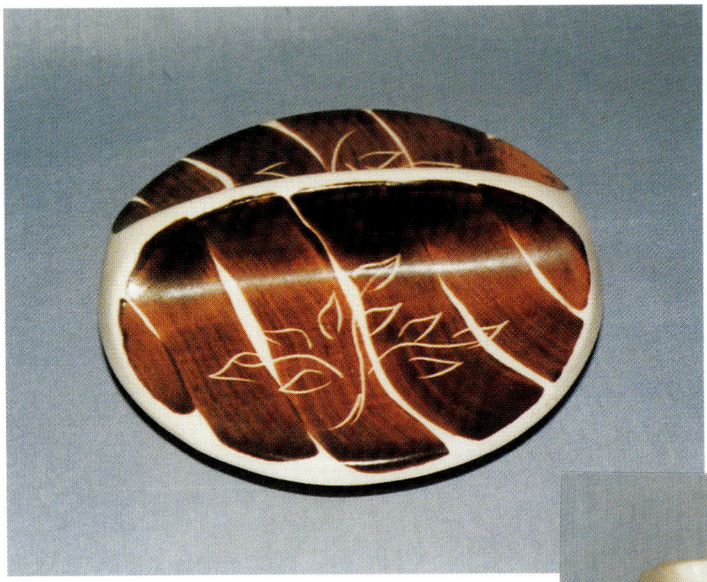

Lid, Rubel individual handled casserole. $25.

Wall pocket. $75. Juice mug with uncommon grapes etch. $40.

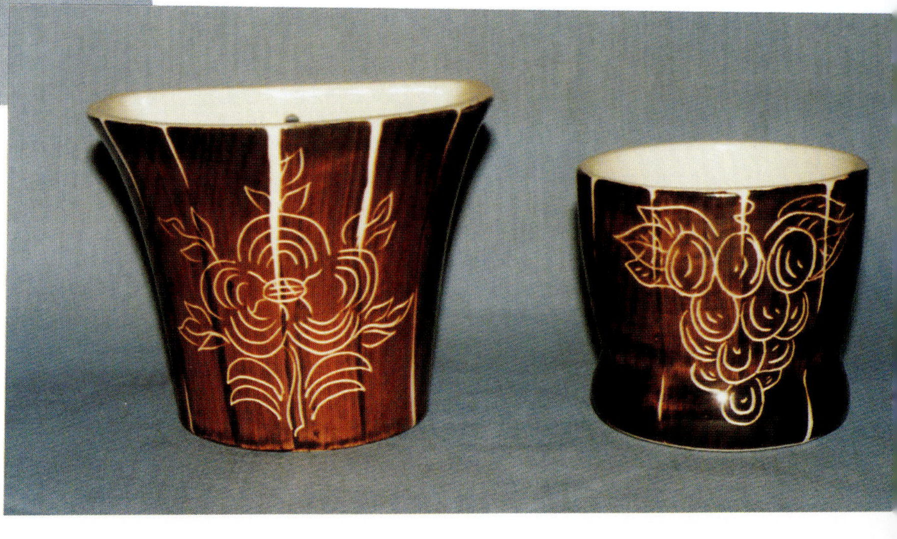

Turquoise Intaglio

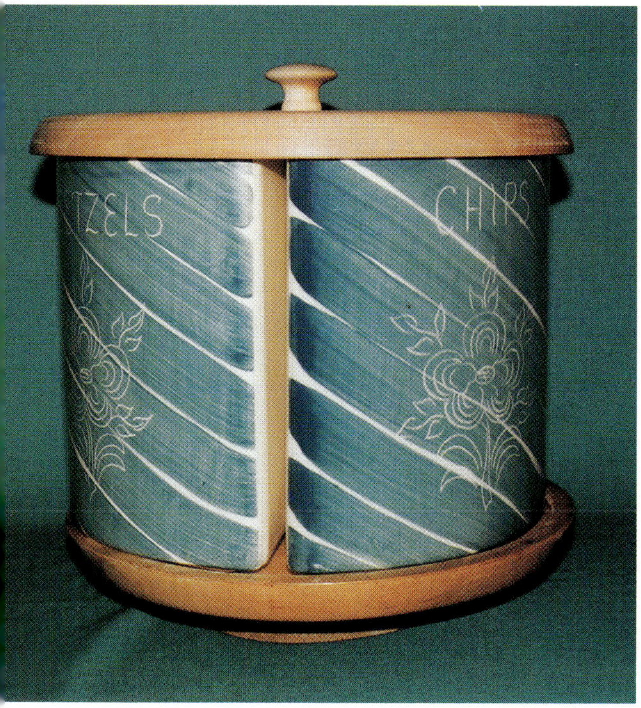

Four-section revolving canister. $200.

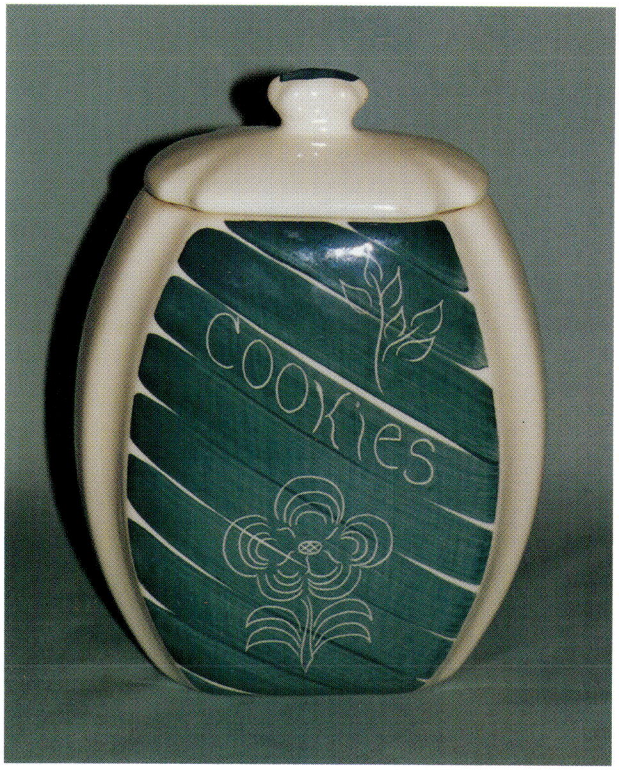

Wide oval cookies jar. $250.

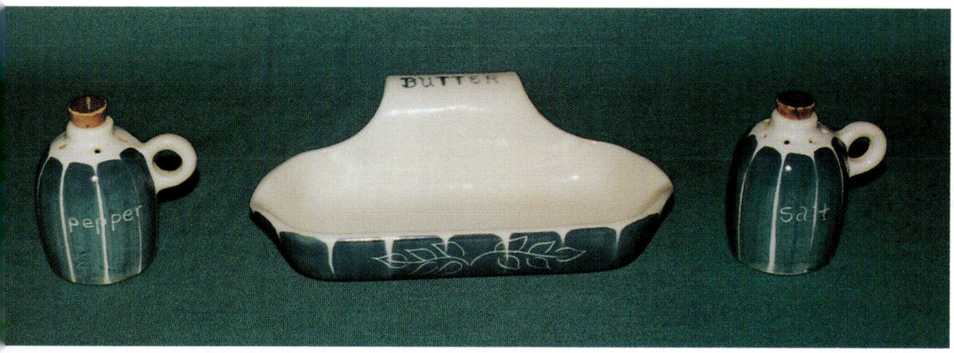

Jug pepper and salt shakers. $50 set. Butter dish. $125.

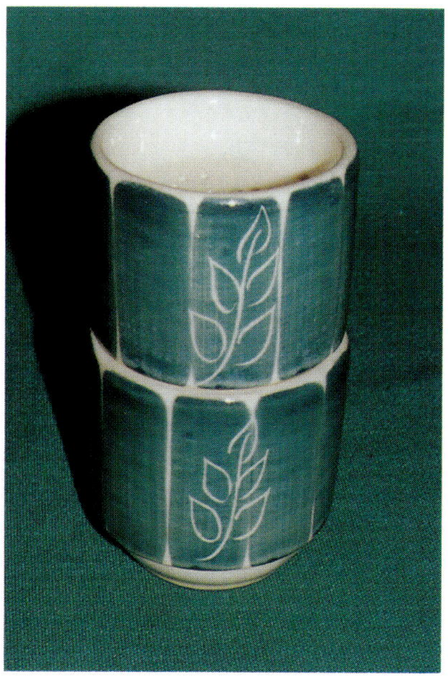

Stacking salt and pepper shakers. $75 set.

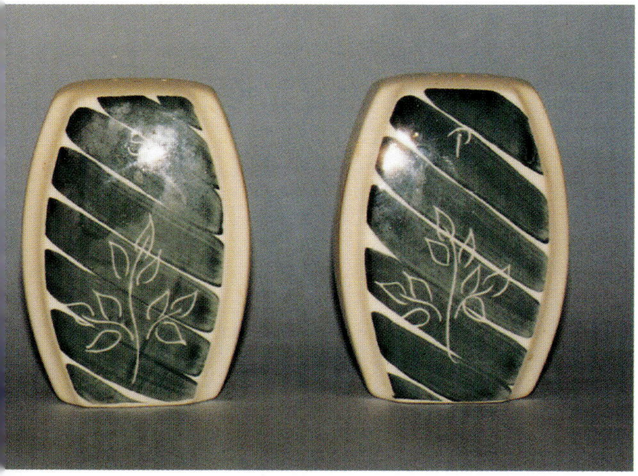

Range salt and pepper shakers. $75 set.

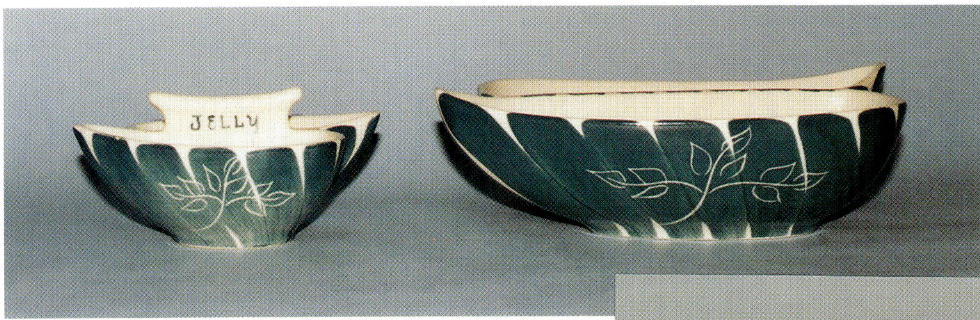

Jam and jelly. $90. Divided vegetable. $50.

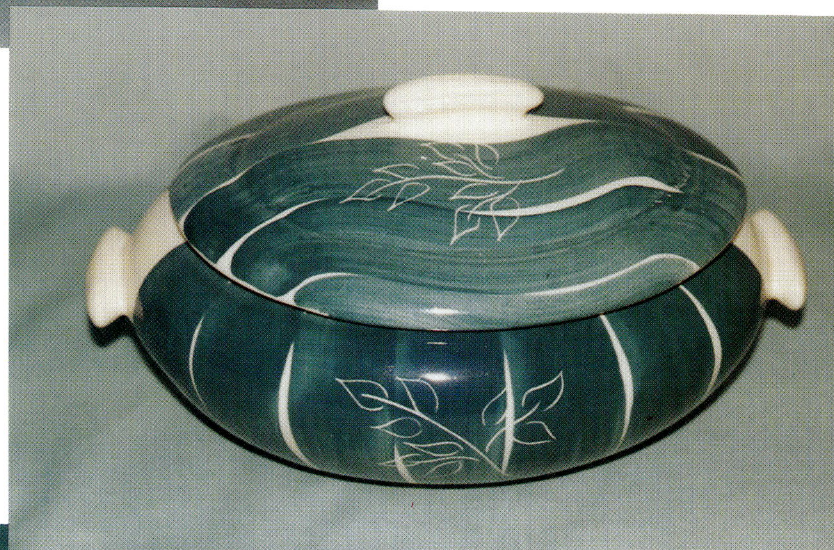

Covered vegetable. $100.

Roll tray. $30.

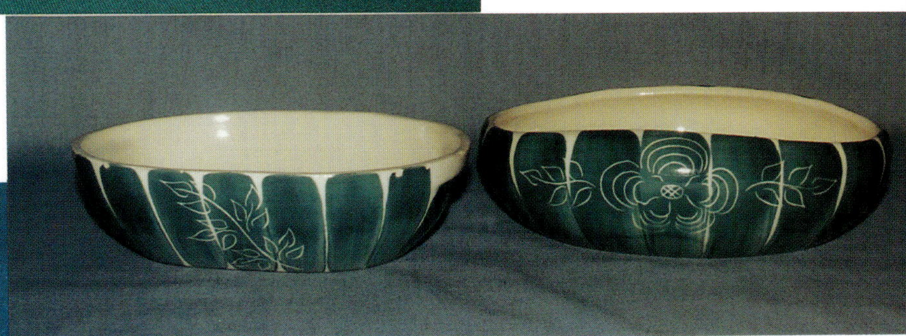

Baker. $30. Open vegetable. $30.

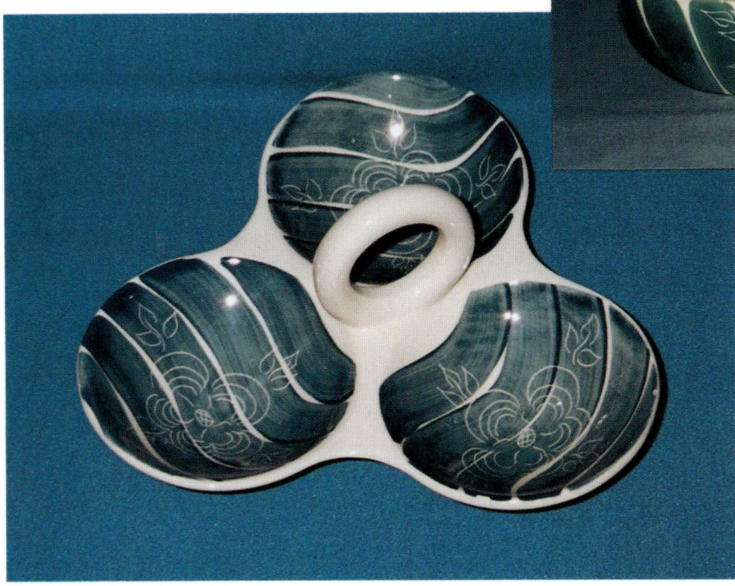

Three part relish with ceramic handle. $75.

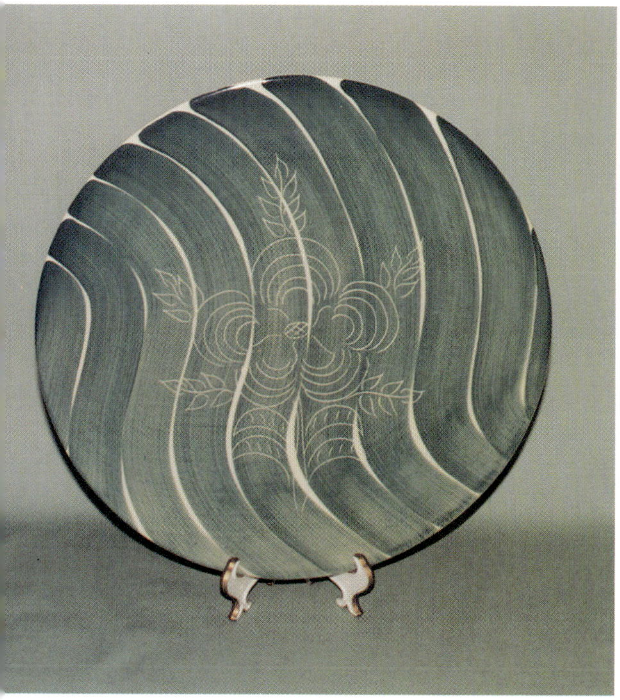

Chop plate. $75.

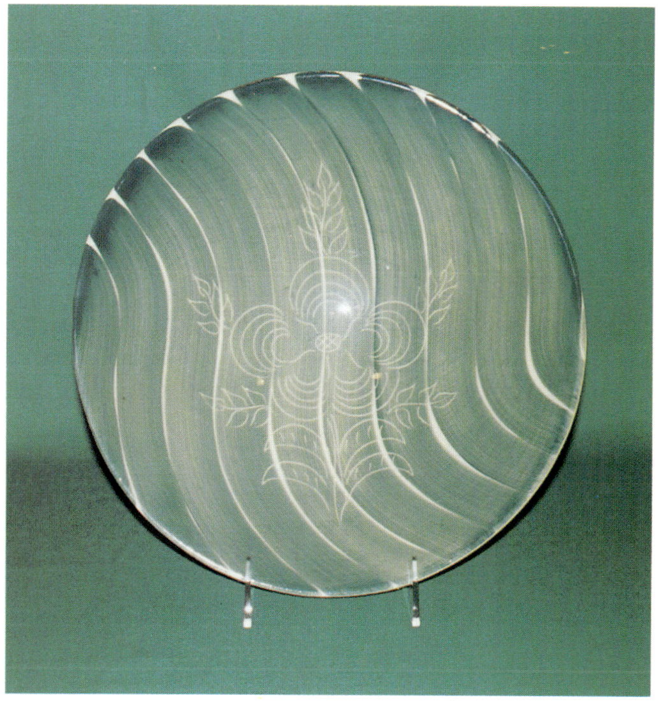

Fruit bowl. $75.

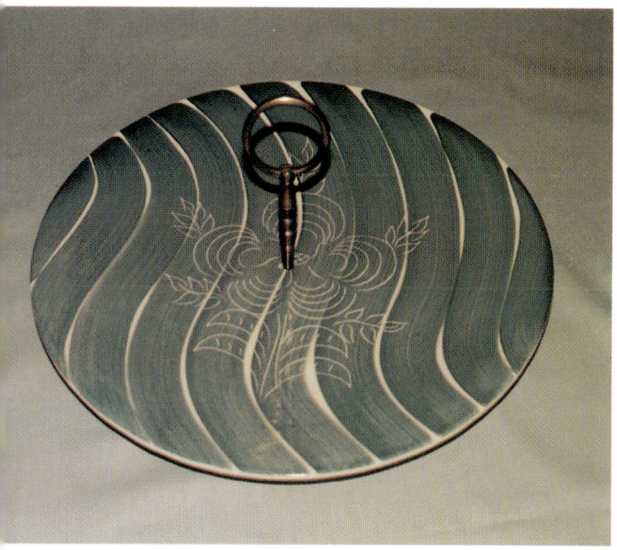

Sandwich plate. $60.

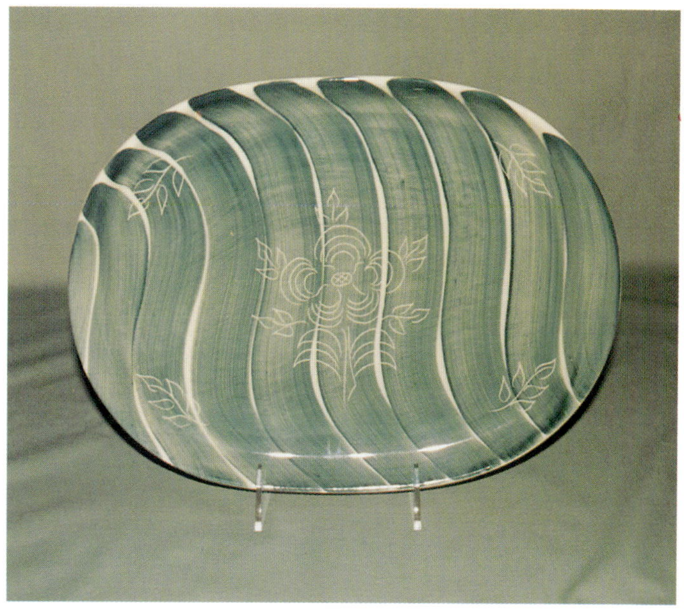

Large platter. $50.

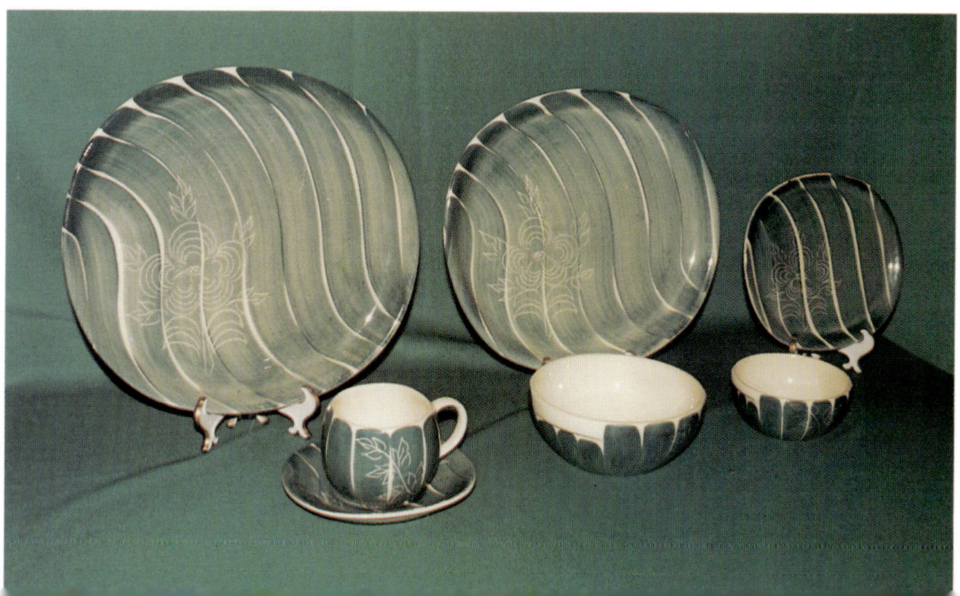

Oversized dinner plate. $30. Dinner plate. $20. Salad plate. $20. Cup. $10. Saucer. $5. Cereal bowl. $10. Dessert bowl. $10.

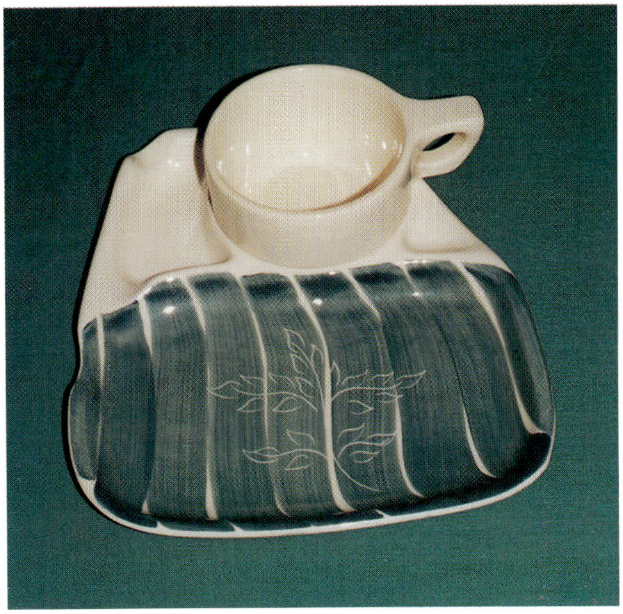

Soup and sandwich plate, Rubel mold, and cup. (Note this cup is plain. It is likely that a Turquoise Intaglio cup was made.) $50 set.

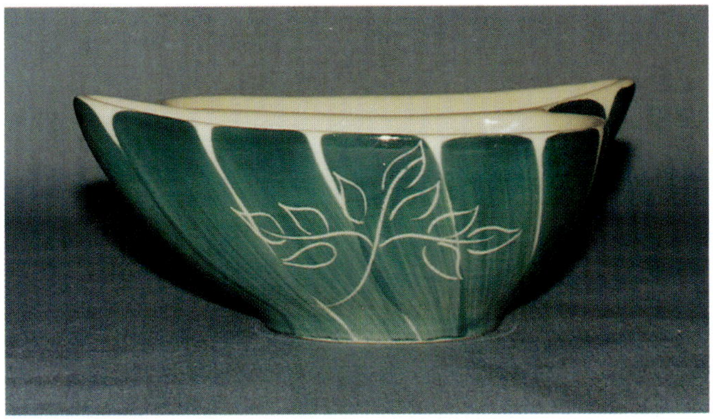

Nut dish. $40.

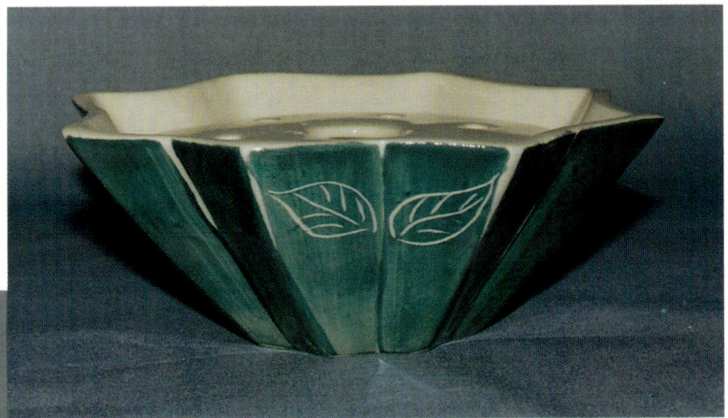

Star candle holder with insert. $40.

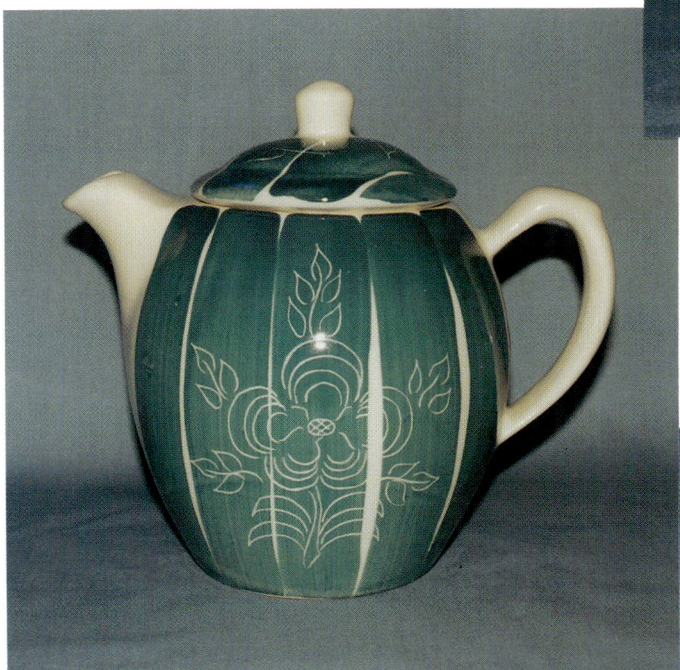

Eight cup coffee pot. $80.

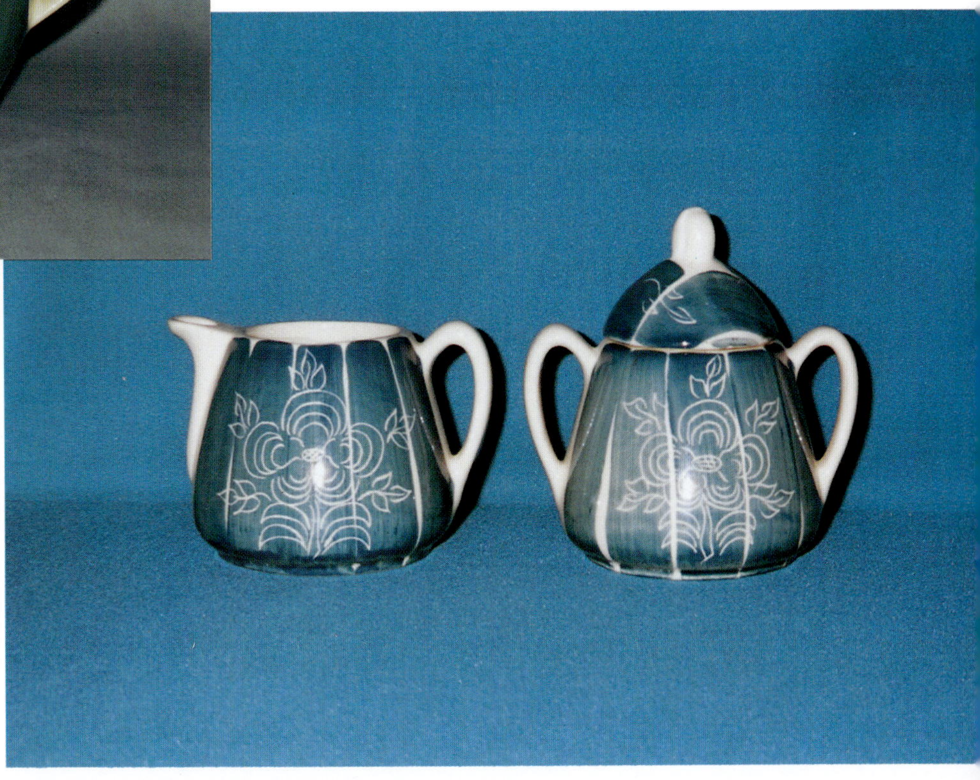

Creamer and covered sugar. $60 set.

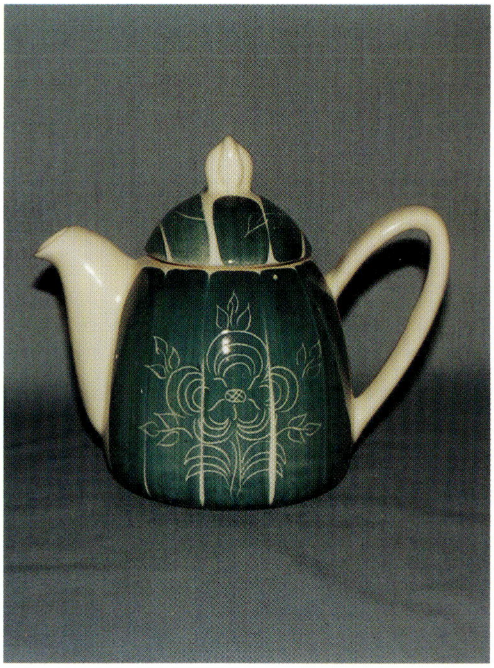

Six cup domed lid teapot. $75.

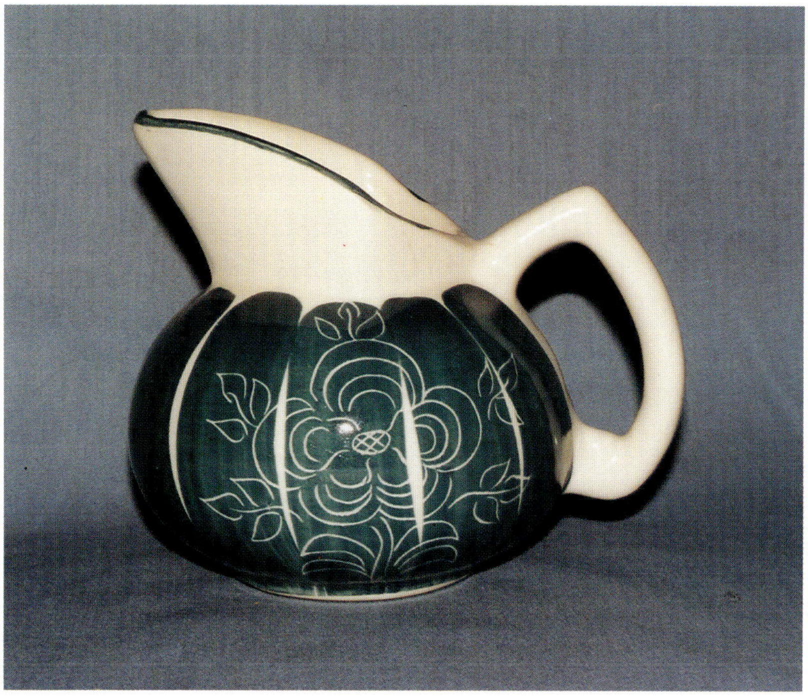

Kent jug. $80.

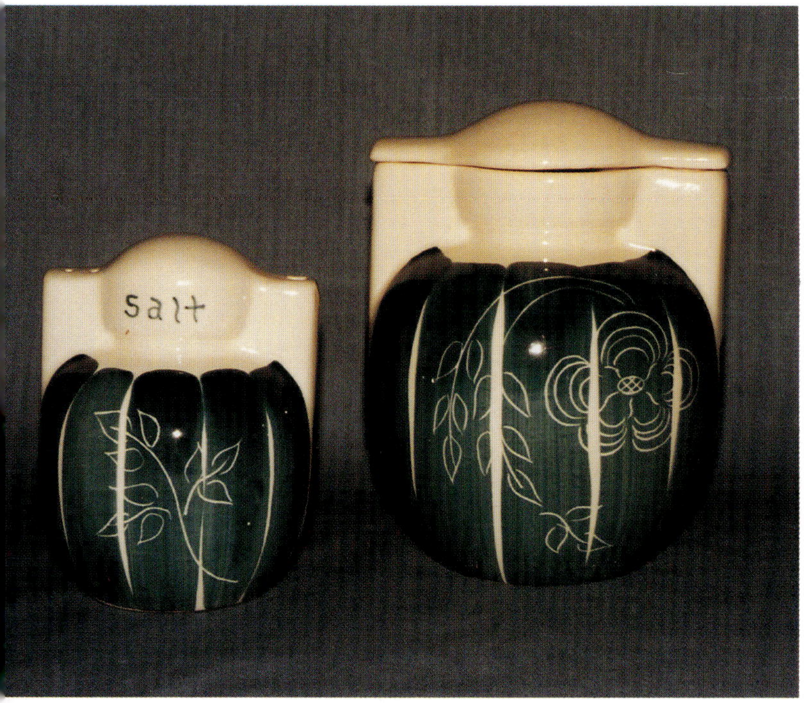

Salt pour and shake shaker. $40. Covered winged grease jar. $70.

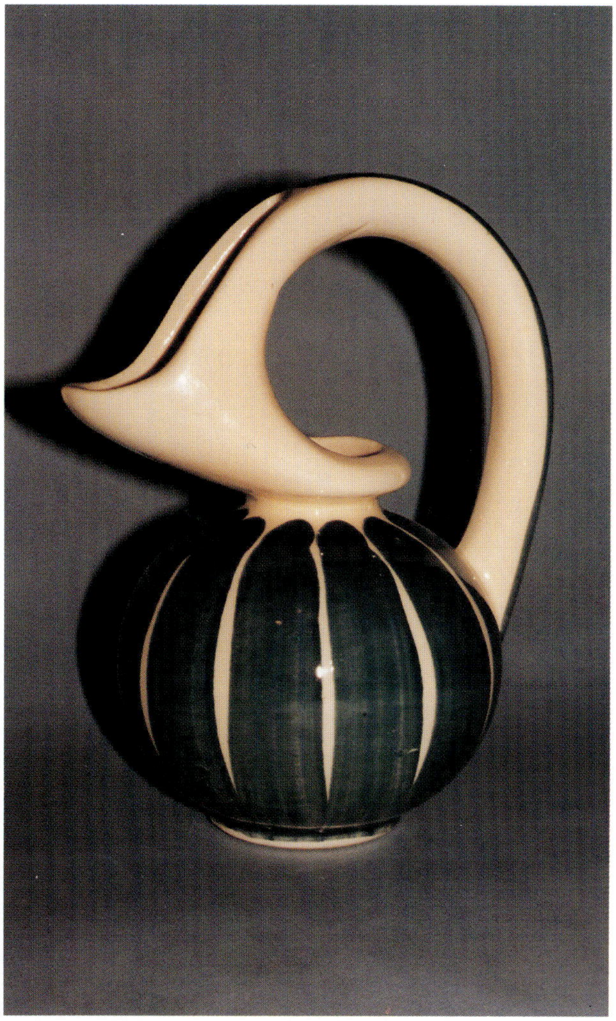

Honey jug. $75.

Golden Brown Intaglio

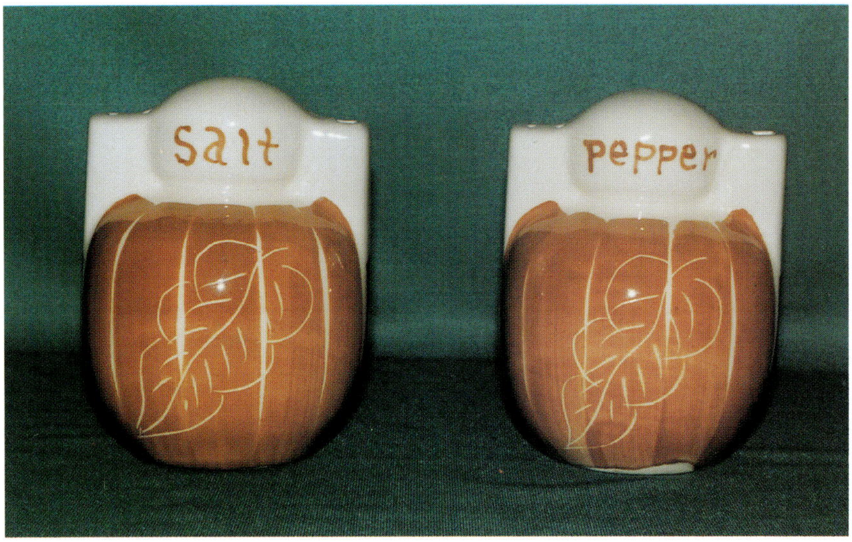

Salt and pepper pour and shake shakers. $100 set.

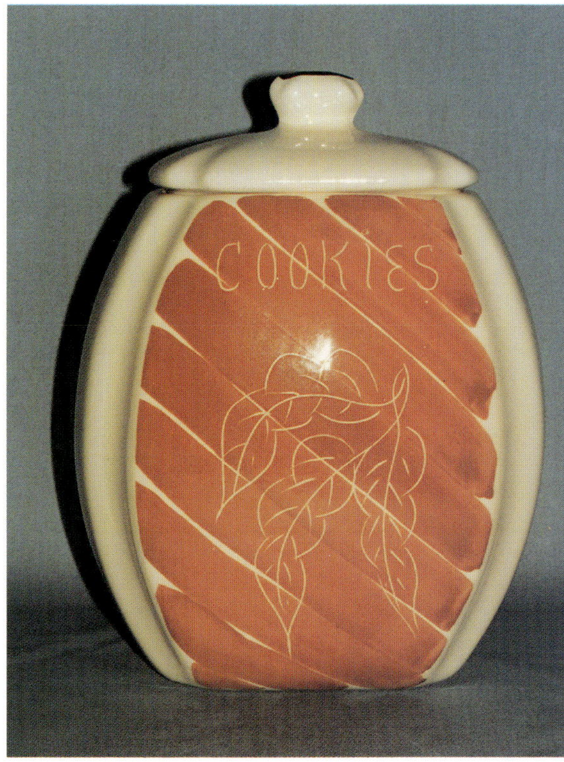

Wide oval cookies jar. $250.

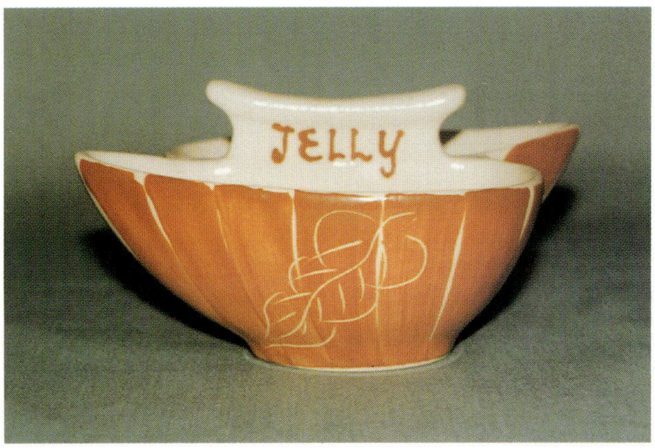

Jam and jelly. $100.

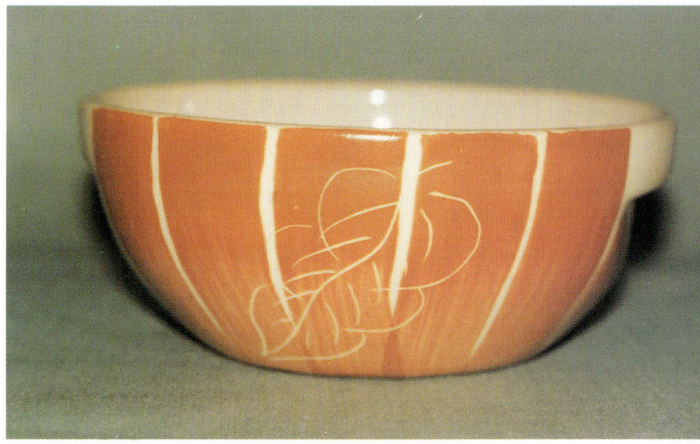

Cereal bowl. $25.

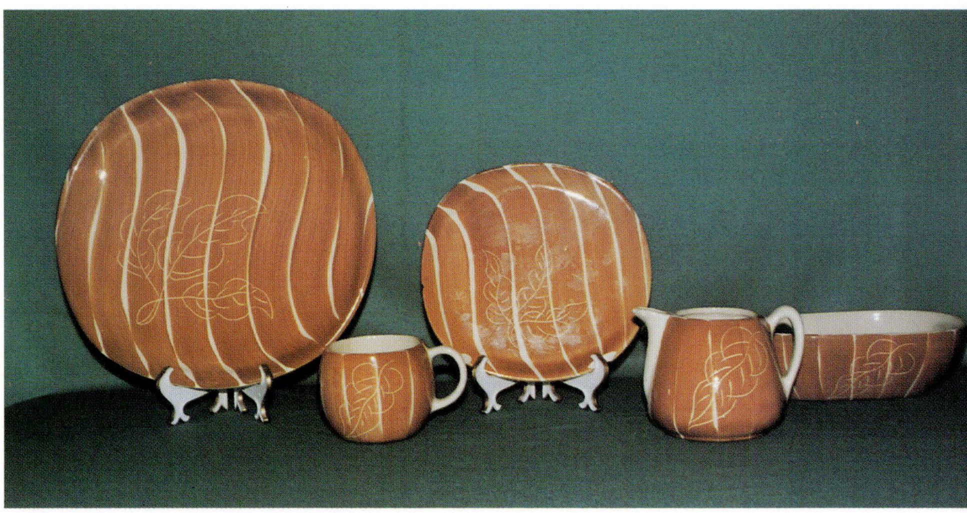

Dinner plate. $40. Salad plate. $25. Cup. $20. Creamer. $40. Baker. $40

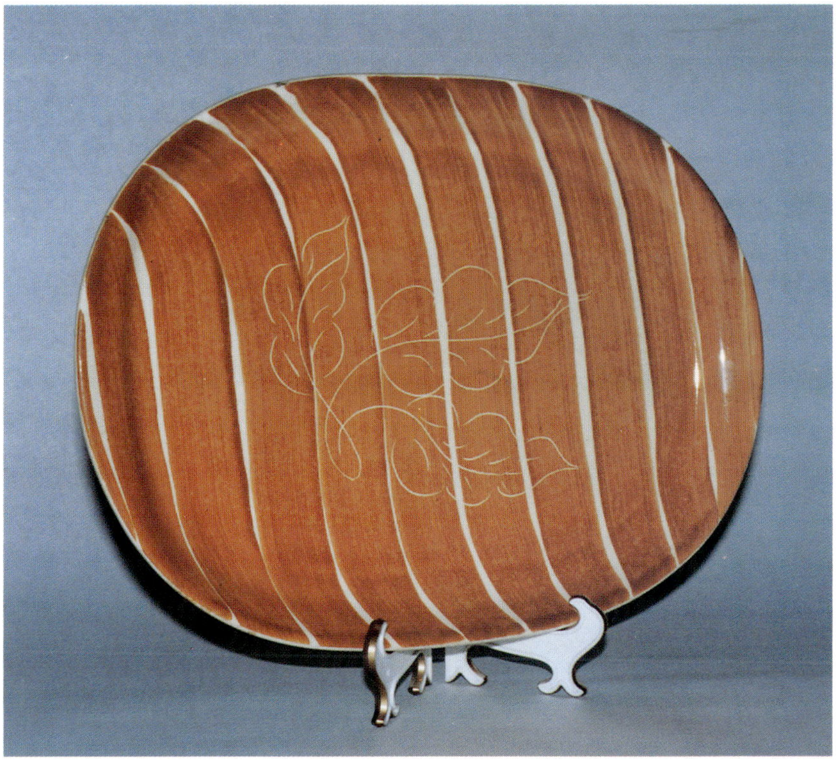

Dinner plates, experimental. $75 each.

Large platter. $75.

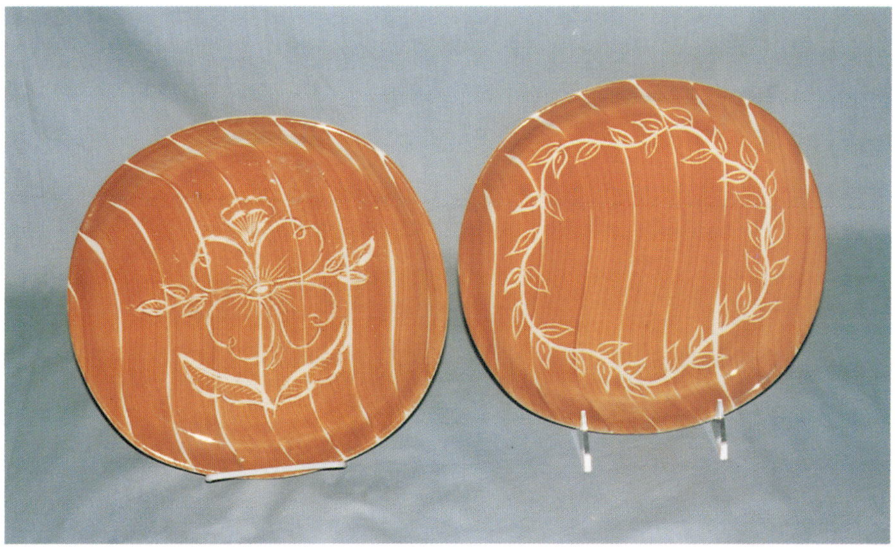

Covered vegetable. $125.

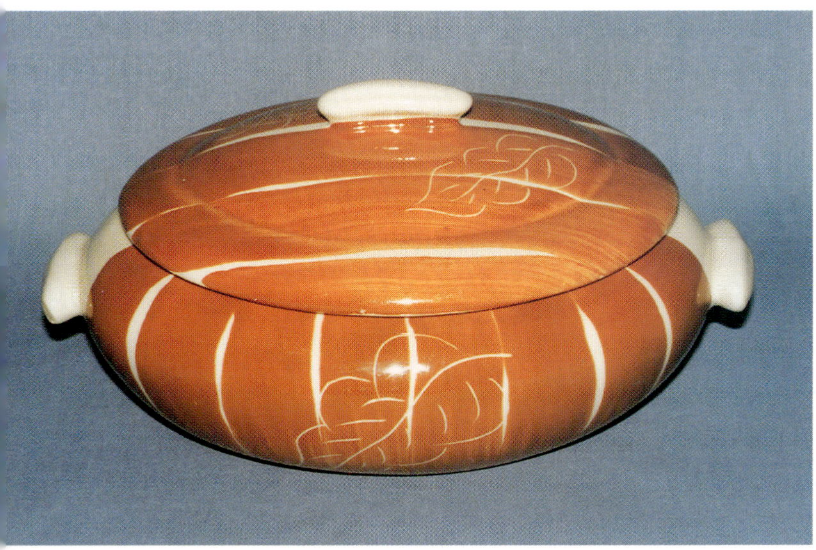

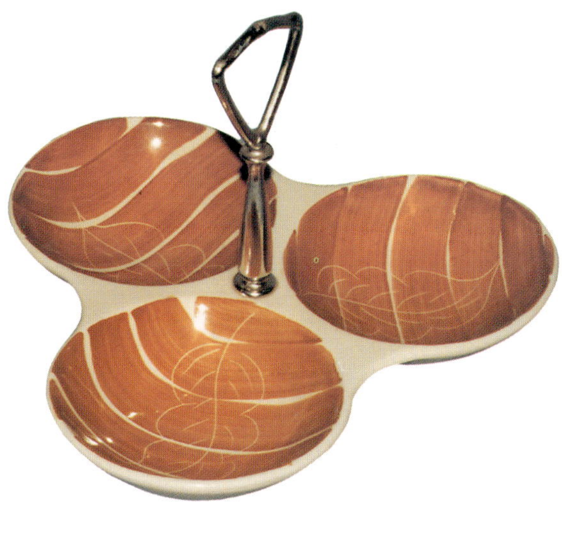

Three part relish with metal handle. $75.

Green Intaglio

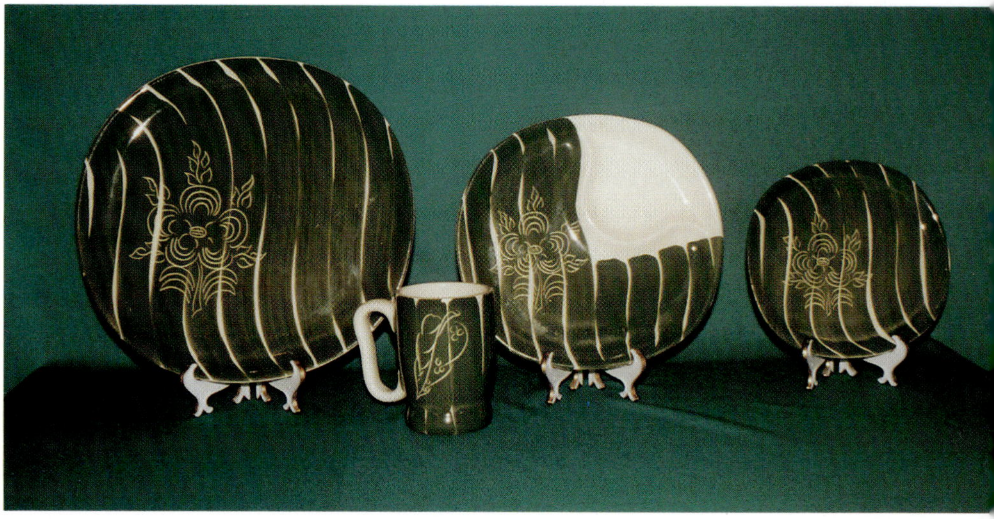

Dinner plate. $30. Coffee mug. $40. Tea and toast plate. $25. Salad plate. $25.

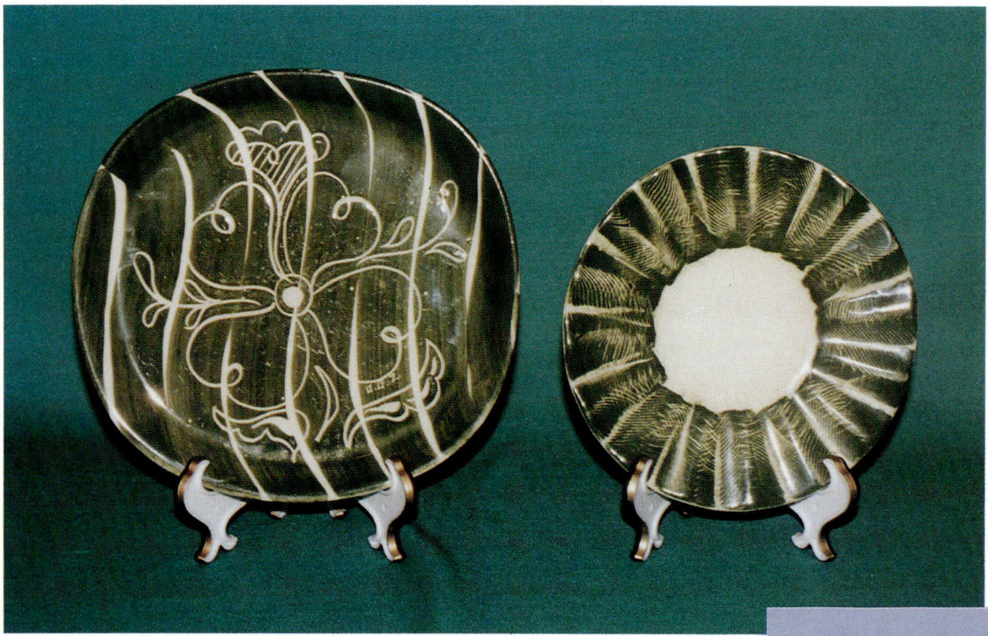

Breakfast plate, experimental. $75. Salad plate, Seaform style, experimental. $50.

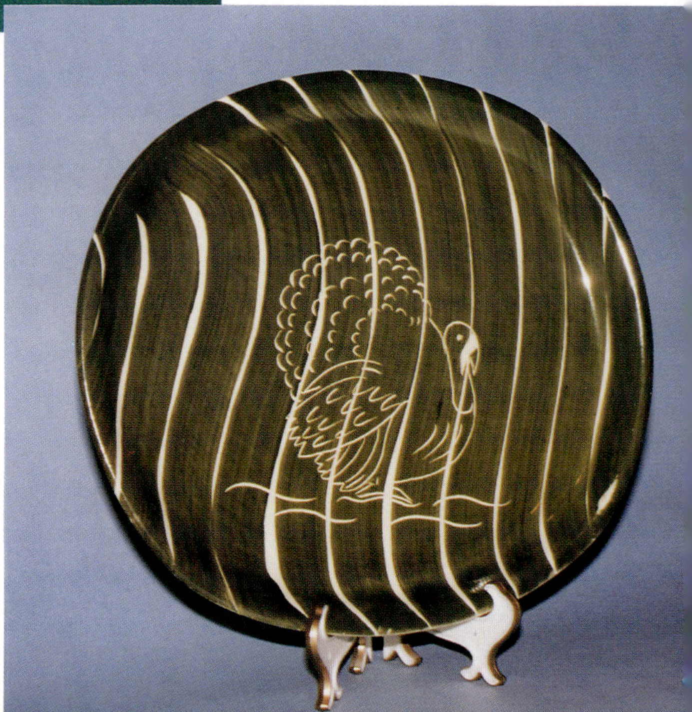

Dinner plate, turkey etch. $250+.

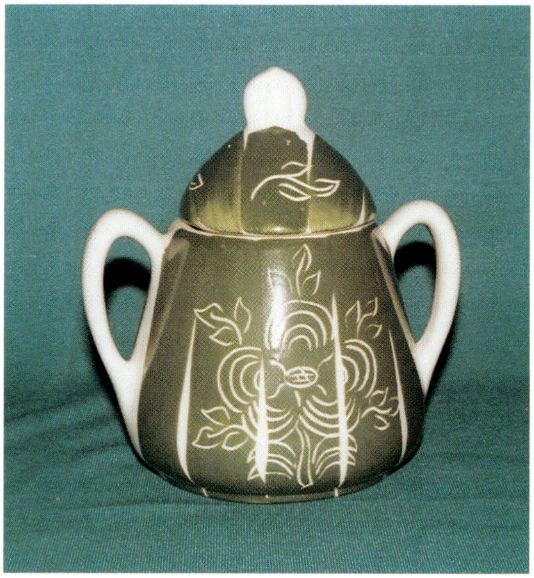

Covered sugar. $35.

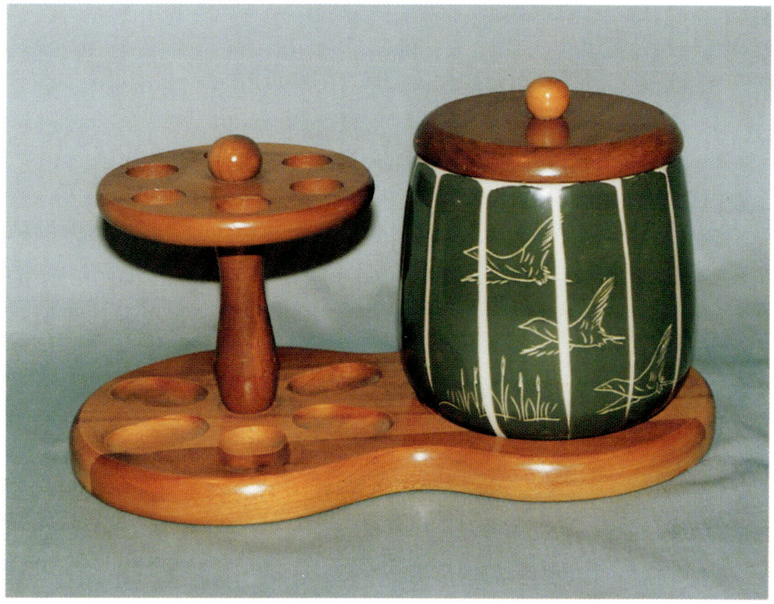

Tobacco humidor, ducks flying, with wooden pipe holder. $175.

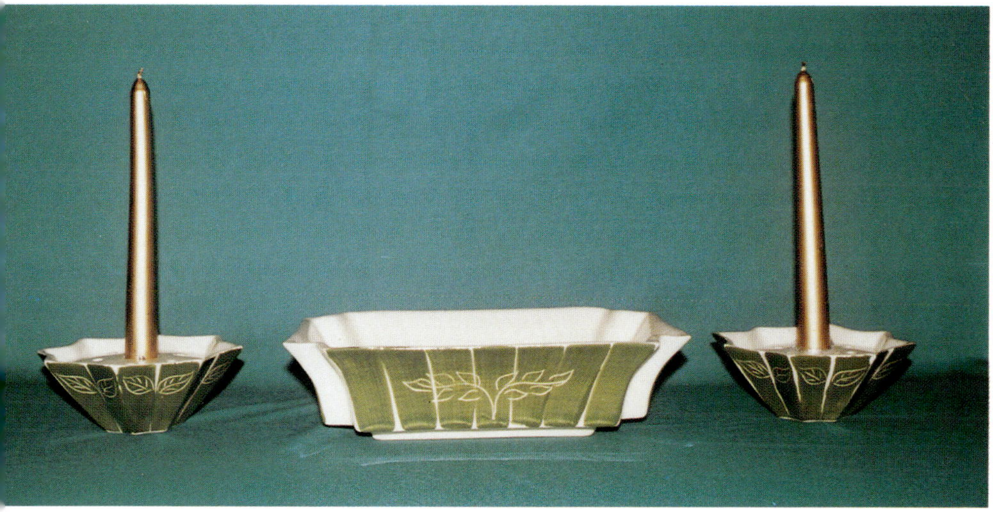

Star candle holders with insert. $125 set. Candy dish, 6" long, NAPCO mold. $50.

Tall vase. $50.

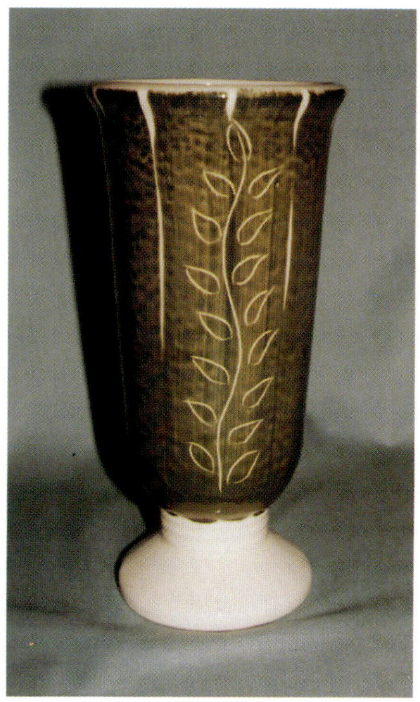

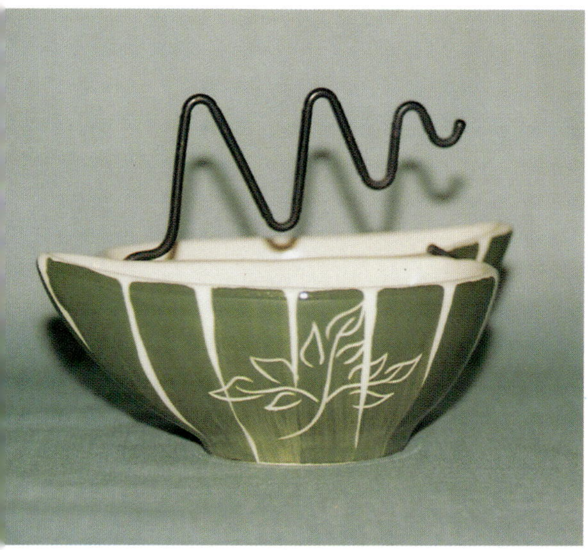

Ashtray. $30.

Coral Intaglio

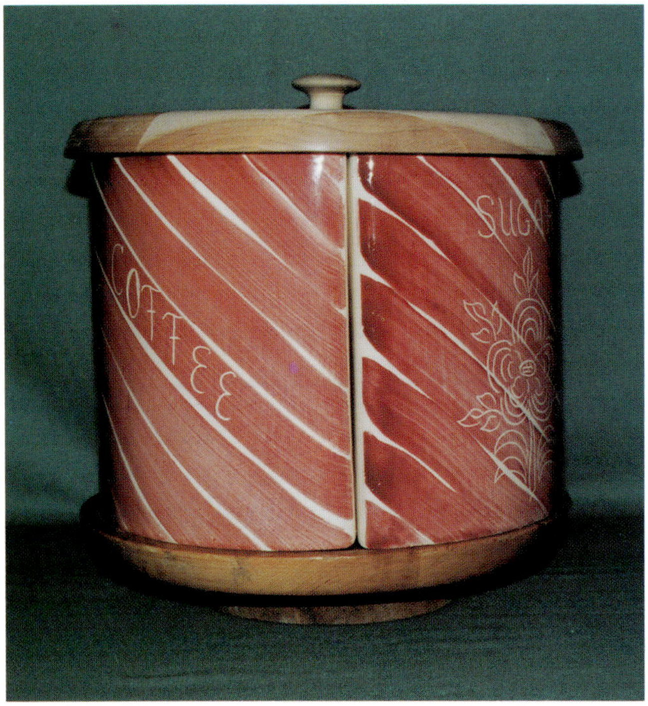

Revolving four-section canister, note different styles of etchings on each piece. $200.

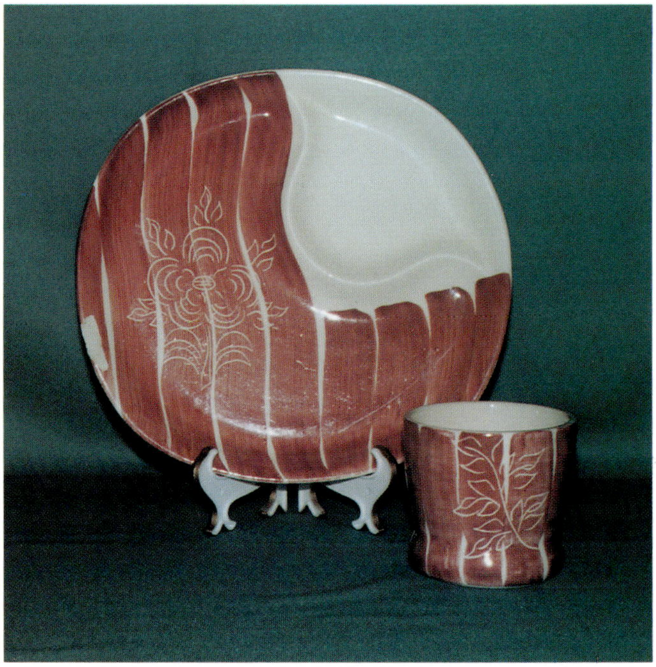

Tea and toast plate. $30. Juice mug. $20.

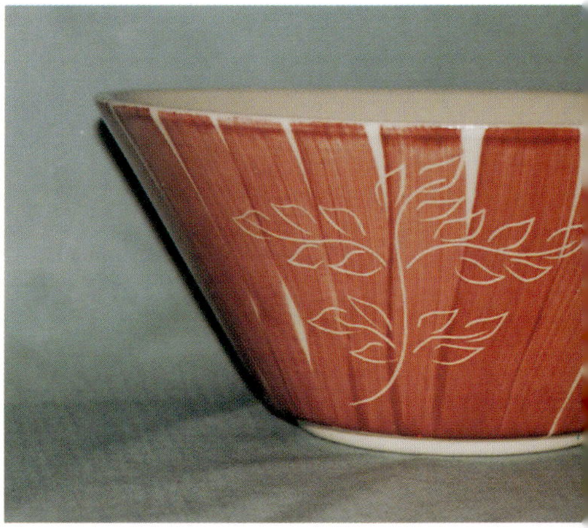

Punch bowl, Rubel mold. $100.

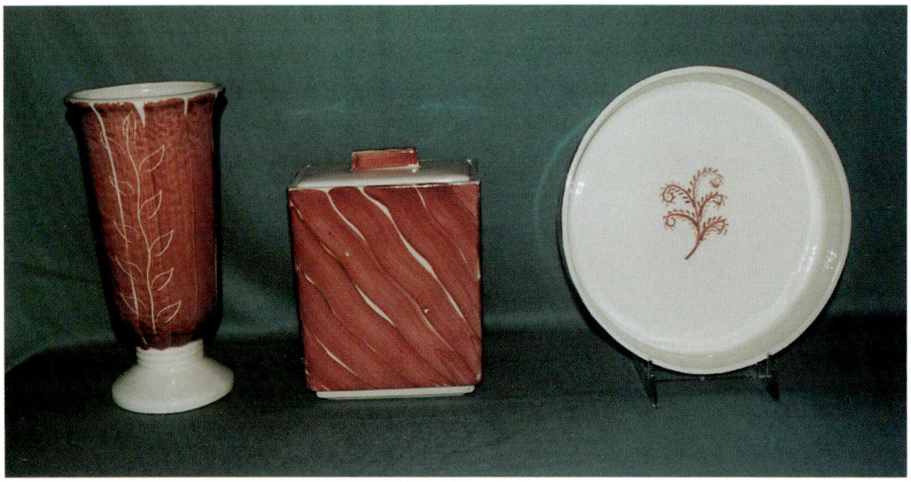

Tall vase. $75. Tall square storage container. $50. Bowl, unknown mold. $40.

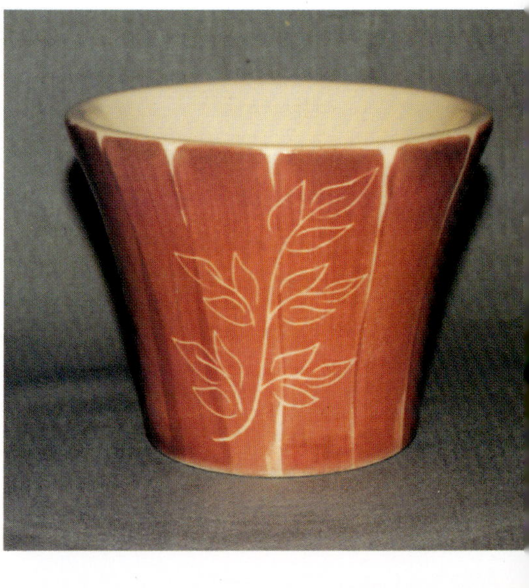

Candy dish, unknown mold, 3.75" diameter, 3" high. $50.

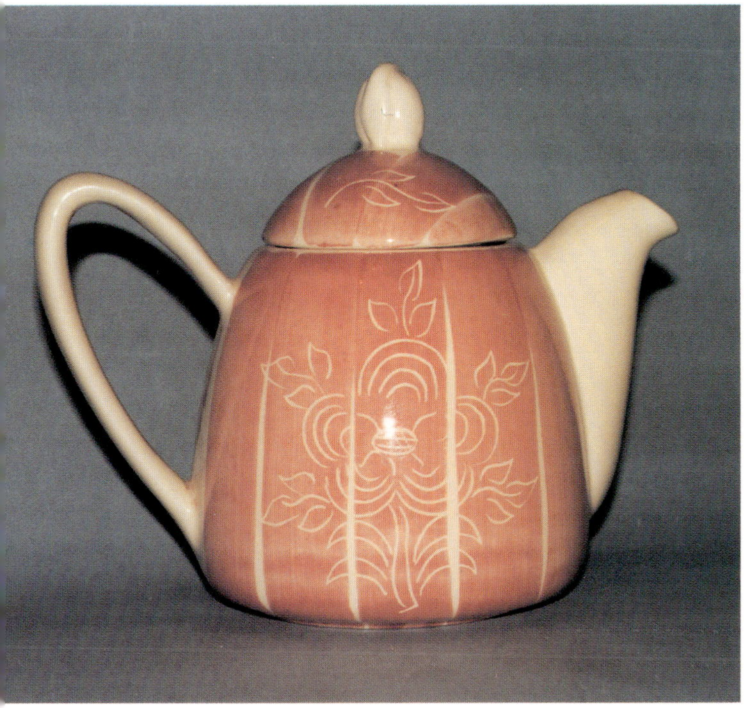

Six cup domed lid teapot. $100.

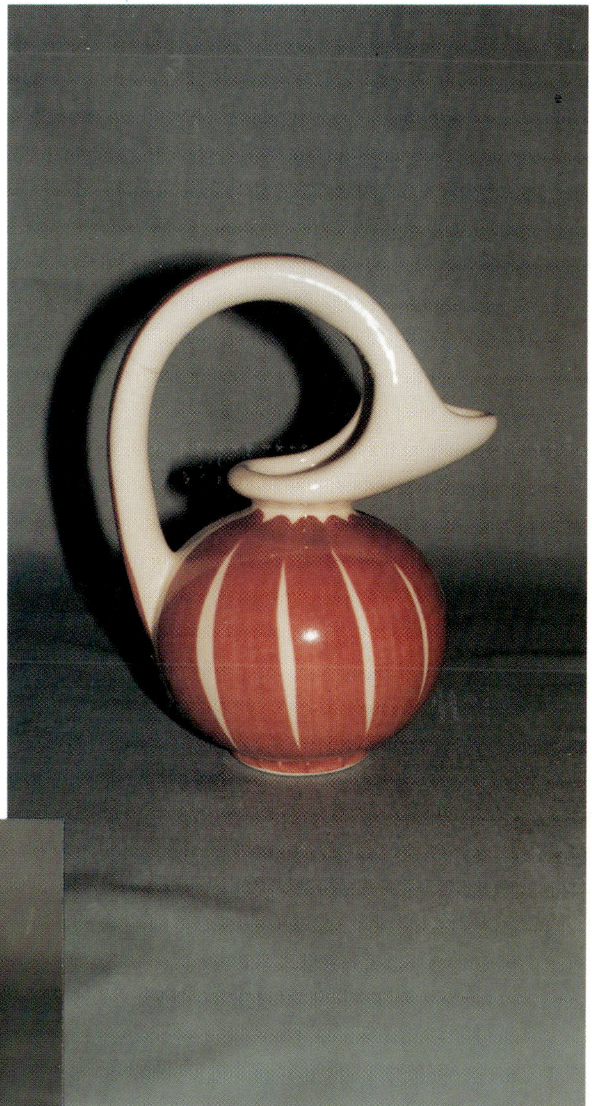

Honey jug. $75.

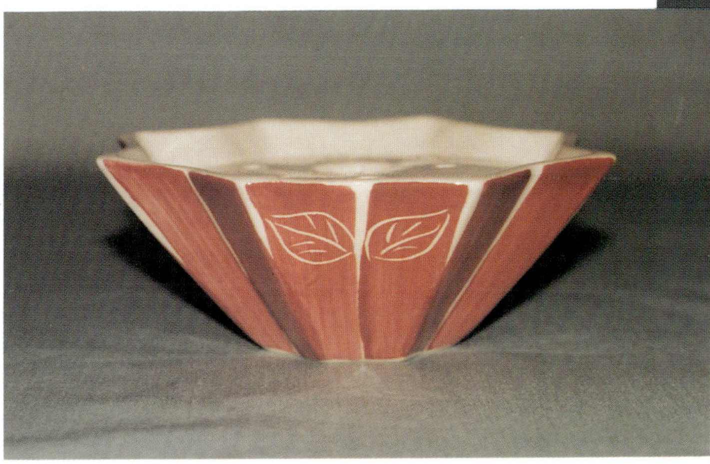

Star candle holder with insert. $50.

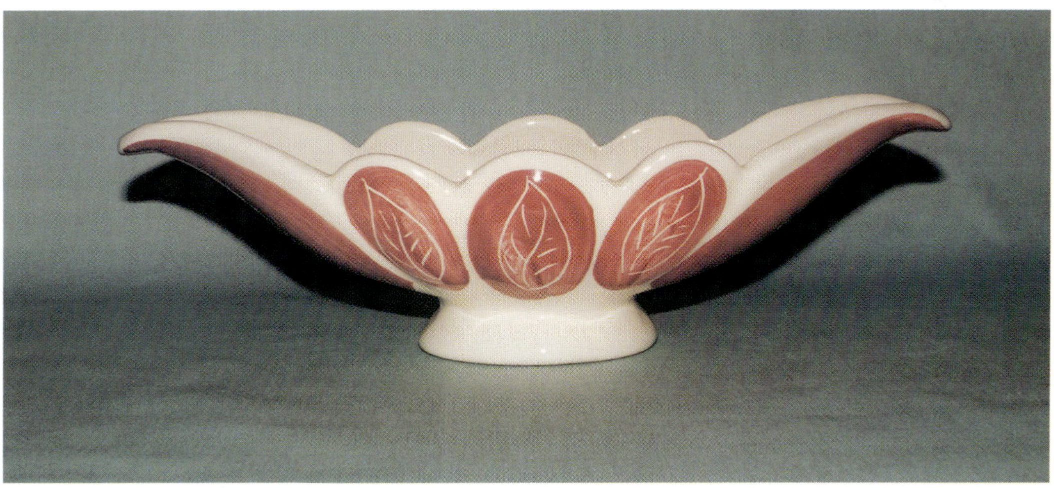

Console bowl, NAPCO mold. $80.

Blue and Black Intaglios

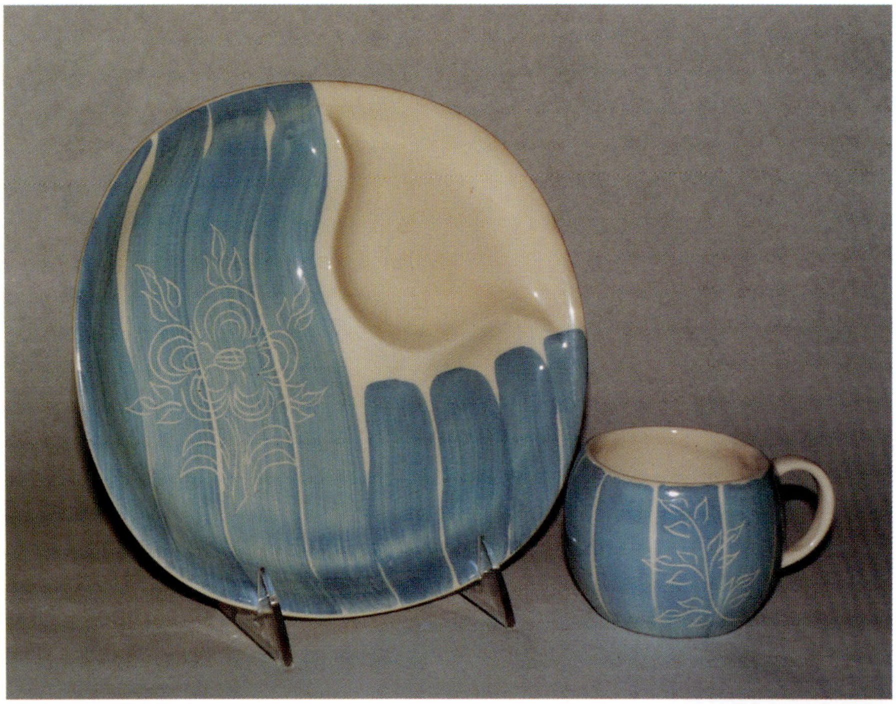

Tea and toast plate, Light Blue Intaglio. $50. Cup, Light Blue Intaglio. $25.

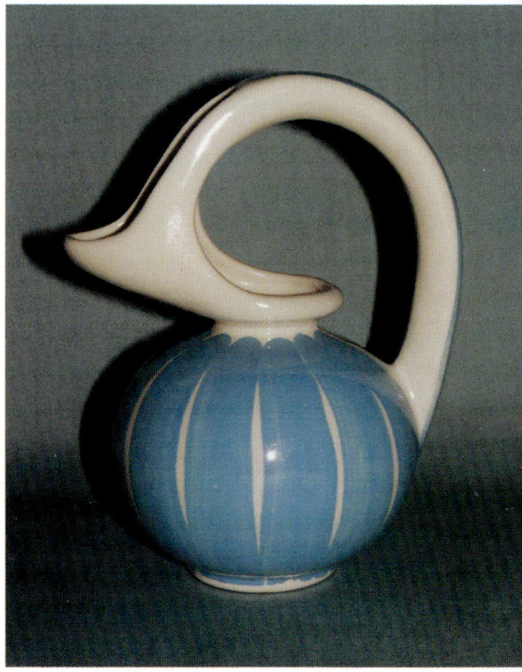

Honey jug, Light Blue Intaglio. $80.

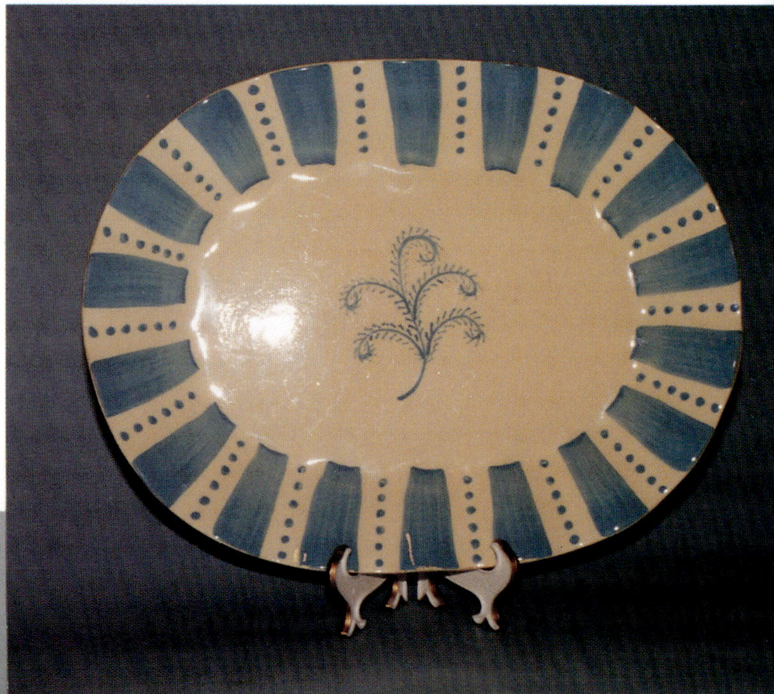

Large platter, Seaform style, experimental, Light Blue Intaglio. $150.

Star candle holder with insert, Light Blue Intaglio. $50.

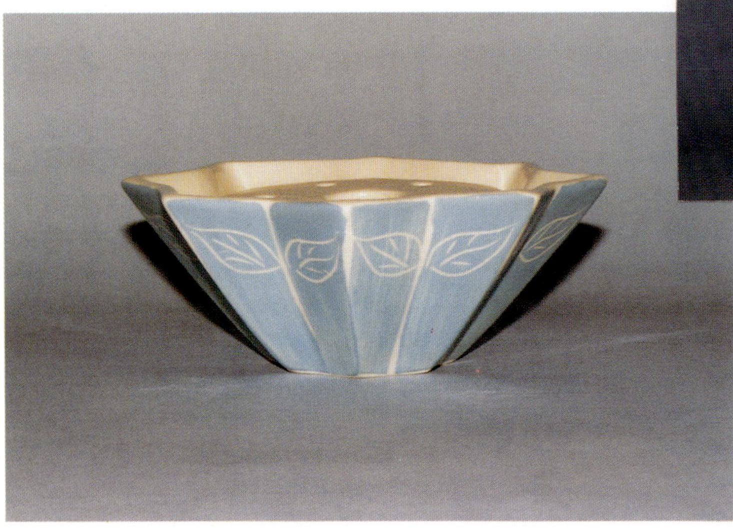

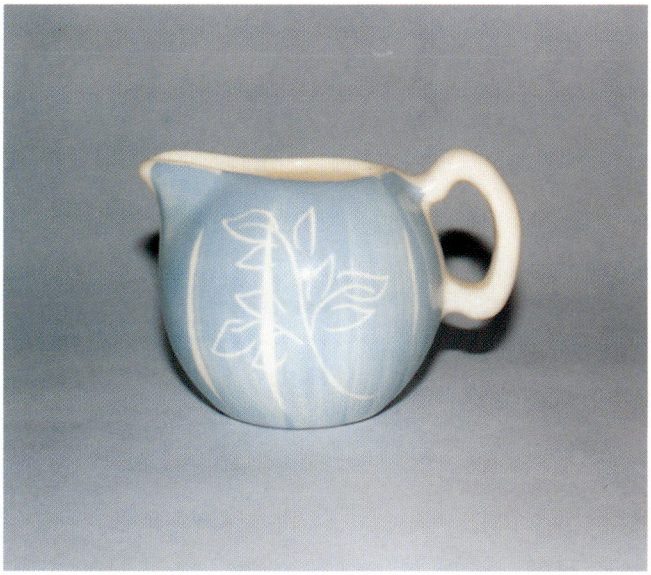

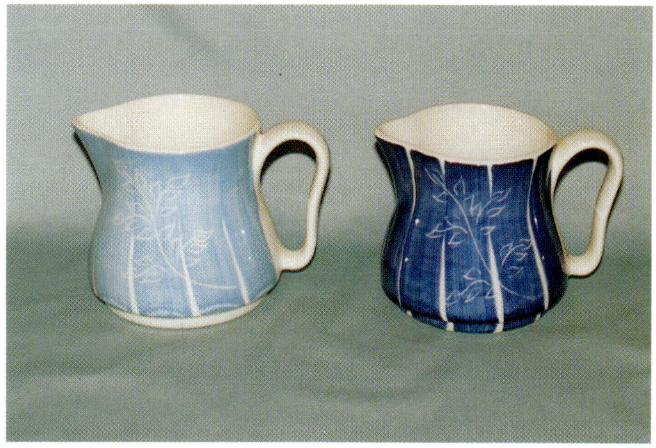

Pitcher, Rubel mold, Light Blue Intaglio. $150. Pitcher, Rubel mold, Cobalt Blue Intaglio. $150.

Individual creamer, Light Blue Intaglio. $50.

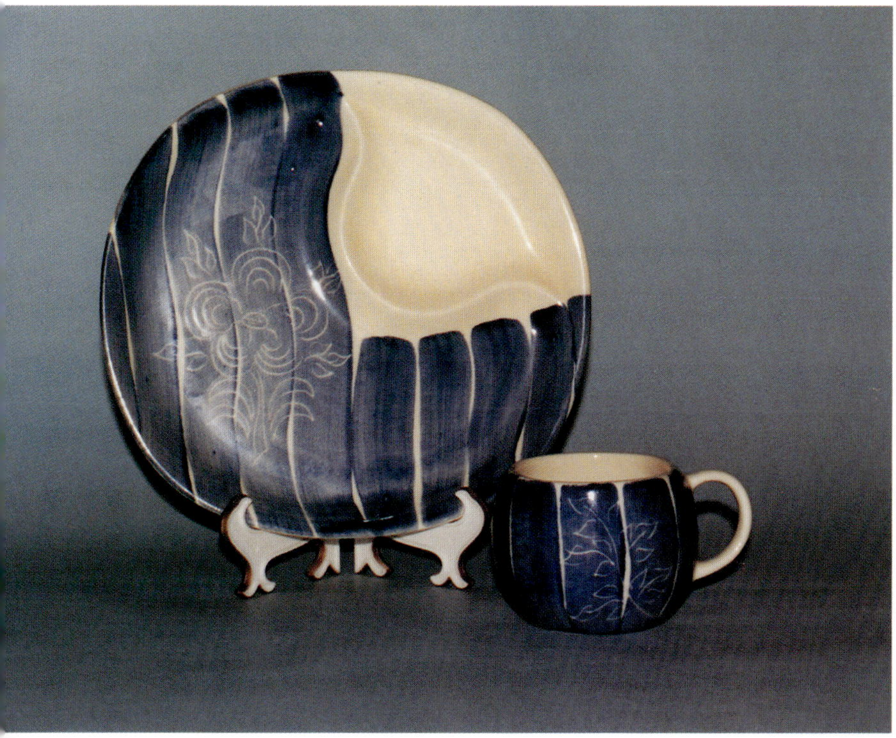

Tea and toast plate, Cobalt Blue Intaglio. $50.
Cup, Cobalt Blue Intaglio. $25.

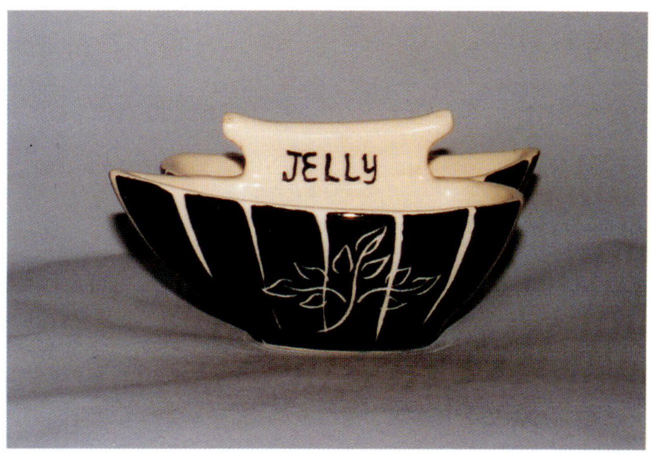

Jam and jelly, Black Intaglio. This is the only item known in Black Intaglio. $150.

Mountain Rose

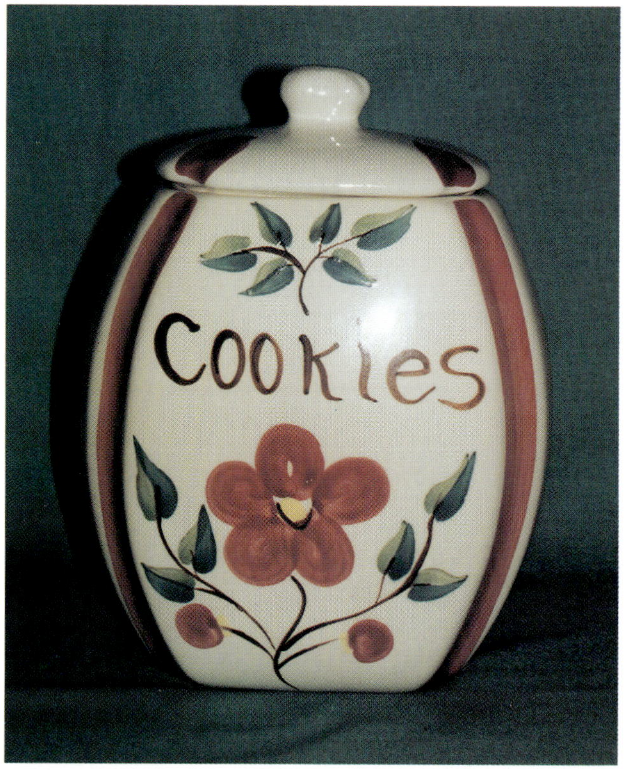

Mountain Rose is most widely seen on two cup teapots made as premiums for the McCormick Tea Company. The Mountain Rose decoration is a four-petal rose with a simple leaf design. You also see this decoration on the basket planter and a few earlier items such as the round creamer and sugar, earlier teapots, and kent jugs. Purinton used this sparingly in the mid-1940s. This pattern was designed for Montgomery Ward, but they did not market it.

The five petal Mountain Rose decoration is more colorful with its two-toned leaves. It was probably introduced in the late 1940s around the time of Chartreuse and Harmony because we see it on the tall and half oval canister sets. Mountain Rose was another item that had a short production run but which decorated a complete dinnerware set with accessory pieces in one body style. Its design is similar to that of Apple with its two-tone leaves and scalloping edges. It required a few more brush strokes to paint.

An abundant supply of the two cup teapots and basket planters made the prices of these items low. Supply for the dinnerware and serving items is limited. Mountain Rose is another Purinton decoration with the country style and is sought after by many collectors. Prices reflect a pattern that is becoming more desirable. More common products include the rum jug planter, rebecca jug, and wall pocket. Cookies jars, canister sets, honey jugs, and oil and vinegar sets are some of the harder to find items.

Mountain Rose wide oval cookies jar. $200.

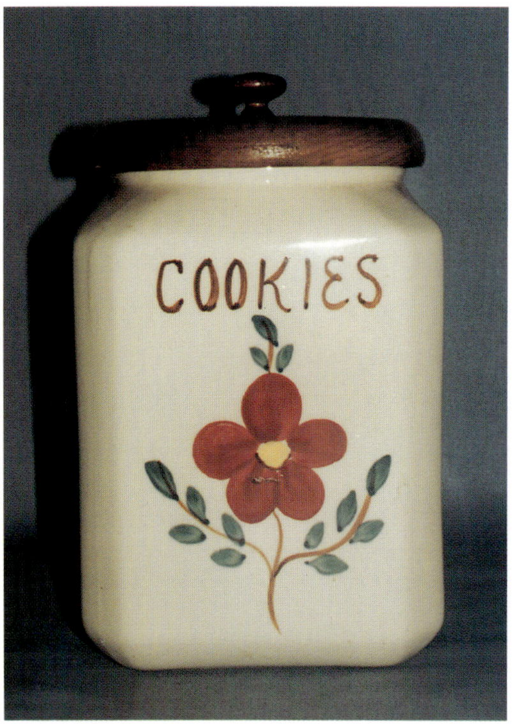

Square cookies jar with a wooden lid. $150.

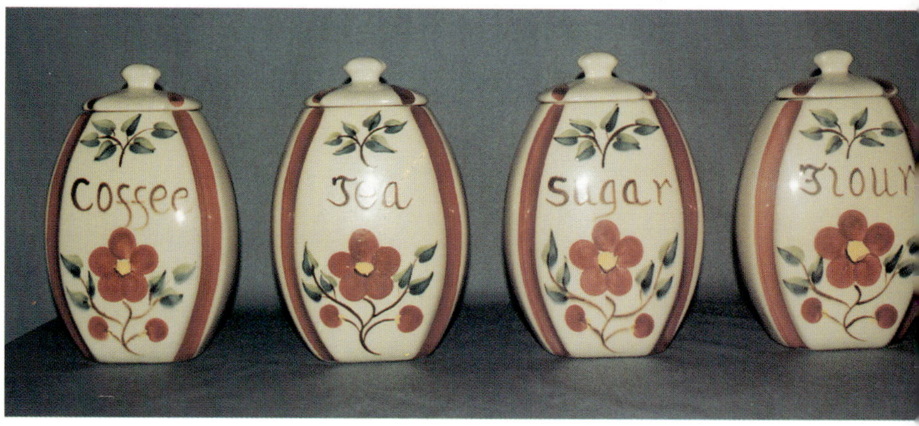

Tall oval four piece canister set. $100 each.

Half oval five piece canister set. $75 each.

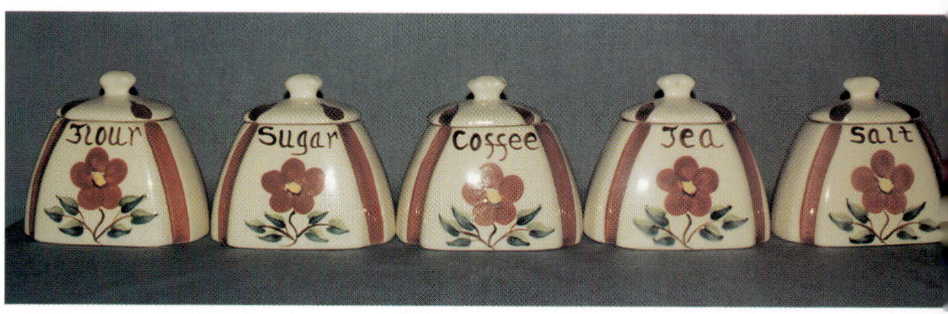

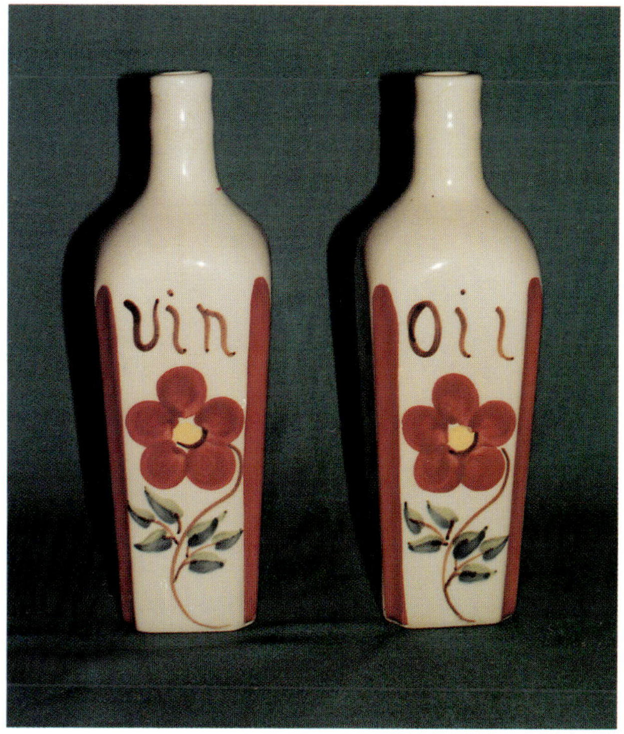

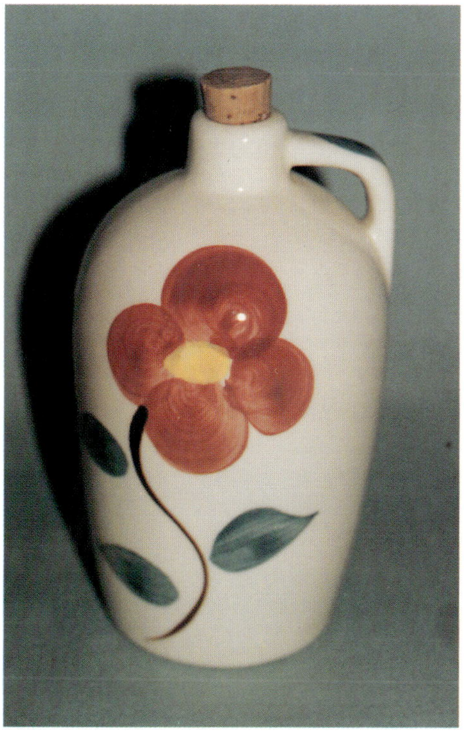

Jug style decanter, 5" high. $40.

Tall oil and vinegar. $125 set.

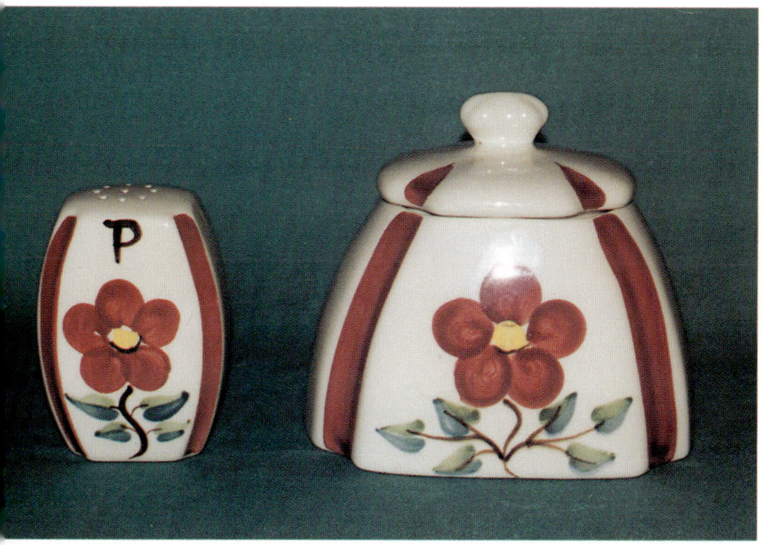

Range pepper shaker. $40. Range covered grease jar. $90.

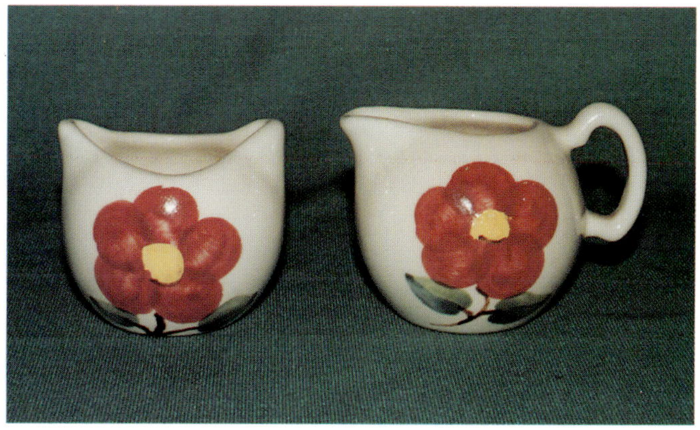

Individual sugar and creamer. $50 set.

Round creamer and covered sugar. $30 set.
Covered sugar and creamer. $70 set.

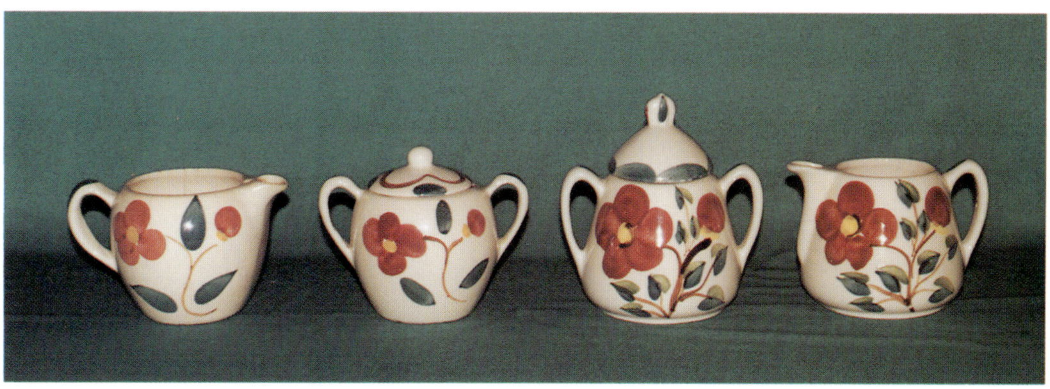

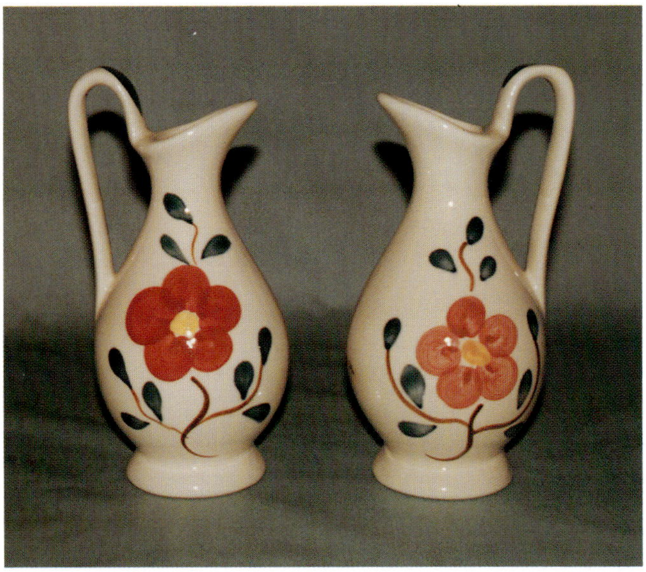

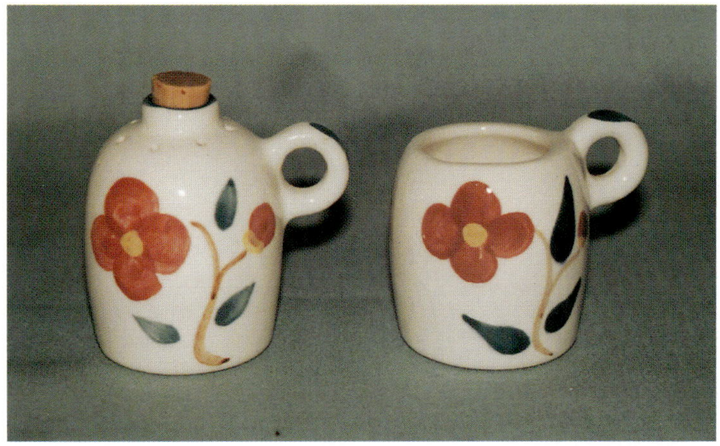

Jug style salt or pepper. $30 each. Jug style whimsy toothpick holder. $50.

Rebecca jugs. $25 each.

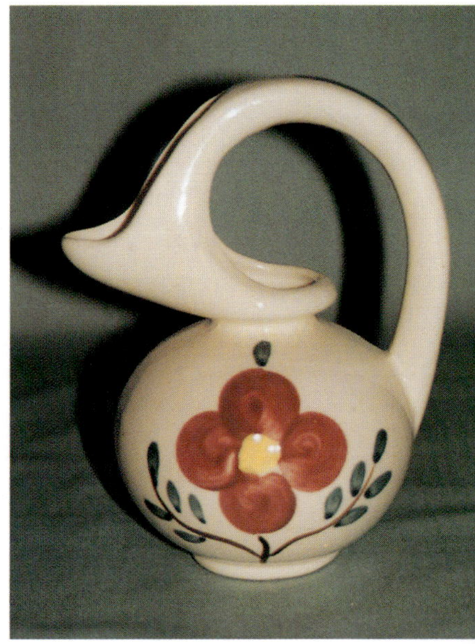

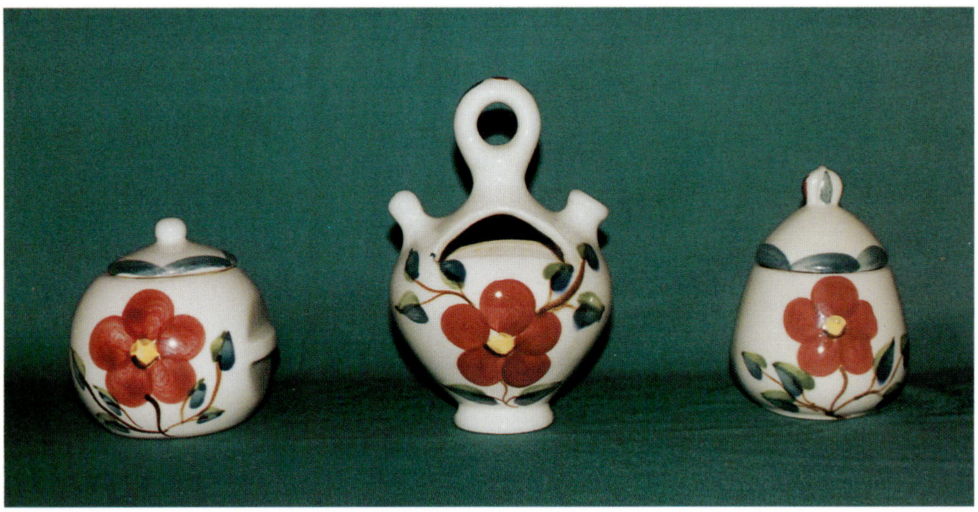

Individual bean pot. $60. Rum jug planter. $50. Marmalade. $70.

Honey jug. $200.

Candy dish. $100.

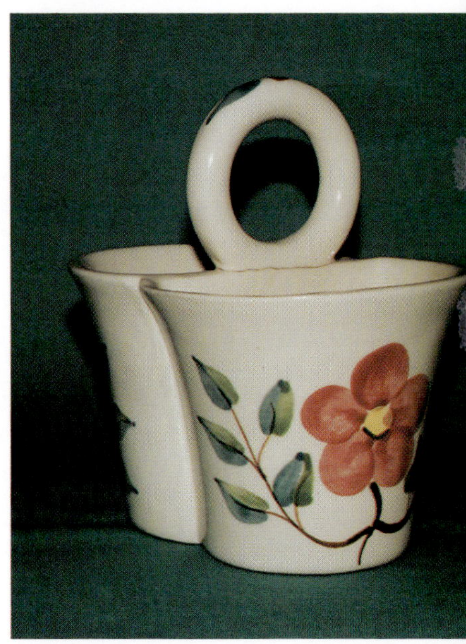

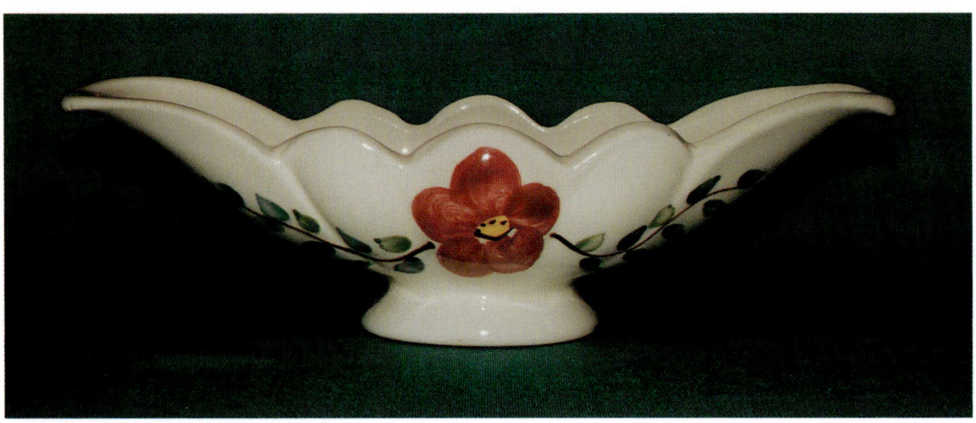

Console bowl, NAPCO mold. $100.

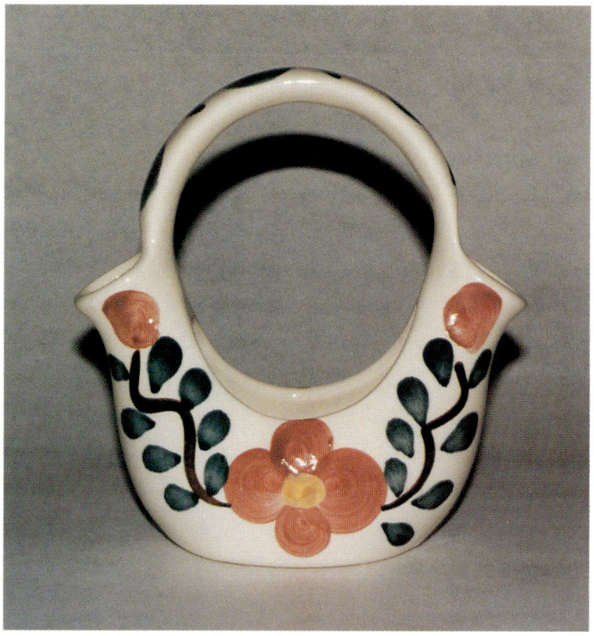

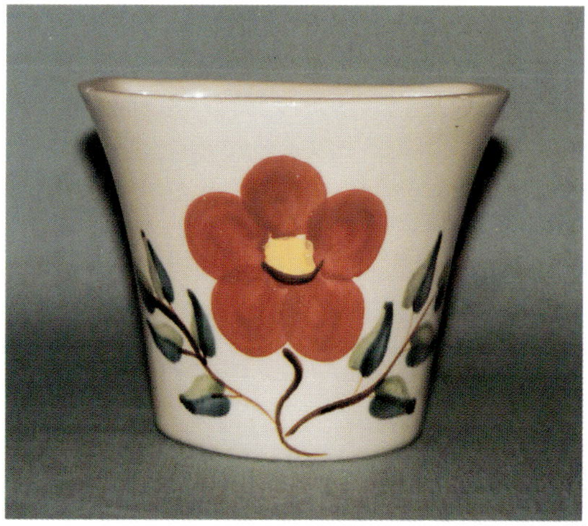

Wall pocket. $60.

Basket planter, this is a very common item. $15.

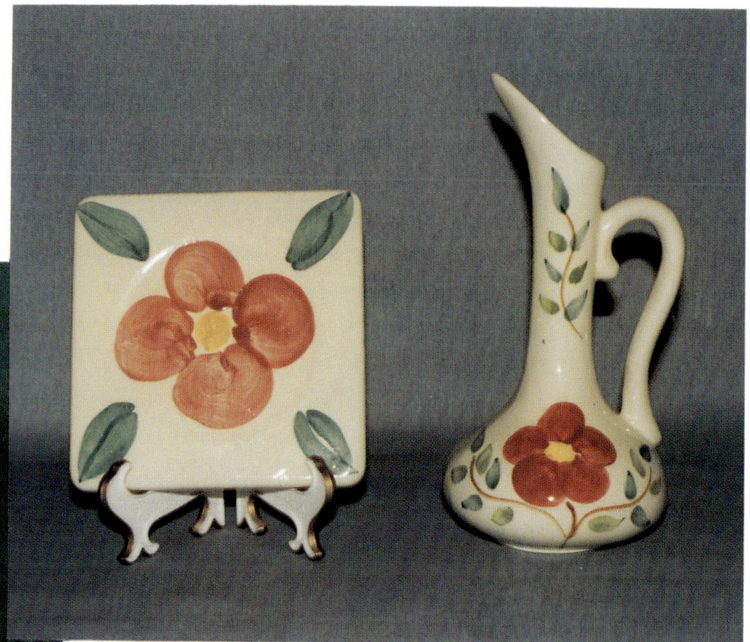

Tea tile. $75. Tall ewer. $80.

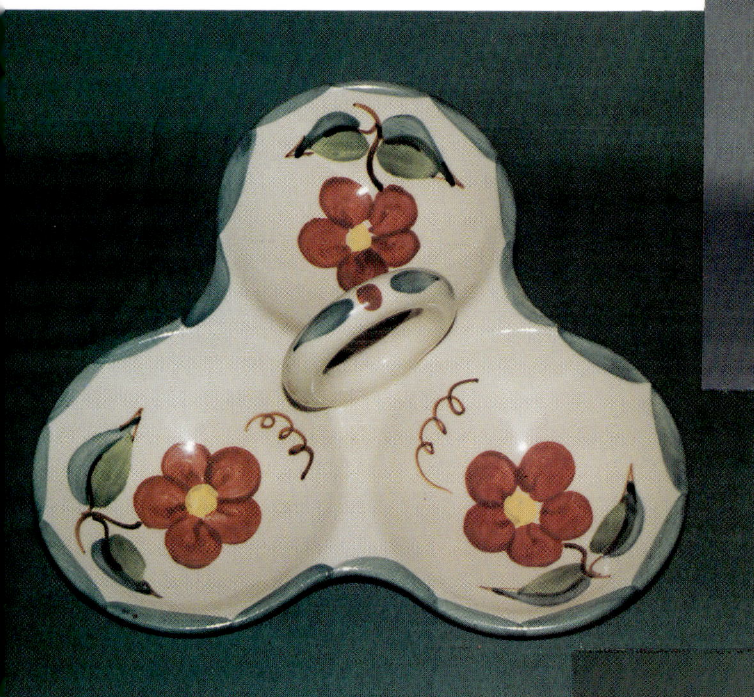

Three part relish with a ceramic handle. $100.

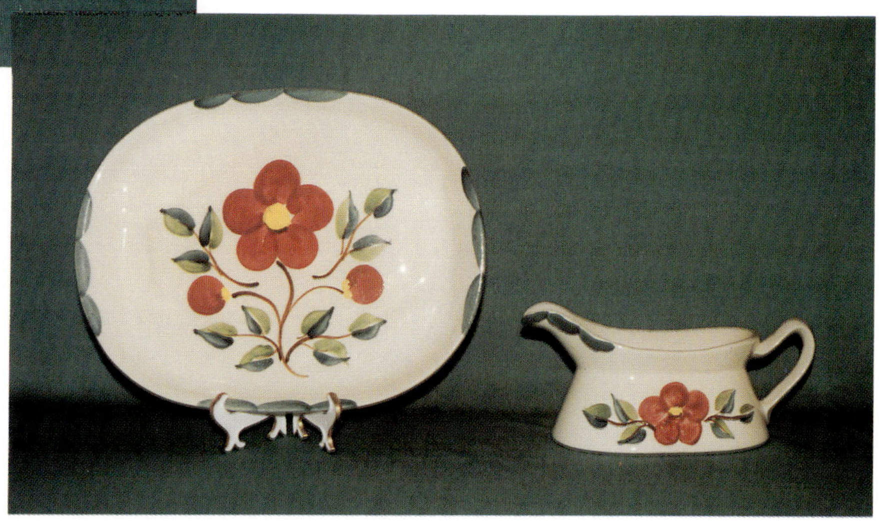

Diamond grill platter. $90. Gravy boat, Taylor Smith Taylor mold. $150.

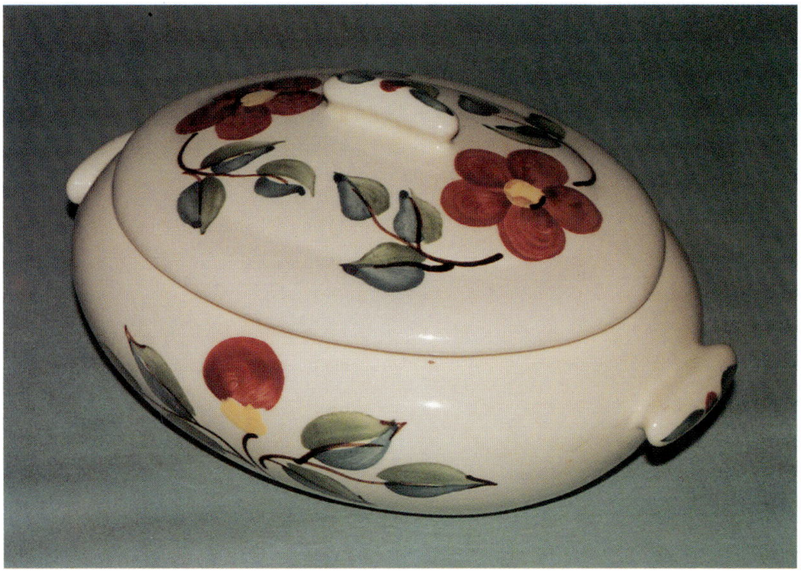

Covered vegetable. $90.

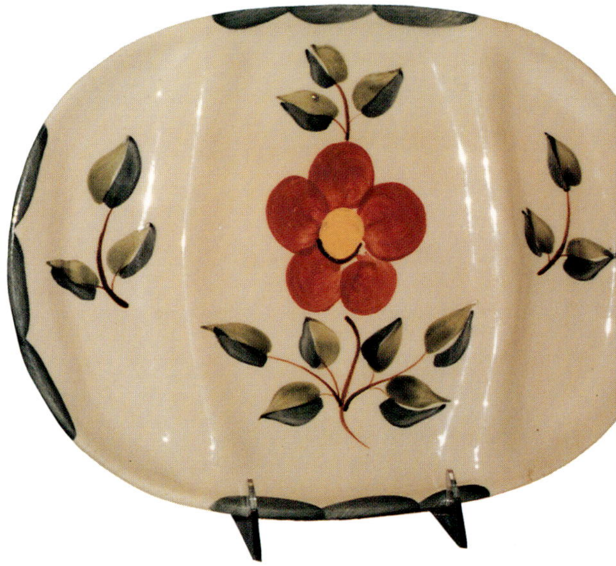

Three section grill platter. $90.

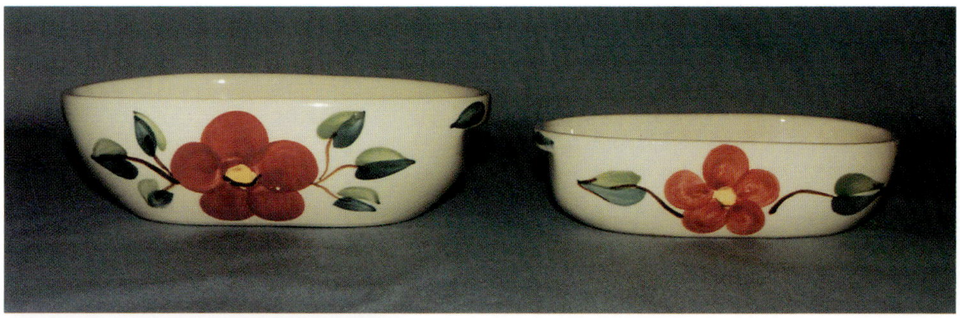

Baker. $60. Pickle. $40.

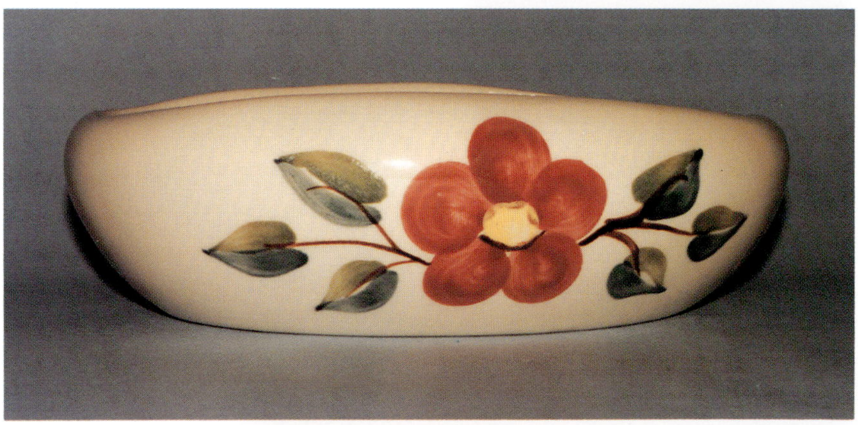

Open vegetable. $60.

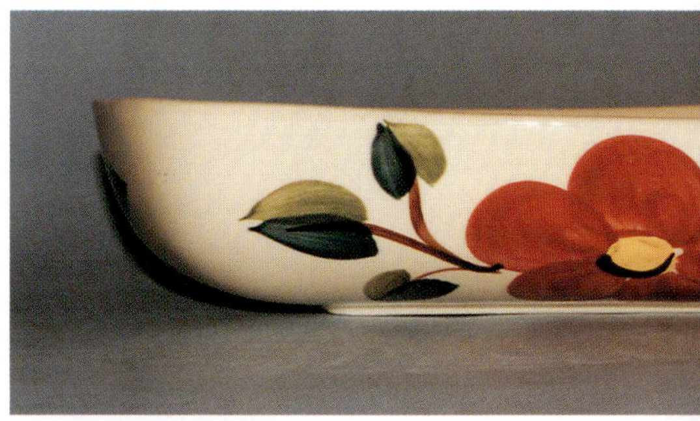

Roll tray. $100.

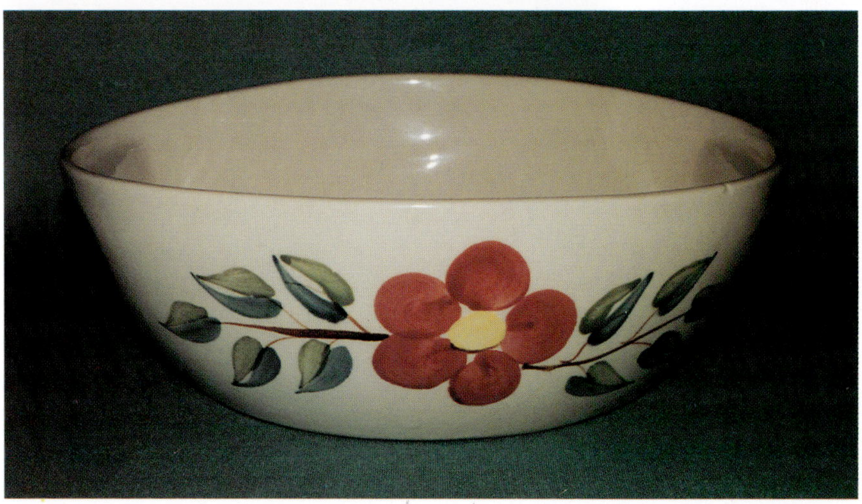

Salad bowl. $100.

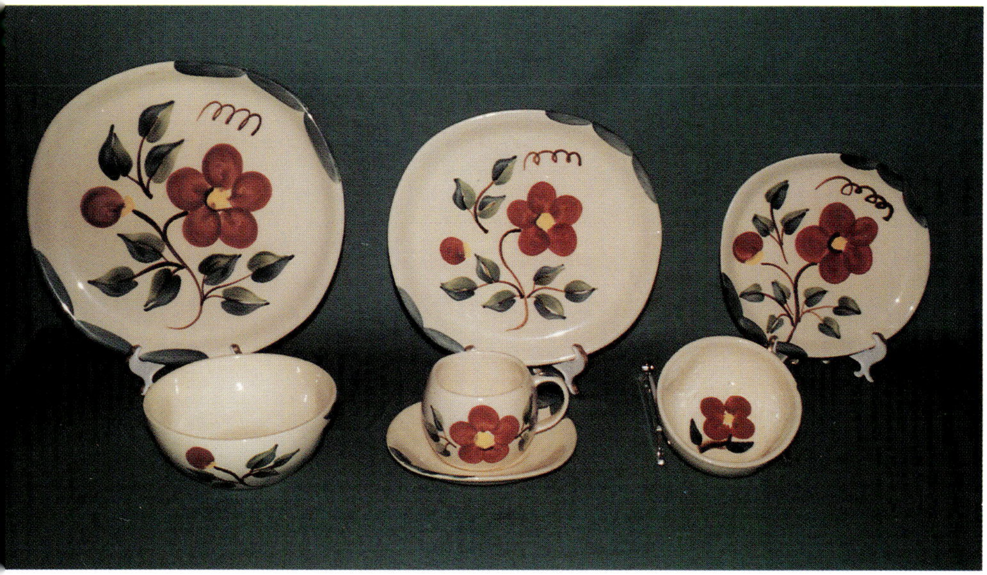

Dinner plate. $40. Breakfast plate. $35. Salad plate. $35. Cereal bowl. $25. Cup. $15. Saucer. $5. Dessert bowl. $25.

Chop plate. $150.

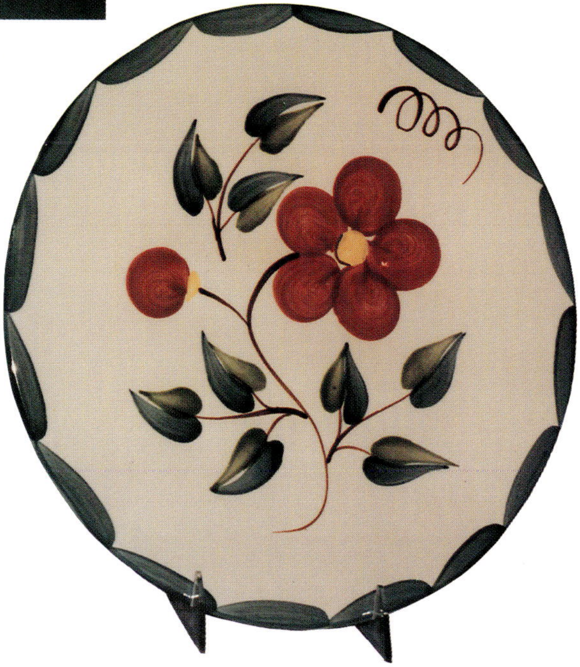

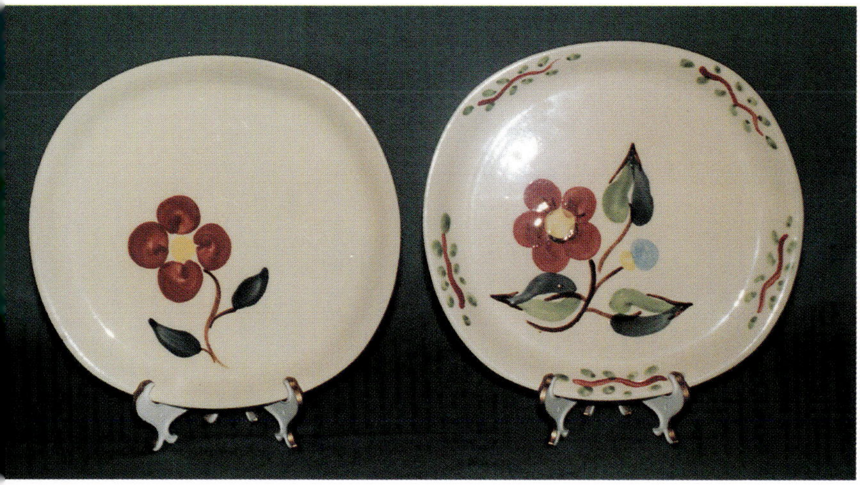

Experimental or variant salad plates. $75 each.

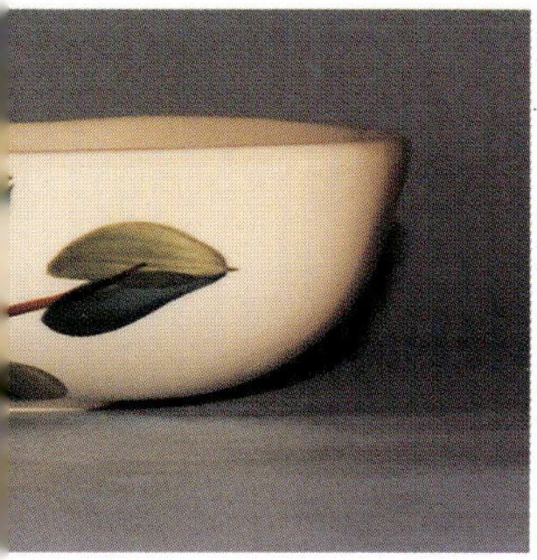

Fruit bowl. $125.

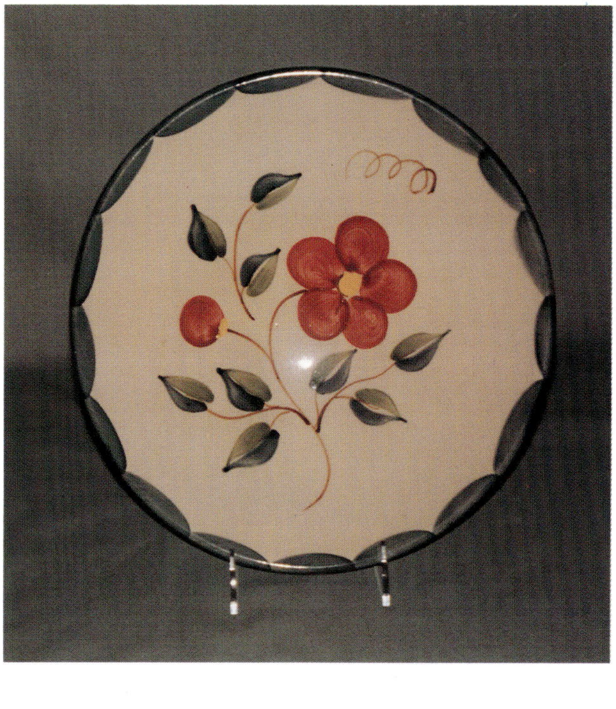

Spaghetti bowl. $200.

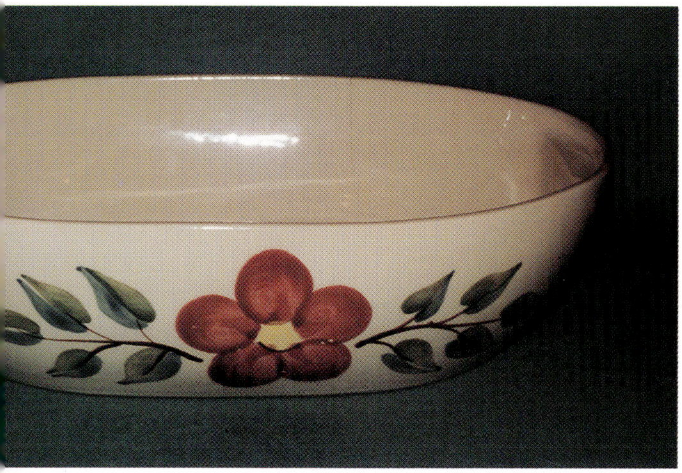

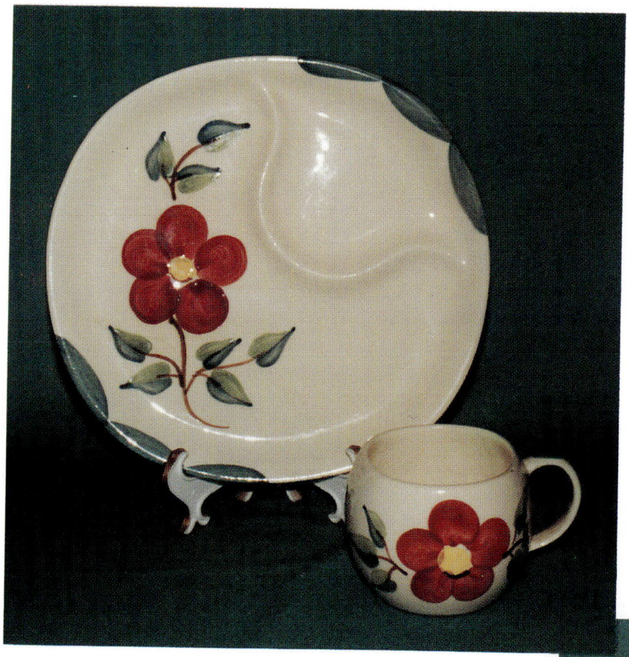

Tea and toast plate. $35. Cup $15.

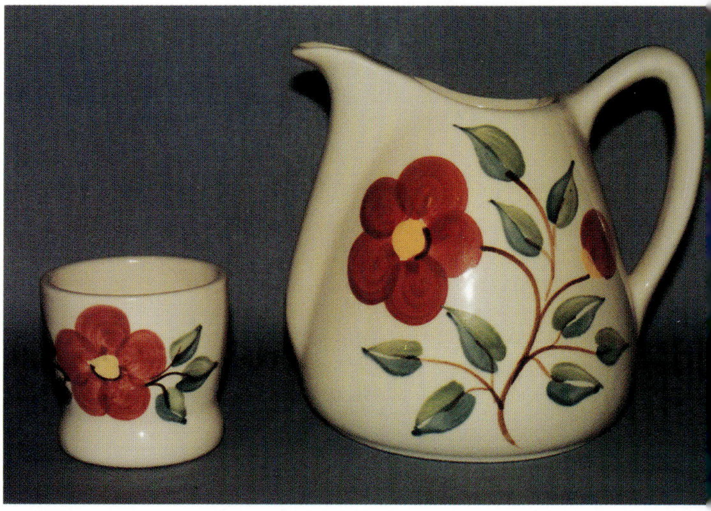

Juice mug. $30. Beverage pitcher. $100.

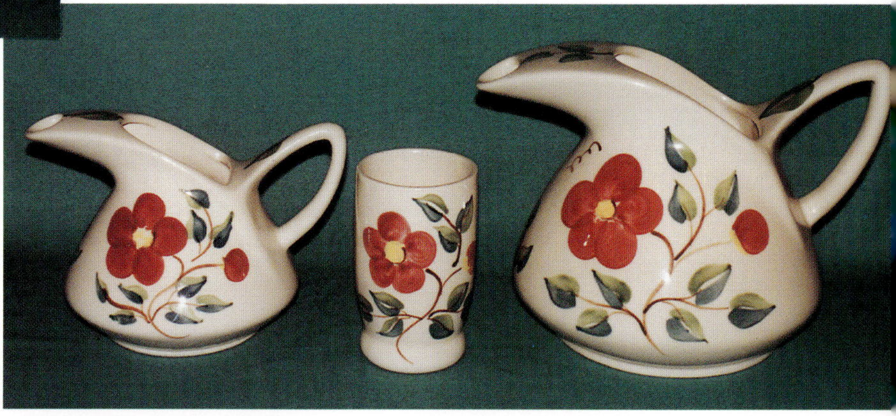

Two pint dutch jug. $100. Tumbler. $50. Five pint dutch jug. $150.

Kent jugs, four petal (notice the variation in decoration). $50. This style of the Mountain Rose decoration is the earlier version of the pattern.

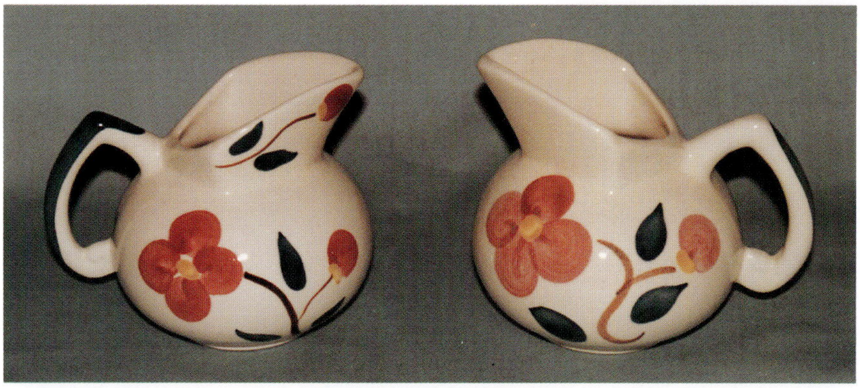

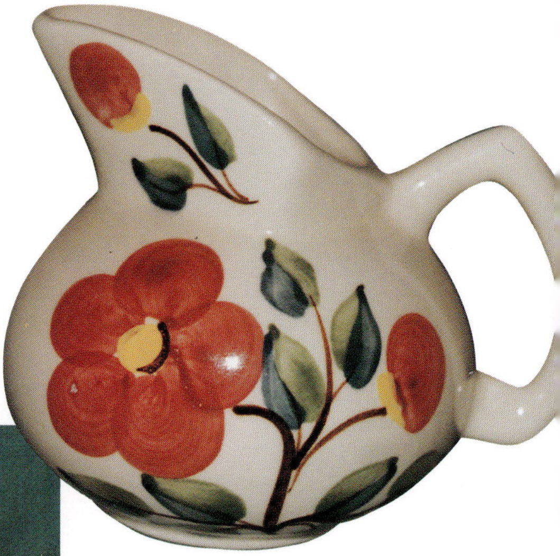

Kent jug, five petal. $50.

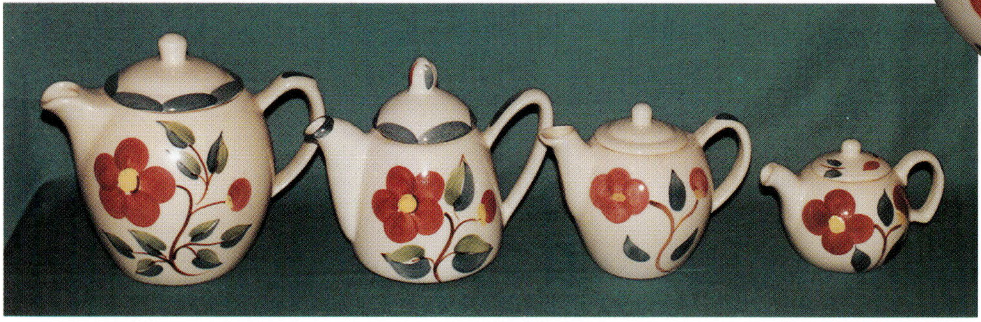

Eight cup coffee pot. $100. Six cup domed lid teapot. $100. Four cup teapot. $40. Two cup teapot (very common, used as a premium for the McCormick Tea Company). $15.

Chartreuse

Chartreuse was presented in a 1949 Crockery and Glass journal as a new design in a 60-piece dinnerware set. As the market for dinnerware grew more competitive, Purinton had to introduce something with a more colorful or vibrant decoration and Chartreuse was one of those decorations. It can be found on most dinnerware and serving pieces. This decoration is striking when seen as a place setting with accessory items.

Prices for Chartreuse are a little higher because of the limited supply of the product. The demand for it is limited more to a specific specialty item that a collector is seeking: such as a cookies jar, candy basket, chop plate, or canister set. The dinnerware line is not found too often and any quantity of dinnerware would be considered a find. We have not seen a butter dish, honey jug, spaghetti bowl, or — surprisingly — any platters.

We believe Chartreuse is a sleeper decoration and will increase in demand. The price is affordable at the time of this writing and will increase as more collectors appreciate its eye appeal.

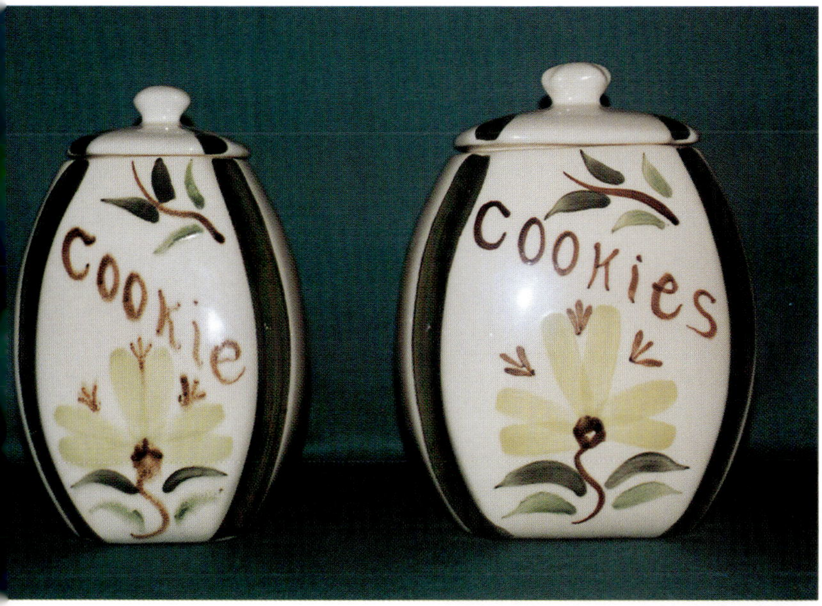

Chartreuse tall oval cookie canister. $90. Wide oval cookies jar. $200.

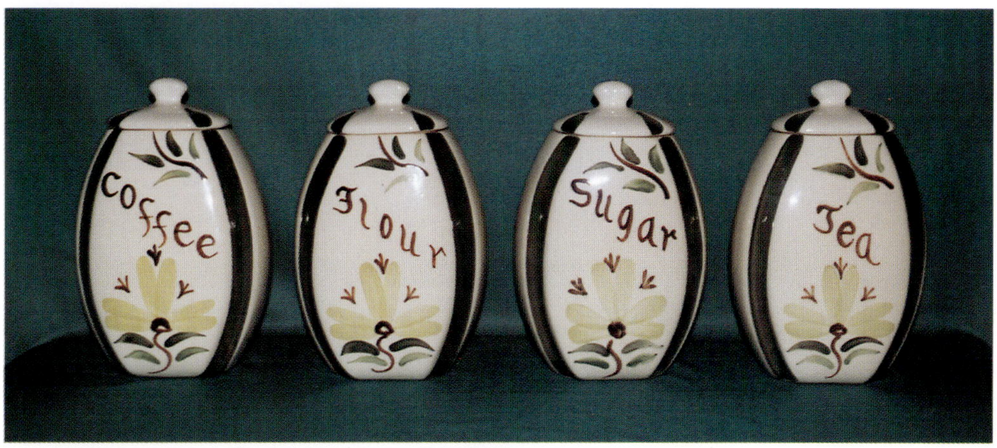

Tall oval four piece canister set. $100 each.

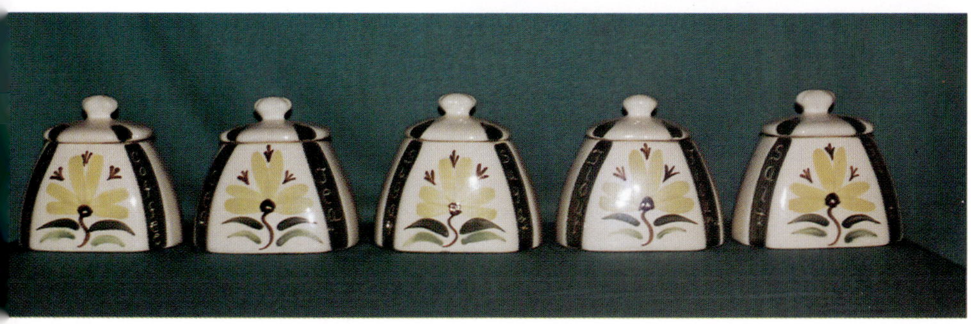

Half oval five piece canister set, incised on trim. $75 each.

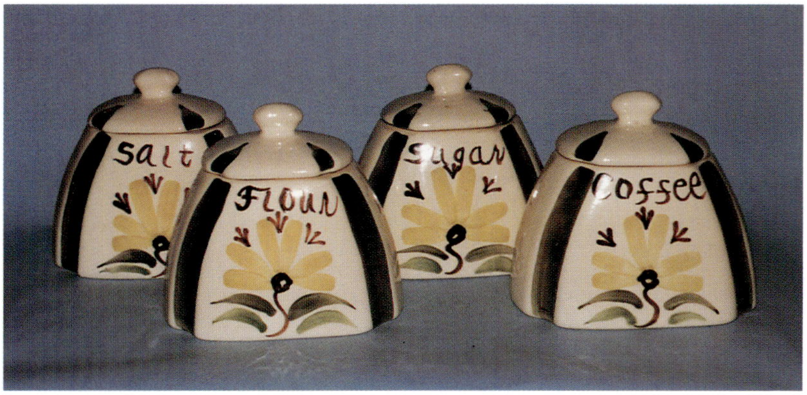

Half oval four piece canister set (missing tea in picture). This set has its contents labeled instead of being incised in like on the previous canister set. $75 each.

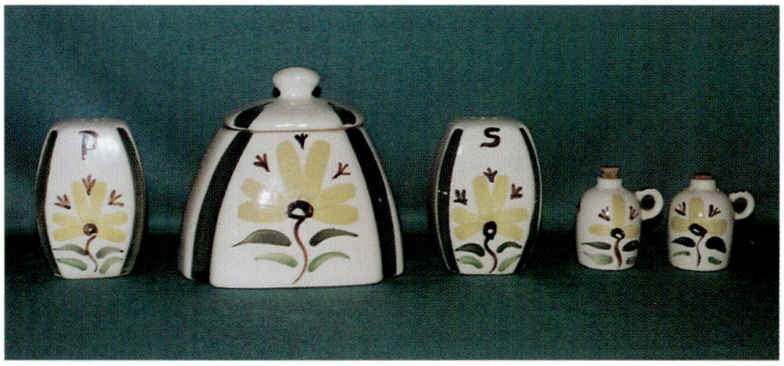

Range salt and pepper shakers. $75 set. Covered range grease jar. $75. Jug style salt and pepper shakers. $50 set.

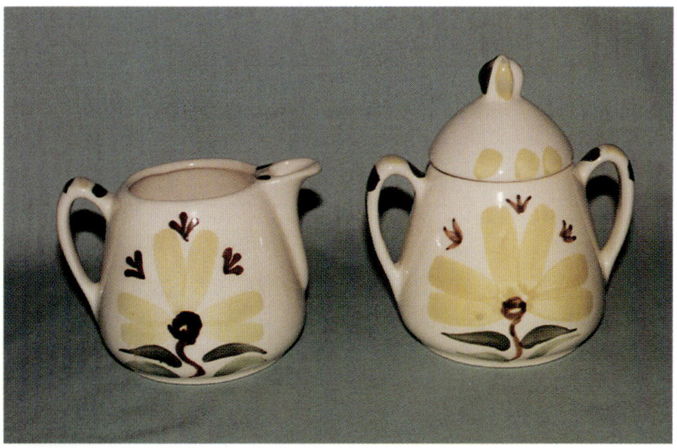

Creamer and covered sugar. $50 set.

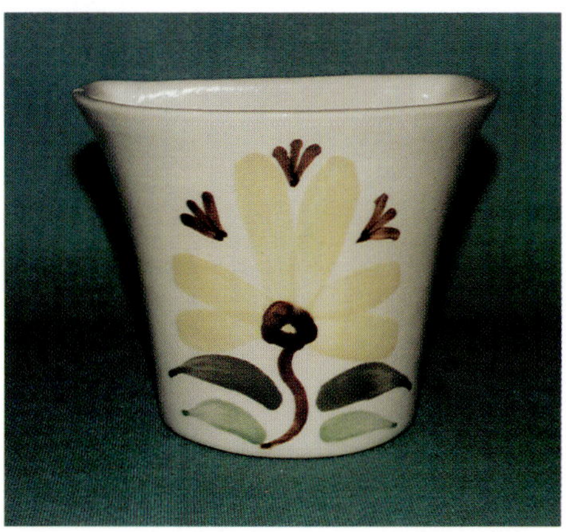

Wall pocket. $90.

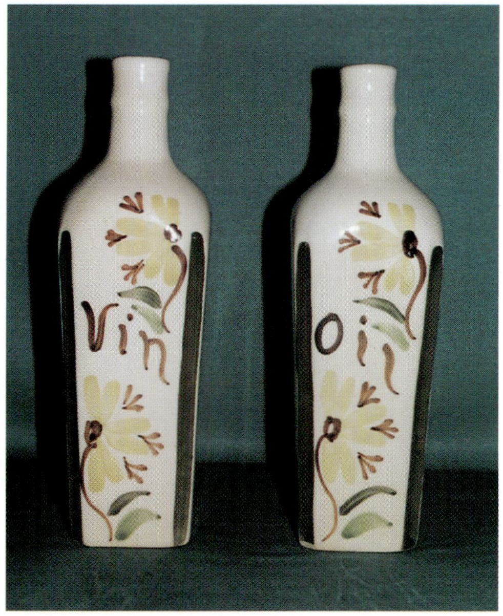

Tall oil and vinegar. $100 set.

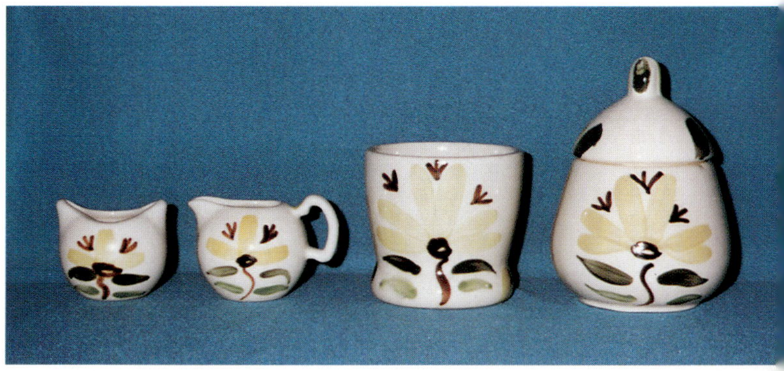

Individual sugar and creamer. $50 set. Juice mug. $20. Marmalade. $7

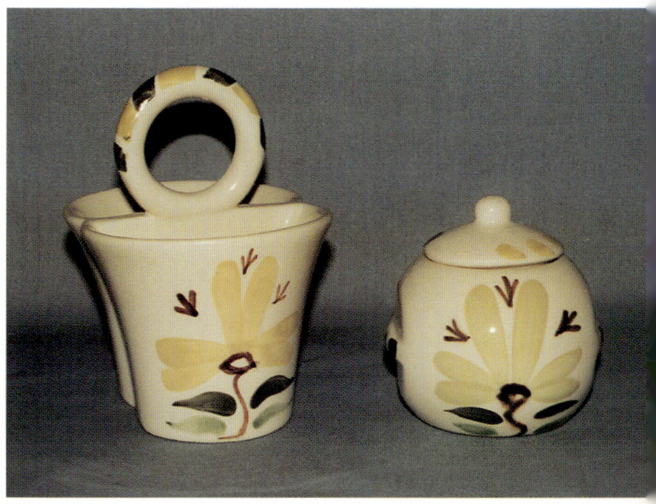

Candy dish. $90. Individual covered bean pot. $50.

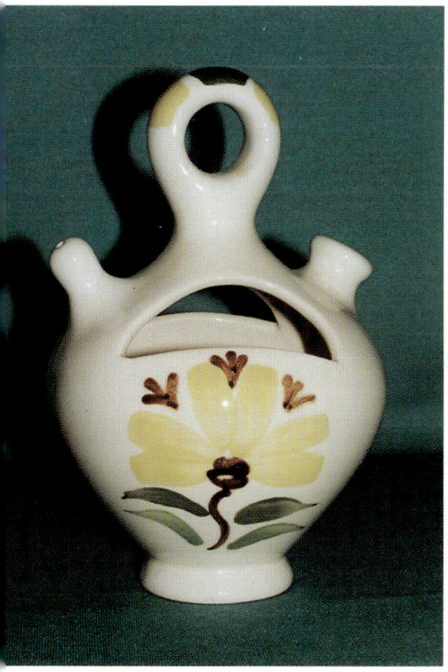

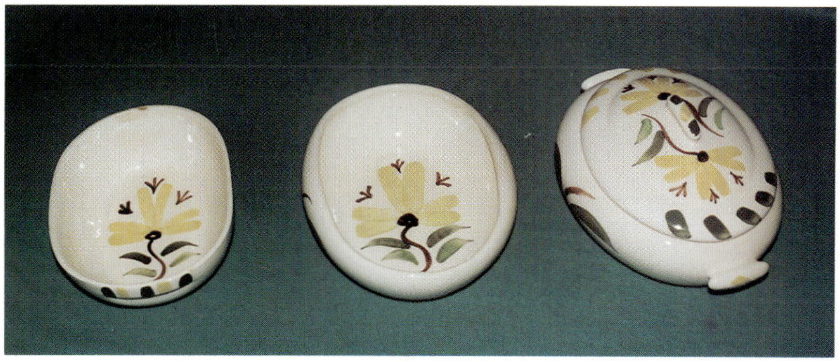

Baker. $30. Open vegetable. $30. Covered vegetable. $75.

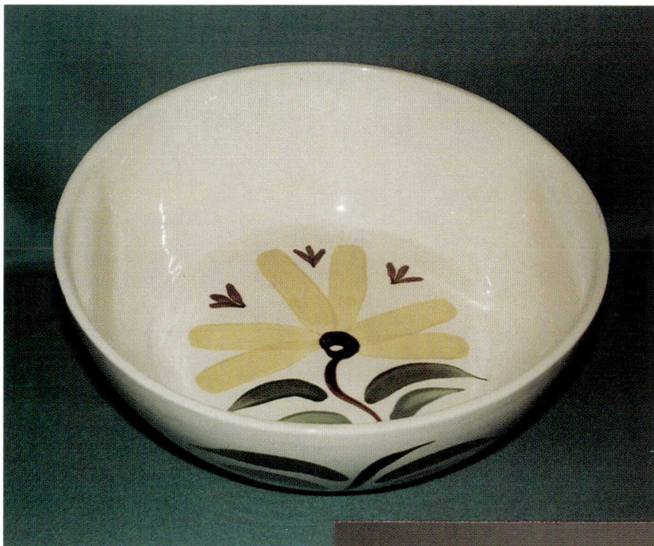

Salad bowl. $75.

Rum jug planter. $75.

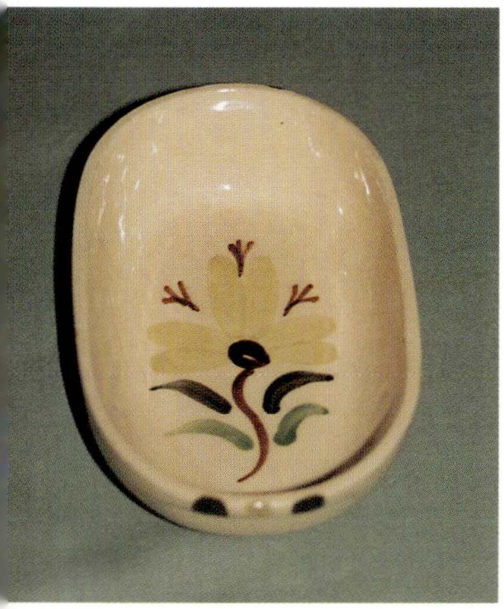

Pickle. $20.

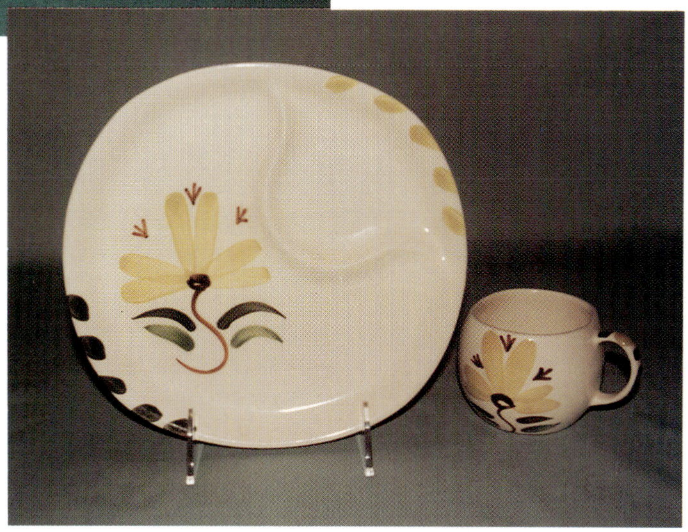

Tea and toast plate. $25. Cup. $10.

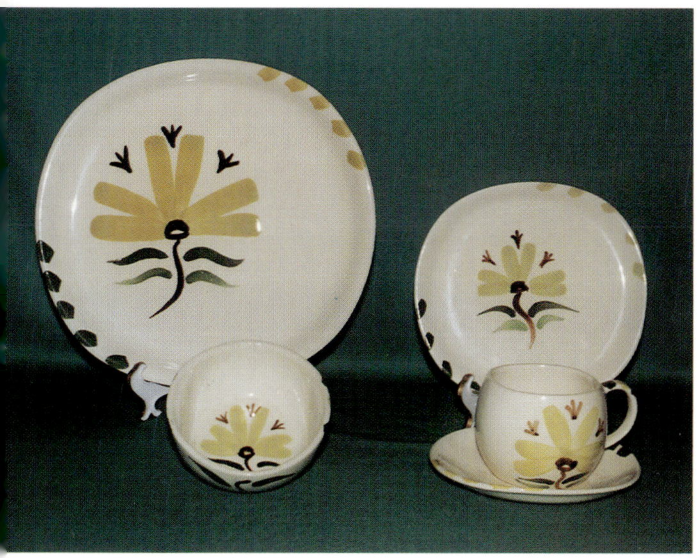

Dinner plate. $25. Salad plate. $15. Dessert bowl. $10. Cup. $10. Saucer. $5.

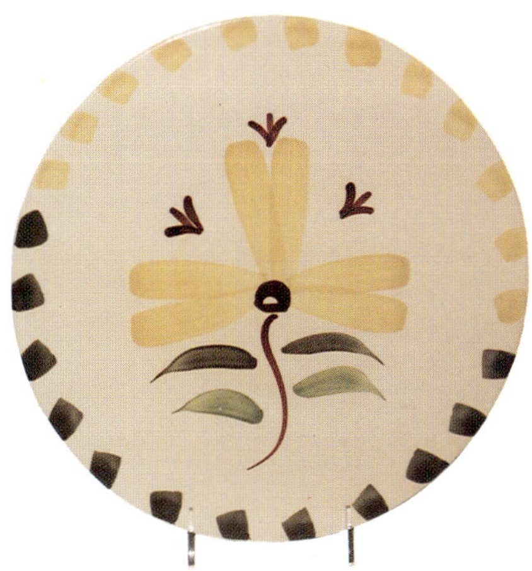

Chop plate. $75.

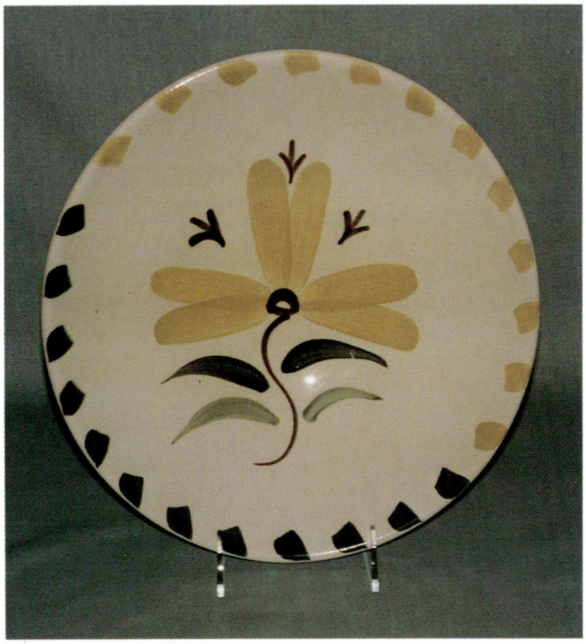

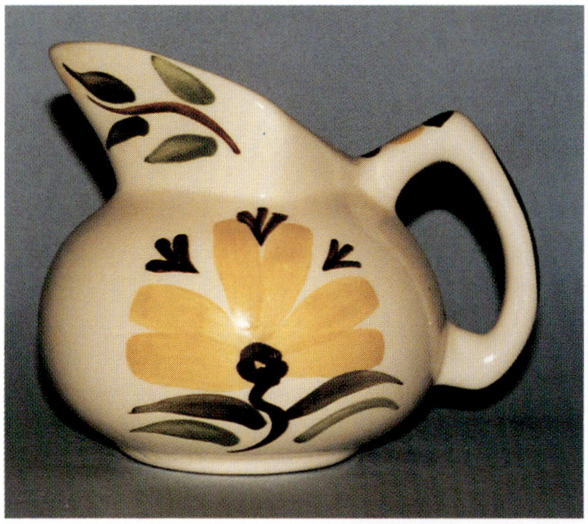

Kent jug. $75.

Fruit bowl. $60.

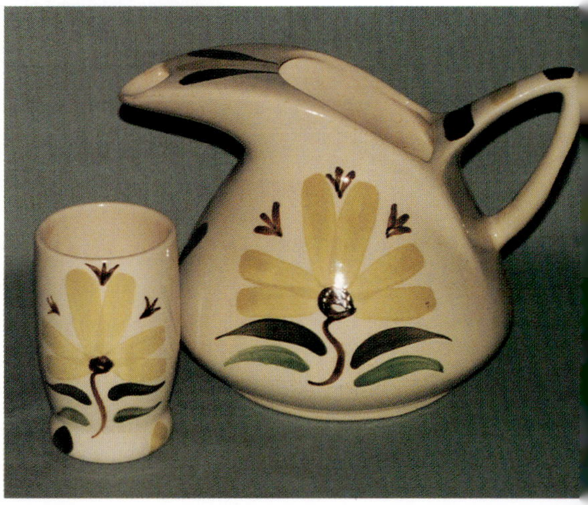

Tumbler. $30. Five pint dutch jug. $75.

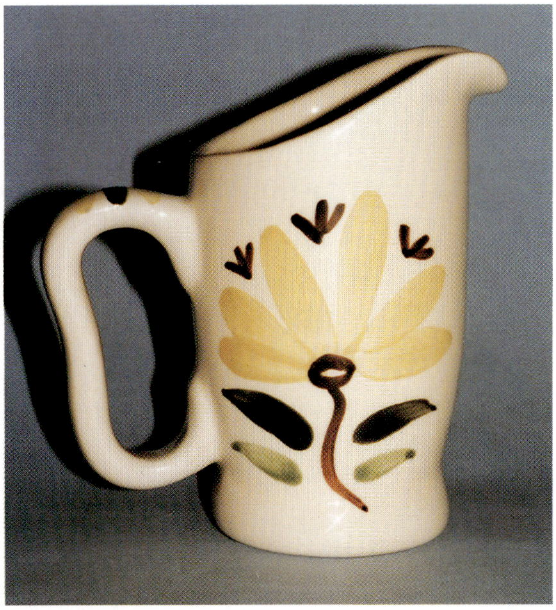

Mug jug. $75.

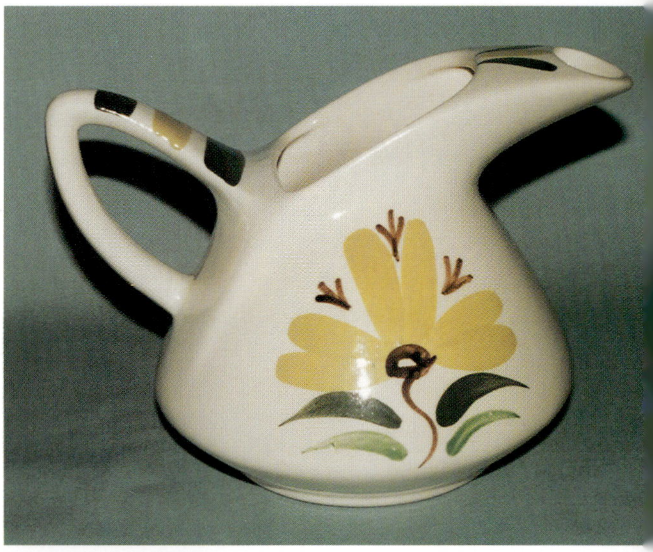

Two pint dutch jug. $60.

Night bottle. $90. Beverage pitcher. $90. Six cup domed lid teapot. $90. Eight cup coffee pot. $90.

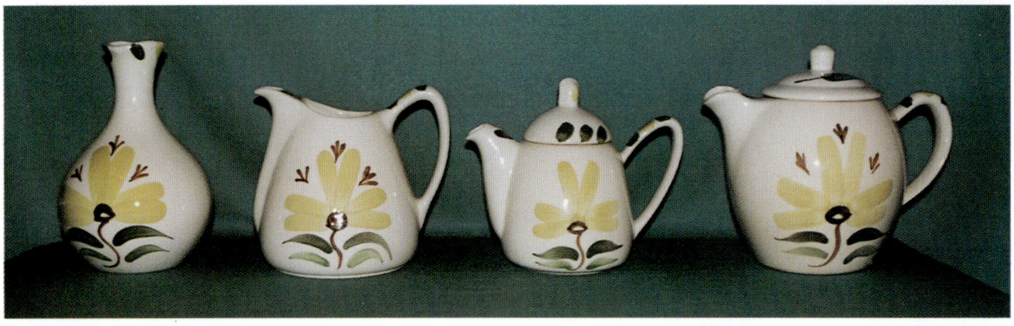

Daisy and Harmony

Daisy and Harmony have been combined into one chapter because of the limited number of items produced for each decoration. Not much information has been found on these products. Both were introduced in the 1940s, Daisy in the mid-1940s and Harmony in 1949.

Daisy was decorated with red or blue trim, red being the harder trim to find. We have only seen Daisy on tall oval canister sets, tall oil and vinegar sets, range shakers, fats storage jars, and rebecca jugs. The prices of rebecca jugs reflect the quantity of such jugs made for the floral industry and the demand for them. Overall, Daisy is not an overly requested pattern today, nor was it very popular in the past. The Daisy supply is limited and to find an item in this decoration would be fairly difficult.

Harmony is decorated with a simple green line and incised leaves. From information we have gathered, Harmony was introduced in 1949 along with Chartreuse. We know it was an open stock item. However, it was not popular and did not see much production. Some items have appeared more recently but on a very limited basis. The decoration for Harmony is very simple and has not been exposed to the market to consider what the demand for it would be. Prices of items pictured reflect the small supply available. Any item in Harmony would be a good find and again certain products such as a wide oval cookies jar would command higher prices. The door is open for this decoration as we see what appears on the market.

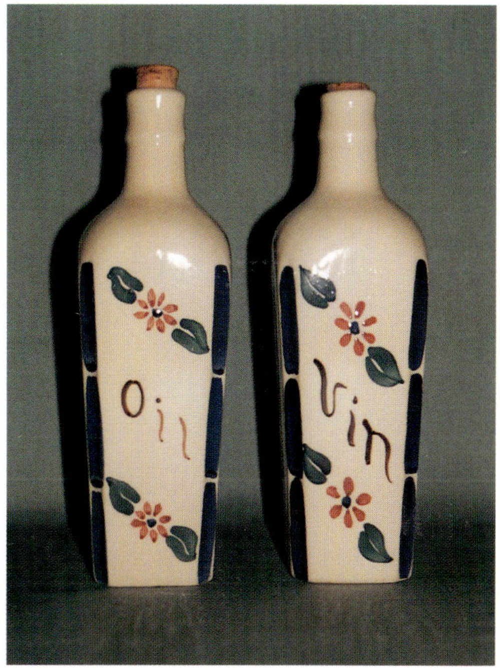

Daisy tall oil and vinegar with cobalt trim. $100 set.

Daisy

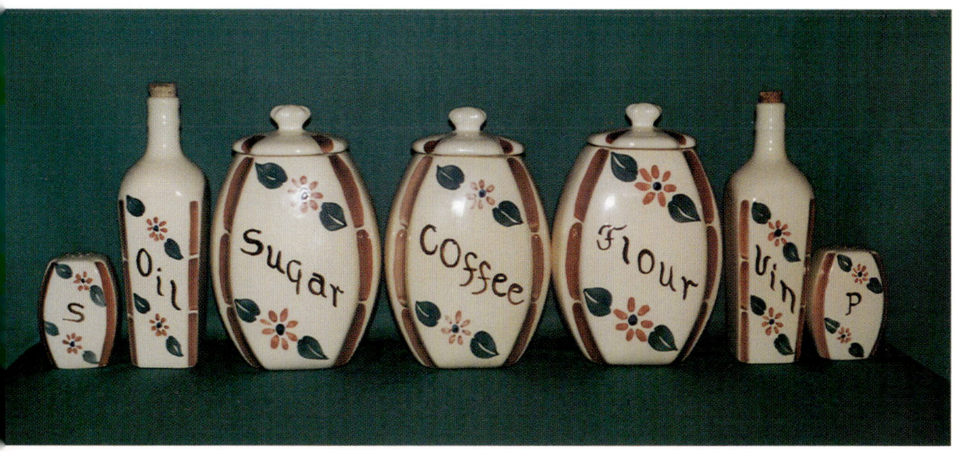

Daisy range salt and pepper shakers with red trim. $75 set. Tall oil and vinegar bottles with red trim. $100 set. Tall oval canister set with red trim, missing tea. $75 each.

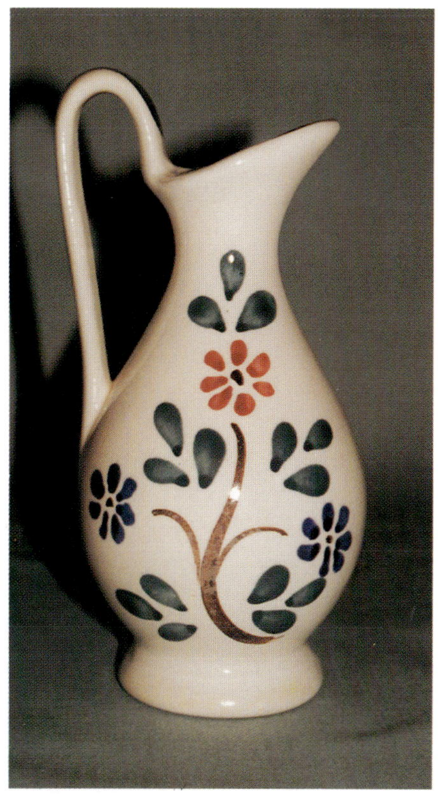

Daisy rebecca jug. $20.

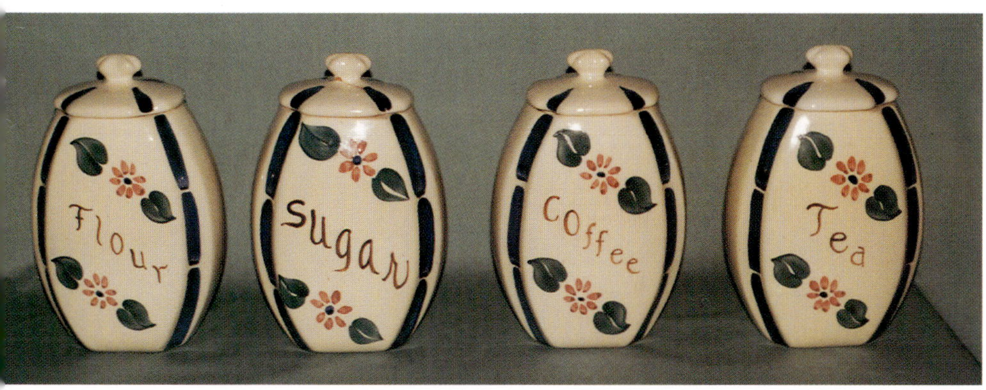

Daisy tall oval four piece canister set with cobalt trim. $75 each.

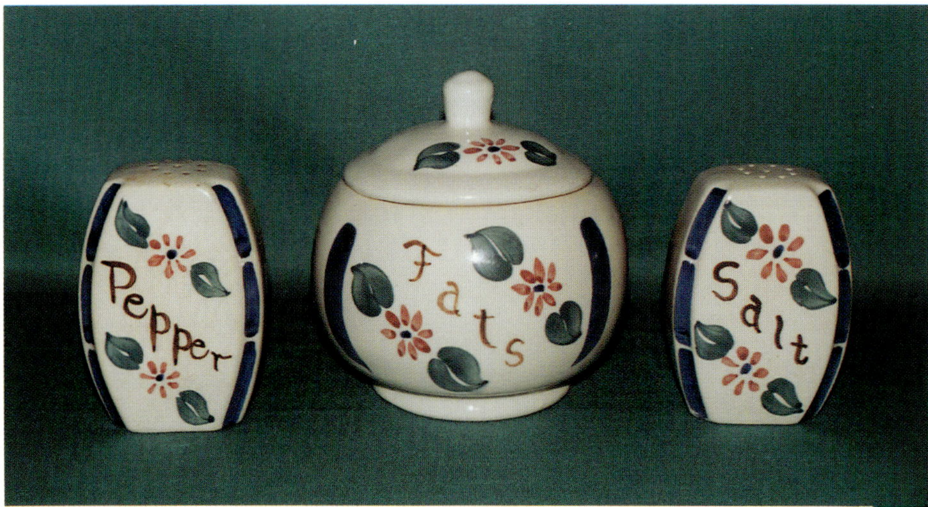

Daisy range salt and pepper shakers with blue trim. $75 set. Fats storage container with blue trim. $60.

Harmony

Harmony wide oval cookies jar. $200.

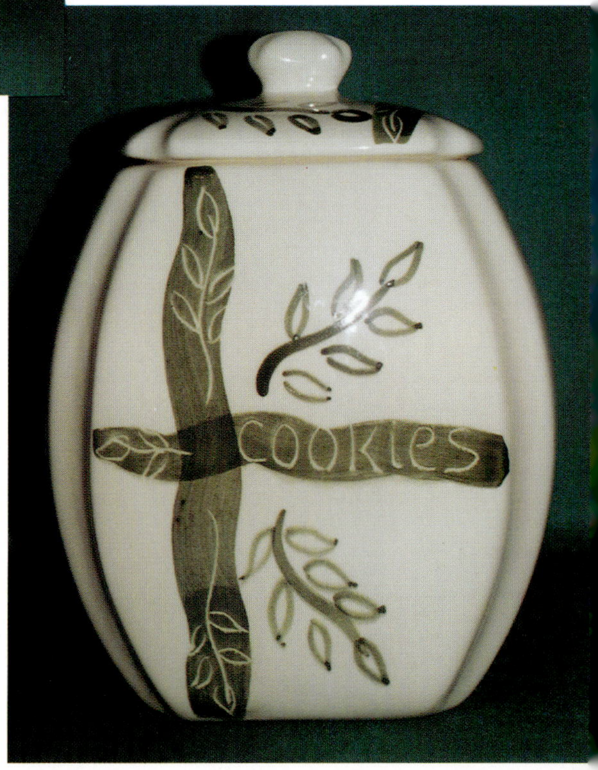

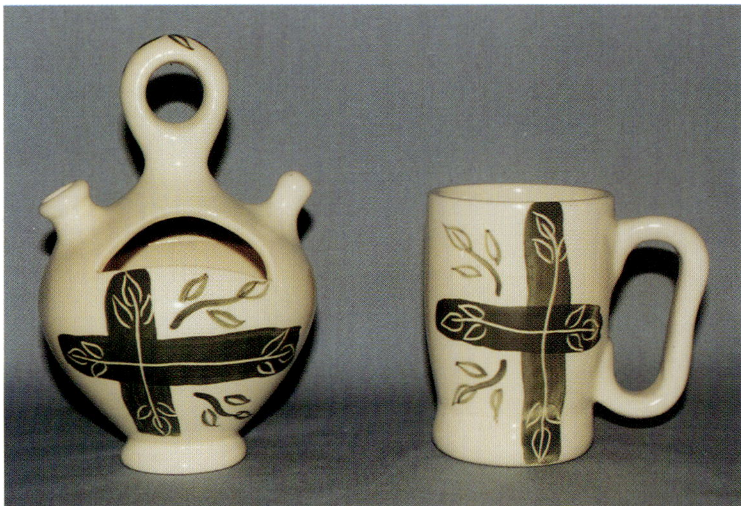

Harmony rum jug planter. $100. Coffee mug. $60.

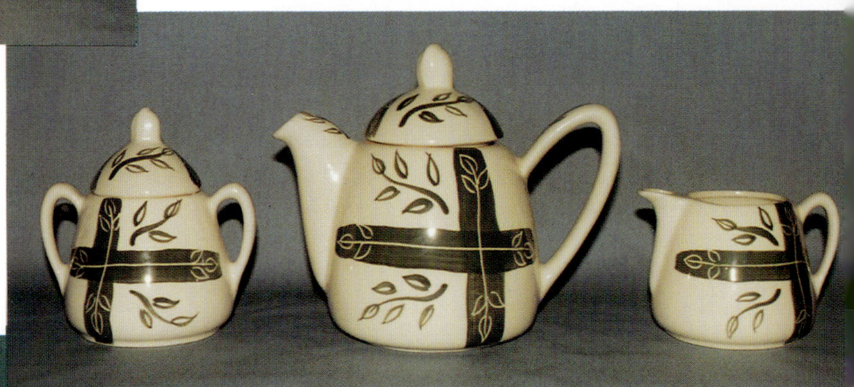

Harmony covered sugar and creamer. $100 set. Six cup domed lid teapot. $100.

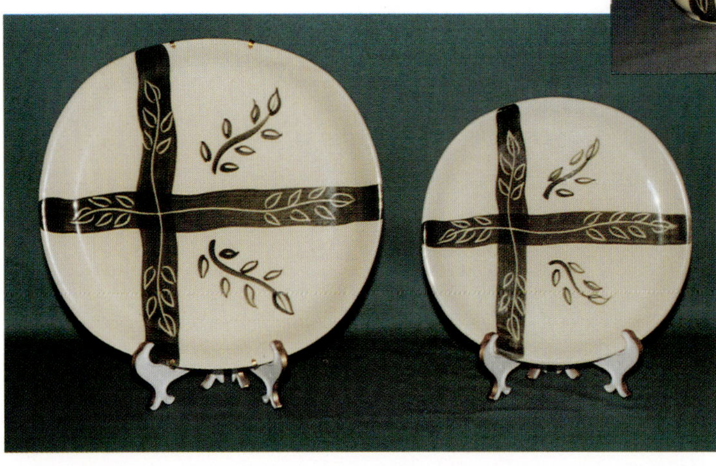

Harmony breakfast plate. $60. Salad plate. $40.

Maywood

Maywood was a unique step for Purinton Pottery. For the first time, a slip other than off-white was introduced as a production decoration. Maywood was presented to the open market in 1950. The green slip with a white dogwood flower on it was an innovative design which proved to be a worthy product for Purinton. Employees recall how difficult it was to fire Maywood and get the slip color just right.

Maywood was an open stock line but the supply of it is far less than other decorations. Demand for the pattern is moderate and Maywood should be considered a harder to find decoration. The canister set and "shake and pours" are very difficult to find. We do not know of a butter dish or spaghetti bowl. There are no common items to be found. Many people probably pass this item when hunting for Purinton, because they are trained to see the off-white slip instead of the green.

Maywood displayed as a table setting with serving pieces is very attractive. The green background with the white dogwood offers a warm, hospitable message. An appreciation for its decoration will increase in the years to come.

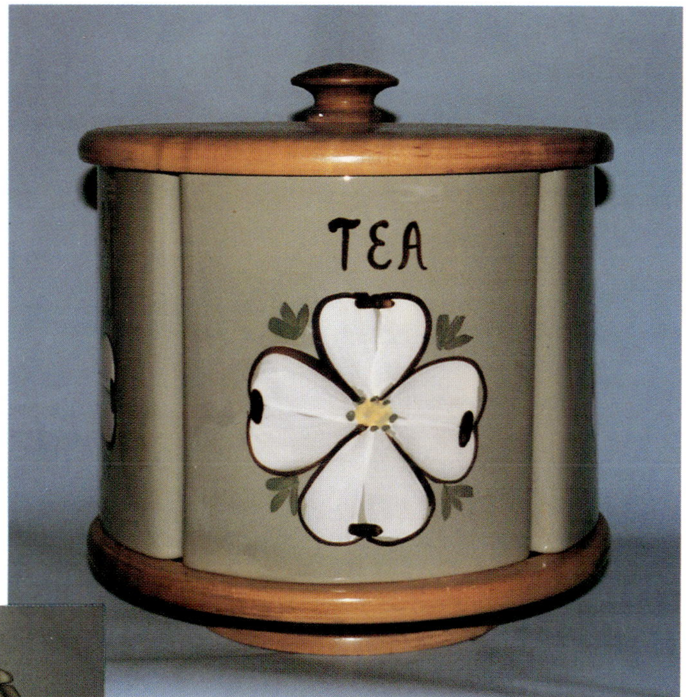

Four-piece revolving canister set. It is rare to find this canister in this pattern. $250 set.

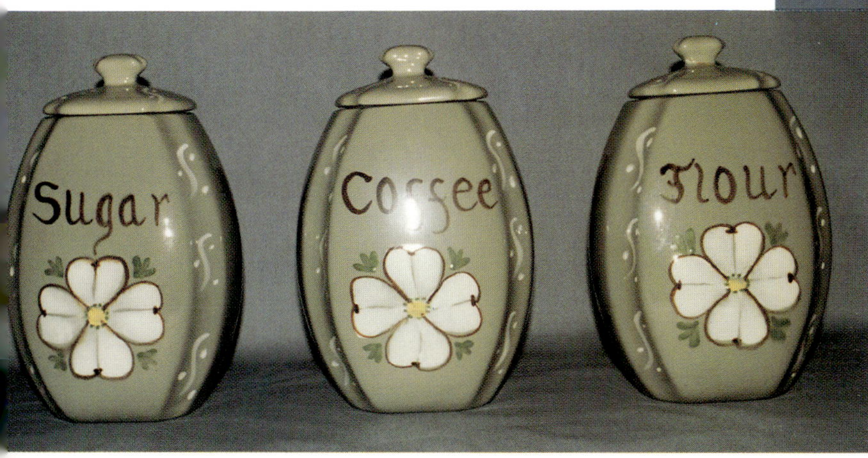

Tall oval canister set, missing tea. $125 each.

All four pieces of the revolving canister set.

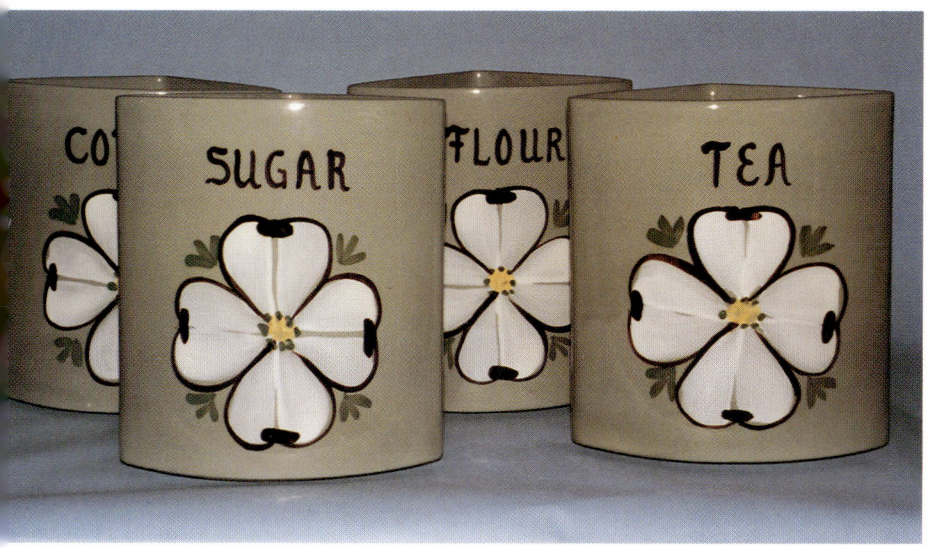

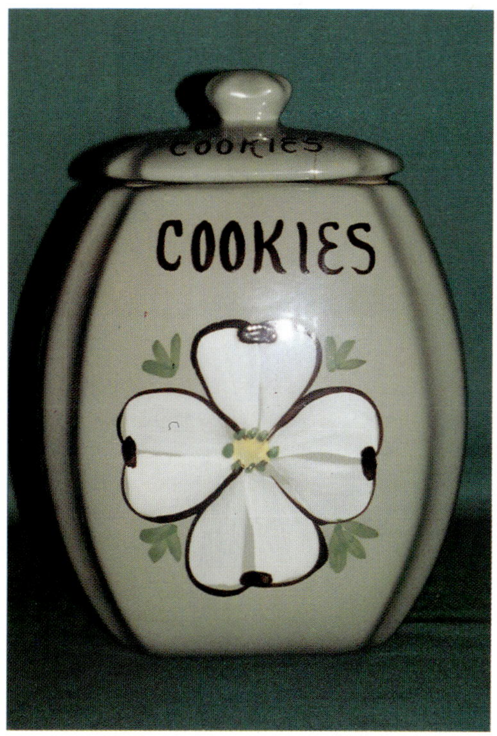

Maywood decorated wide oval cookies jar. $200.

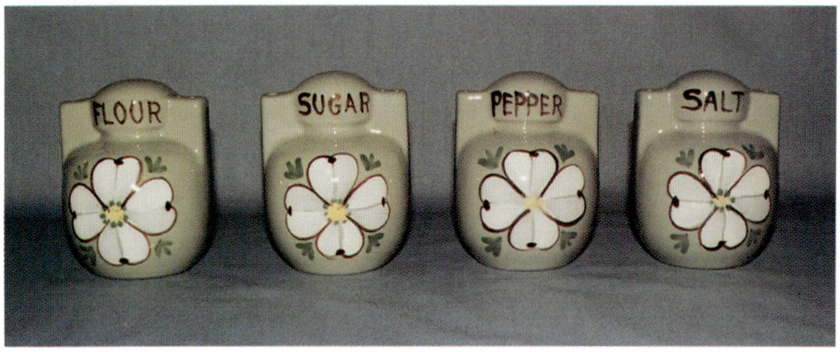

Pour and shake shakers: flour $100, sugar $100, pepper $75, salt $75.

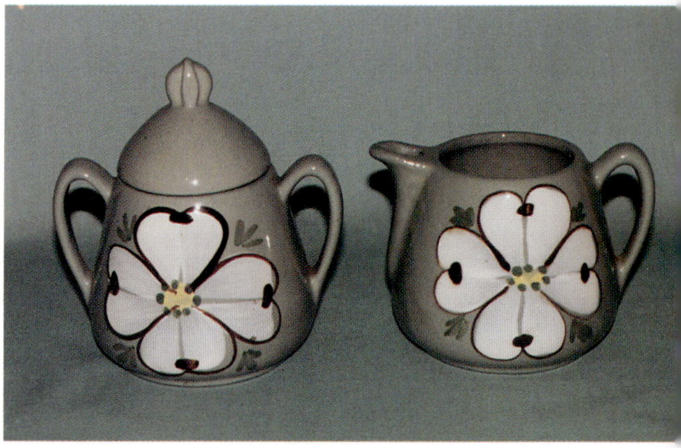

Covered sugar and creamer. $50 set.

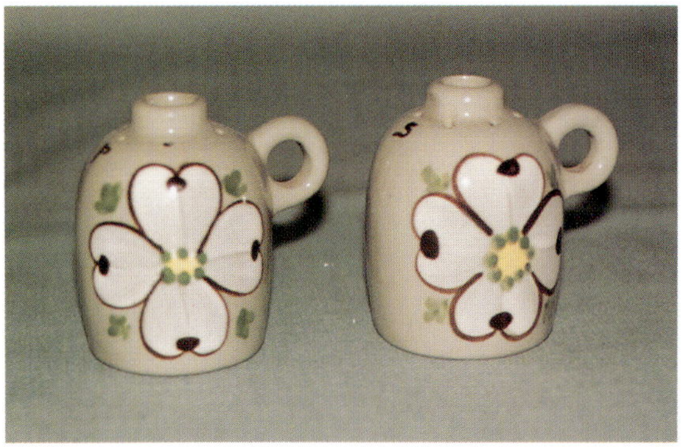

Jug style salt and pepper shakers. $30 set.

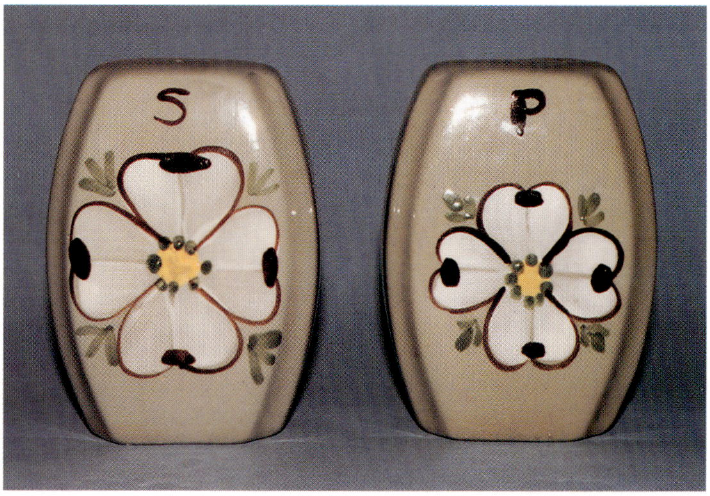

Range salt and pepper shakers. $50 set.

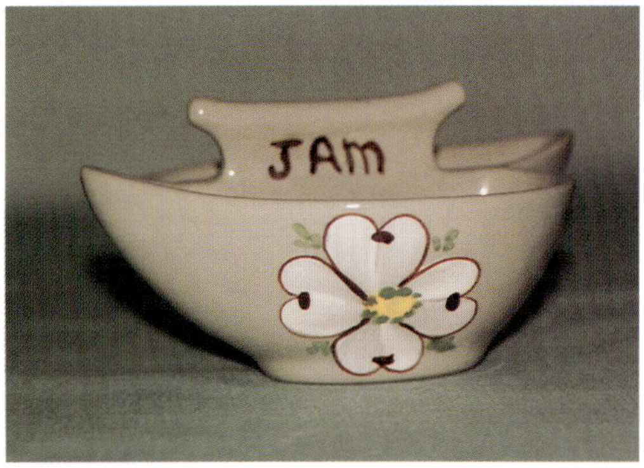

Jam and jelly. $60.

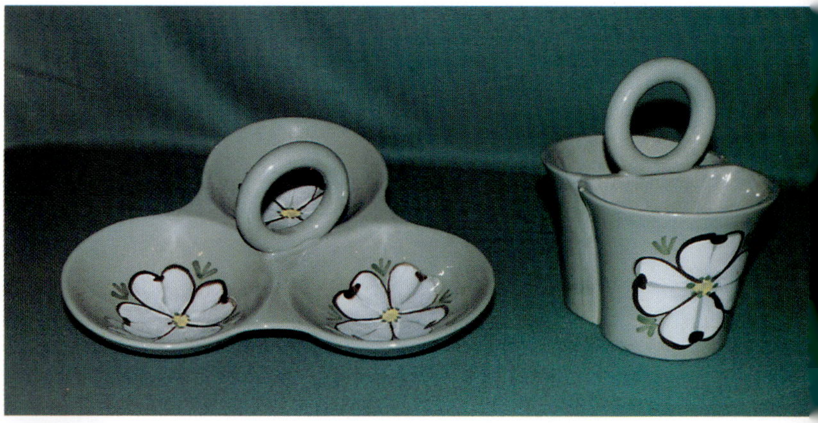

Three part relish with ceramic handle. $75. Candy dish. $75.

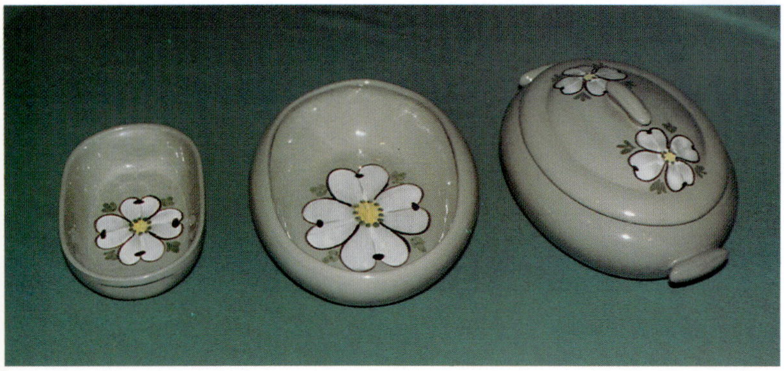

Pickle. $25. Open vegetable. $30. Covered vegetable. $75.

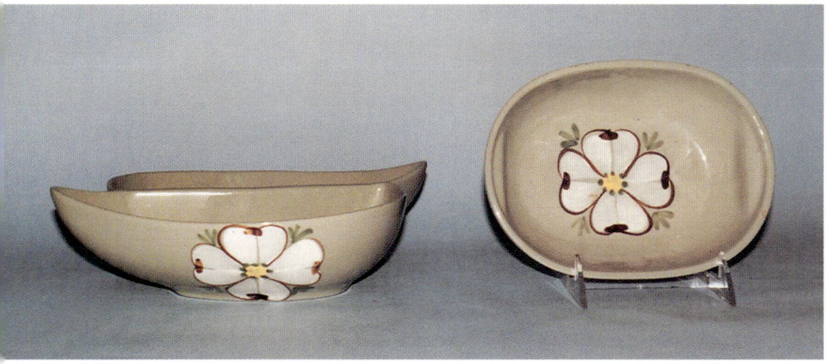

Divided vegetable. $35. Baker. $30.

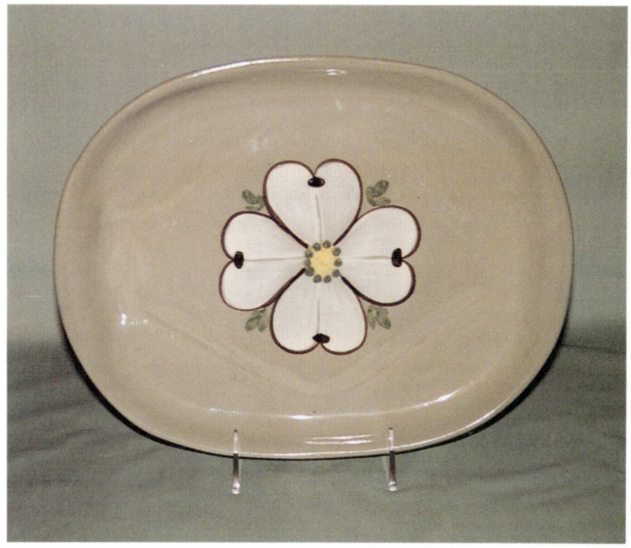

Diamond grill platter. $50.

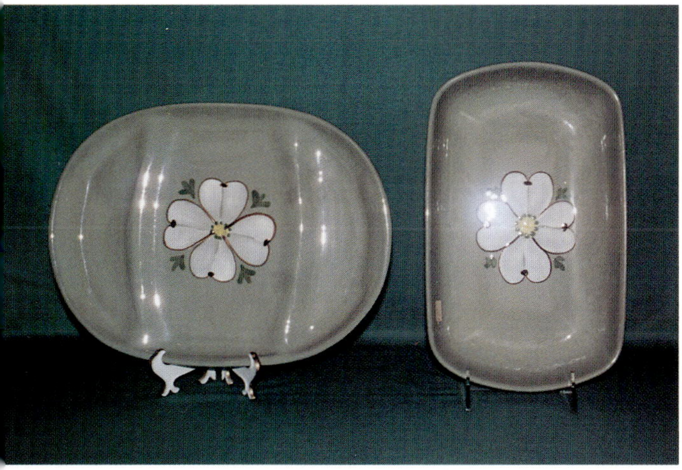

Three section grill platter. $50. Roll tray. $35.

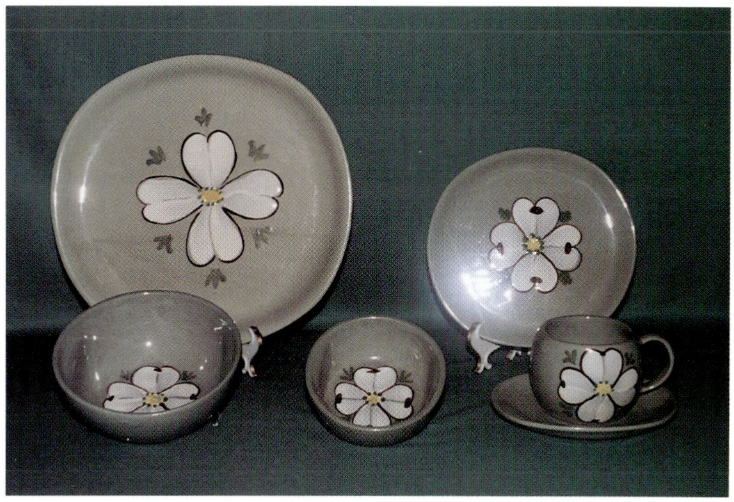

Dinner plate. $25. Salad plate. $15. Cereal bowl. $15. Dessert bowl. $12. Cup. $10. Saucer. $5.

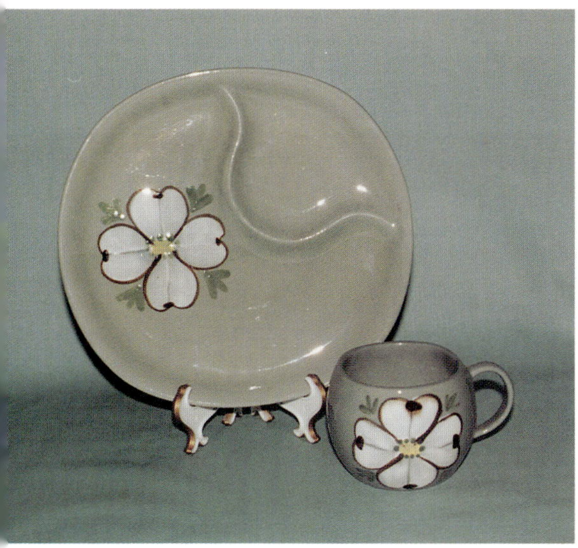

Tea and toast plate. $15. Cup. $10.

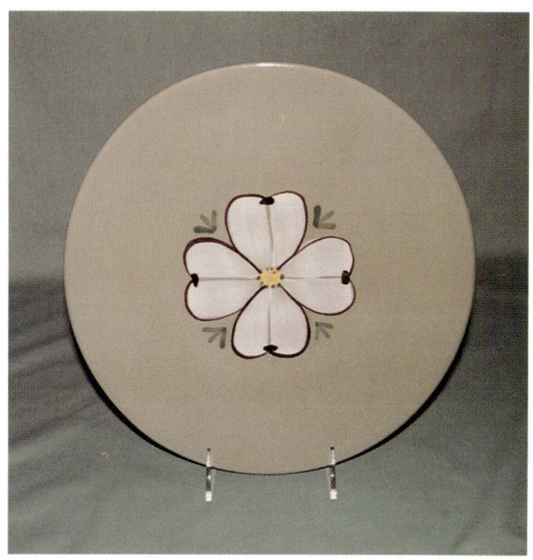

Chop plate. $80.

Sandwich plate. $70.

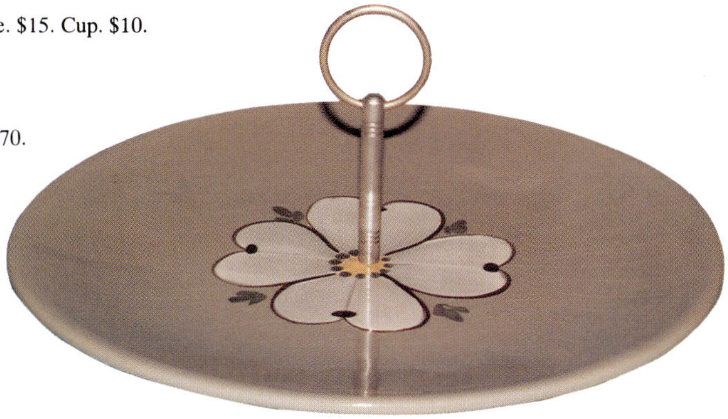

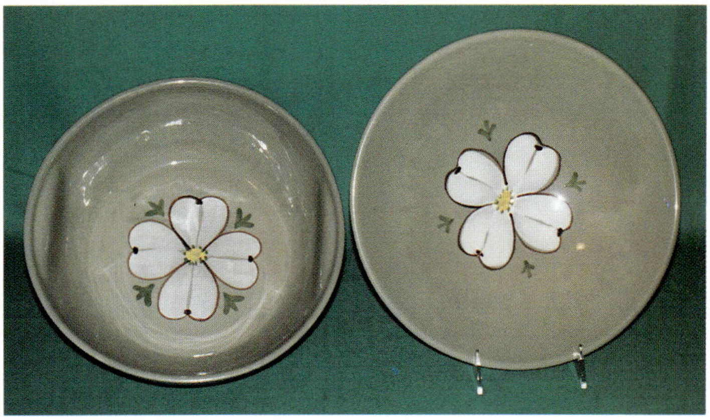

Salad bowl. $75. Fruit Bowl. $75.

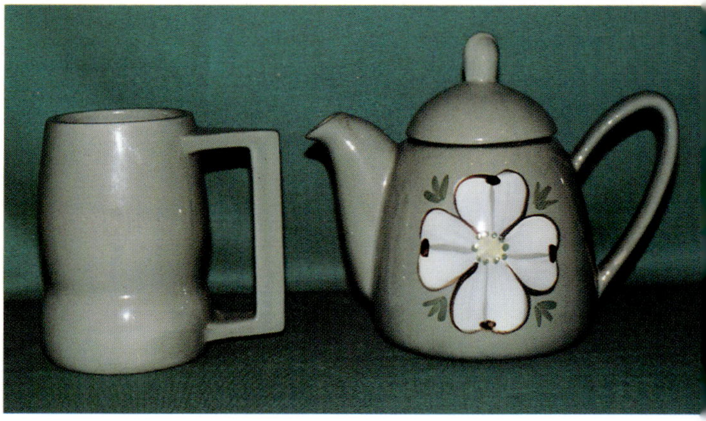

Beer mug, no decoration. $20. With Maywood decoration. $60. Six cup domed lid teapot. $60.

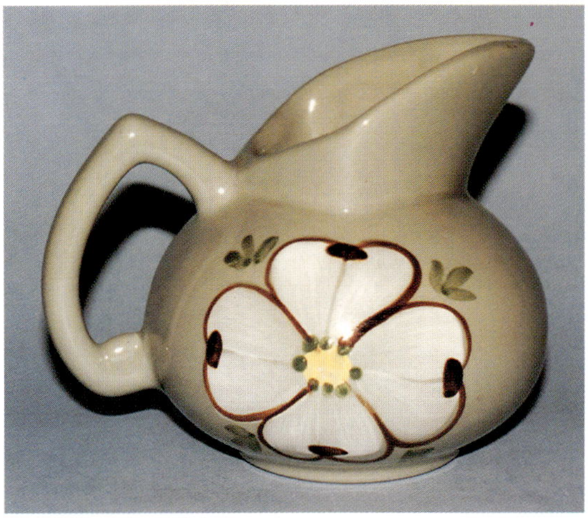

Kent jug. $50.

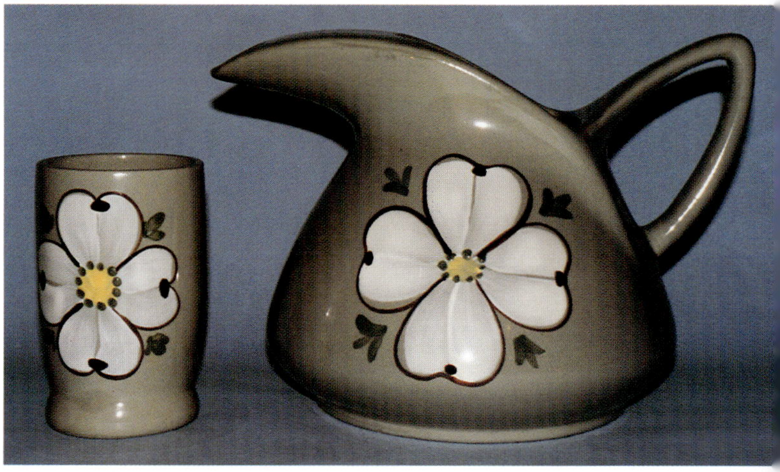

Tumbler. $40. Five pint dutch jug. $90.

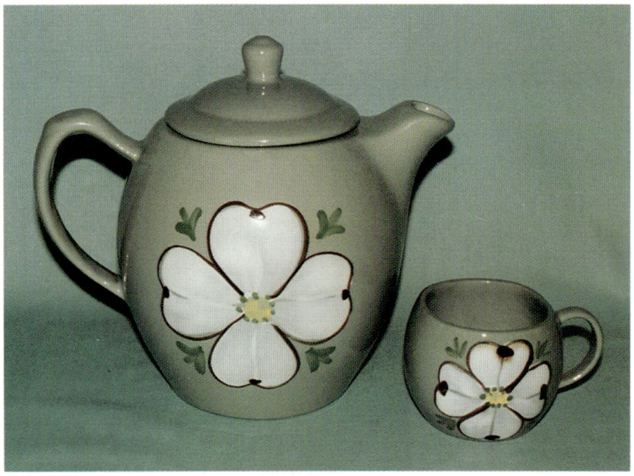

Eight cup coffee pot. $70. Cup. $10.

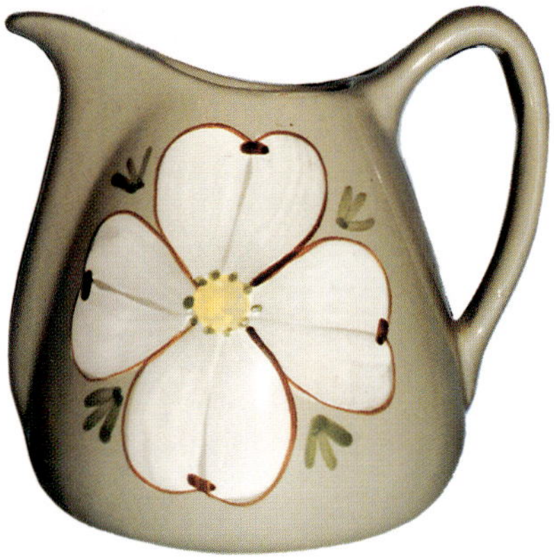

Beverage pitcher. $90.

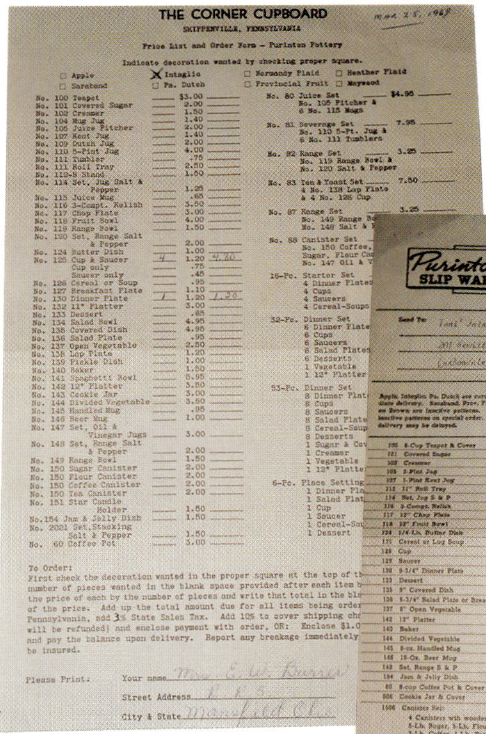

THE CORNER CUPBOARD
SHIPPENVILLE, PENNSYLVANIA
Mar. 25, 1969

Price List and Order Form – Purinton Pottery

Indicate decoration wanted by checking proper square.

☐ Apple ☒ Intaglio ☐ Normandy Plaid ☐ Heather Plaid
☐ Saraband ☐ Pa. Dutch ☐ Provincial Fruit ☐ Maywood

No. 100 Teapot $3.00
No. 101 Covered Sugar 2.00
No. 102 Creamer 1.50
No. 104 Mug Jug 1.40
No. 105 Juice Pitcher 2.00
No. 107 Kent Jug 1.40
No. 109 Dutch Jug 2.00
No. 110 5-Pint Jug 4.00
No. 111 Tumbler .75
No. 111 Roll Tray 2.50
No. 112-B Stand 1.50
No. 114 Set, Jug Salt & Pepper 1.25
No. 115 Juice Mug .65
No. 116 3-Compt. Relish 3.50
No. 117 Chop Plate 3.00
No. 118 Fruit Bowl 4.00
No. 119 Range Bowl 1.50
No. 120 Set, Range Salt & Pepper 2.00
No. 124 Butter Dish 1.00
No. 125 Cup & Saucer 4 1.20 4.80
Cup only .75
Saucer only .45
No. 126 Cereal or Soup .95
No. 127 Breakfast Plate 1.10
No. 130 Dinner Plate 1 1.20 1.20
No. 132 11" Platter 3.00
No. 133 Dessert .65
No. 134 Salad Bowl 4.95
No. 135 Covered Dish 4.95
No. 136 Salad Plate .95
No. 137 Open Vegetable 2.50
No. 138 Lap Plate 1.20
No. 139 Pickle Dish 1.00
No. 140 Baker 1.50
No. 141 Spaghetti Bowl 5.95
No. 142 12" Platter 3.50
No. 143 Cookie Jar 3.00
No. 144 Divided Vegetable 3.50
No. 145 Handled Mug .95
No. 146 Beer Mug 1.00
No. 147 Set, Oil & Vinegar Jugs 3.00
No. 148 Set, Range Salt & Pepper 2.00
No. 149 Range Bowl 1.50
No. 150 Sugar Canister 2.00
No. 150 Flour Canister 2.00
No. 150 Coffee Canister 2.00
No. 150 Tea Canister 2.00
No. 151 Star Candle Holder 1.50
No. 154 Jam & Jelly Dish 1.50
No. 2021 Set, Stacking Salt & Pepper 1.50
No. 60 Coffee Pot 3.00

No. 80 Juice Set $4.95
No. 105 Pitcher & 6 No. 115 Mugs
No. 81 Beverage Set 7.95
No. 110 5-Pt. Jug & 6 No. 111 Tumblers
No. 82 Range Set 3.25
No. 119 Range Bowl & No. 120 Salt & Pepper
No. 83 Tea & Toast Set 7.50
4 No. 138 Lap Plate & 4 No. 126 Cup
No. 87 Range Set 3.25
No. 149 Range Bo…
No. 148 Salt & …
No. 88 Canister Set
No. 150 Coffee, Sugar, Flour Ca…
No. 147 Oil & V…
16-Pc. Starter Set
4 Dinner Plates
4 Cups
4 Saucers
4 Cereal-Soups
32-Pc. Dinner Set
6 Dinner Plate…
6 Cups
6 Saucers
6 Salad Plates
6 Desserts
1 Vegetable
1 12" Platter
53-Pc. Dinner Set
8 Dinner Plat…
8 Cups
8 Saucers
8 Salad Plate…
8 Cereal-Soup…
8 Desserts
1 Sugar & Cov…
1 Creamer
1 Vegetable
1 12" Platte…
6-Pc. Place Setting
1 Dinner Pla…
1 Salad Plat…
1 Cup
1 Saucer
1 Cereal-Sou…
1 Dessert

To Order:
First check the decoration wanted in the proper square at the top of th… number of pieces wanted in the blank space provided after each item b… the price of each by the number of pieces and write that total in the bla… of the price. Add up the total amount due for all items being order… Pennsylvania, add 3% State Sales Tax. Add 10% to cover shipping ch… will be refunded) and enclose payment with order, OR: Enclose $1.0… and pay the balance upon delivery. Report any breakage immediately… be insured.

Please Print: Your name Mrs. E. W. Burrer
Street Address R. R. 5.
City & State Mansfield Ohio

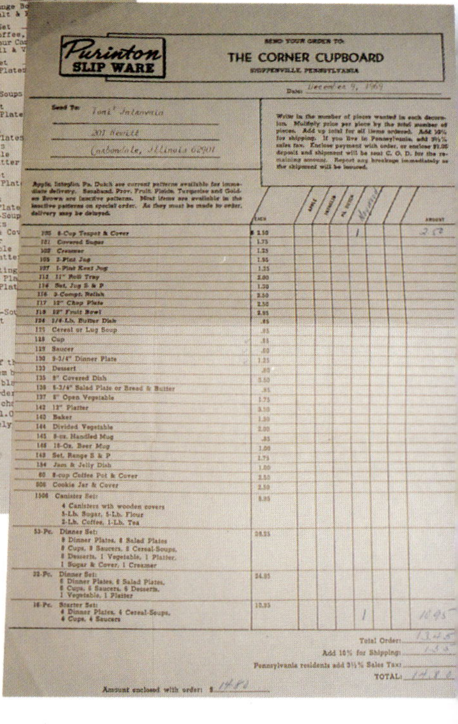

Purinton SLIP WARE

SEND YOUR ORDER TO:
THE CORNER CUPBOARD
SHIPPENVILLE, PENNSYLVANIA

Date: December 9, 1969

Send To: Toni Intanvaia
301 Beville
Carbondale, Illinois 62901

Write in the number of pieces wanted in each decoration. Multiply price per piece by the total number of pieces. Add up total for all items ordered. Add 10% for shipping. If you live in Pennsylvania, add 3½% sales tax. Enclose payment with order, or enclose $1.00 deposit and shipment will be sent C. O. D. for the remaining amount. Report any breakage immediately as the shipment will be insured.

Apple, Intaglio, Pa. Dutch are current patterns available for immediate delivery. Saraband, Prov. Fruit, Plaids, Turquoise and Golden Brown are inactive patterns. Most items are available in the inactive patterns on special order. As they must be made to order, delivery may be delayed.

	Item	Each	Apple	Intaglio	Pa. Dutch	Maywood			Amount
100	6-Cup Teapot & Cover	$ 2.50				1			2.50
101	Covered Sugar	1.75							
102	Creamer	1.25							
105	2-Pint Jug	1.95							
107	1-Pint Kent Jug	1.25							
112	11" Roll Tray	2.00							
114	Set, Jug S & P	1.30							
116	3-Compt. Relish	2.50							
117	12" Chop Plate	2.50							
119	12" Fruit Bowl	2.95							
124	1/4-Lb. Butter Dish	.85							
126	Cereal or Lug Soup	.95							
128	Cup	.85							
129	Saucer	.60							
130	9-3/4" Dinner Plate	1.25							
133	Dessert	.80							
135	9" Covered Dish	3.50							
136	6-3/4" Salad Plate or Bread & Butter	.95							
137	8" Open Vegetable	1.75							
142	12" Platter	3.50							
140	Baker	1.50							
144	Divided Vegetable	2.00							
145	8-oz. Handled Mug	.85							
146	16-Oz. Beer Mug	1.00							
148	Set, Range S & P	1.75							
154	Jam & Jelly Dish	1.00							
60	8-cup Coffee Pot & Cover	2.50							
508	Cookie Jar & Cover	2.50							
1506	Canister Set: 4 Canisters with wooden covers 5-Lb. Sugar, 5-Lb. Flour 2-Lb. Coffee, 1-Lb. Tea	8.85							
53-Pc.	Dinner Set: 8 Dinner Plates, 8 Salad Plates 8 Cups, 8 Saucers, 8 Cereal-Soups, 8 Desserts, 1 Vegetable, 1 Platter, 1 Sugar & Cover, 1 Creamer	38.25							
32-Pc.	Dinner Set: 6 Dinner Plates, 6 Salad Plates, 6 Cups, 6 Saucers, 6 Desserts, 1 Vegetable, 1 Platter	24.95							
16-Pc.	Starter Set: 4 Dinner Plates, 4 Cereal-Soups, 4 Cups, 4 Saucers	10.95				1			10.95

Total Order: 13.45
Add 10% for Shipping: 1.35
Pennsylvania residents add 3½% Sales Tax:
TOTAL: 14.80
Amount enclosed with order: $ 14.80

Another order blank for The Corner Cupboard. It's fun to look at the prices.

Corner Cupboard order form. This person ordered a Maywood six cup teapot with cover for $2.50 and a four piece starter set for $10.95. Those were the days!

Saraband

Saraband, a "love it or hate it" decoration, was painted like the Intaglio pattern. Saraband combines brown, green, and chartreuse. Introduced in the early 1950s, it was a consistent seller for Purinton throughout the decade.

Items decorated with Saraband are not in great supply; however, the demand for this pattern is low and it does not dictate a high price. Some harder to find shapes that people collect will bring a higher price. Harder to find items are the wide oval cookies jars, kent jugs, butter dishes, canister sets, tumblers, and five pint dutch jugs. Dinnerware items are fairly common and can be found at a reasonable price.

Saraband may not demand the higher prices of some other patterns, but is still a decoration which some will find enjoyable to collect and use.

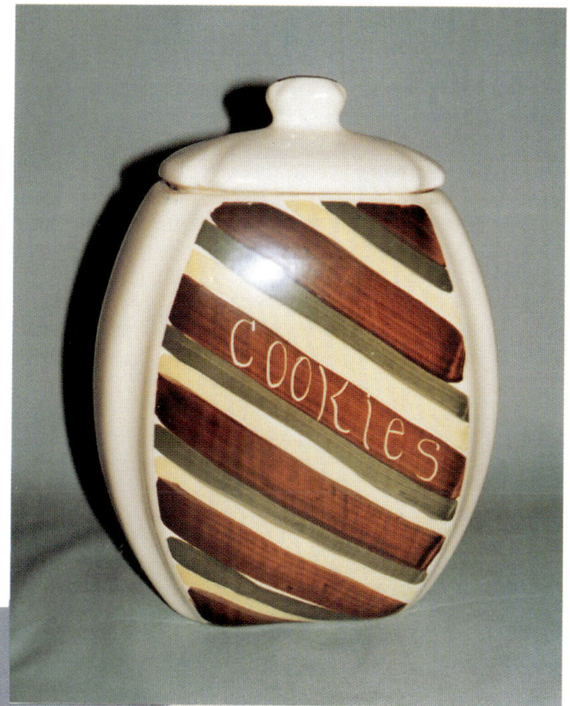

Wide oval cookies jar. $150.

Saraband decorated four piece apartment canister set. $30 each.

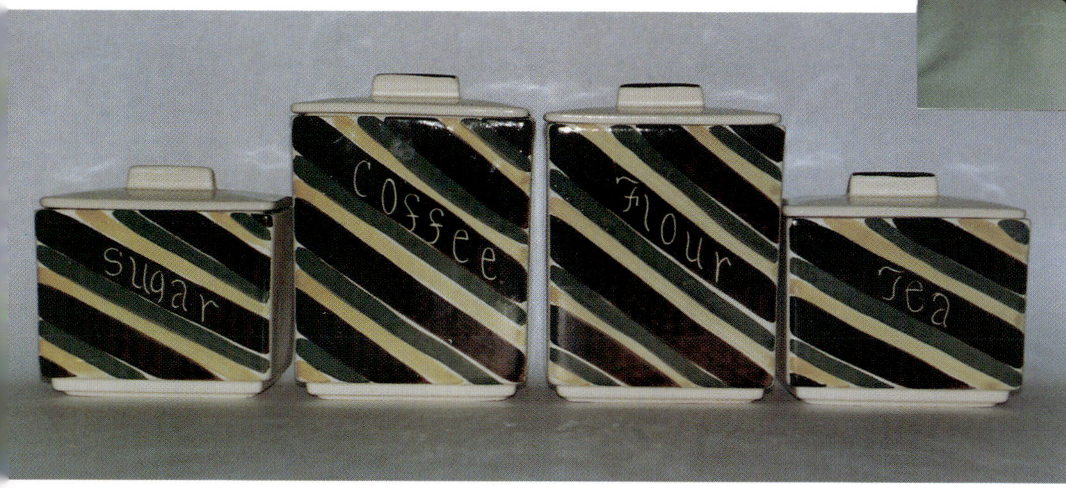

Revolving canister wedge. $20.

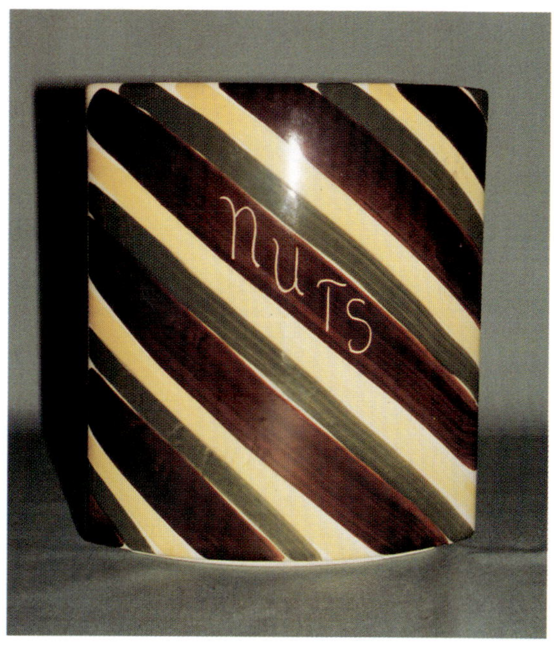

Revolving canister set with wooden base and lid. $100.

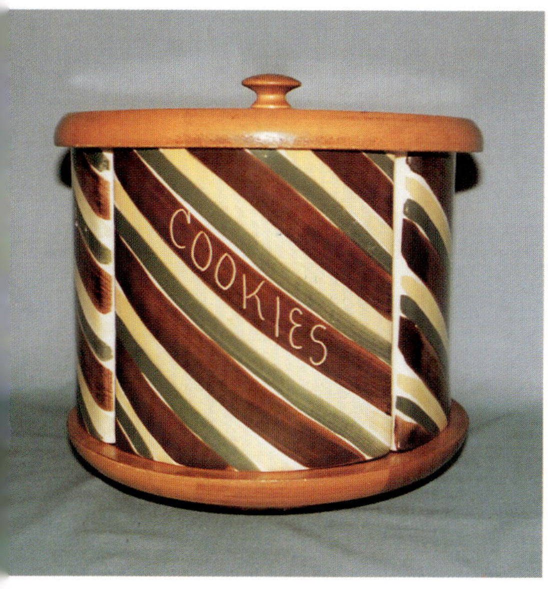

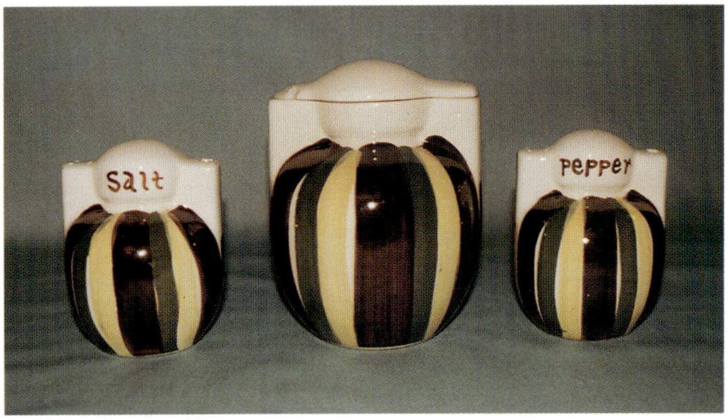

Salt and pepper pour and shake shakers. $40 set. Covered winged grease jar. $50.

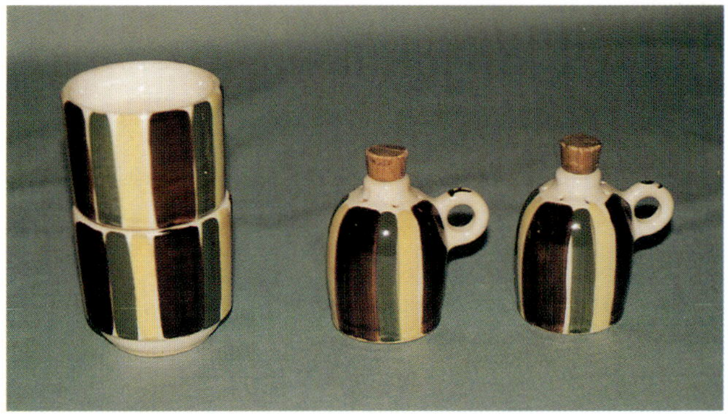

Stacking salt and pepper shakers. $40 set. Jug style salt and pepper shakers. $20 set.

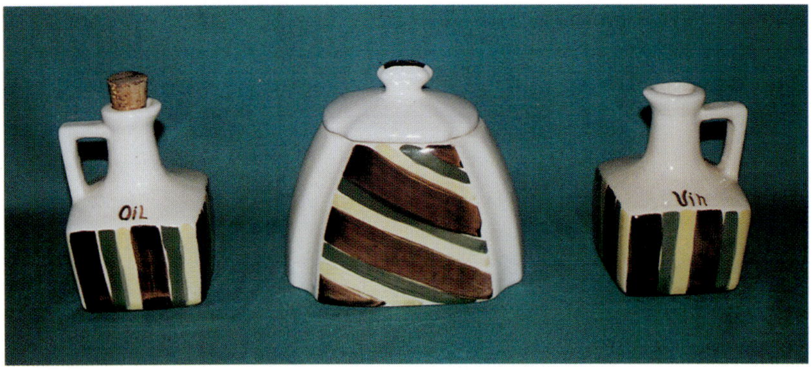

Square oil and vinegar. $40 set. Range covered grease jar. $40.

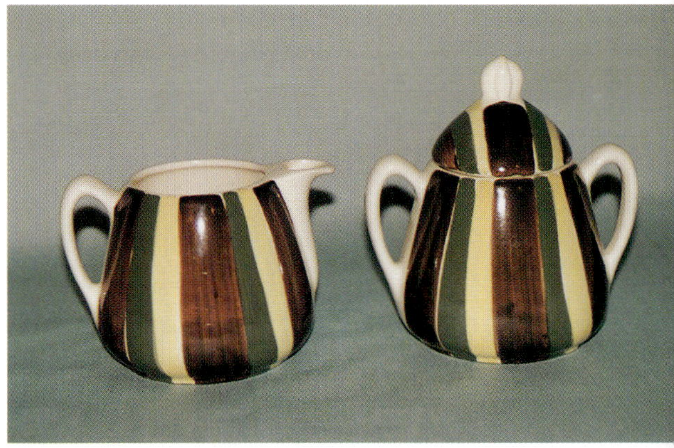

Creamer and covered sugar. $20 set.

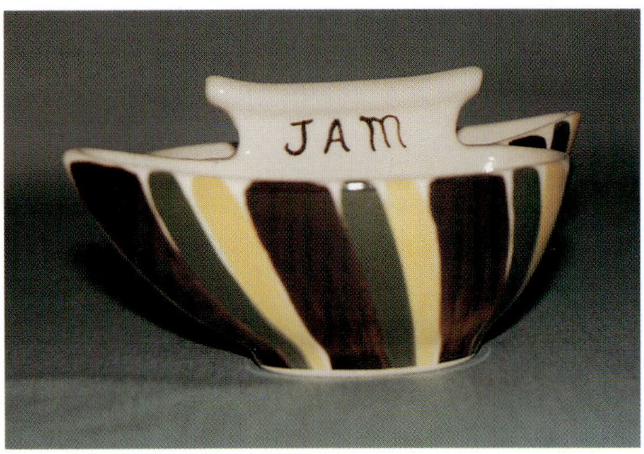

Jam and jelly. $30.

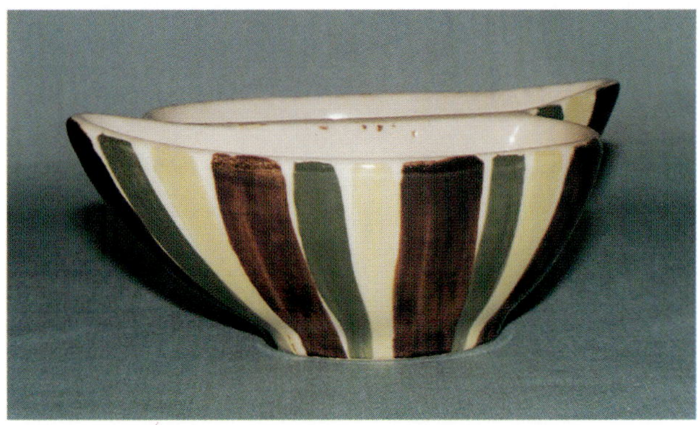

Nut dish (which is actually a jam and jelly that had the handle cut off before it was glazed and fired.) $30.

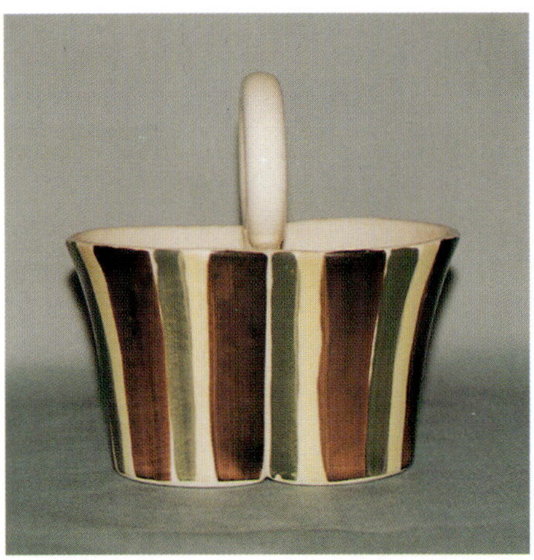

Candy dish. $75.

Star candle holder with insert. $35.

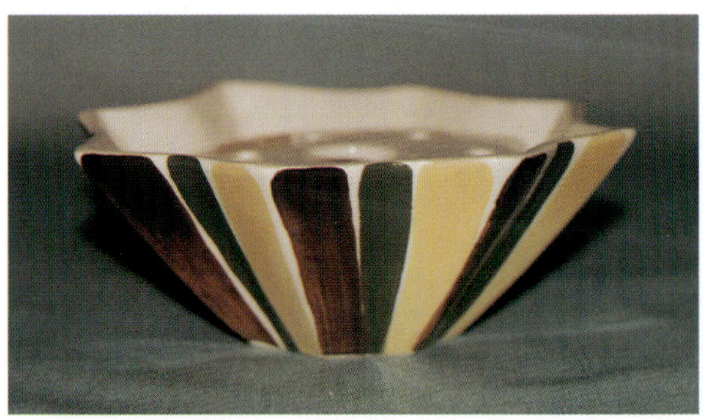

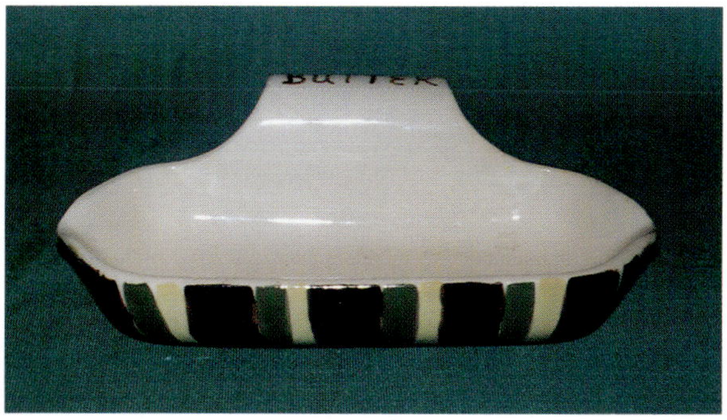

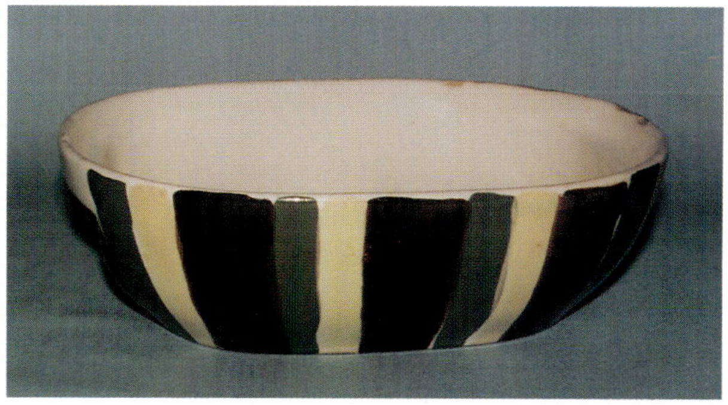

Baker. $25.

Butter dish. $75.

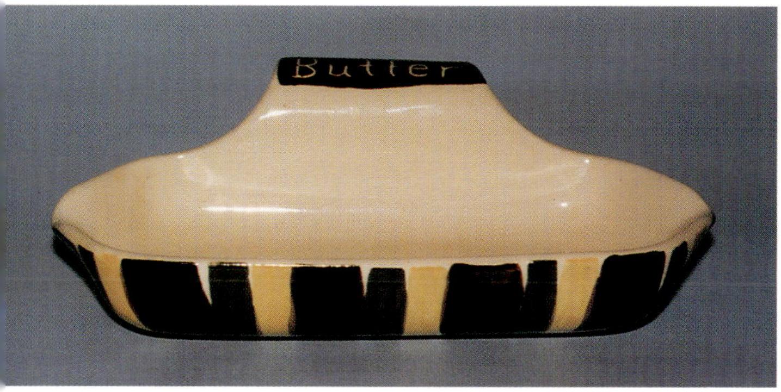

Butter dish with a variation on the handle. Initialed on reverse side by Dorothy Purinton. $200+.

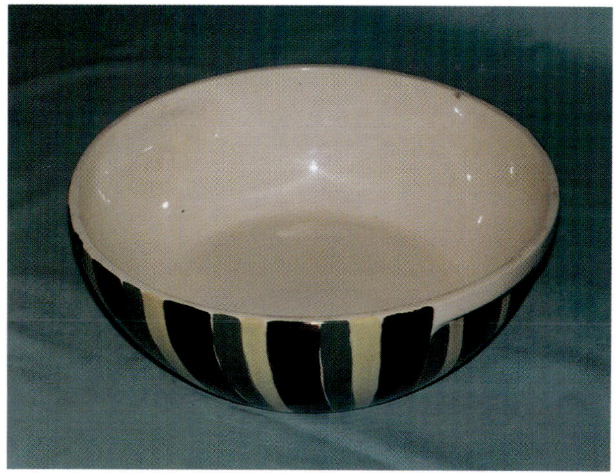

Salad bowl. $50.

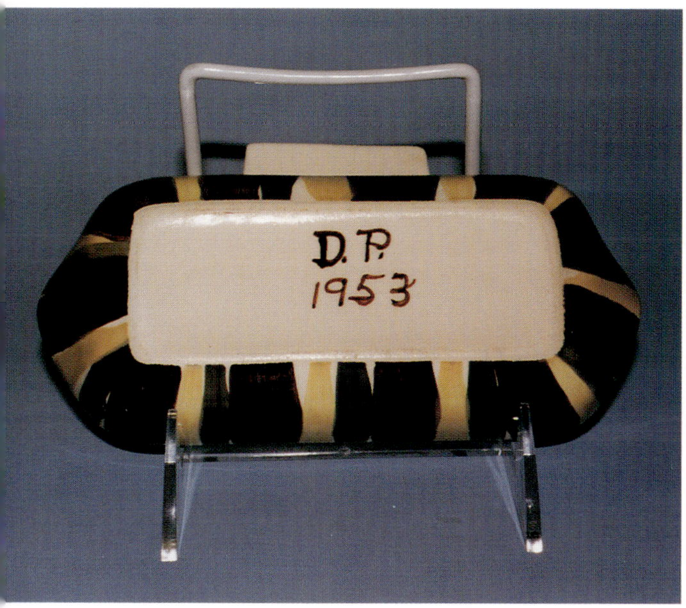

Reverse side of Saraband butter.

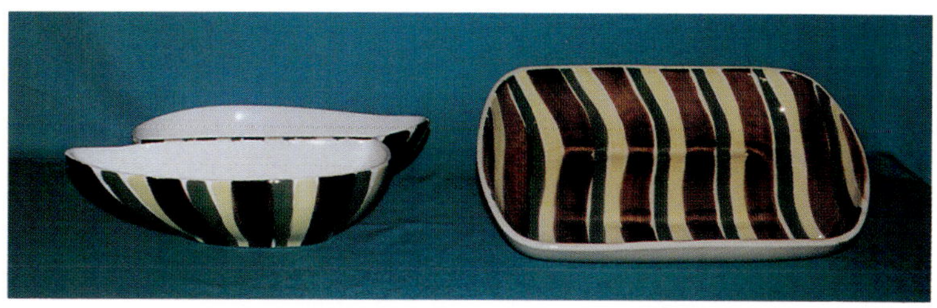

Divided vegetable. $25. Roll tray. $25.

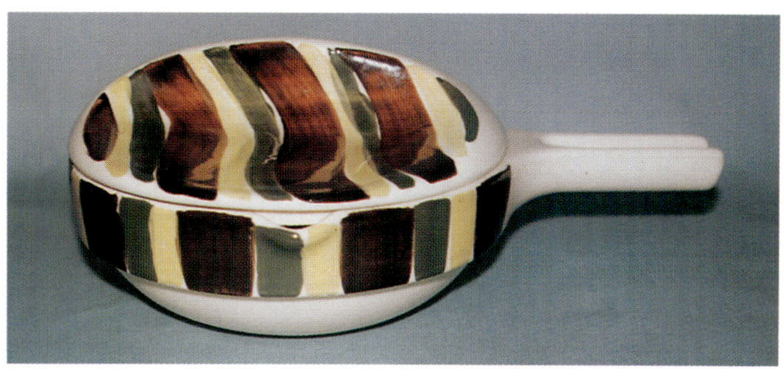

One quart handled casserole with lid, Rubel mold. $50.

Pickle dish. $15.

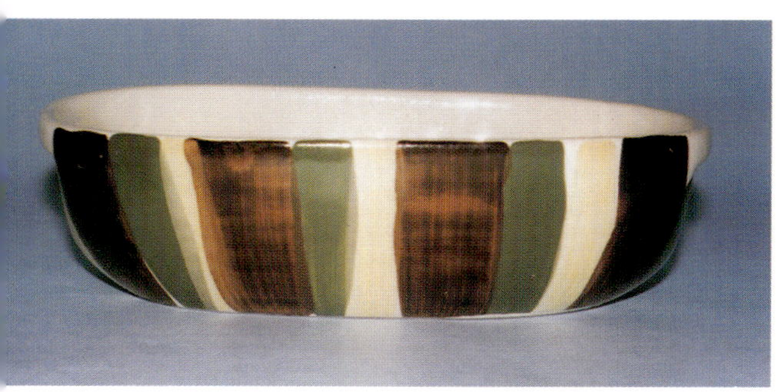

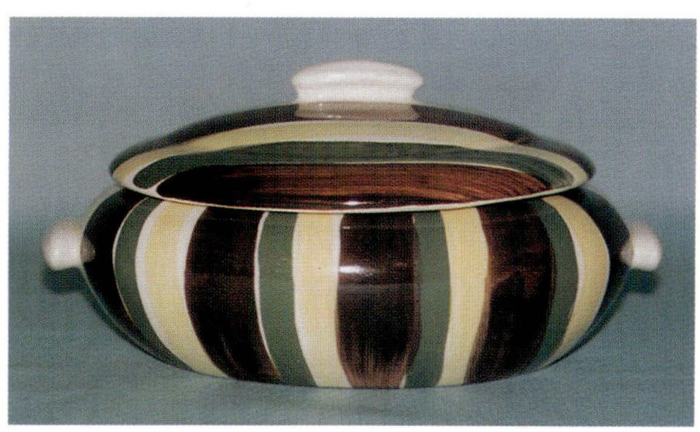

Covered vegetable. $50.

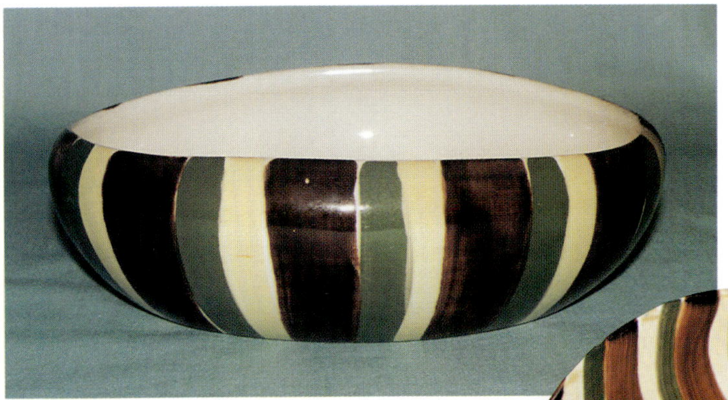

Fruit bowl. $50.

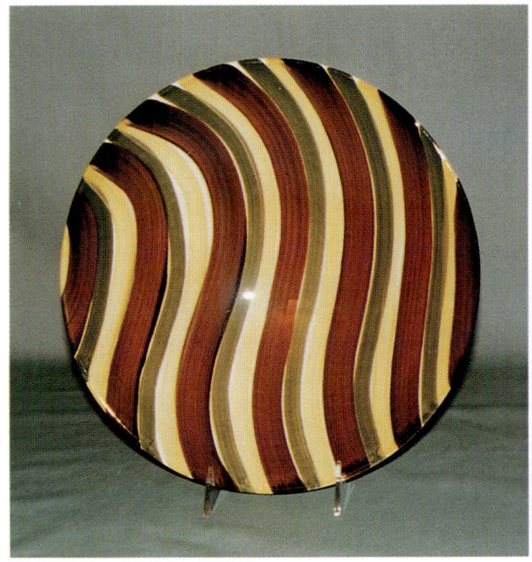

Open vegetable. $20.

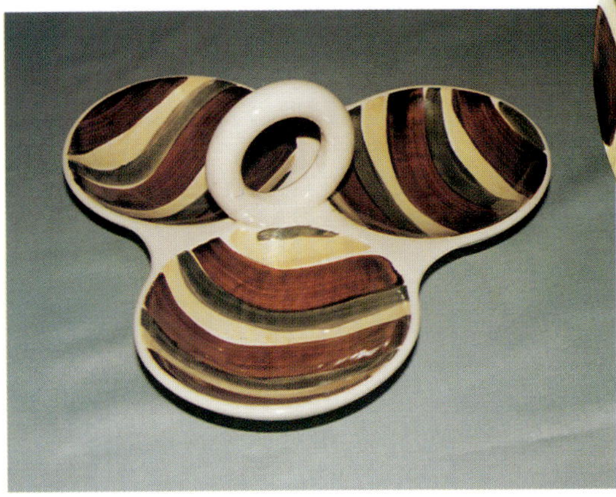

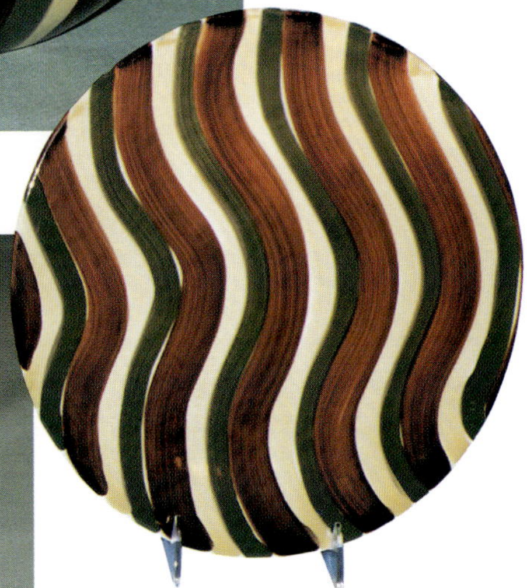

Chop plate. $50.

Sandwich plate. $35.

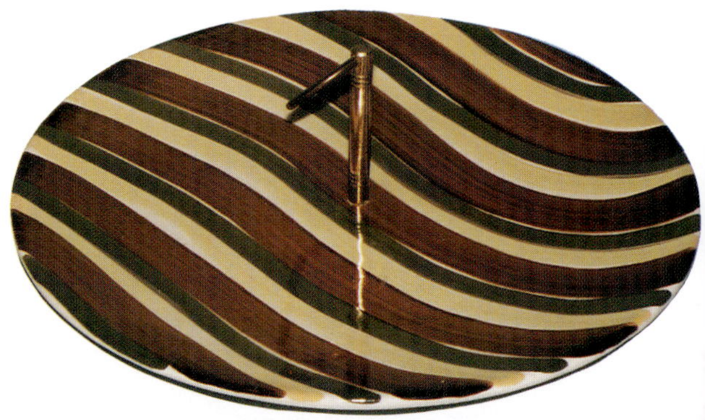

Three part relish with ceramic handle. $40.

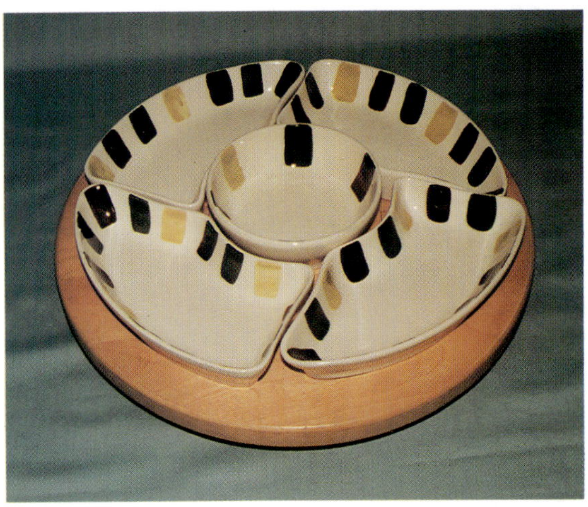

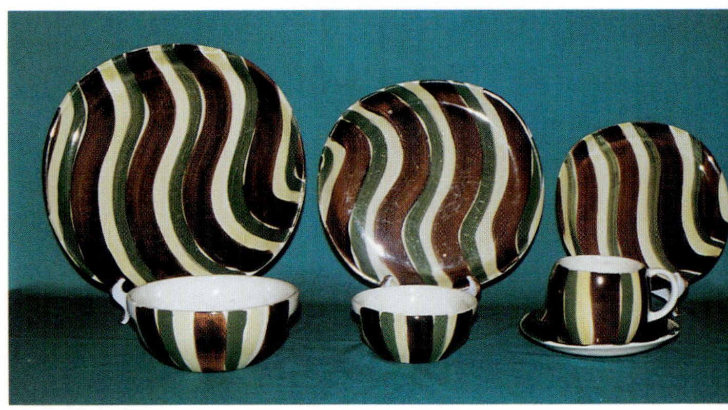

Lazy susan. $40.

Large platter. $25. Small platter. $25.

Dinner plate. $10. Breakfast plate. $7. Salad plate. $7. Cereal bo
$5. Dessert bowl. $5. Cup. $5. Saucer. $2.

Tea and toast plate. $15. Cup. $5.

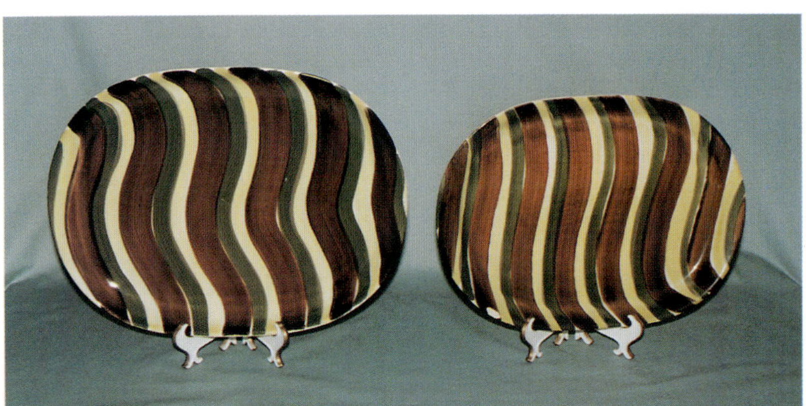

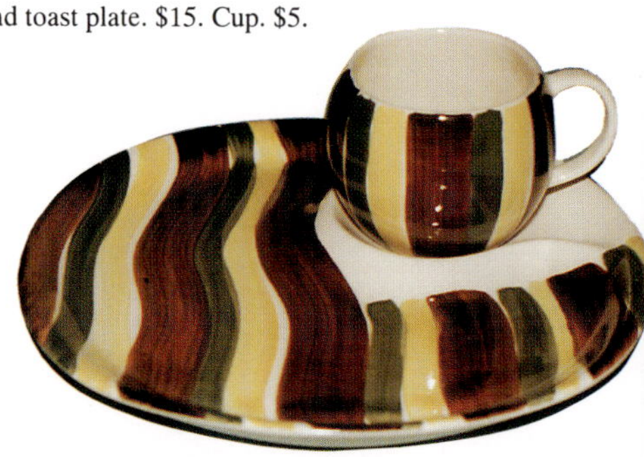

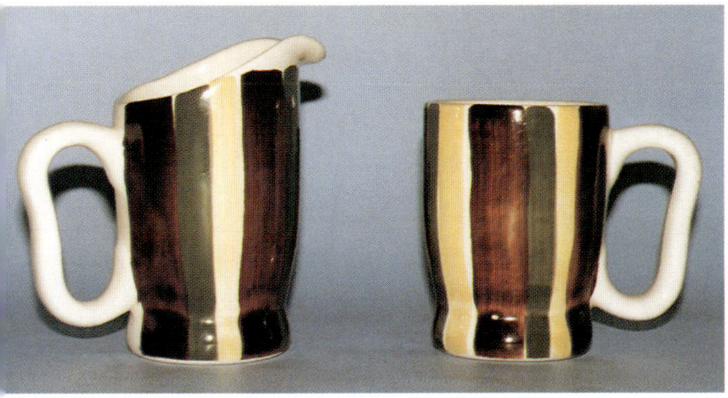

Mug jug. $40. Coffee mug. $35.

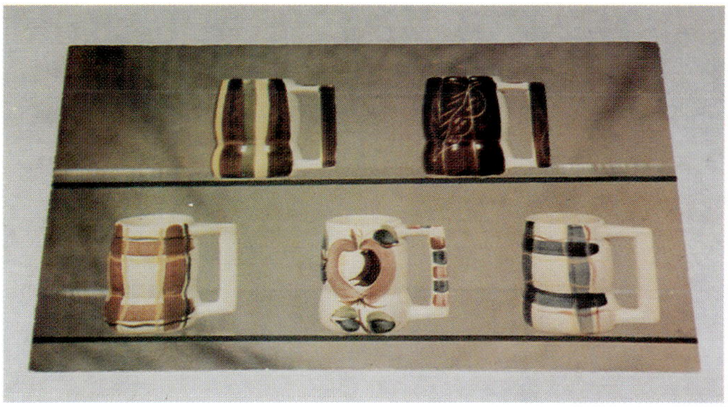

Postcard illustrating Purinton beer mugs.

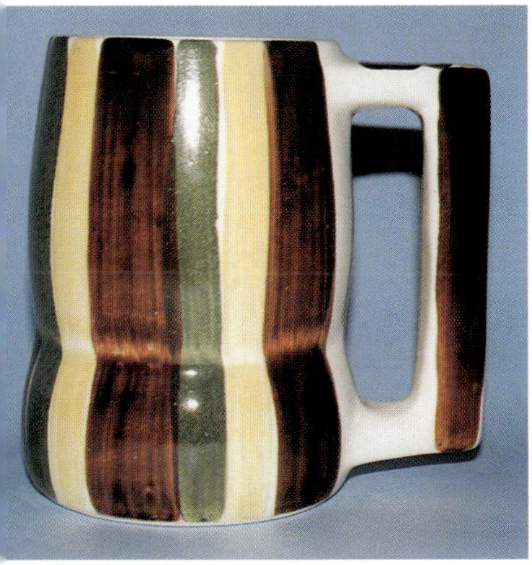

Beer mug. $40.

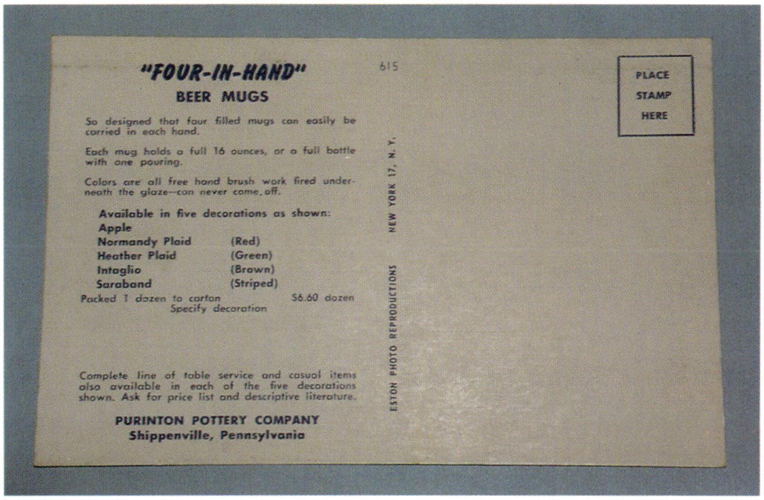

"FOUR-IN-HAND"

BEER MUGS

So designed that four filled mugs can easily be carried in each hand.

Each mug holds a full 16 ounces, or a full bottle with one pouring.

Colors are all free hand brush work fired underneath the glaze—can never come off.

Available in five decorations as shown:

Apple	
Normandy Plaid	(Red)
Heather Plaid	(Green)
Intaglio	(Brown)
Saraband	(Striped)

Packed 1 dozen to carton $6.60 dozen
Specify decoration

Complete line of table service and casual items also available in each of the five decorations shown. Ask for price list and descriptive literature.

PURINTON POTTERY COMPANY
Shippenville, Pennsylvania

615

ESTON PHOTO REPRODUCTIONS NEW YORK 17, N. Y.

PLACE STAMP HERE

Reverse side of the beer mug postcard.

Individual bean pot. $40. Five pint dutch jug. $75.

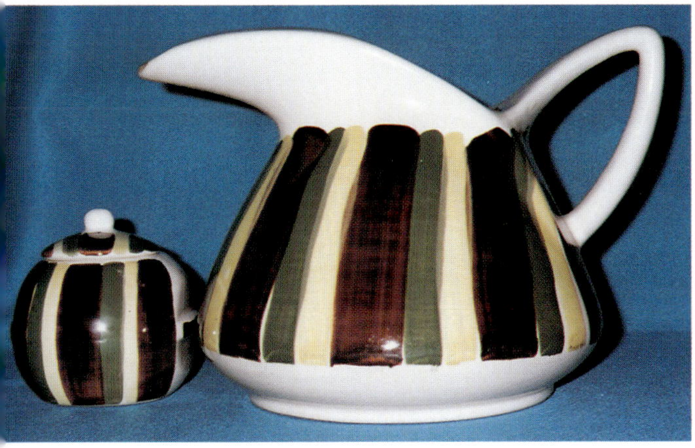

Two pint dutch jug. $50. Juice mug. $10.

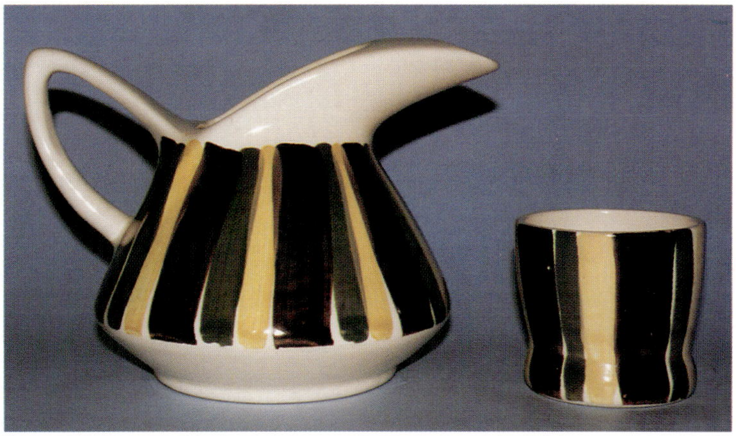

Six cup domed lid teapot. $50.

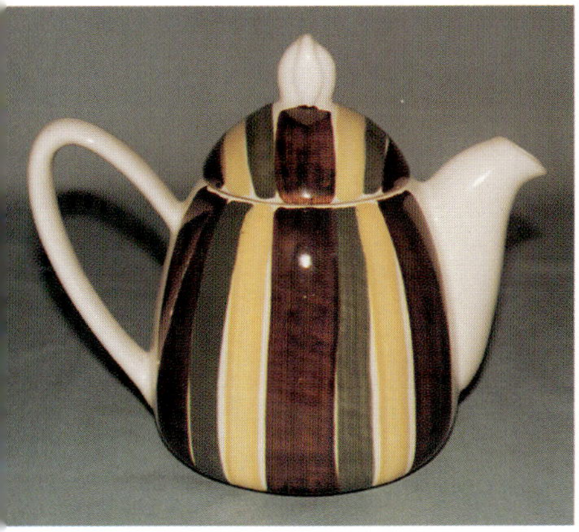

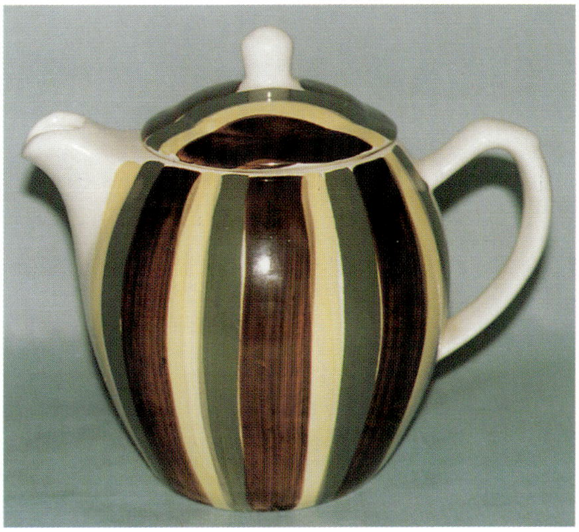

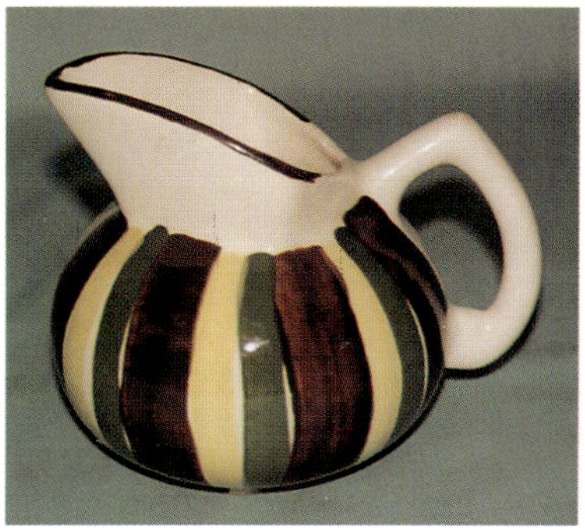

Kent jug. $75.

Eight cup coffee pot. $40.

Normandy and Heather Plaids

The Plaids consist of Normandy and Heather. Although designed by Bill Blair, the Plaids were not introduced until the 1950s. Normandy is painted with red and trimmed in green and chartreuse. Heather is a teal green with red and chartreuse trim. The Plaids continued through the 1950s as open stock items and were strong sellers for Purinton.

Both items can be found in great numbers, Normandy more so than Heather. Demand for the Plaids is lower as can be seen in the pricing. The Plaids represent the more modernistic 1950s style. With styles of that time becoming more popular with baby boomers, an opportunity for collectors to purchase this decoration at a reasonable price will be short lived.

Dinnerware and serving items can be found with reasonable ease. Harder to find items are the canister sets, butter dishes, shake and pour shakers other than salt and pepper, and round candle holders. Items found other than those pictured are rare.

At the end of the chapter, a few designs utilizing other colors are pictured. None of these were production items, except for the chartreuse plaid pillow vase which was made for NAPCO at the Tionesta plant. Finding a different color plaid on any shape would be considered a great find.

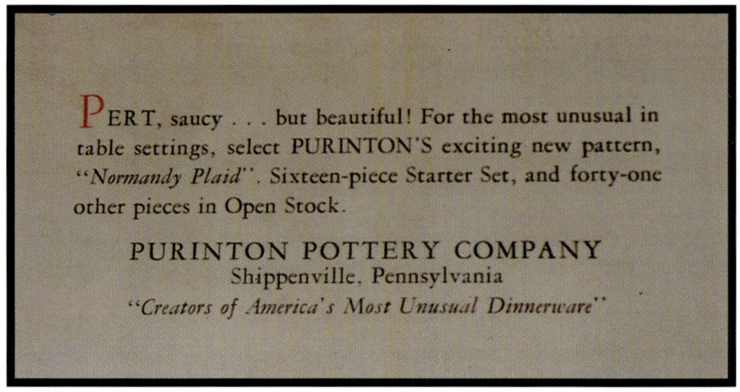

PERT, saucy . . . but beautiful! For the most unusual in table settings, select PURINTON'S exciting new pattern, *"Normandy Plaid"*. Sixteen-piece Starter Set, and forty-one other pieces in Open Stock.

PURINTON POTTERY COMPANY
Shippenville, Pennsylvania
"Creators of America's Most Unusual Dinnerware"

Normandy Plaid pattern description.

Normandy Plaid

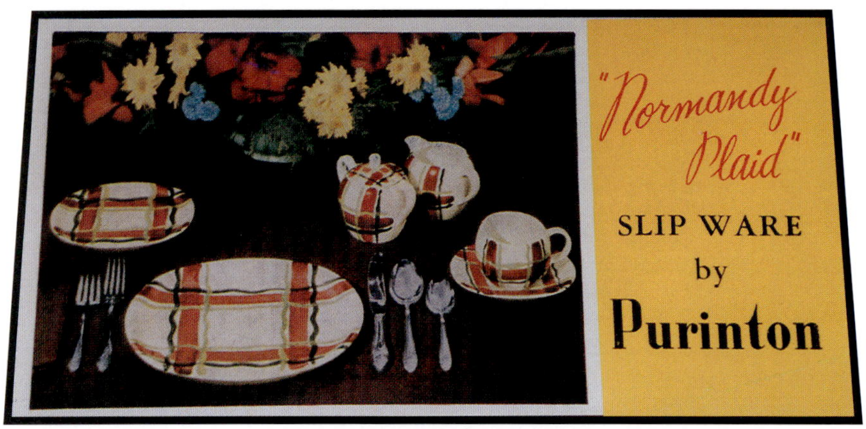

Normandy Plaid product card.

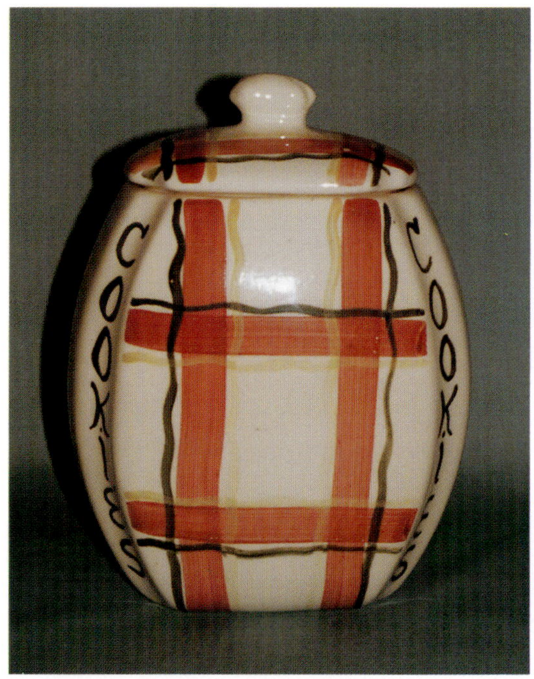

Wide oval cookies jar. $75.

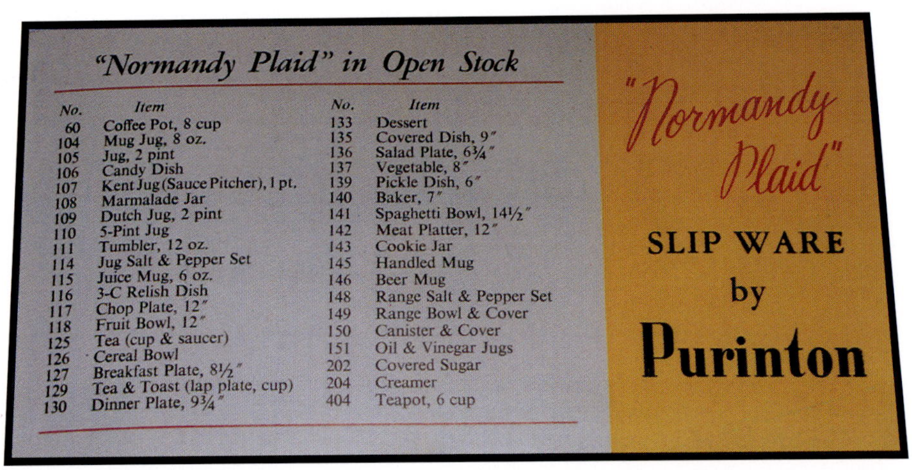

"Normandy Plaid" in Open Stock

No.	Item	No.	Item
60	Coffee Pot, 8 cup	133	Dessert
104	Mug Jug, 8 oz.	135	Covered Dish, 9″
105	Jug, 2 pint	136	Salad Plate, 6¾″
106	Candy Dish	137	Vegetable, 8″
107	Kent Jug (Sauce Pitcher), 1 pt.	139	Pickle Dish, 6″
108	Marmalade Jar	140	Baker, 7″
109	Dutch Jug, 2 pint	141	Spaghetti Bowl, 14½″
110	5-Pint Jug	142	Meat Platter, 12″
111	Tumbler, 12 oz.	143	Cookie Jar
114	Jug Salt & Pepper Set	145	Handled Mug
115	Juice Mug, 6 oz.	146	Beer Mug
116	3-C Relish Dish	148	Range Salt & Pepper Set
117	Chop Plate, 12″	149	Range Bowl & Cover
118	Fruit Bowl, 12″	150	Canister & Cover
125	Tea (cup & saucer)	151	Oil & Vinegar Jugs
126	Cereal Bowl	202	Covered Sugar
127	Breakfast Plate, 8½″	204	Creamer
129	Tea & Toast (lap plate, cup)	404	Teapot, 6 cup
130	Dinner Plate, 9¾″		

Normandy Plaid open stock offerings.

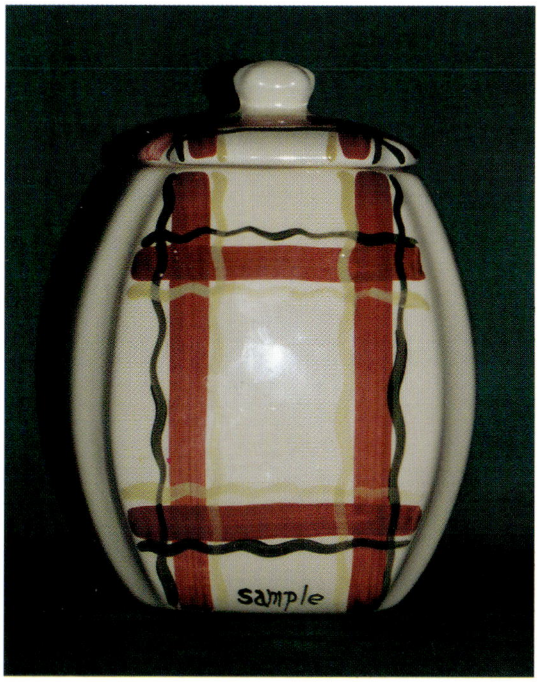

Wide oval canister with "sample" written on the bottom. Probably used as a sample for the decorators. $200.

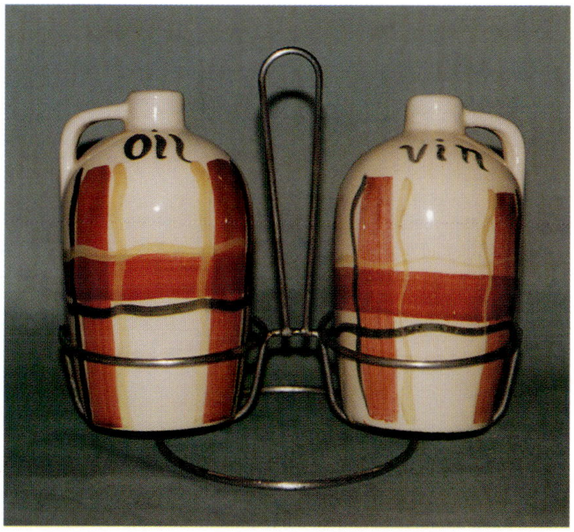

Jug style oil and vinegar in wire rack. $75 set.

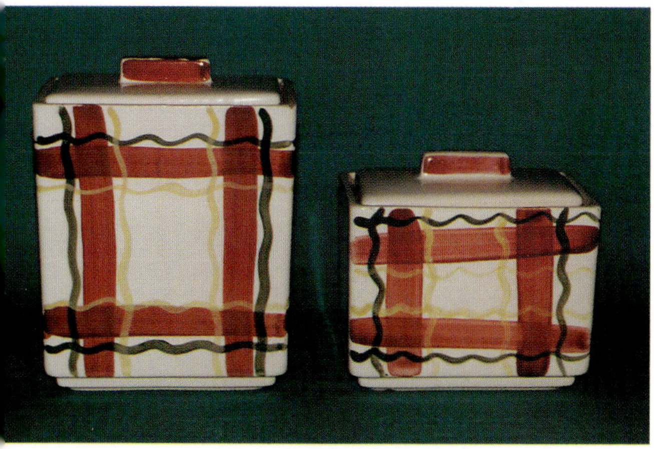

Storage canisters. $50 each.

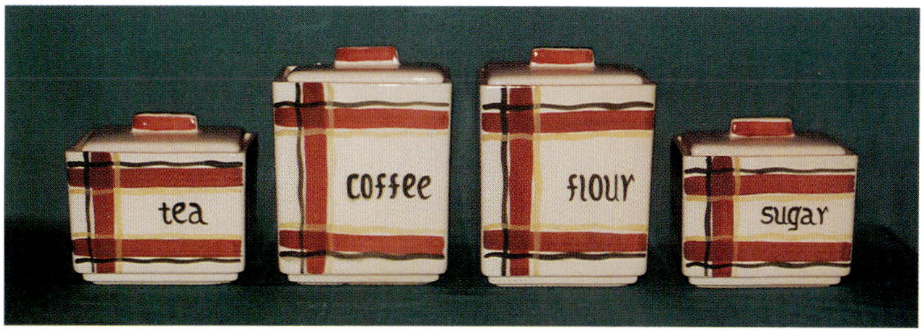

Four piece apartment canister set. $30 each.

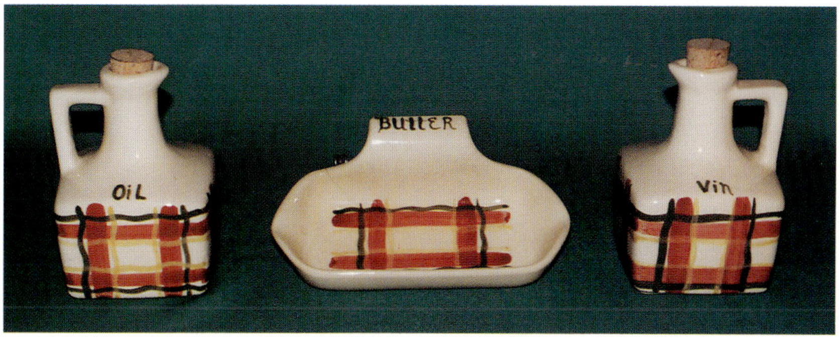

Square oil and vinegar. $30 set. Butter dish. $100.

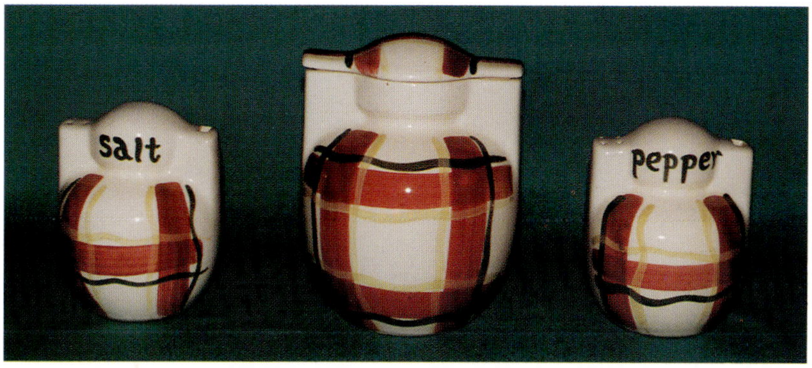

Pour and shake salt and pepper shakers. $35 set. Winged covered grease jar. $45.

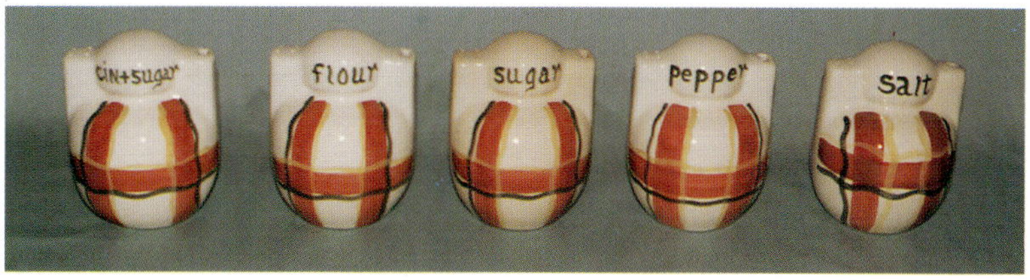

Pour and shake shaker set: cin. + sugar $75, flour $75, sugar $75, pepper and salt $35 set.

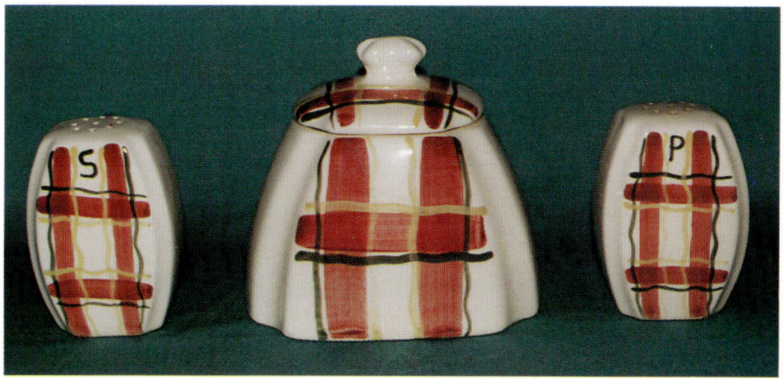

Range salt and pepper shakers. $50 set. Range covered grease jar. $40.

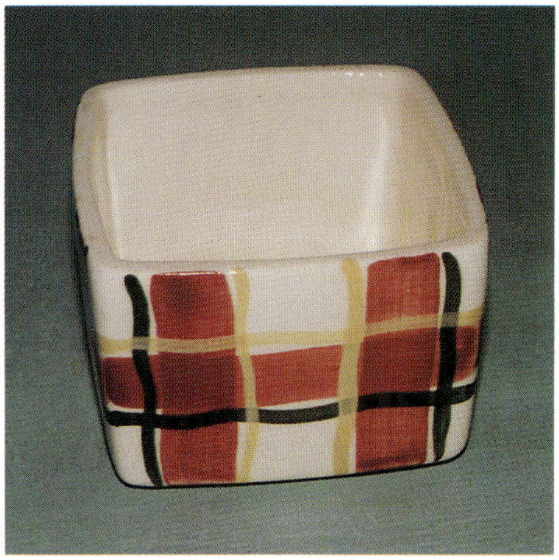

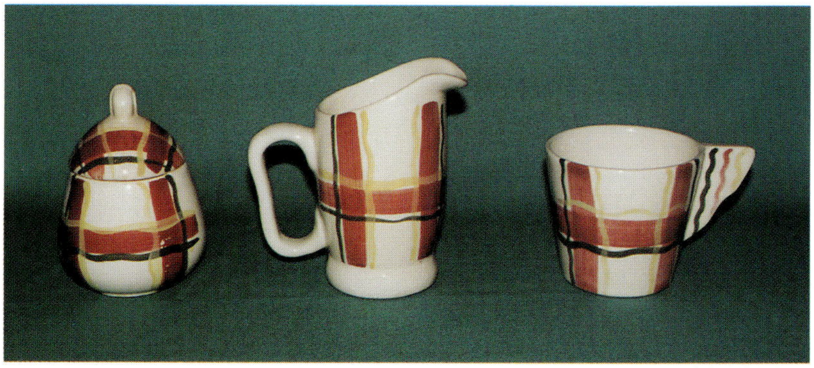

Marmalade jar. $40. Mug jug. $50. Odd handled cup, experimental mold. $75.

Whimsy bottom from square oil or vinegar. $40.

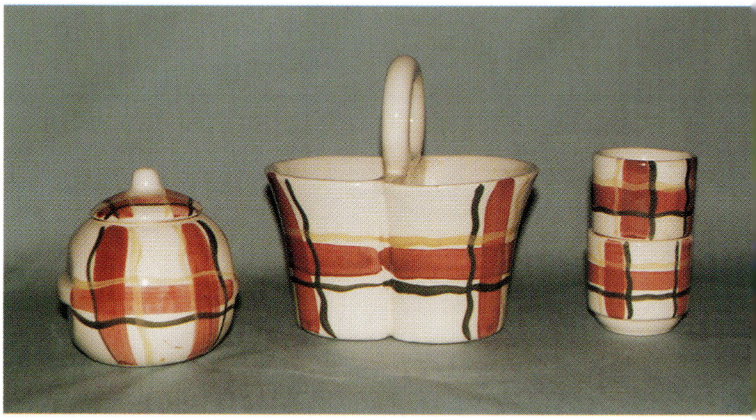

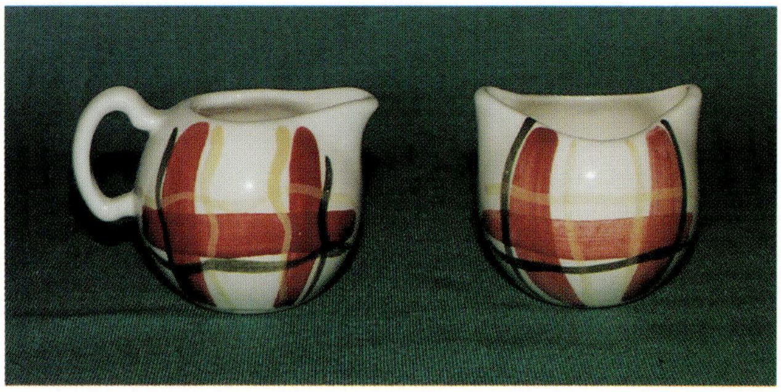

Individual bean pot. $40. Candy dish. $75. Stacking salt and pepper. $50 set.

Individual creamer and sugar. $25 set.

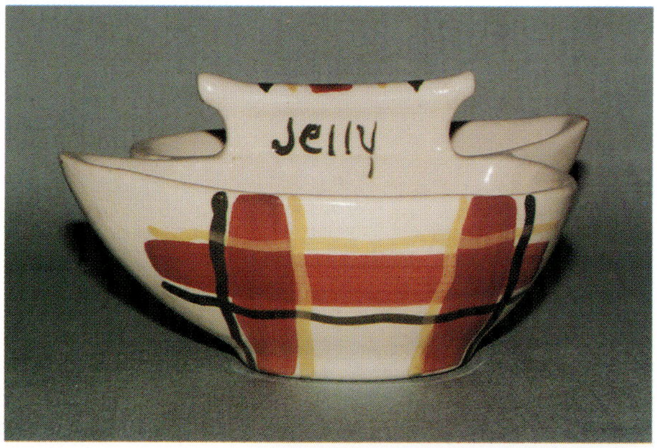

Jam and jelly. $40.

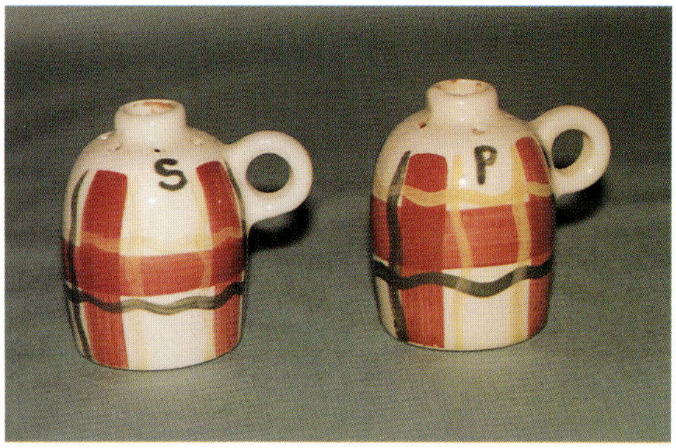

Jug style salt and pepper shakers. $20 set.

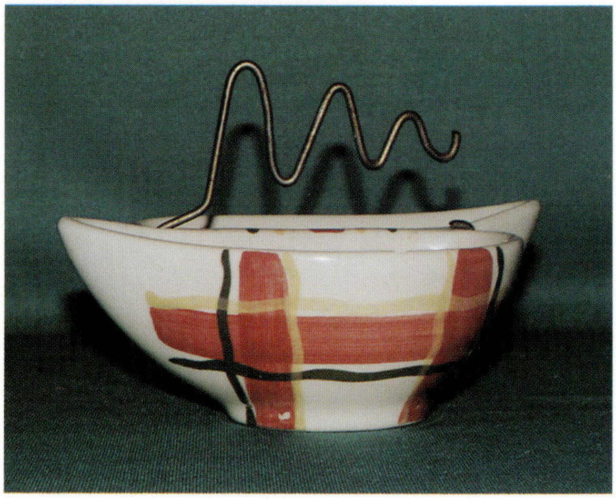

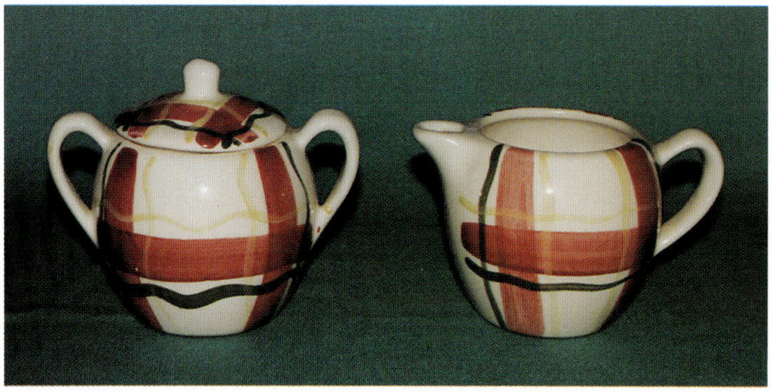

Round covered sugar and creamer. $25 set.

Ashtray. $35.

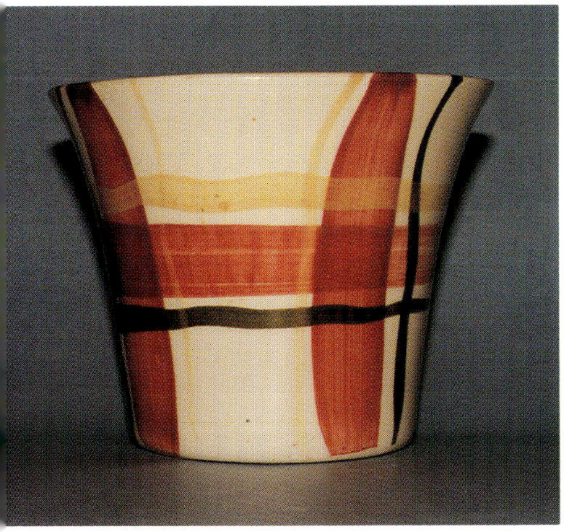

Wall pocket. $75.

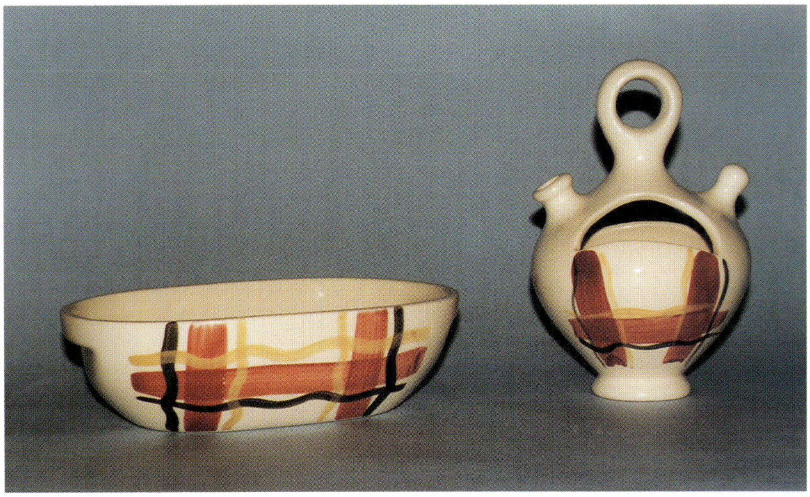

Baker. $25. Rum jug planter. $60.

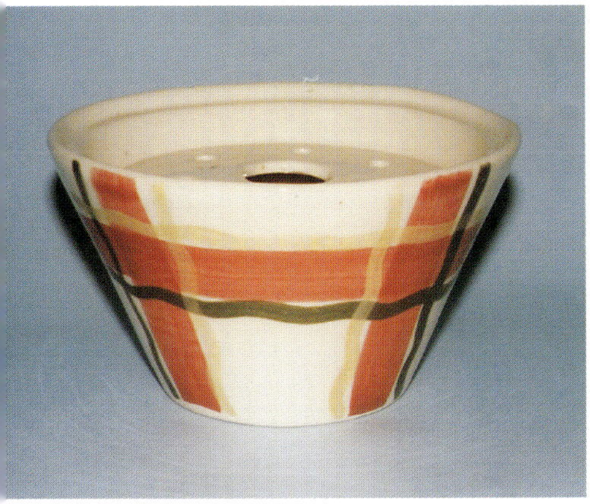

Round candle holder with insert. $150.

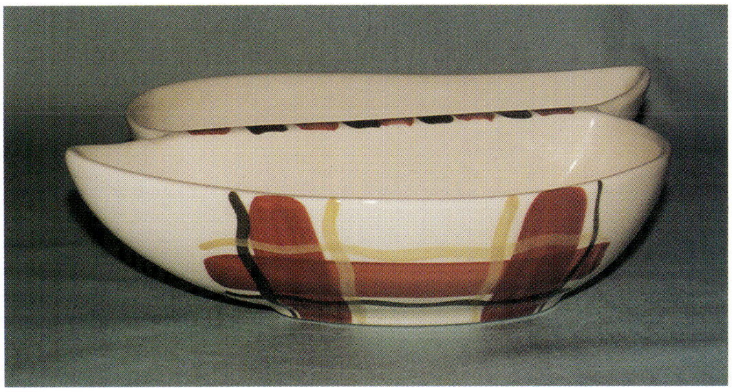

Divided vegetable. $20. Divided vegetable with "sample" painted on bottom as illustrated. $75.

Divided vegetable used as a model for the decorators.

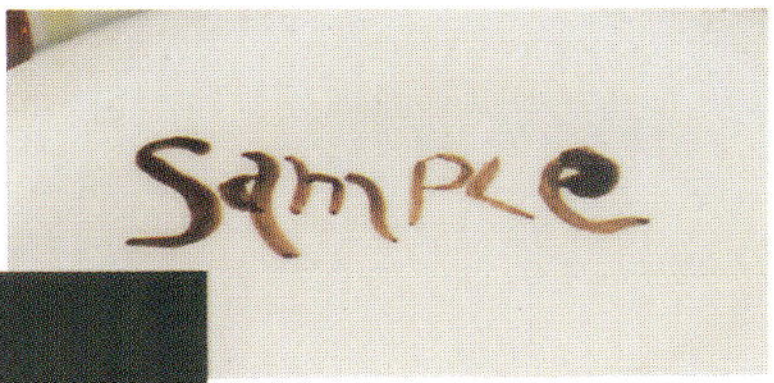

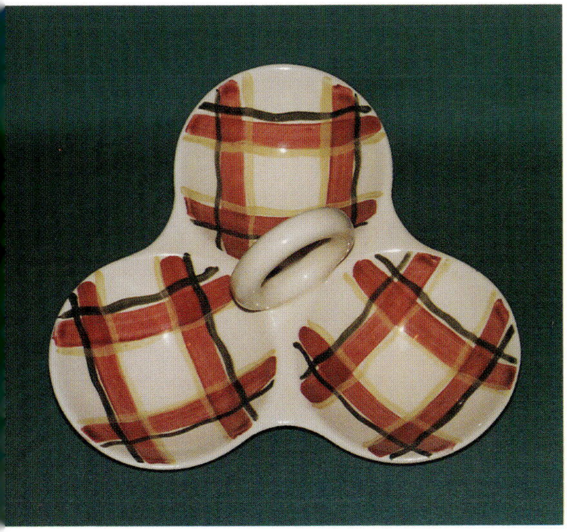

Three part relish with ceramic handle. $30.

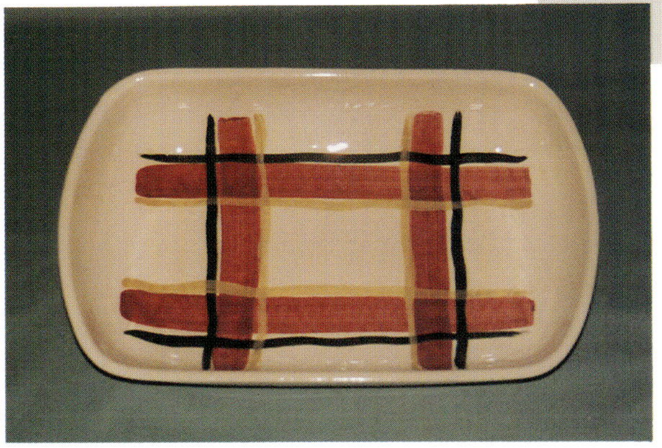

Roll tray. $20.

Spaghetti bowl. $125.

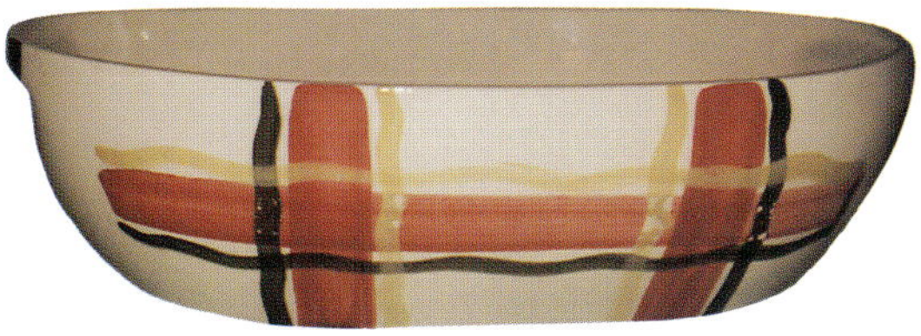

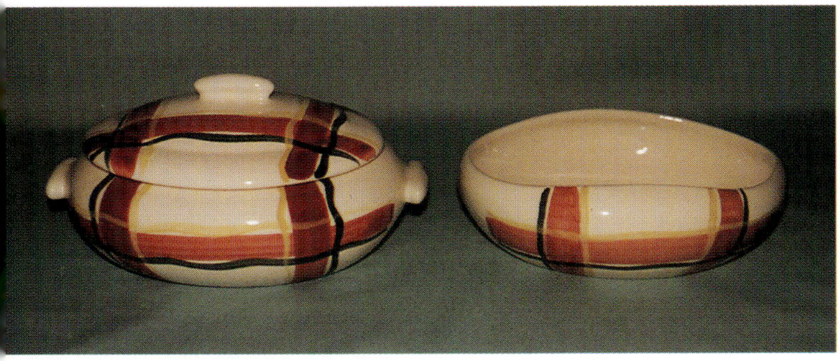

Covered vegetable. $50. Open vegetable. $20.

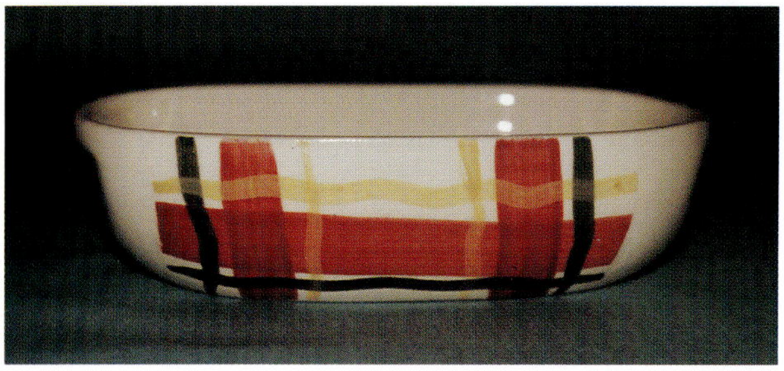
Pickle. $15.

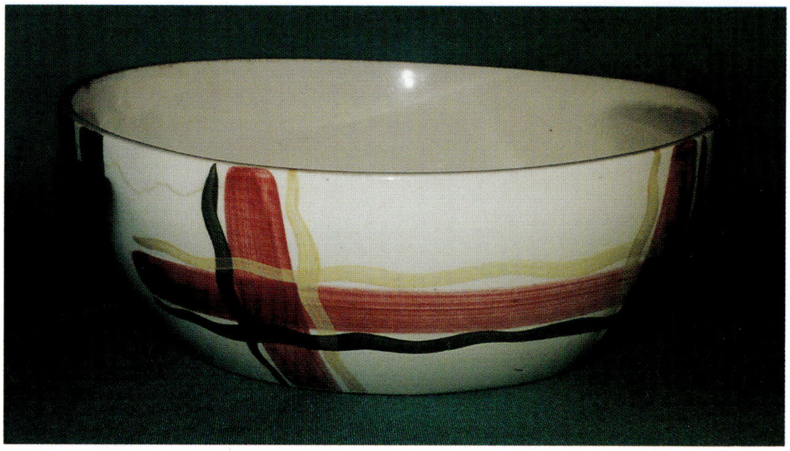
Salad bowl. $95.

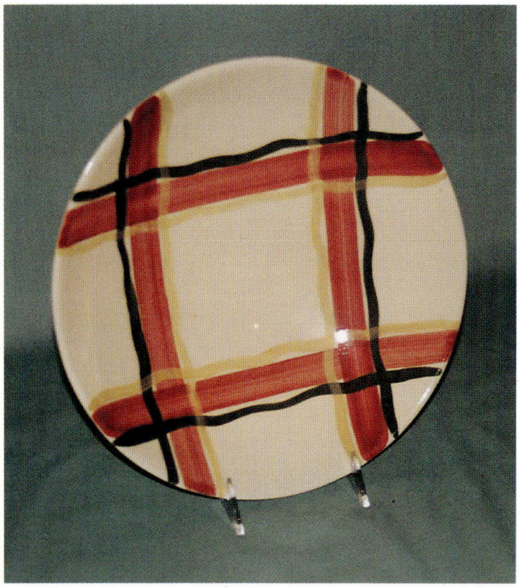
Fruit Bowl. $35.

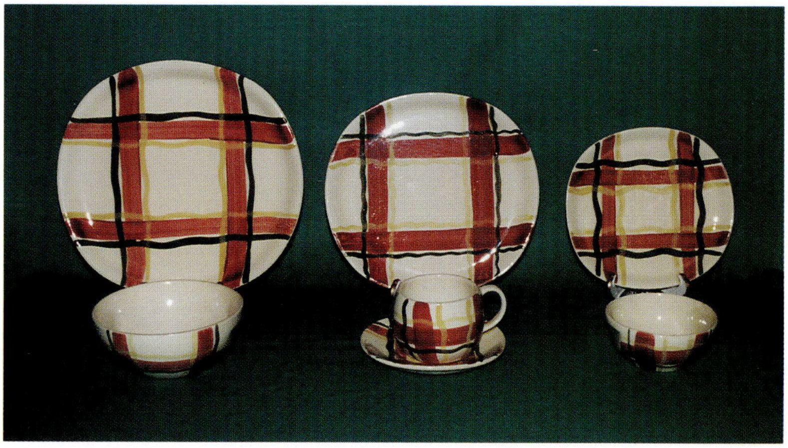
Dinner plate. $10. Breakfast plate. $10. Salad plate. $7. Cereal bowl. $7. Cup. $5. Saucer. $2. Dessert bowl. $5.

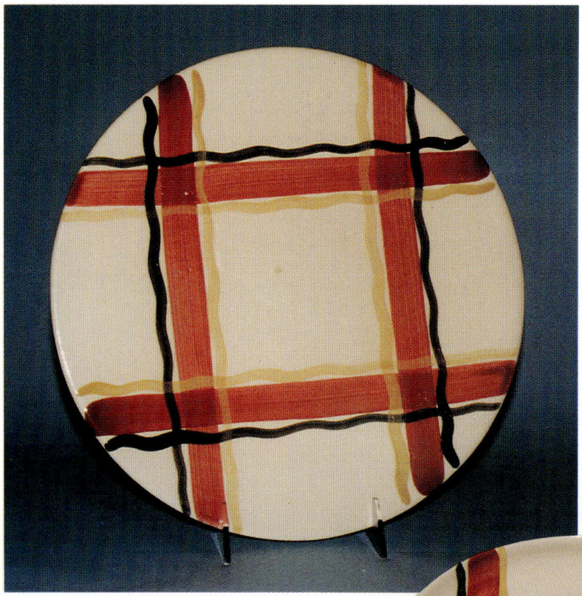
Chop plate. $40.

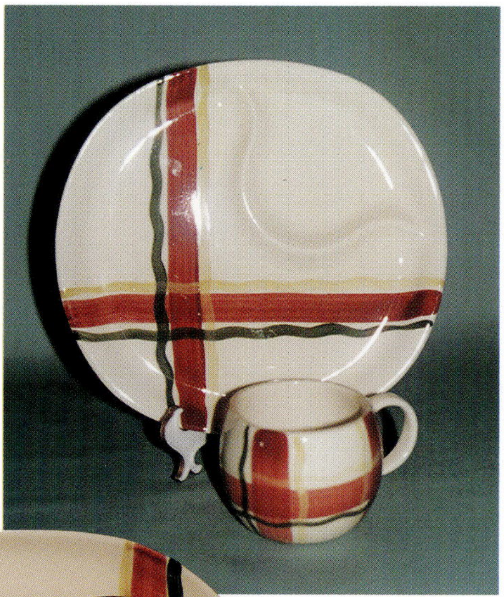
Tea and toast plate. $10. Cup. $5.

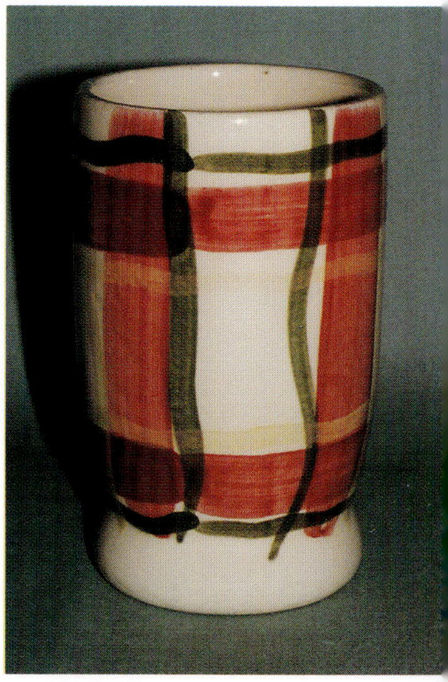
Tumbler. $20.

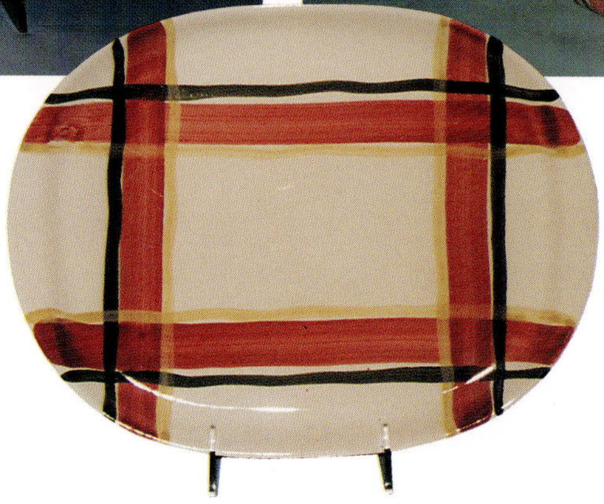
Large platter. $25.

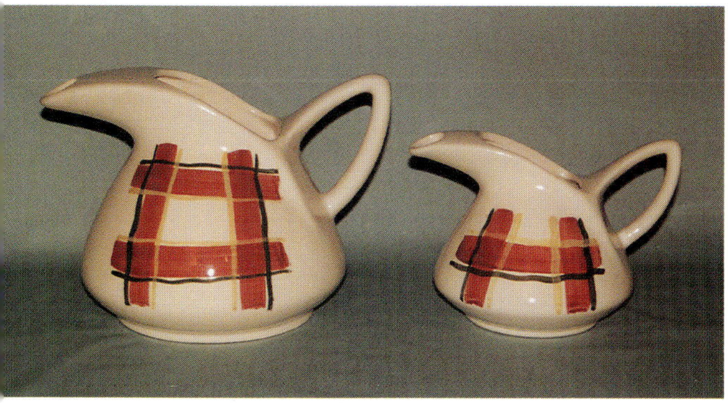

Five pint dutch jug. $60. Two pint dutch jug. $35.

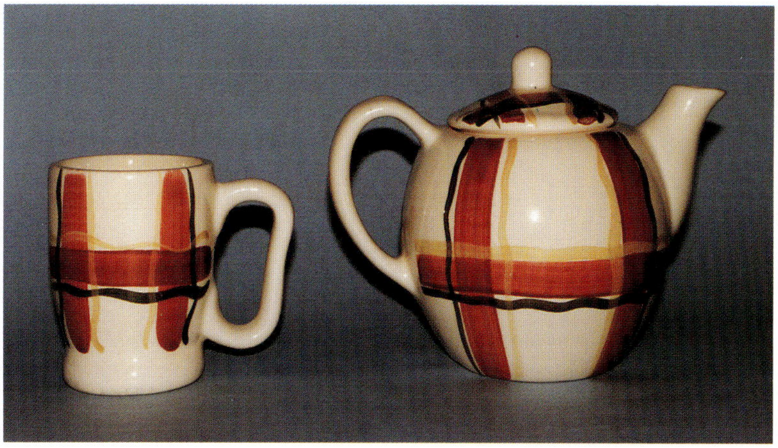

Coffee mug. $40. Six cup teapot. $20.

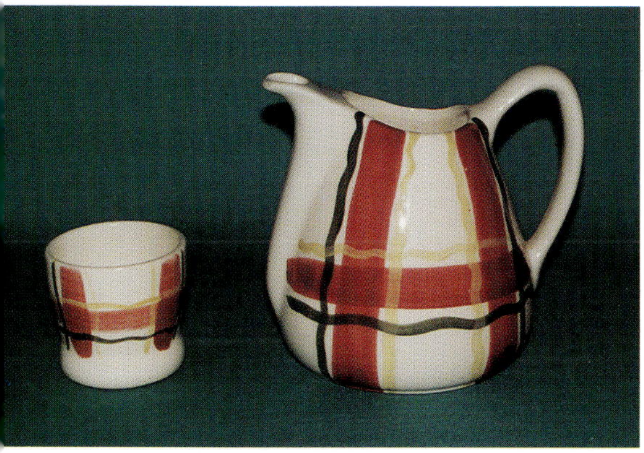

Juice mug. $15. Beverage pitcher. $50.

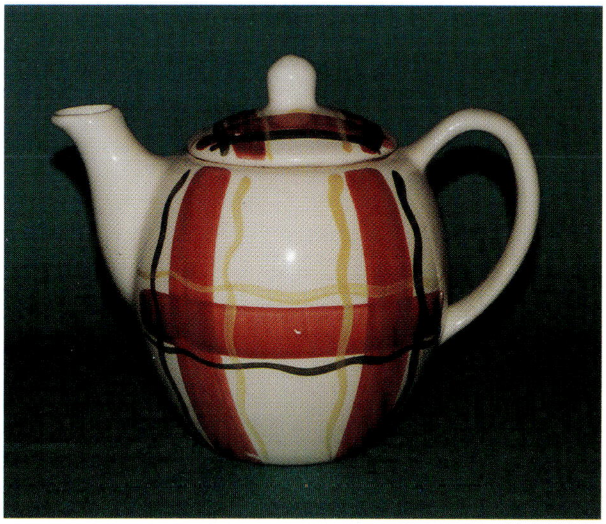

Four cup teapot. $20.

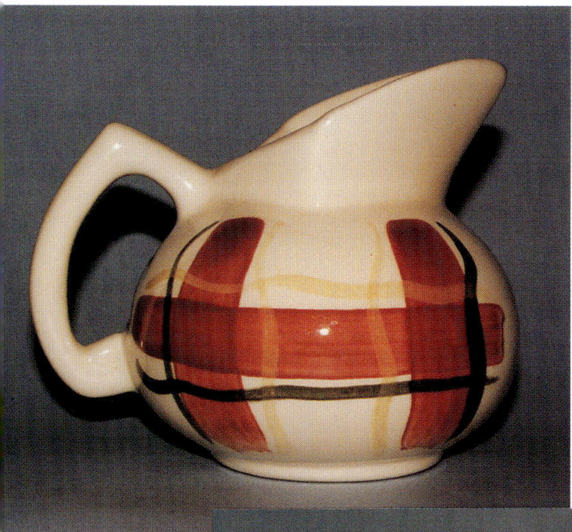

Kent jug. $35.

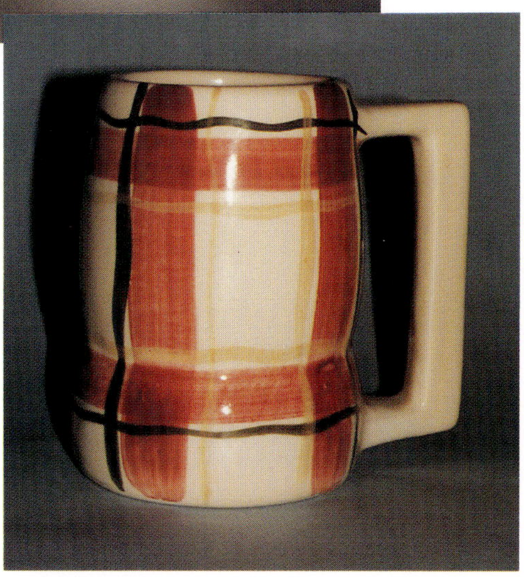

Beer mug. $50.

Heather Plaid

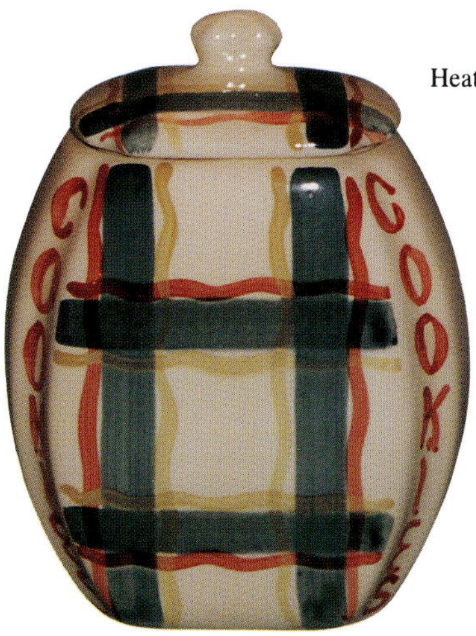

Heather Plaid wide oval cookies jar. $75.

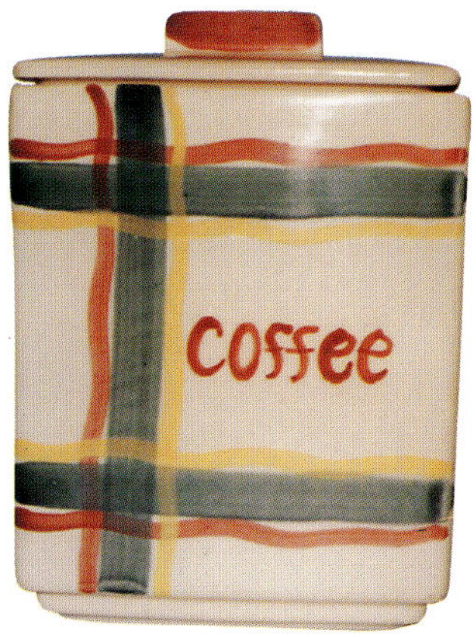

Coffee canister from square apartment canister set. $30 each.

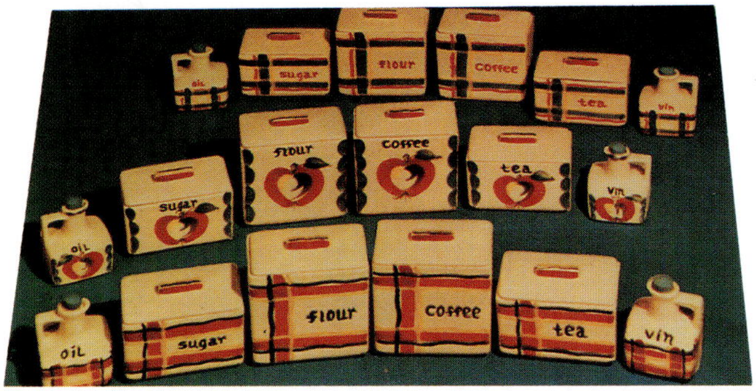

The number 88 canister set product card.

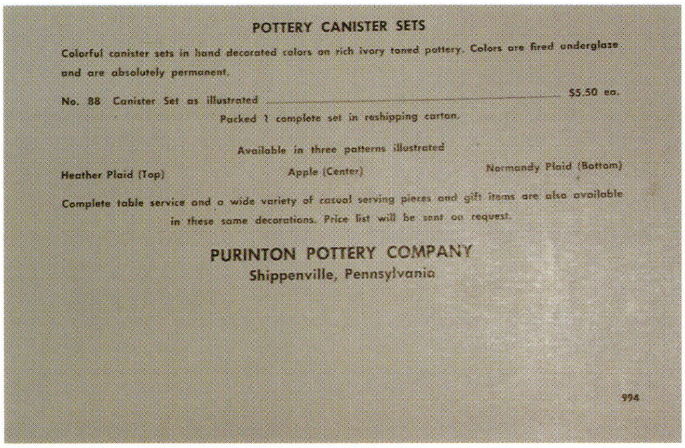

POTTERY CANISTER SETS

Colorful canister sets in hand decorated colors on rich ivory toned pottery. Colors are fired underglaze and are absolutely permanent.

No. 88 Canister Set as illustrated ______ $5.50 ea.

Packed 1 complete set in reshipping carton.

Available in three patterns illustrated

Heather Plaid (Top) Apple (Center) Normandy Plaid (Bottom)

Complete table service and a wide variety of casual serving pieces and gift items are also available in these same decorations. Price list will be sent on request.

PURINTON POTTERY COMPANY
Shippenville, Pennsylvania

994

Reverse side of canister set product card.

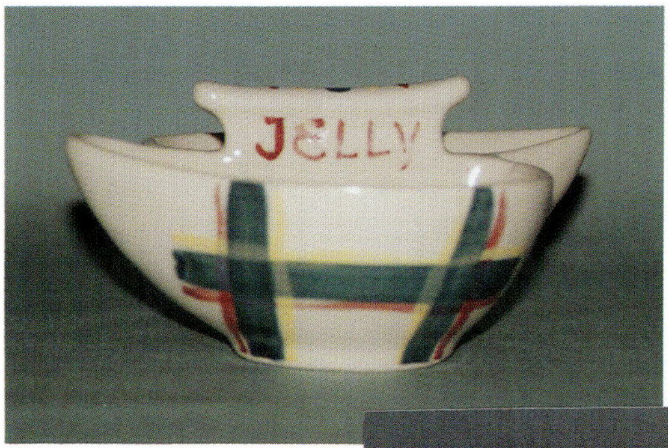

Jam and jelly. $50.

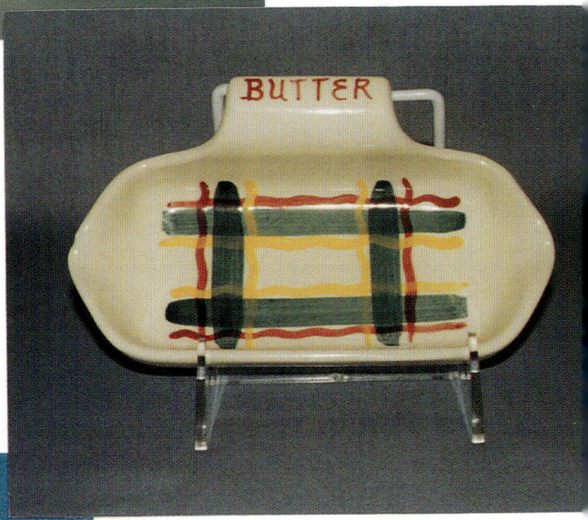

Butter dish. $90.

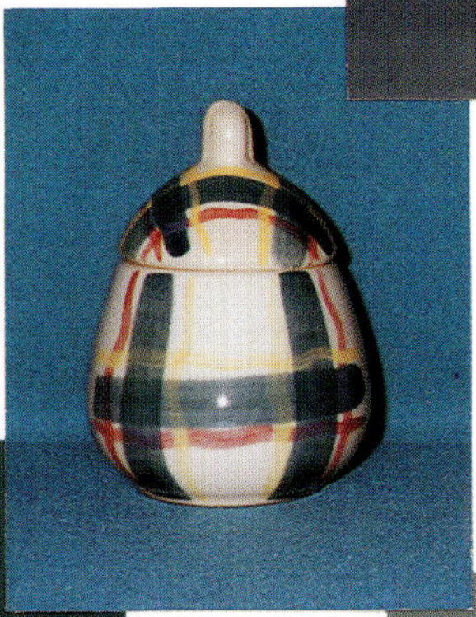

Marmalade jar. $50.

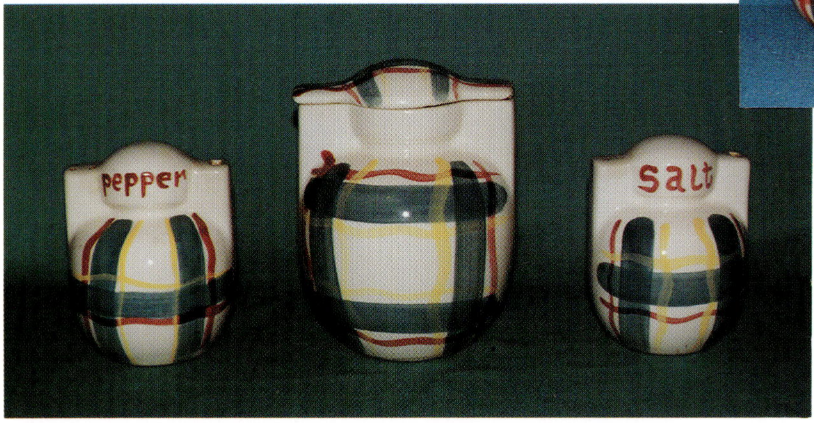

Pour and shake salt and pepper shakers. $40 set. Covered winged grease jar. $40.

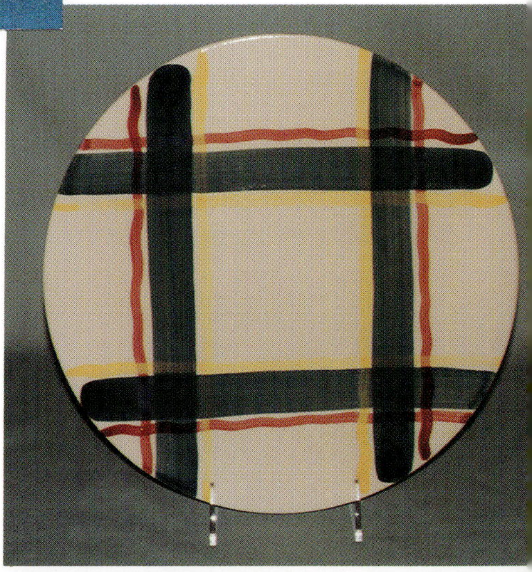

Chop plate. $40.

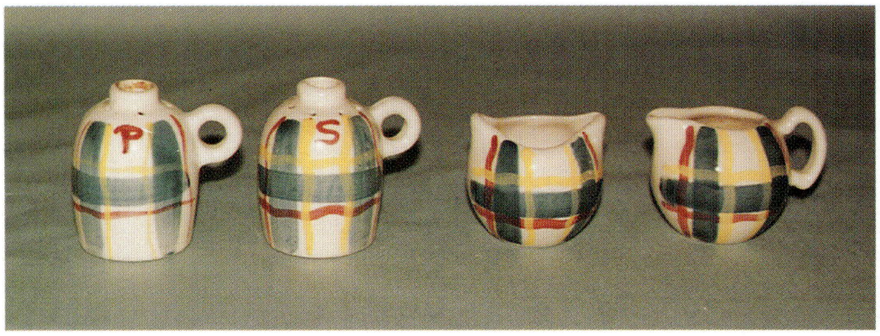

Jug style salt and pepper shakers. $20 set. Individual sugar and creamer. $30 set.

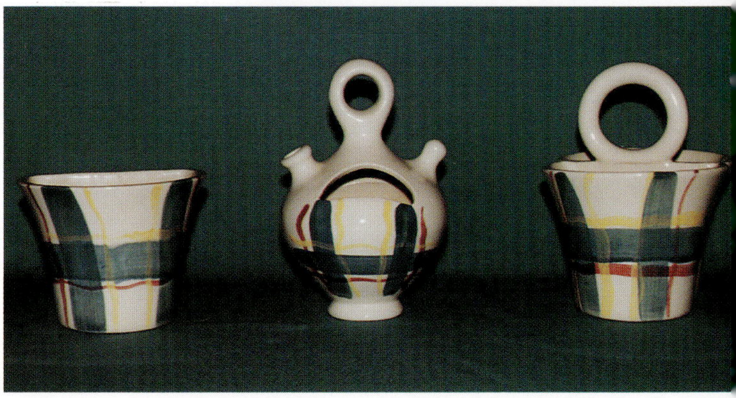

Wall pocket. $75. Rum jug planter. $50. Candy dish $50.

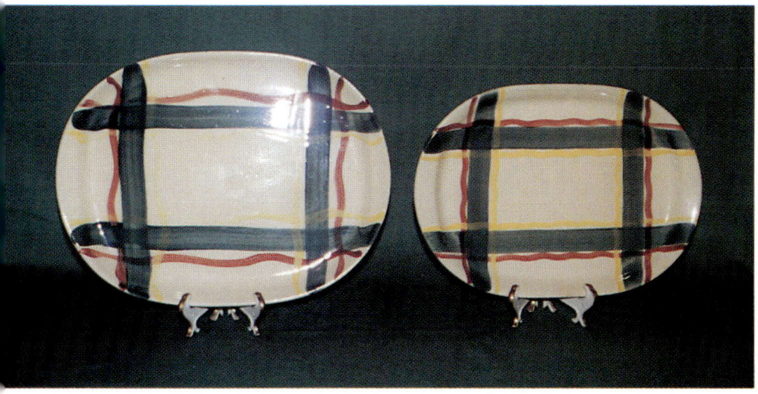

Large platter. $25. Small platter. $25.

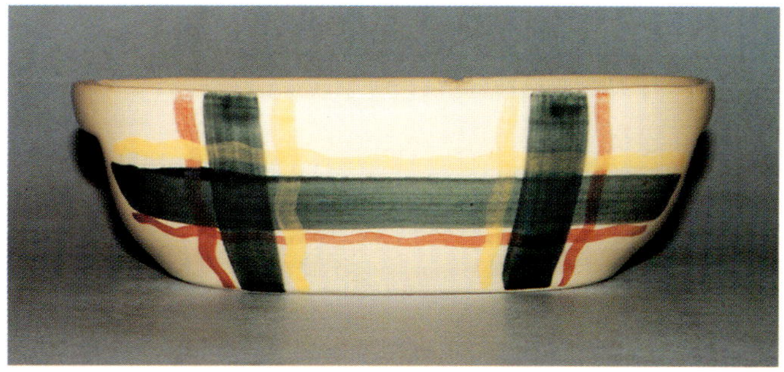

Pickle dish. $20.

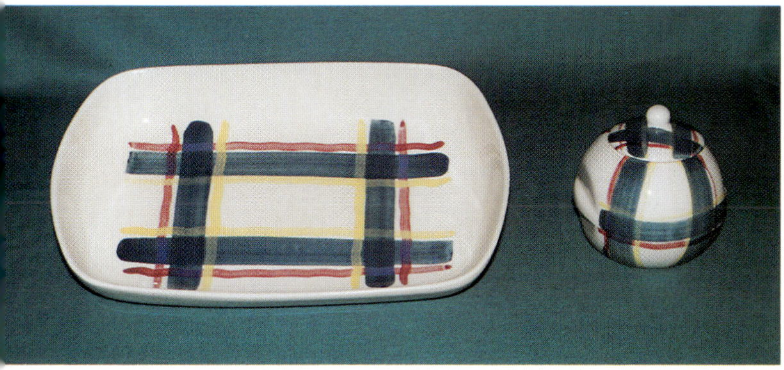

Roll tray. $20. Individual bean pot. $30.

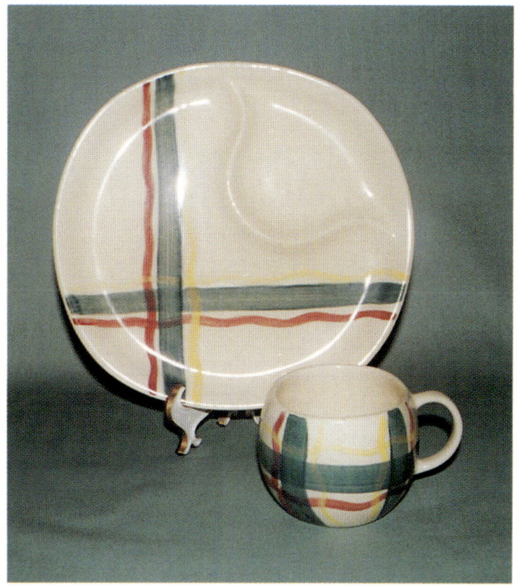

Tea and toast plate. $10. Cup. $5.

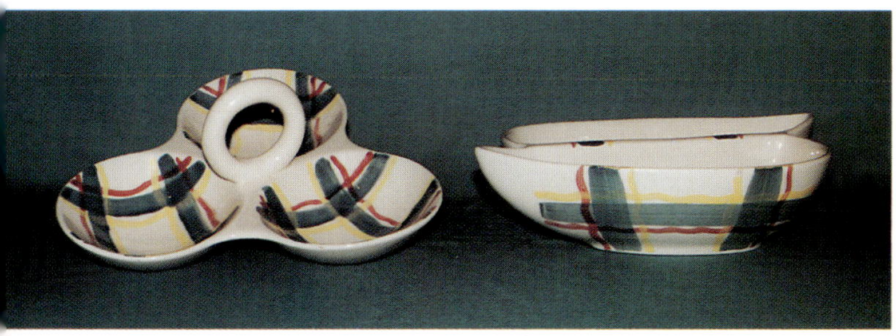

Three part relish with a ceramic handle. $30. Divided vegetable. $20.

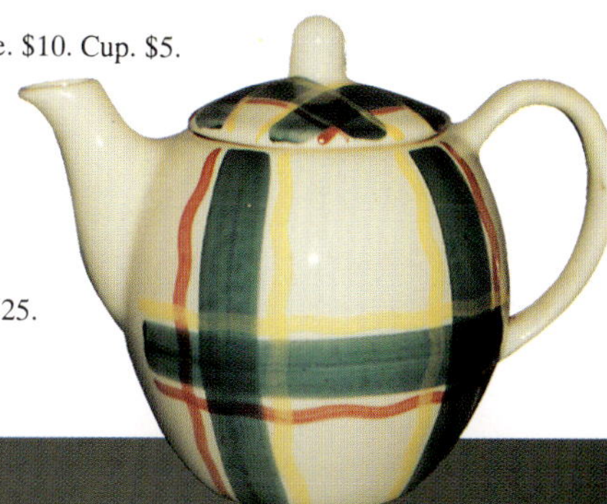

Four cup teapot. $25.

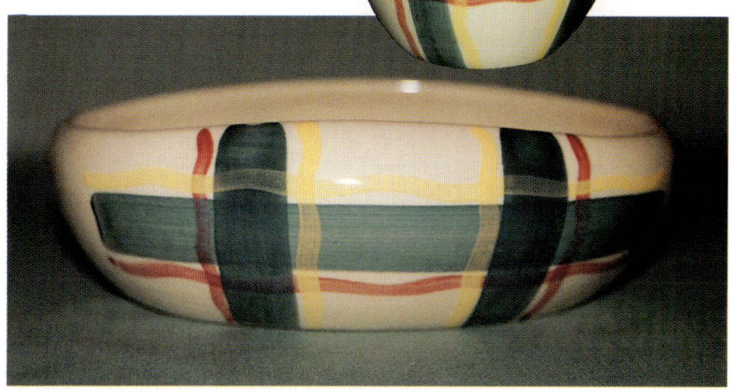

Open vegetable. $15.

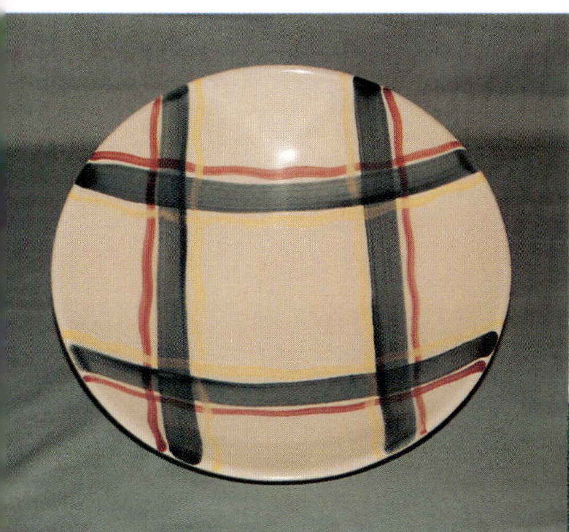

Fruit bowl. $40.

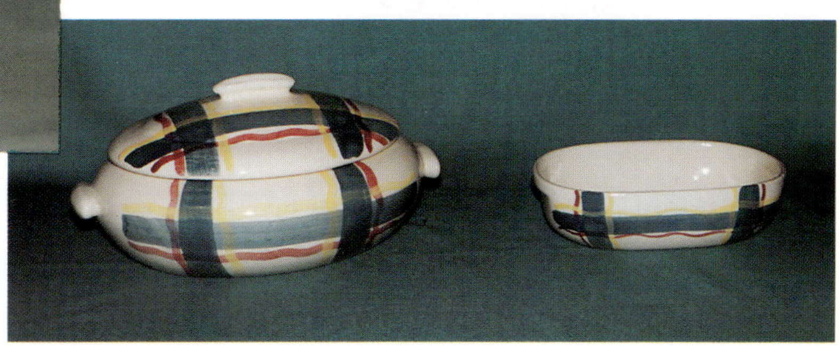

Covered vegetable. $50. Baker. $20.

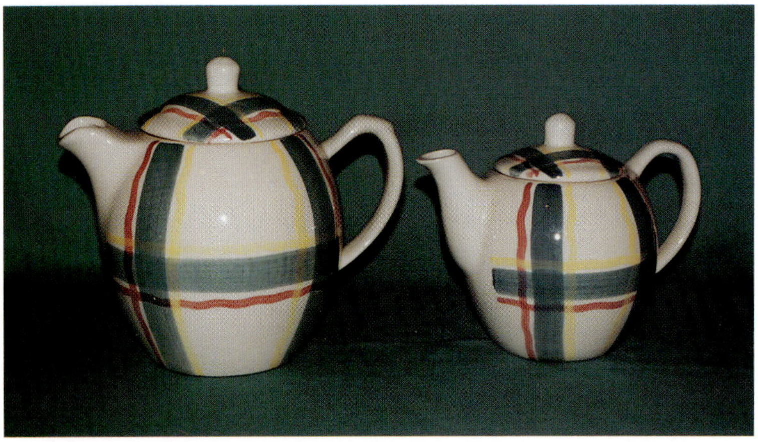

Eight cup coffee pot. $40. Six cup teapot. $25.

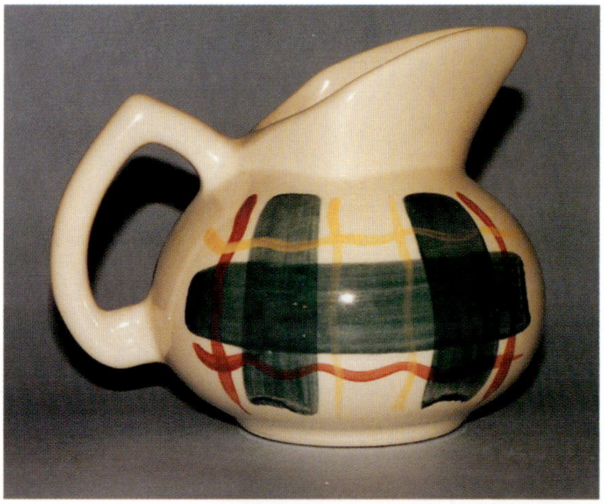

Kent jug. $30.

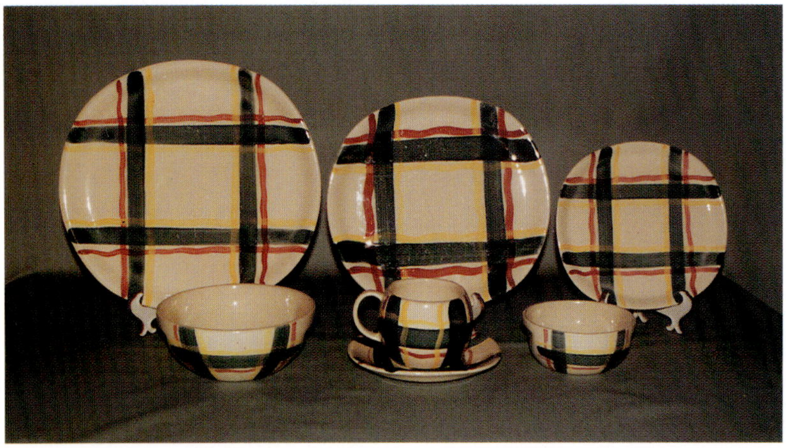

Dinner plate. $10. Breakfast plate. $10. Salad plate. $7. Cereal bowl. $7. Cup. $5. Saucer $2. Dessert bowl. $5.

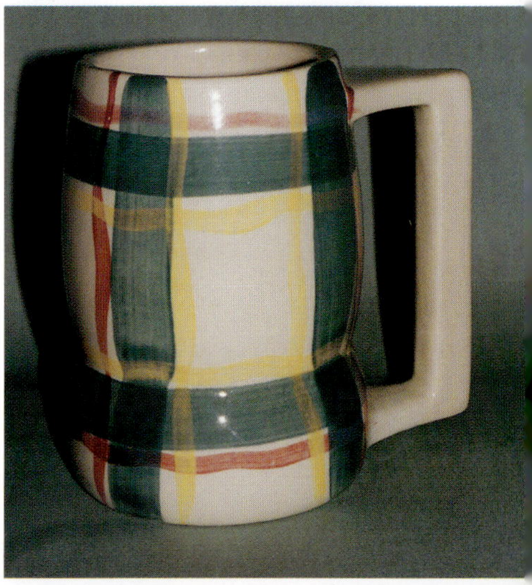

Beer mug. $40.

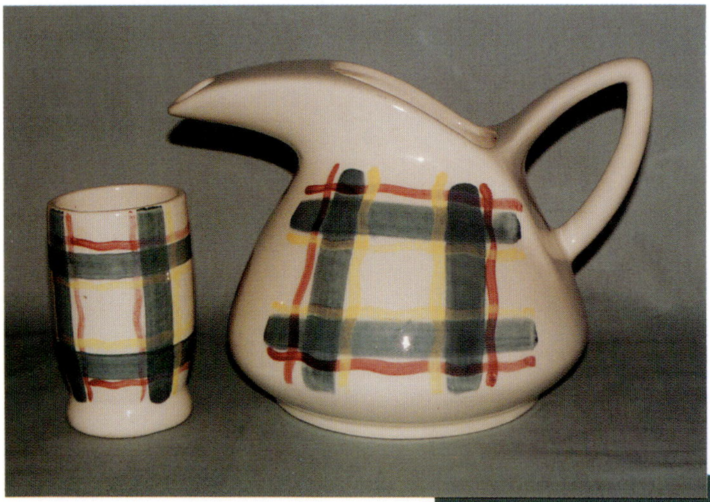

Tumbler. $20. Five pint dutch jug. $75.

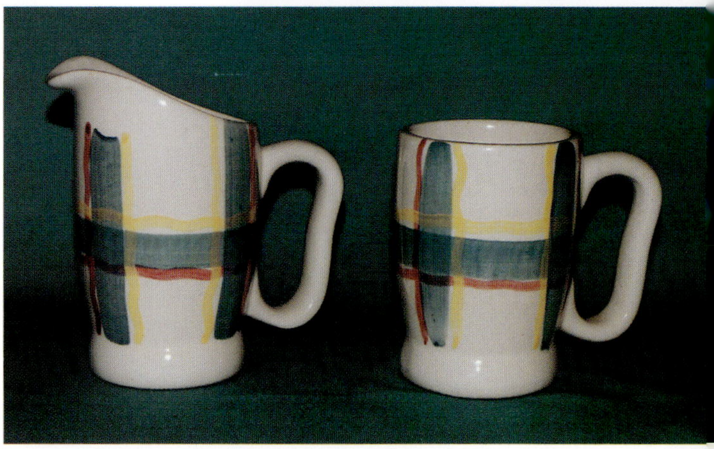

Mug jug. $50. Coffee mug. $50.

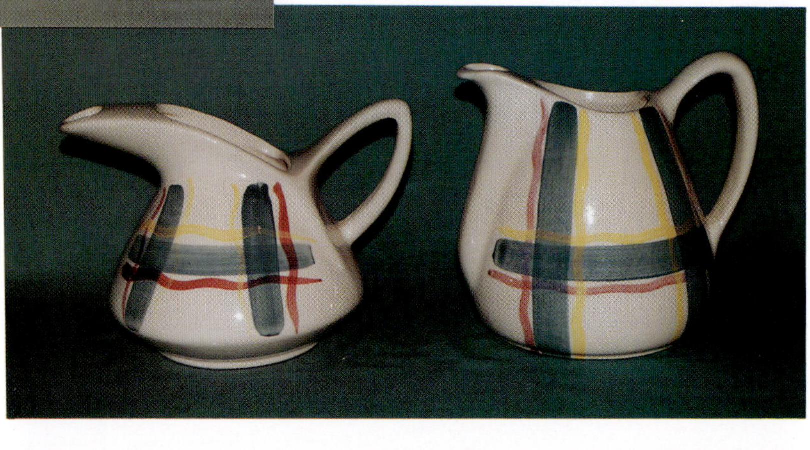

Two pint dutch jug. $45. Beverage pitcher. $50.

Miscellaneous Plaids

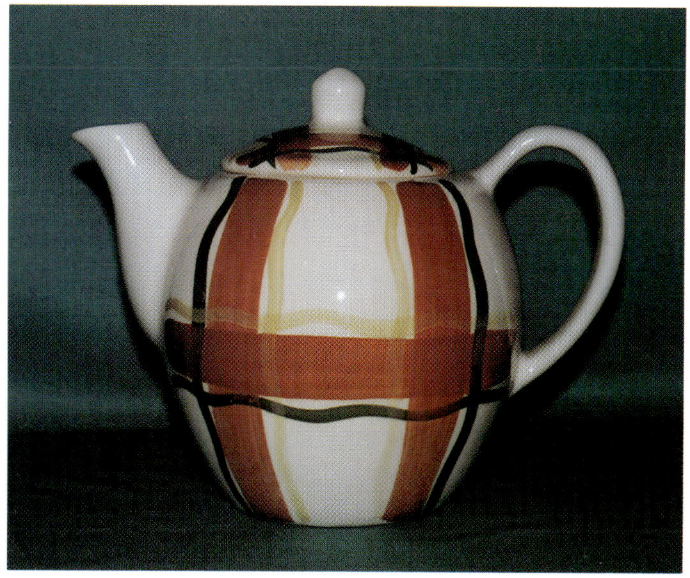

Golden Brown plaid six cup teapot. $75.

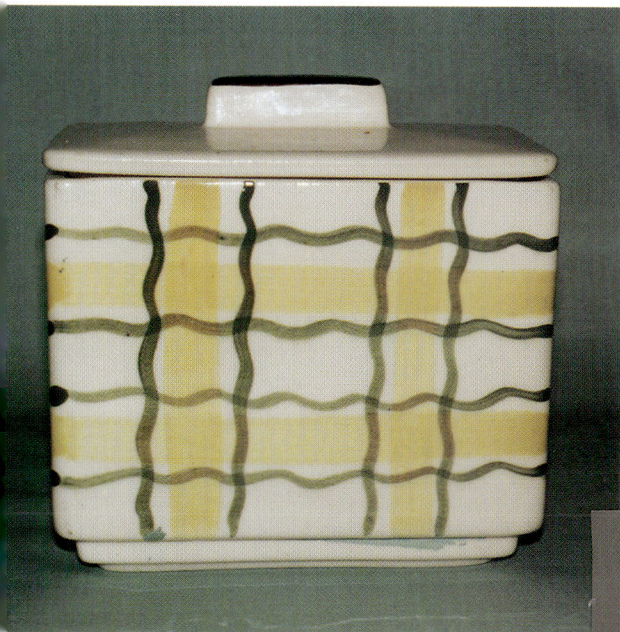

Chartreuse plaid pillow vase, short, with lid. $35.

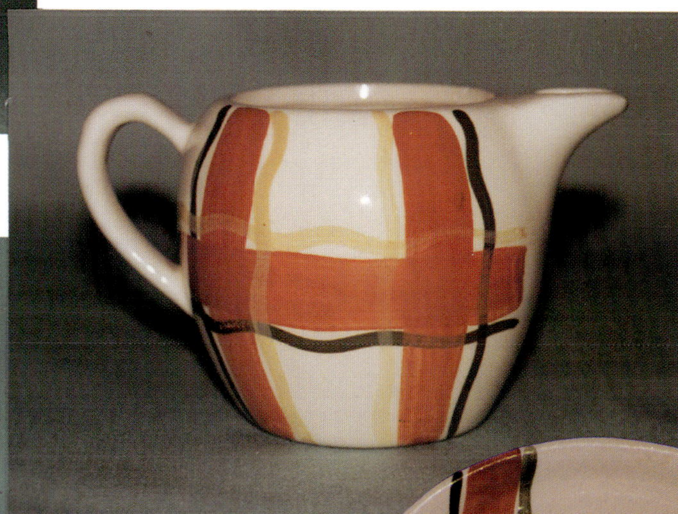

Golden Brown plaid round creamer. $35.

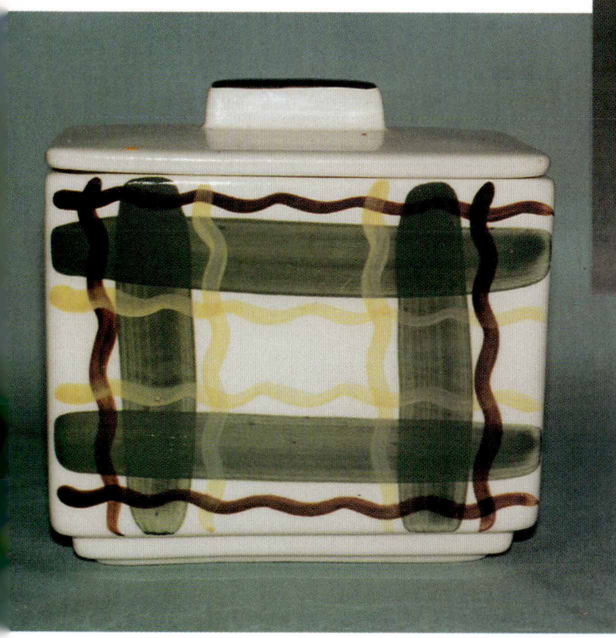

Gay Plaid pillow vase, short, with lid. $50.

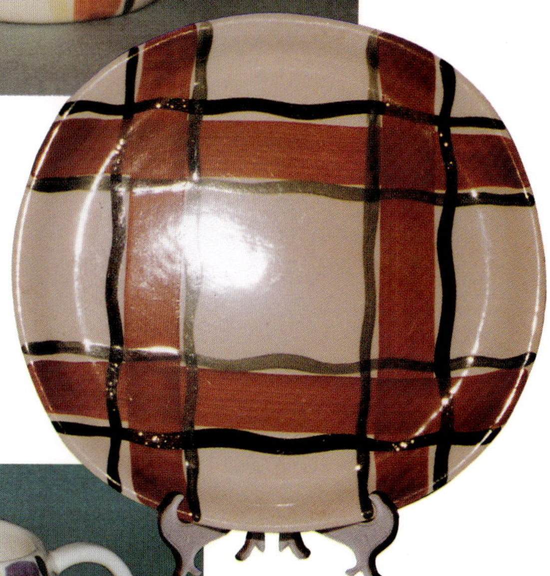

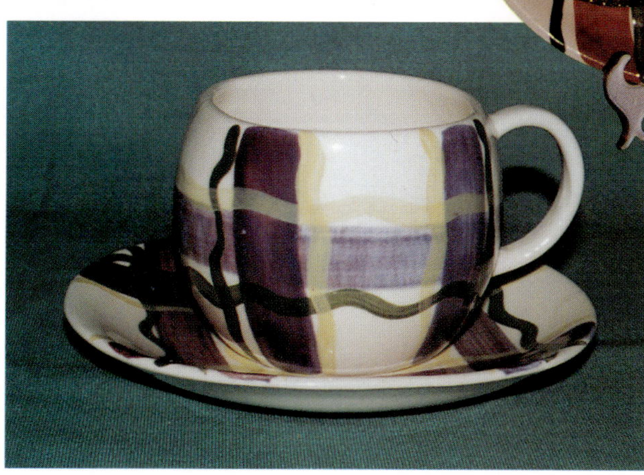

Purple plaid cup and saucer. $40 set.

Petals

The Petals pattern was made to fill a contract with Sears, Roebuck and Company. However, a new Sears buyer subsequently rejected the pattern, buying only what had been boxed and shipped. The Tionesta plant was responsible for the contract work and not much was made after the contract was lost. Its cobalt blue and red flower with teal leaves make it an attractive and desirable pattern.

The supply is limited and demand is fairly strong. The dinnerware is very difficult to find and only a few pieces are known, most of which are dinner plates. Any of the serving items are in demand. Ironically, the Petals honey jug was mass produced as a floral vase and is very common. Finding any item beyond what is pictured would be rare.

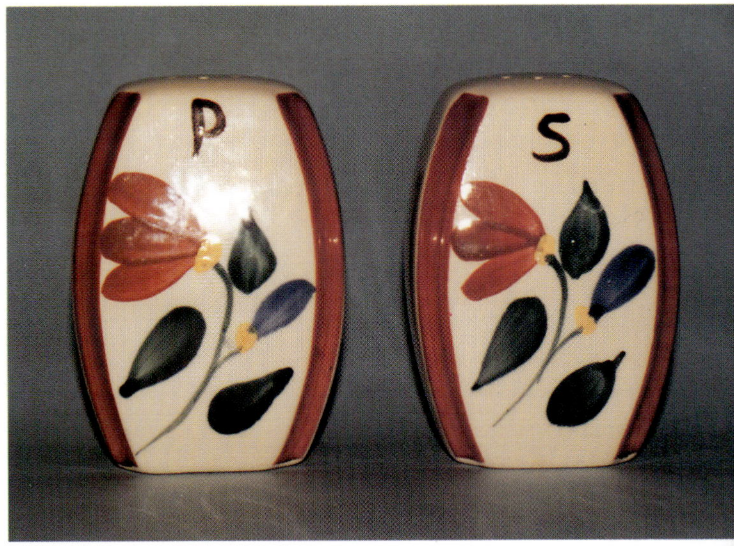

Range salt and pepper shakers. $100 set.

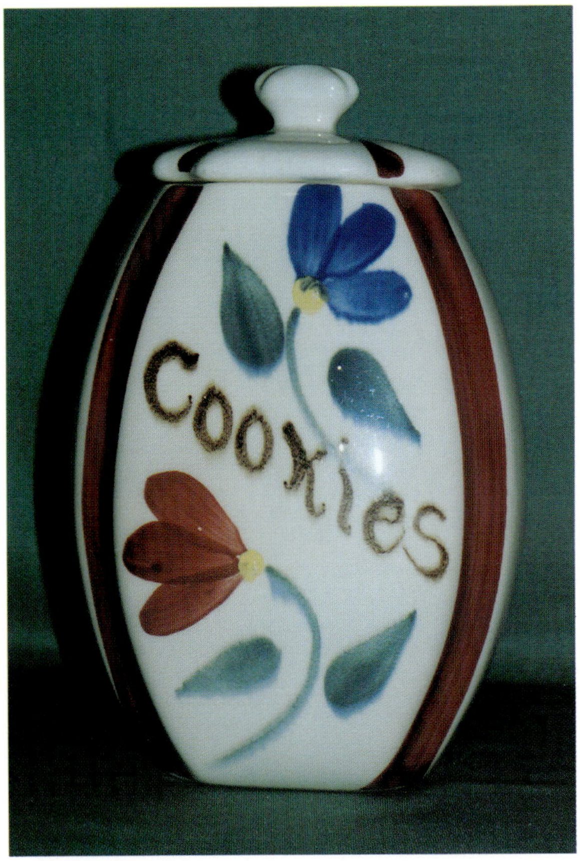

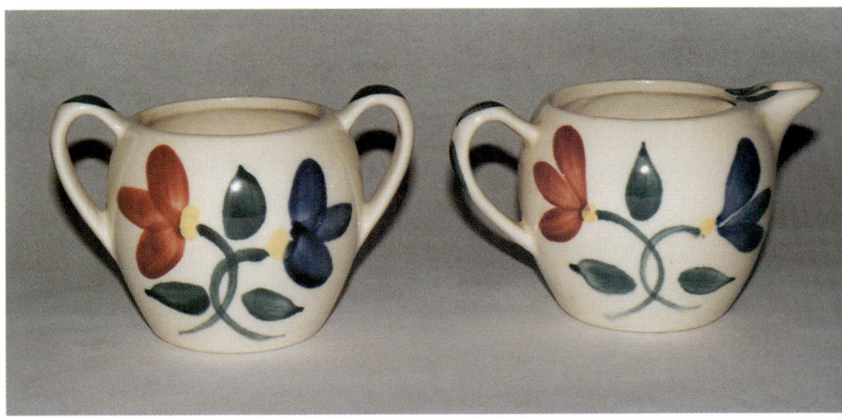

Round sugar (lid not pictured) and creamer. $75 set.

Petals tall oval cookies jar. $125.

Jug style salt and pepper shakers. $50 set.

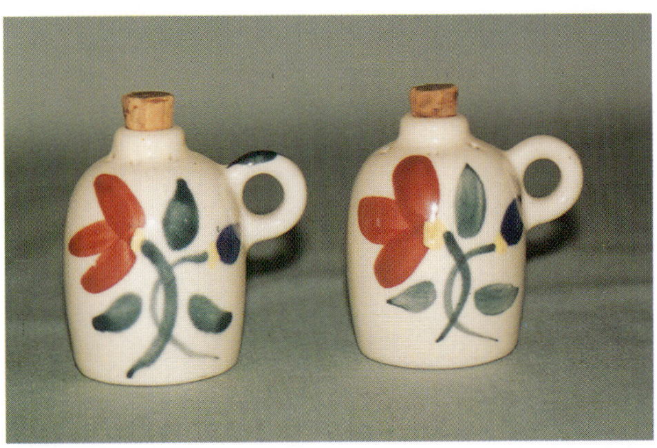

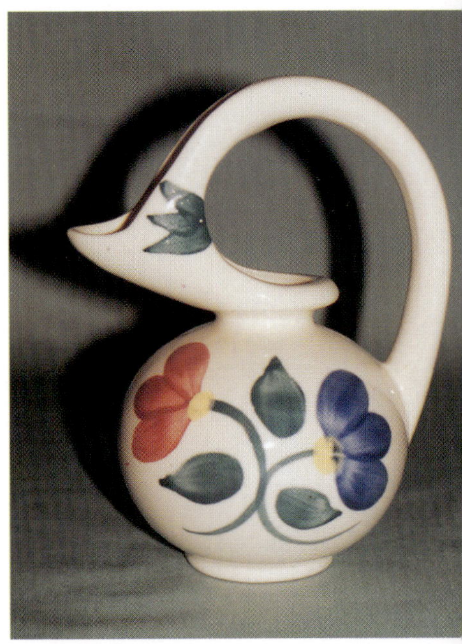

Honey jug, very common. $15.

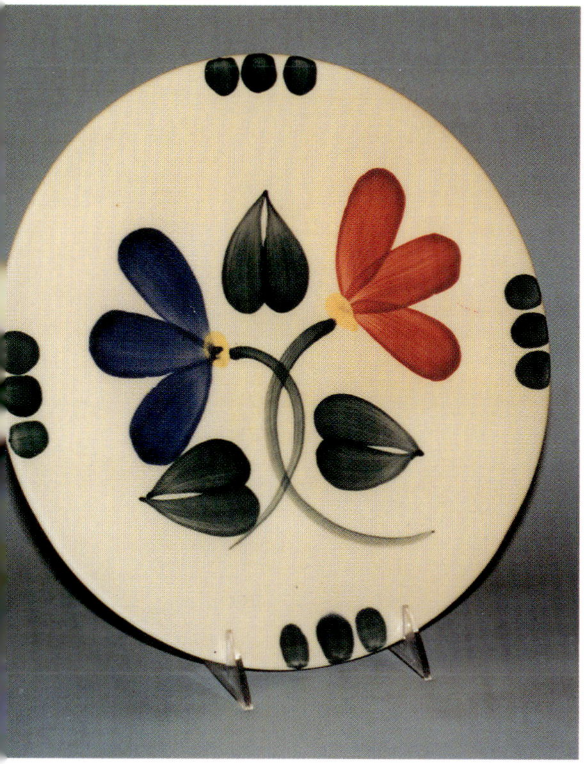

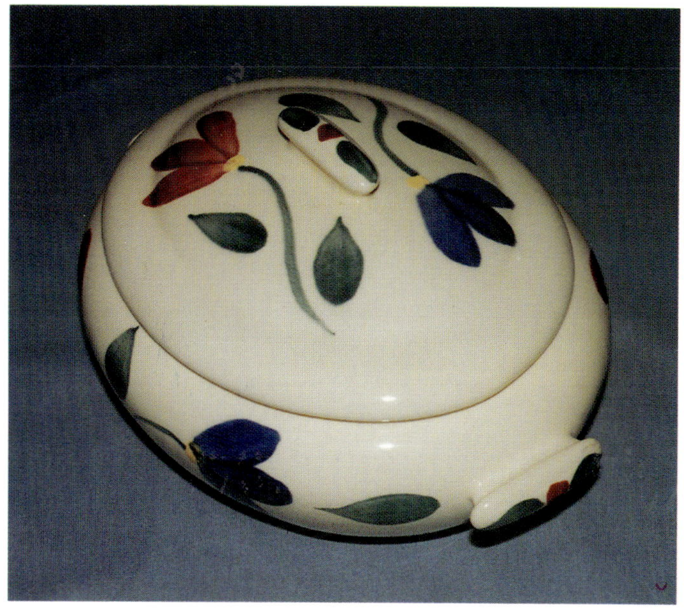

Covered vegetable. $150.

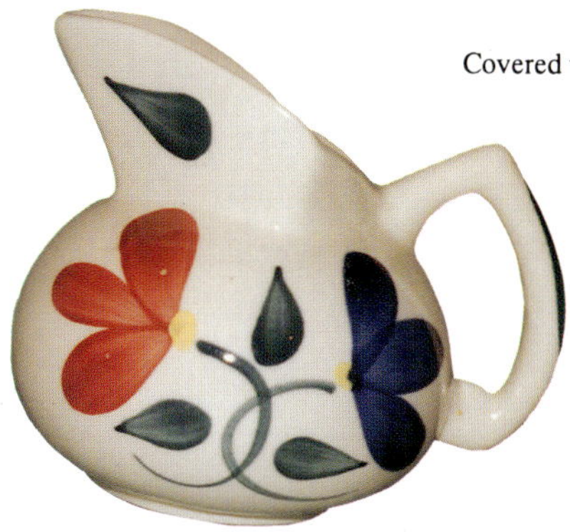

Chop plate. $250.

Kent jug. $100.

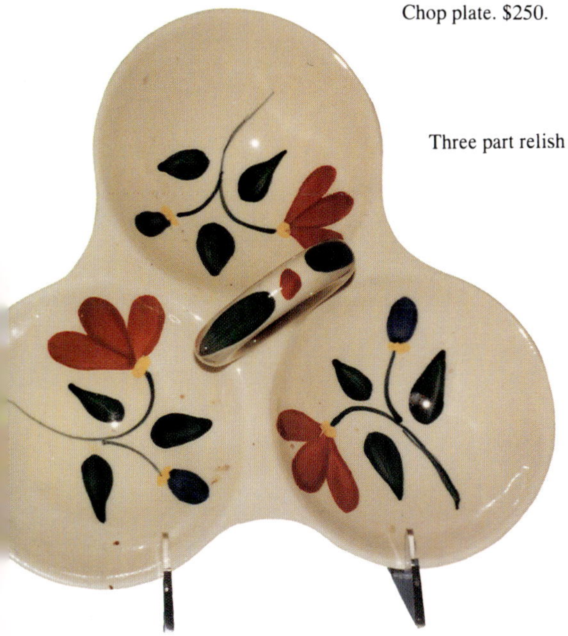

Three part relish with a ceramic handle. $100.

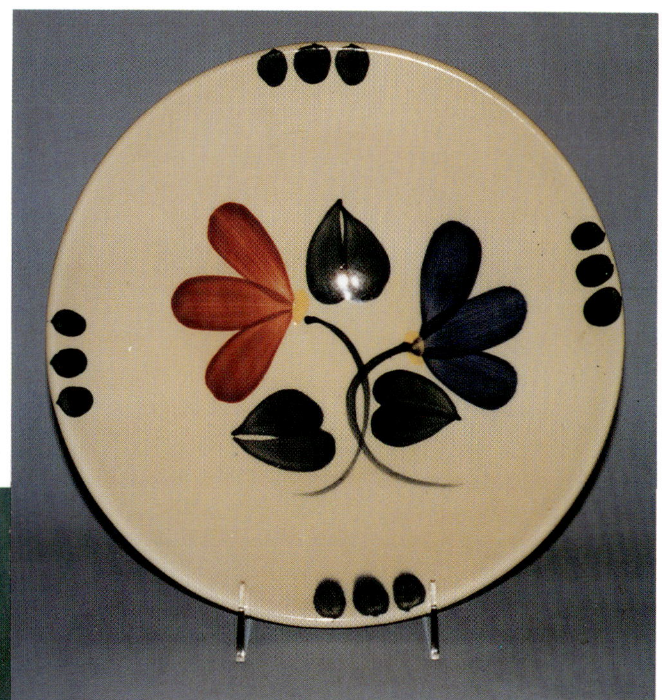

Fruit bowl. $150.

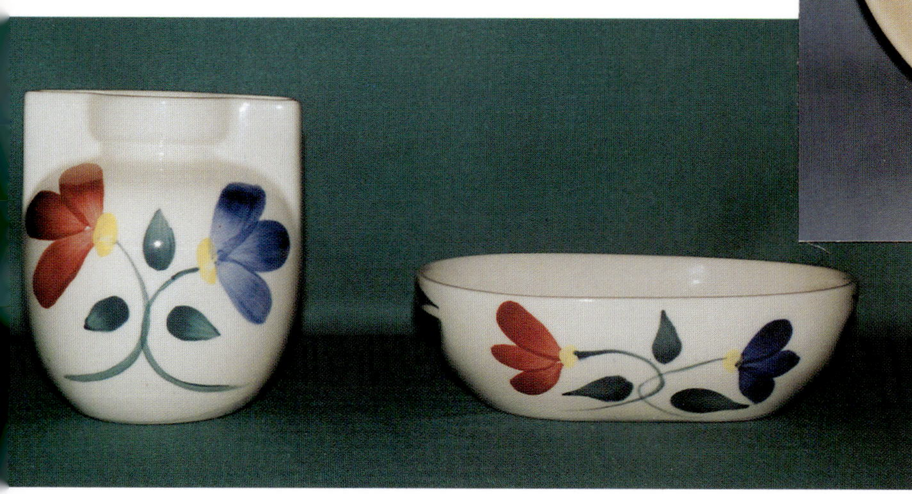

Winged vase (with lid would be grease jar). $75.
Baker. $50.

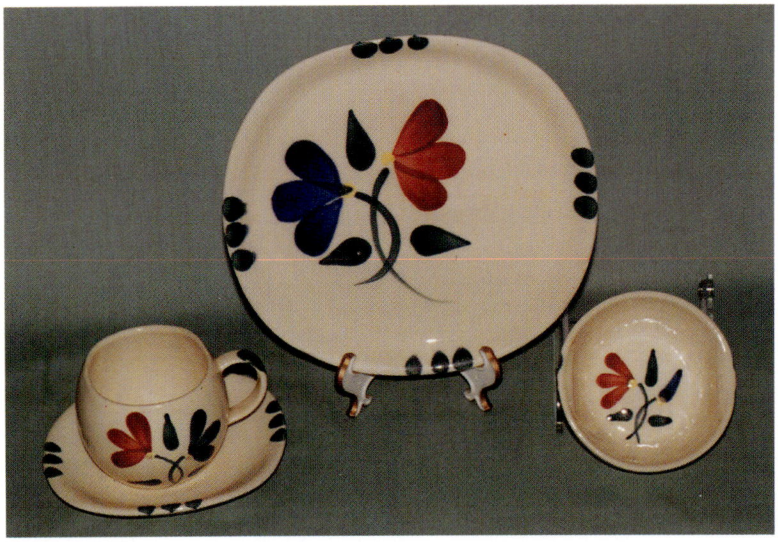

Cup. $50. Saucer. $10. Breakfast plate. $60. Dessert bowl. $40.

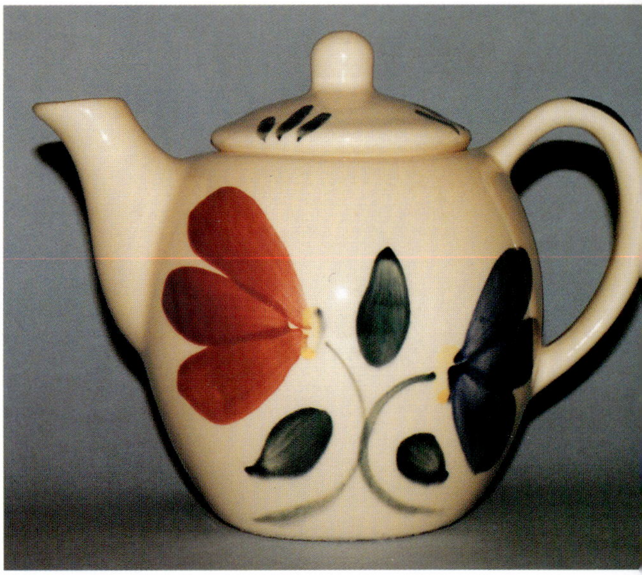

Six cup teapot. $70.

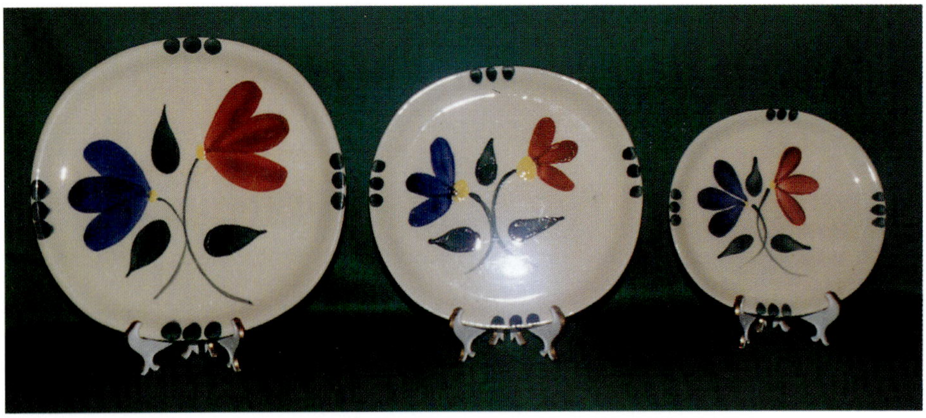

Dinner plate (rare). $75. Breakfast plate. $60. Salad plate. $50.

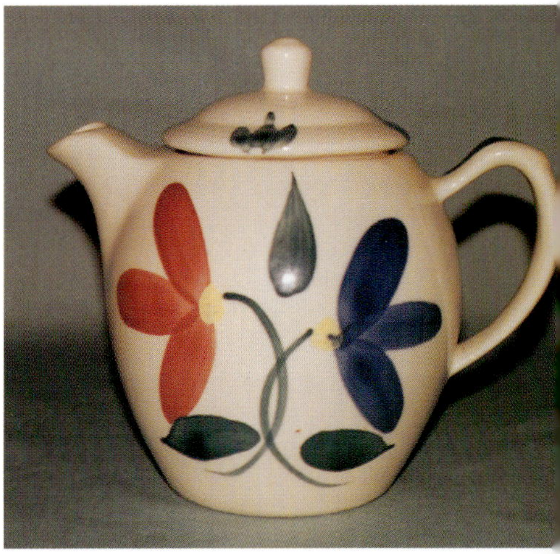

Eight cup coffee pot. $100.

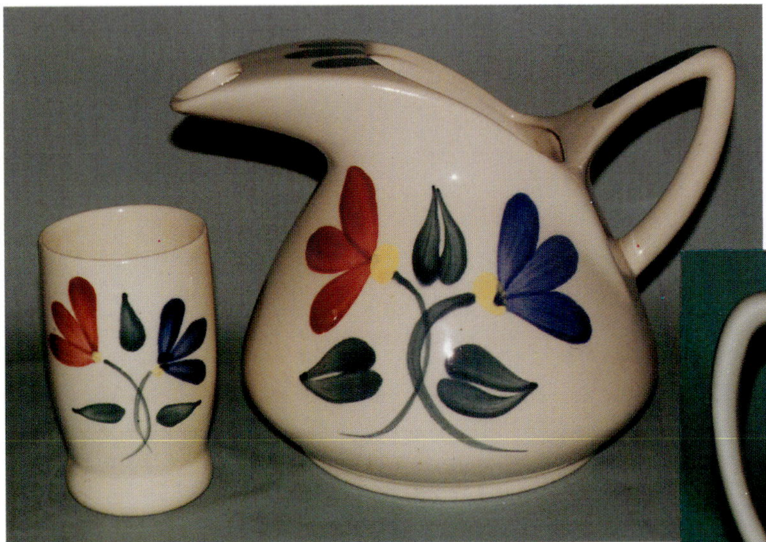

Tumbler. $35. Five pint dutch jug. $125.

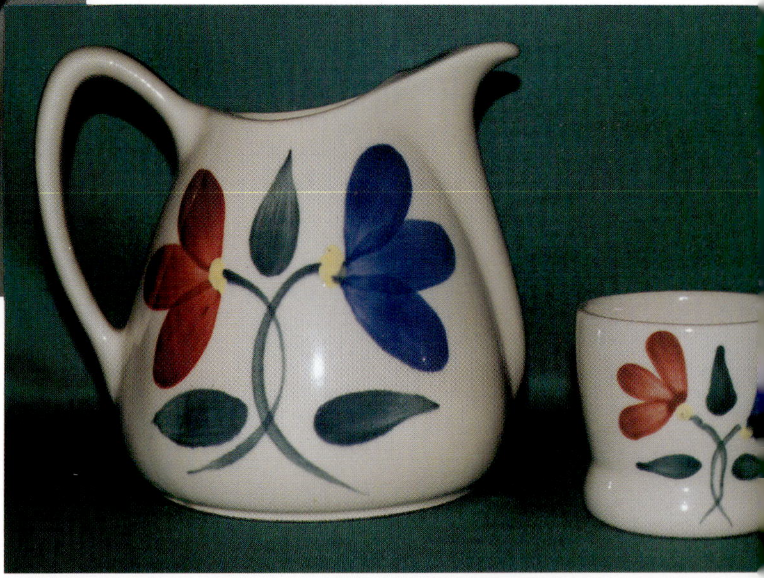

Beverage pitcher. $125. Juice mug. $25.

Pennsylvania Dutch

Pennsylvania Dutch is probably the most collected pattern next to Apple. Purinton introduced a few variations in the late 1940s but not until the early 1950s did we see the pink and blue design. Developed by Dorothy Purinton, Pennsylvania Dutch offers a warm country folk art look that Dorothy used in many of her decorations. Pennsylvania Dutch demand has increased in recent years and it is being sought after by even more collectors because of its appealing design.

The heart and tulip are synonymous with the pattern. The heart is seen less on products and commands a slightly higher price. Dinnerware has become more available but people demand the accessory pieces. Some pricing has been open ended as the market for it changes. Desirable pieces include the canister sets, wide oval cookies jars, coffee pots, six cup domed lid teapots, and beverage pitchers. Dinner plates with the heart are also very difficult to find. More common items include the honey jug, jug style salt and pepper shaker, and the square cookie canister with the wooden lid. A few odd pieces have surfaced and were not made for production. They were probably either experimental items or employee "take home" pieces.

Variation in color is also a factor. Some of the older wares were painted with a darker blue and red color. Some designs have variations including added hearts or birds familiar to Pennsylvania Dutch history.

Prices for the Pennsylvania Dutch pattern are very high as it is in low supply and high demand. Some items have open ended prices in anticipation of market changes. Prices attained in the past may begin to drop as more items are discovered. Either way, Pennsylvania Dutch will continue to be a favorite pattern among collectors.

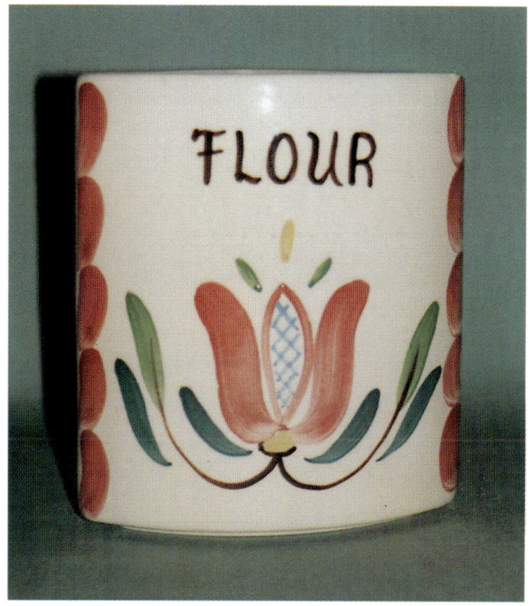

Revolving canister wedge. $100 *If complete, a four section set of Pennsylvania Dutch canister set with a wooden base and lid is worth $600+.

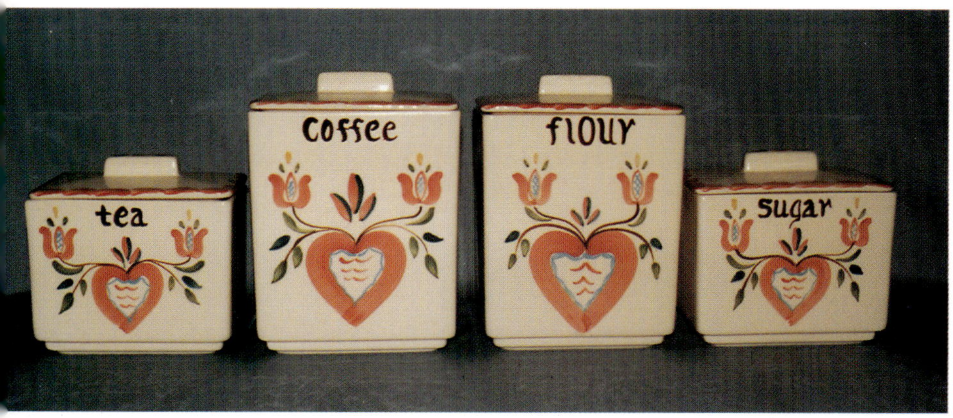

Pennsylvania Dutch four piece apartment canister set. $250+ each.

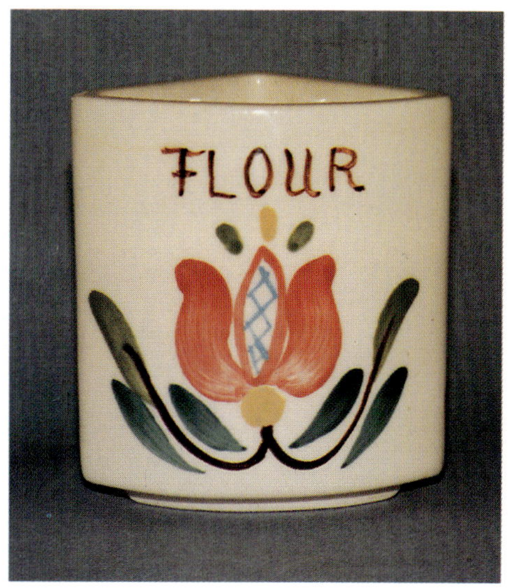

Miniature revolving canister wedge. Only miniature section known. $200.

Four piece square canister set with wooden lids. $125 each.

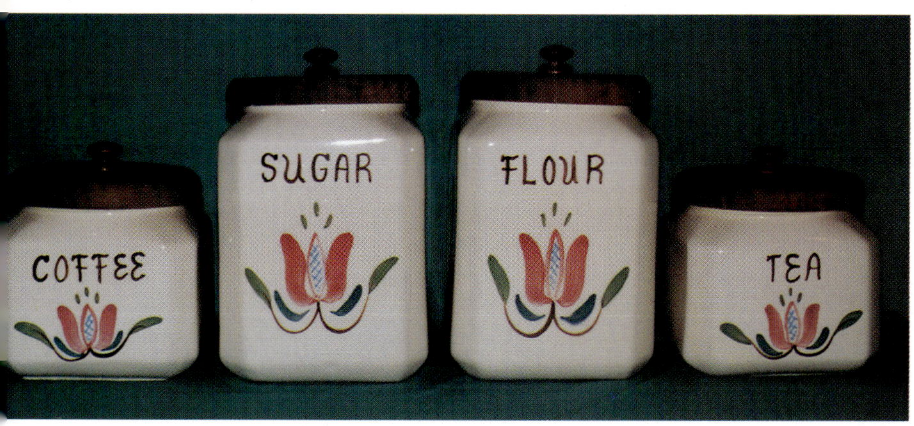

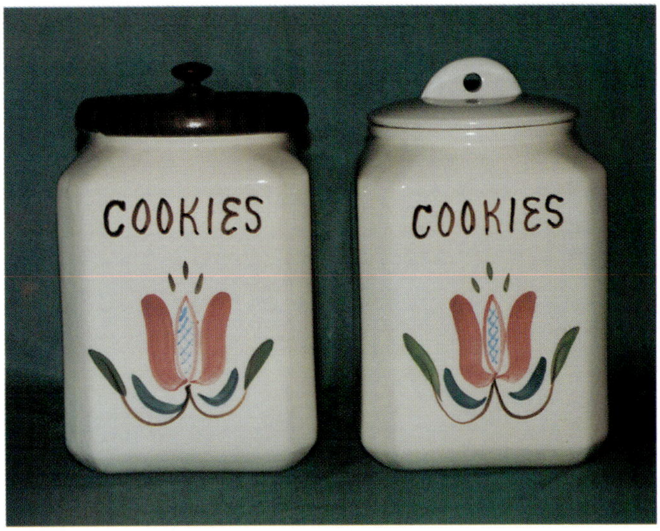

Square cookies jar with a wooden lid. $100. Square cookies jar with a ceramic lid. $125.

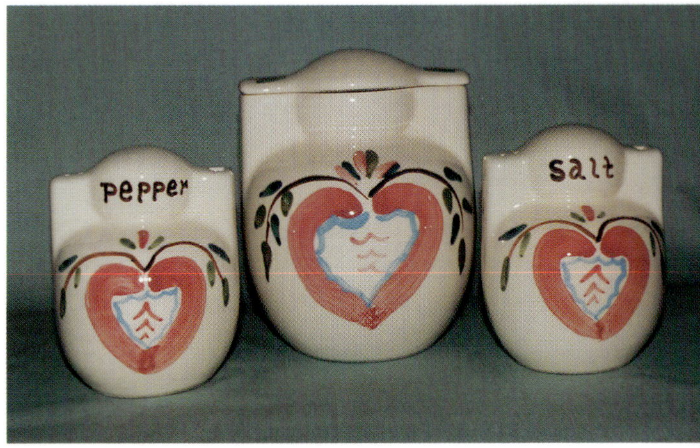

Pour and shake salt and pepper. $125 set. Covered winged grease jar. $175.

Five piece pour and shake set: salt and pepper $125 set, sugar $150, cin. + sugar $150, flour $150.

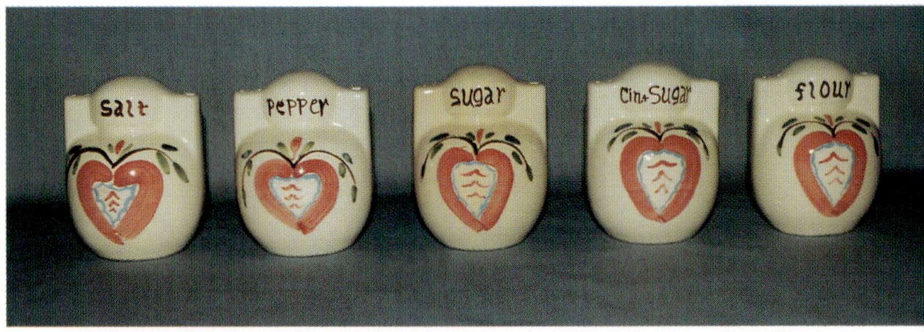

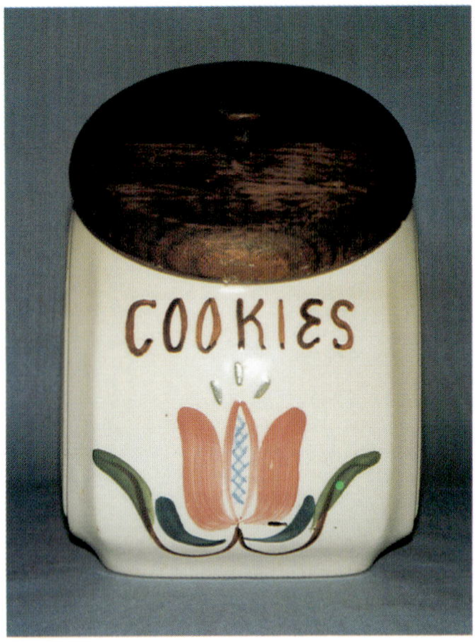

Slant front cookies jar with a wooden lid, unknown mold. $250.

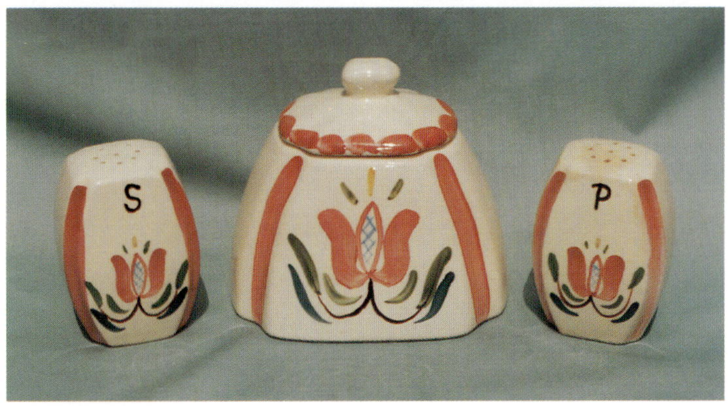

Range salt and pepper shakers. $175 set. Range covered grease jar. $175.

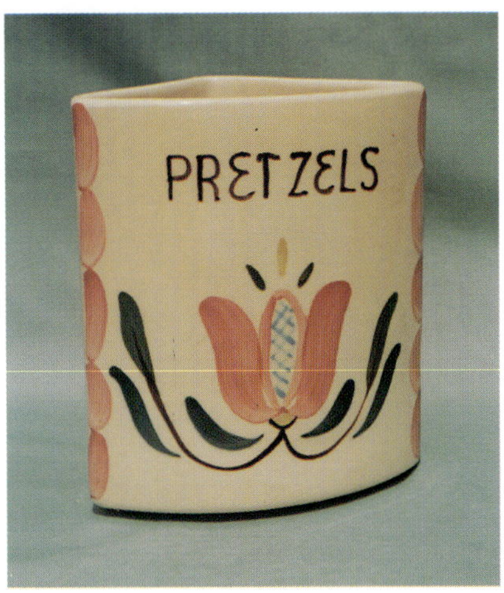

Revolving canister wedge. $100.

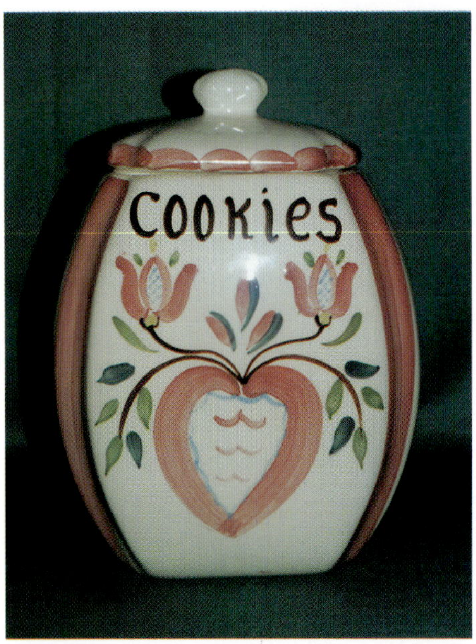

Wide oval cookies jar. $500+.

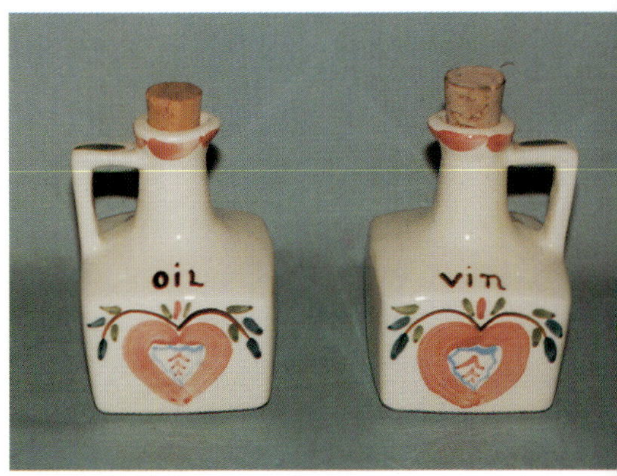

Square oil and vinegar. $150 set.

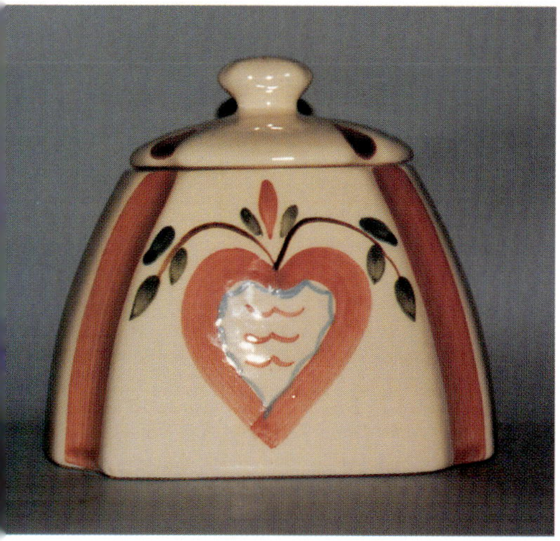

Range covered grease jar with heart decoration. $225.

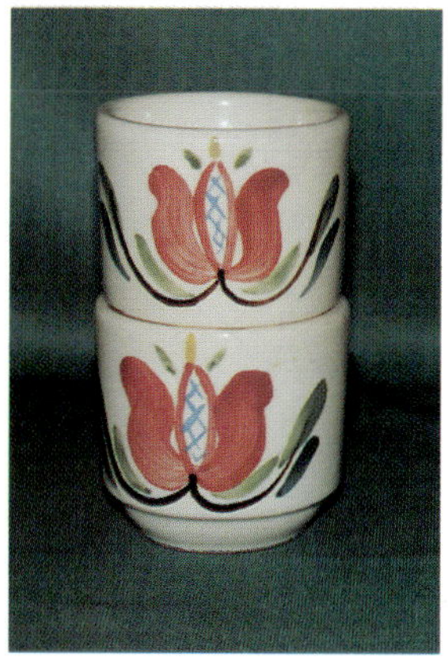

Stacking salt and pepper. $150 set.

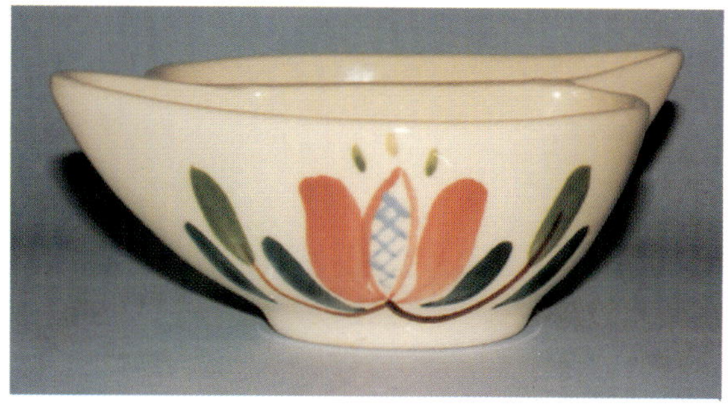

Nut dish. $125.

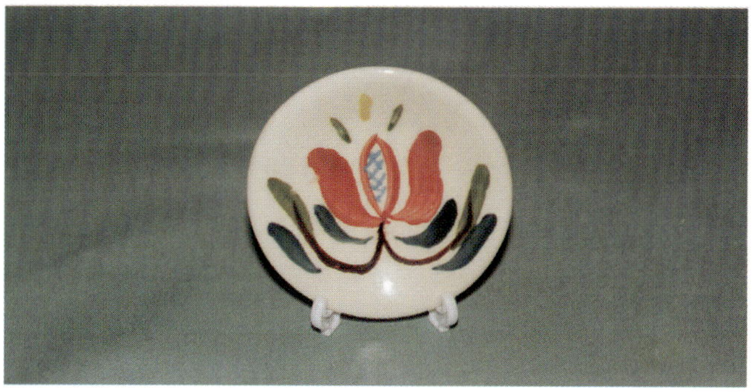

Whimsy butter pat. Dated 9-16-59 on the back. The significance of this date is unknown at this time. $100.

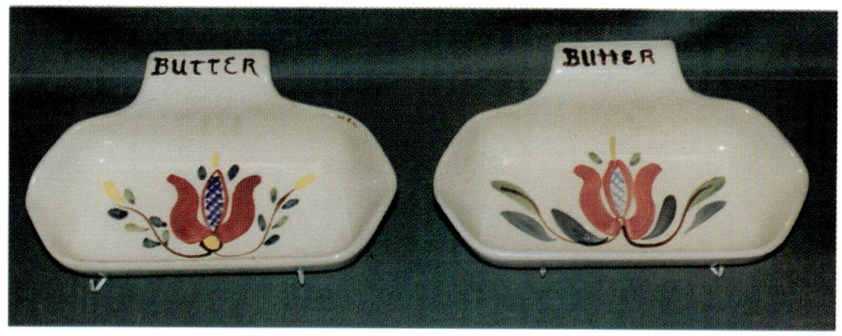

Butter dish with Pennsylvania Dutch variation. $300+. Butter dish. $300+.

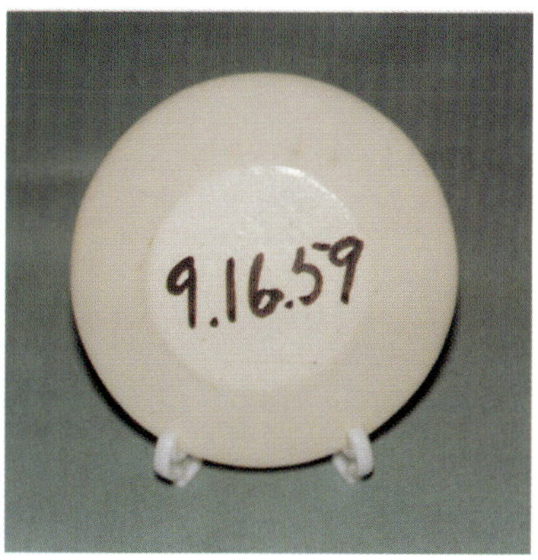

Reverse of whimsy butter pat. Dated 9-16-59.

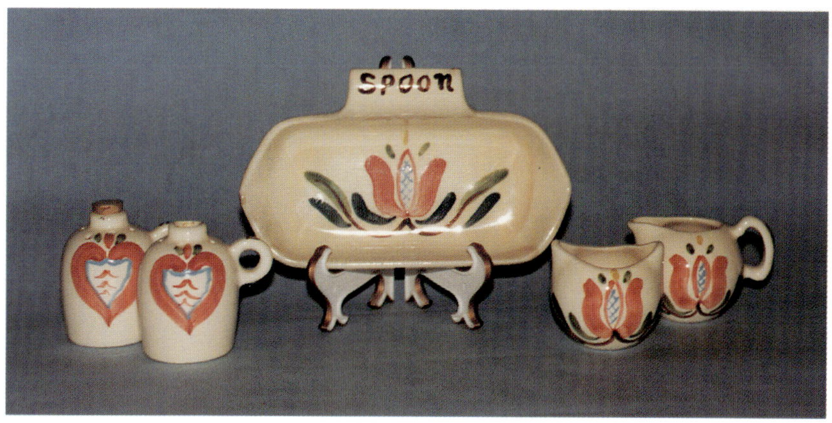

Jug style salt and pepper shakers. $80 set. Spoon rest made out of a butter dish. $400+. Individual sugar and creamer. $125 set.

Covered sugar and creamer. $125 set.

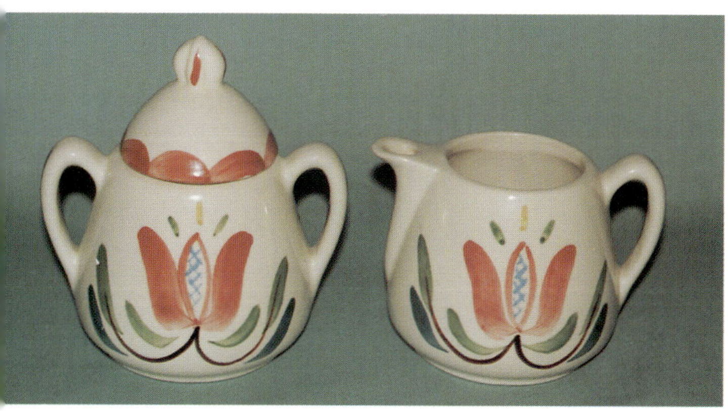

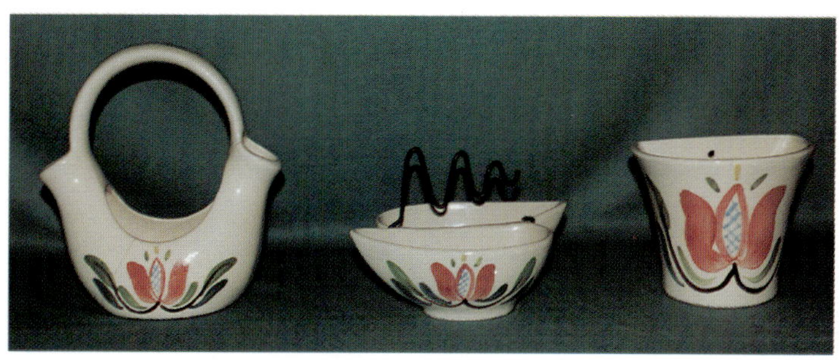

Basket planter. $150. Ashtray. $125. Wall pocket. $175.

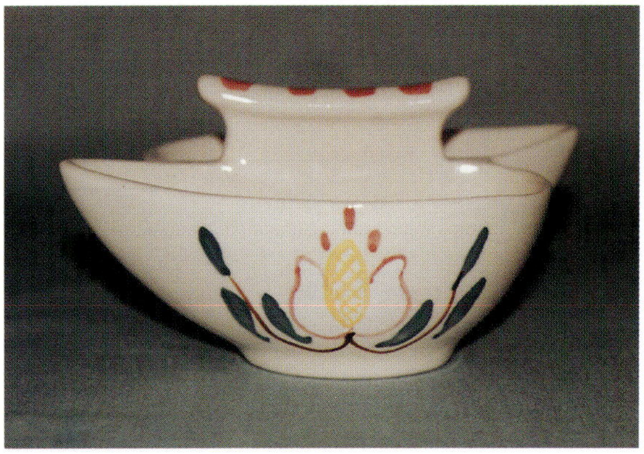

Jam and jelly with white coloration inside the tulip (a variation). $200.

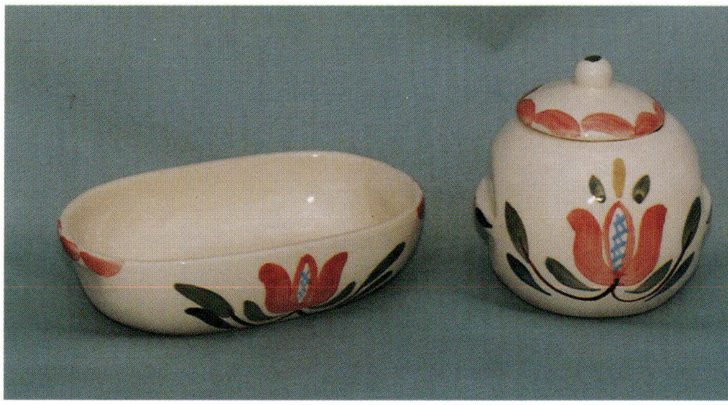

Pickle. $75. Individual bean pot. $150.

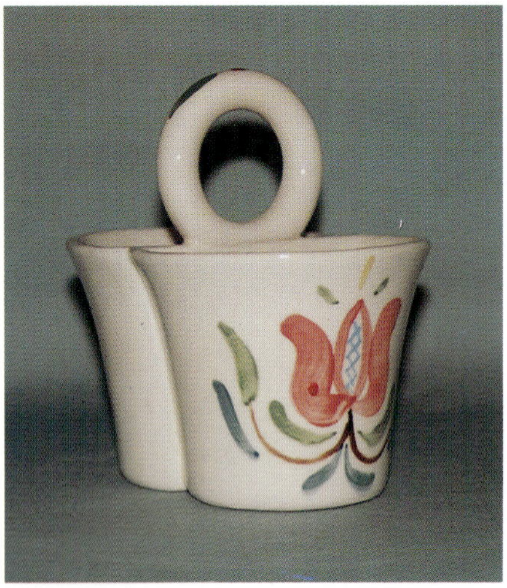

Candy dish. $150+.

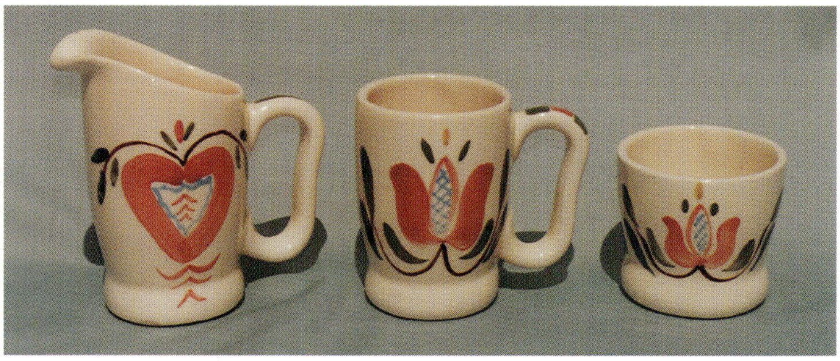

Mug jug. $200. Coffee mug. $100. Juice mug. $50.

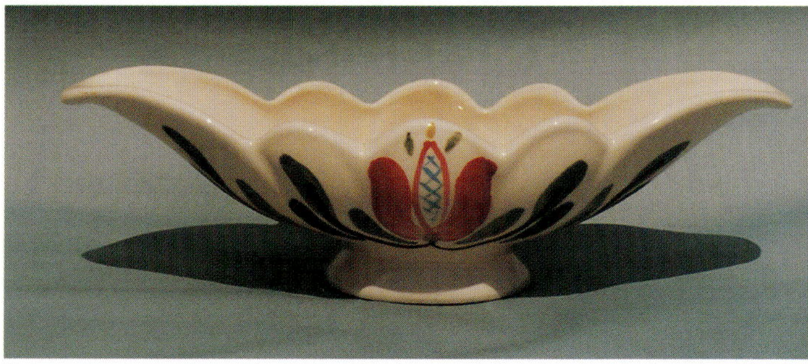

Console bowl, NAPCO mold. $300.

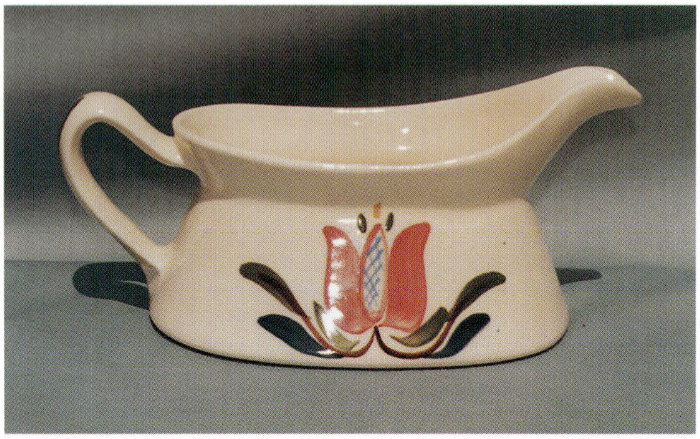

Gravy boat, Taylor Smith Taylor mold. $200+.

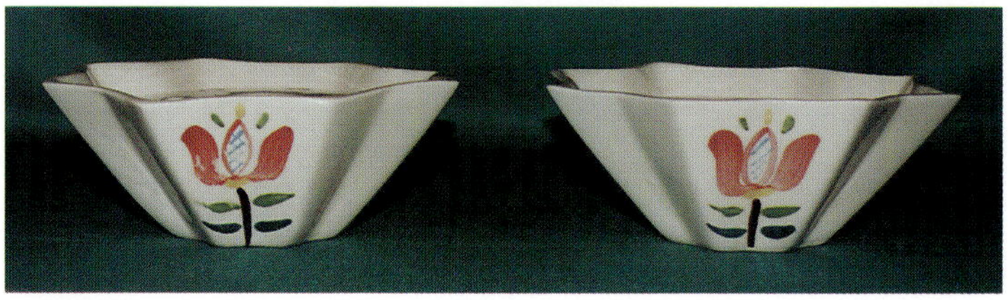

Star candle holders with inserts. $500 set.

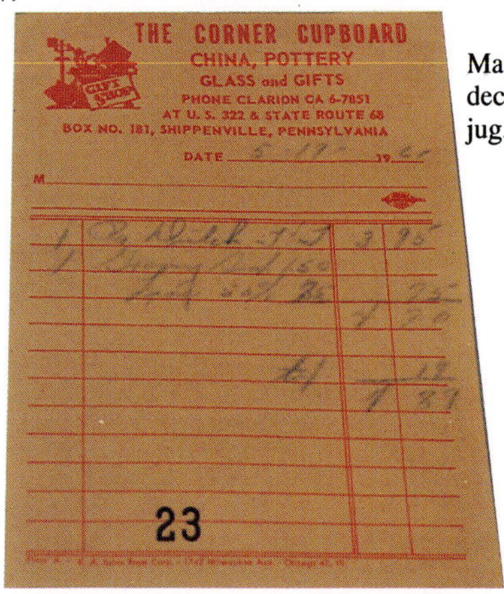

THE CORNER CUPBOARD
CHINA, POTTERY
GLASS and GIFTS
PHONE CLARION CA 6-7851
AT U. S. 322 & STATE ROUTE 68
BOX NO. 181, SHIPPENVILLE, PENNSYLVANIA

DATE 5-19- 19 61

M

23

Original receipt for a Pennsylvania Dutch tea and toast plate ($3.95) and gravy boat (only $.75 at half price). Sold at the Corner Cupboard in Shippenville, Pennsylvania. Notice the date of May 19, 1961, almost two years after the closing of the plant.

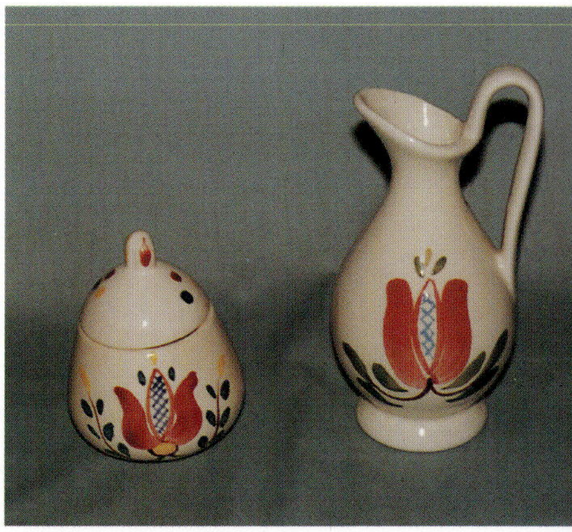

Marmalade jar with variant decoration. $150. Rebecca jug. $200.

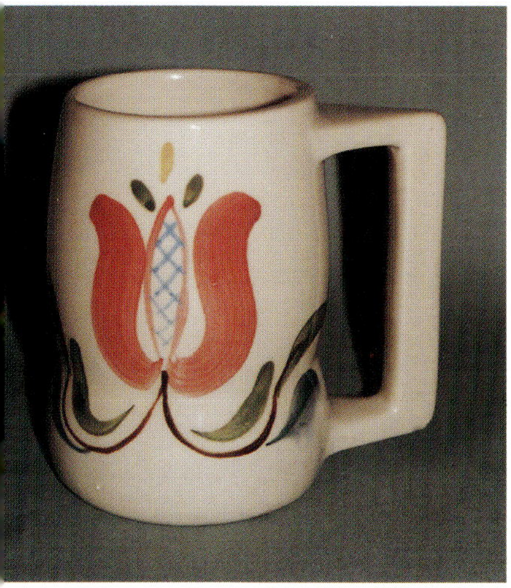

Beer mug. $125.

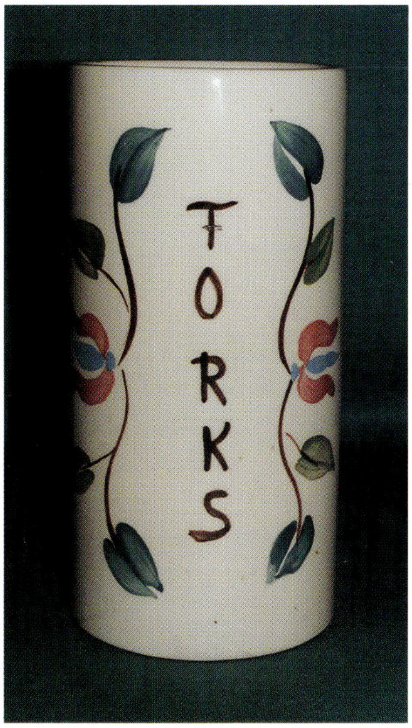

Whimsy "forks" holder. $150.

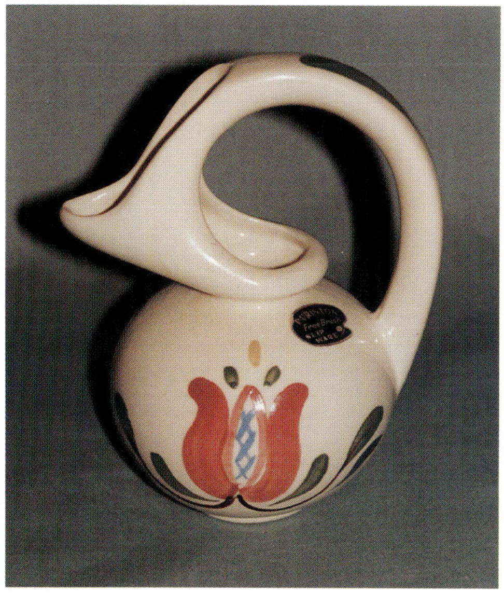

Honey jug. Note original sticker. $100.

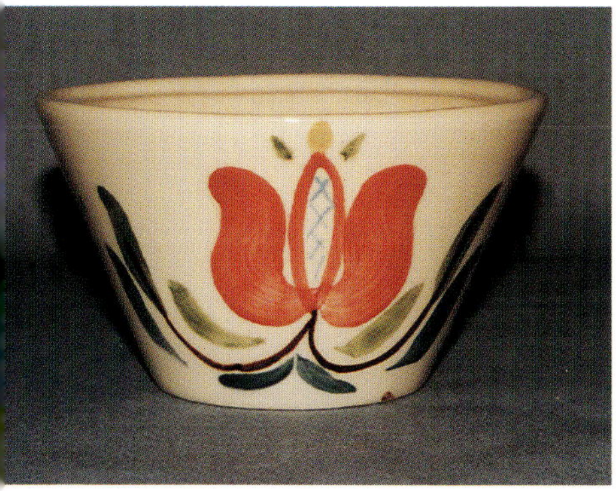

Round candle holder with insert. $300.

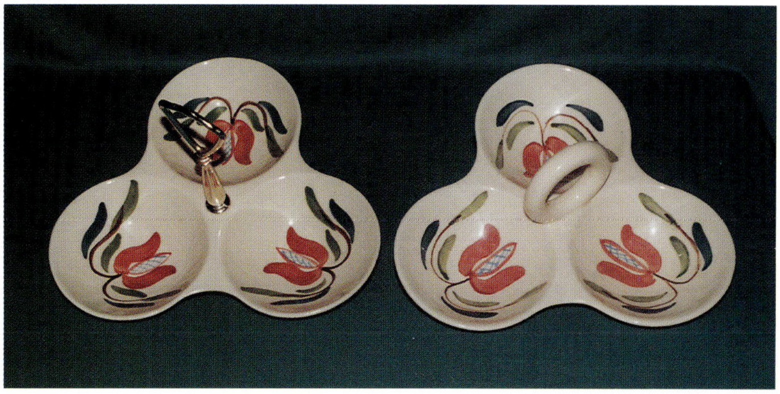

Three part relish with a metal handle. $125. Three part relish with ceramic handle. $125.

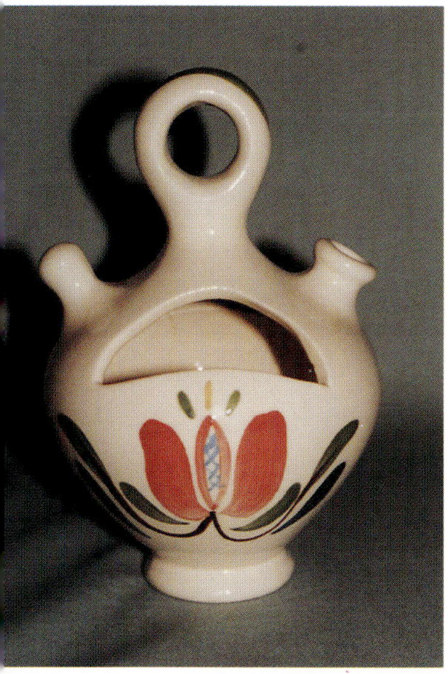

Rum jug planter. $250.

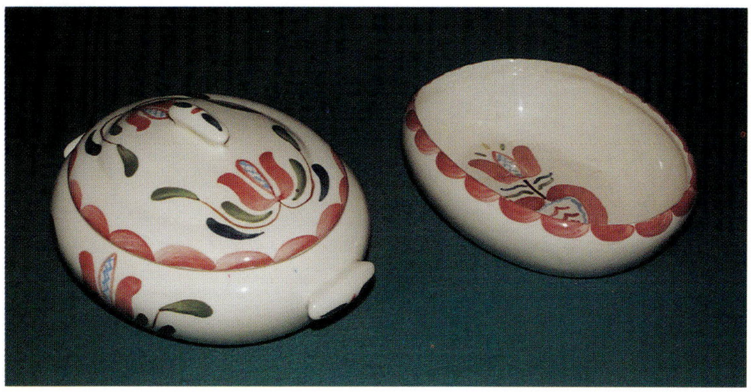

Covered vegetable. $300+. Open vegetable. $100.

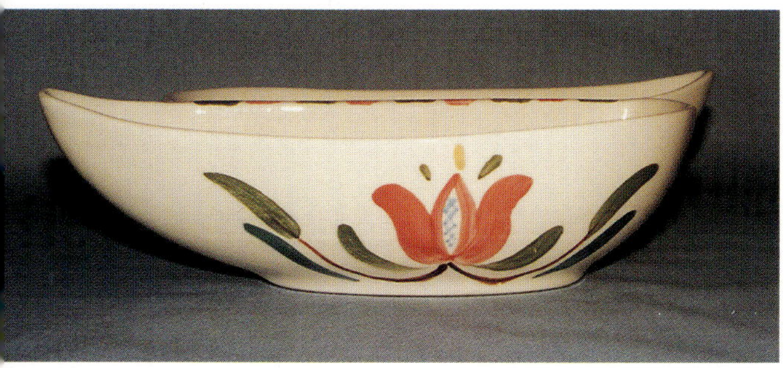

Divided vegetable. $125.

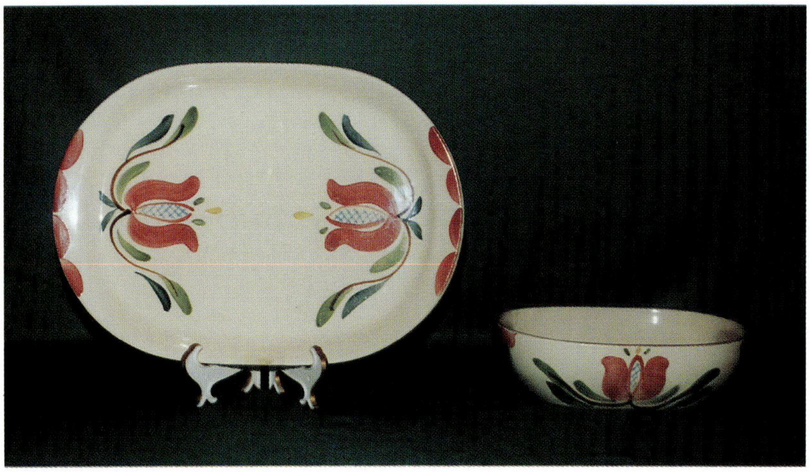

Large platter. $175. Baker. $125.

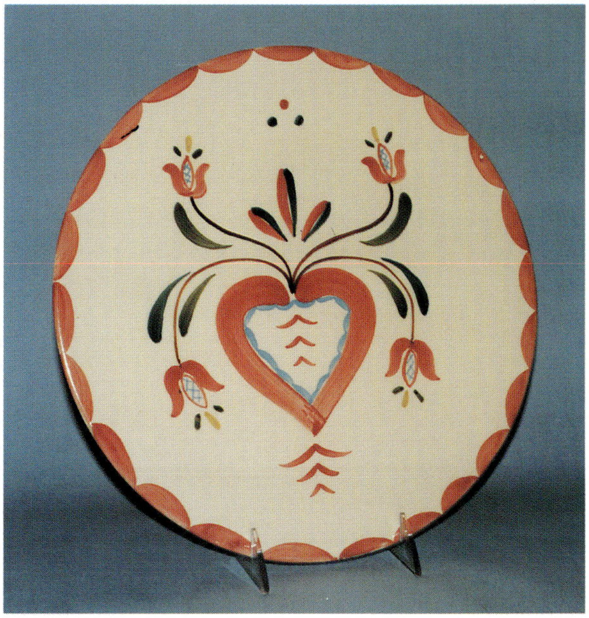

Chop plate, Pennsylvania Dutch variant. $450+.

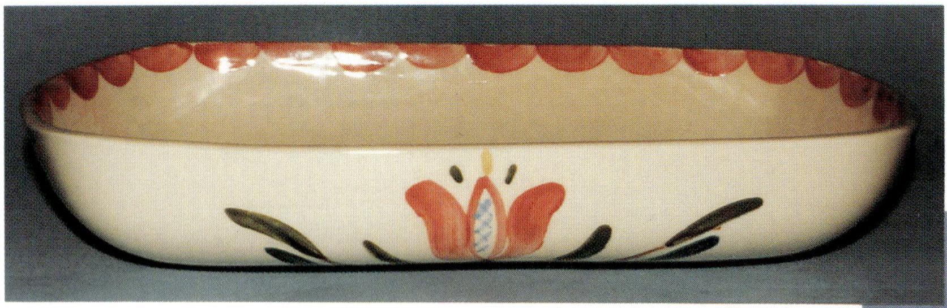

Roll tray. $125.

Sandwich plate. $150.

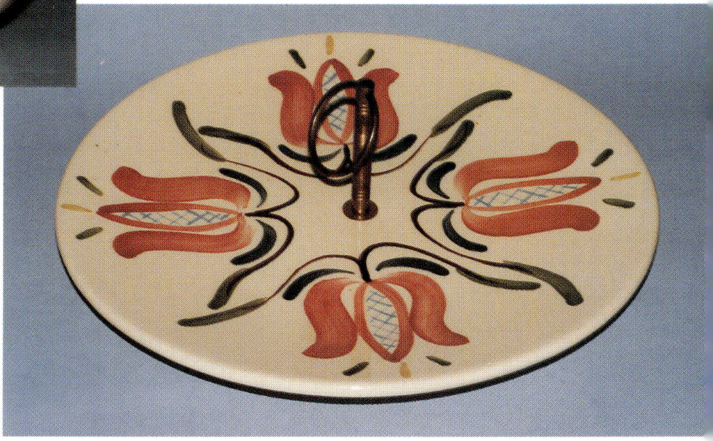

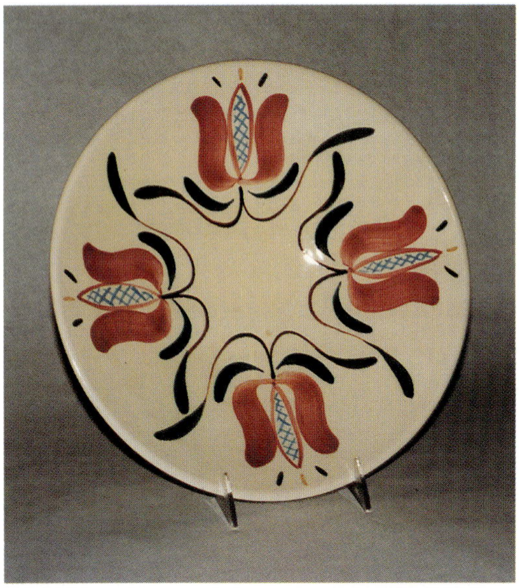

Fruit bowl. $300+.

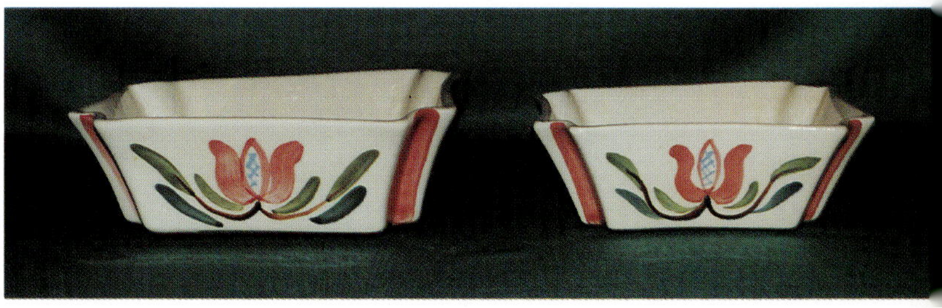

Candy dish, 6", NAPCO mold. $150. Candy dish, 5", NAPCO mold. $150.

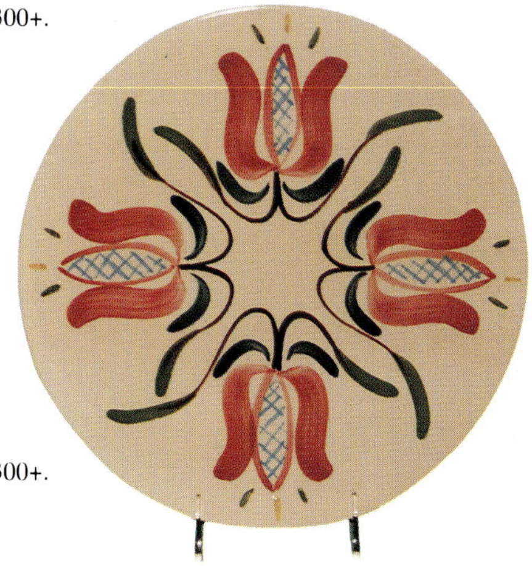

Chop plate. $300+.

Oblong planter, NAPCO mold. $250.

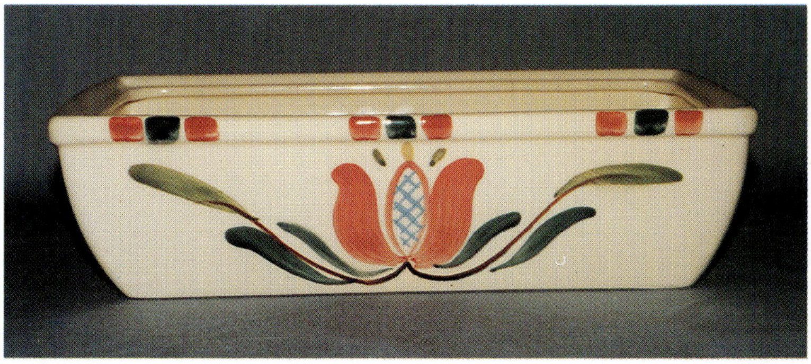

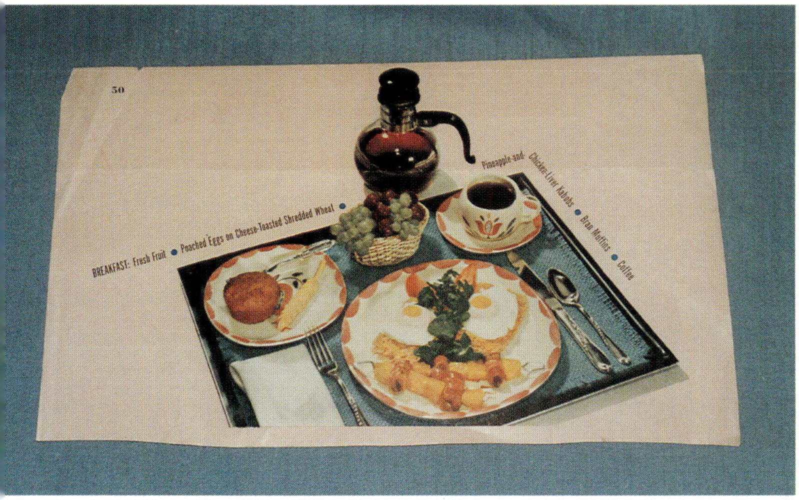

Advertisement utilizing a Pennsylvania Dutch place setting. Luckily their menu preference did not seem to influence sales ... how would you like to start your day with fresh fruit, poached eggs on cheese-toasted shredded wheat, pineapple-and-chicken-liver kabobs, bran muffins, and coffee?

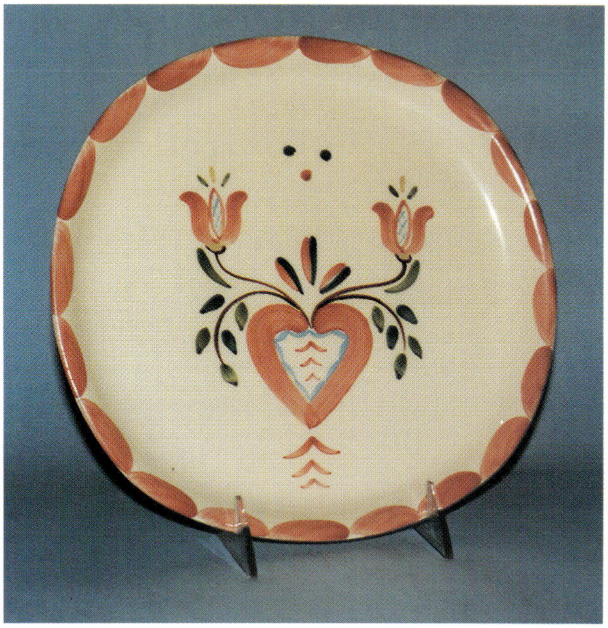

Dinner plate, Pennsylvania Dutch variant. $200.

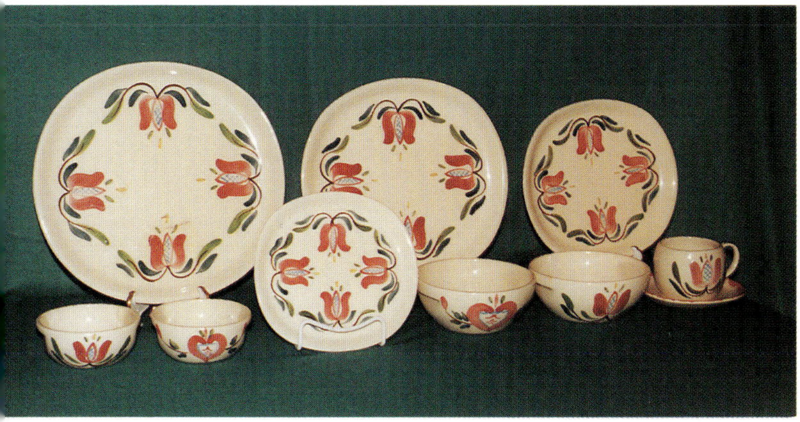

Oversized dinner plate. $50. Dinner plate. $30. Breakfast plate. $30. Tulip dessert bowl. $25. Heart dessert bowl. $30. Salad plate. $25. Heart cereal bowl. $30. Tulip cereal bowl. $25. Cup. $25. Saucer. $5.

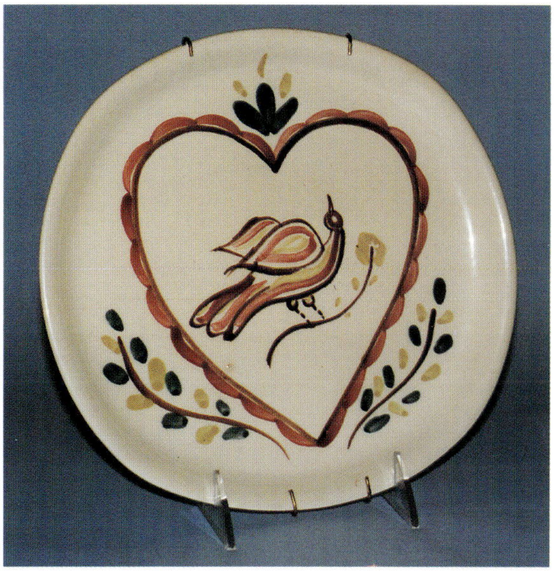

Dinner plate, heart with distalfink. $300.

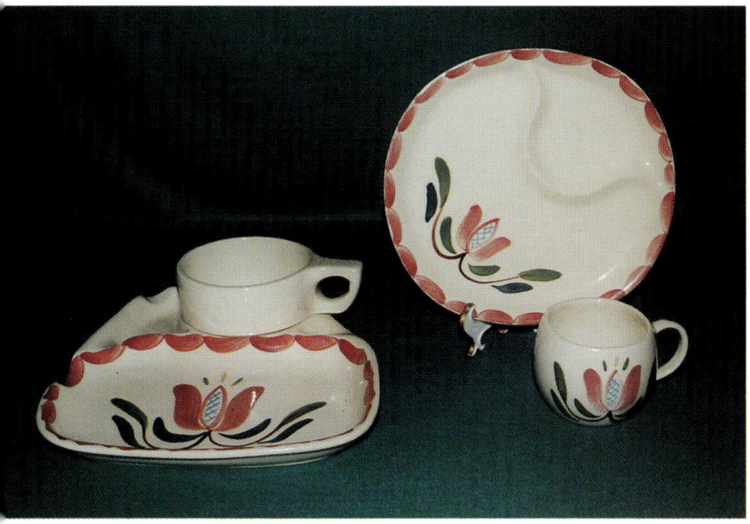

Rubel soup and sandwich set. (Photograph shows a plain cup.) $200. Tea and toast plate. $40. Cup $25.

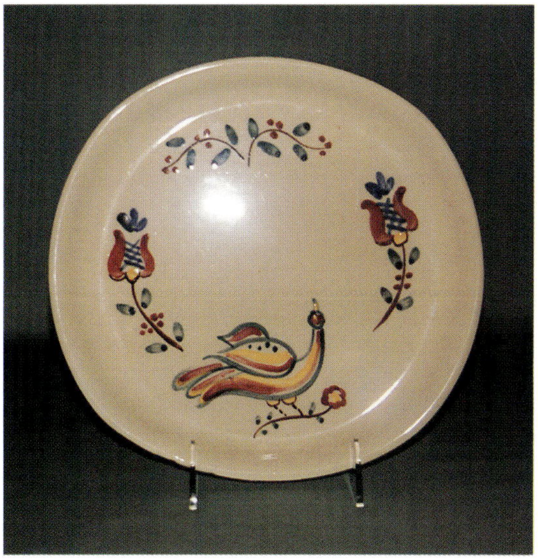

Dinner plate, Pennsylvania Dutch variant with distalfink. "Distalfink" is a Pennsylvania Dutch term for a stylized bird. $300.

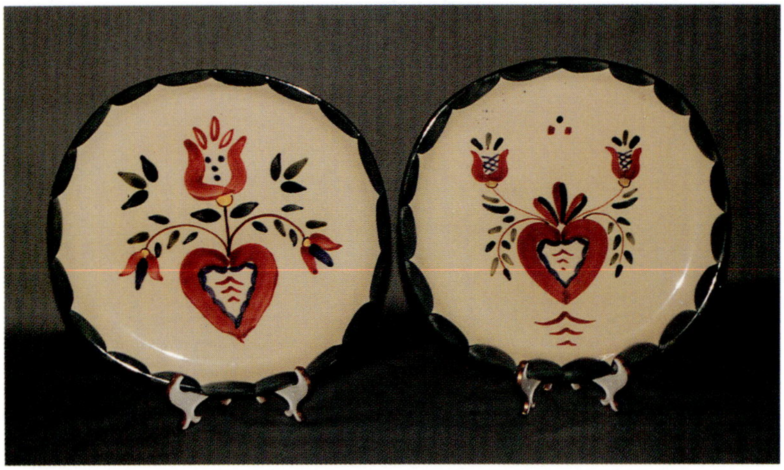

Dinner plates, Pennsylvania Dutch variant, painted with red and cobalt. $200 each.

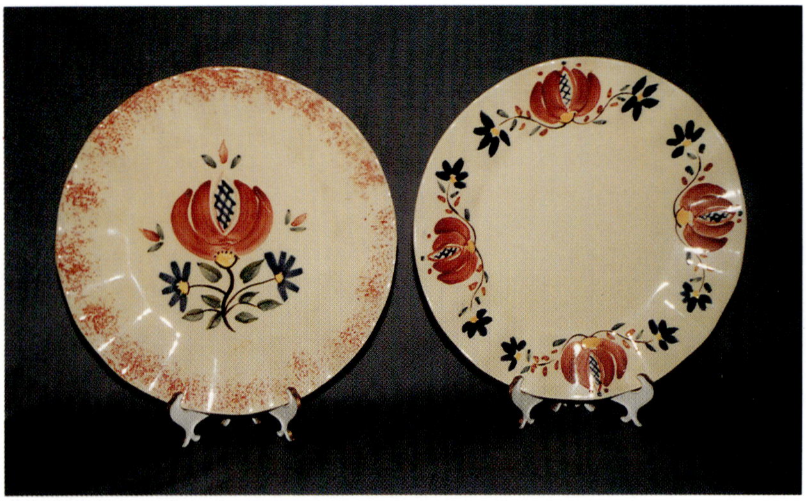

Dinner plates, Seaform style, Pennsylvania Dutch variant, experimental. $250 each.

Two cup teapot. $200+.

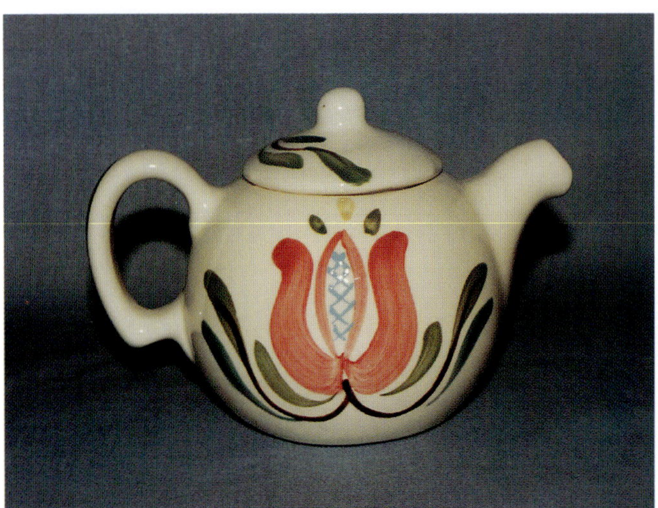

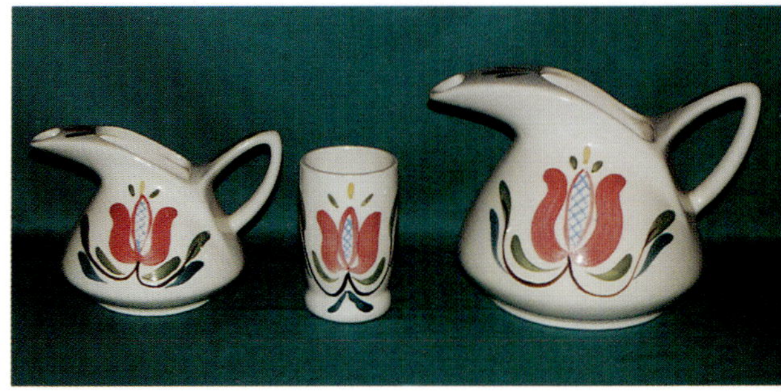

Two pint dutch jug. $250. Tumbler. $75+. Five pint dutch jug. $300+.

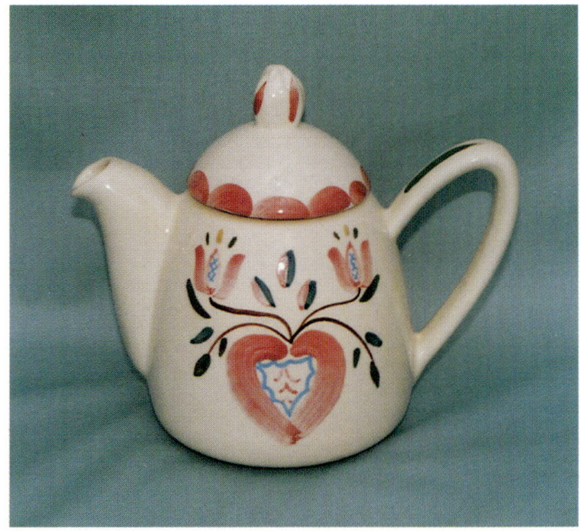

Six cup domed lid teapot. $300+.

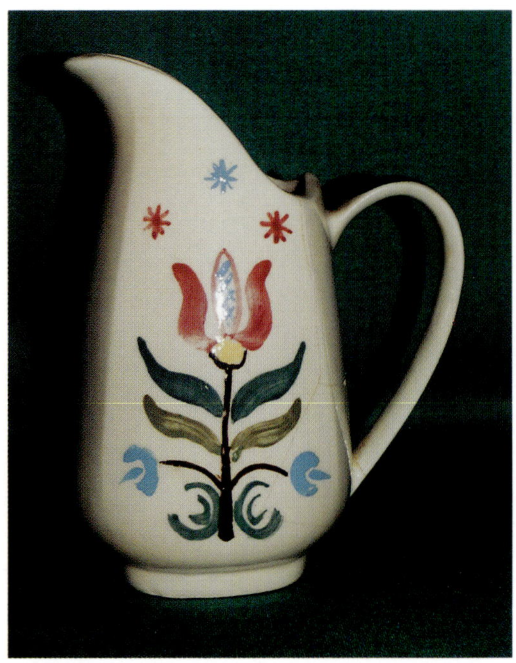

Milk pitcher, 7.5" high, not a production piece. $300.

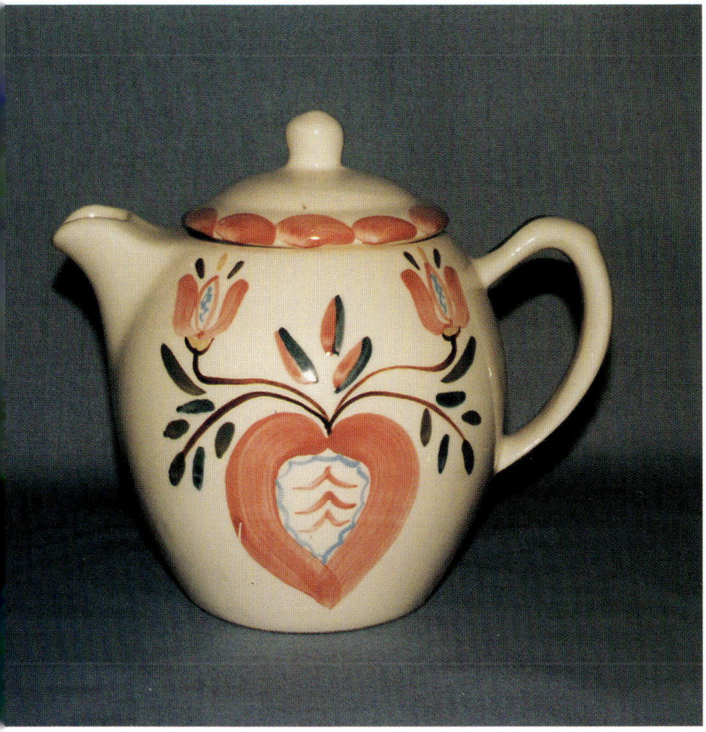

Eight cup coffee pot. $500+.

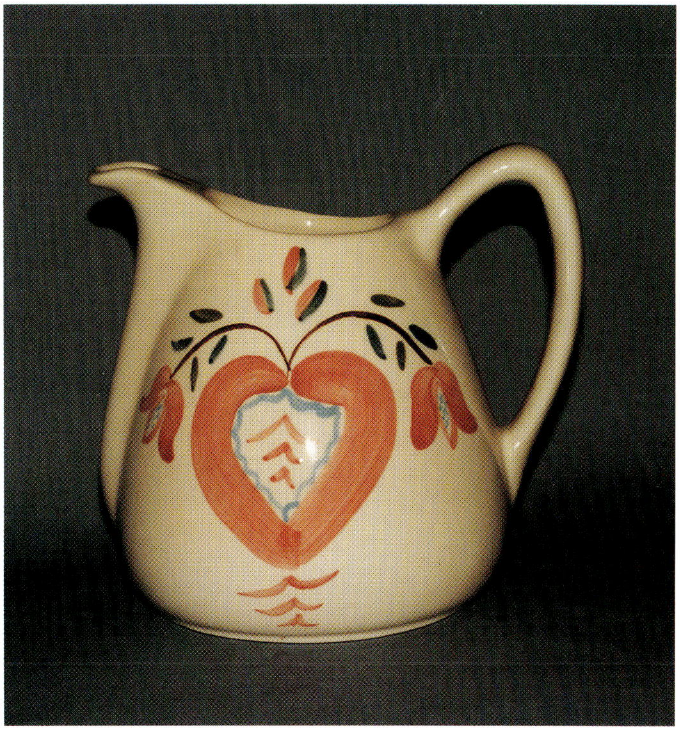

Beverage pitcher. $400+.

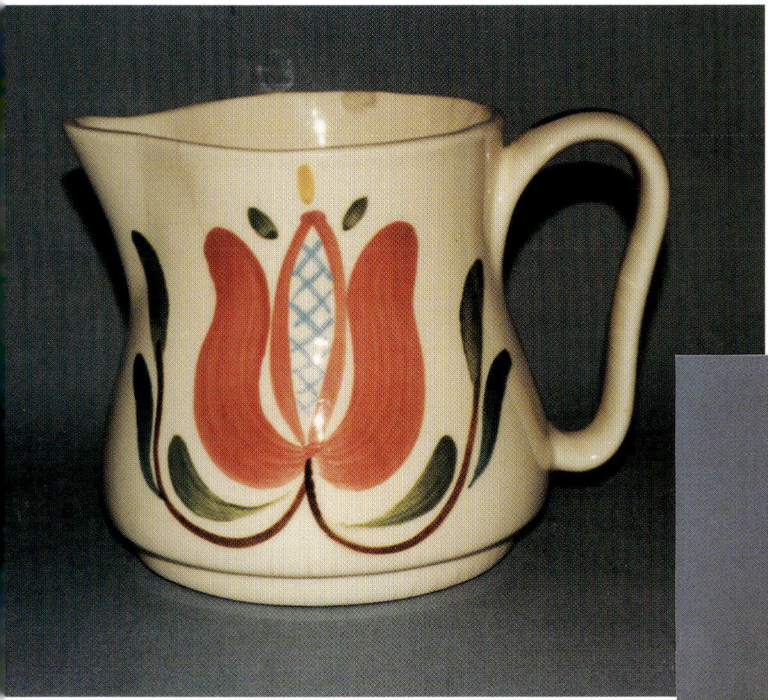

Pitcher, Rubel mold. $500+.

Kent jug. $150.

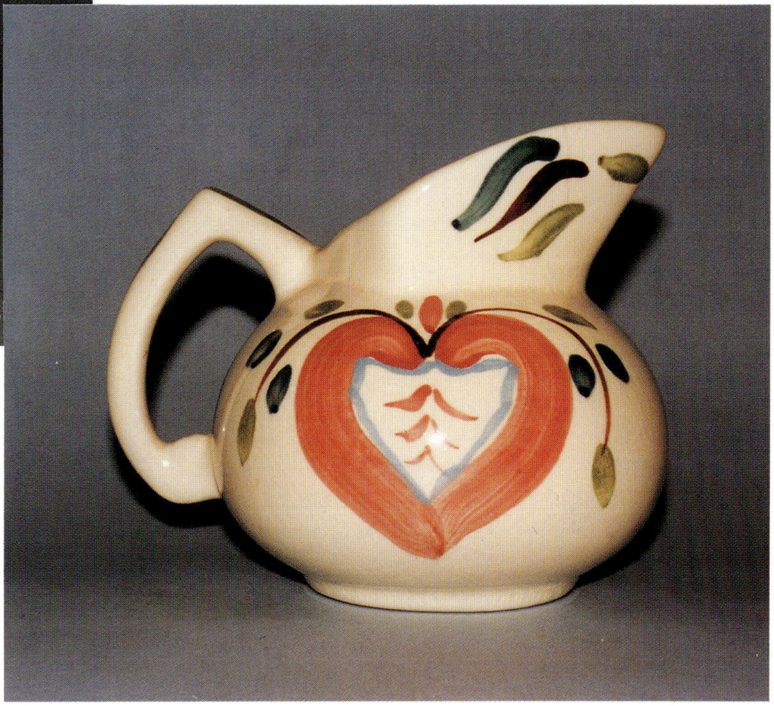

Ming Tree

Ming Tree decoration was first used by NAPCO on jardinieres and vases made at the Tionesta plant. Purinton offered it on open stock items in the 1950s, but it turned out to be a "short run" pattern. The Ming Tree design is commonly seen on other potteries' products and is not limited to Purinton. The burnt orange coloring with black trim is a bold decoration. Collectors either love it or hate it.

Pieces most commonly found with Ming Tree decoration are the floral items from NAPCO, but they are even scarce compared to other floral patterns. You will also find NAPCO vases with an entirely green Ming Tree decoration which will bring a slightly higher price. The dinnerware and serving pieces are very difficult to find. The supply of these items is limited and the demand has increased. These dining and serving pieces command a higher price than the average Purinton ware.

The items pictured are what is known to carry the Ming Tree decoration and some are the only ones known to the authors. Finding a canister set, cookies jar, butter dish, or any item in a harder to find shape would be rare.

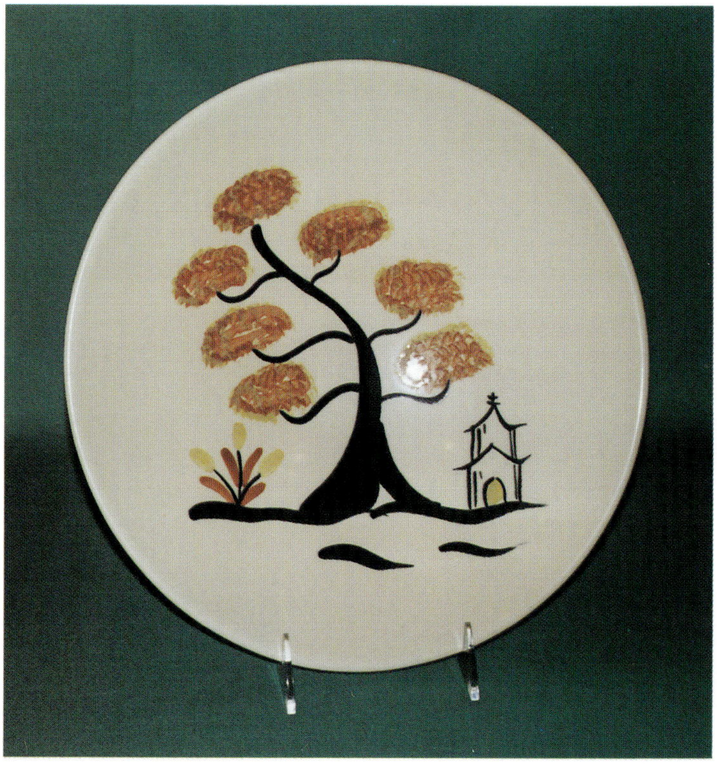

Fruit bowl. $150+.

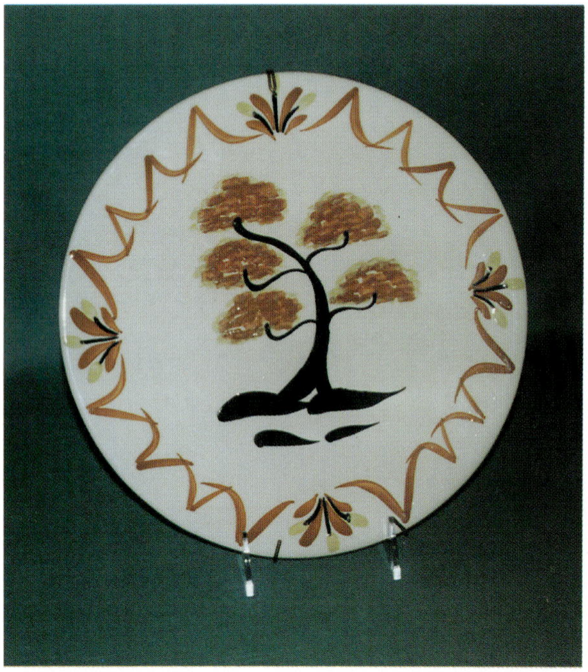

Ming Tree decorated chop plate. $150+.

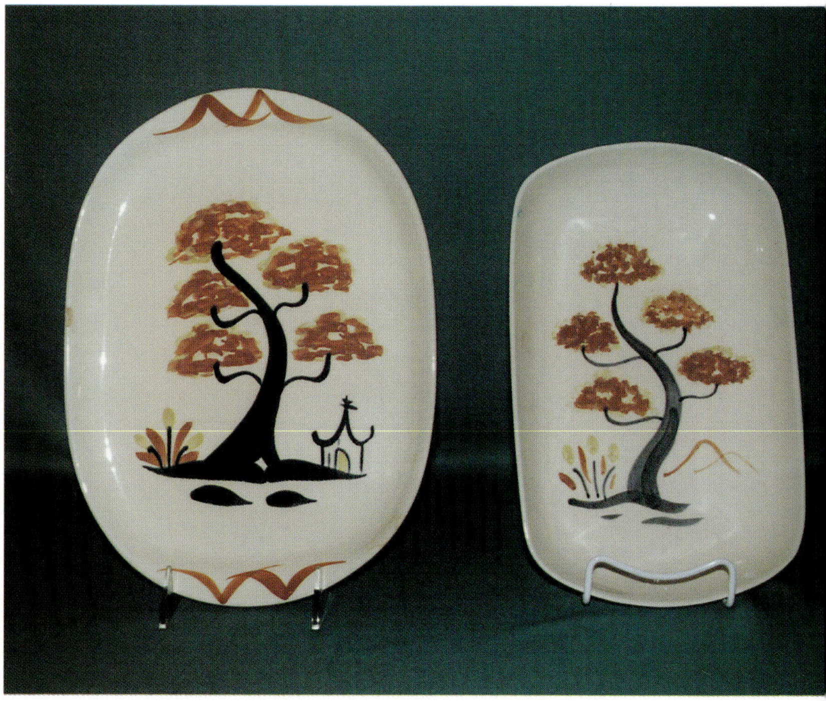

Large platter. $150. Roll tray. $100.

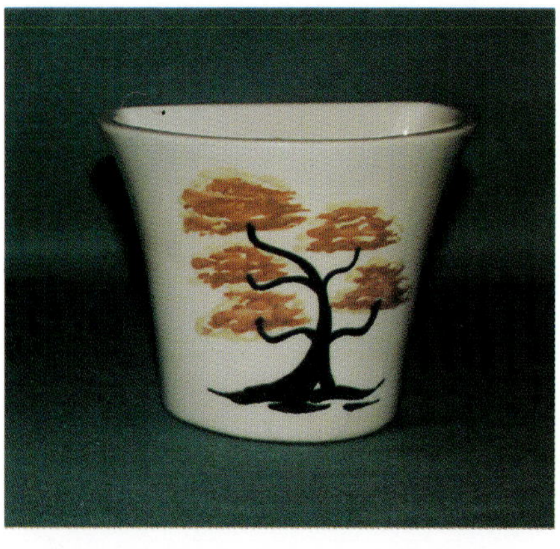

Wall pocket. $150.

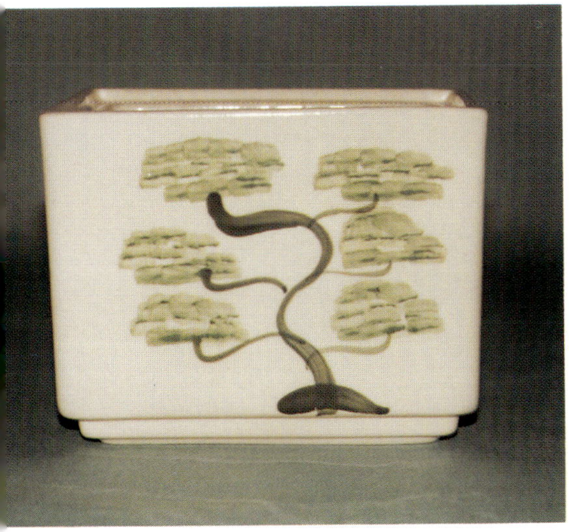

Small pillow vase, NAPCO mold, green Ming Tree decoration. $75.

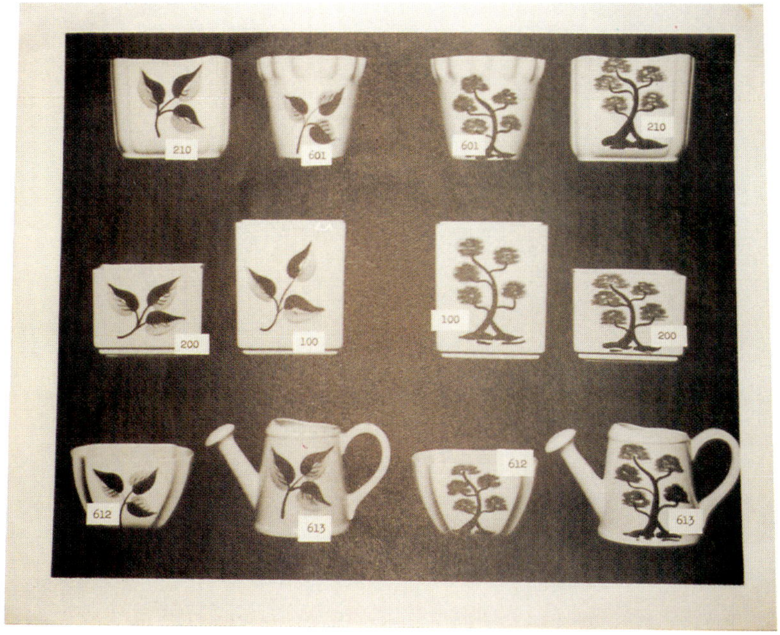

Product card for NAPCO planters, vases, and sprinklers produced by the Purinton Pottery Company.

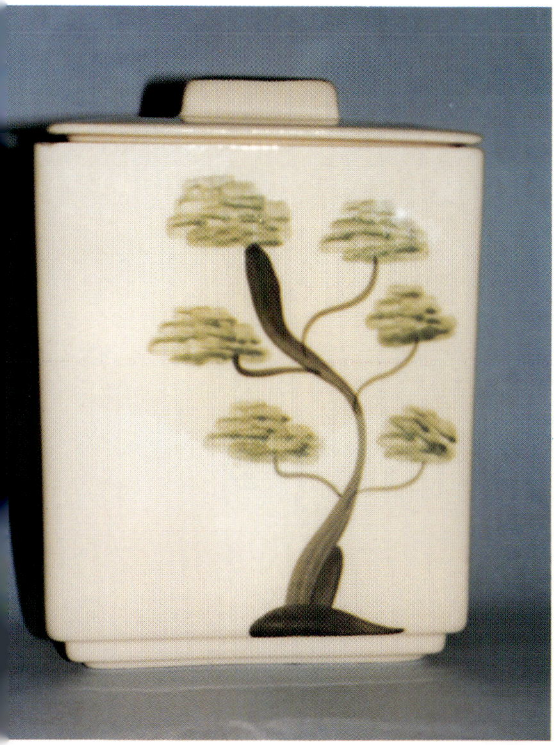

Large pillow vase, NAPCO mold, green Ming Tree decoration (shown with lid), $ 75.

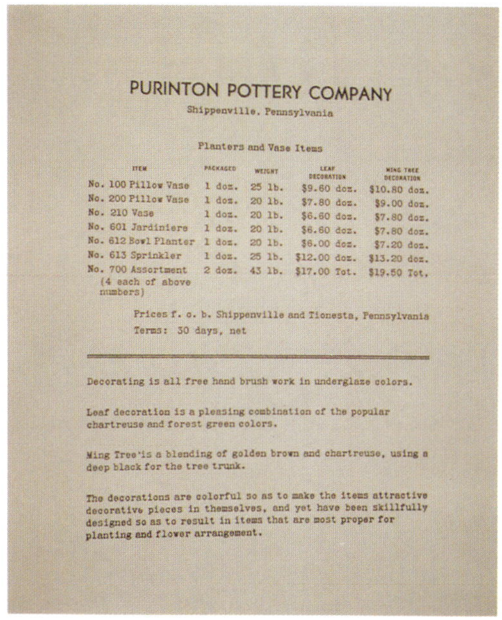

PURINTON POTTERY COMPANY

Shippenville, Pennsylvania

Planters and Vase Items

ITEM	PACKAGED	WEIGHT	LEAF DECORATION	MING TREE DECORATION
No. 100 Pillow Vase	1 doz.	25 lb.	$9.60 doz.	$10.80 doz.
No. 200 Pillow Vase	1 doz.	20 lb.	$7.80 doz.	$9.00 doz.
No. 210 Vase	1 doz.	20 lb.	$6.60 doz.	$7.80 doz.
No. 601 Jardiniere	1 doz.	20 lb.	$6.60 doz.	$7.80 doz.
No. 612 Bowl Planter	1 doz.	20 lb.	$6.00 doz.	$7.20 doz.
No. 613 Sprinkler	1 doz.	25 lb.	$12.00 doz.	$13.20 doz.
No. 700 Assortment (4 each of above numbers)	2 doz.	43 lb.	$17.00 Tot.	$19.50 Tot.

Prices f. o. b. Shippenville and Tionesta, Pennsylvania

Terms: 30 days, net

Decorating is all free hand brush work in underglaze colors.

Leaf decoration is a pleasing combination of the popular chartreuse and forest green colors.

Ming Tree is a blending of golden brown and chartreuse, using a deep black for the tree trunk.

The decorations are colorful so as to make the items attractive decorative pieces in themselves, and yet have been skillfully designed so as to result in items that are most proper for planting and flower arrangement.

Reverse side of product card for planters, vases, and sprinklers produced in the Leaf and Ming Tree patterns. Their description says that Leaf is a combination of chartreuse and forest green, while Ming Tree is a blending of chartreuse and golden brown.

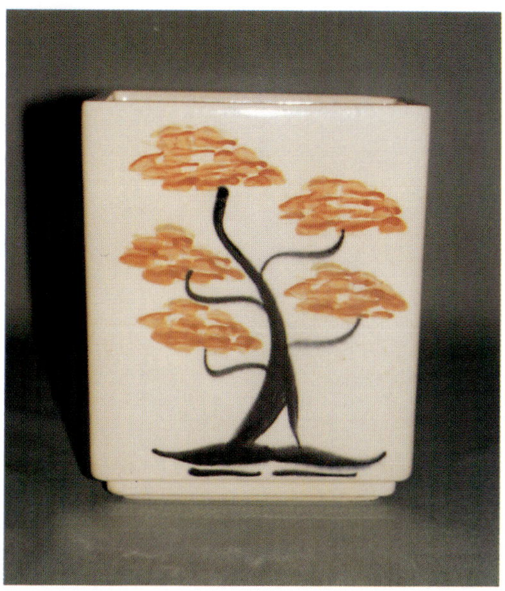

Large pillow vase, NAPCO mold. $60.

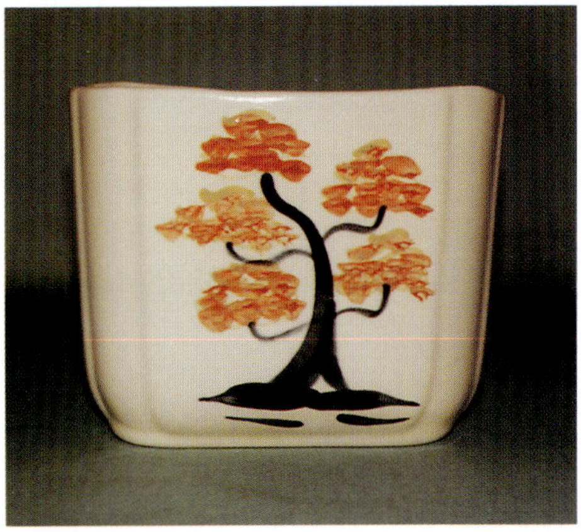

Vase. $75.

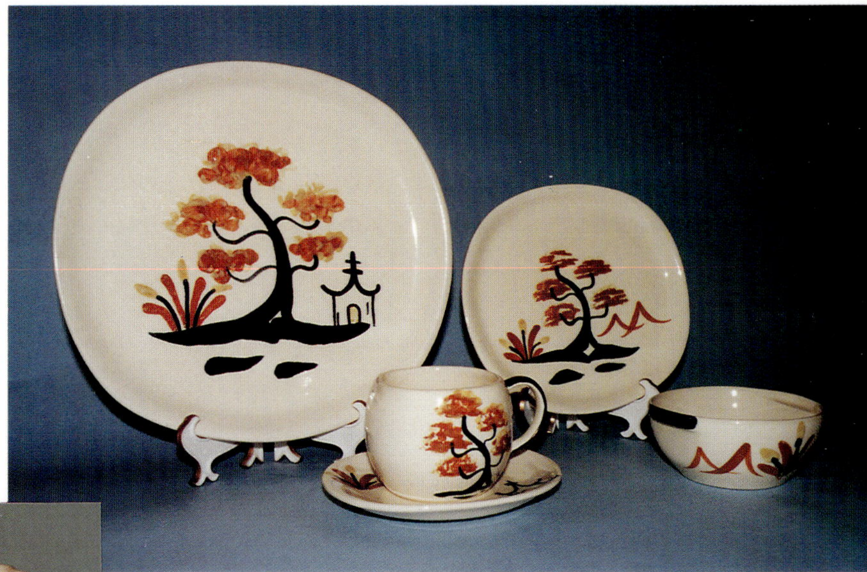

Dinner plate. $50. Salad plate. $50. Cup. $40. Saucer. $25. Dessert bowl. $30.

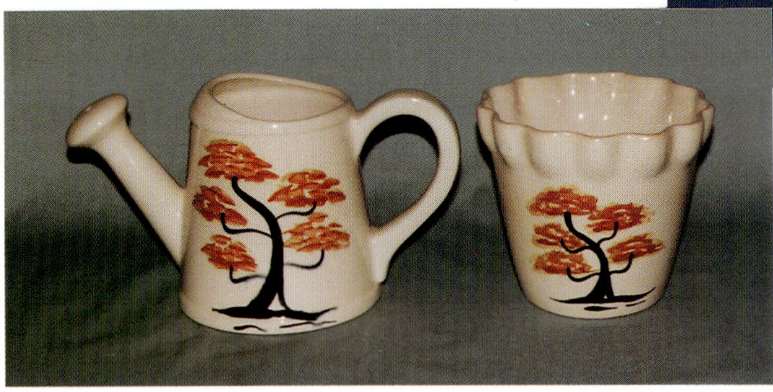

Sprinkler. $100. Jardiniere, 5" high. $75.

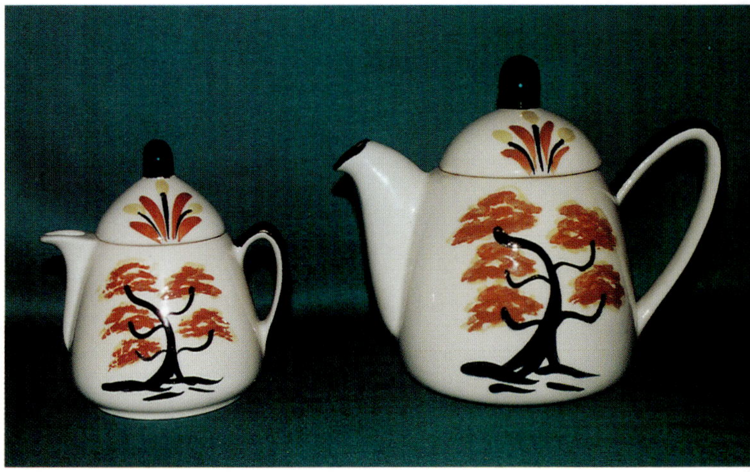

Covered creamer. $75. Six cup domed lid teapot. $150.

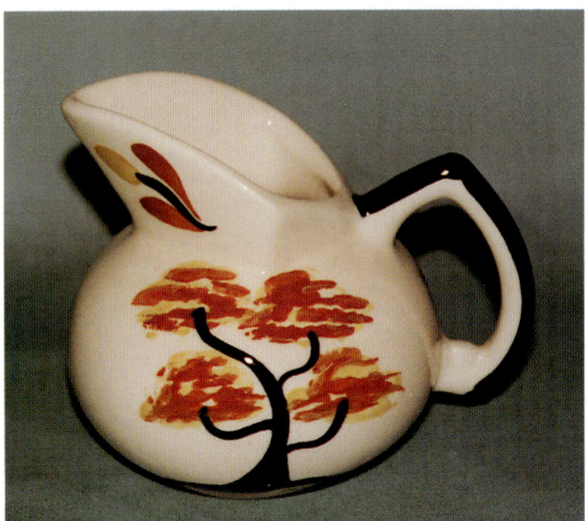

Kent jug. $150+.

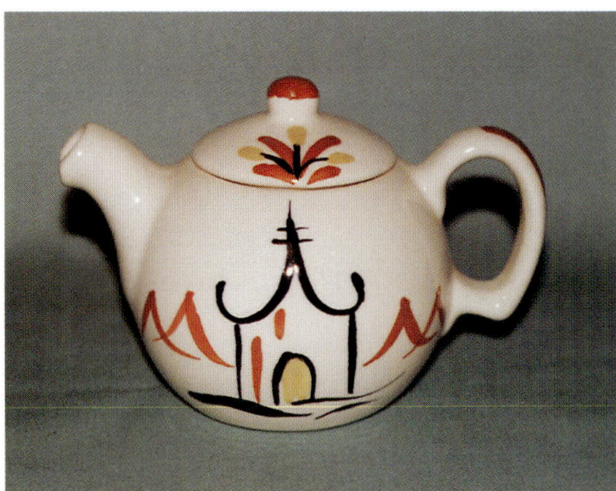

Two cup teapot with pagoda decoration. Sometimes the Ming Tree decoration has a pagoda within the decoration. $150+

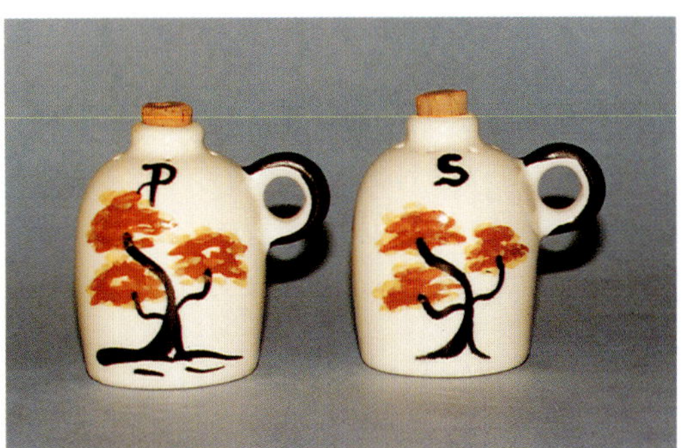

Jug style salt and pepper shakers. $100+ set.

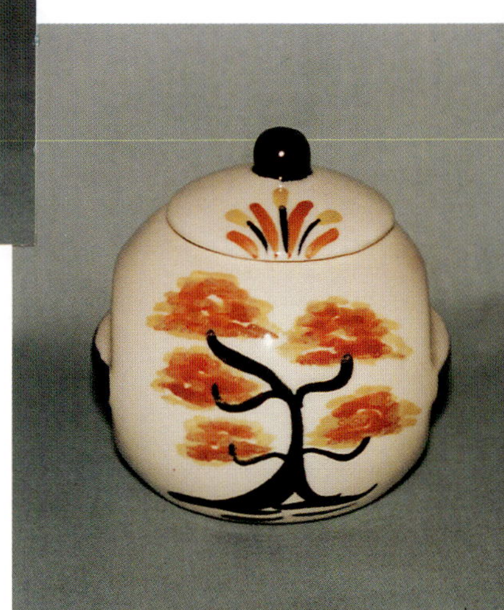

Individual bean pot. $100.

Palm Tree

Purinton produced Palm Tree for John "Pete" Purinton, the son of Bernard and Dorothy. He operated an outlet in Ft. Myers, Florida. Palm Tree was especially made for this shop. Dorothy designed Palm Tree and it is found painted on off-white slip or incised in intaglio in a variety of colors.

Palm Tree is most commonly found on honey jugs and salt and pepper shake and pours. Prices for these are much lower than for other pieces. Other items with the Palm Tree decoration command a high price and many pieces are open ended in pricing as it is hard to determine the market for them. Most of the intaglio is found on dinnerware plates and certain colors demand a higher price. Palm Tree Intaglio patterned dining wares may have been made as place settings because cups and cereal bowls have been located.

Palm Tree is probably the most elusive decoration and in the highest demand. Prices vary and it is very rare to find pieces other than the honey jugs and shake and pours.

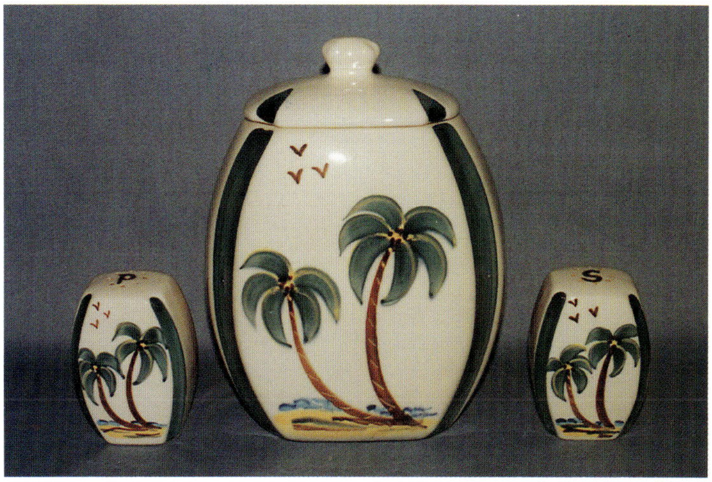

Palm Tree range salt and pepper shakers. $200+. Wide oval canister. $400+.

Palm Tree

Beverage pitcher. $300+. Beer mug. $250.

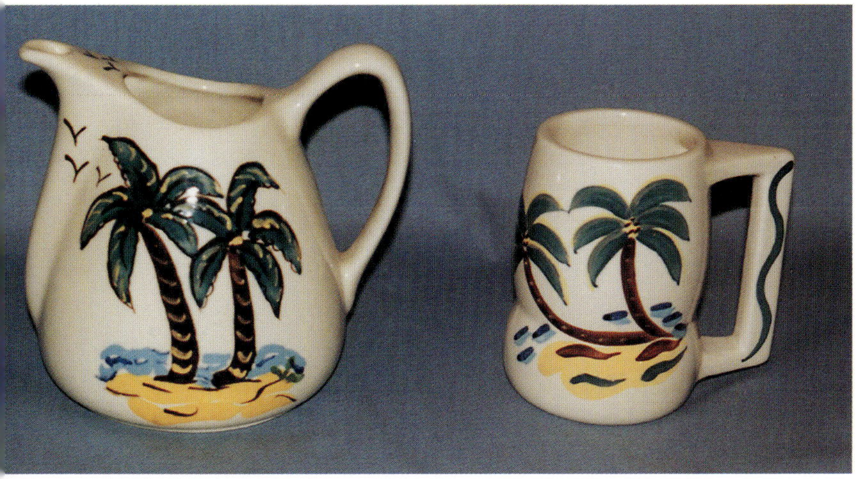

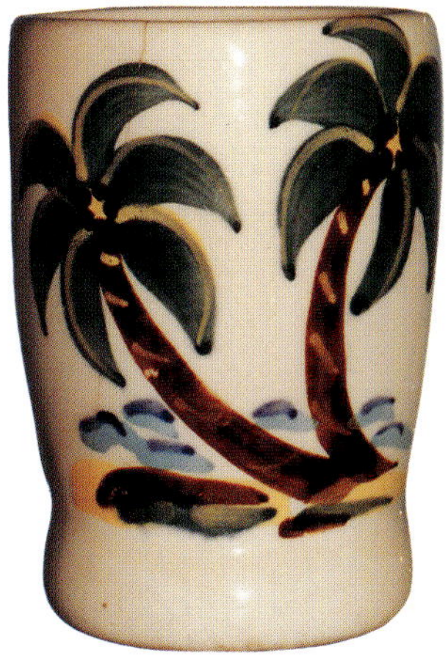

Tumbler, 3.75" high. This is a coffee mug that had its handle removed before it was glazed. $200.

Marmalade. $200+. Two pint dutch jug. $300+.

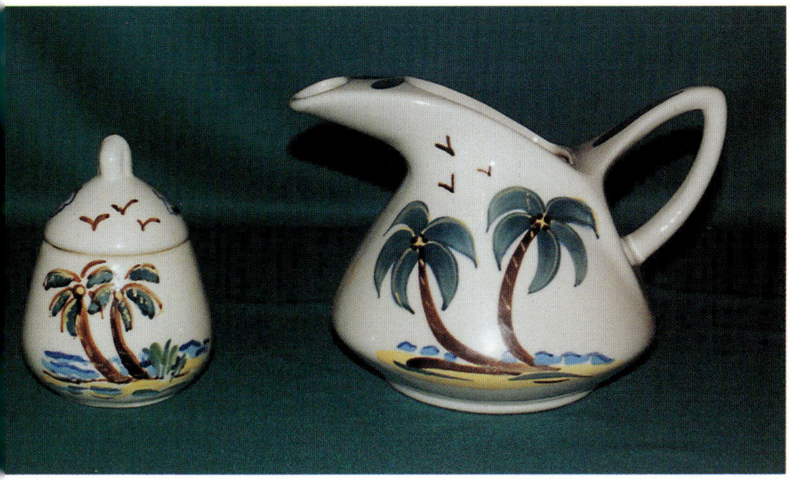

Mug jug. $200+.

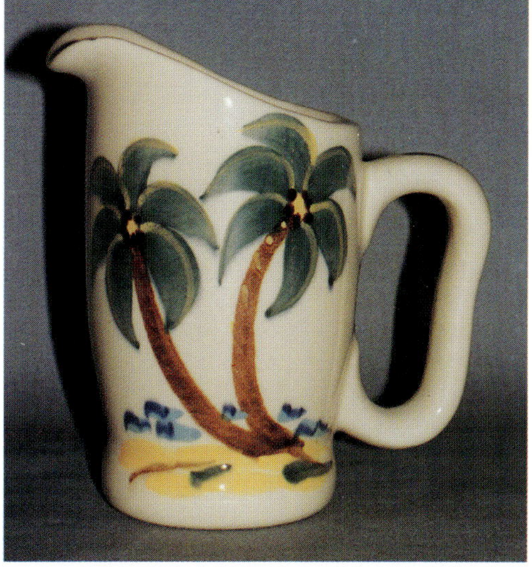

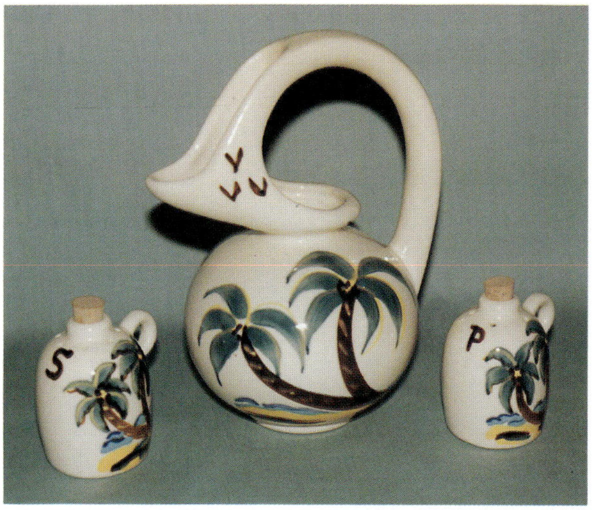

Jug style salt and pepper shakers. $200 set. Honey jug. $150.

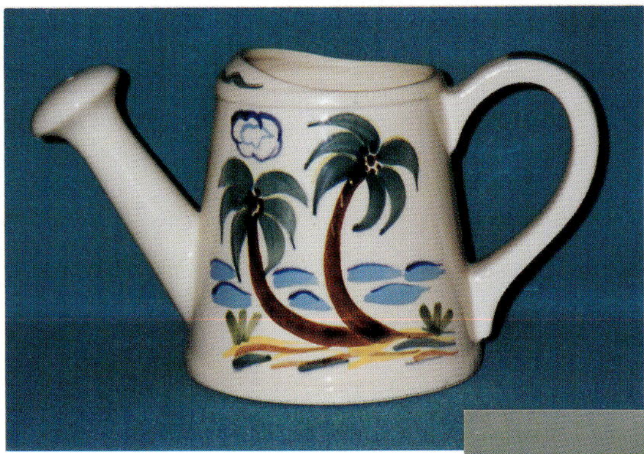

Sprinkler. $350+.

Pour and shake salt and pepper shakers. $150 set.

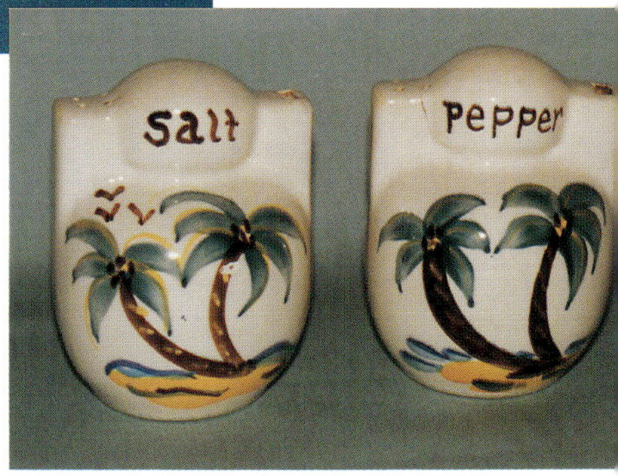

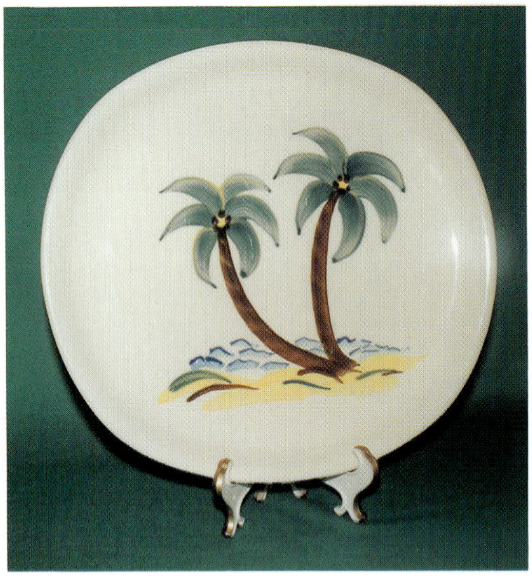

Dinner plate. $200+.

Palm Tree Intaglio

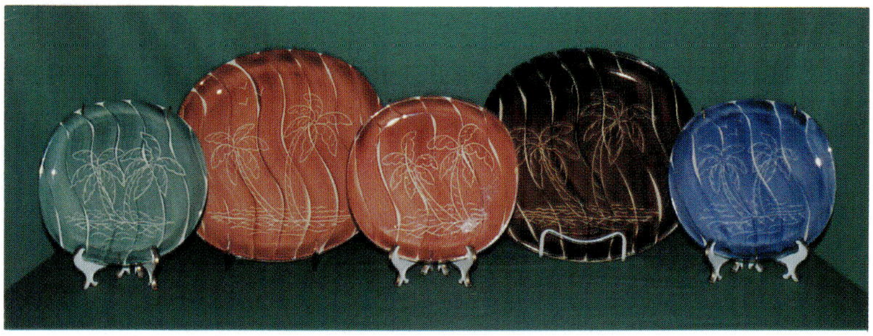

Palm Tree Intaglio decorates each of these plates. Salad plate, turquoise. $150. Dinner plate, coral. $250. Salad plate, coral. $150. Dinner plate, brown. $250. Salad plate, cobalt. $200.

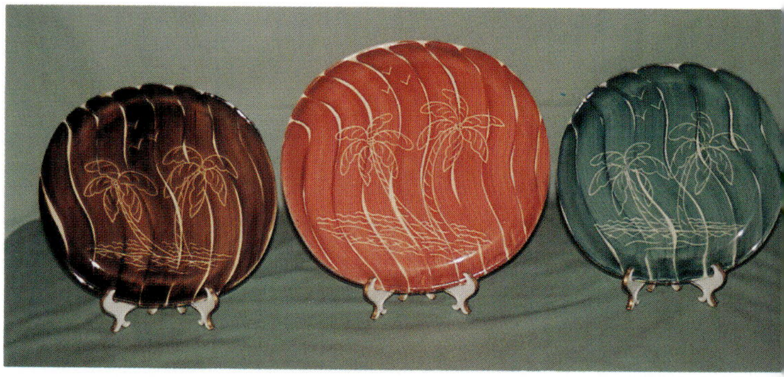

Breakfast plate, brown. $150. Dinner plate, coral. $250. Breakfast plate, turquoise. $200.

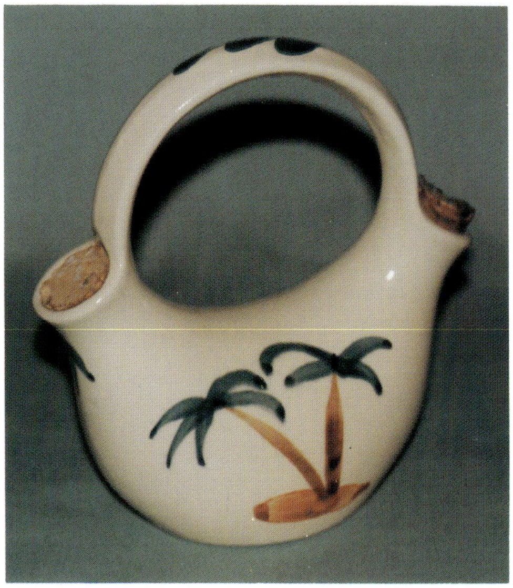

Variation of the basket planter, no large opening and a simple palm tree design. $125.

Cereal bowl, coral. $75.

Beer mug, purple. $200+.

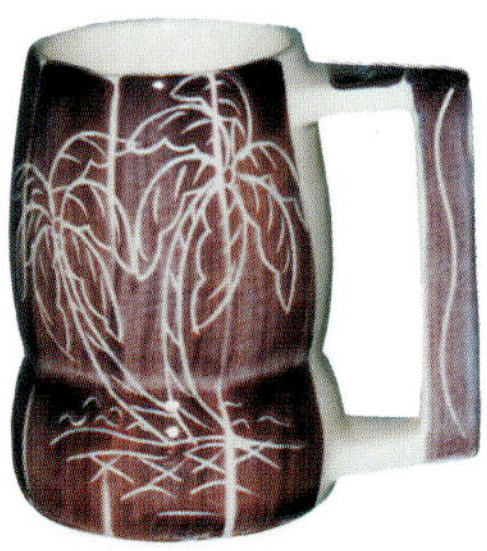

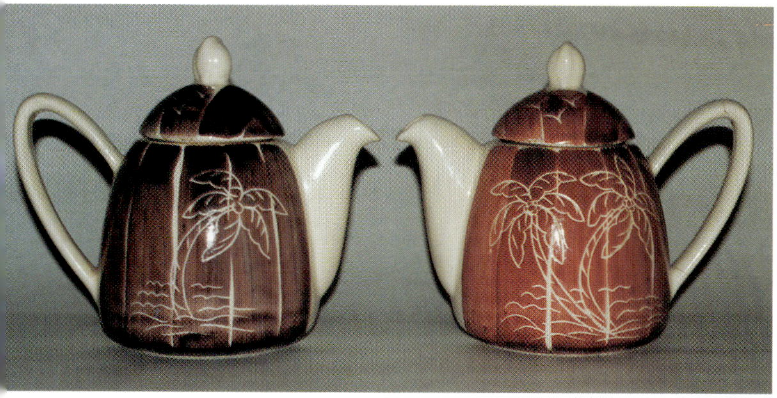

Six cup domed lid teapot, purple. $300+. Six cup domed lid teapot, coral. $300+.

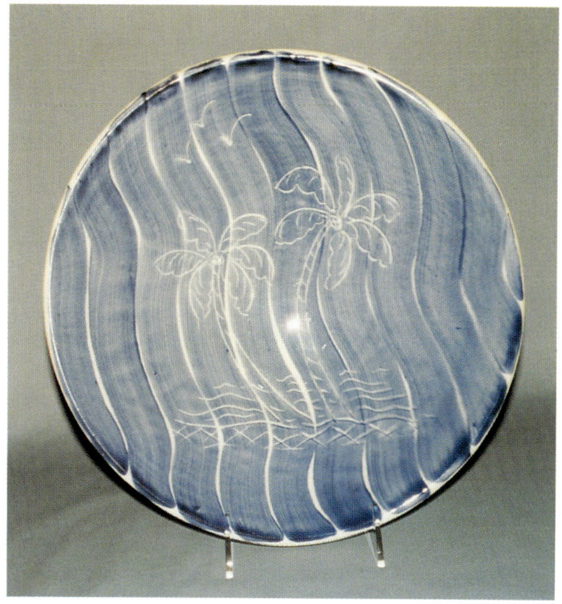

Fruit bowl, cobalt. $500+.

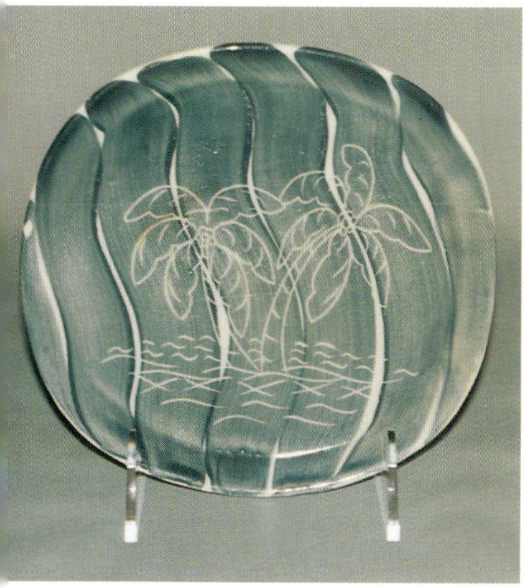

Salad plate, turquoise. $150.

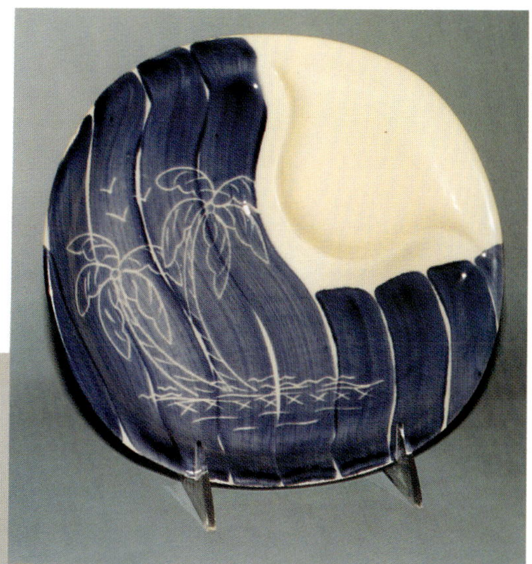

Tea and toast plate, cobalt. $200.

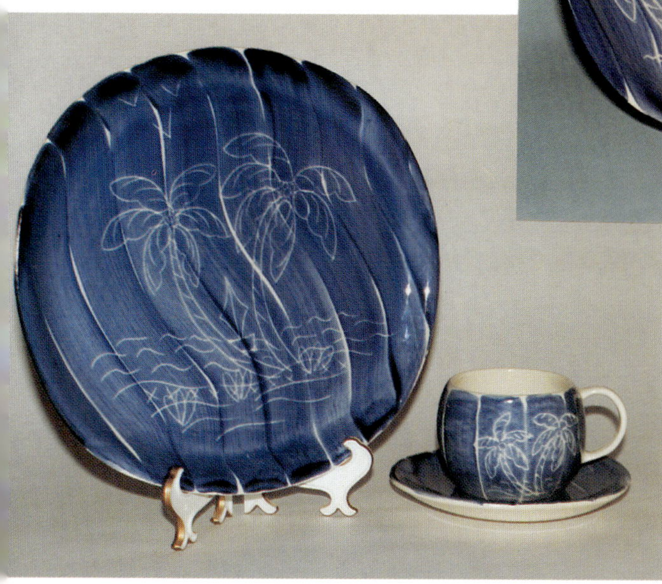

Dinner plate, cobalt. $300. Cup, cobalt. $125. Saucer, cobalt. $50.

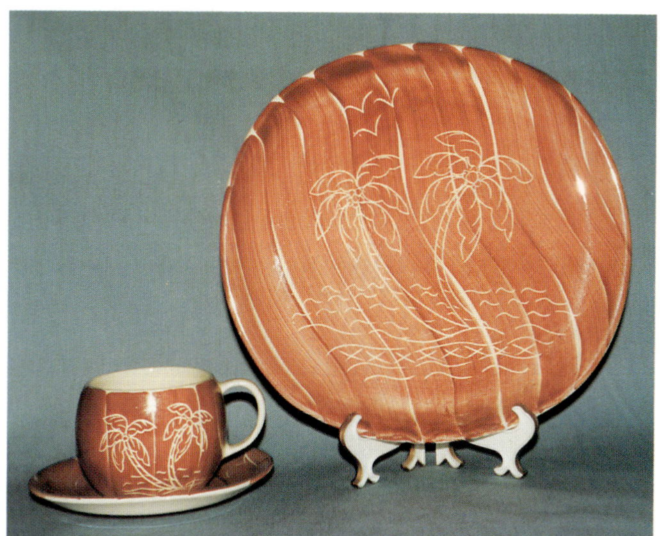

Cup, coral $125. Saucer, coral. $25. Dinner plate, coral. $250.

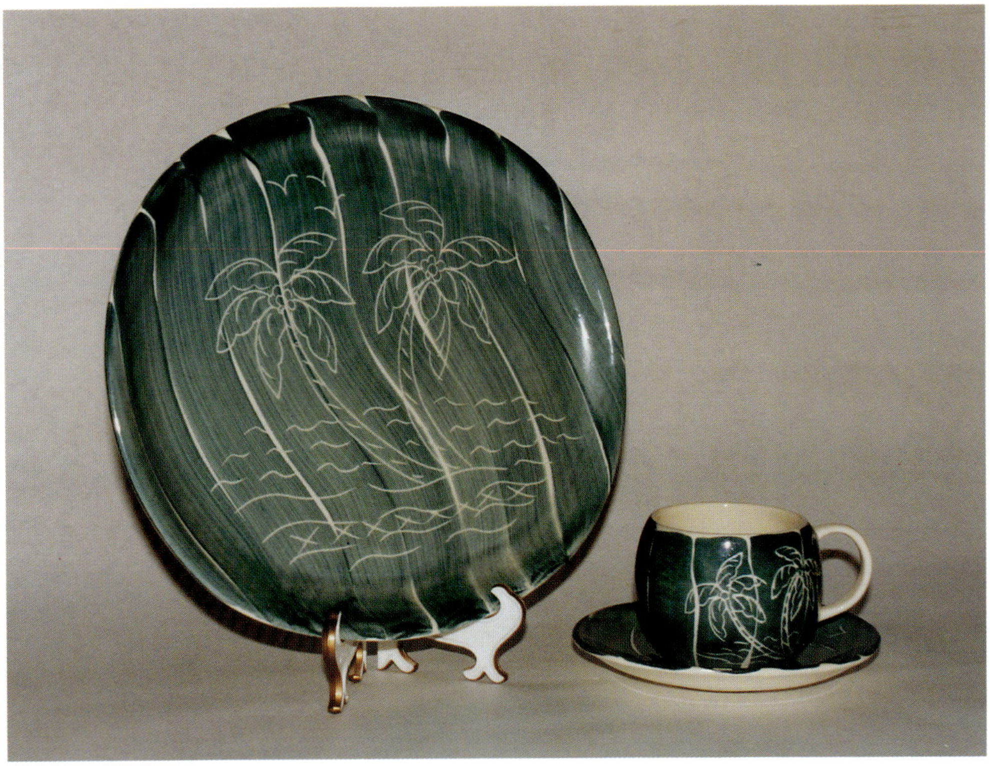

Dinner plate, turquoise. $250. Cup, turquoise. $125. Saucer, turquoise. $25.

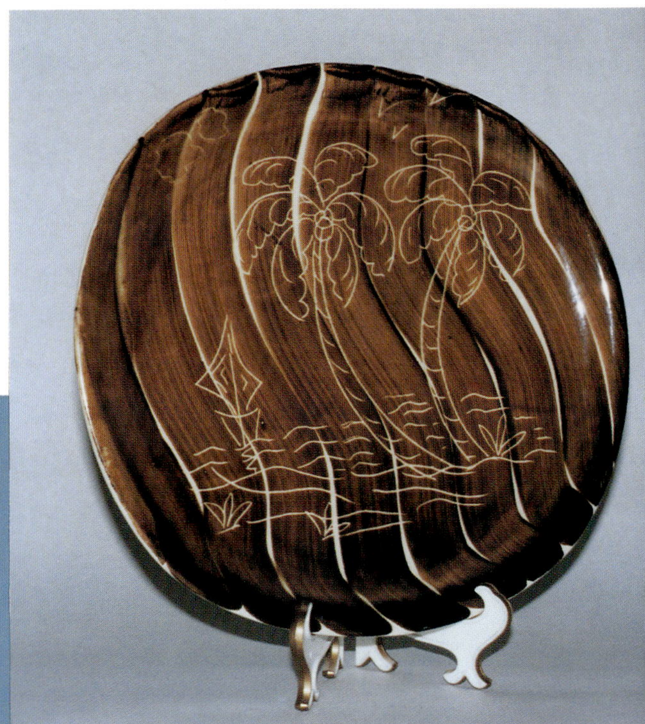

Dinner plate, brown, notice the sailboat. $250.

Tea and toast plate, brown. $175. Cup. $100.

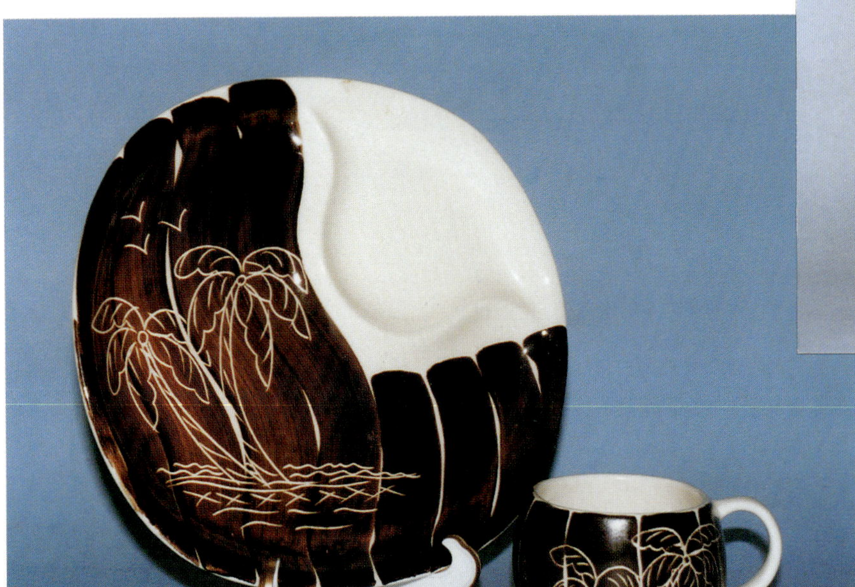

Peasant Garden

Peasant Garden should not be confused with Peasant Ware. Peasant Garden was not introduced until the 1950s, but was derived from the decoration on the peasant lady candle holder. It was a short-lived product line featuring a bold red stripe surrounded by green leaves. Some detailing had small flowers on the items.

Finding Peasant Garden is difficult as the supply is limited. Dinnerware items are scarce. Some accessory pieces pictured are the only ones known. Demand for this pattern is high because of its association with the Wellsville years. Prices on some items are open ended because of the limited amount found in this decoration.

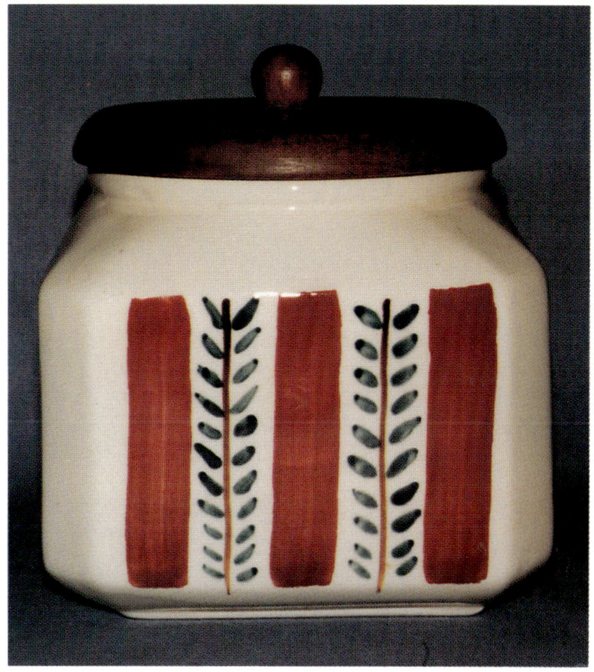

Peasant Garden decorated square storage canister with a wooden lid. $150.

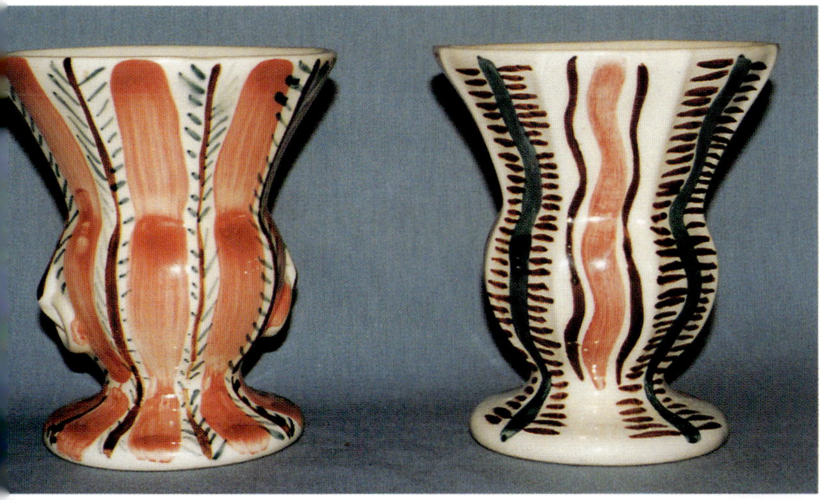

Vases, variation of the Peasant Garden decoration, unknown molds. $75+.

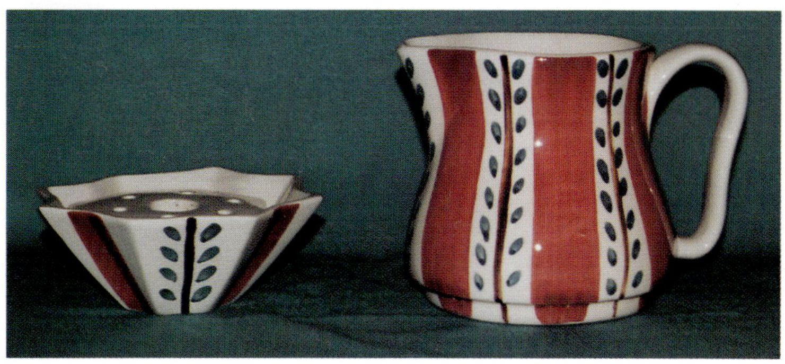

Peasant Garden pattern on a star candle holder with insert. $150. Pitcher, Rubel mold. $300.

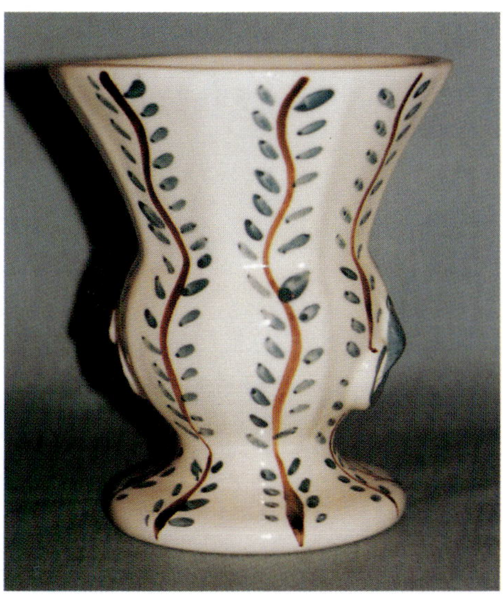

Vase, variation of the Peasant Garden decoration, unknown mold. Painted and initialed DP by Dorothy Purinton and given as a gift to an employee. $400+.

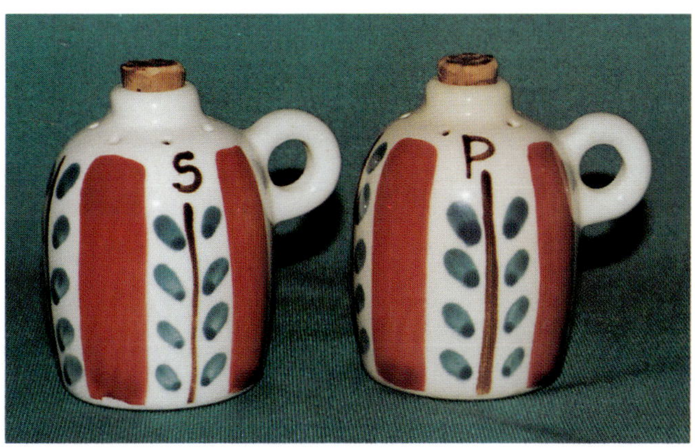

Jug style salt and pepper shakers. $100 set.

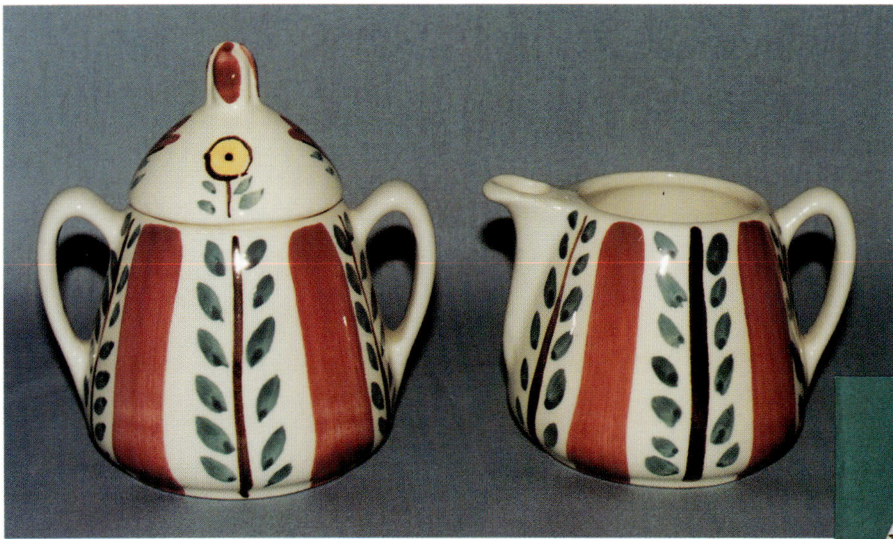

Covered sugar and creamer. $125 set.

Tea and toast plate. $75. Cup. $40.

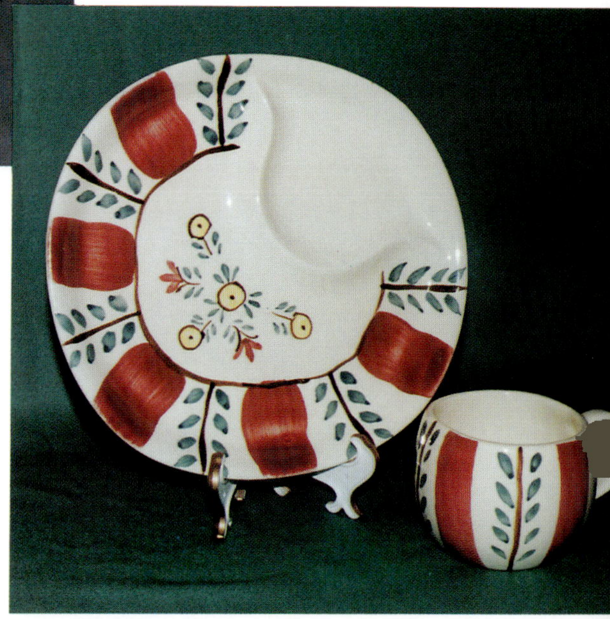

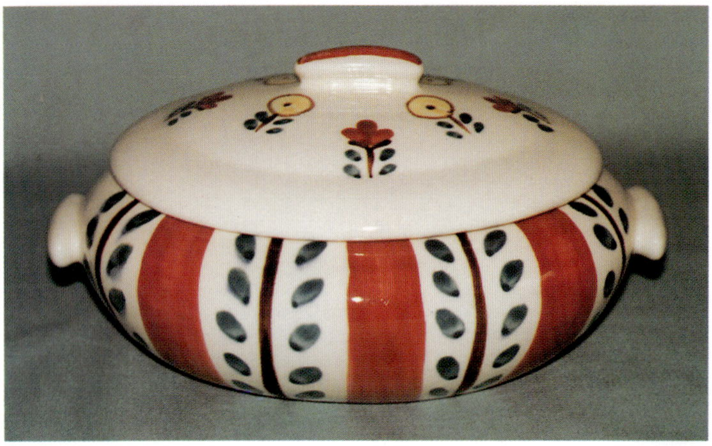

Covered vegetable. $200.

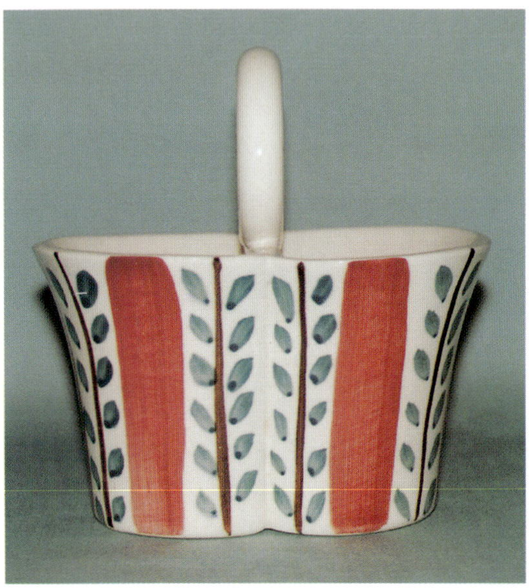

Candy dish. $200.

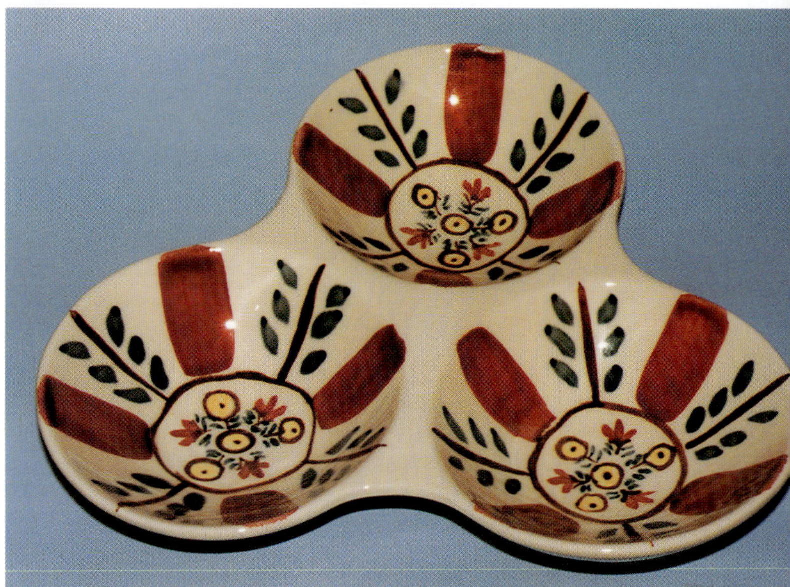

Three part relish, no handle. $100.

Baker. $100. Pickle. $40.

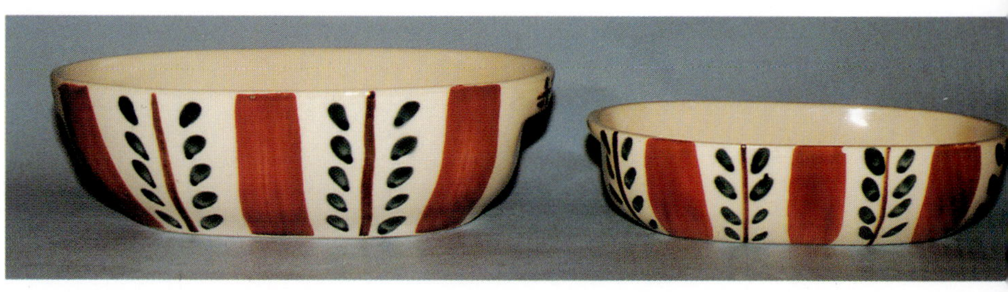

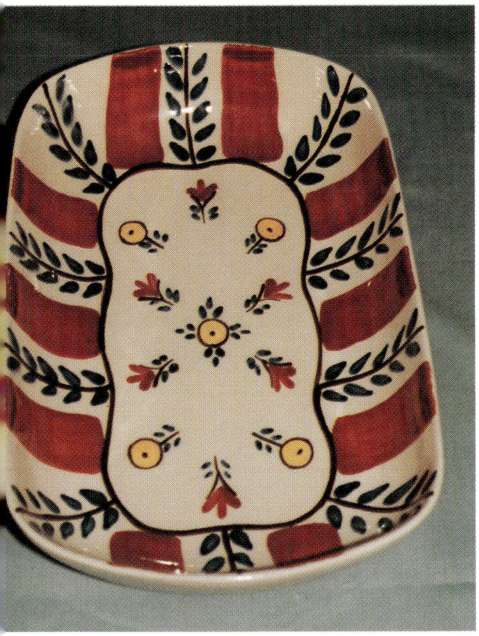

Roll tray. $200.

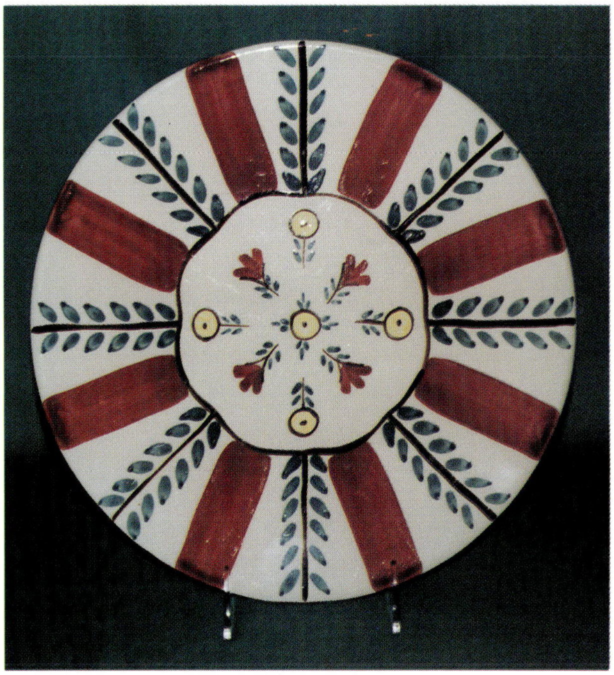

Chop plate. $300+.

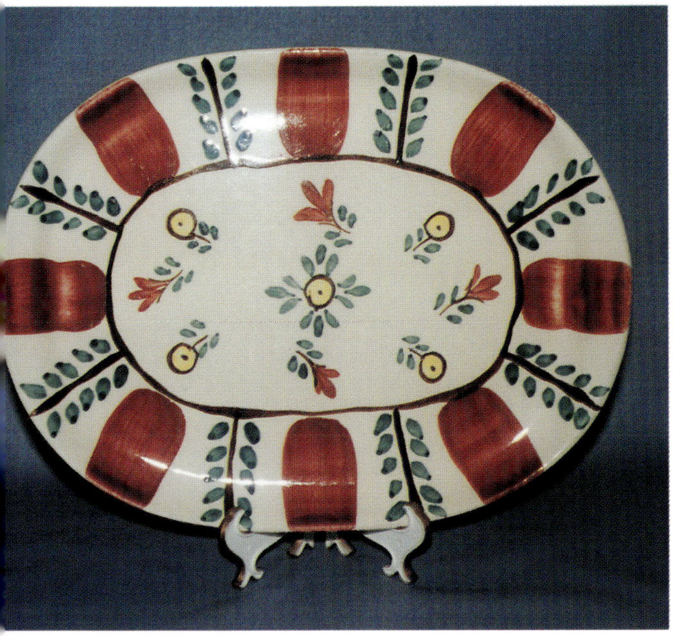

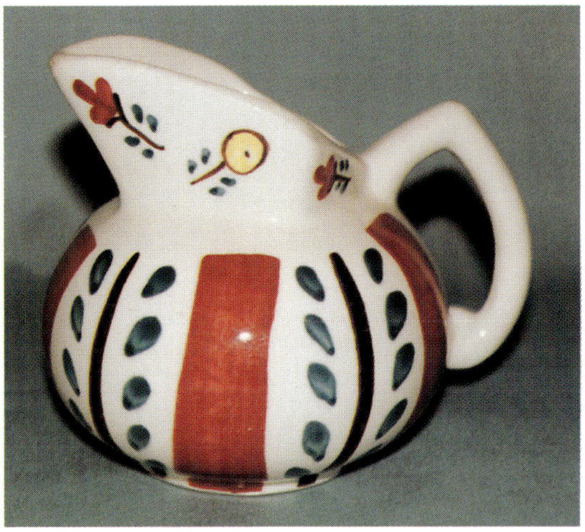

Kent jug. $200.

Fruit Bowl. $275+.

Large platter. $200+.

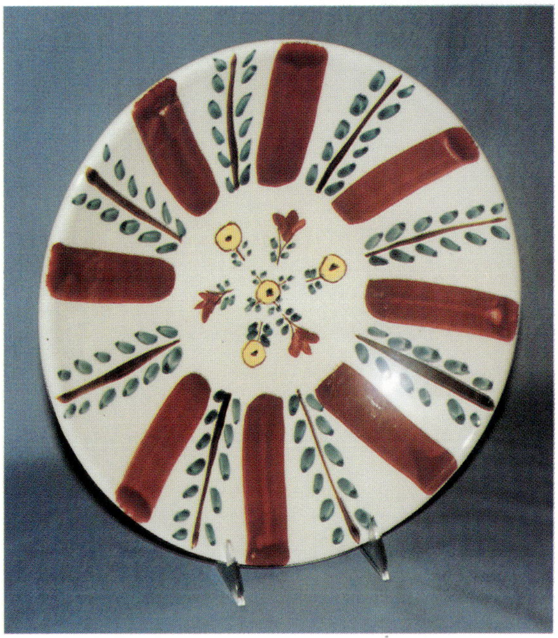

Dinner plate. $60. Salad plate. $50. Cereal bowl. $40. Cup. $40. Saucer. $30. Dessert bowl. $40.

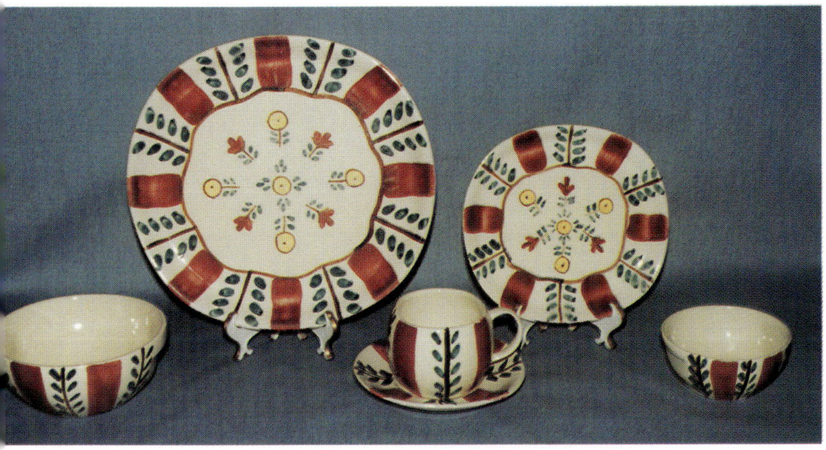

Provincial Fruit

Provincial Fruit was introduced in the 1950s. Designed by Dorothy Purinton, its stylistic fruit design of aqua, rose, yellow and charcoal was a decoration which appealed to the changing modern world. Some employees even called it "modern fruit." Provincial Fruit was an open stock item.

The supply of Provincial Fruit is limited. Some dinnerware items have been found and the locating of accessory pieces is more difficult. We have not seen a canister set or a spaghetti bowl, and we have only seen a few items in what should be common shapes. Some items are found with only the pear or the apple decoration; however, it seems the pear is the more common decorative motif. The demand for Provincial Fruit is increasing. It is an attractive pattern, all the more so because of its charcoal trim.

Prices are high for Provincial Fruit and climbing. Among the open stock items, there are probably many items yet to be found. Discovering an item not pictured would be desirable.

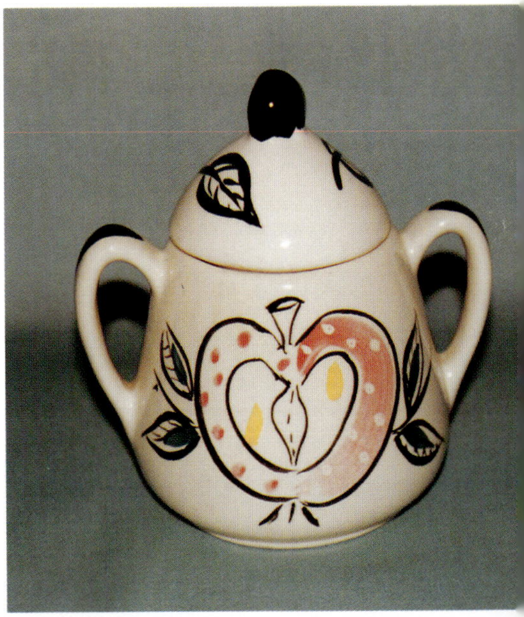

Covered sugar, apple decoration. $75.

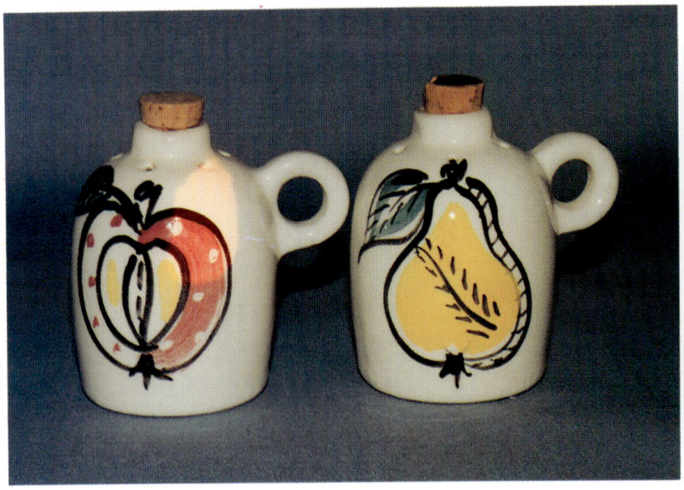

Jug style salt and pepper shakers, separate apple and pear decorations. $100 set.

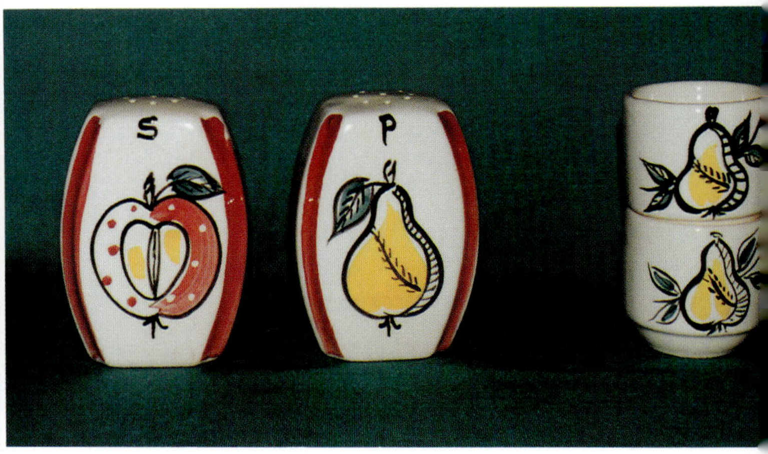

Range salt and pepper shakers. $100 set. Stacking salt and pepper shakers. $100 set.

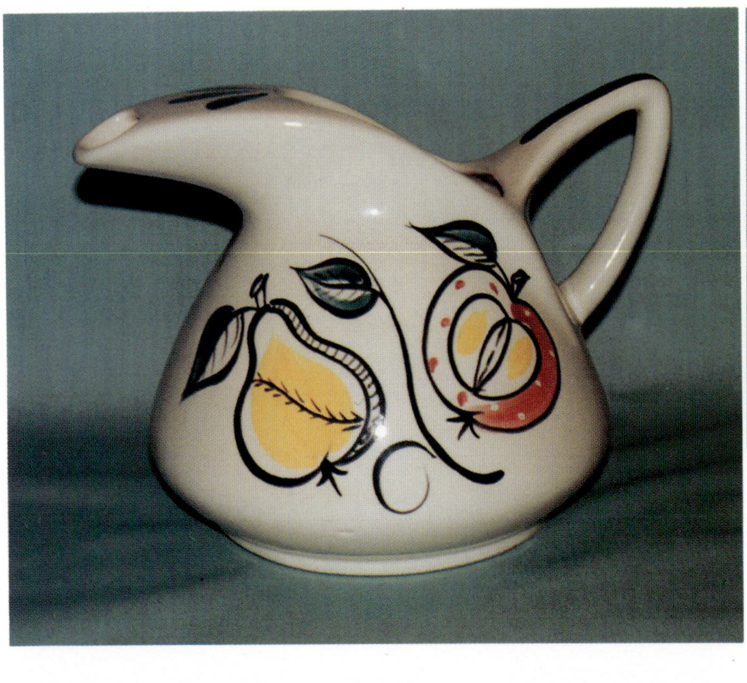

Five pint dutch jug. $300+.

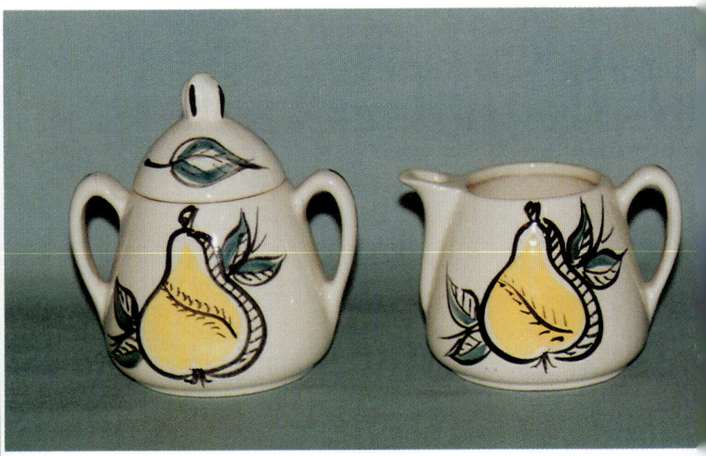

Provincial Fruit covered sugar and creamer. $125 set.

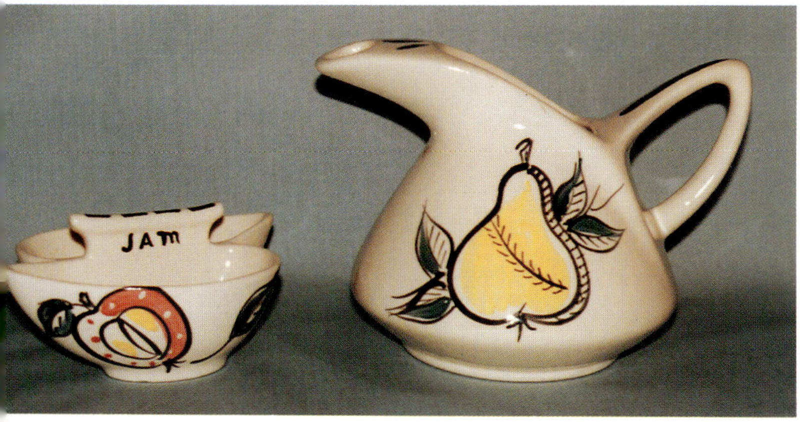

Jam and jelly. $125. Two pint dutch jug. $200.

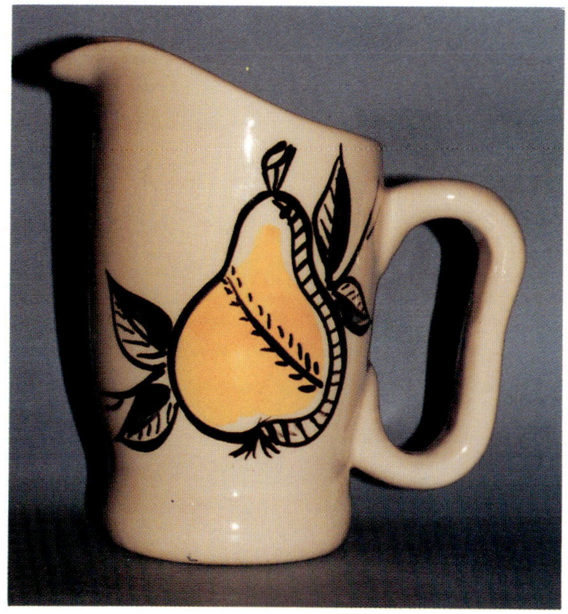

Mug jug. $200.

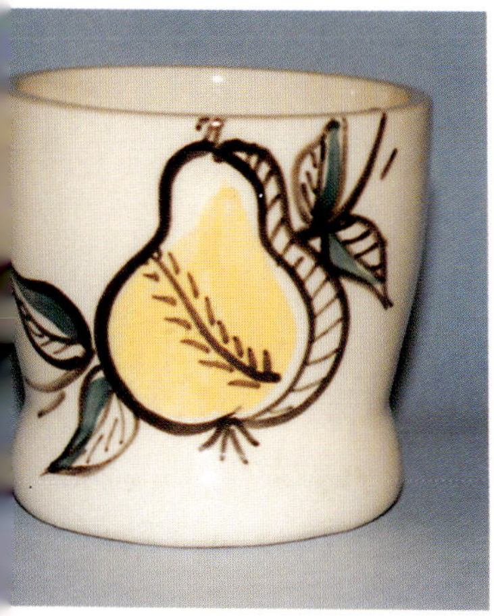

Juice mug. $40.

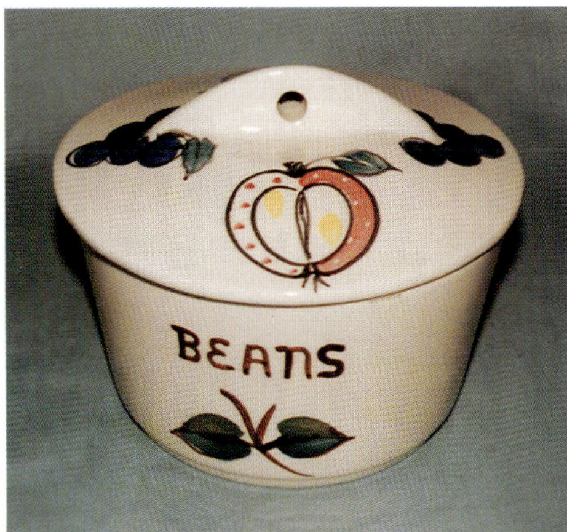

Beans pot. $100.

Three part relish with a ceramic handle. $125.

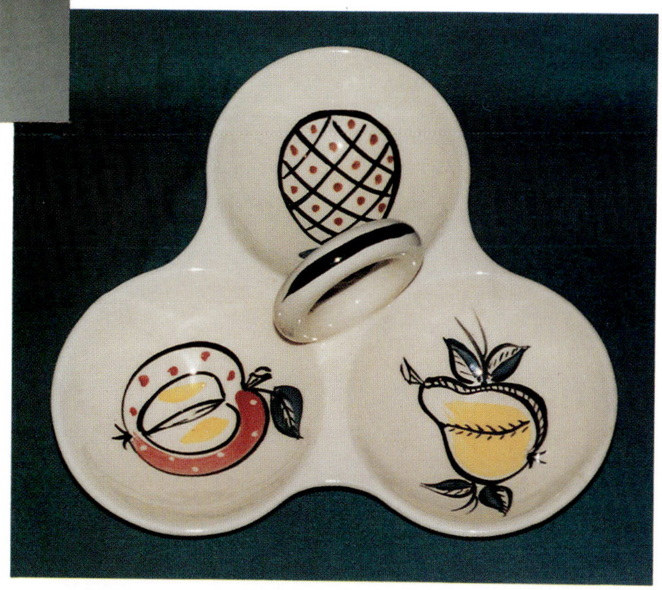

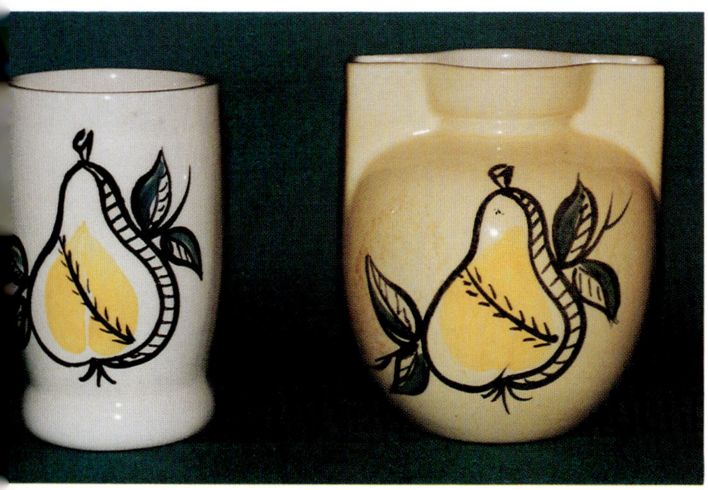

Tumbler. $75. Winged vase (with a lid this would be a grease jar). $100.

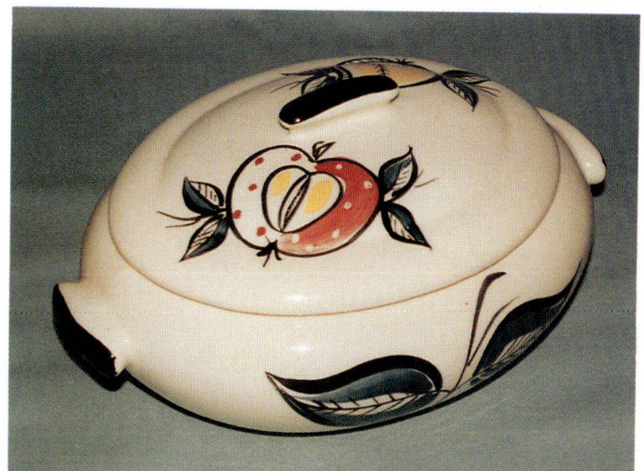

Covered vegetable. $125.

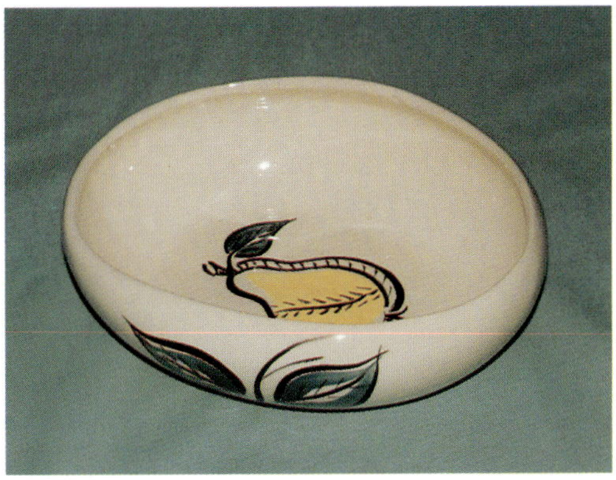

Open vegetable. $75.

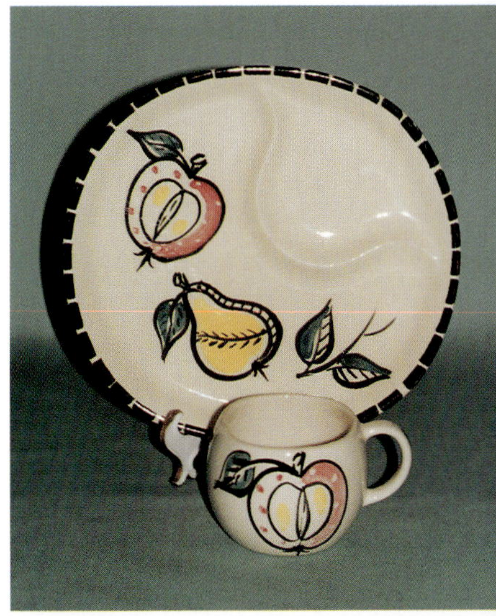

Tea and toast plate. $40. Cup. $25.

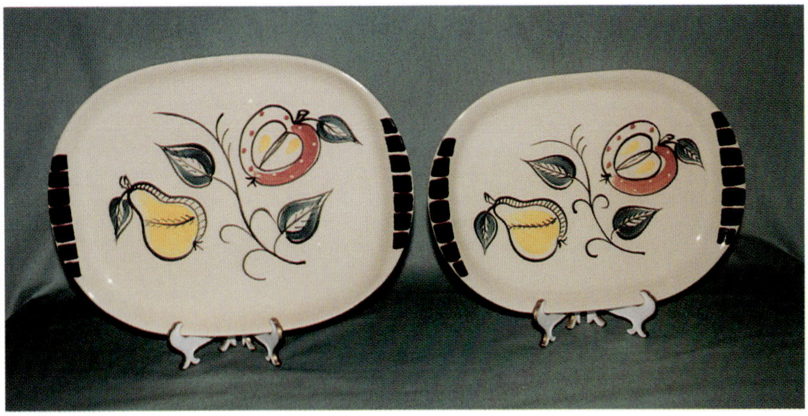

Large platter. $125. Small platter. $125.

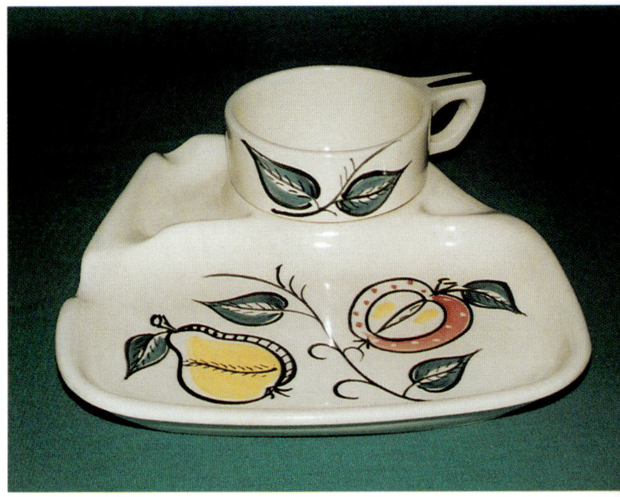

Soup and sandwich, Rubel mold. $100 set.

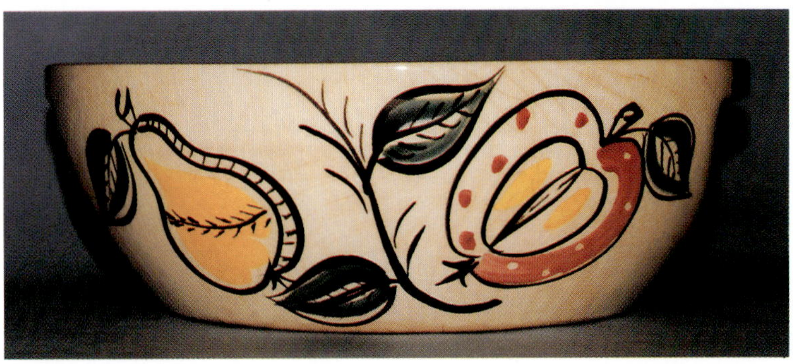

Salad bowl. $150.

Fruit Bowl. $200+.

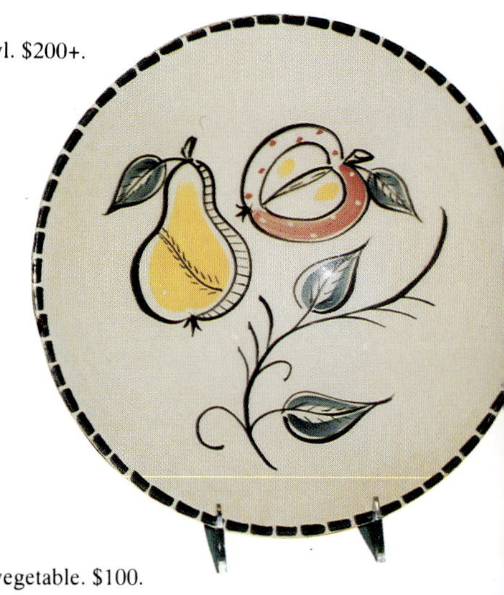

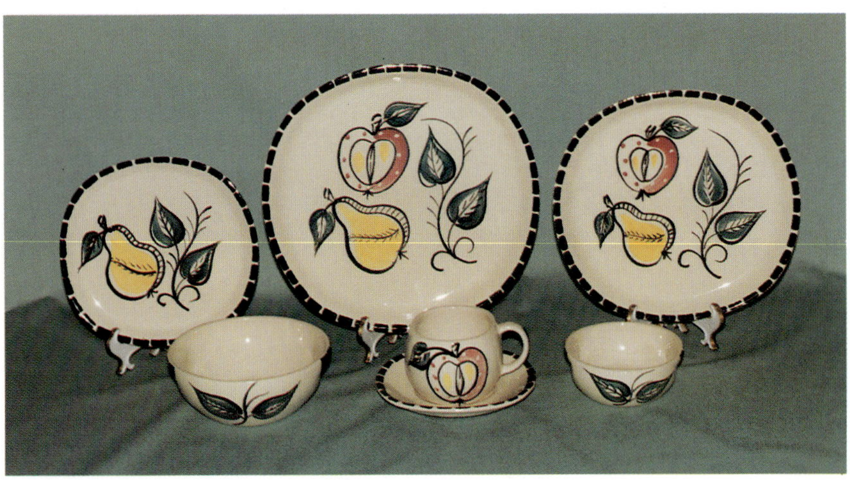

Salad plate. $40. Dinner plate. $50. Breakfast plate. $50. Cereal bowl. $30. Cup. $25. Saucer. $10. Dessert bowl. $25.

Divided vegetable. $100.

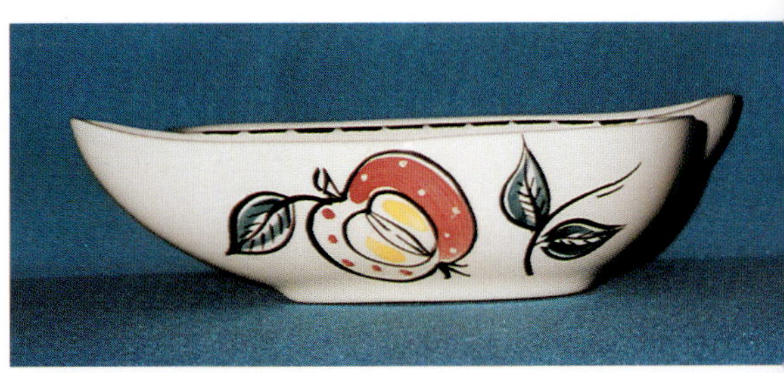

Seaform

Introduced in the mid-1950s, Seaform presented a new decorative style to the regular Purinton shapes. The ruffled edge shape offered a new look that Purinton hoped would be popular in homes. The pink flower with small green leaves was more difficult to paint. The combination of painting challenges and casting difficulties presented by the ruffled edges made Seaform another short run pattern. Purinton introduced a new style creamer and sugar with under plate in the Seaform decoration. They also utilized the Seaform style in some other production items.

Seaform is found only in limited quantities. With its more colorful and brighter decoration, the demand is moderate. Seaform offers a desirable decoration that is very attractive. Dinnerware is hard to find in mint condition. The most desirable serving pieces include the coffee server, teapot, butter dish, and star candle holders. The Seaform flower is painted in full bloom or as a half flower (half of a whole blossom) on some items. This variation makes it desirable to have more than one of a specific item.

Prices are higher for Seaform than for most other patterns. Seaform presents a variation in color and shape that would be a charming addition to any home or collection.

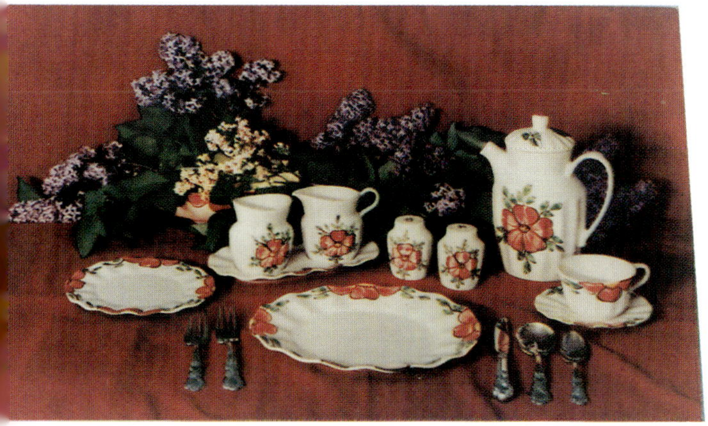

Seaform dinnerware product advertising card.

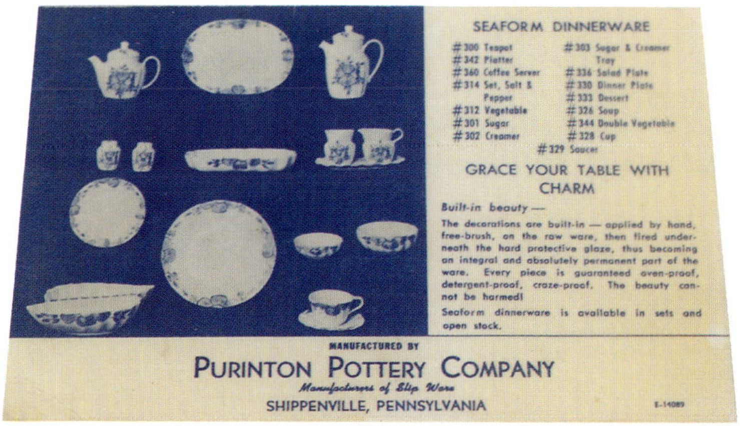

Reverse side of the Seaform dinnerware product advertising card.

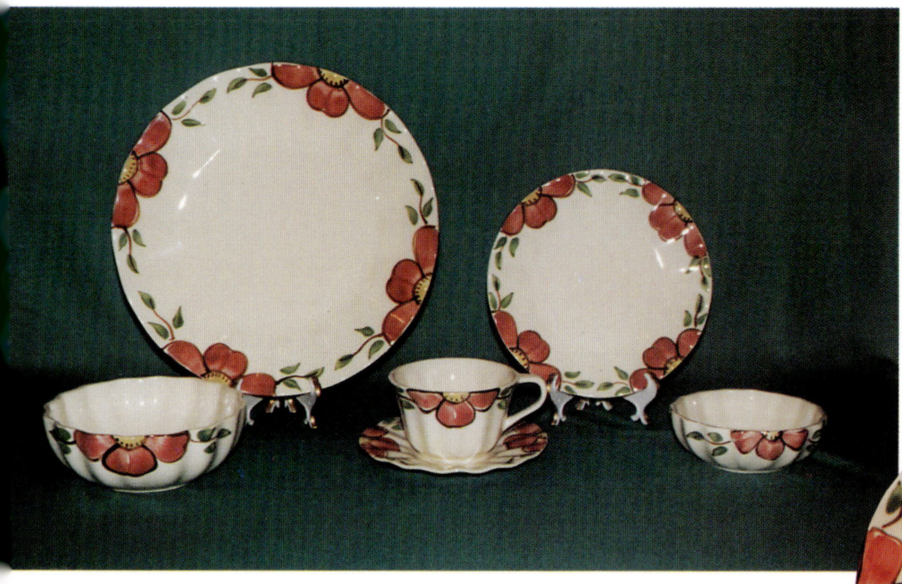

Dinner plate. $20. Salad plate. $15. Cereal bowl. $10. Cup. $15. Saucer. $10. Dessert bowl. $15.

Large platter. $60.

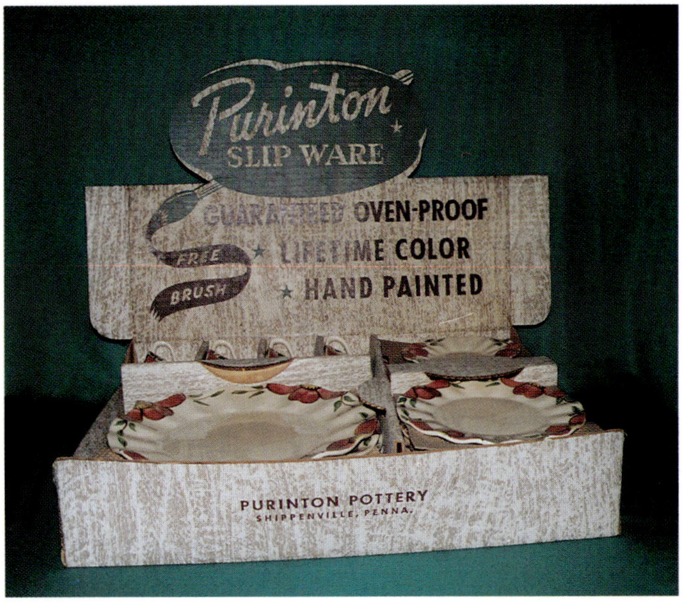

Original box containing a four piece place setting of Seaform dinnerware.

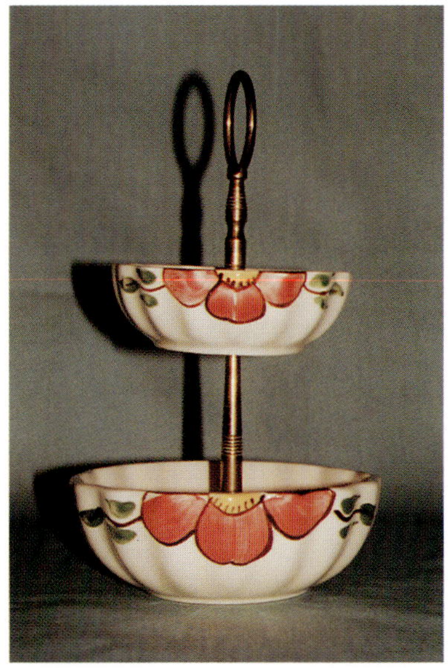

Tidbit tray utilizing dessert and cereal bowls. $60.

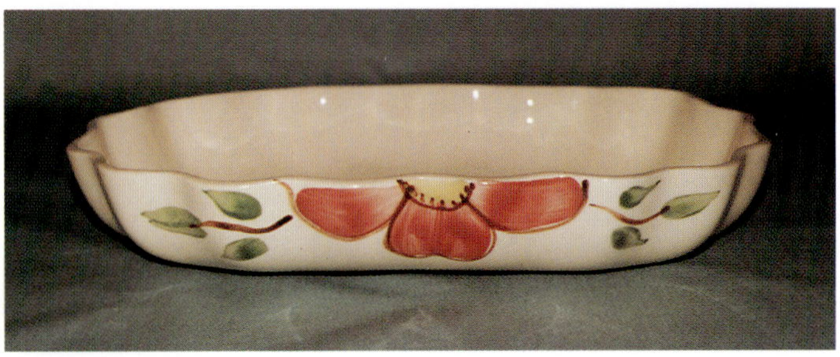

Roll tray. $50.

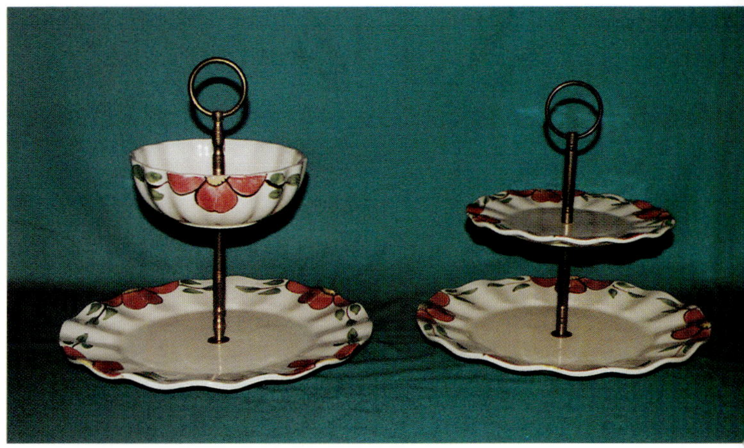

Tidbit tray utilizing cereal bowl and dinner plate. $60. Tidbit tray utilizing salad and dinner plates. $60.

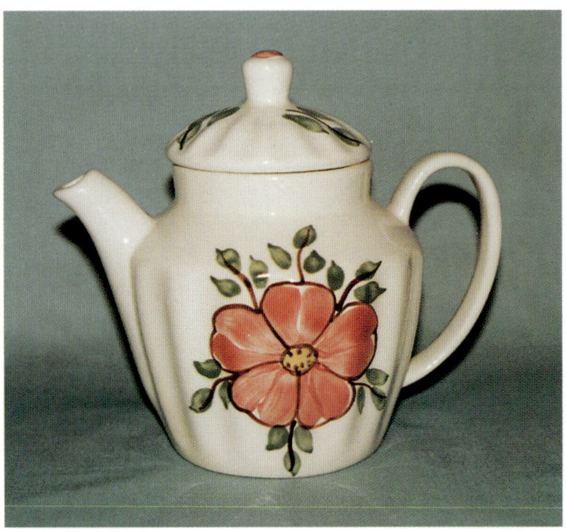

Teapot. $200+.

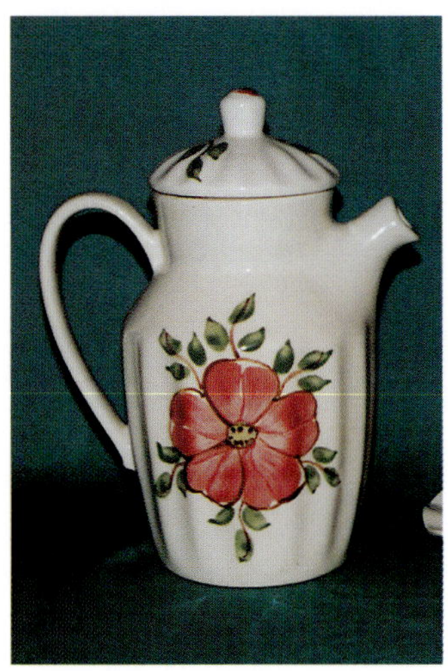

Coffee server. $250+.

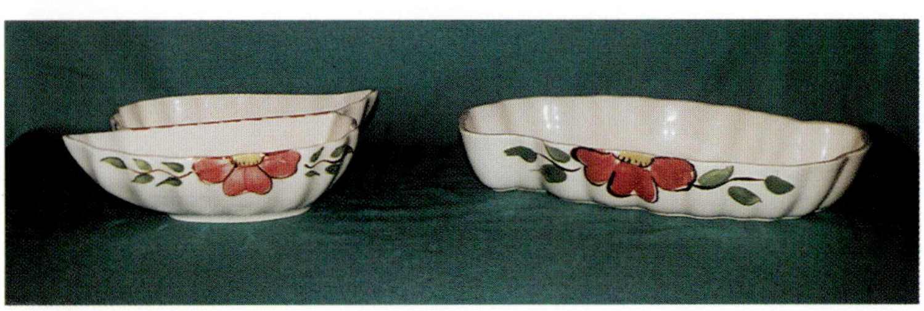

Divided vegetable. $40. S shaped bowl. $60.

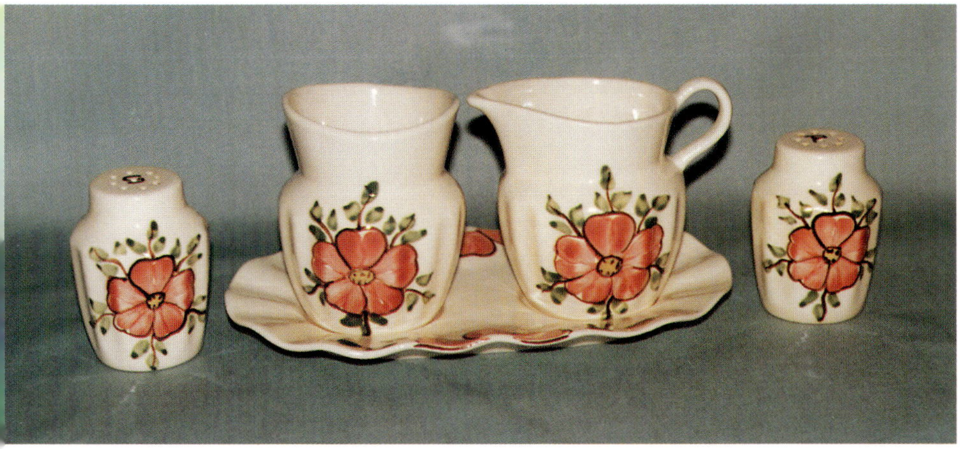

Seaform style salt and pepper shakers. $25 set. Creamer and sugar with tray. $100 set.

Jam and jelly. $75.

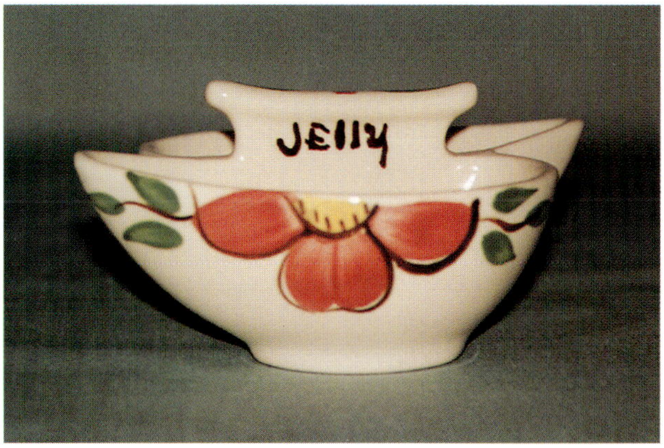

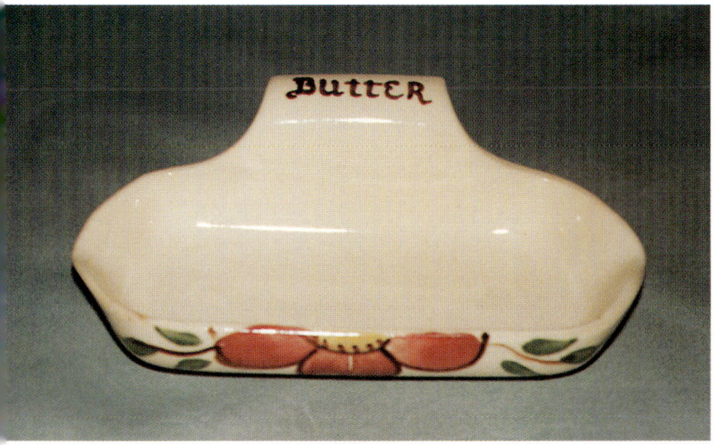

Butter dish. $125.

Star candle holder with insert. $100.

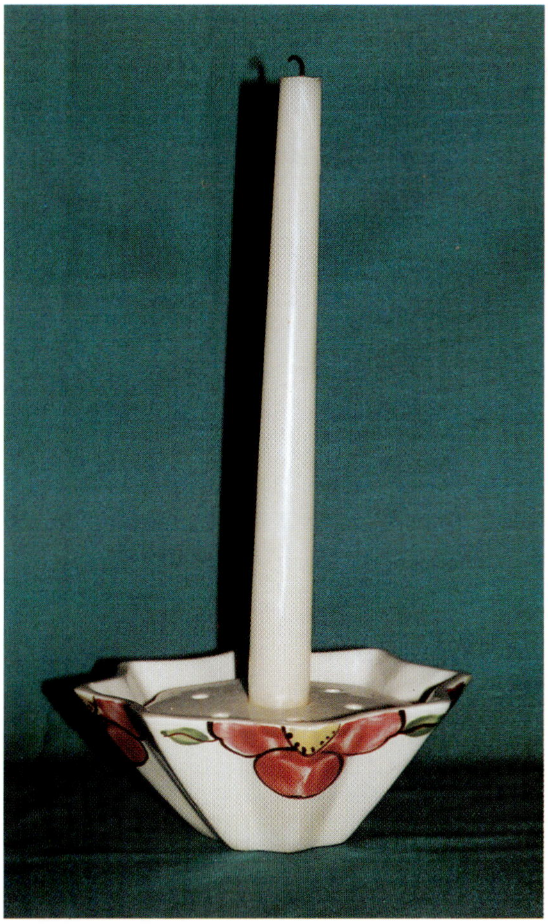

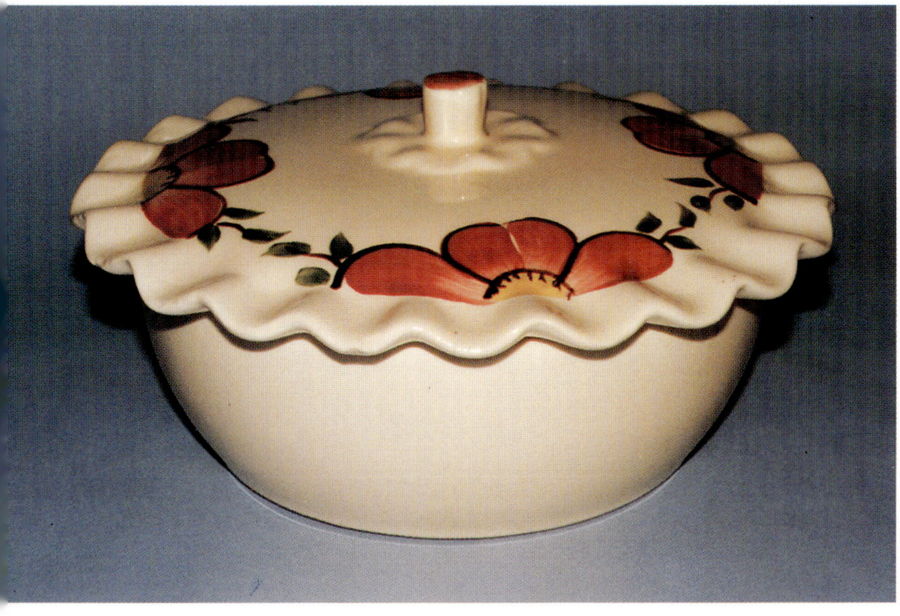

Covered casserole for a lazy susan. $125.

Tea Rose and Miniature Tea Rose

Tea Rose is an elusive pattern introduced in the mid-1950s. Its vibrant pink flower and green leaves use the same colors as the Seaform pattern. We do not know if this was a production pattern limited to dinnerware or a pattern sold only locally in the Shippenville area. Most of the items pictured were purchased as a group with a number of place settings and accessory pieces. Creamer and sugar sets and some miscellaneous pieces have been found outside the Clarion County area.

Supply is very limited and items are priced accordingly. The creamer and sugar set is the most common accessory item. A few dinner and salad plates have been found.

Mini Tea Rose was also a limited-run decoration. Few items are found.

Tea Rose

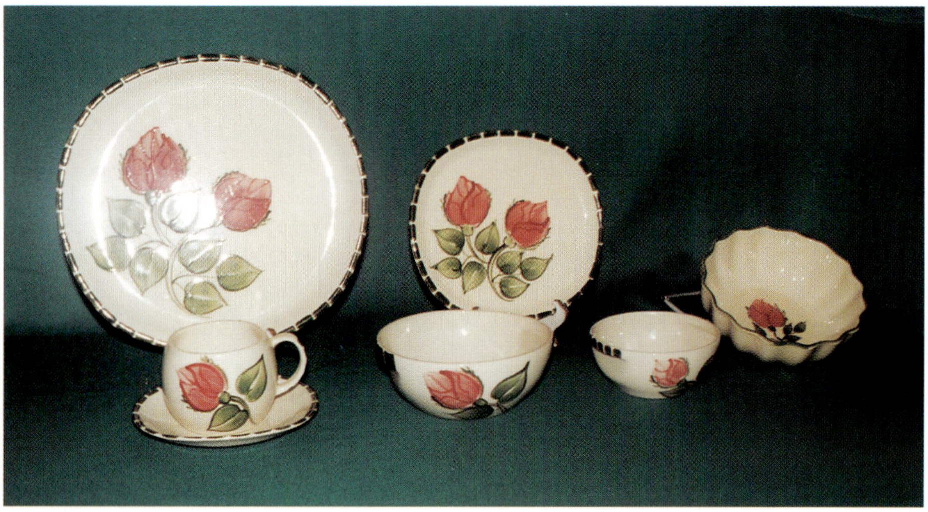

Tea Rose decorated wares. Dinner plate. $75. Salad plate. $50. Cup. $40. Saucer. $15. Cereal bowl. $50. Dessert bowl. $50. The cereal bowl is in the Seaform style. $50.

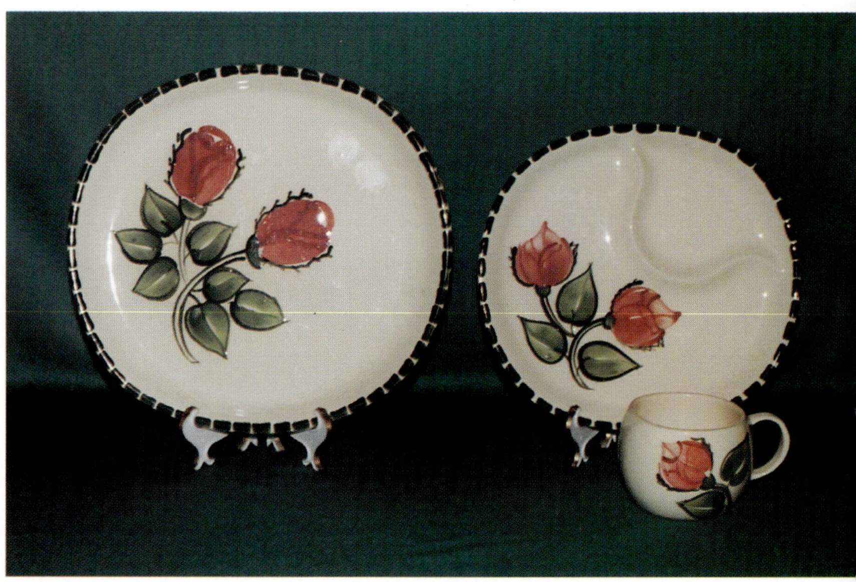

Dinner plate. $75. Tea and toast plate. $100. Cup. $40.

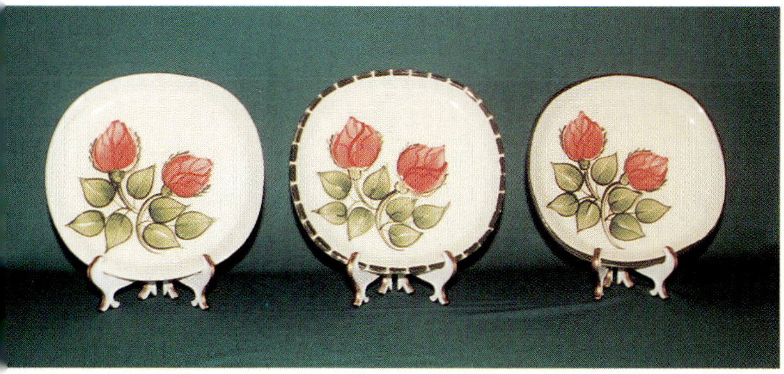

Salad plate, no outside trim. $50. Salad plate, regular outside trim. $50. Salad plate, solid outside trim. $50.

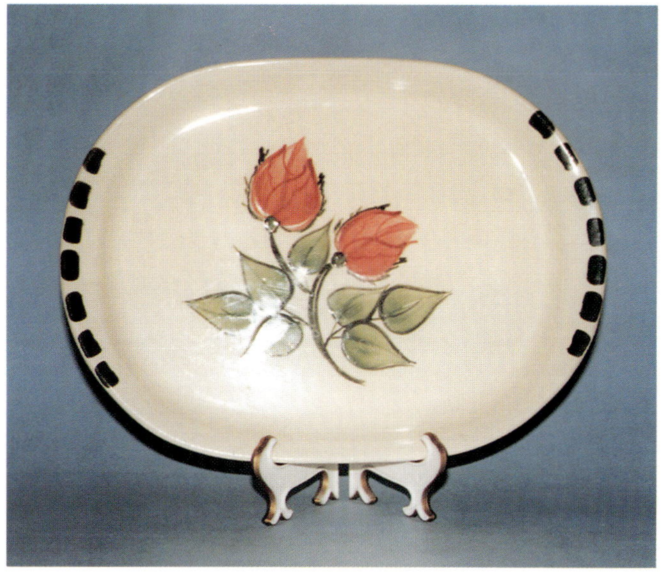

Small platter. $200.

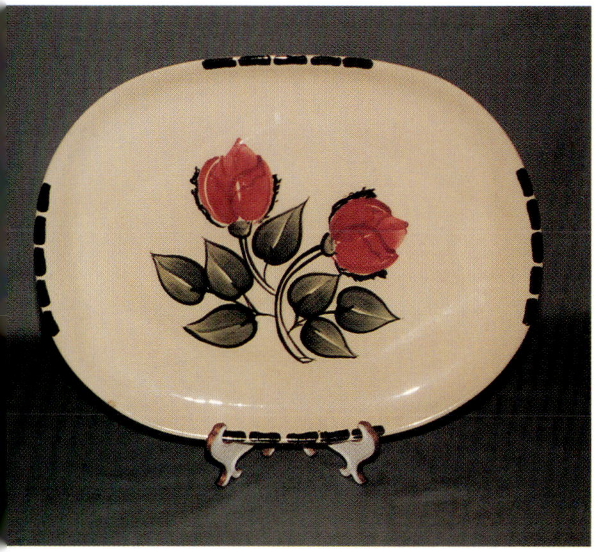

Diamond grill platter. $200.

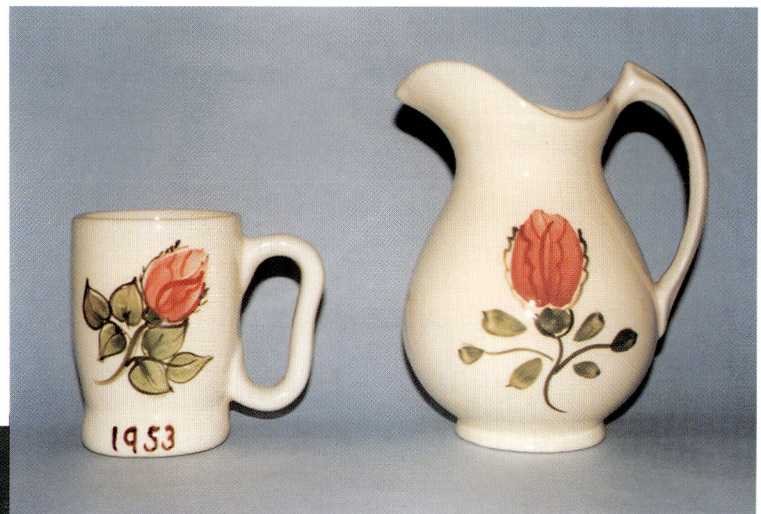

Coffee mug dated 1953. $200+. Pitcher, 6.5" high. $250+.

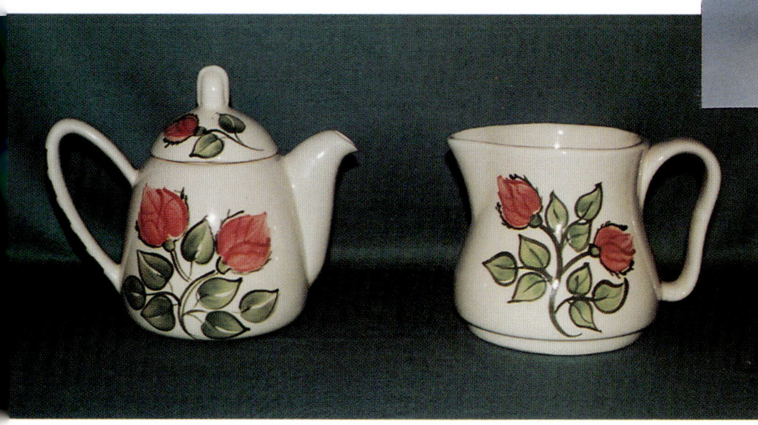

Six cup domed lid teapot. $200+. Pitcher, Rubel mold. $300+.

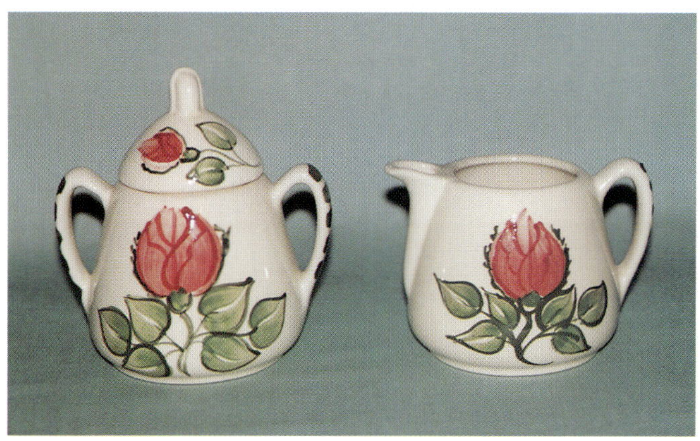

Covered sugar and creamer. $125 set.

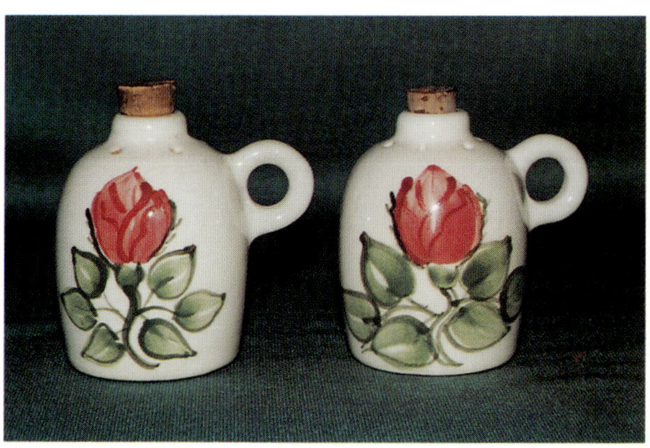

Jug style salt and pepper shakers. $75 set.

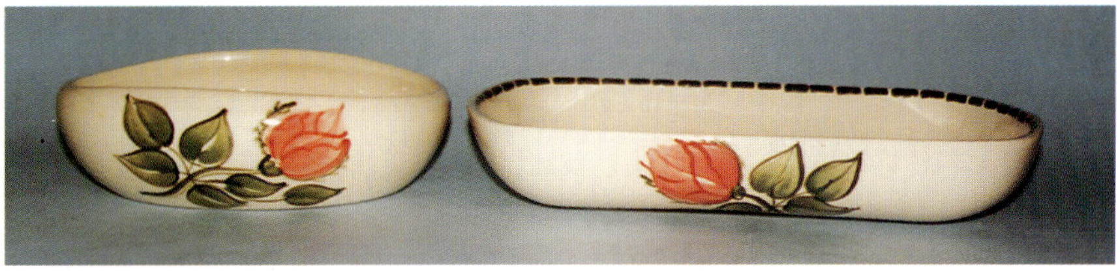

Open vegetable. $125. Roll tray. $200.

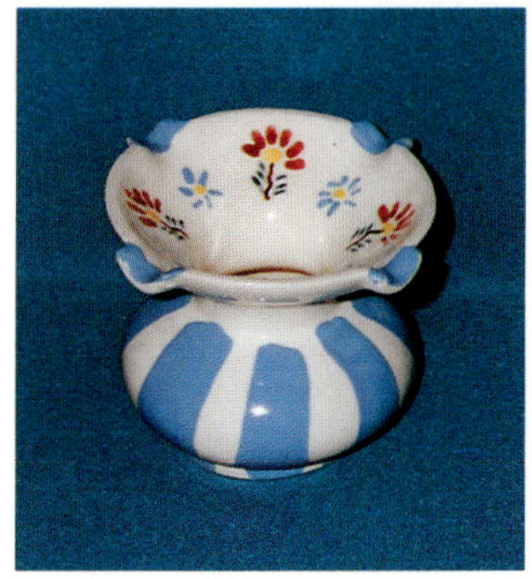

Whimsy ashtray spittoon shape with Miniature Daisy decoration, 3" high. $100.

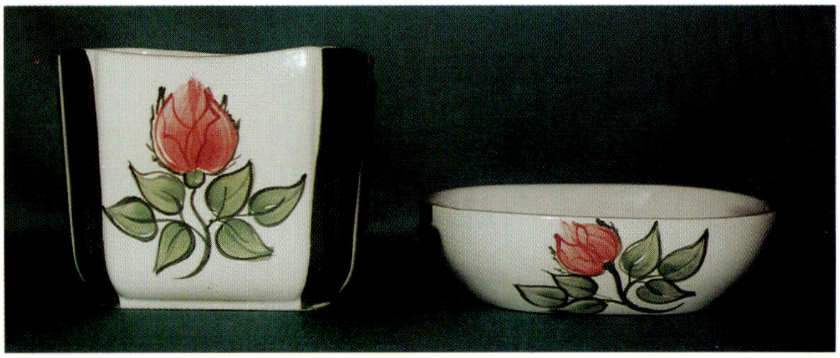

Vase, NAPCO mold. $100+. Baker. $75.

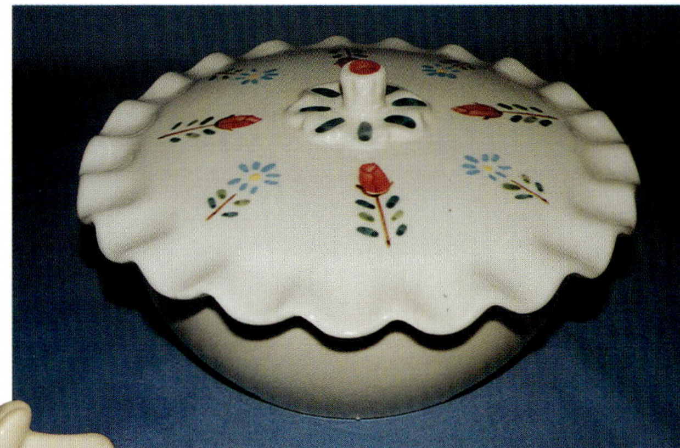

Casserole bowl with Miniature Tea Rose lid. $100.

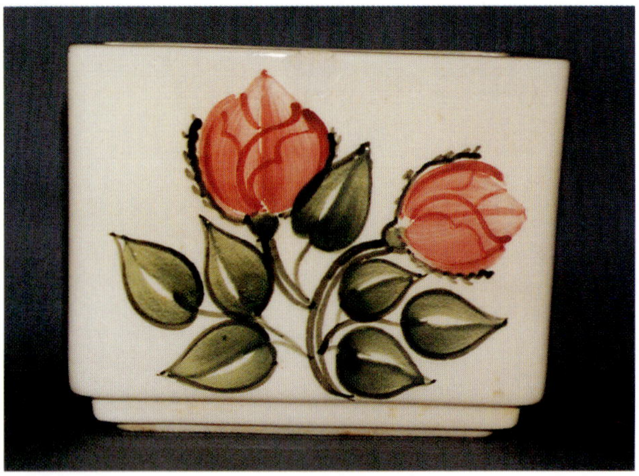

Pillow vase, short, NAPCO mold. $100+

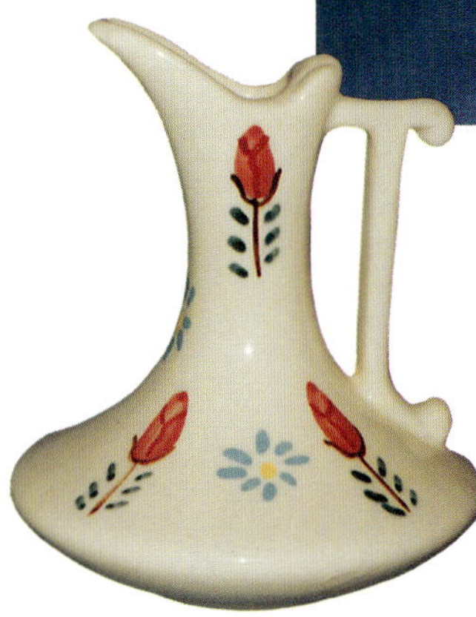

Small ewer. $75.

Miniature Tea Rose

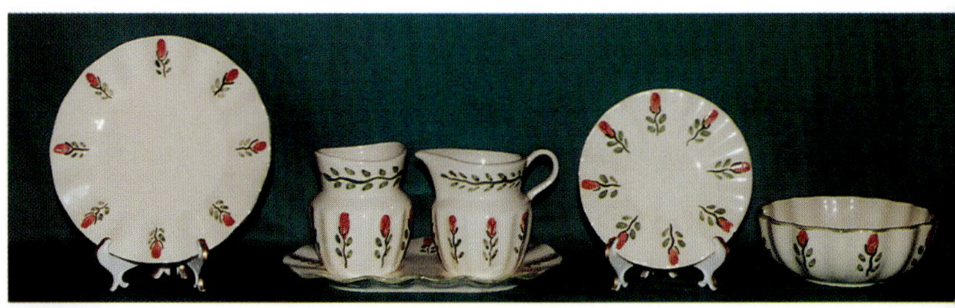

Salad plate, Seaform style. $45. Sugar and creamer on tray, all Seaform style. $125 set. Saucer, Seaform style. $25. Cereal bowl, Seaform style. $35.

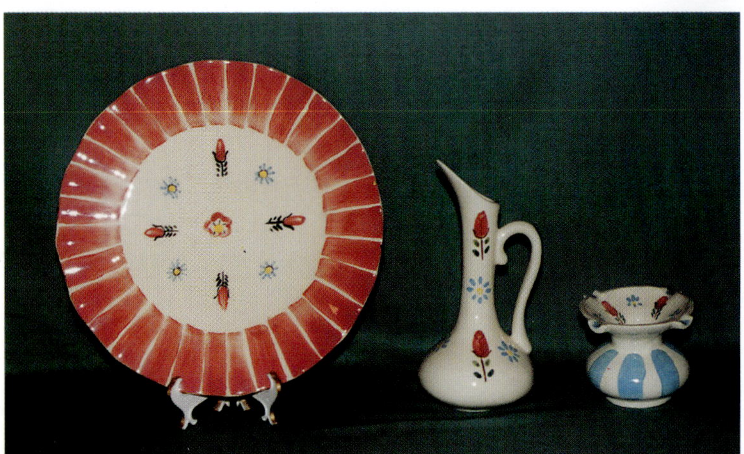

Miniature Tea Rose dinner plate in the Seaform style, signed Dorothy Purinton. $300+. Tall ewer. $75. Whimsy ashtray spittoon shape, 3" high. $100.

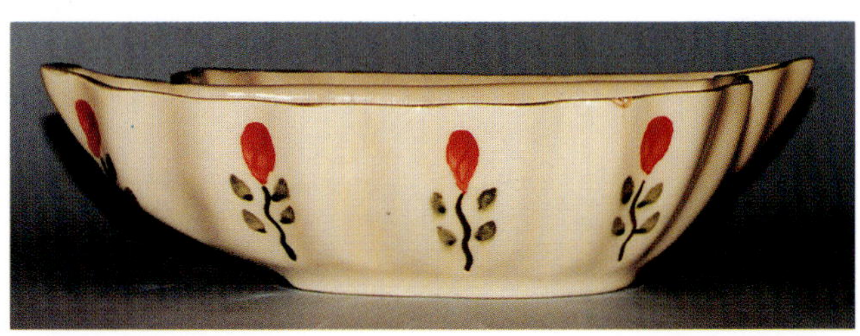

Divided vegetable, Seaform style. $75.

Miscellaneous

This miscellaneous chapter covers many decorations produced by Purinton Pottery. One of their biggest contracts was to make floral items for other companies. Items pictured in this chapter include pieces made for other companies, decorations made on limited pieces, and solid glaze items, among others. Most of the items, like the floral vases, have been mass produced. The honey jug, cornucopia vase, and winged vase (a smaller version of a winged grease jar without the lid) were made for floral shops and distributors. A taller vase with a foot was made in the Tionesta plant and the tall, oval canister was used as a vase before being produced as a canister set.

Starflower and Woodflowers are two decorations that were mainly seen on a pitcher set. Morning Glory is found mostly on a honey jug. Half Blossom, Sunny, Pussy Willow, Shooting Star, Windflower, and Blue Pansy are seen on floral items.

Rubel, Taylor Smith Taylor, and NAPCO products are shown. Familiar decorations made for these companies include Tulip and Vine and Autumn Leaves. These decorations are painted on limited products.

Kay Kraft jewelry was made for Kay Purinton, daughter-in-law of Bernard and Dorothy. Pieces were sold in the outlet with Palm Tree in Ft. Myers, Florida.

Some solid glaze items are pictured. Purinton made items in Wellsville, Shippenville, and Tionesta with a solid glaze. These are not desirable and are listed more for the identification of their shapes. If they are found with a decoration on them, like Apple or Pennsylvania Dutch, they could command a high price.

Items pictured vary in supply and demand and the prices reflect this. An explanation of each product is given in the caption. Harder to find items include the Tulip and Vine fruit bowl, Oriental individual bean pot, Morning Glory wide oval cookies jar, and the Starflower square cookie canister.

Kay Kraft Jewelry

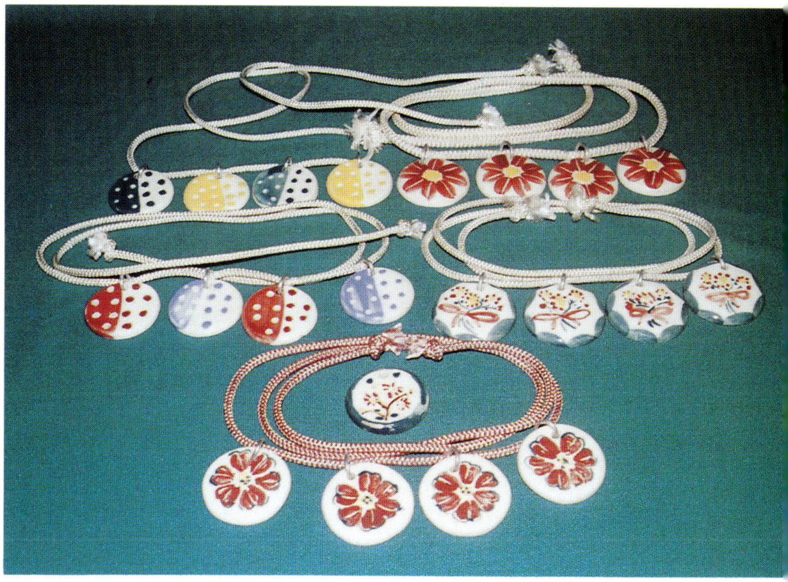

Here is a dazzling array of Kay Kraft necklaces; Kay Kraft was manufactured by Purinton Pottery and sold in Florida by Kay Purinton, the wife of Dorothy and Bernard's son Pete. $50 each.

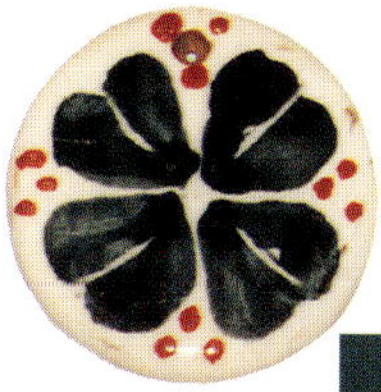

Kay Kraft four leaf clover charm. $10.

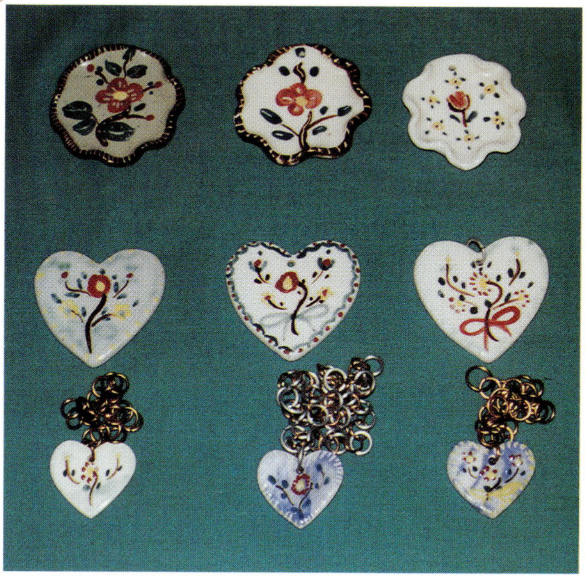

Variety of Kay Kraft pieces and bracelets. $10 each.

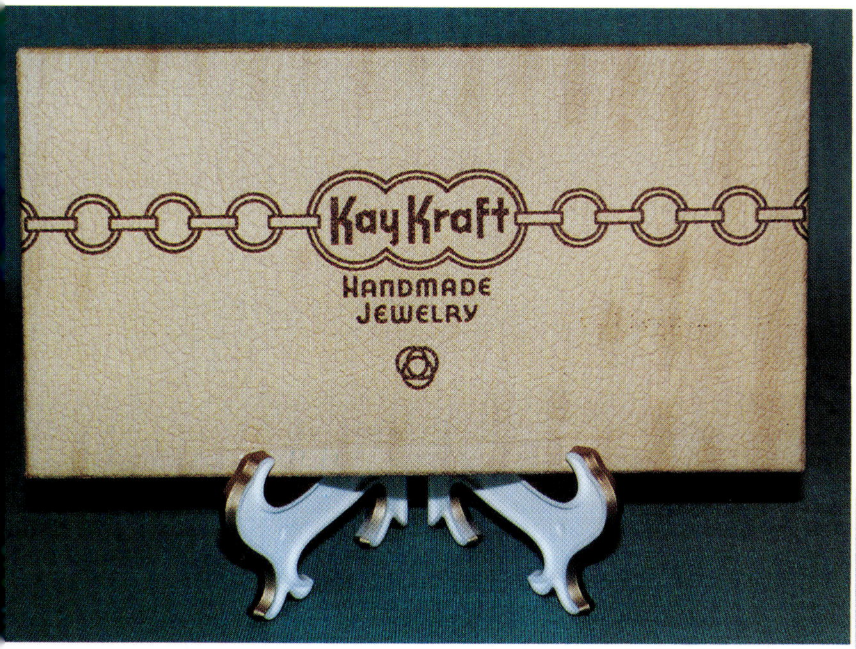

Kay Kraft jewelry box. $50.

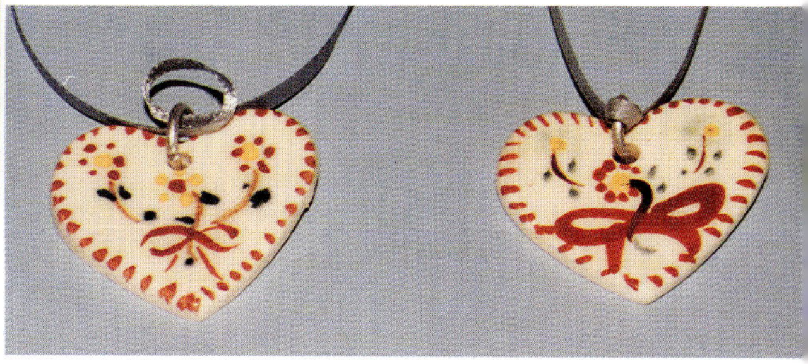

Kay Kraft hearts. $10 each.

Morning Glory

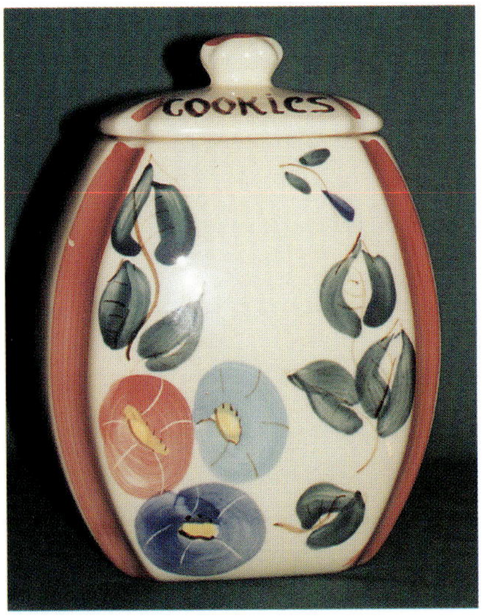

Morning Glory wide oval cookies jar. $250.

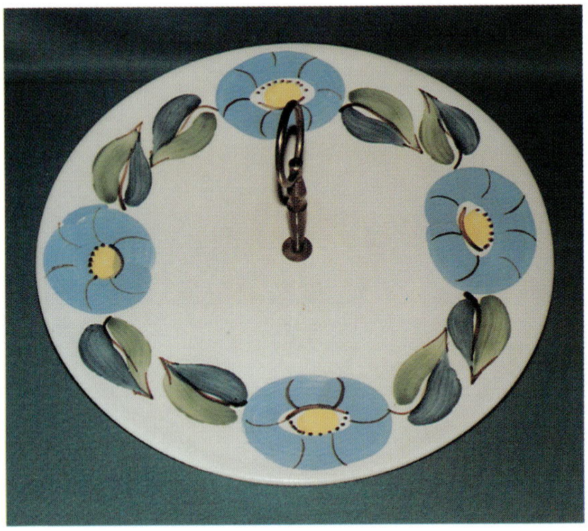

Morning Glory sandwich plate. $100.

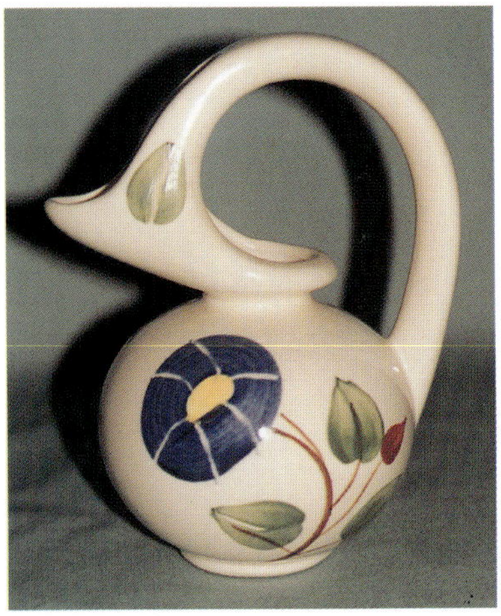

Morning Glory honey jug. $30.

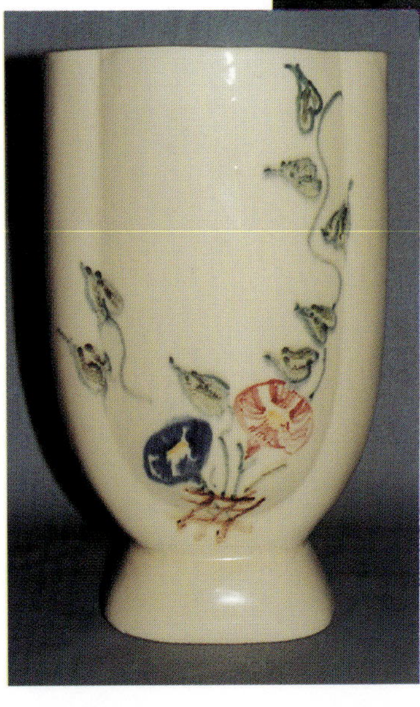

Morning Glory vase, 9" high. $40.

Oriental

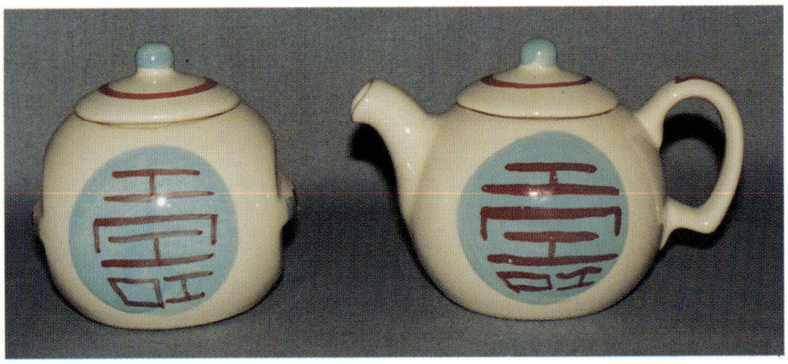

Light blue Oriental individual bean pot or sugar bowl. $100 (rare). Two cup teapot. $25. Produced for Epicurio Tea Company.

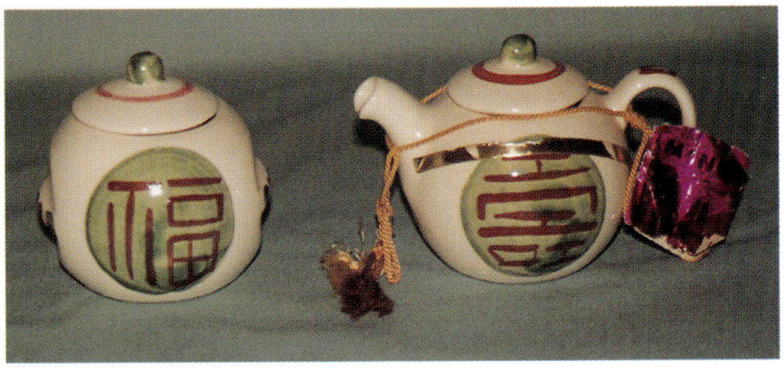

Green Oriental individual bean pot or sugar bowl. $100 (rare). Two cup teapot with an original Ming Tea label. $25. Produced for Epicurio Tea Company.

Tulip and Vine

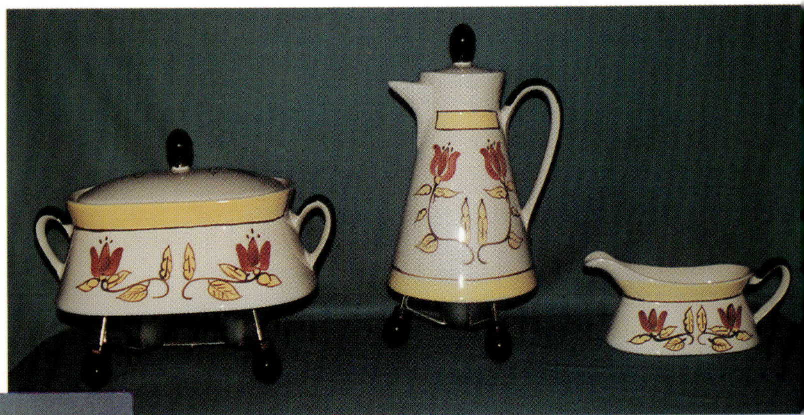

Tulip and Vine pattern produced for Taylor Smith Taylor. Covered tureen. $50 Coffee server. $70. Gravy boat. $50.

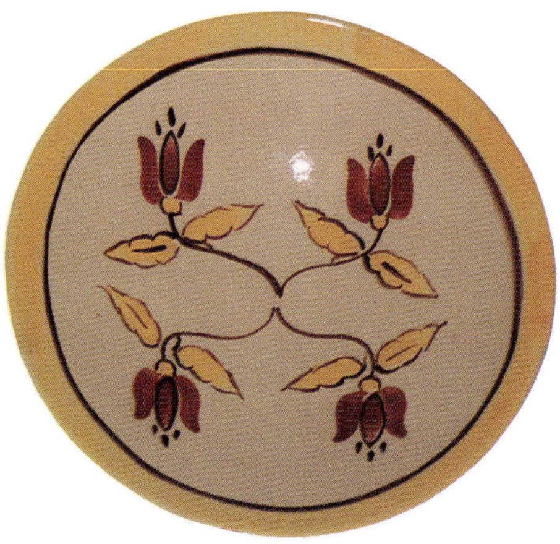

Tulip and Vine fruit bowl — it is very unusual to find this decoration on anything except the three Taylor Smith Taylor serving pieces. This piece was discovered at a yard sale in Tionesta. $150

Southwestern

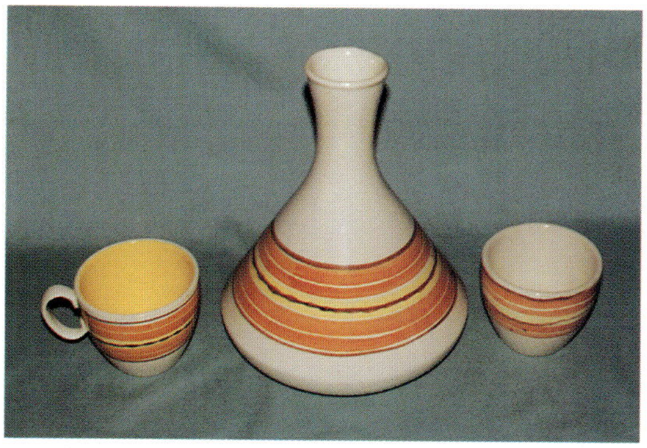

The Southwestern pattern was made for Taylor Smith Taylor. Cup. $30. Water bottle. $30. Sugar bowl. $30

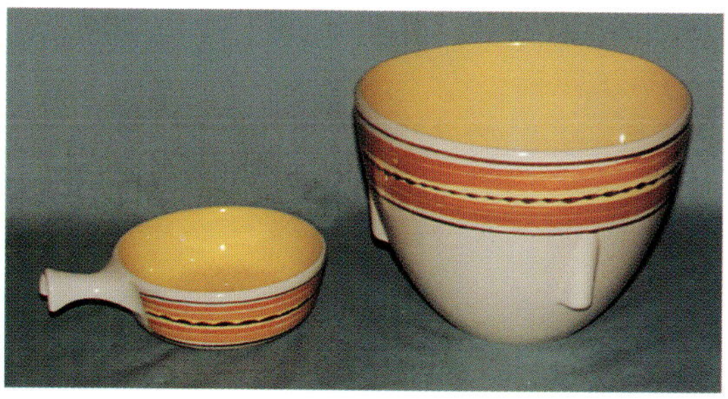

Southwestern individual handled casserole. $10. Bowl. $30.

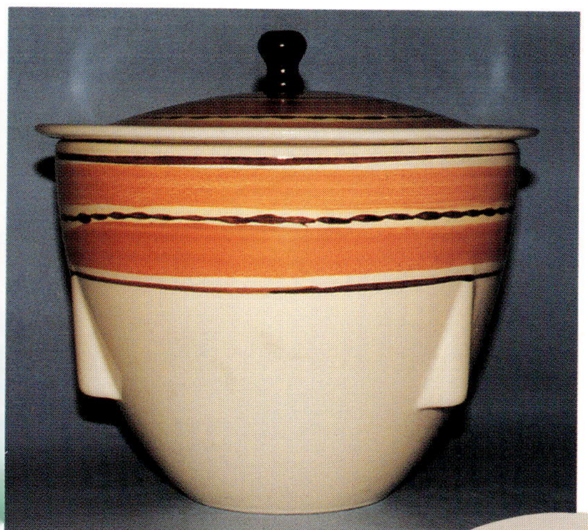

Southwestern ice bucket with lid. $50.

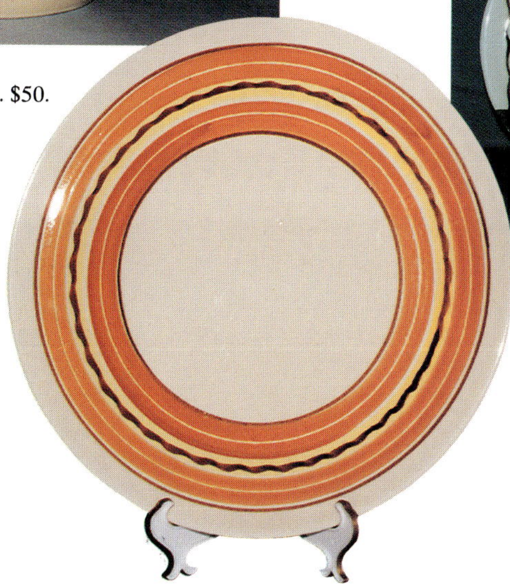

Southwestern dinner plate. $30.

Autumn Leaves

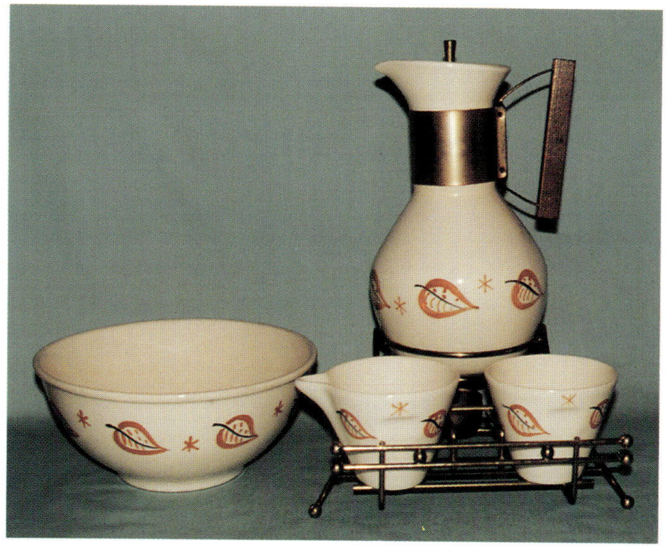

Autumn Leaves bowl 8.5" diameter. $25. Autumn Leaves coffee server with a metal handle. $40. Autumn Leaves creamer and sugar. $60 set (uncommon). Add $10 to the price with the metal rack. These pieces are from Rubel molds.

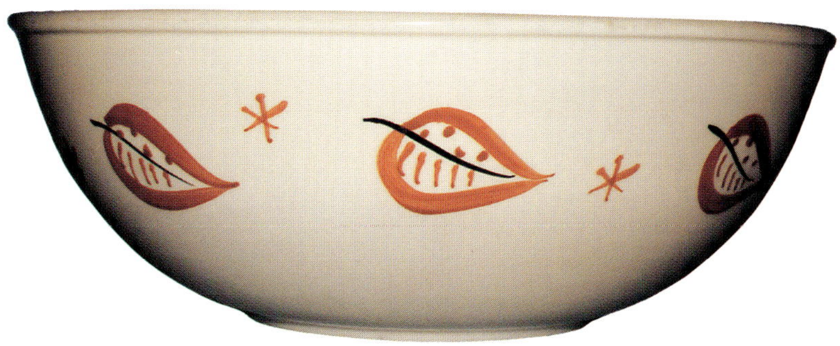

Autumn Leaves bowl, 10" diameter. $25.

Leaf

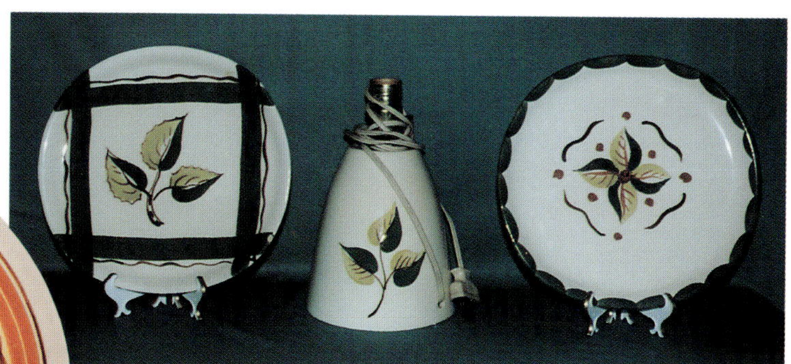

Leaf dinner plate, experimental. $75. Lamp. $50. Dinner plate, signed Dorothy Purinton. $250+.

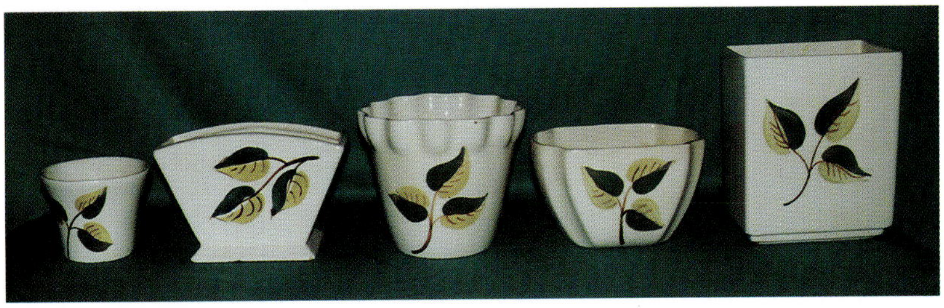

Leaf candy dish, 3" high. $30. Fan shaped vase, 4" high. $30. Jardiniere, 5" high. $20. Vase, NAPCO mold. $25. Large pillow vase, NAPCO mold. $25.

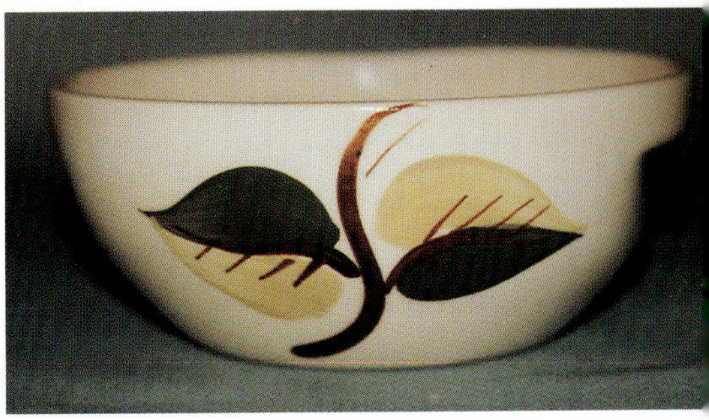

Leaf cereal bowl. $10.

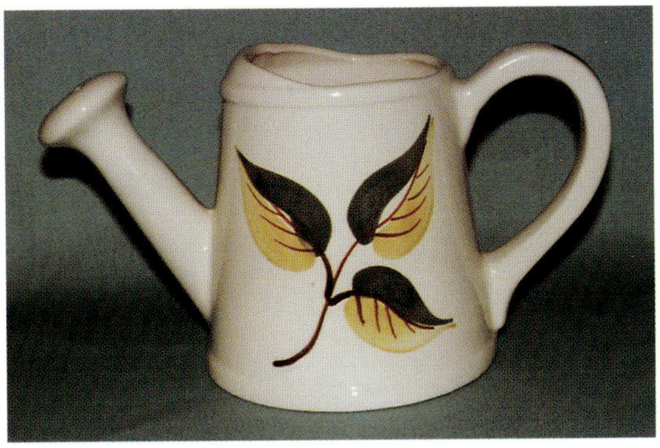

Leaf sprinkler, NAPCO mold. $40.

Starflower

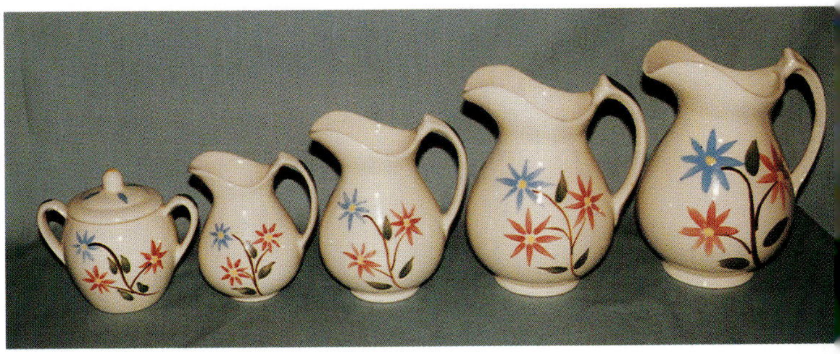

Starflower sugar with lid. $25. Creamer, 5" high. $25. Pitcher, 5.5" high. $40. Pitcher, 6" high. $40. Pitcher, 6.5" high. $40.

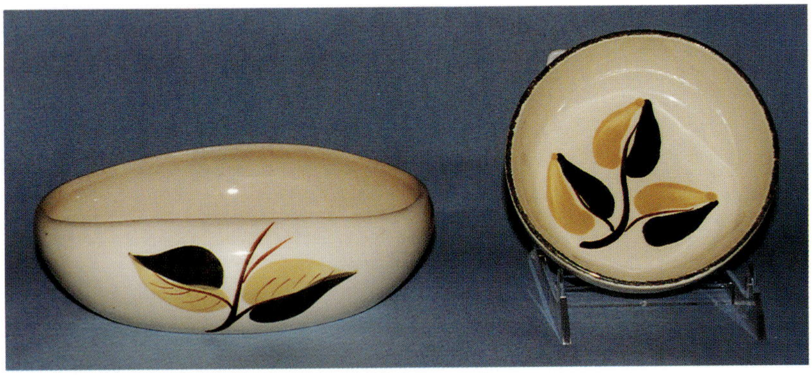

Leaf open vegetable. $20. Center bowl for lazy susan. $10.

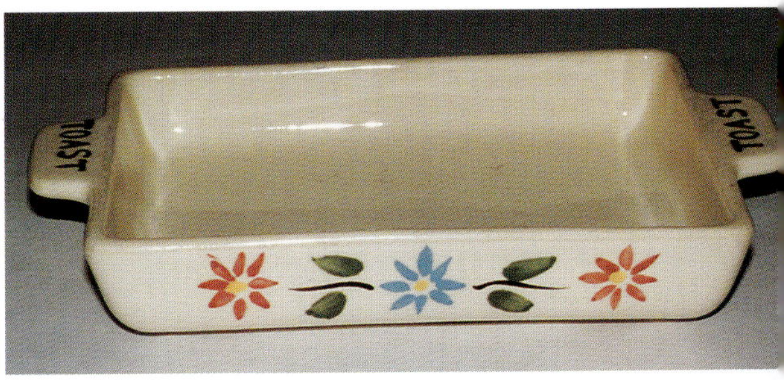

Starflower toast plate, whimsy piece. This is a rectangular three part relis with the dividers removed. $85.

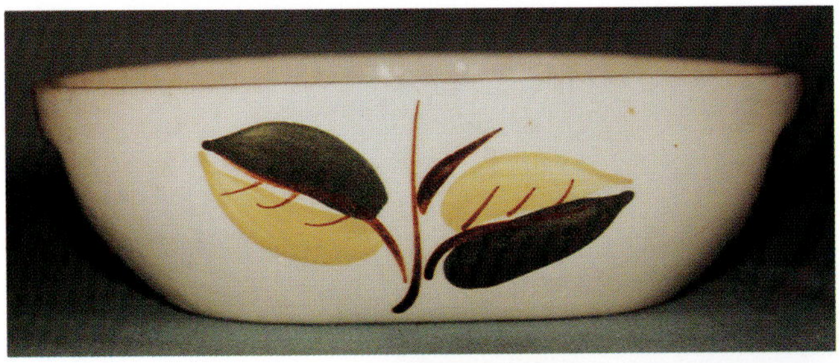

Leaf baker. $20.

Starflower square cookies jar with a wooden lid. $200.

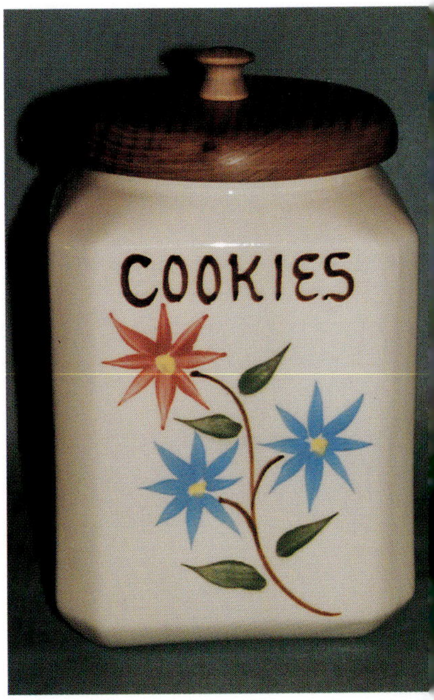

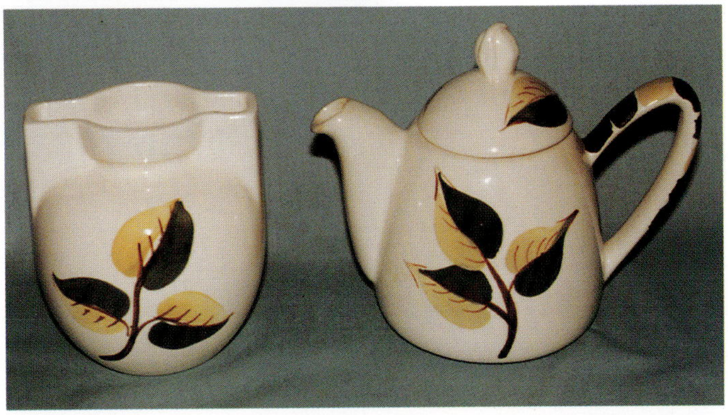

Leaf winged vase. $30. Six cup domed lid teapot. $40.

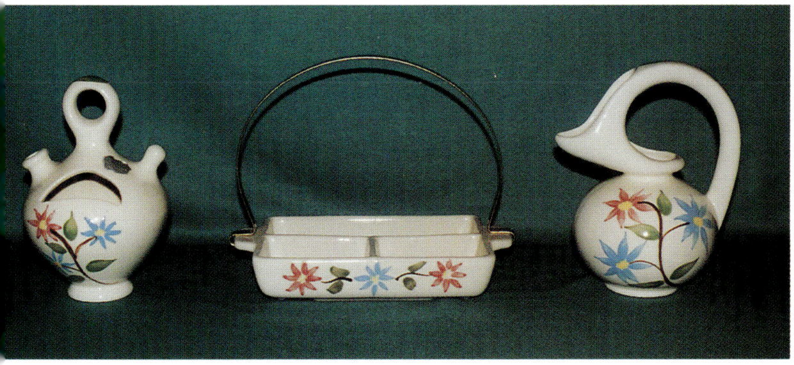

Starflower rum jug planter. $65. Rectangular three part relish with a metal handle. $50. Honey jug. $150 (uncommon).

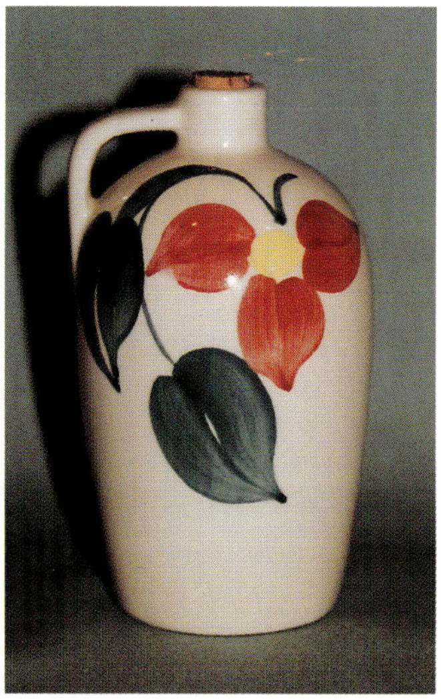

Half Blossom jug decanter. $30.

Woodflowers

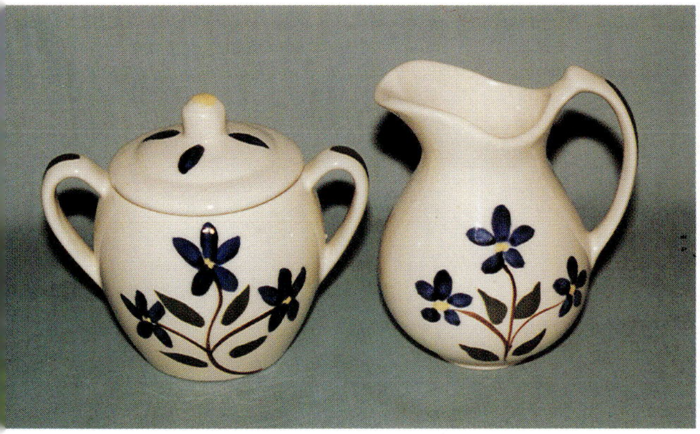

Woodflowers round covered sugar and creamer. $50 set.

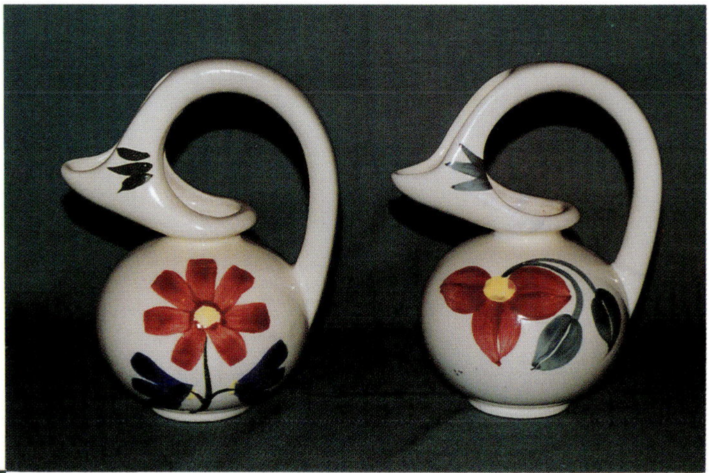

Honey jug with decoration. $75. Honey jug with Half Blossom decoration. (uncommon). $100.

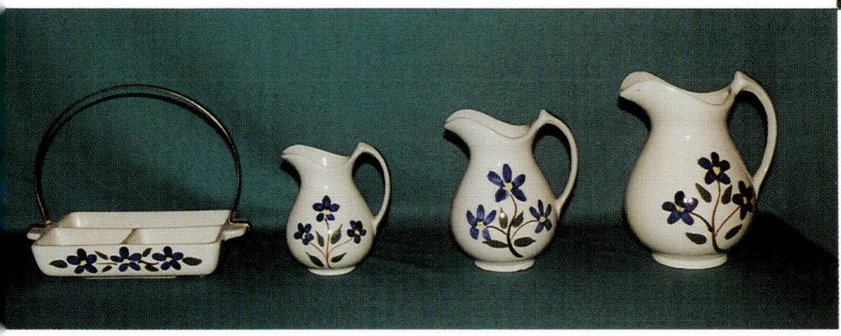

Woodflowers rectangular three part relish with a metal handle. $50. Pitcher, 5.5" high. $40. Pitcher, 6" high. $40. Pitcher, 6.5" high. $40.

General Miscellaneous

Shooting Star variant honey jugs. $25 each.

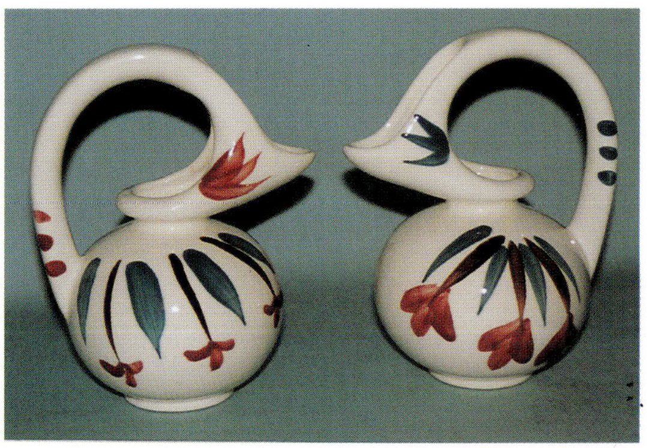

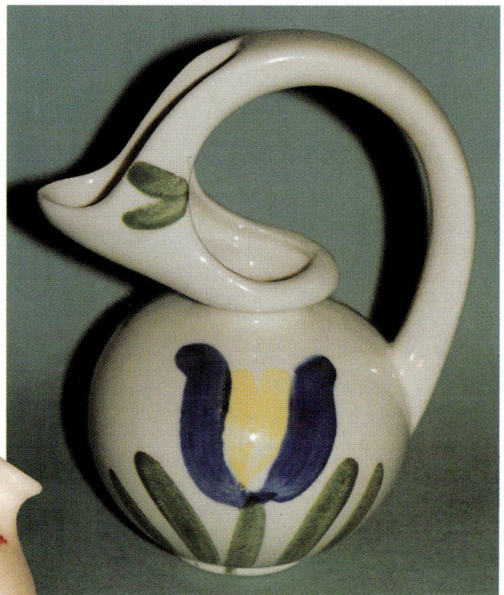

Blue and Yellow Tulip honey jug. $75.

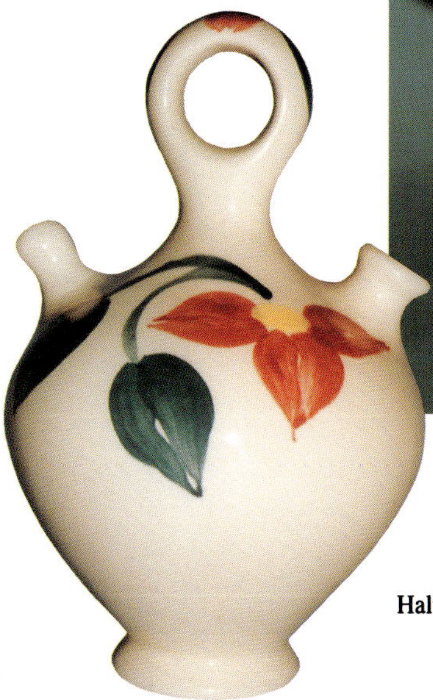

Half Blossom rum jug planter without the cut-out. $60.

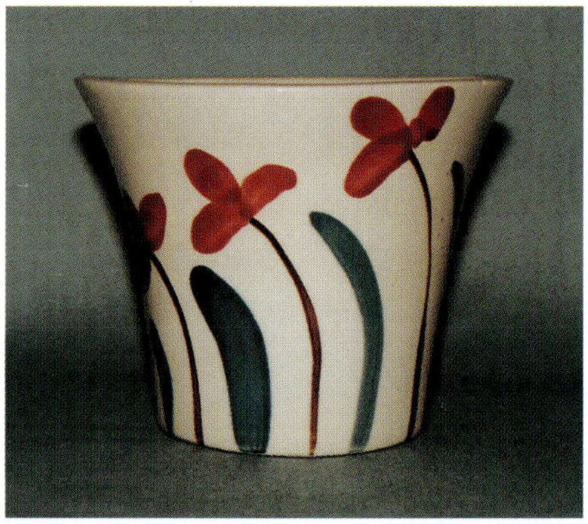

Wall pocket with Shooting Star decoration. $75.

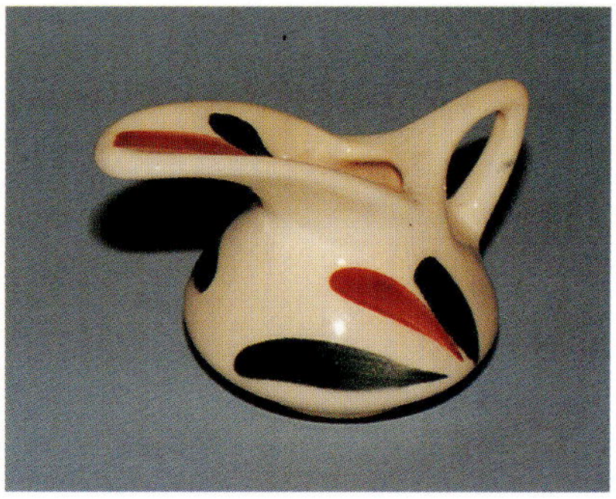

Jigger jug, three lines. $25.

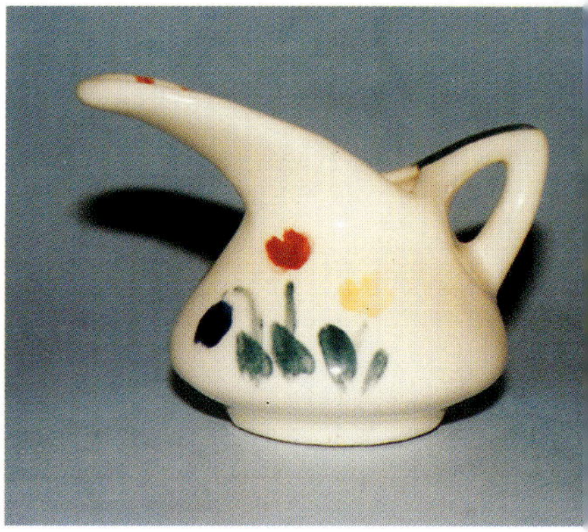

Jigger jug, multi-colored tulips. $25.

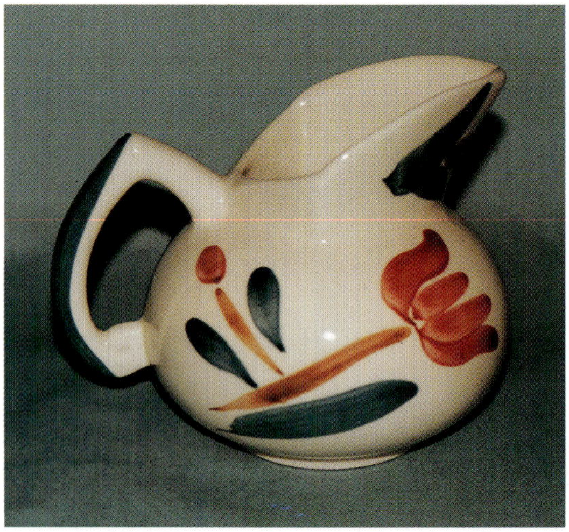

Kent jug with pronged flower. $50.

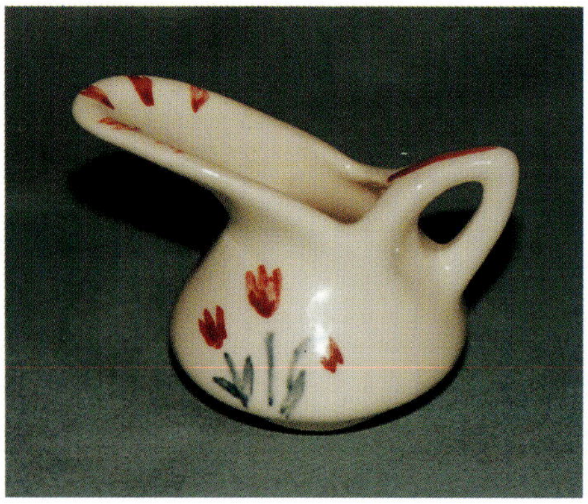

Jigger jug, red tulips. $25.

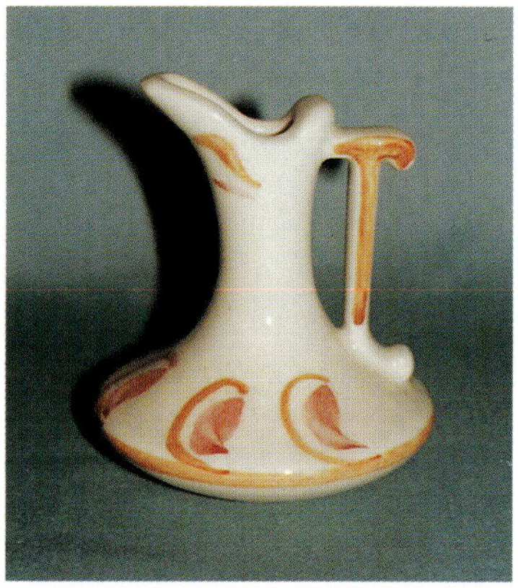

Small ewer. $25.

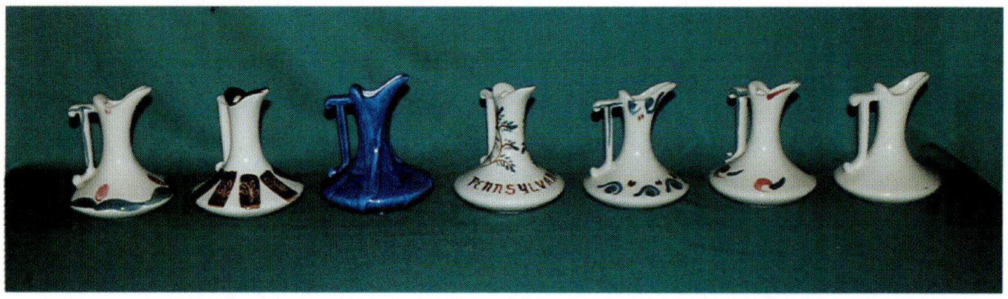

Small ewers. $25 each. A small Pennsylvania souvenir ewer is located in the middle. $150.

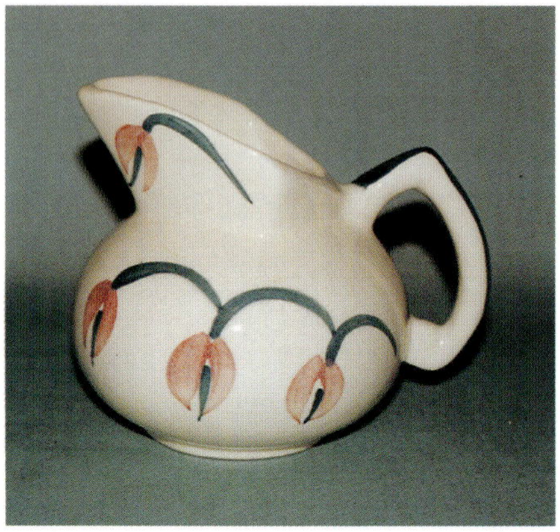

Kent jug with Fuscia decoration. $45.

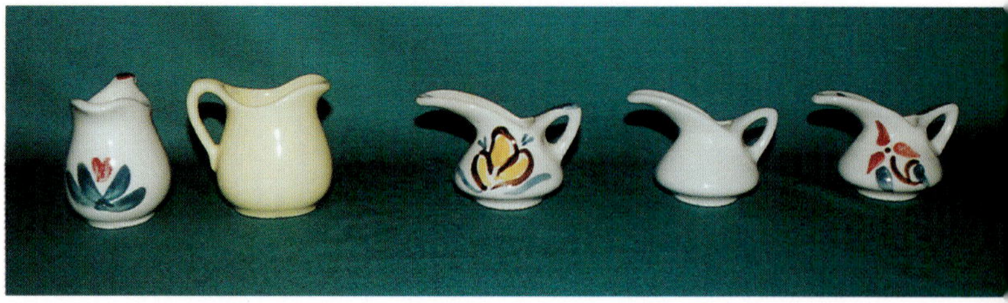

Miniature pitchers. $15 each. Jigger jugs. Cactus flower. $50. Plain. $5. Starflower. $30.

Jigger jug, Fuscia decoration. $30.

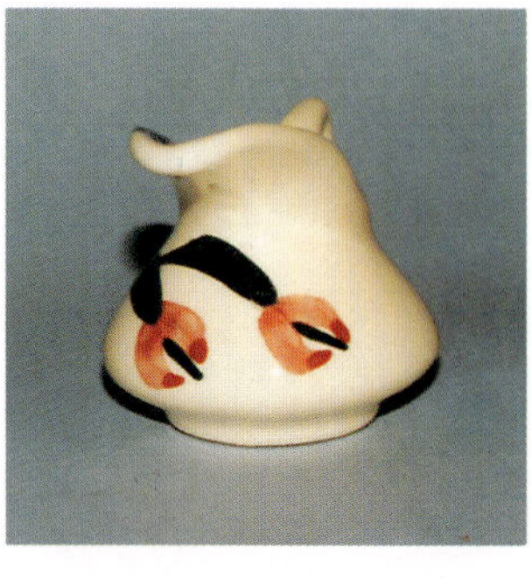

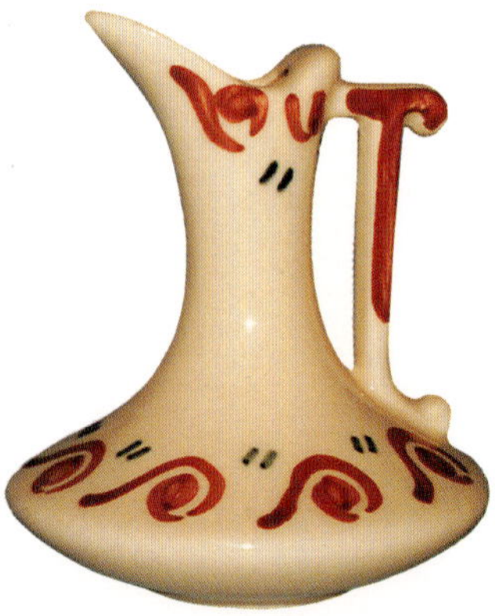

Small ewer. $25.

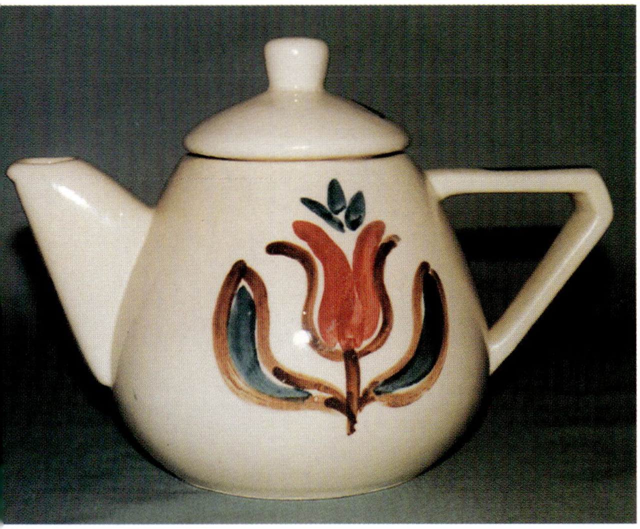

Angle handled teapot with red tulip decoration. $100.

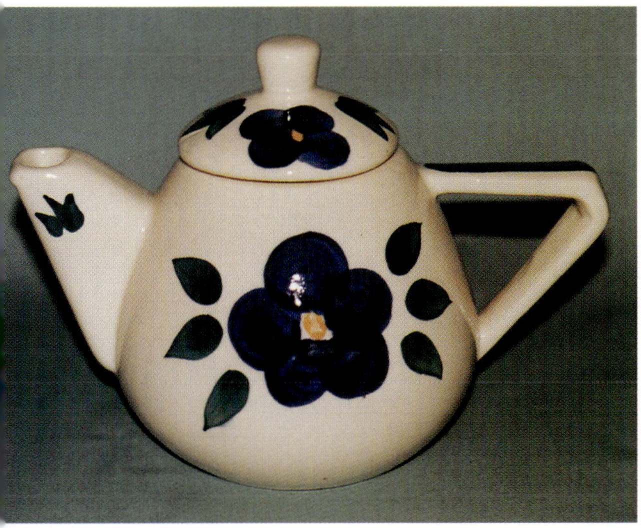

Angle handled teapot with Blue Pansy decoration. $75.

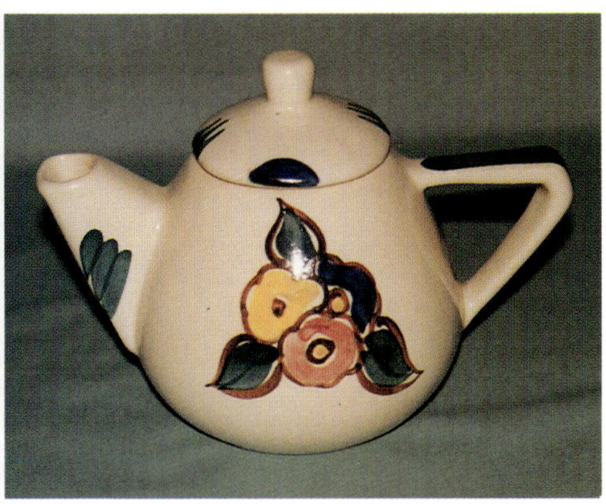

Angle handled teapot with Three Pansies decoration. $100.

Angle handled teapot with Flower Garden decoration. $100.

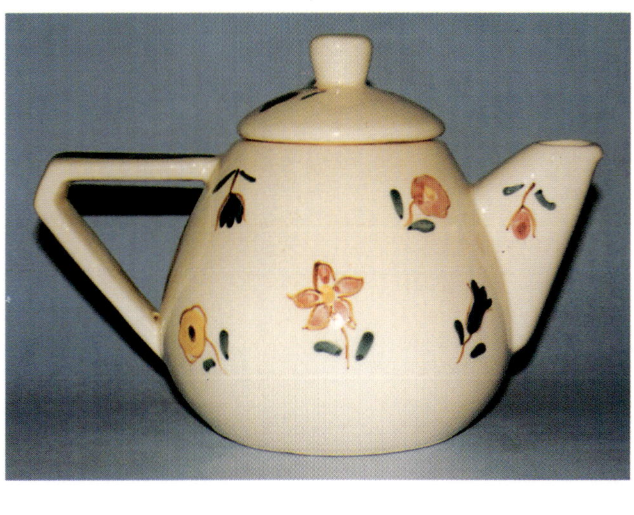

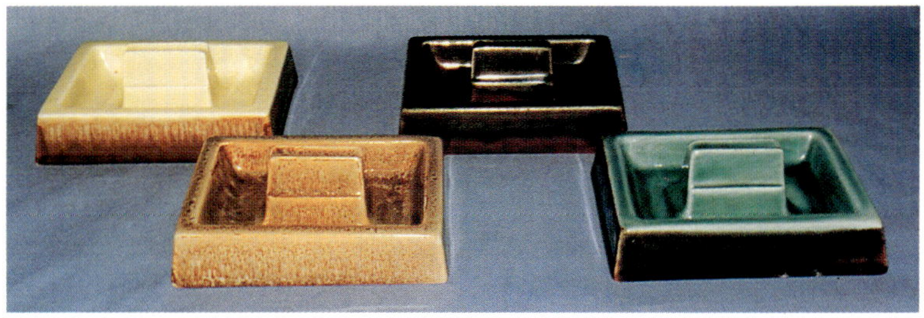

Various blind man's ashtrays. $20 each.

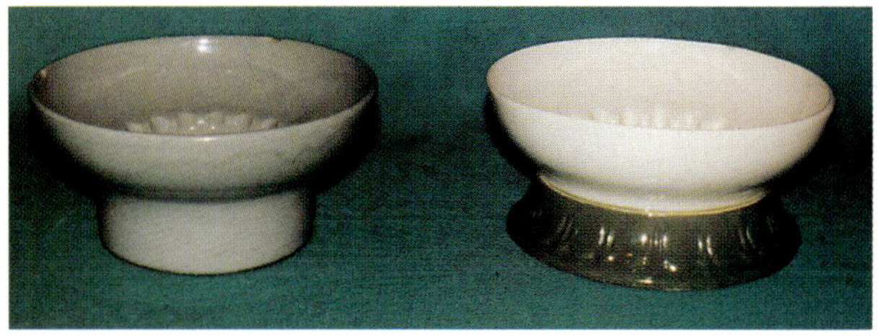

Experimental ashtrays, similar shape to SIDIX ashtray pictured in the Brown Intaglio section. $20 each.

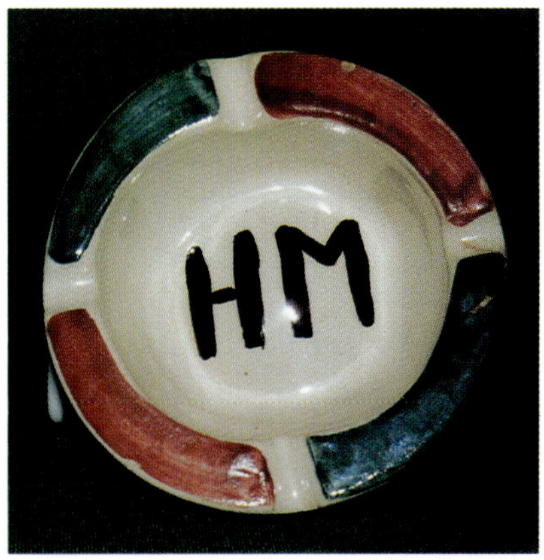

Round ashtray, personalized with the initials HM. $30.

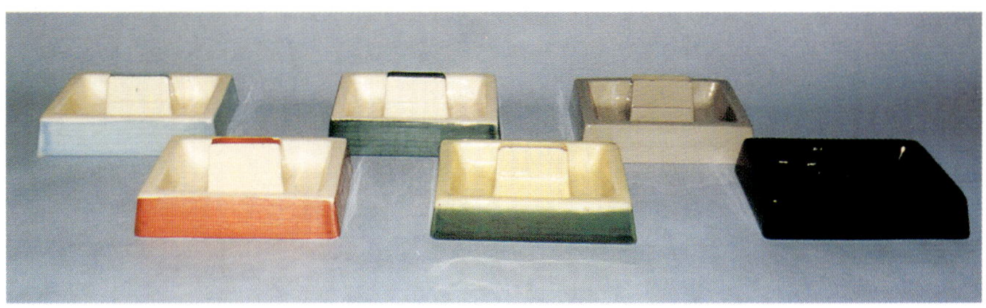

Blind man's ashtrays. $20 each.

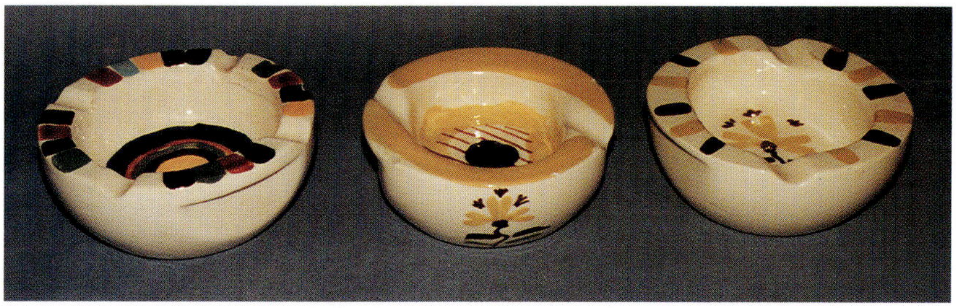

Experimental ashtrays. $40 each.

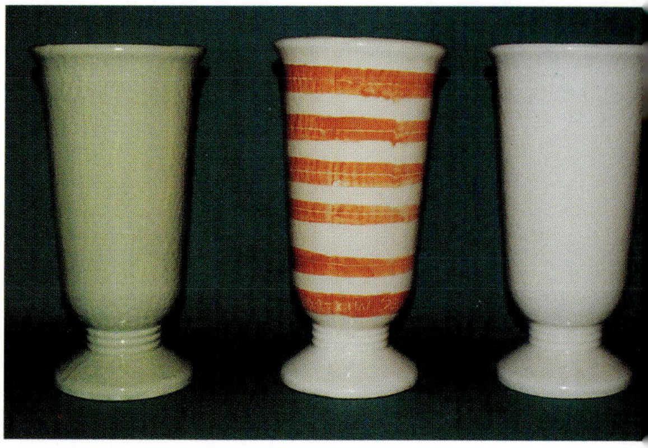

Vases, 9" high. $15 each.

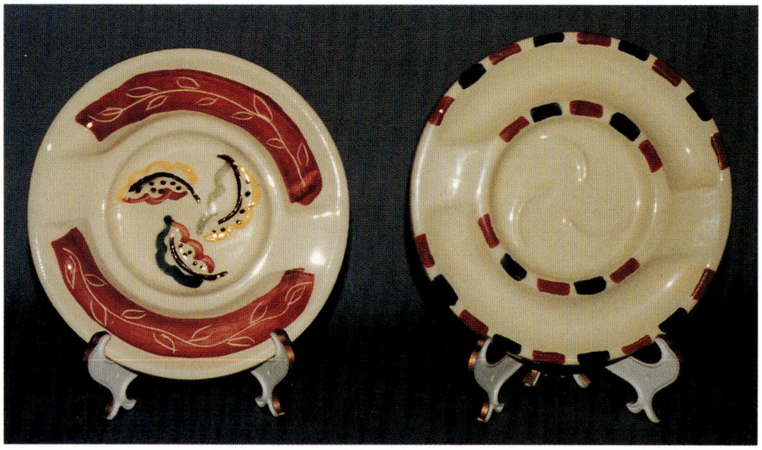

Experimental ashtrays. $40 each.

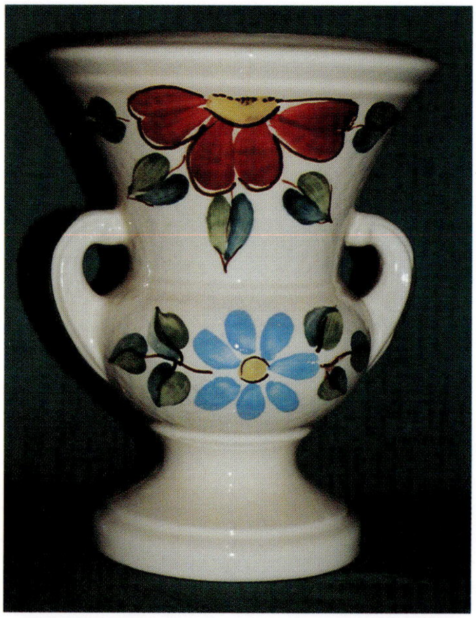

Handled vase with Seaform type decoration in Morni Glory colors, 9" higl $75.

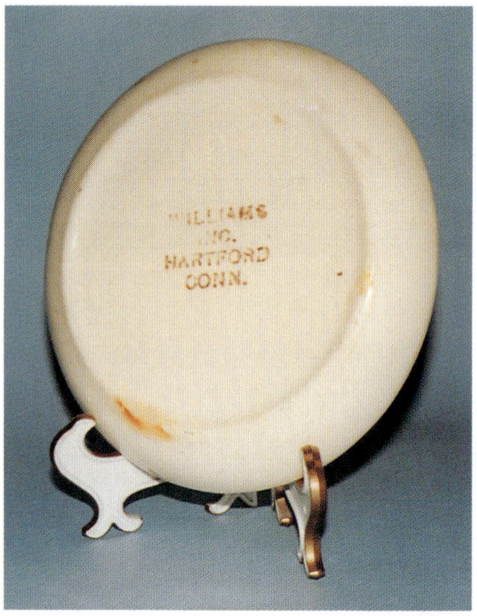

Reverse side of the round ashtray has Williams Inc. Hartford, Conn., stamped on it. Perhaps it was a contracted job.

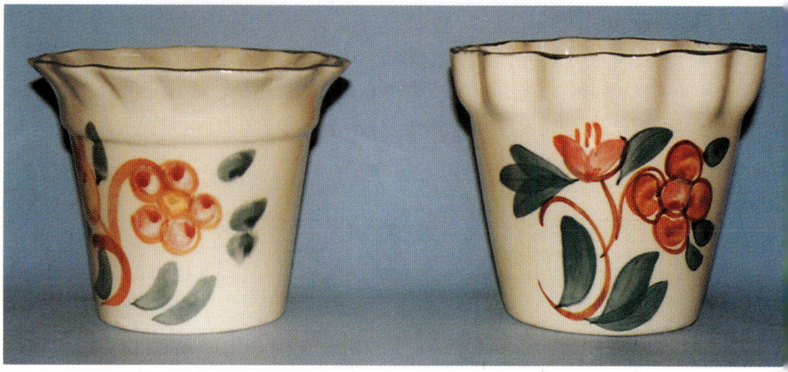

Experimental individual ashtray. $30.

Jardinieres with floral decorations, 5" high. $30 each.

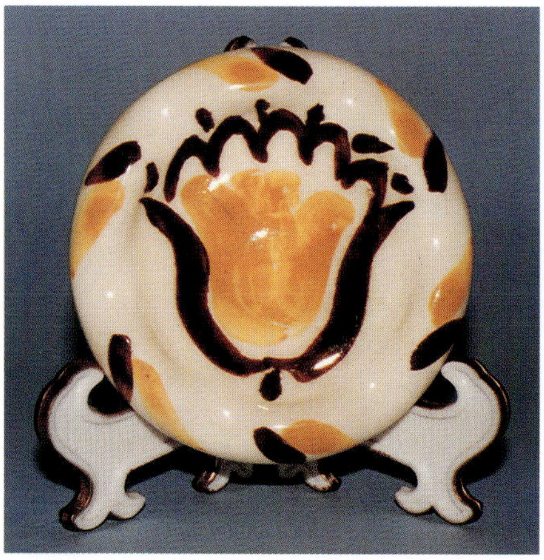

Handled vases, 9" high. $15.

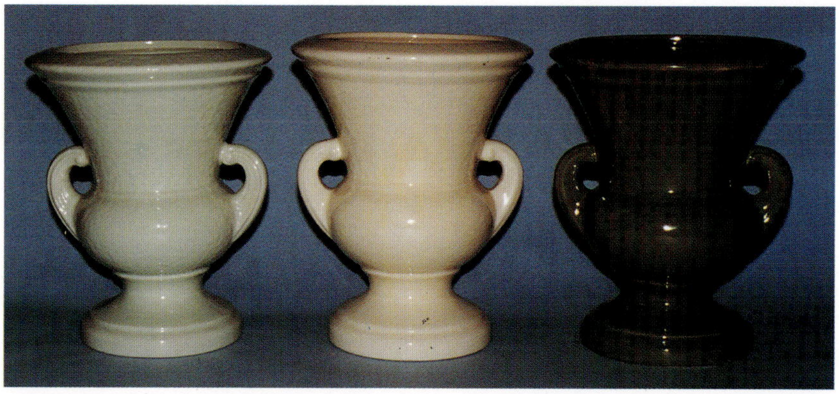

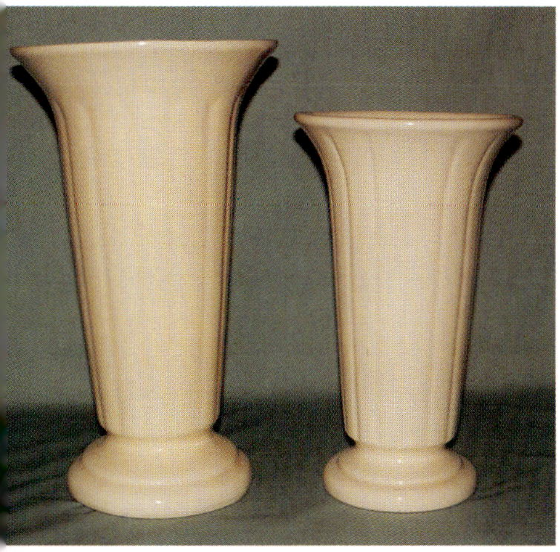

duced at the Tionesta Plant: ribbed vase, 13.75" high. $15.
bed vase, 11.5" high. $15.

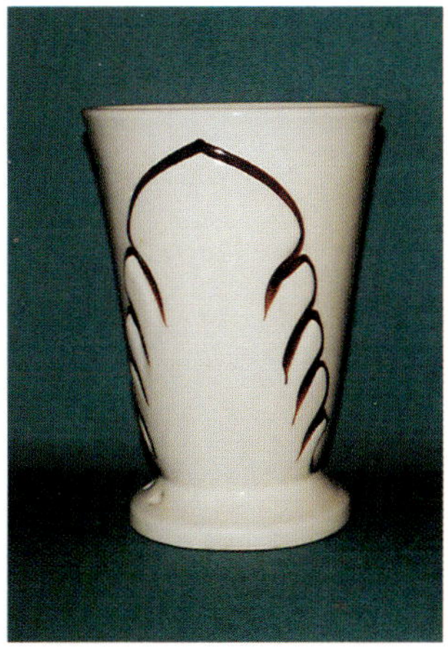

TV feather lamp with brown trim, 8.5" high. $40.

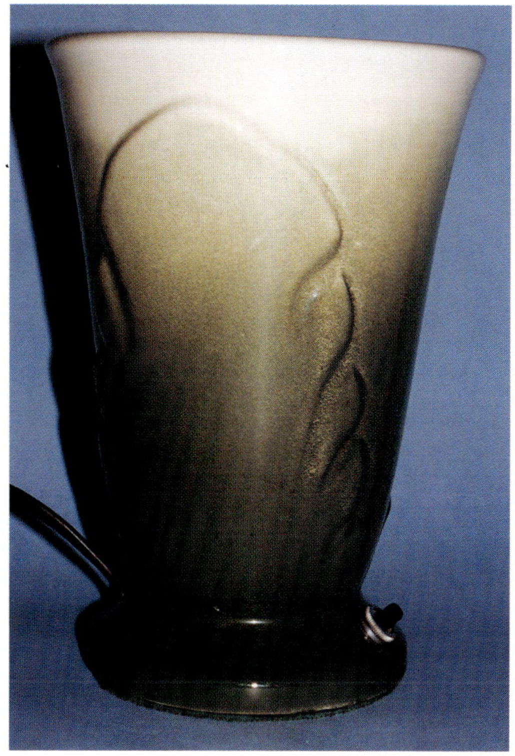

TV feather lamp with green air brush decoration. $40.

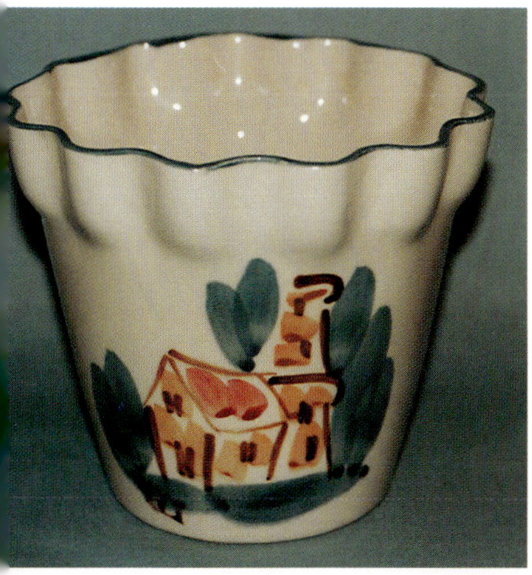

Jardiniere, house decoration. $60.

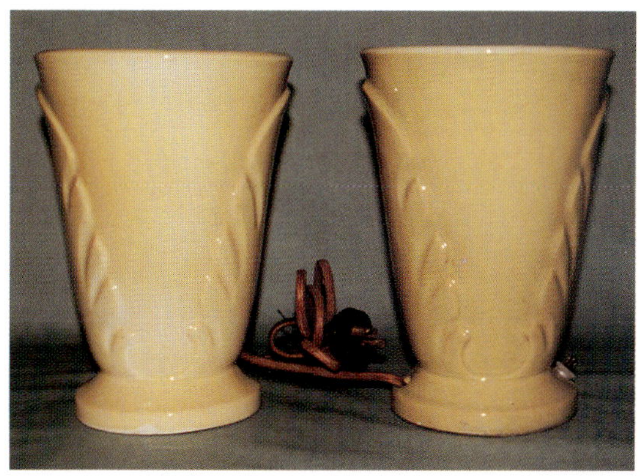

Feather vase with yellow glaze. $35. Matching TV feather lamp with yellow glaze. $40.

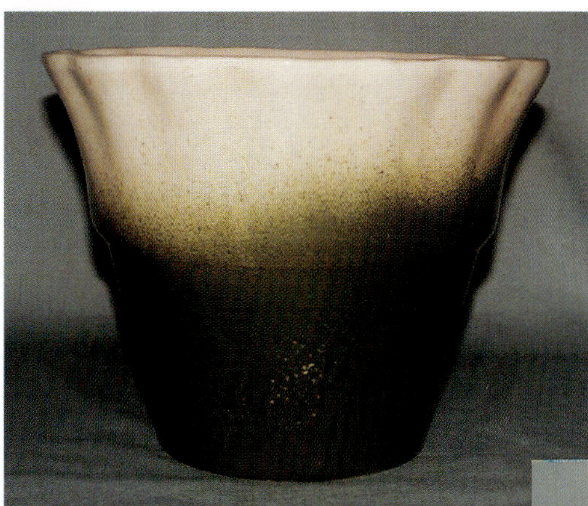

ardiniere, 7" high, green spray. $20.

Basket planter with green scallops. $20. Basket planter in solid teal glaze. $20. Basket planter with Blue Pansy decoration. $20.

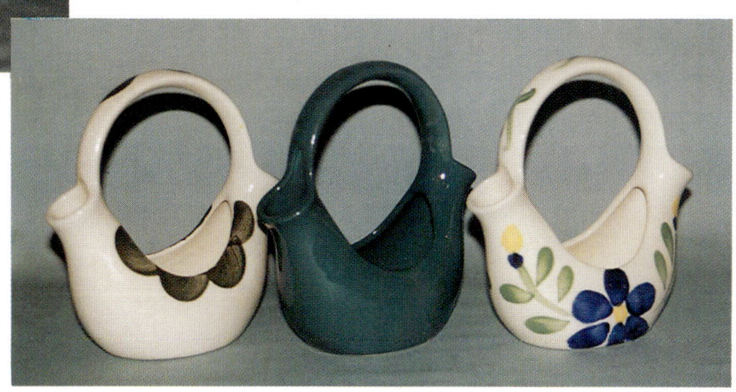

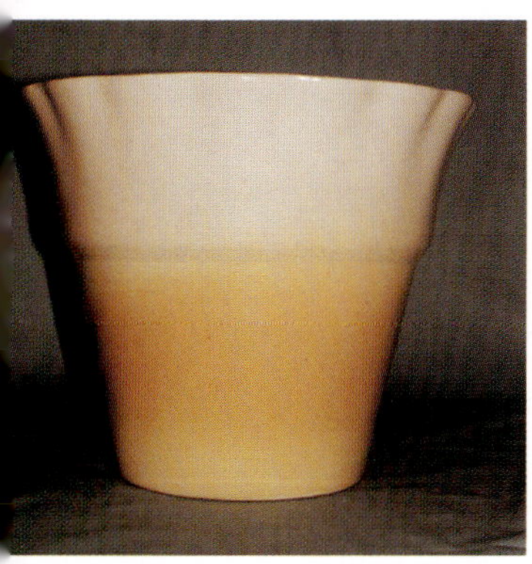

Jardiniere, 7" high with chartreuse spray. This airbrush technique was only performed at the Tionesta Plant. $20.

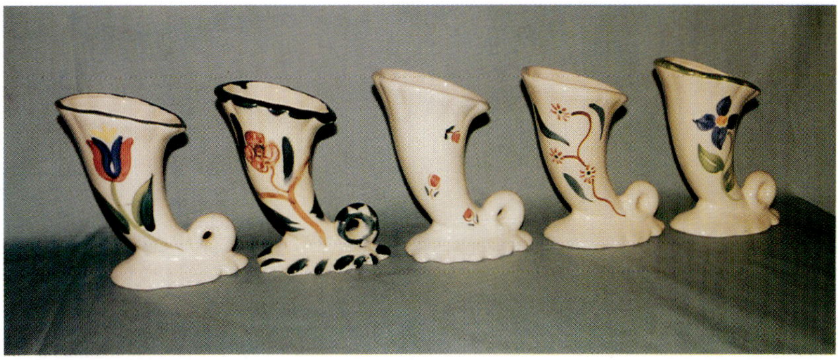

Cornucopia vases. $20 each.

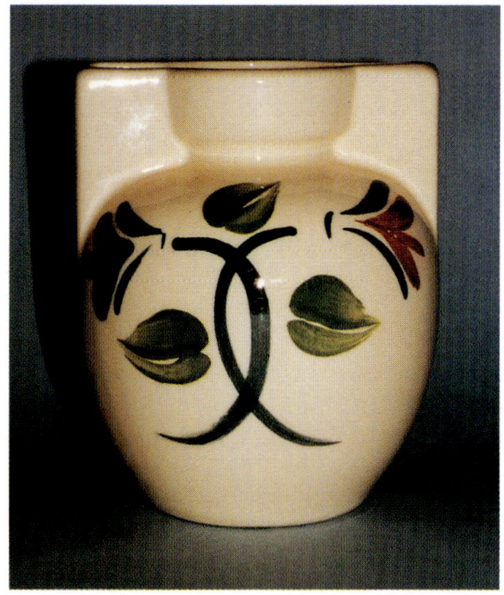

Winged vase with blue and red flower decoration. $35.

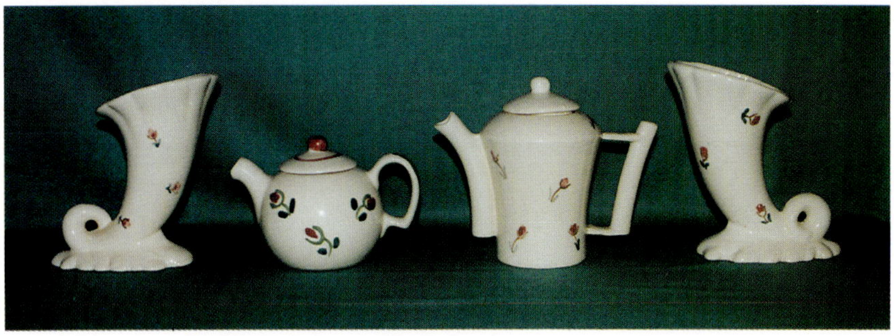

Cornucopia vases with Rosebud decoration. $25 each. Two cup teapot with Rosebud decoration. $40. Teapot, 5.25" high, Taylor Smith Taylor mold with Rosebud decoration. $40.

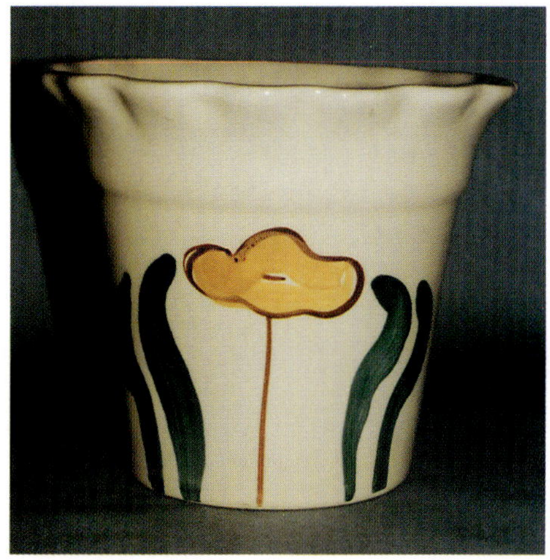

Sunny jardiniere, 5" high. $35.

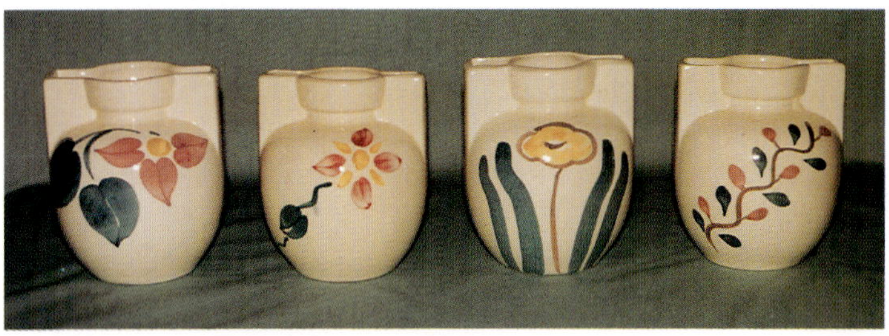

Half Blossom winged vase. $10. Blossom winged vase. $10. Sunny winged vase. $30. Pussy Willow winged vase. $10.

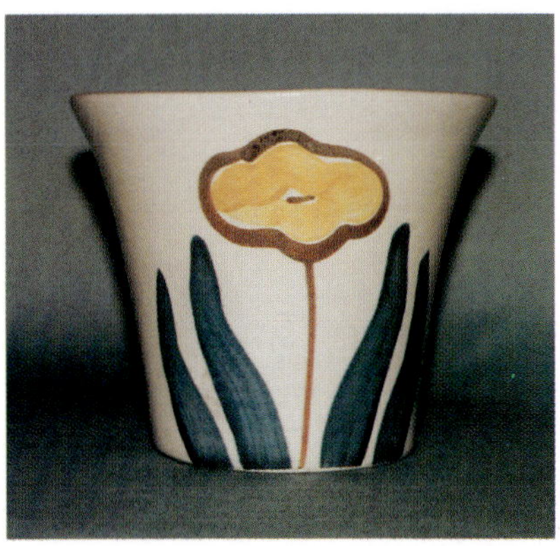

Sunny wall pocket. $50.

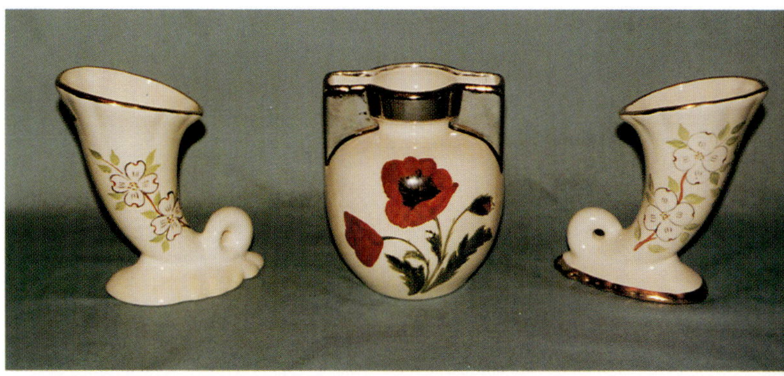

Purinton cornucopia and winged vase blanks decorated by the Lenoir Company. $10 each.

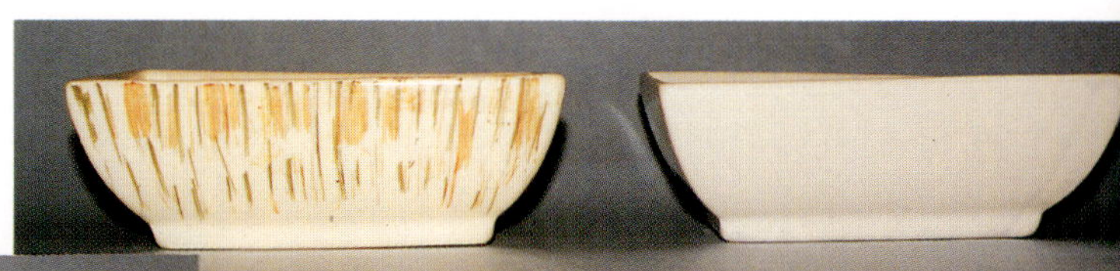

Planters, NAPCO mold. $10 each.

Planters, yellow, coral, and green decorated, NAPCO mold. $30 each.

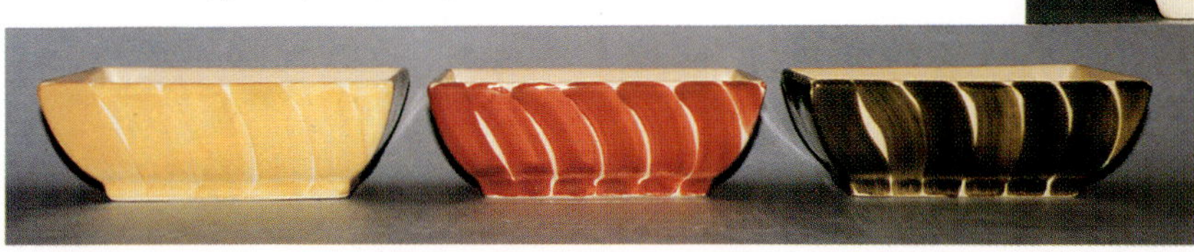

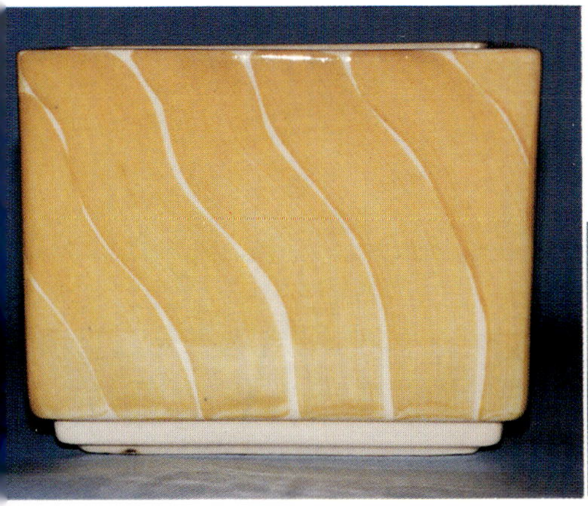

Chartreuse Intaglio short pillow vase, NAPCO mold. $40.

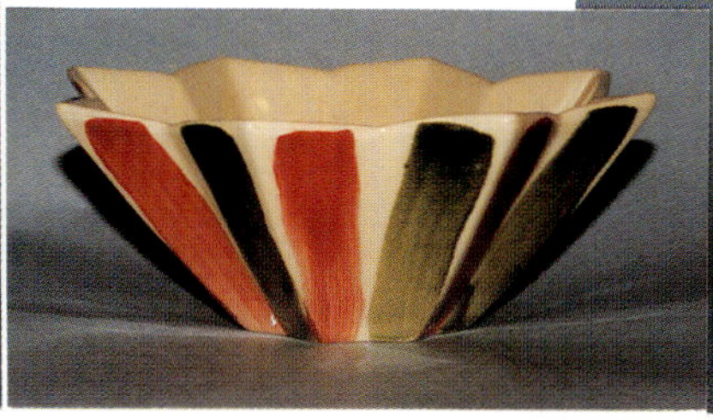

Star candy dish, green and coral. $35.

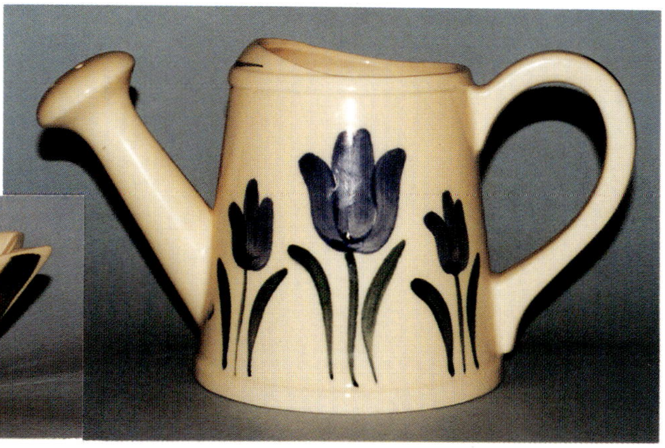

Sprinkler, Cobalt Blue Tulip decoration. $50.

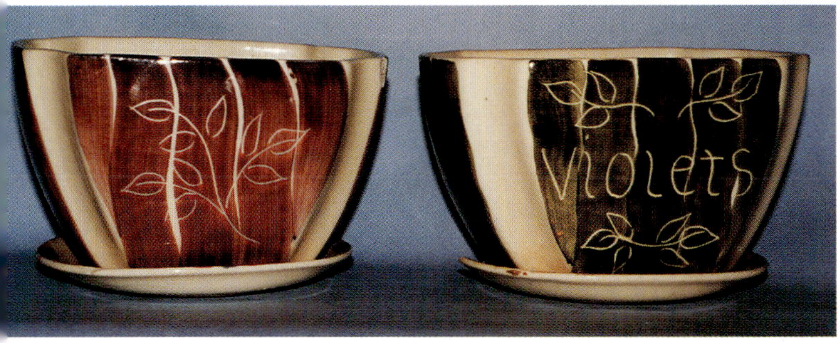

Purple Intaglio planter. $35. Green Intaglio violets planter. $40. These planters are inverted half canisters adhered to saucers.

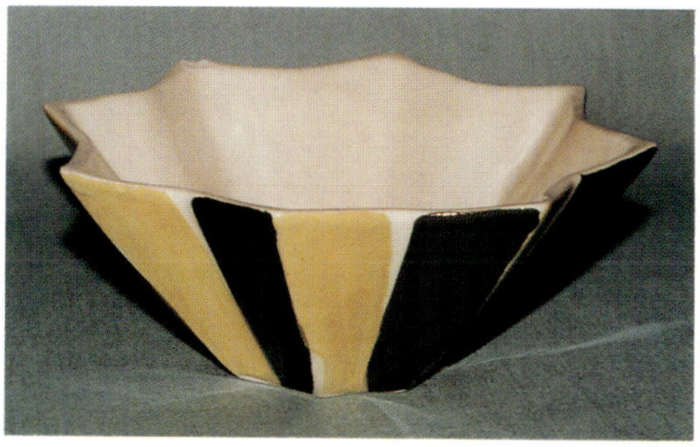

Star candy dish, green and yellow. $35.

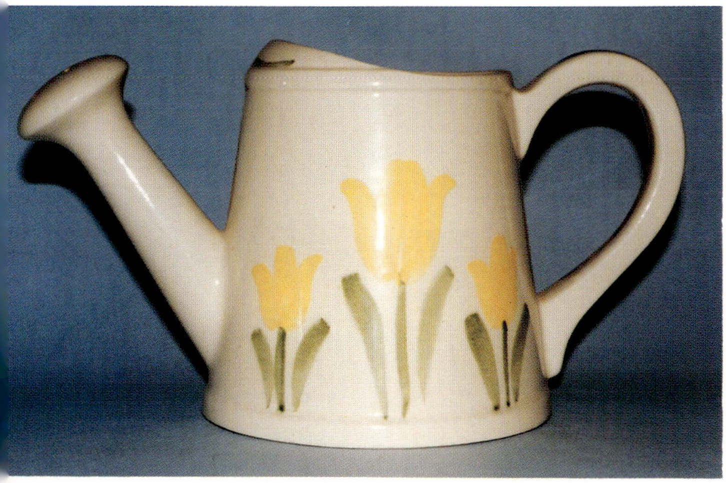

Sprinkler, Yellow Tulip decoration. $50.

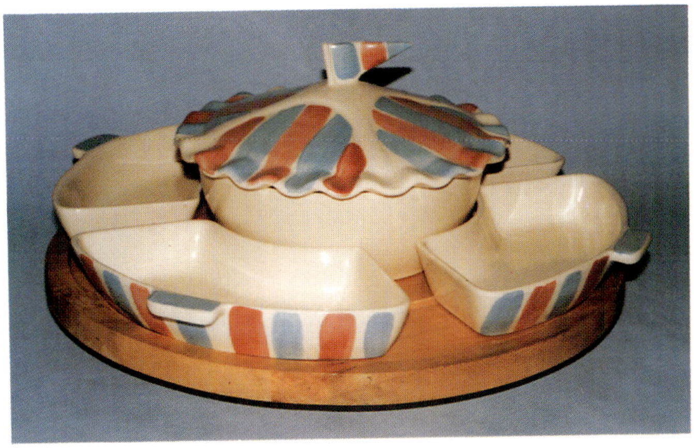

Esmond big top lazy susan. This is the most difficult to find of all of the lazy susans. $150. A collector from Michigan has one with wooden horses that fill the spaces between the pieces to make it look like a carousel.

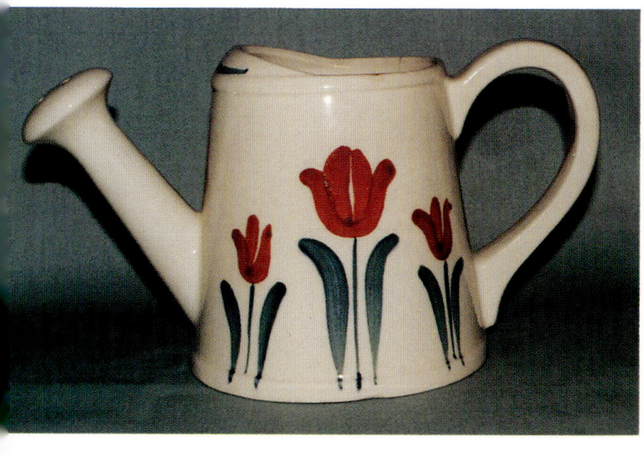

Sprinkler, Red Tulip decoration. $50.

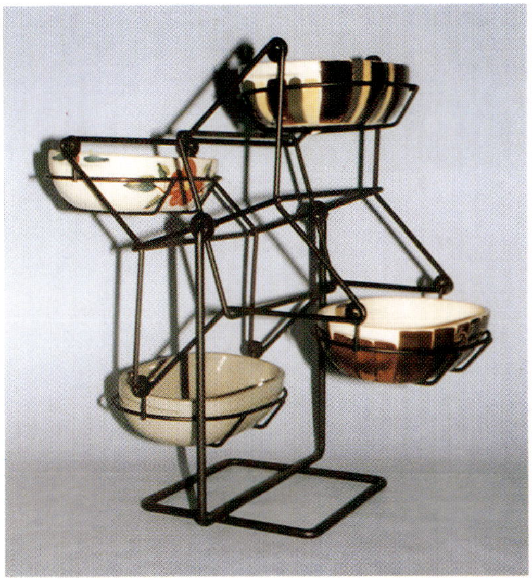

Ferris wheel designed to hold four pickle dishes. Very unusual. $100.

Solid Colors

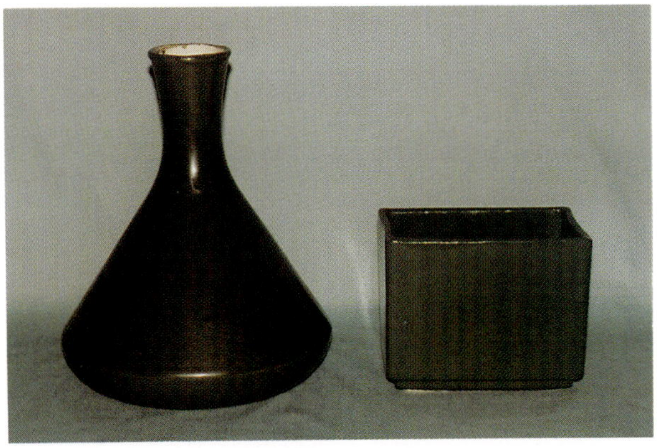

Water bottle, green. $10. Small pillow vase, green, NAPCO mold. $5.

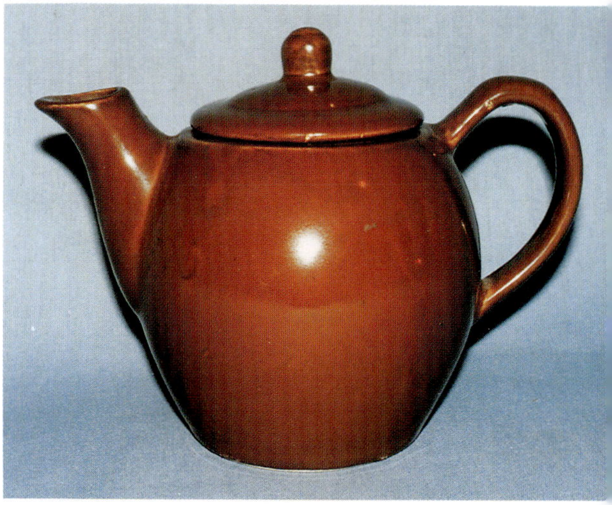

Six cup teapot, golden brown. $10.

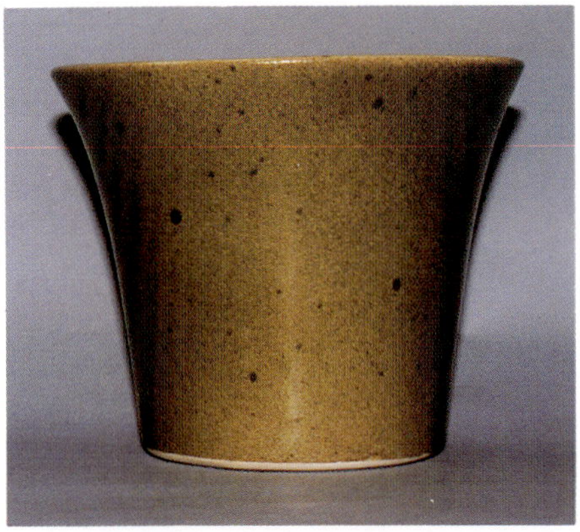

Wall pocket, green. $25.

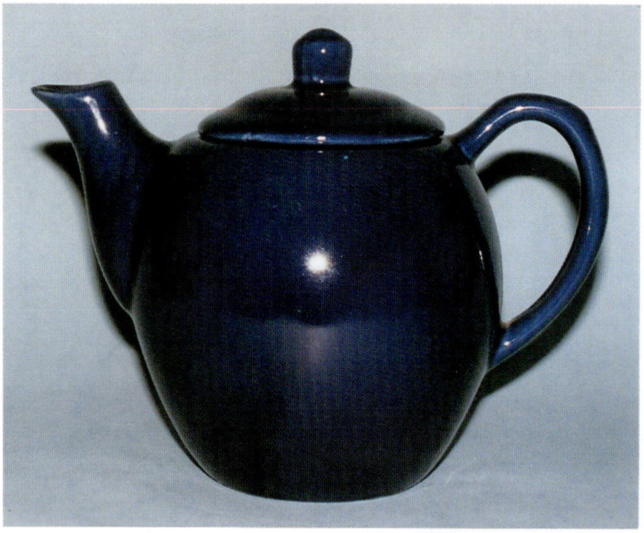

Six cup teapot, cobalt blue. $20.

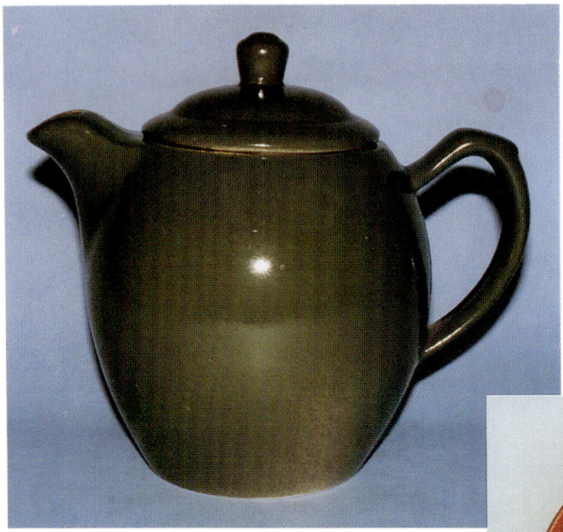

Eight cup coffee pot, sprayed green. $10.

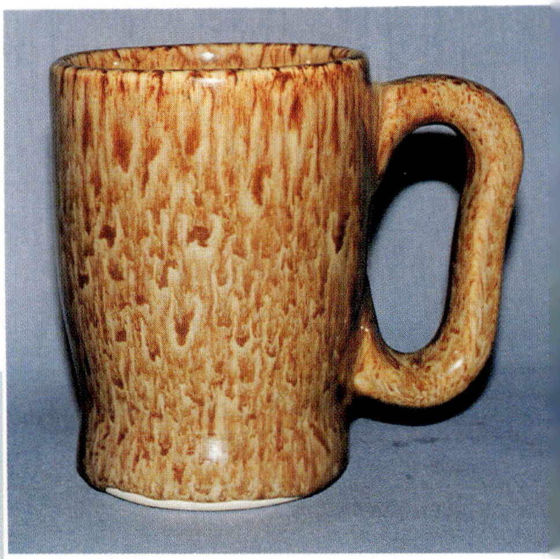

Coffee mug, brown spatterware. $5.

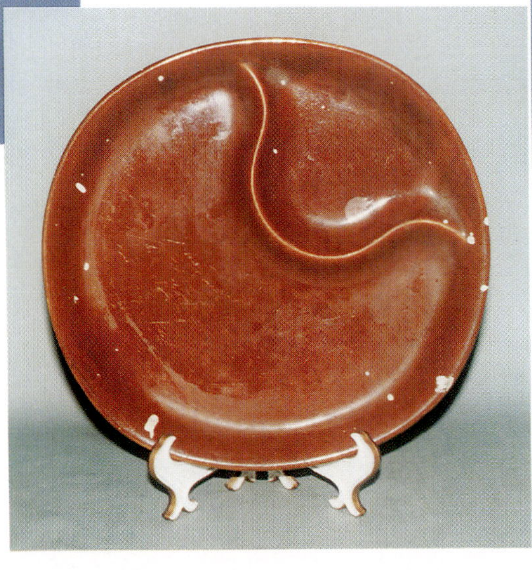

Tea and toast plate, golden brown. $5.

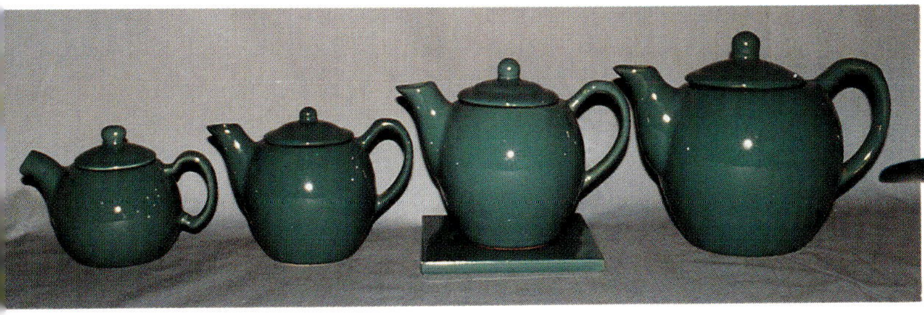

Teal colored teapots: two cup, Wellsville style, $20; two cup, $15; four cup, $15; tea tile, $15; six cup, $15.

Black console bowl, NAPCO mold. $10.

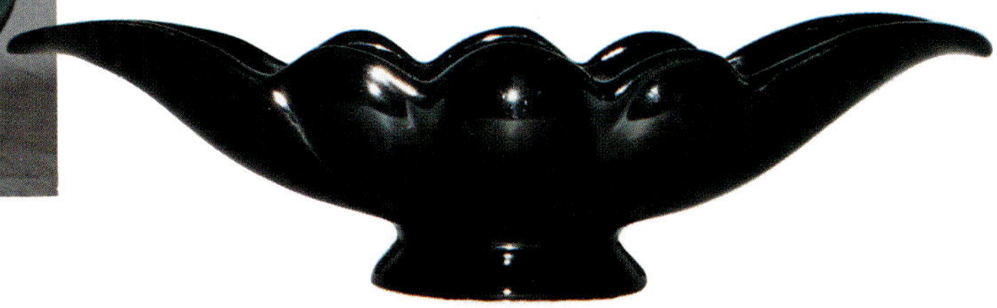

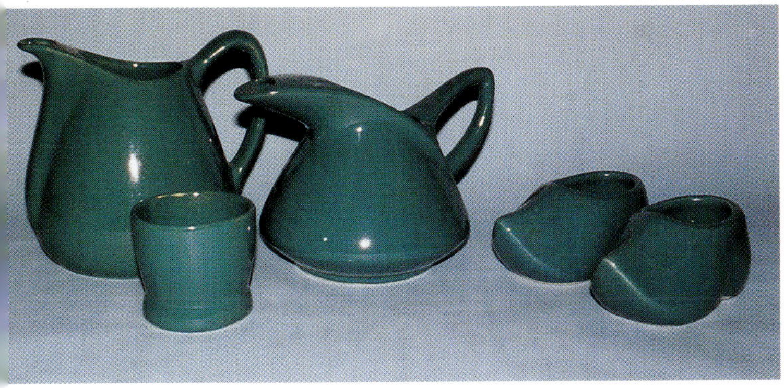

Teal colored items: beverage pitcher, $25; juice mug, $5; two pint dutch jug, $25; dutch shoe planters, $5 set.

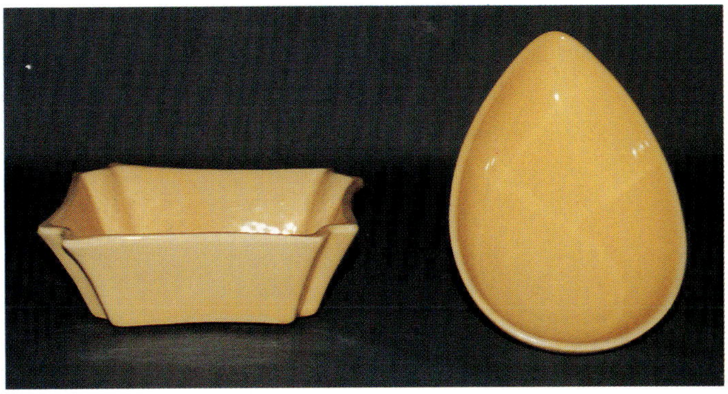

Solid yellow NAPCO bowl. $5. Rubel teardrop shaped bowl. $5.

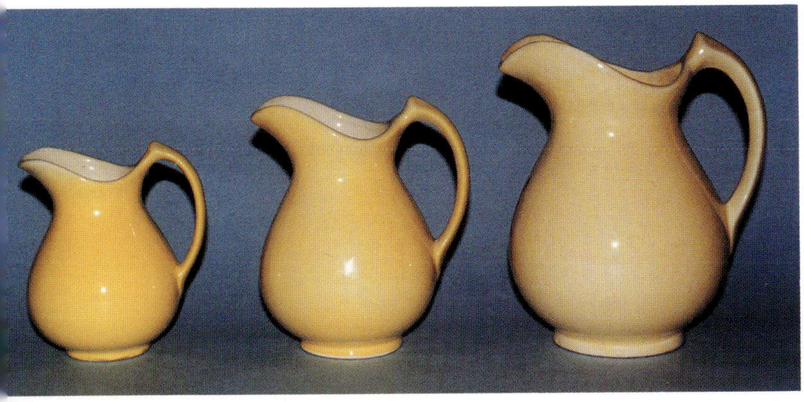

Solid yellow: pitcher, 5" high, $10; pitcher, 5.5" high, $10; pitcher, 6.5" high, $10.

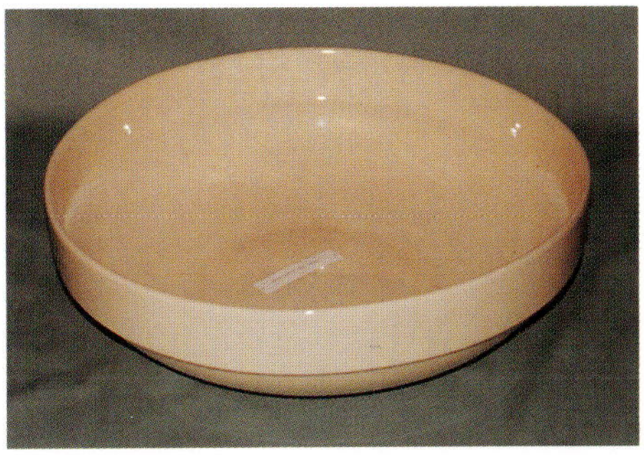

Plain salad bowl, 13.5" diameter, Rubel mold. $20.

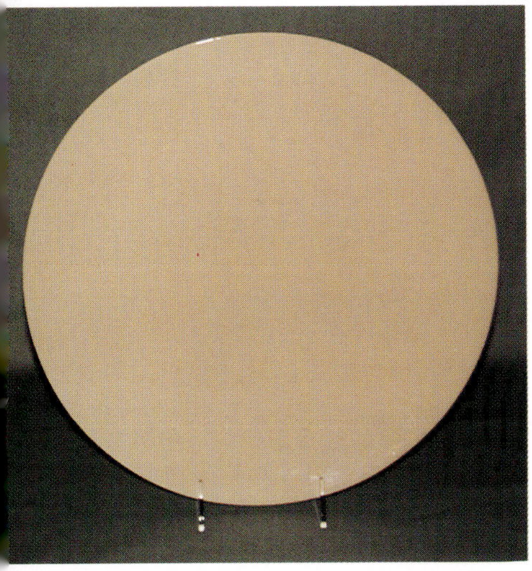

Plain chop plate, 14" diameter, Rubel mold. $25.

Plain individual sugar and creamer. $10 set. Basket planter. $10.

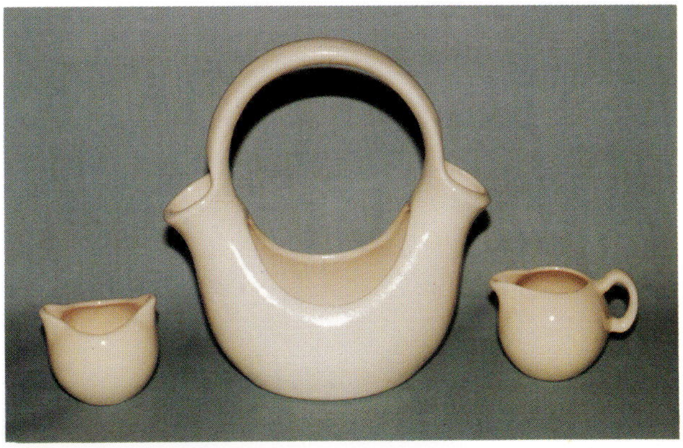

Plain beverage pitcher. $20. Tumbler. $20. Two pint dutch jug. $20.

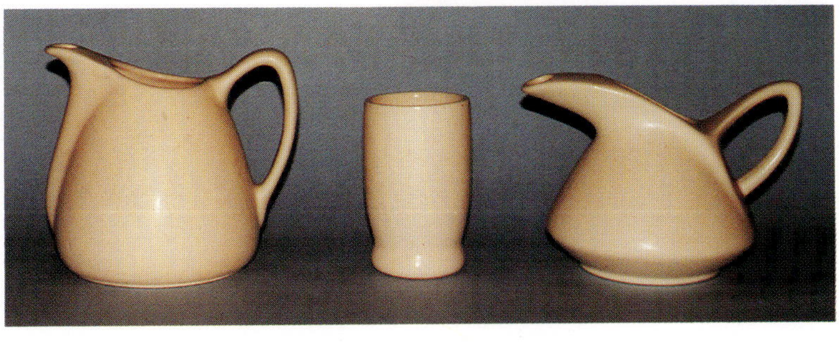

Signed Items

Dorothy Purinton and William Blair are the two people who developed the Purinton patterns and trained the decorators in Wellsville, Shippenville, and Tionesta. They are two of the most important people affiliated with Purinton Pottery. William Blair's history goes beyond Purinton and should be known. It is about time that he was more widely recognized and a greater appreciation for his talents was developed among collectors. Dorothy Purinton requires the same.

It is a rare opportuny to own one of their special pieces and these pieces are highly desired. Prices have increased dramatically as the demand for these items has appreciated. Each of their items is a work of art. Many pieces can be attributed to each of them. Having a signed pattern is like having an artist's signature on a painting.

William H. Blair

Born in 1909, Bill Blair was the youngest brother of Dorothy Blair Purinton. His artistic talents emerged at an early age, and he pursued his education at the Cleveland School of Art. After graduation, he continued his studies in Europe.

He returned to Ohio with the dream of achieving success through his oils and watercolors. While they received high praise, monetary success was elusive and for a short while Blair painted children's portraits as a steady income.

During this time, Bernard Purinton, his brother-in-law, offered Bill a job decorating items at the Wellsville plant. During the pottery's early stages, it produced a limited number of items in solid glazes. Bill did not like the traditional dinnerware form, with its round plates and decal decoration. He preferred the use of hand-painted underglaze decoration. Most, if not all, of Purinton's hand decorated patterns can be attributed to Bill Blair. His style is evident in the early Peasant Ware patterns. He was also influential in the design of Purinton's off round plates.

Bill's nephew, Bart Higgins, was also employed at Purinton. In their spare time, Bill and Bart experimented, making red clay figures. They eventually left Purinton and set up a small operation called Ceramicraft in East Liverpool, Ohio. The company produced red clay planters and figurines, including angels, little children, and animals. Production stopped in late 1942 or early 1943 due to the war and was never resumed.

Purinton Pottery had relocated to Shippenville and Bill went back to work for Purinton for a short period. Bill designed Purinton's most famous pattern, the open Apple. He also originated the Brown Intaglio decoration, using it first in Wellsville with stylized animals and cherubs.

Bill always had an interest in producing his own line of hand decorated underglaze dinnerware, and by 1945 he and his nephew Bart pursued that dream. In 1946 they opened Blair Ceramics, Inc. in Ozark, Missouri.

His disdain for dinnerware popular at that time is clearly evident in the style of Blair Ceramics. Most round forms were replaced with square shapes. Handles were typically twisted rope fashion. His hand-decorated wares were untraditional, ranging from the bold green and brown Gay Plaid to the watercolor look of gray and green Pear to the white washed Brick redware.

Demand was high for the dinnerware and, at times, orders were backlogged. In 1952 the plant was struck by lightening and destroyed in the ensuing fire. It was never reopened.

Bill Blair remained in the ceramics industry for the rest of his career, working for companies that produced glazes, kilns, and other related products. Bill passed away in 1968.

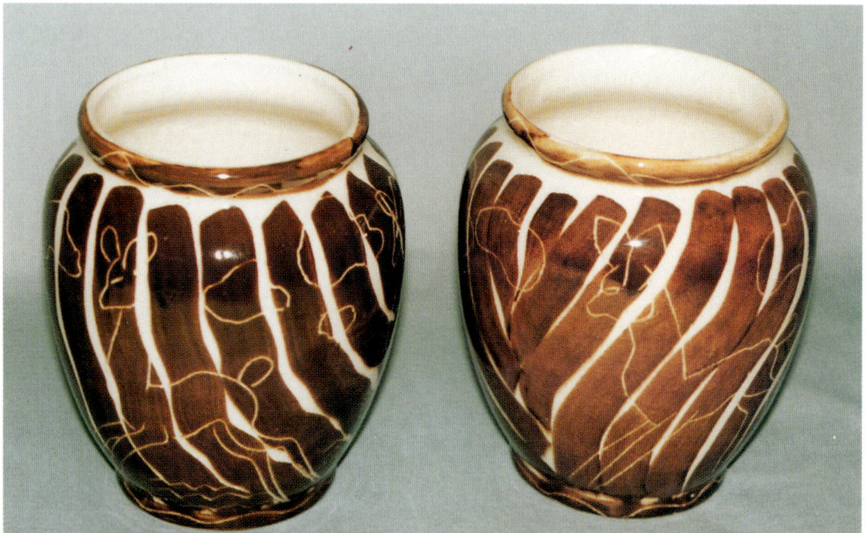

Brown Intaglio vases with incised deer, signed Wm. H. Blair. $500+ each.

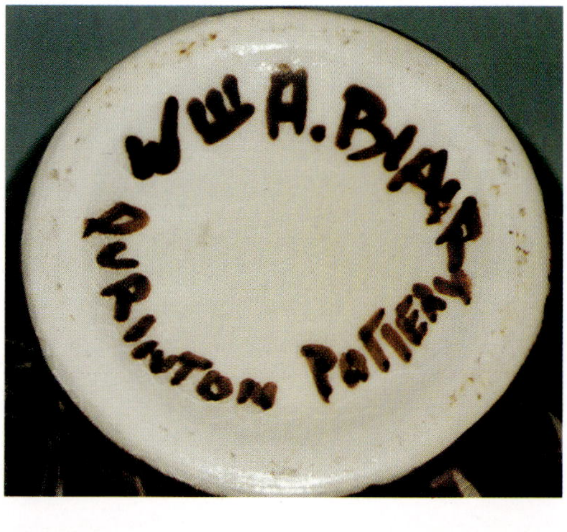

Signature of William H. Blair as it appears on the bottom of the vase.

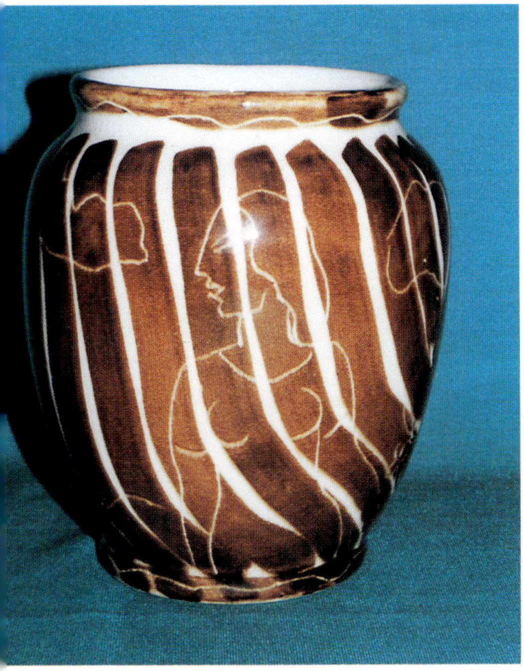

Brown Intaglio vase with an incised woman. Signed Wm. H. Blair. $500+.

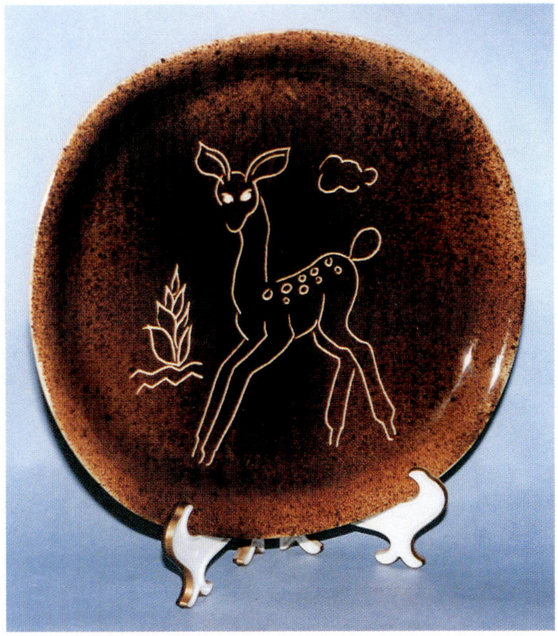

Brown glazed breakfast plate with an incised deer. Attributed to Wm. H. Blair. $400+.

Wm. H. Blair signature.

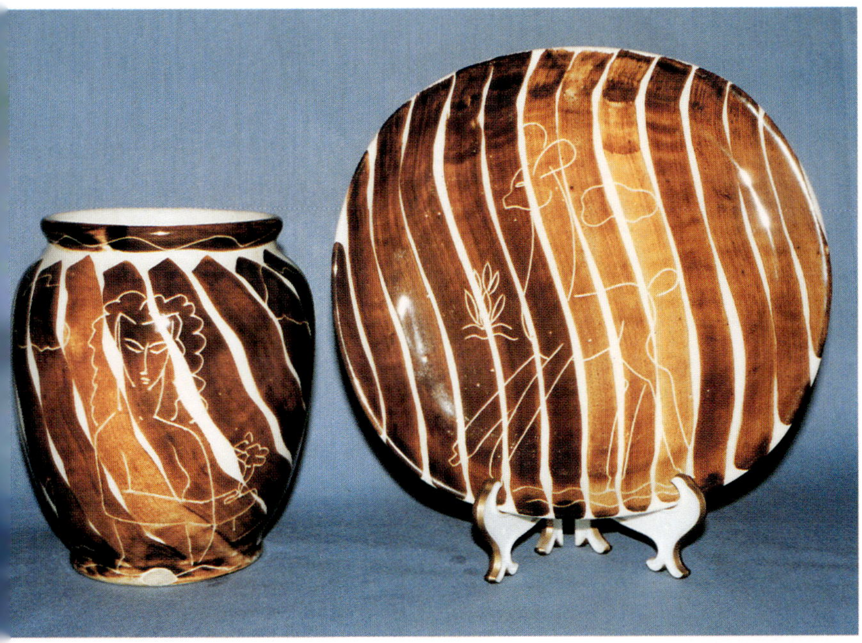

Brown Intaglio vase with incised woman. Signed Wm. H. Blair. $500+. Brown Intaglio breakfast plate with incised deer. Signed Wm. H. Blair. $500+.

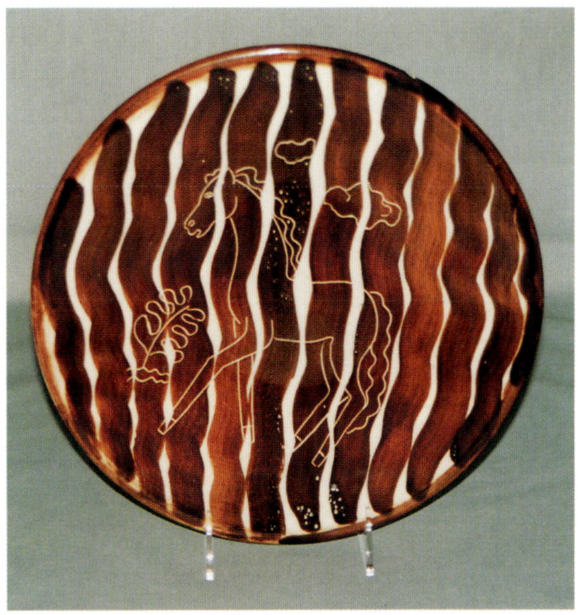

Brown Intaglio chop plate with an incised horse. Signed Wm. H. Blair. $750+.

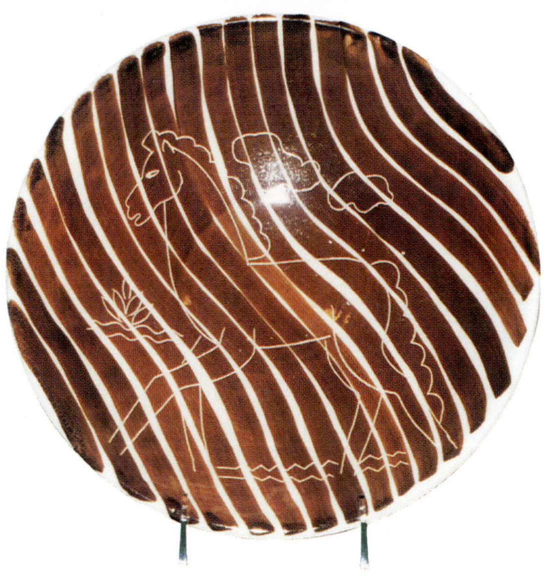

Brown Intaglio fruit bowl with incised horse. Signed Wm. H. Blair. $750+.

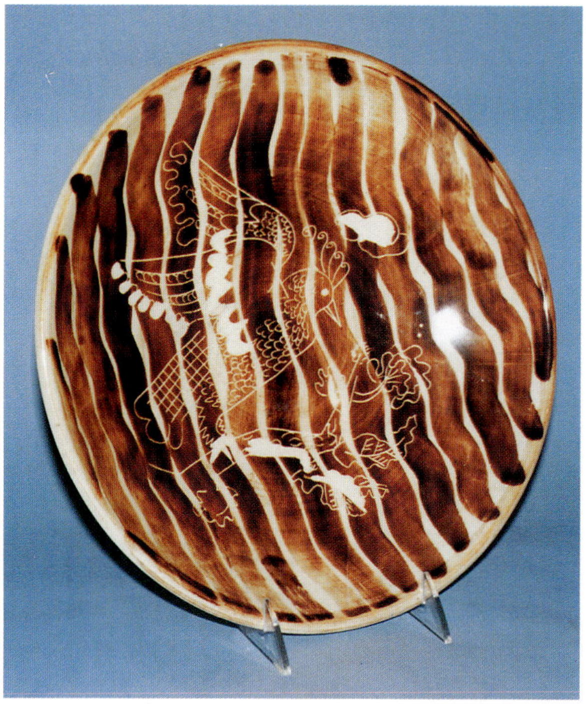

Fruit bowl with elegant bird incised. Signed Wm. H. Blair. $750+.

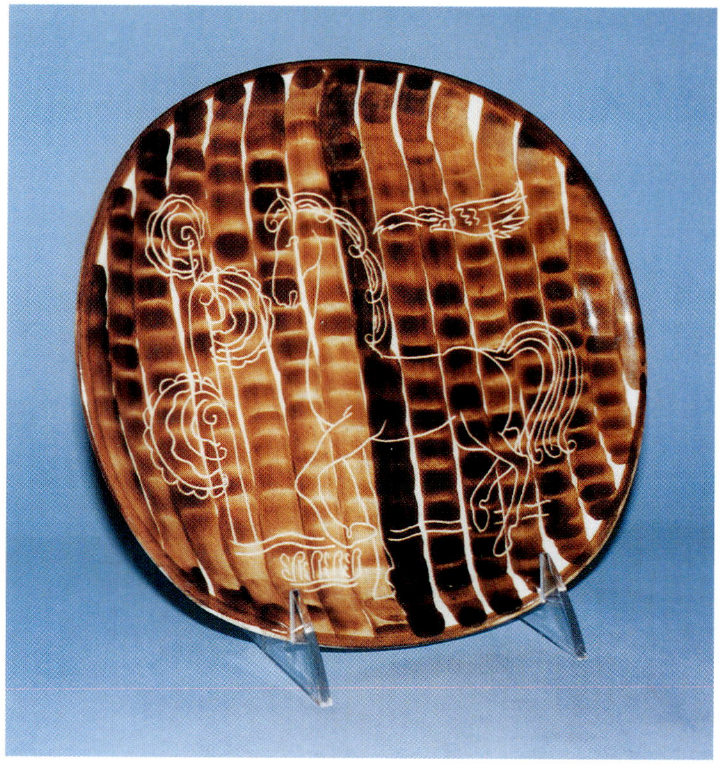

Brown Intaglio breakfast plate with incised horse and eagle. Signed R.C. Anderten. Anderten was an employee at the Wellsville Purinton plant. $500+.

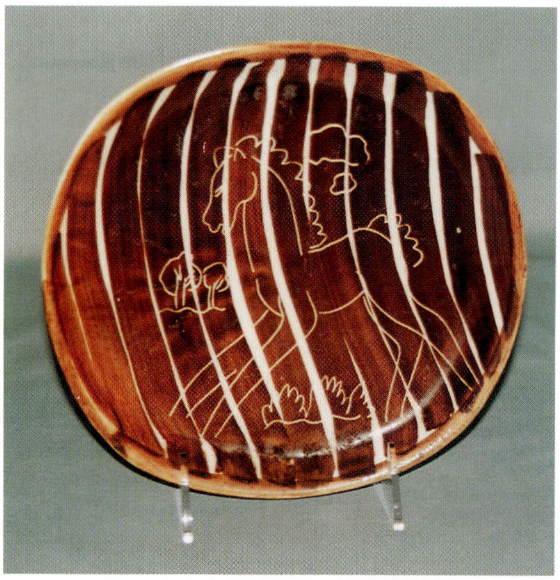

Brown Intaglio breakfast plate with incised horse. Signed Wm. H. Blair. $500+.

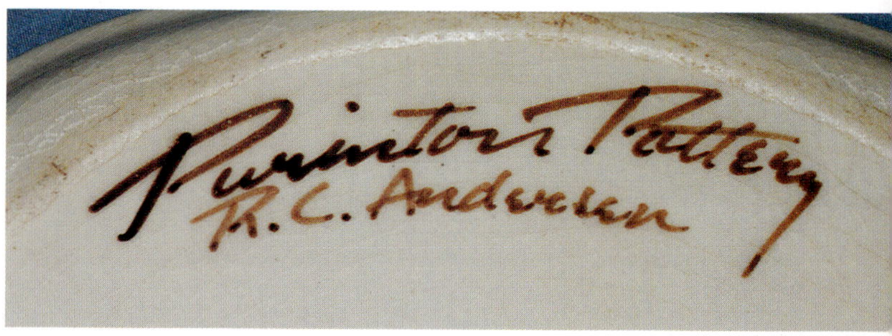

R.C. Anderten signature.

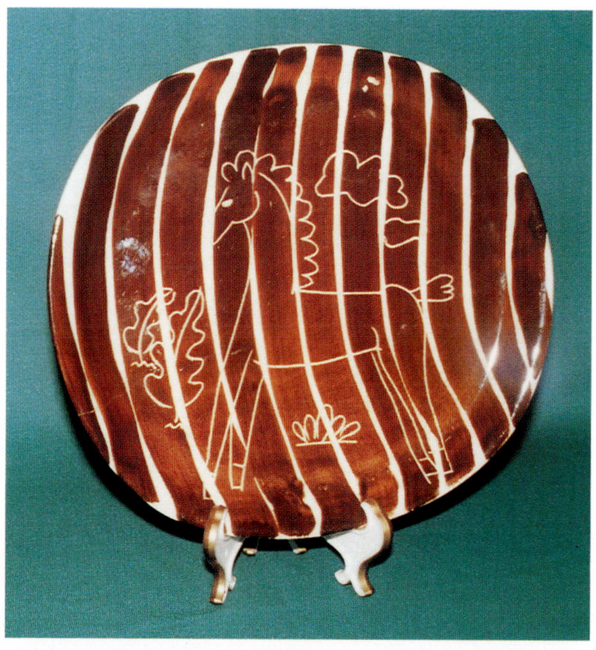

Brown Intaglio breakfast plate with incised horse. Signed Wm. H. Blair. $500+.

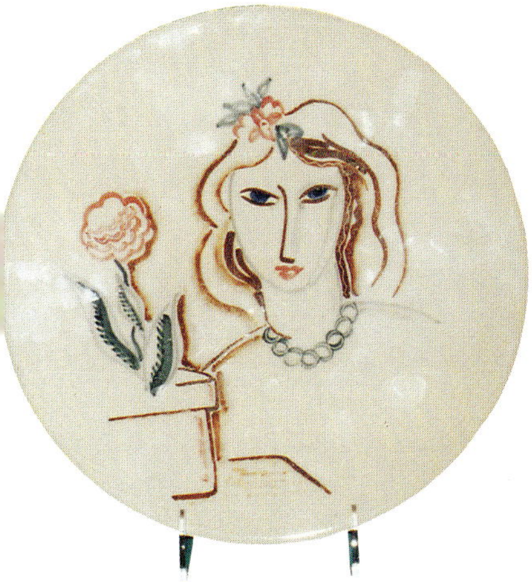

Chop plate with woman decoration. Signed Wm. H. Blair. $750+.

Chop plate with giraffe decoration. Signed Wm. H. Blair. $750+.

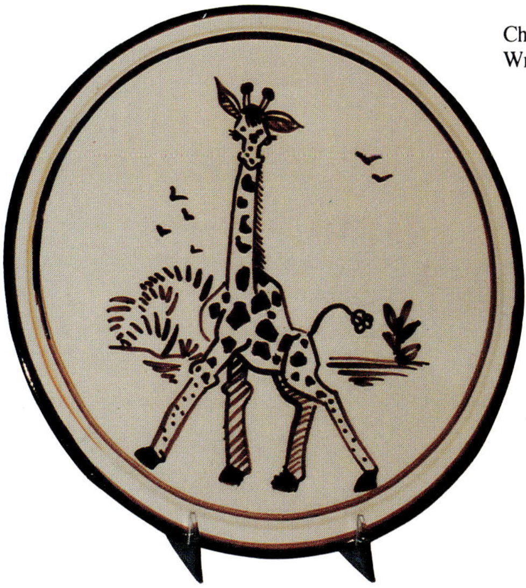

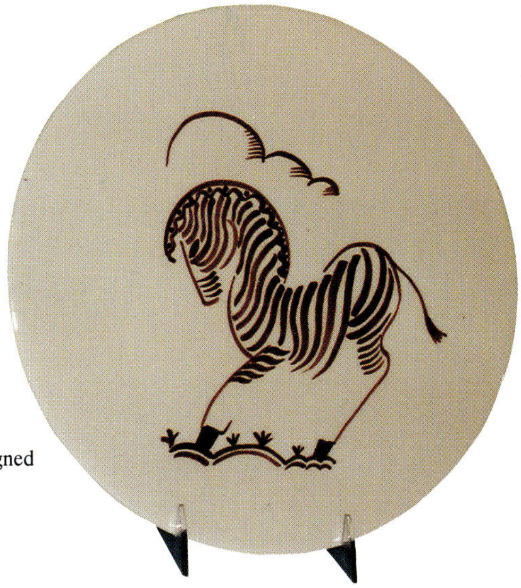

Chop plate with zebra decoration. Signed Wm. H. Blair. $750+.

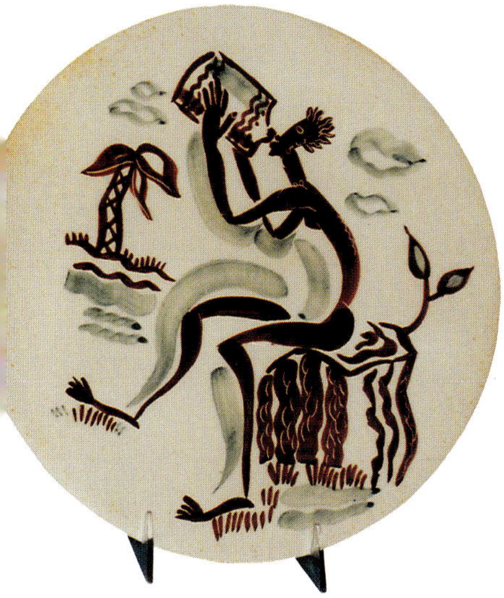

Chop plate with native drinking from a jug. Signed Wm. H. Blair. $750+.

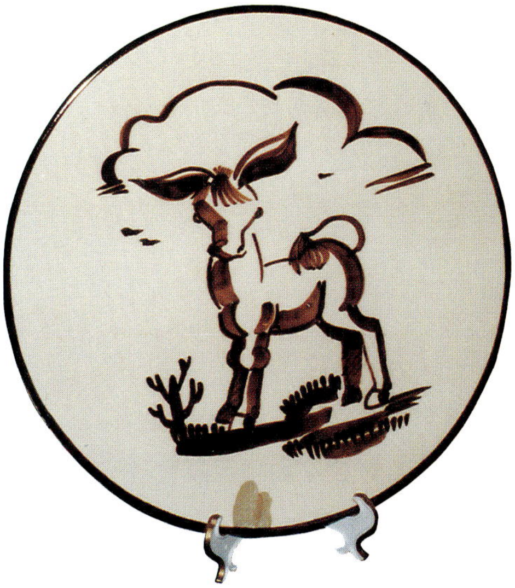

Chop plate with burro decoration. Signed Wm. H. Blair. $750+.

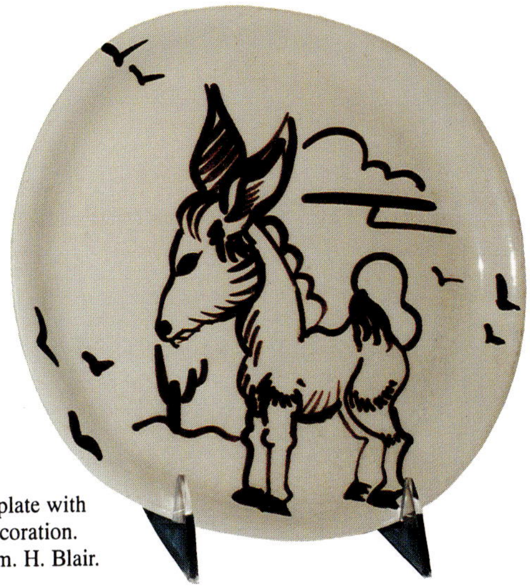

Breakfast plate with donkey decoration. Signed Wm. H. Blair. $500+.

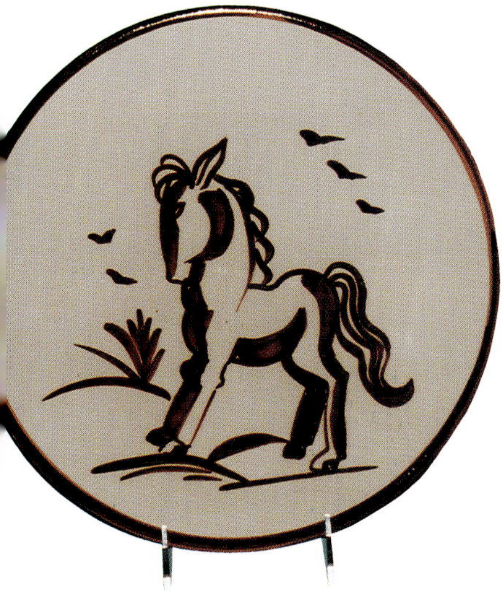

Chop plate with horse decoration. Signed Wm. H. Blair. $750+.

Chop plate with deer decoration. Signed Wm. H. Blair. $750+.

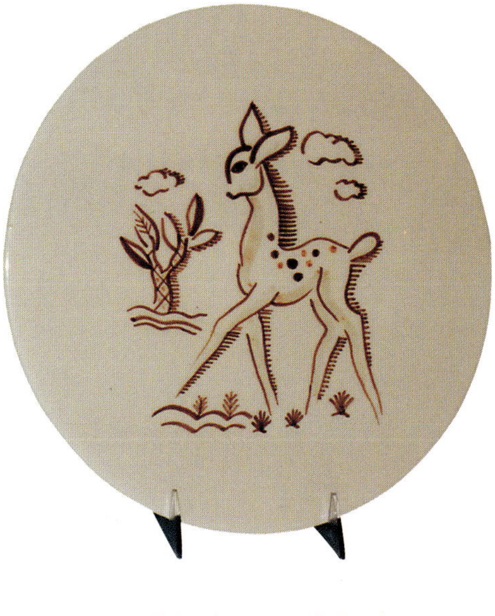

Breakfast plate with sailboat decoration. Signed Wm. H. Blair. $500+.

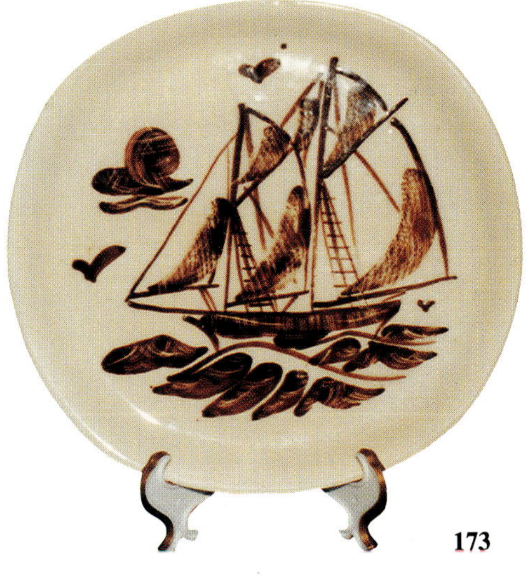

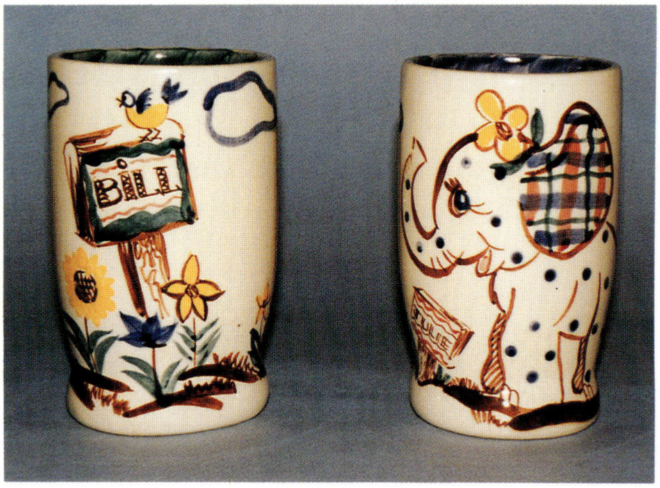

Tumblers decorated by Wm. Blair for Bill Bower's children Bill and Julie. $150+ each.

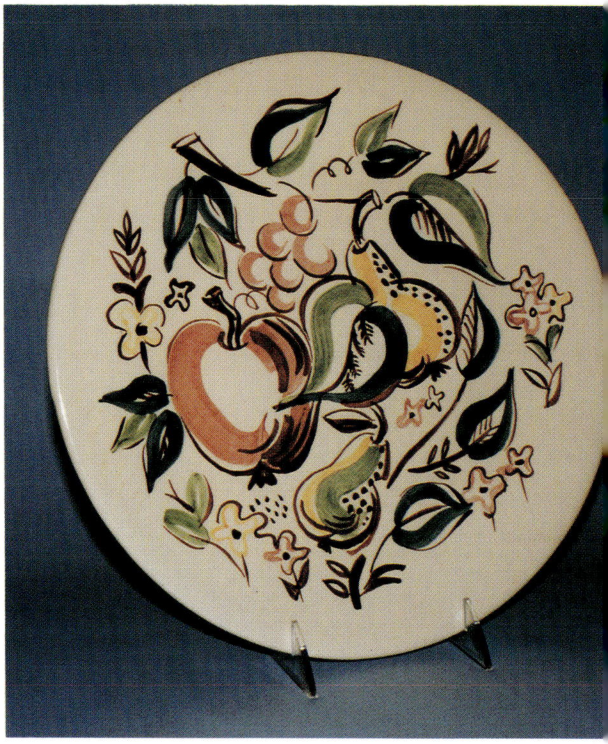

Chop plate, signed Wm. H. Blair, completed in Wellsville before the plant moved to Shippenville. This piece may have been the inspiration for the Apple pattern. $750+.

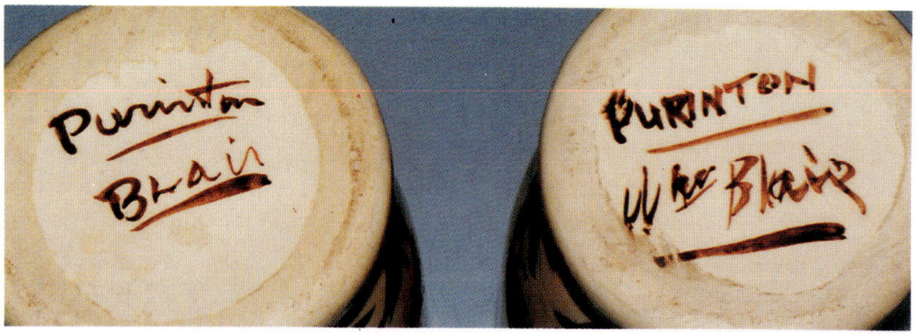

Signature of Wm. Blair on the bottom of the tumblers painted for Bill Bower's children.

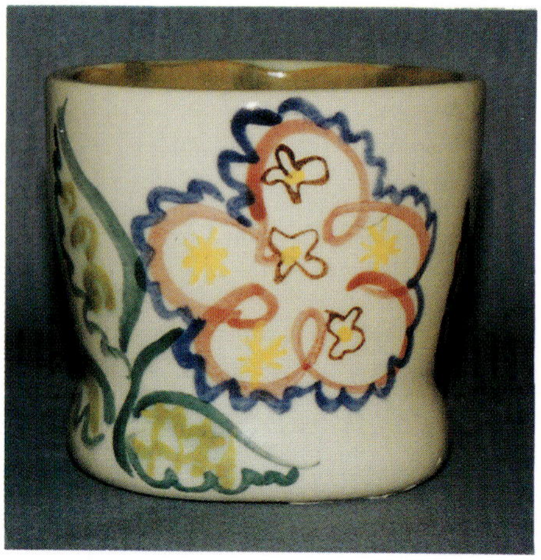

Juice mug painted by William Blair. $150+.

Blair signature on the bottom of juice mug.

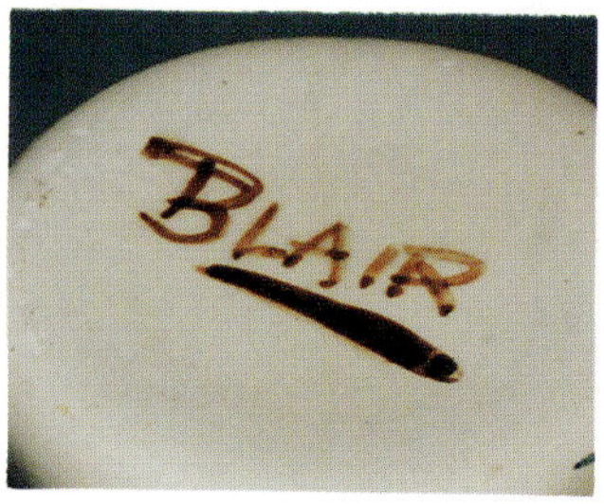

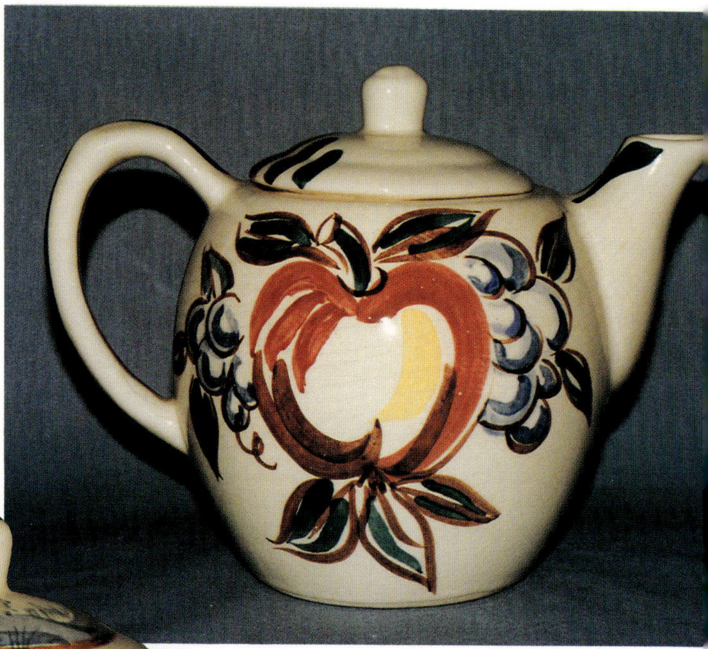

Six cup teapot with open apple and grapes decoration. Attributed to Wm. Blair. $300+.

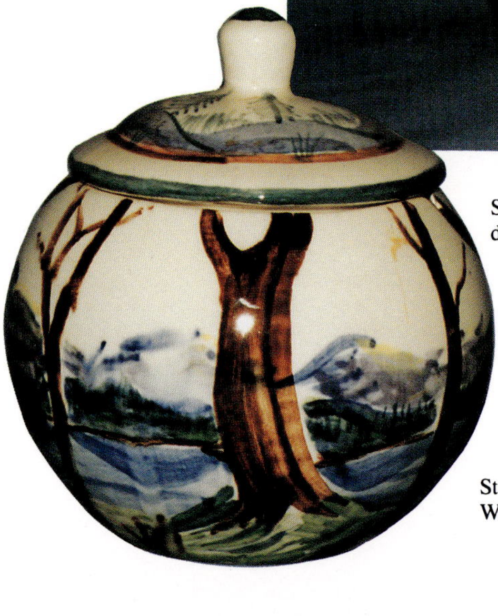

Storage jar with scenic decoration. Attributed to Wm. Blair. $150+.

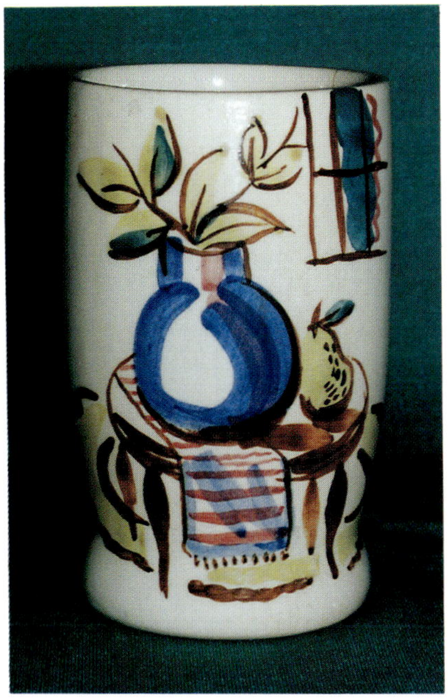

Tumbler with vase on table decoration. Signed Wm. Blair. $300+.

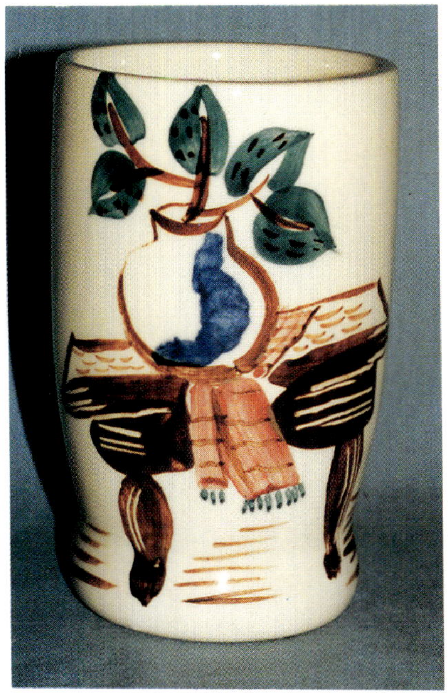

Tumbler with vase on table decoration. Attributed to Wm. Blair. $200+.

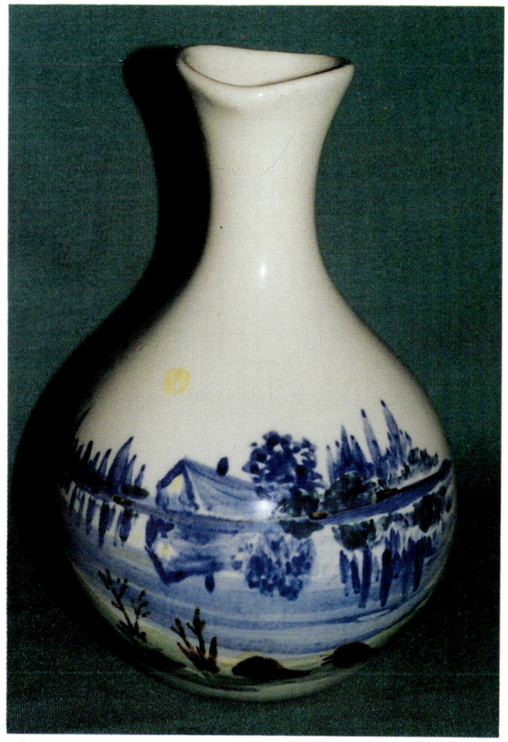

Night bottle with lake scene. Attributed to Wm. Blair. $150+.

Dorothy Purinton

Dorothy Blair was born in Mt. Vernon, Ohio, and married Bernard Purinton in 1917. Her artistic talent came naturally. She received no formal training, but this may have benefited Purinton Pottery. Her simple designs were the backbone of Purinton's decorations. She is credited with designing all the patterns at Shippenville except Intaglio, Apple, and the Plaids.

Dorothy worked at the plant but was not a paid employee. She not only developed new patterns but was responsible for training the decorators at Shippenville and Tionesta.

Many of her design ideas came from her interest in the Pennsylvania Dutch culture. A friend recalls that Dorothy was fascinated with the Pennsylvania Dutch Amish. On trips in the area, she would always remark about their simple lives as well as their dedication to God and hard work. From this influence, she created her special blessing plates. Many of them have a Pennsylvania Dutch design and/or blessing. She also painted plates featuring Amish or peasant people.

These blessing plates were made for friends at special occasions such as anniversaries. She also gave them as gifts at birthdays and Christmas. Dorothy had a habit of getting the anniversary date wrong or misspelling a name, but she was always willing to correct her mistake with a new plate. Bill Bower, secretary/treasurer of Purinton Pottery, tells how Dorothy put July 25 as his wedding anniversary date. When he told her of the mistake, his anniversary was the 24th, she painted another one with the 25th! Bill did not get a third one. Her two most famous anniversary plates are for President Eisenhower and Charles Lindbergh (she spelled Lindbergh without the h). Blair Purinton, her son, recalls that her opportunity to create these special plates was her payment for working at the plant.

Some plates marked special occasions or membership for organizations in the local area, such as the Clarion Chapter of the Eastern Star and Womans Club of Clarion Pennsylvania. Also difficult to find are the plates Dorothy made commemorating the Clarion Autumn Leaf Festival. This is an annual event which still exists in Clarion. You can also see her work on Intaglio plates marked Pennsylvania. Some of those were not signed but can be attributed to her. Plates such as these, and a few blessing plates, were sold at the Corner Cupboard.

Neither William Blair's nor Dorothy Purinton's items are the hardest to find Purinton Pottery wares, but they are in the biggest demand. These are unique pieces from two people who made Purinton Pottery an appreciated part of the history of American dinnerware.

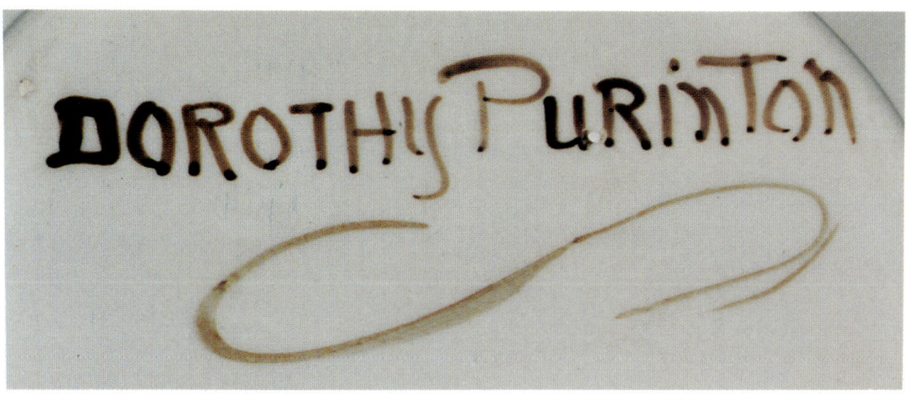

The Dorothy Purinton signature, a highly sought after mark by collectors. Dorothy's signature or initials on a piece of pottery adds tremendously to the desirability and value of the piece.

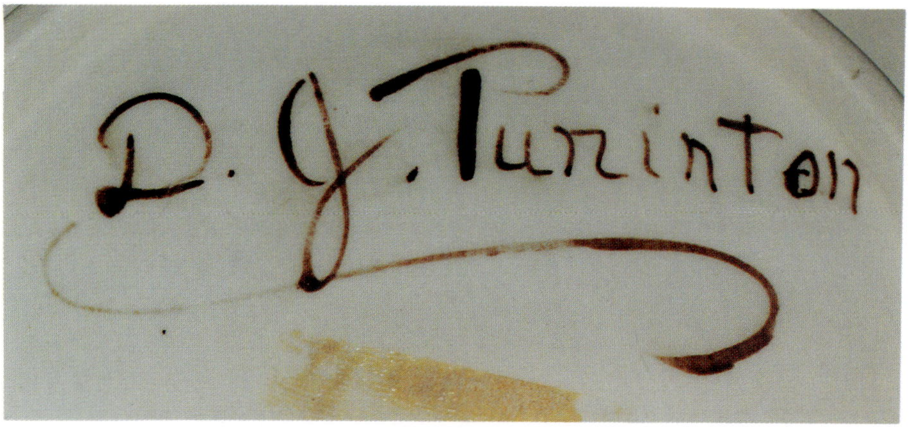

Dorothy Purinton's signature with her middle initial.

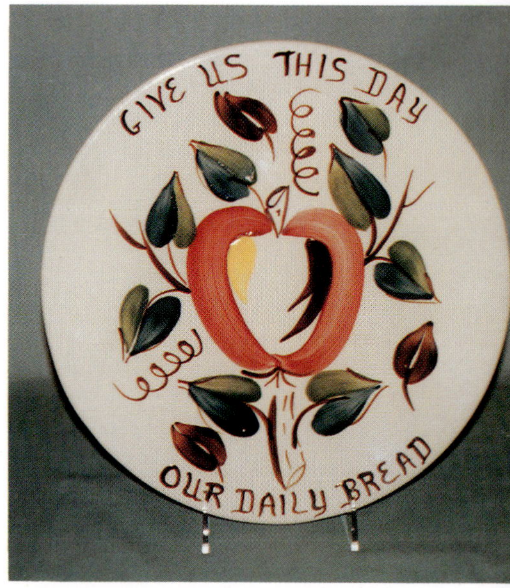

Chop plate with "Give us this day our daily bread" blessing, Apple decoration. Signed by Dorothy Purinton. $1000+.

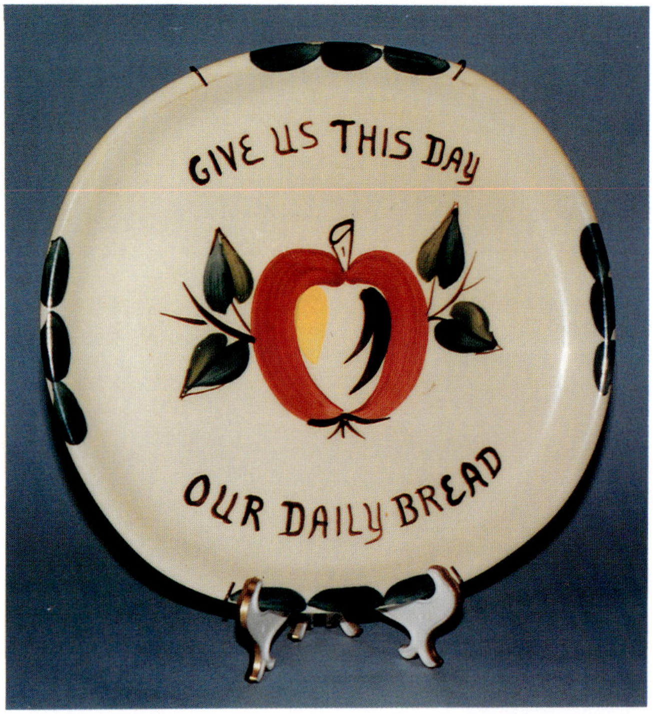

Dinner plate with "Give us this day our daily bread" blessing, Apple decoration. Signed by Dorothy Purinton. $500+.

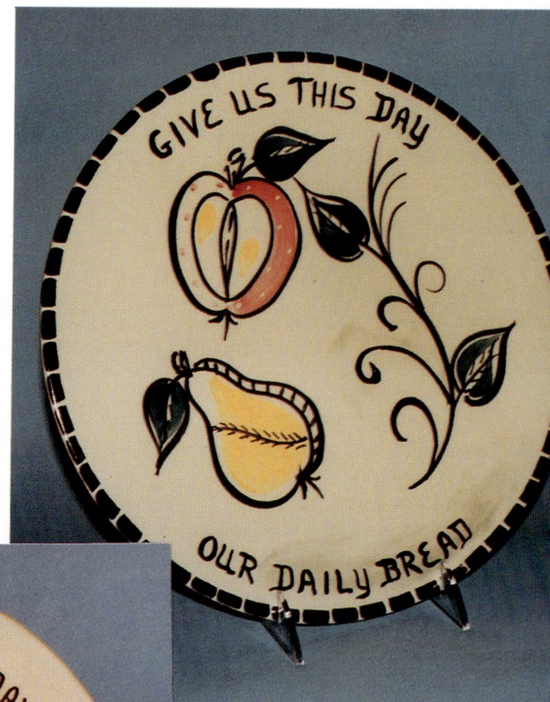

Chop plate with "Give us this day our daily bread" blessing, Provincial Fruit decoration. Signed by Dorothy Purinton. $1000+.

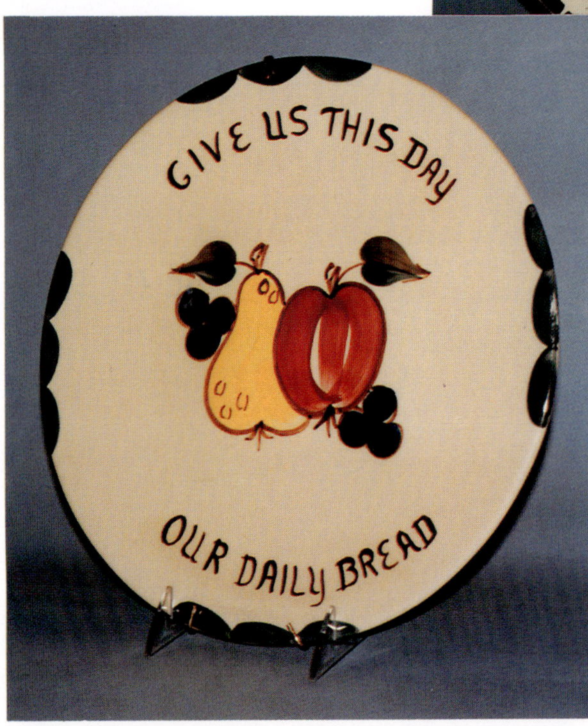

Chop plate with "Give us this day our daily bread" blessing, Esmond Fruit decoration. Signed by Dorothy Purinton. $1000+.

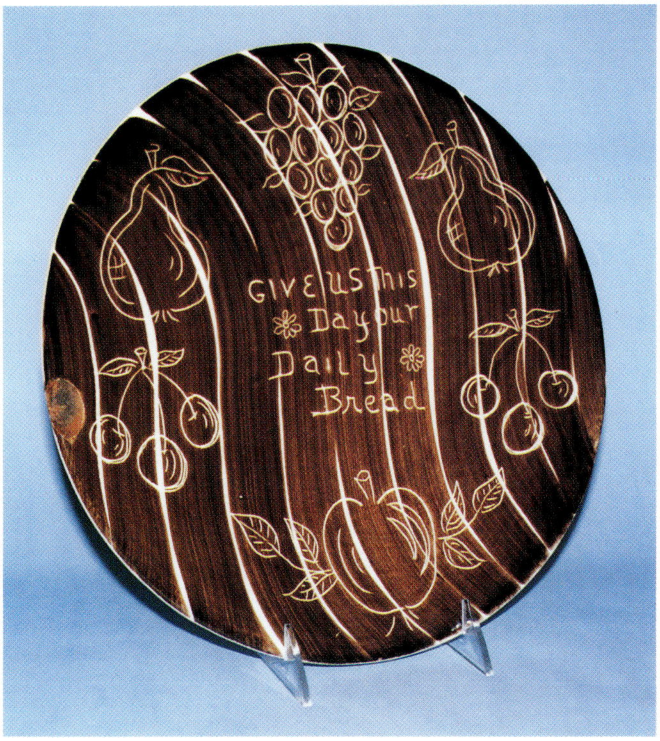

Chop plate with "Give us this day our daily bread" blessing, Brown Intaglio incised decoration. Signed by Dorothy Purinton. $750+.

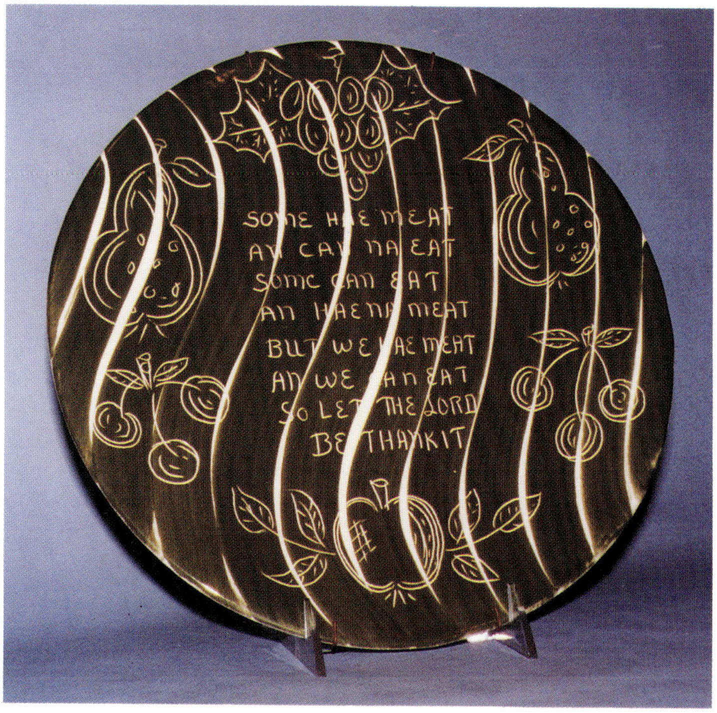

Chop plate with "Some hae meat an can na eat, some can eat an hae na meat. But we hae meat an we can eat. So let the Lord be thankit" blessing, Green Intaglio incised decoration. Signed by Dorothy Purinton. $750+.

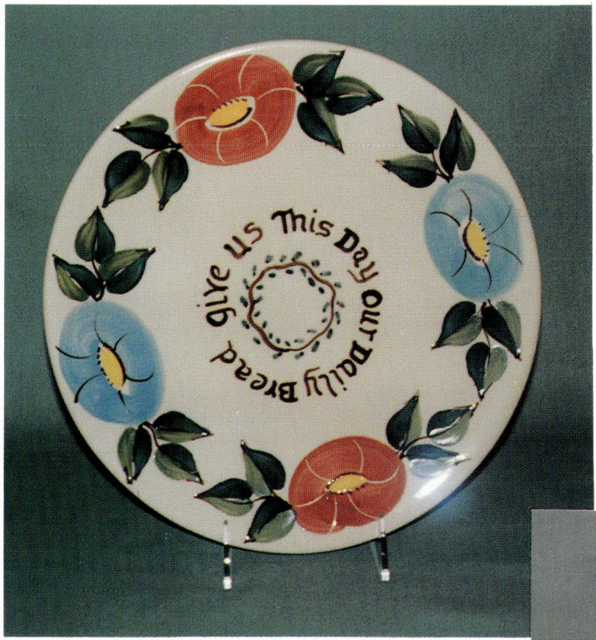

Chop plate with "Give us this day our daily bread" blessing, Morning Glory decoration. Signed by Dorothy Purinton. $750+.

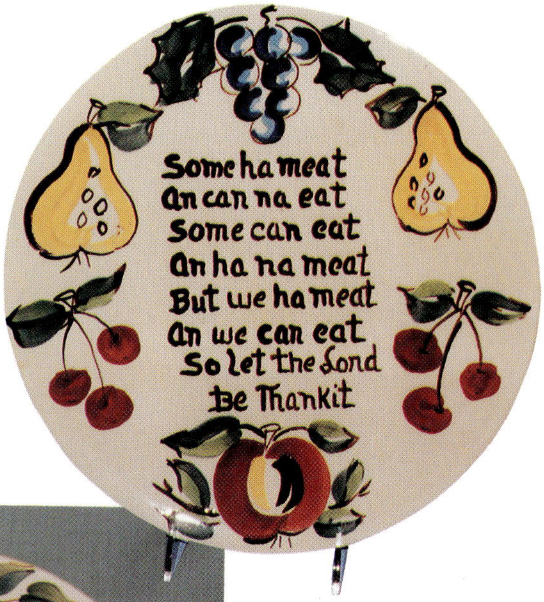

Chop plate with "Some hae meat an can na eat, some can eat an hae na meat. But we hae meat an we can eat. So let the Lord be thankit" blessing, Fruit decoration. Signed by Dorothy Purinton. $750+.

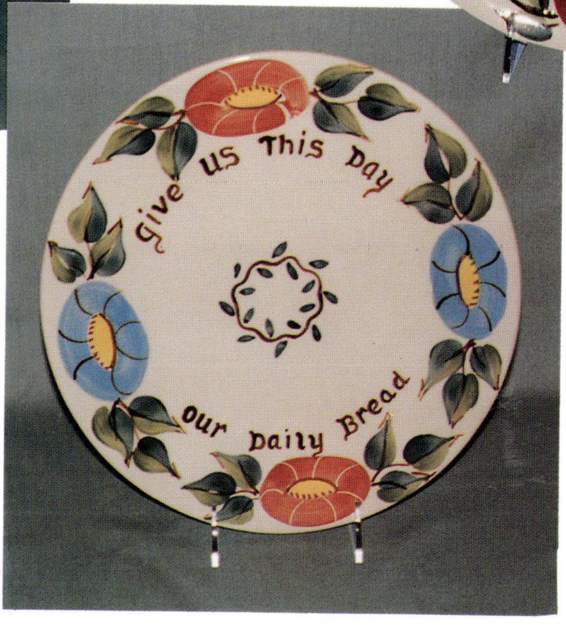

Chop plate with "Give us this day our daily bread" blessing, Morning Glory decoration. Signed by Dorothy Purinton. $750+.

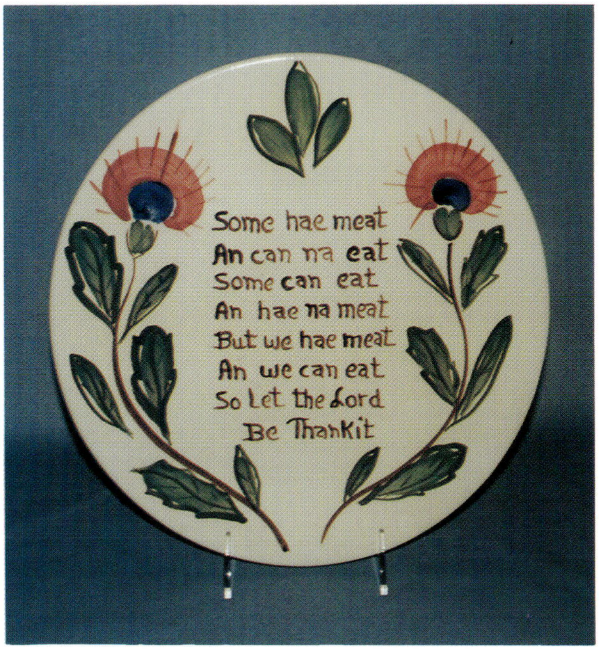

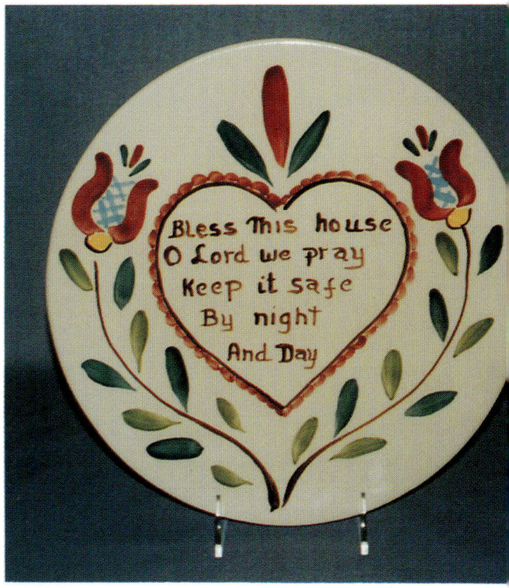

Chop plate with "Bless this house O Lord we pray keep it safe by night and day" blessing, with Pennsylvania Dutch decoration. Signed by Dorothy Purinton. $750+

Chop plate with "Some hae meat an can na eat, some can eat an hae na meat. But we hae meat and we can eat. So let the Lord be thankit" blessing, Thistle decoration. Signed by Dorothy Purinton. $1000+.

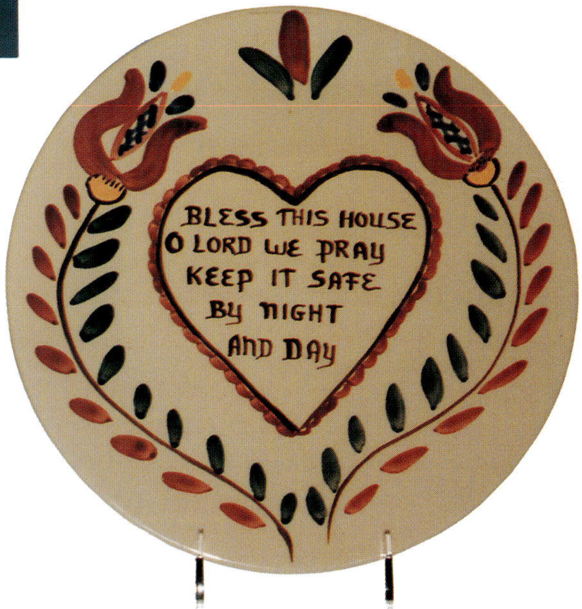

Chop plate with "Bless this house O Lord we pray keep it safe by night and day" blessing, Pennsylvania Dutch decoration using darker colors. Signed by Dorothy Purinton. $750+.

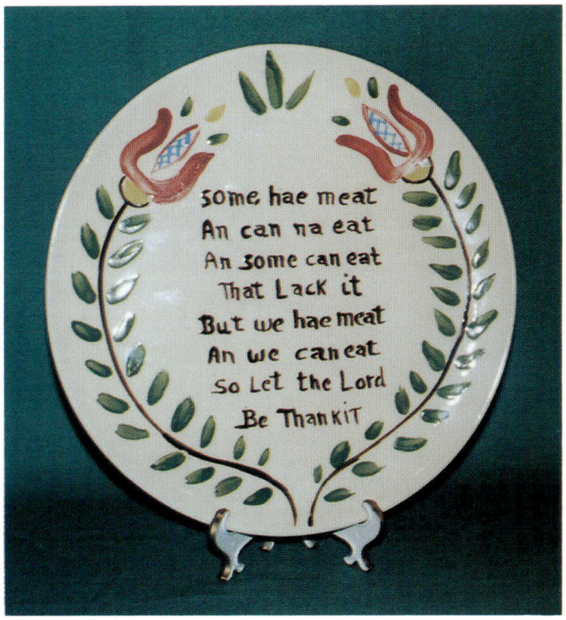

Chop plate with "Some hae meat and can na eat. An some can eat that lack it. But we hae meat an we can eat. So let the Lord be thankit" blessing with Pennsylvania Dutch decoration. Signed by Dorothy Purinton. $1000+.

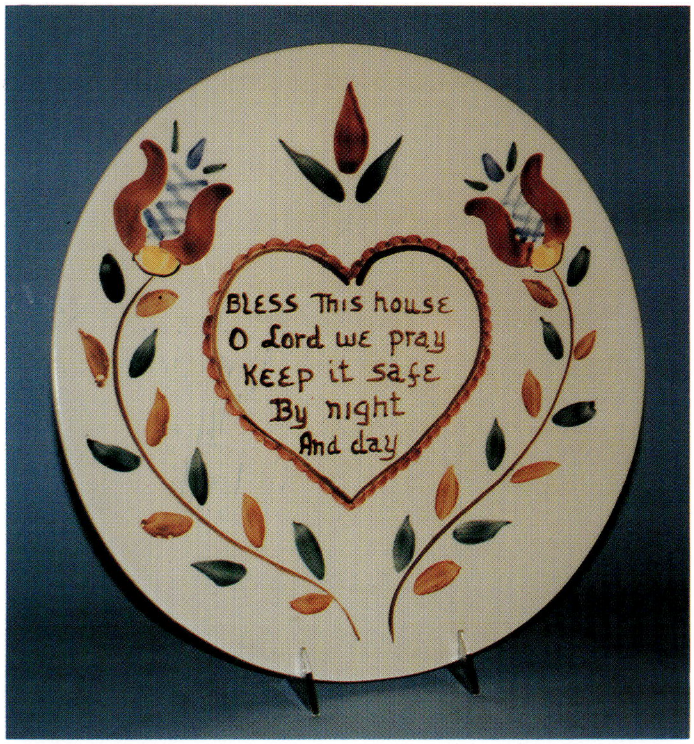

Chop plate, 14" Rubel mold with "Bless this house O Lord we pray keep is safe by night and day" blessing, Pennsylvania Dutch decoration. Signed by Dorothy Purinton. $1000+.

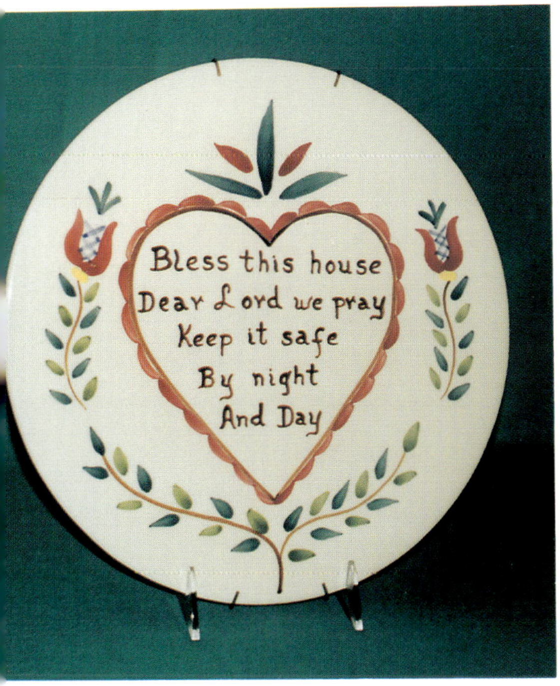

Chop plate with "Bless this house Dear Lord we pray keep it safe by night and day" blessing, Pennsylvania Dutch decoration. Signed by Dorothy Purinton. $750+.

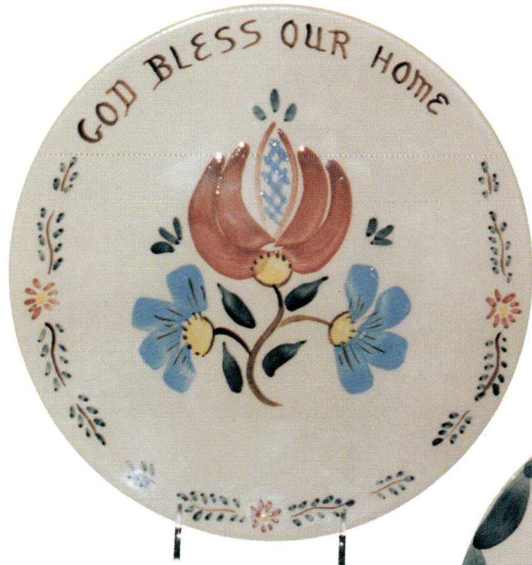

Chop plate with "God Bless Our Home" blessing, Pennsylvania Dutch variant decoration. Signed by Dorothy Purinton. $750+.

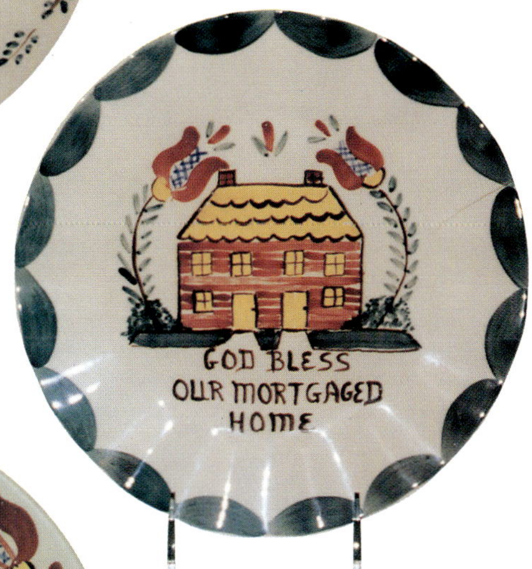

Dinner plate, Seaform style with "God bless our mortgaged home" blessing Pennsylvania Dutch decoration with house. Signed by Dorothy Purinton. $600+.

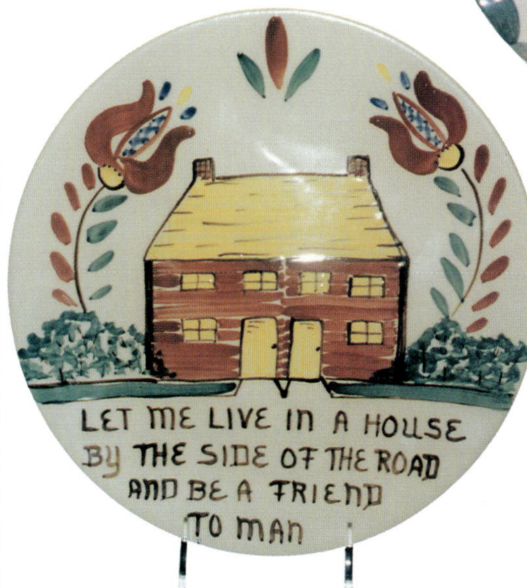

Chop plate with "Let me live in a house by the side of the road and be a friend to man" blessing, Pennsylvania Dutch decoration with house. Signed by Dorothy Purinton. $1000+.

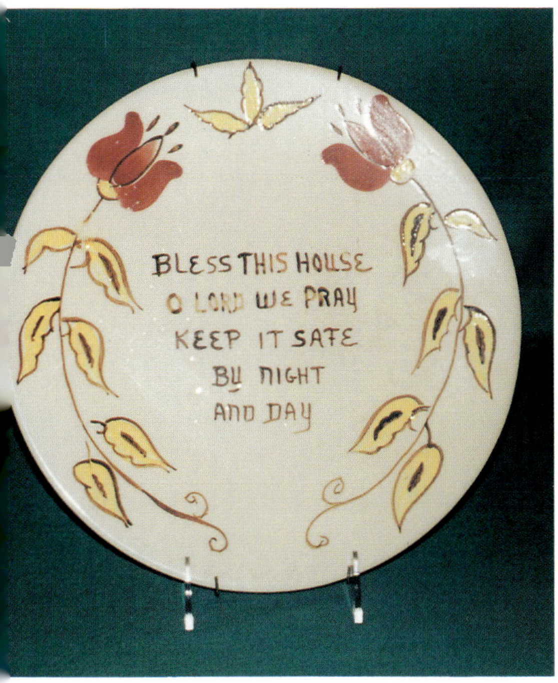

Chop plate with "Bless this house O Lord we pray keep it safe by night and day" blessing, Tulip and Vine decoration. Signed by Dorothy Purinton. $750+.

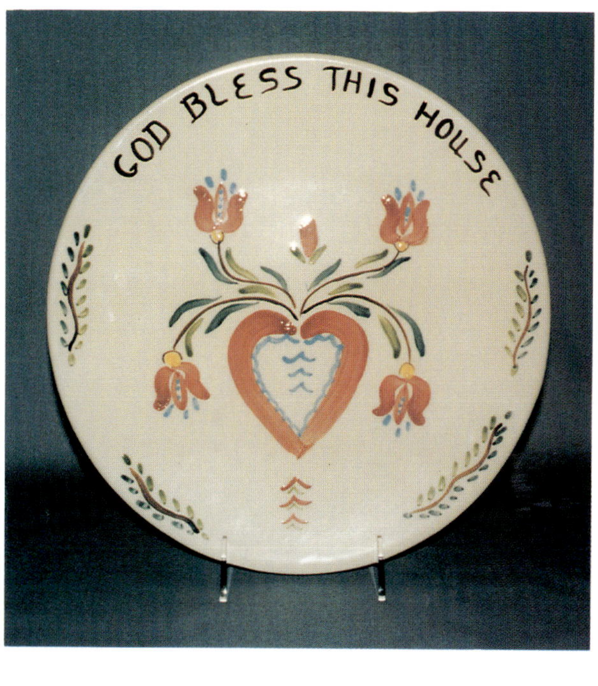

Chop plate with "God bless this house" blessing, Pennsylvania Dutch decoration. Signed by Dorothy Purinton. $1000+.

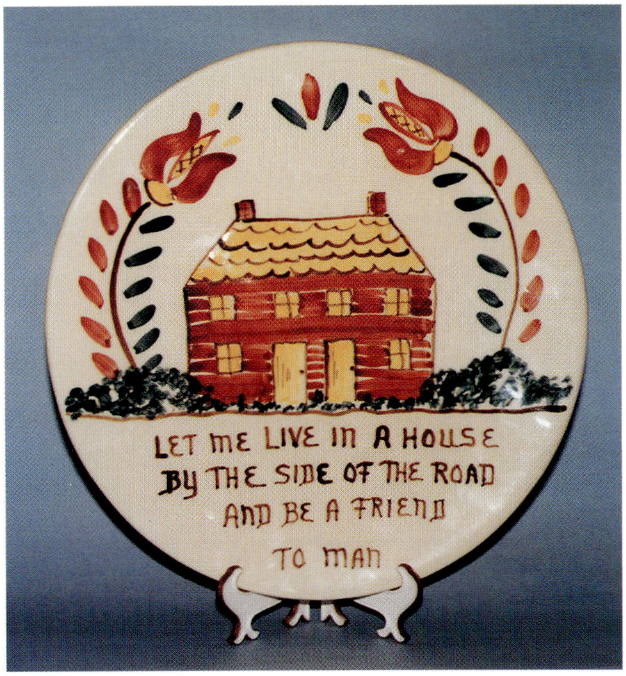

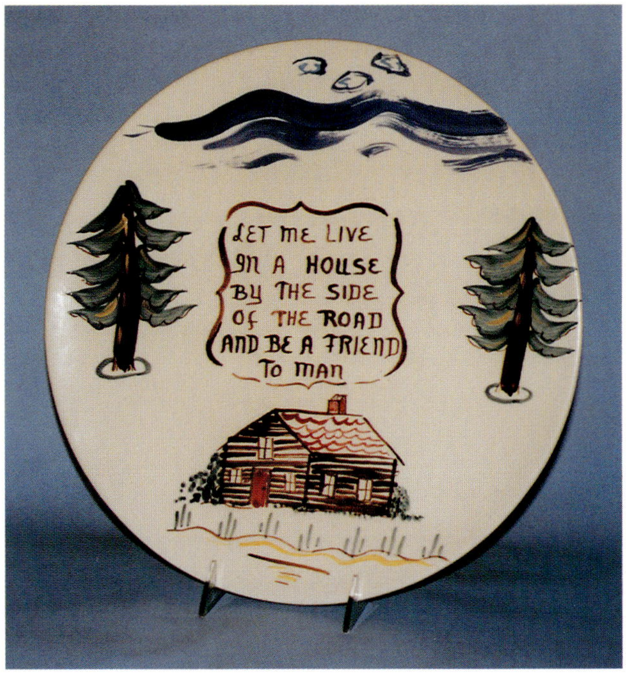

Chop plate with "Let me live in a house by the side of the road and be a friend to man" blessing, Pennsylvania Dutch decoration with house. Signed by Dorothy Purinton. $1000+.

Chop plate, 14" Rubel mold with "Let me live in a house by the side of the road and be a friend to man" blessing, cabin and tree decoration. Signed by Dorothy Purinton. $1200+.

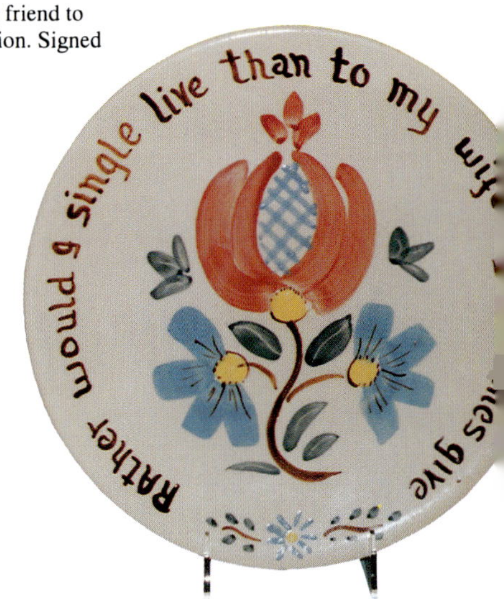

Chop plate with "Rather would I single live than to my wife my breeches give" saying, Pennsylvania Dutch variant decoration. Signed by Dorothy Purinton. $750+.

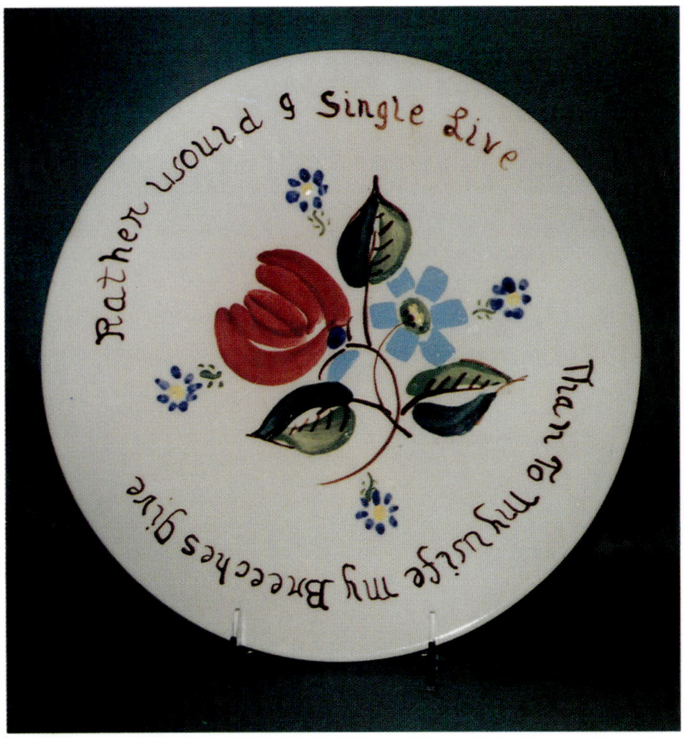

Chop plate with "Rather would I single live than to my wife my breeches give" saying, Pennsylvania Dutch variant decoration. Signed by Dorothy Purinton. $750+.

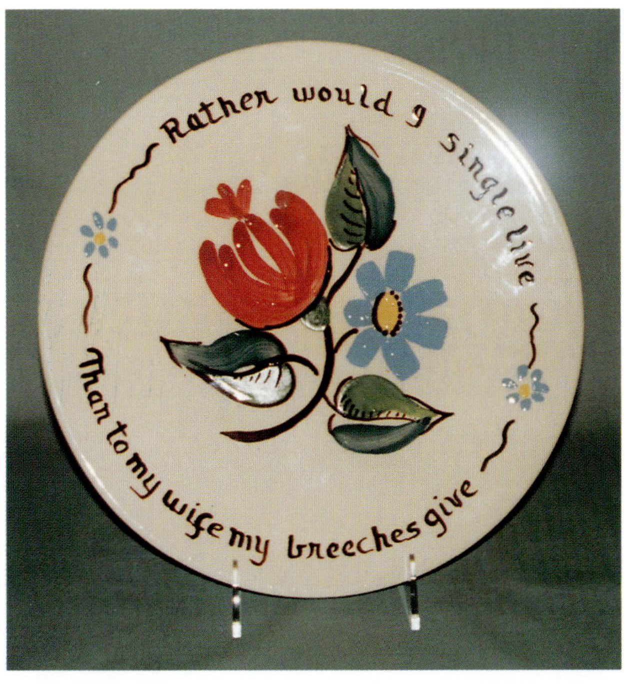

Chop plate with "Rather would I single live than to my wife my breeches give" saying, Pennsylvania Dutch variant decoration. Signed by Dorothy Purinton. $750+.

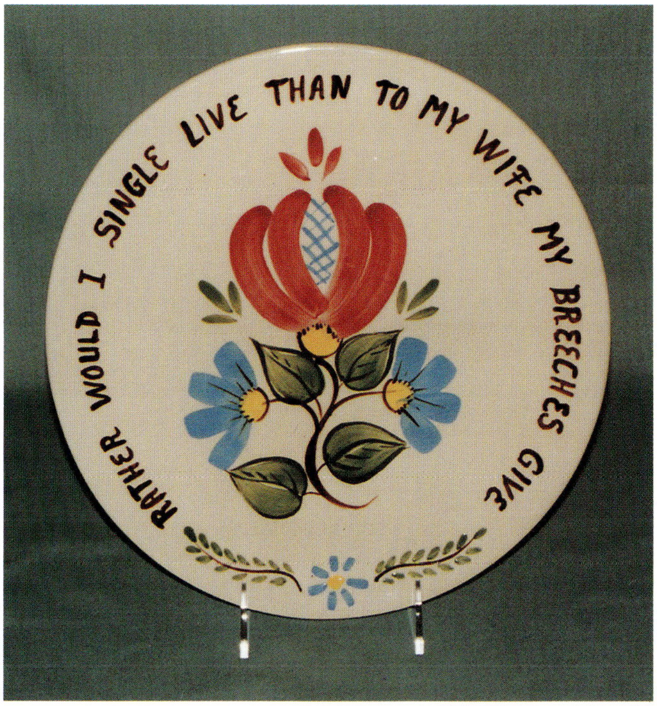

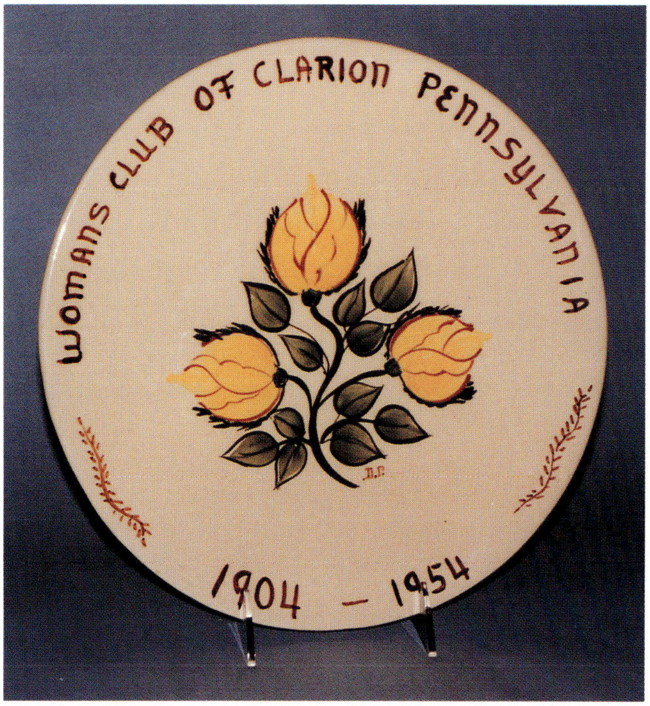

Chop plate with "Rather would I single live than to my wife my breeches give" saying, Pennsylvania Dutch variant decoration. Signed by Dorothy Purinton. $750+.

Chop plate presented to Mary Smathers, President of the Womans Club of Clarion Pennsylvania on their 50th anniversary, 1904-1954, Yellow Tea Rose design with DP initials below the flowers. Signed by Dorothy Purinton. $1000+.

Chop plate commemorating the 37th wedding anniversary of Dwight Eisenhower and Mamie Doud. Dorothy was an avid admirer of President Eisenhower and Mamie. She sent them one for their anniversary and received a thank you for her gift, Pennsylvania Dutch variant decoration on Maywood slip. Signed by Dorothy Purinton. $1500+.

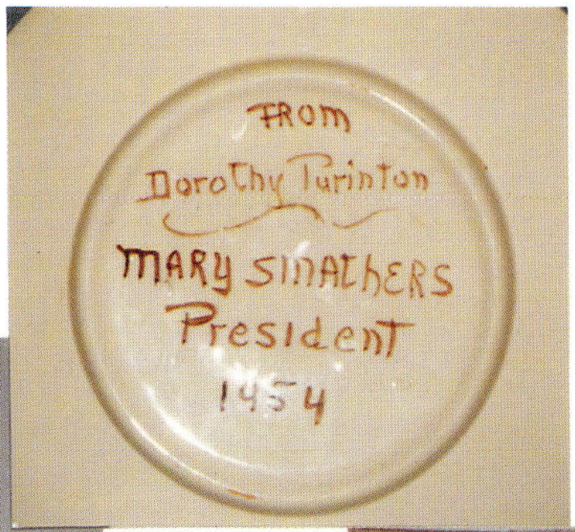

Reverse side of the Clarion Womans Club plate.

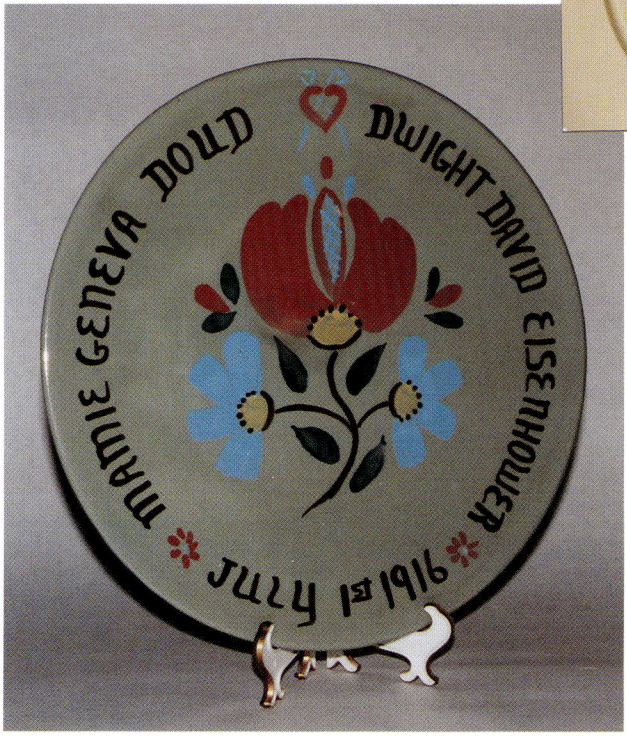

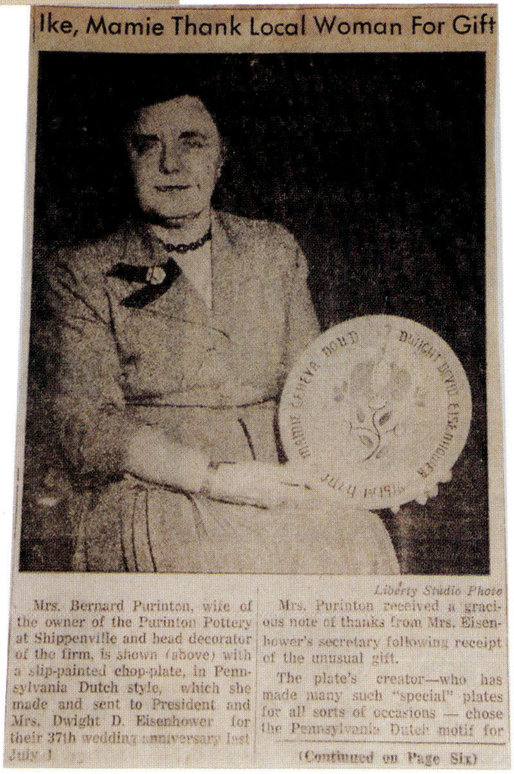
Ike, Mamie Thank Local Woman For Gift

Liberty Studio Photo

Mrs. Bernard Purinton, wife of the owner of the Purinton Pottery at Shippenville and head decorator of the firm, is shown (above) with a slip-painted chop-plate, in Pennsylvania Dutch style, which she made and sent to President and Mrs. Dwight D. Eisenhower for their 37th wedding anniversary last July 1.

Mrs. Purinton received a gracious note of thanks from Mrs. Eisenhower's secretary following receipt of the unusual gift.

The plate's creator—who has made many such "special" plates for all sorts of occasions — chose the Pennsylvania Dutch motif for

(Continued on Page Six)

Newspaper clipping showing Dorothy Purinton holding the Eisenhower plate. It is speculated that the president is unable to accept gifts, so the chop plate was returned to the Purinton family.

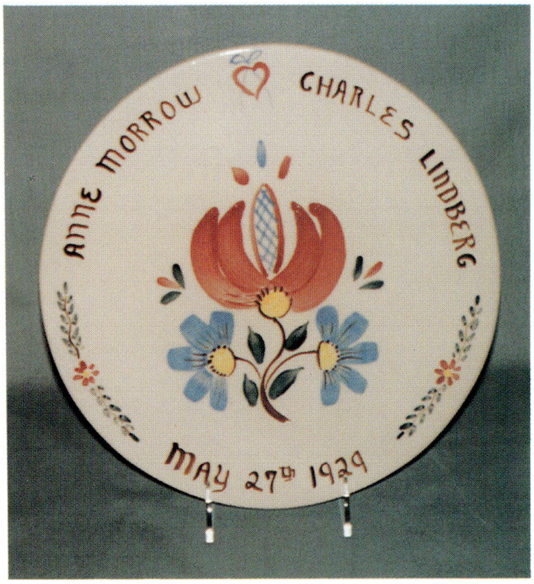

Chop plate commemorating the wedding anniversary of Charles Lindbergh and Anne Morrow. Dorothy was an admirer of Anne Morrow. (Note in the photograph that Lindbergh is spelled incorrectly.) This plate resurfaced after the death of Mrs. Lindbergh. Signed by Dorothy Purinton. $1500+.

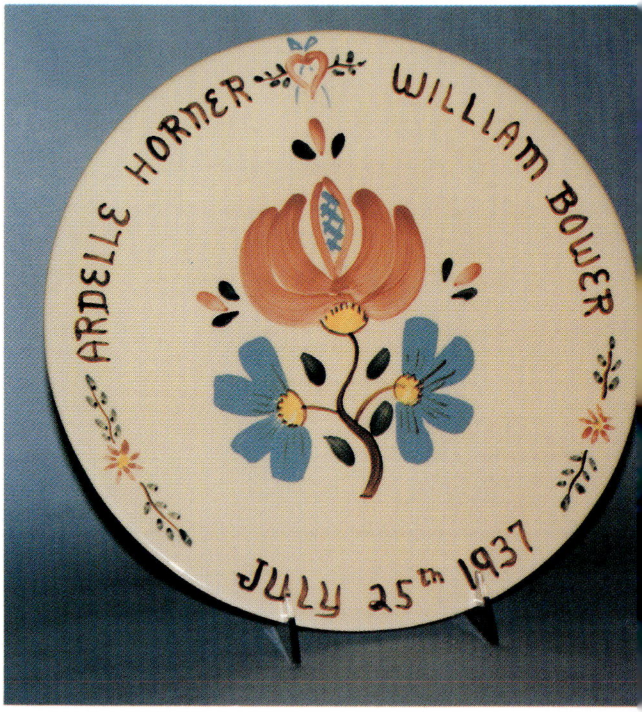

Chop plate commemorating the wedding anniversary of William Bower, Secretary and Treasurer of Purinton Pottery, and his wife Ardelle, Pennsylvania Dutch variant decoration. Signed by Dorothy Purinton. $750+.

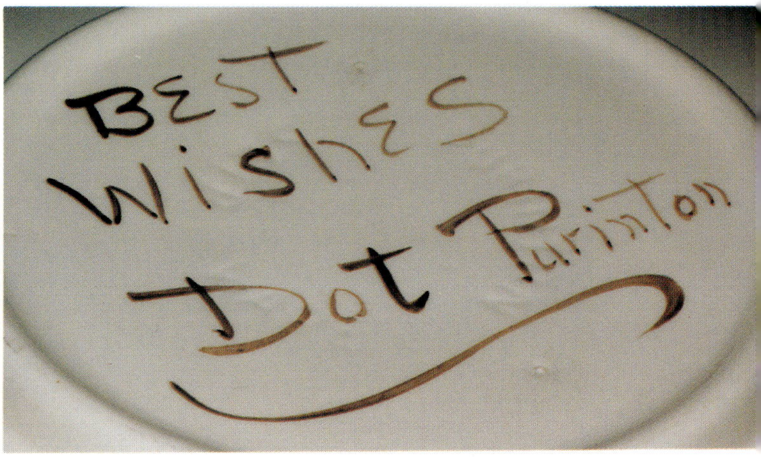

Dorothy Purinton signature on the back of Bill Bower's anniversary plate.

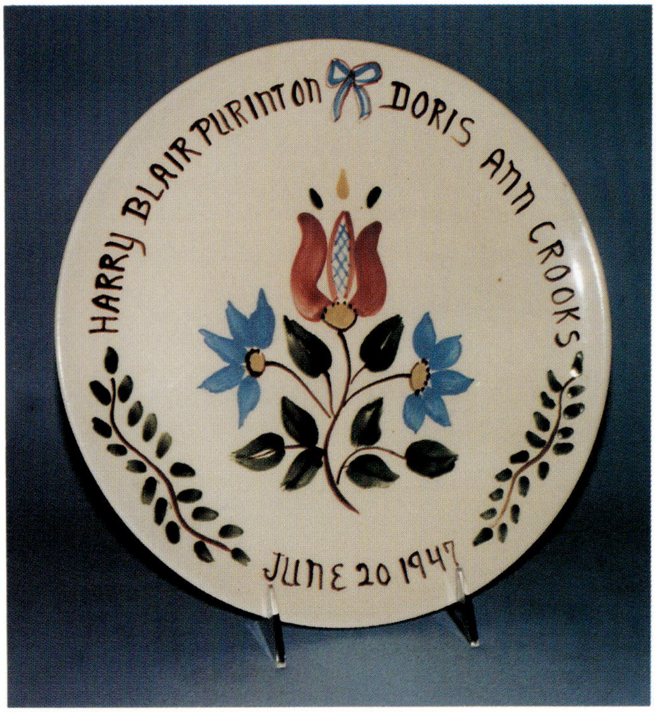

Chop plate commemorating the wedding anniversary of Blair Purinton (son of Dorothy and Bernard) and his wife Dorie. Signed by Dorothy Purinton. $750+.

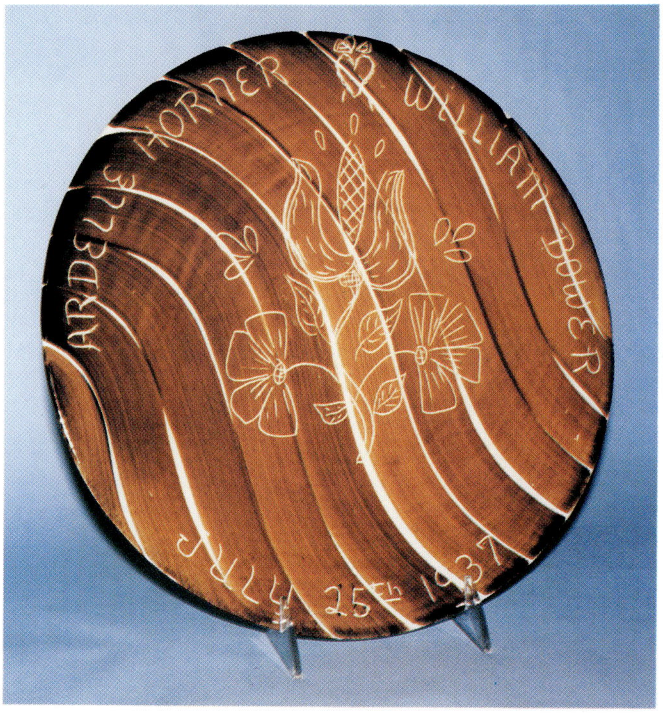

Chop plate commemorating the anniversary of William Bower, Secretary/Treasurer of Purinton Pottery, and his wife Ardelle. This is one of two Dorothy made for Bill and both had the wrong anniversary date (The correct date is July 24, 1937.), Brown Intaglio with incised Pennsylvania Dutch variant decoration. Signed by Dorothy Purinton. $750+.

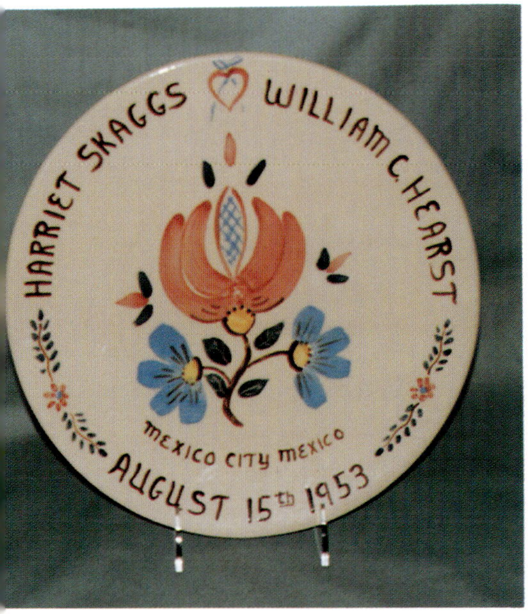

Chop plate commemorating the wedding anniversary of Harriet Skaggs and William C. Hearst. Mr. Hearst owned the Clarion newspaper. Mrs. Hearst told us that Dorothy was fascinated with the fact that she got married in Mexico City, so she added it to the plate. Signed by Dorothy Purinton. $750+.

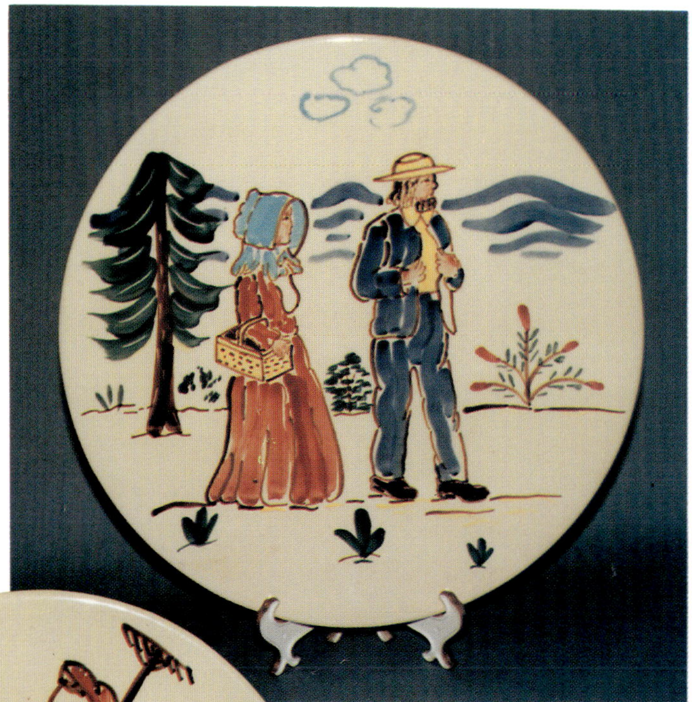

Chop plate with Amish couple. Signed by Dorothy Purinton. $1000+.

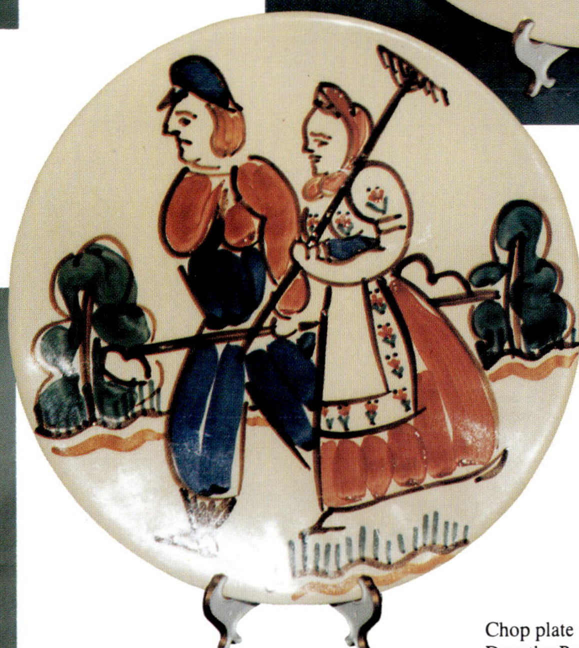

Chop plate with peasant couple. Signed by Dorothy Purinton. $1000+.

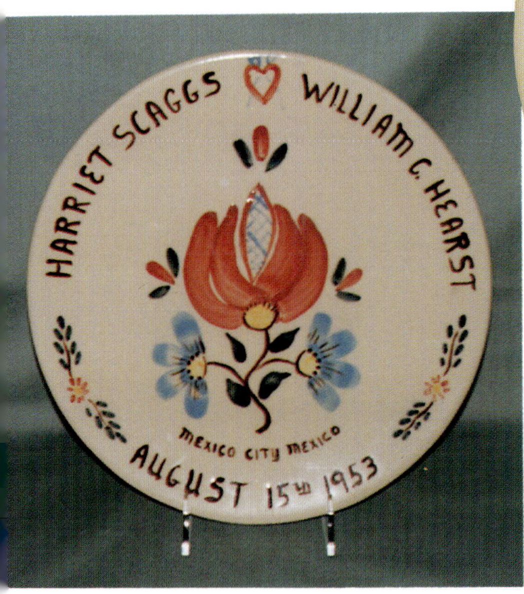

Note that Scaggs is not the correct spelling on this plate. It is rumored that there were often two plates anniversary plates presented since the first one often had some type of error. Signed by Dorothy Purinton. $750+.

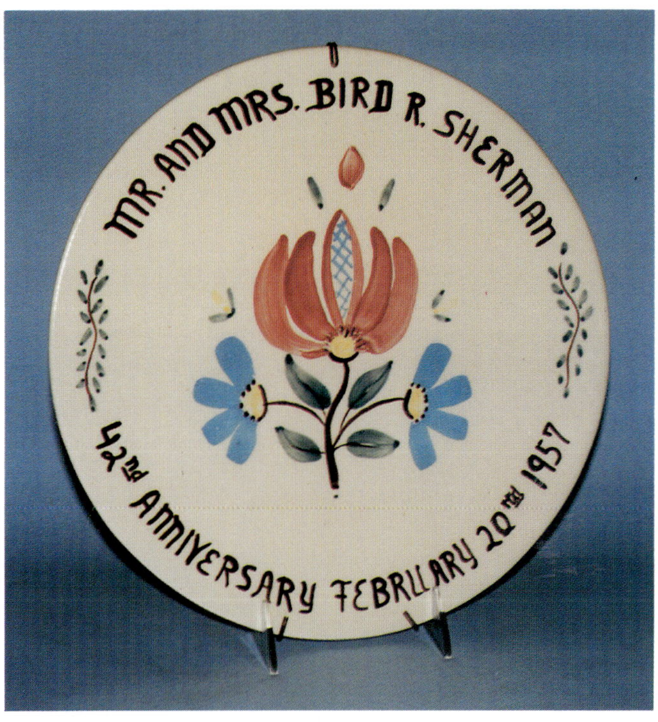

Chop plate commemorating the wedding anniversary of Mr. and Mrs. Bird Sherman. Signed by Dorothy Purinton. $750+.

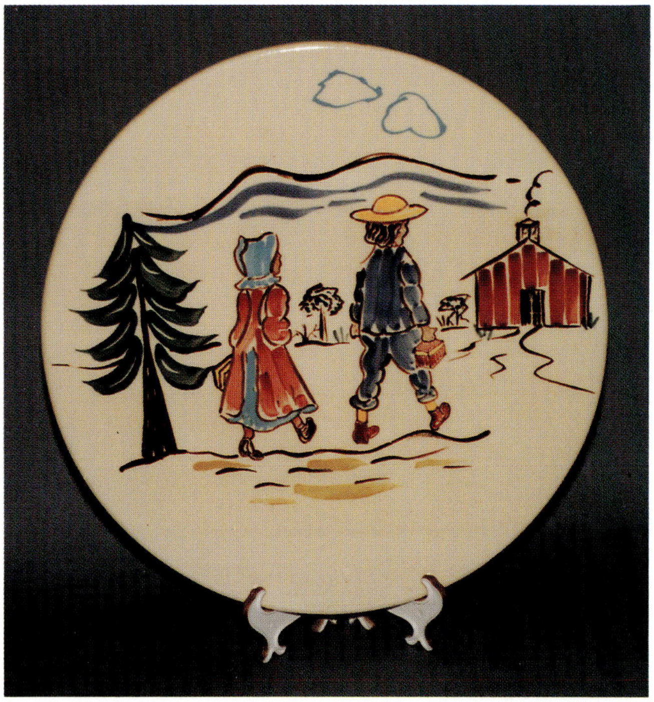

Chop plate with Amish children. Signed by Dorothy Purinton. $1000+.

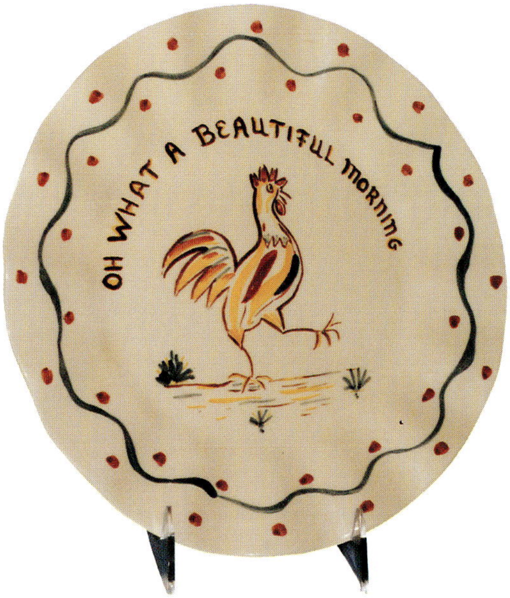

Dinner plate, Seaform style with "Oh what a beautiful morning" saying and rooster. Signed by Dorothy Purinton. $600+.

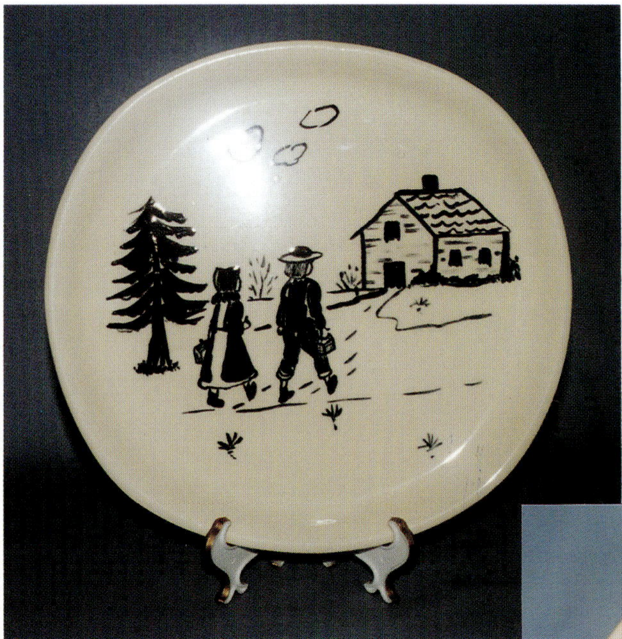

Dinner plate with Amish children going to school. Signed by Dorothy Purinton. $500+.

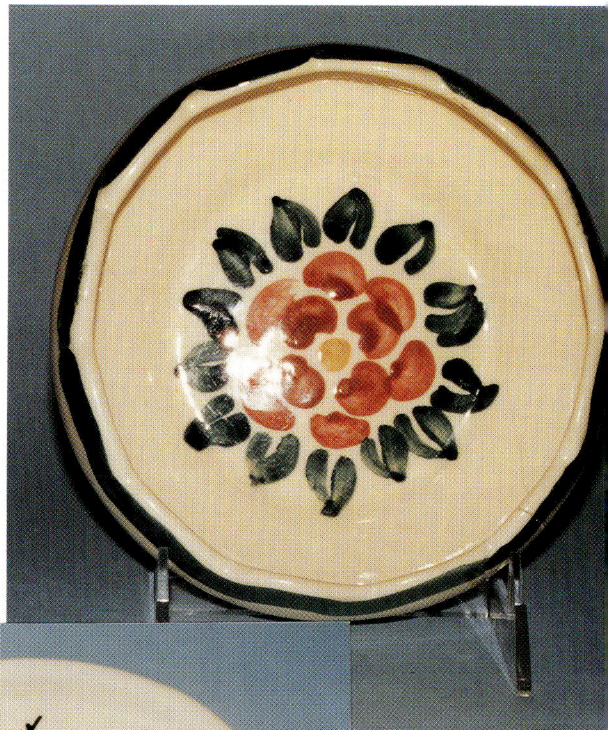

Unusual bowl, initialed DP. $100+.

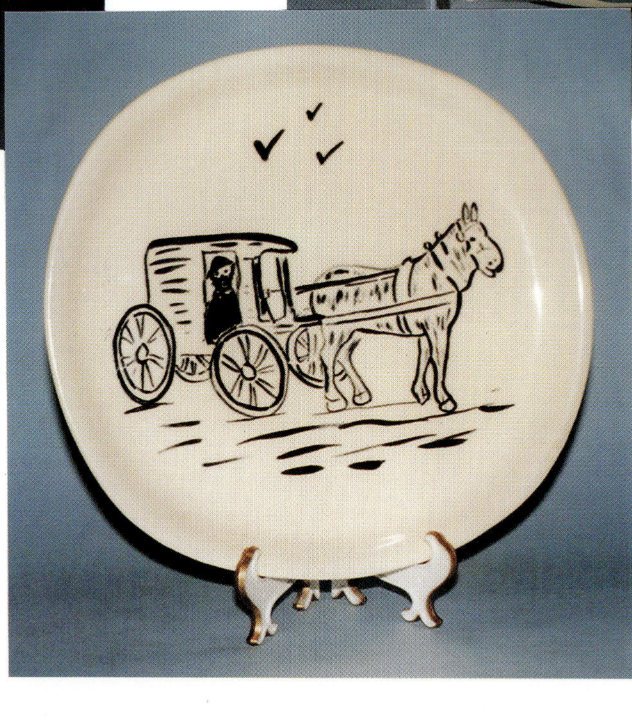

Dinner plate with an Amish man in a horse drawn buggy. Signed by Dorothy Purinton. $500+.

Souvenir Items

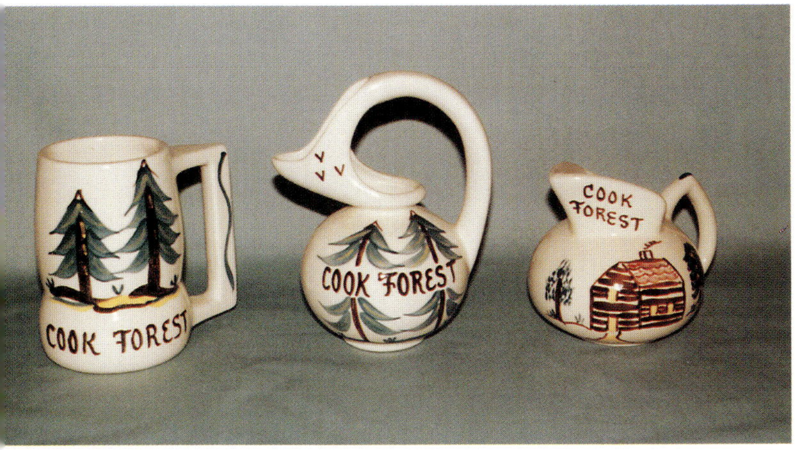

Cook Forest beer mug. $250. Cook Forest honey jug. $250. Cook Forest kent jug. $250.

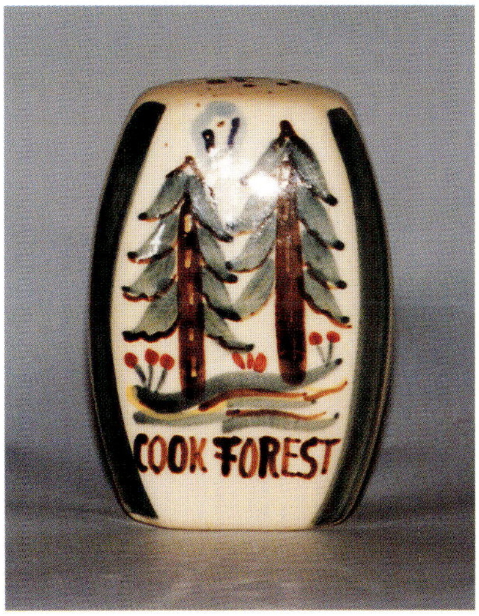

Cook Forest range shaker. $100 each.

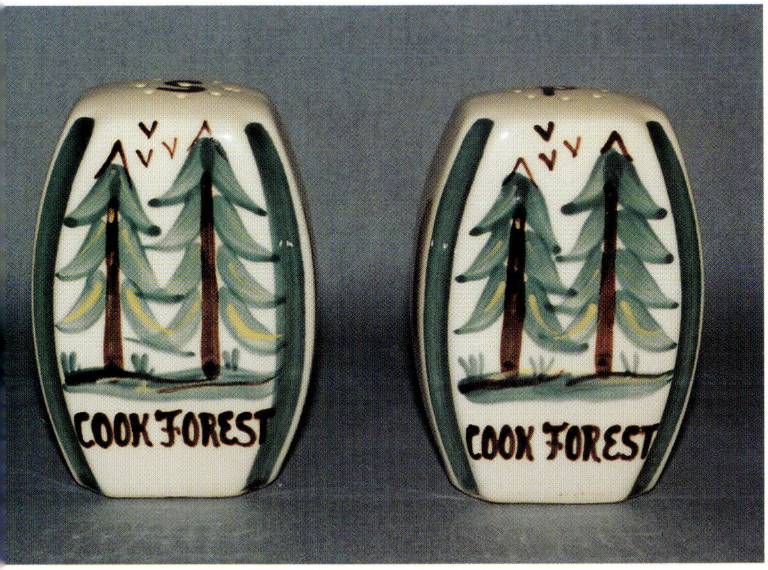

Cook Forest range salt and pepper shakers. $200 set.

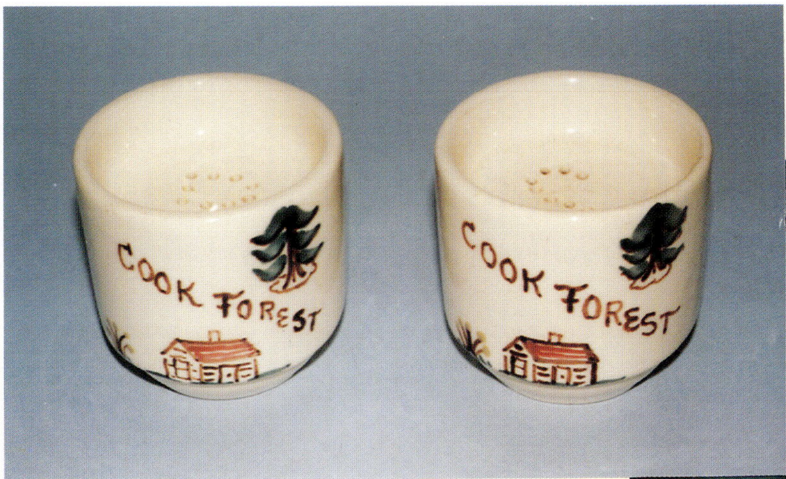

Cook Forest stacking salt and pepper shakers. $200.

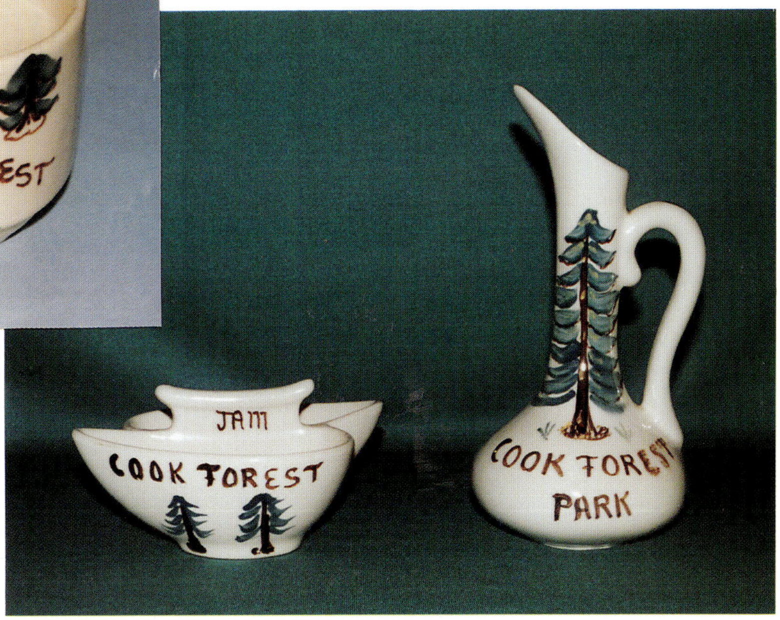

Cook Forest jam and jelly. $200. Cook Forest Park tall ewer. $200.

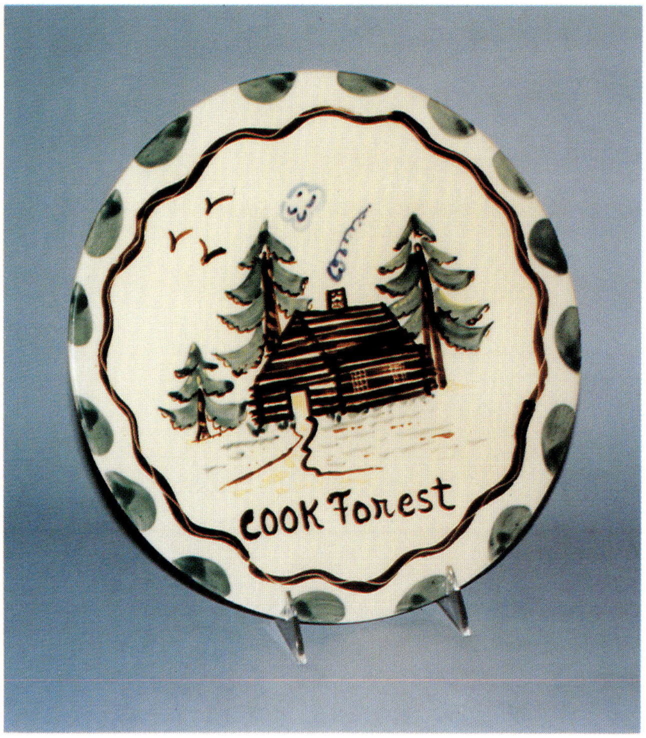

Cook Forest chop plate with log cabin in the forest. Signed by Dorothy Purinton. $1000+.

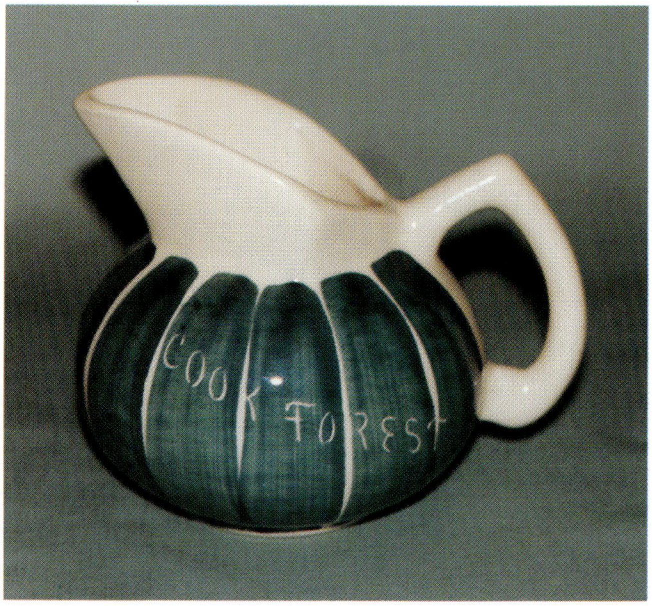

Cook Forest kent jug, Turquoise Intaglio. $200.

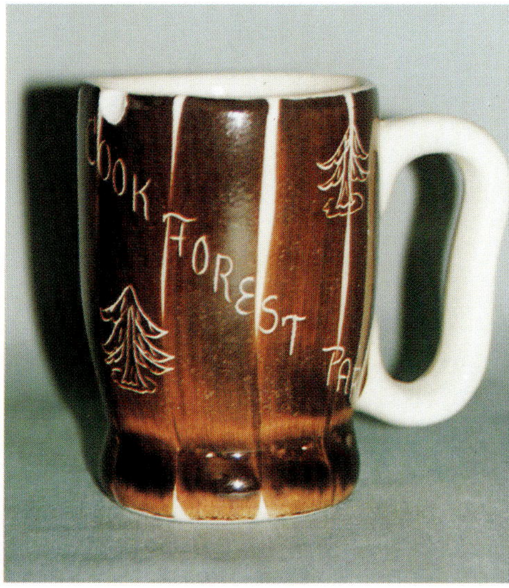

Cook Forest Park coffee mug, Brown Intaglio. $150.

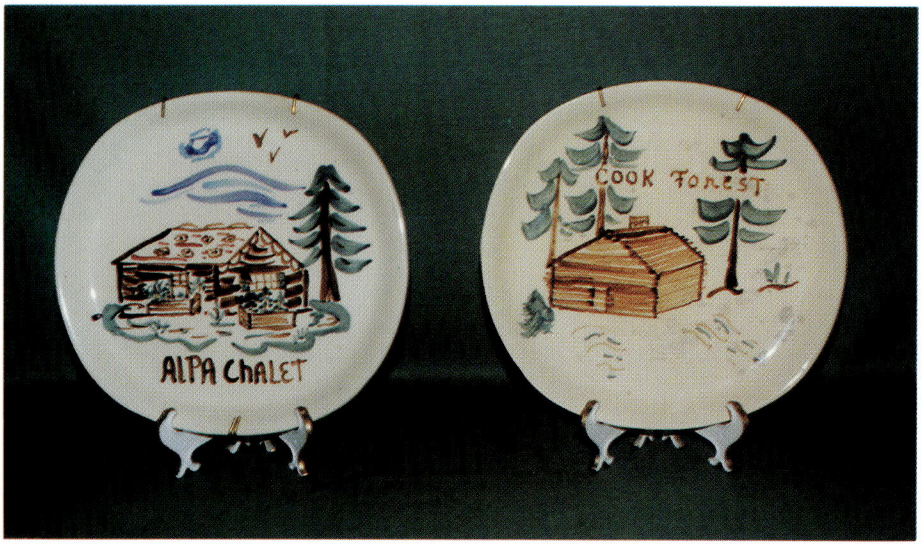

ALPA Chalet breakfast plate, probably given to a friend of Dorothy Purinton. $300+. Cook Forest breakfast plate. $300+.

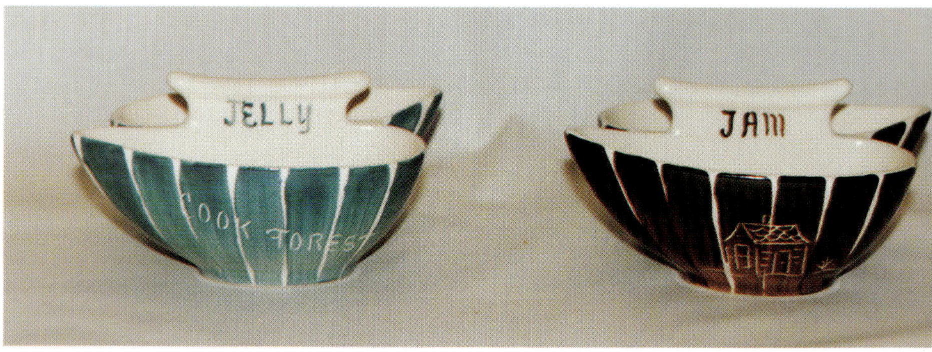

Cook Forest Intaglio jam and jelly (the Brown Intaglio jam and jelly is showing the reverse side). $125 each.

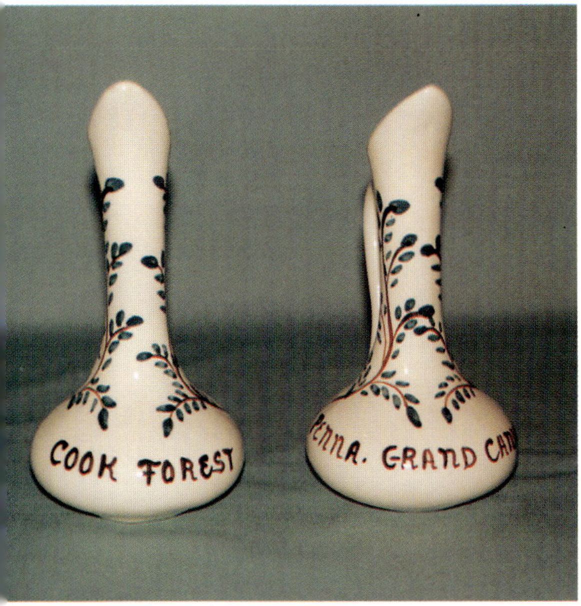

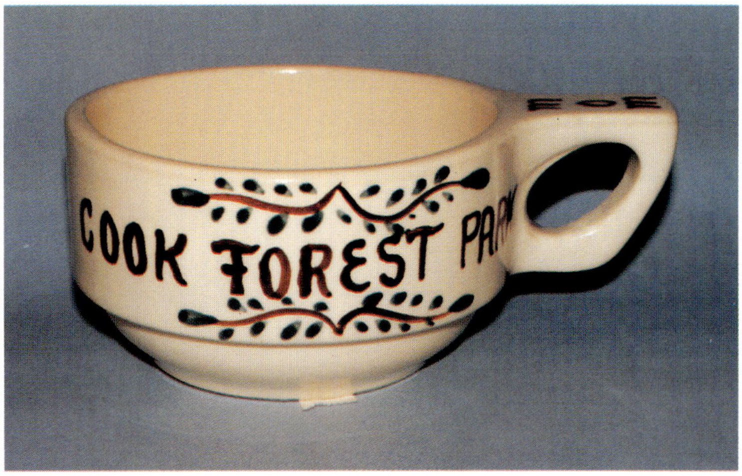

Cook Forest Park soup mug, Rubel mold, personalized Mom. $150.

Cook Forest tall ewer. $100. Penna. Grand Canyon tall ewer. $100.

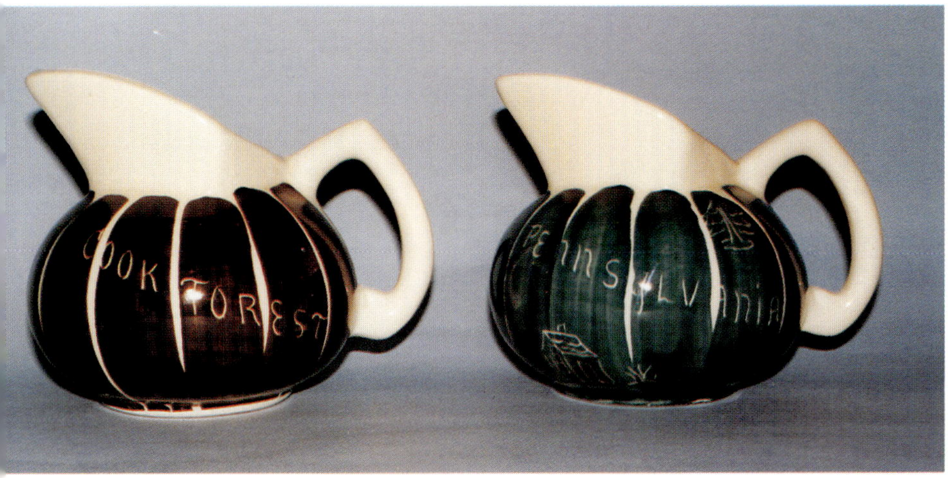

Cook Forest kent jug, Brown Intaglio. $200. Pennsylvania kent jug, Turquoise Intaglio. $200.

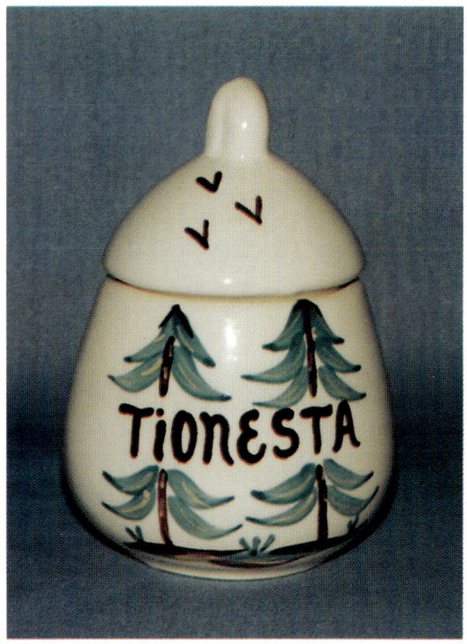

Tionesta marmalade jar. $200+.

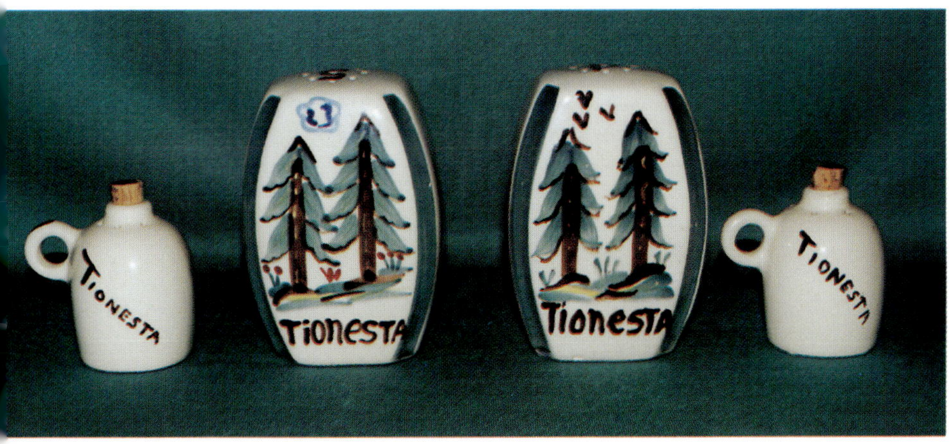

Tionesta jug style salt and pepper shakers. $100 set. Tionesta range salt and pepper shakers. $200 set.

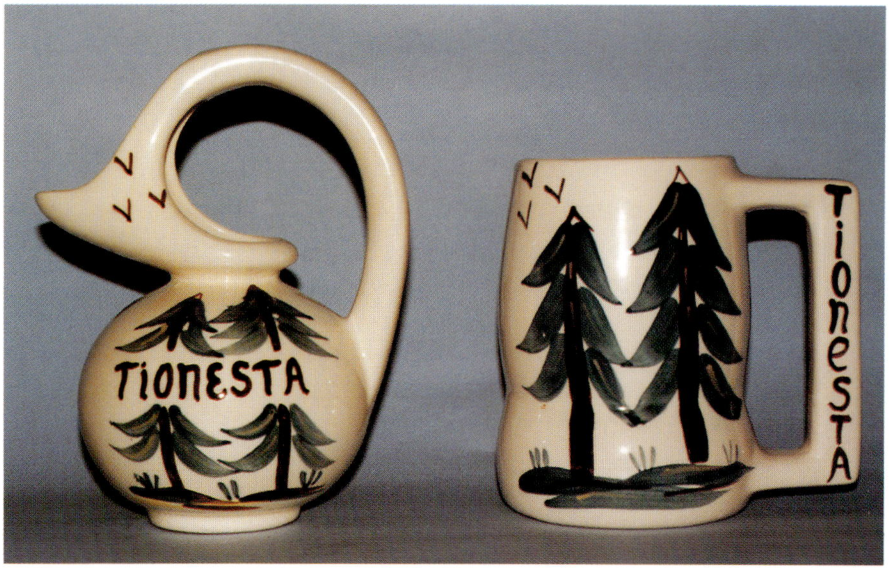

Tionesta honey jug. $300+. Tionesta beer mug. $300+.

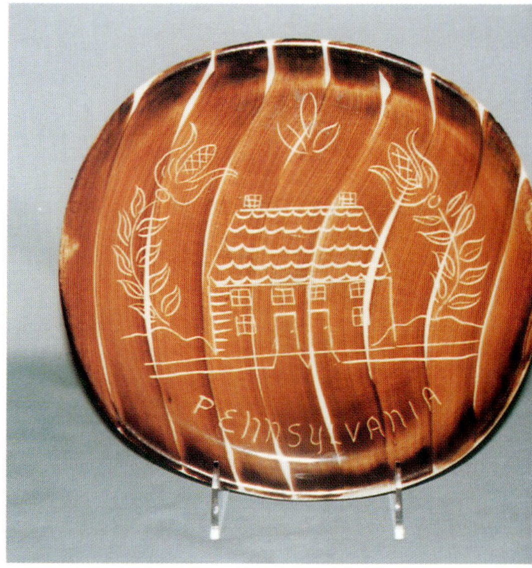

Pennsylvania dinner plate with a house and tulips incised on it, Brown Intaglio. Attributed to Dorothy Purinton. $400. If it were signed by Dorothy Purinton, it would be worth $500+.

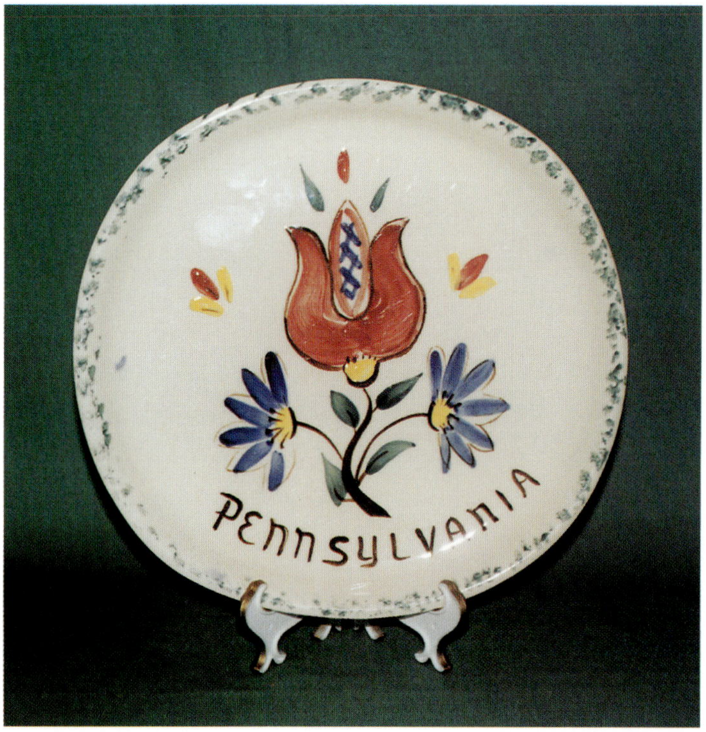

Pennsylvania dinner plate with Pennsylvania Dutch variant flower. Signed by Dorothy Purinton. $400+.

Pennsylvania dinner plate with a log house in the forest, Brown Intaglio. Signed by Dorothy Purinton. $500+.

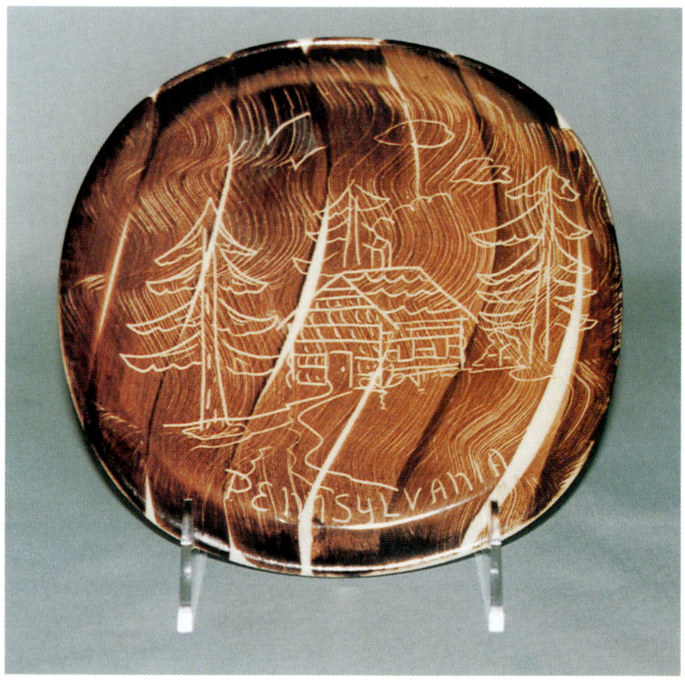

Brown Intaglio: Emlenton blind man's ashtray, used by the Emlenton, Pennsylvania, Men's Club. $75. Pennsylvania candy dish 5" long, NAPCO mold. $150. Pennsylvania jug salt shaker. $75.

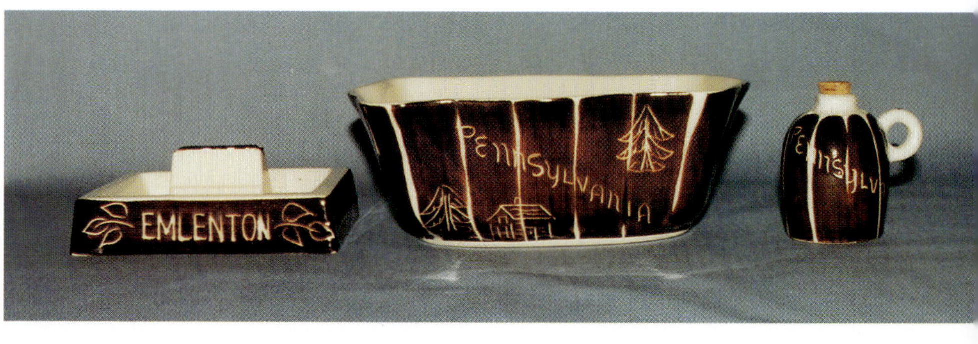

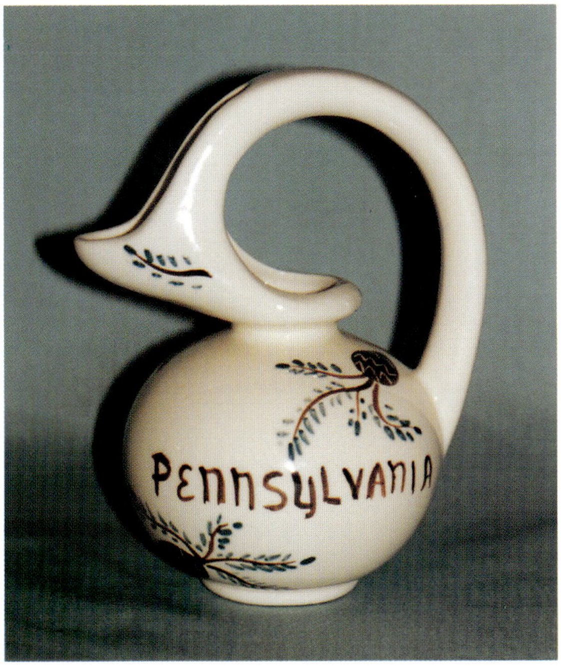

Pennsylvania honey jug with pine cones and branches on it (unusual). $300+.

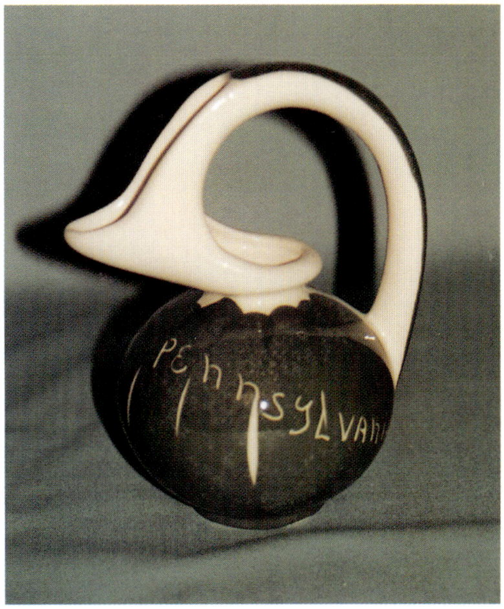

Pennsylvania honey jug, Green Intaglio. $150.

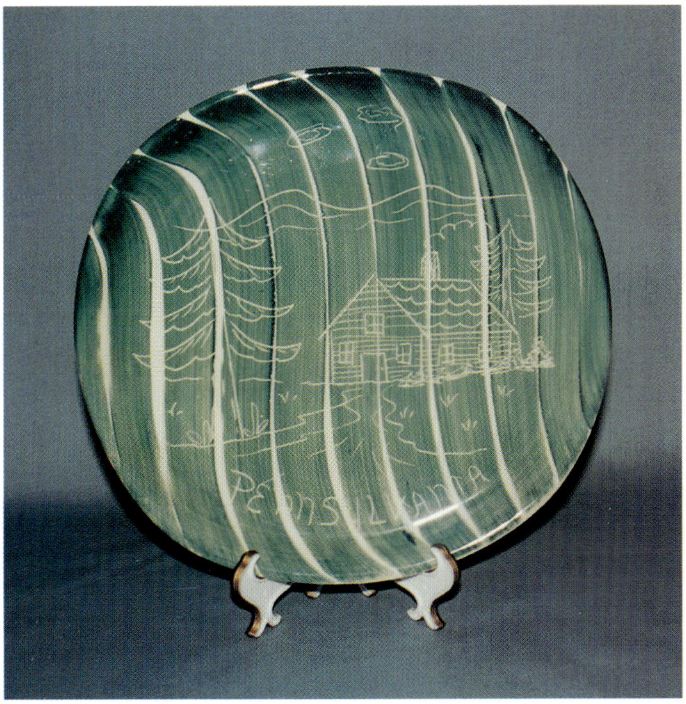

Pennsylvania dinner plate with a log house in the forest incised on it, Turquoise Intaglio. Attributed to Dorothy Purinton. $400. Signed by Dorothy Purinton. $500+.

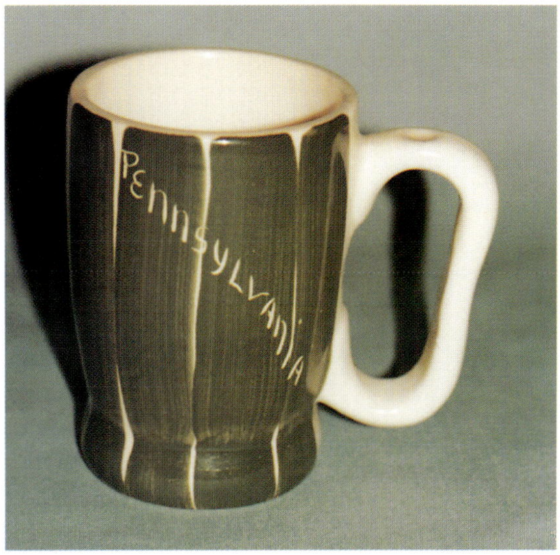

Pennsylvania coffee mug, Green Intaglio. $150.

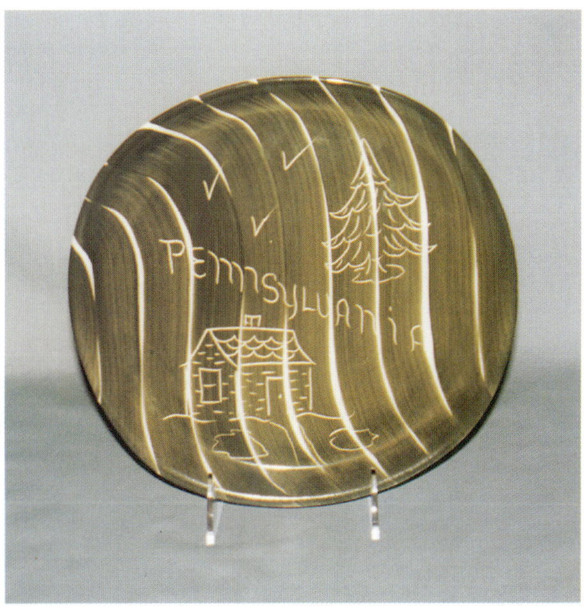

Pennsylvania dinner plate with a log cabin, Green Intaglio. Attributed to Dorothy Purinton. $400+. Signed by Dorothy Purinton. $500+.

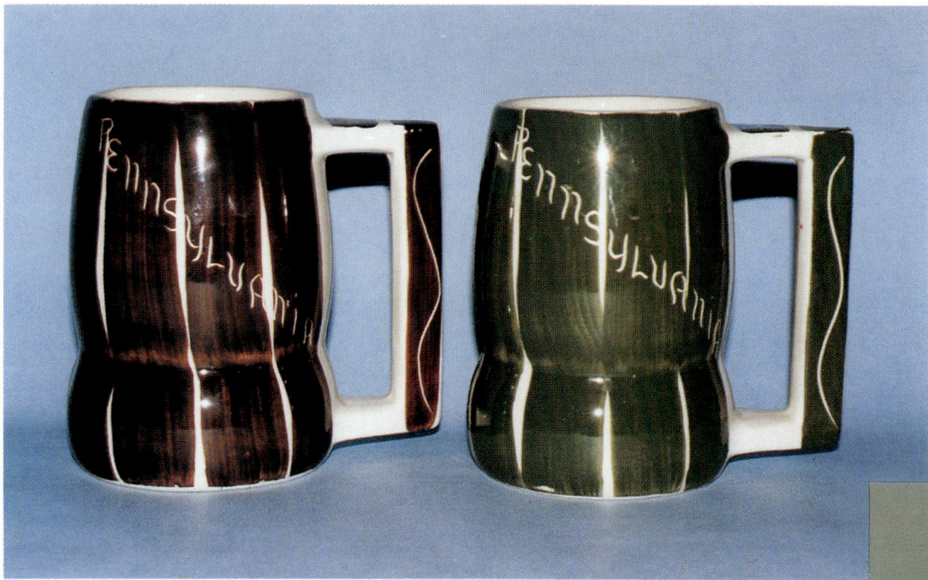

Pennsylvania beer mug, Brown Intaglio. $200. Pennsylvania beer mug, Green Intaglio. $200.

Penna. Grand Canyon kent jug, Green Intaglio. $200.

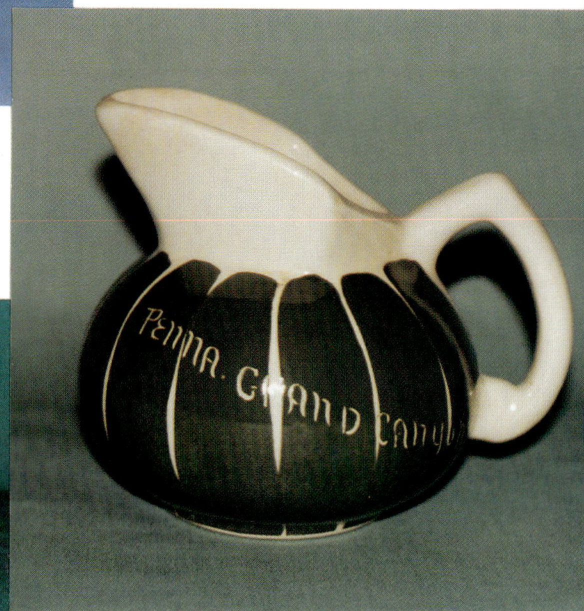

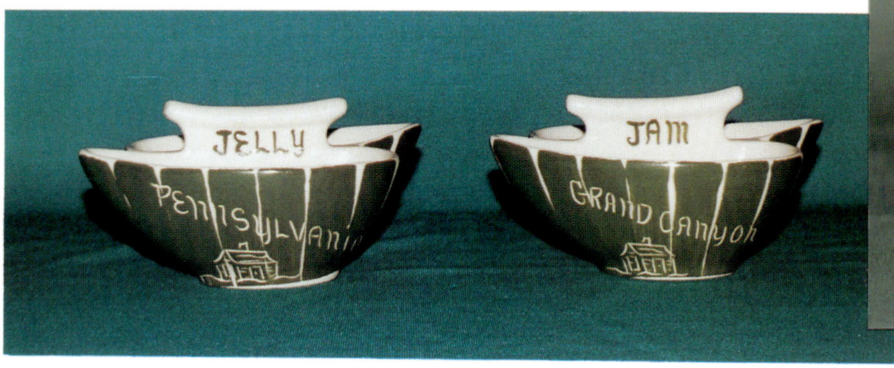

Jam and jellies, Pennsylvania on one side and Grand Canyon on the other, Green Intaglio. $150 each.

"Oil's 1st Centennial, 1859-1959, Titusville, Pa" inscription and incised first oil well humidor with a wooden lid, Brown Intaglio. $300+.

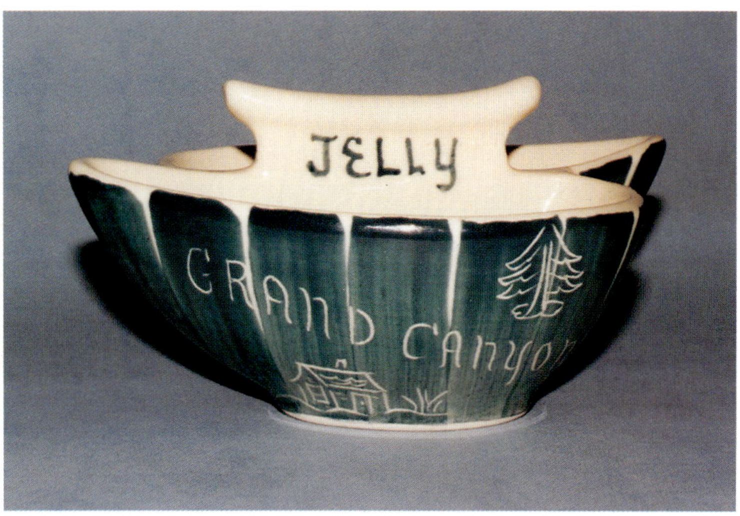

Jam and jelly. Grand Canyon on one side and Pennsylvania on the other, Turquoise Intaglio. $150.

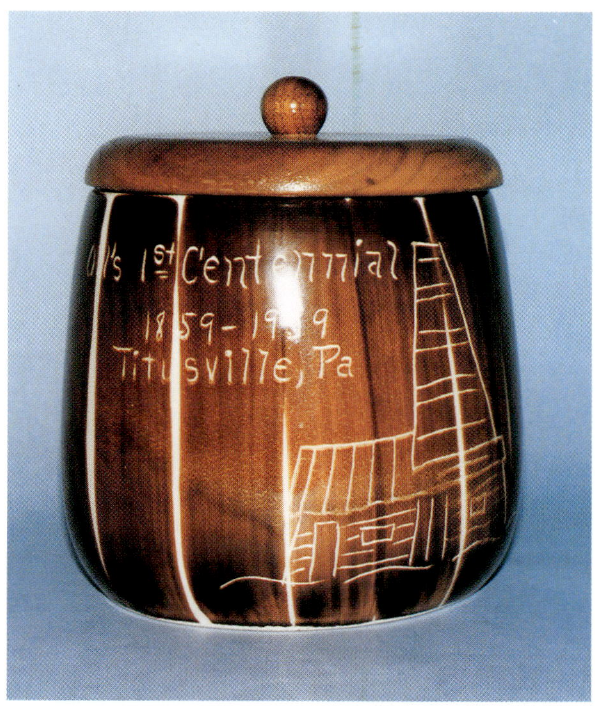

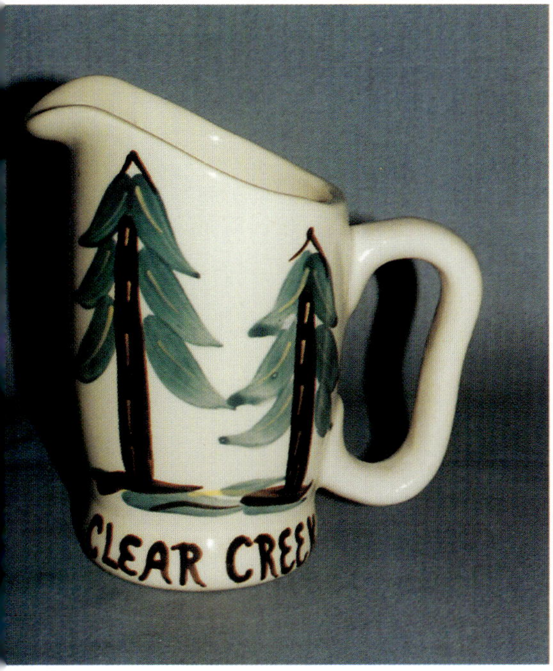

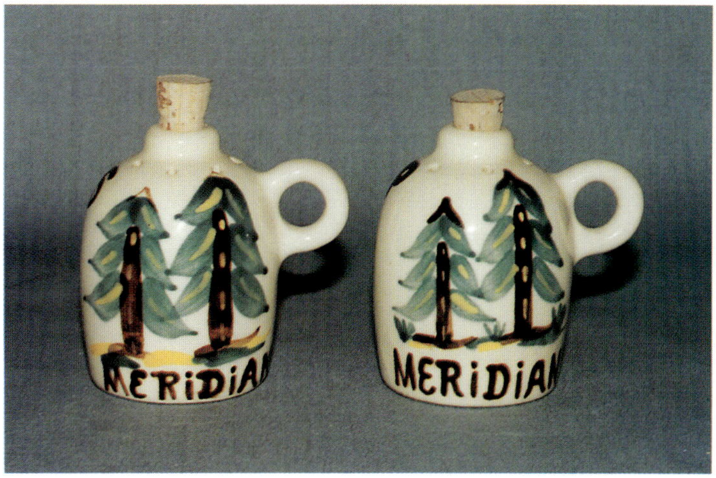

Meridian jug salt and pepper shakers. $200 set. Meridian is a town about 50 miles south of Shippenville, Pennsylvania.

Clear Creek mug jug. $250+. Clear Creek is a state park about 25 miles Northeast of Shippenville, Pennsylvania.

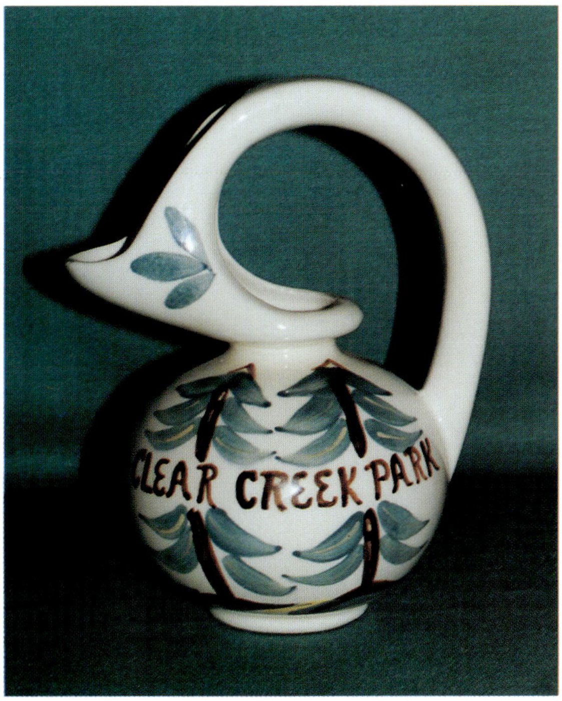

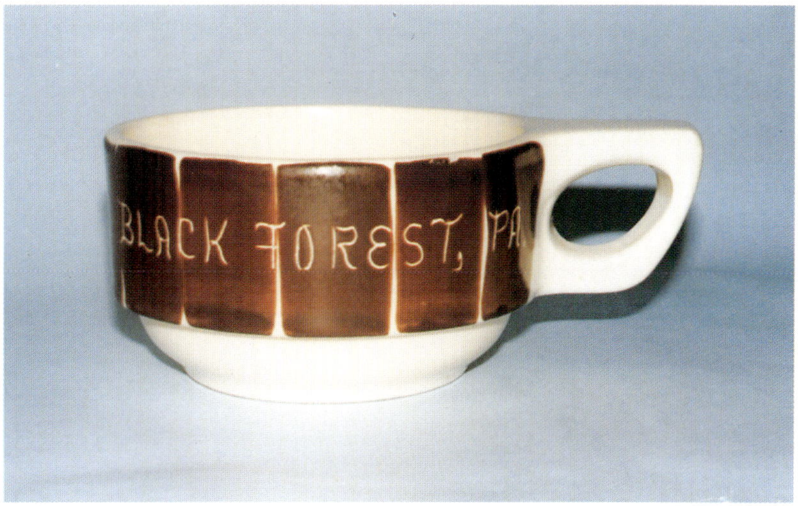

"Black Forest, PA" soup cup, Rubel mold, Brown Intaglio. $200+. Black Forest is near Coudersport, Pennsylvania.

Clear Creek Park honey jug. $300+.

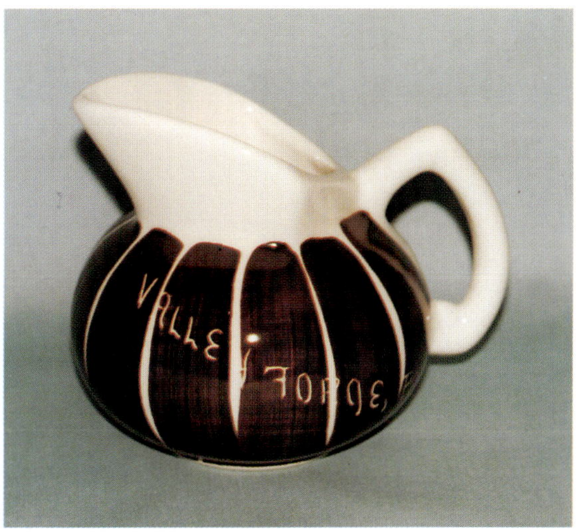

Valley Forge kent jug, Brown Intaglio. $200+.

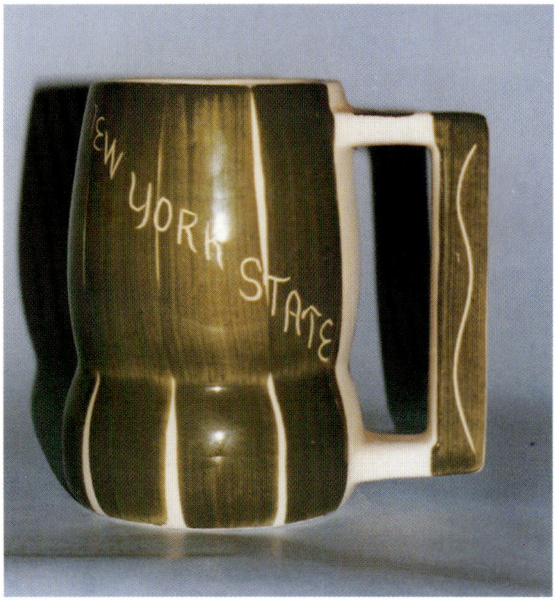

New York State beer mug, Green Intaglio. $250.

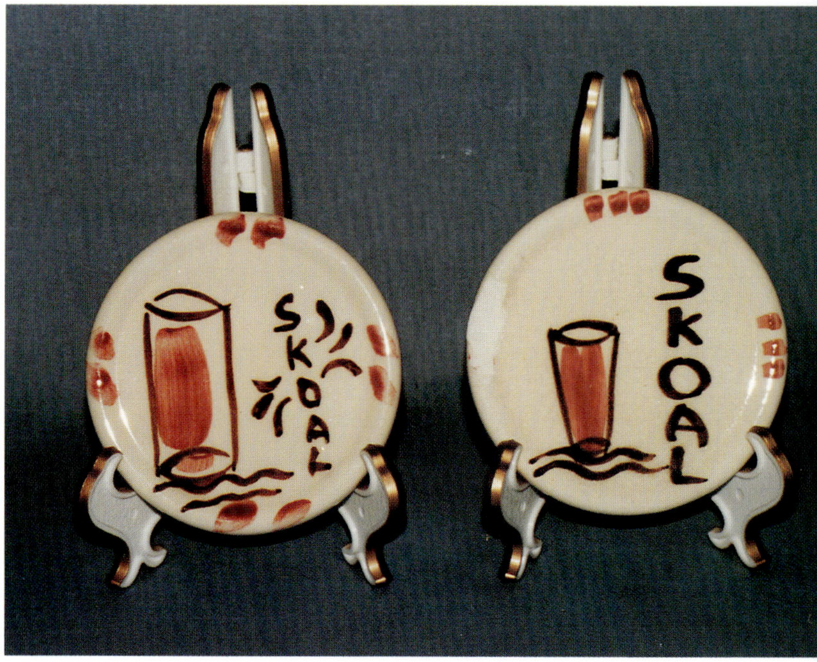

SKOAL coasters with a filled glass on them. These are "take home" pieces from the plant. $75 each.

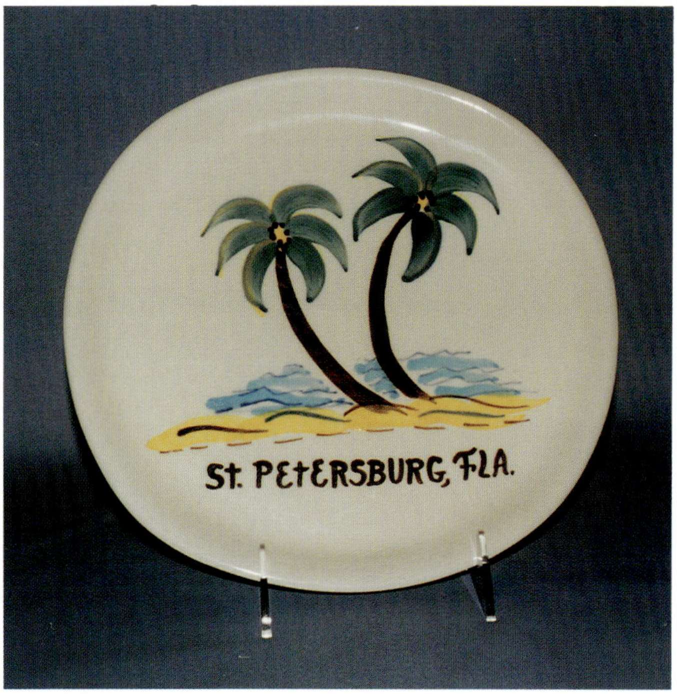

"St. Petersburg, Fla." Palm Tree dinner plate. $300+.

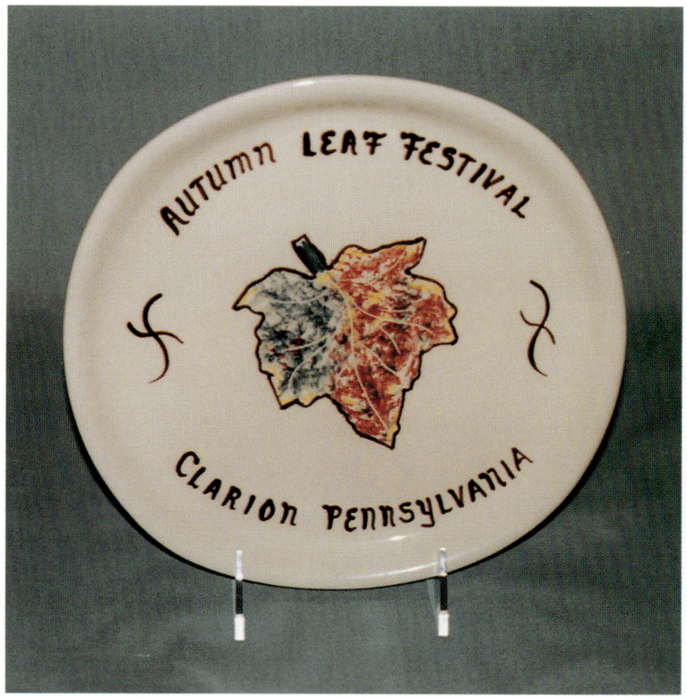

"Autumn Leaf Festival, Clarion Pennsylvania" dinner plate with a sponged leaf. Attributed to Dorothy Purinton. $500+.

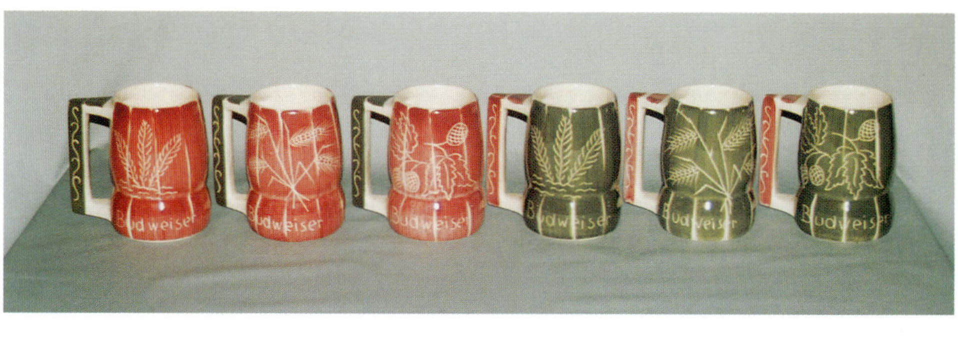

Budweiser beer mugs, sold as a set of six as a premium for a distributor in the Pittsburgh area. Each one is incised with Budweiser and a picture of barley, wheat, or hops. Three are Coral Intaglio with green handles and three are Green Intaglio with coral handles. $125 each.

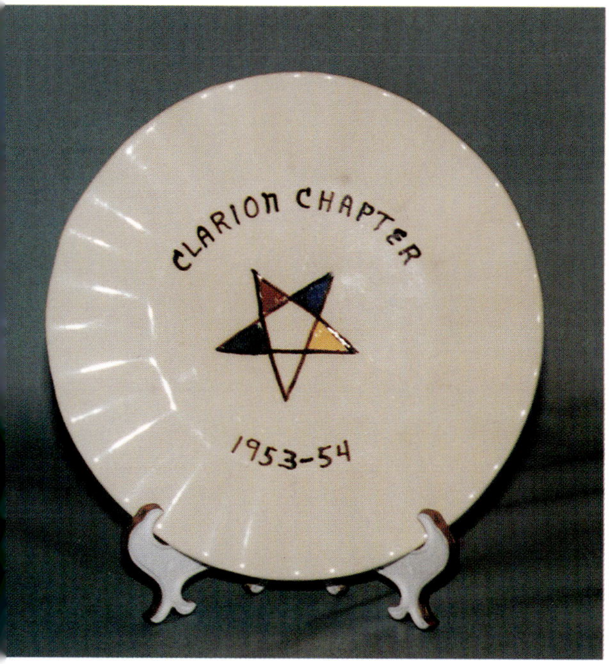

Eastern Star Clarion Chapter, 1953-54 salad plate, Seaform style. Made for the members of the Clarion chapter of the Eastern Star. Signed by Dorothy Purinton. $300+.

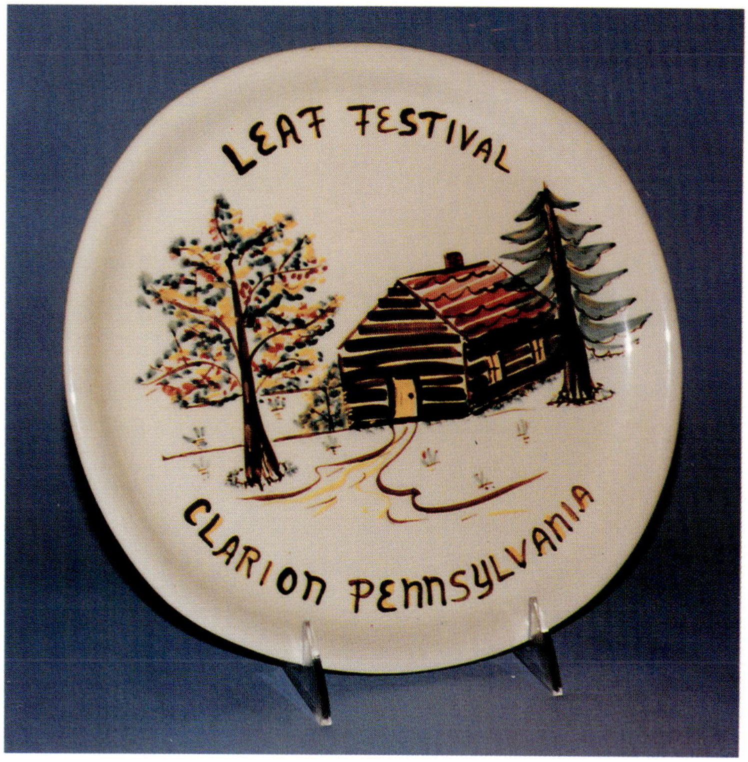

"Leaf Festival, Clarion Pennsylvania" dinner plate with a log cabin in a forest. Signed by Dorothy Purinton. $750+.

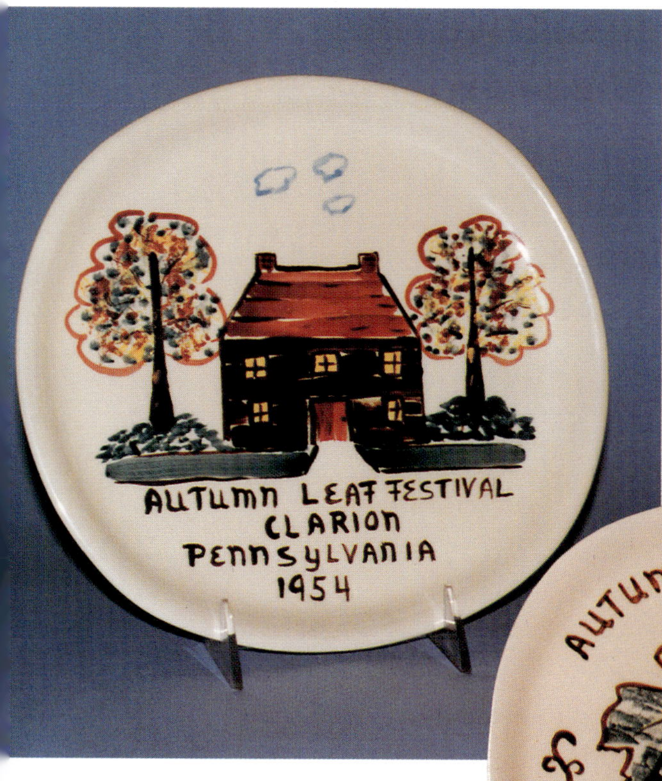

"Autumn Leaf Festival, Clarion Pennsylvania 1954" dinner plate with log house. Signed by Dorothy Purinton. $750+.

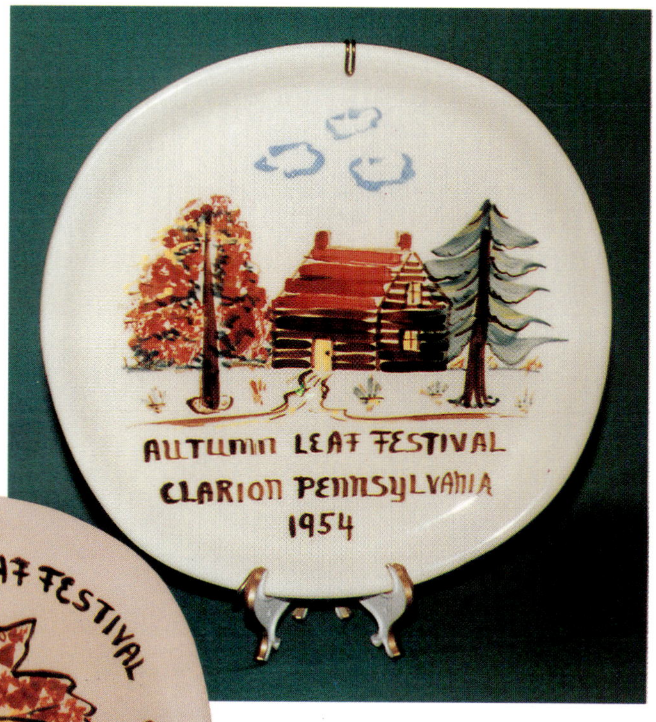

"Autumn Leaf Festival, Clarion Pennsylvania, 1954" dinner plate with a log cabin. Signed by Dorothy Purinton. $750+.

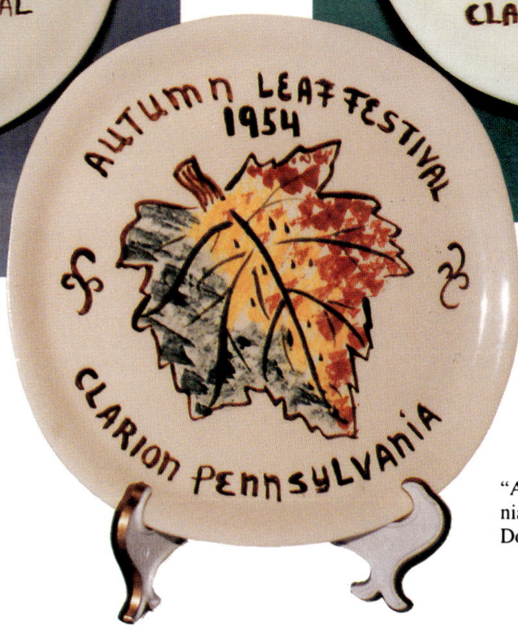

"Autumn Leaf Festival, 1954, Clarion Pennsylvania" salad plate with a sponged leaf. Signed by Dorothy Purinton. $700+.

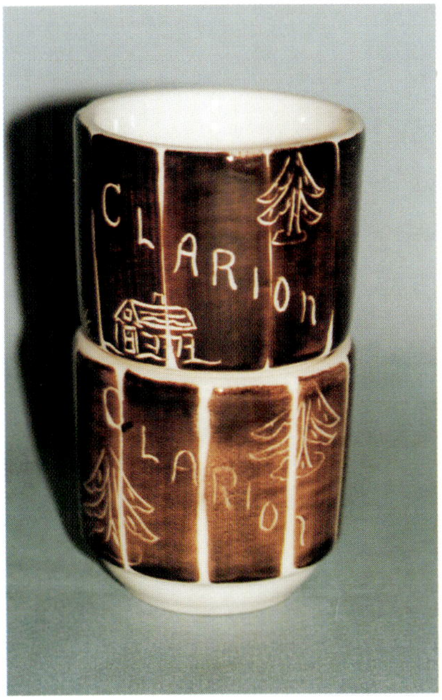

Clarion stacking salt and pepper shakers, Brown Intaglio. $200+.

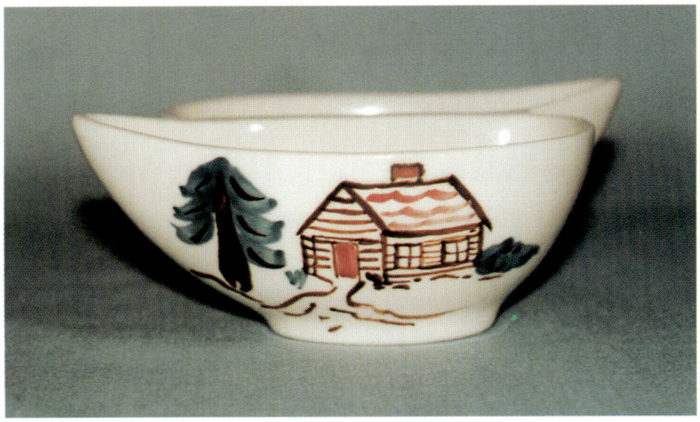

Nut dish with log cabin. $150.

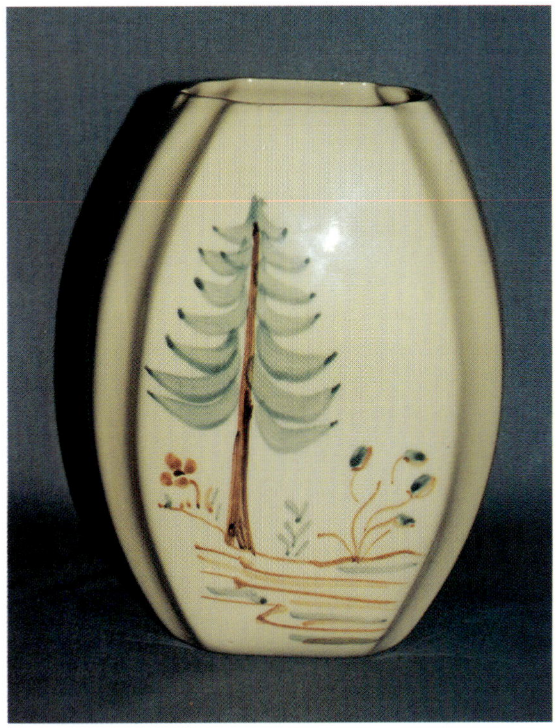

Tall oval vase with a pine tree, shrub, and flower. $100.

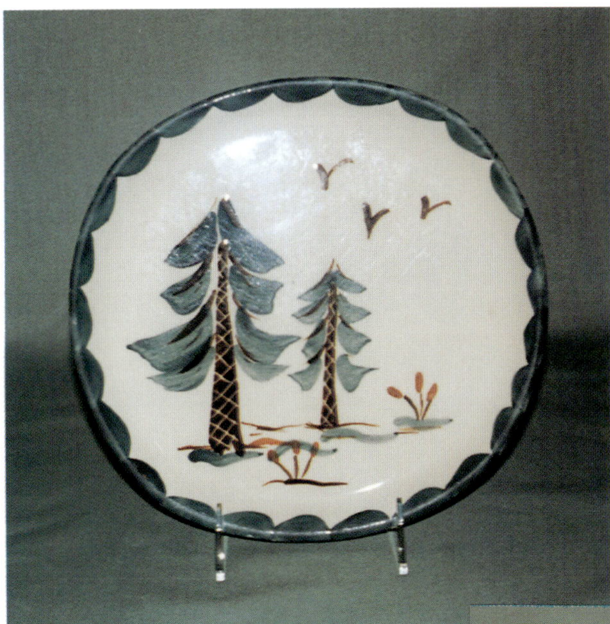

Dinner plate with pine trees, experimental. $150.

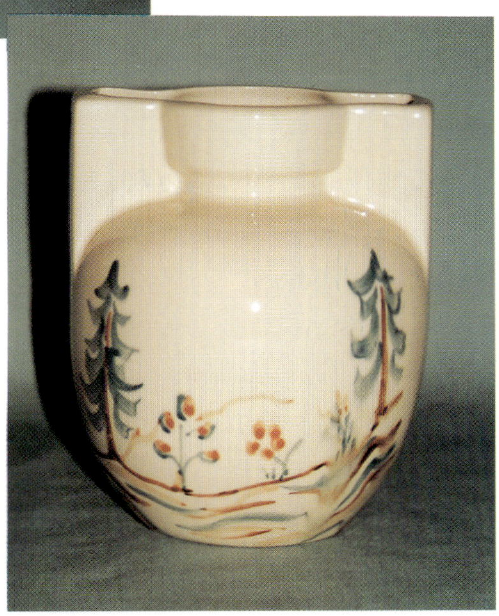

Winged vase with pine trees, shrubs, and flowers. $100.

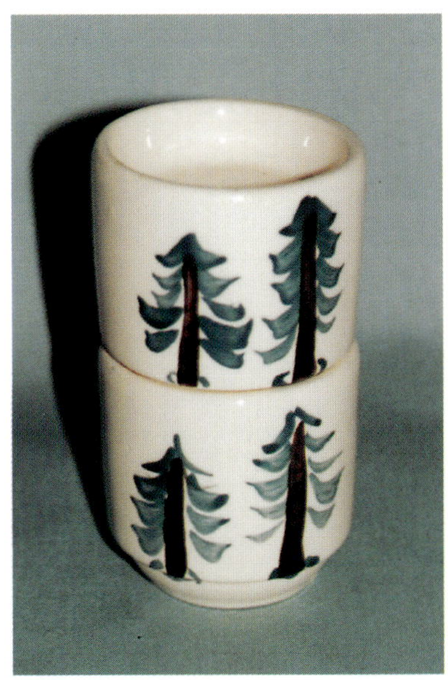

Stacking salt and pepper shakers with pine trees. $100.

Children's Items

Purinton made few children's items. The items which were made were sold in limited amounts, few of which have survived. Many of the pieces which have survived are in poor condition. Children's items are unique and very pleasing. Some are found personalized because they were made for employees' children or grandchildren. Decorations were painted on a breakfast plate, mug, and bowl. These were probably sold as a set. Some tea and toast plates have been found decorated.

Plates are the most difficult to find, followed by mugs, and bowls. The dog is the most common decoration followed by the duck. The cat, reindeer, lamb, and elephant are all equally difficult to locate.

Children's items are very desirable and locating even one of them is difficult. Damage to an item will reduce the price considerably.

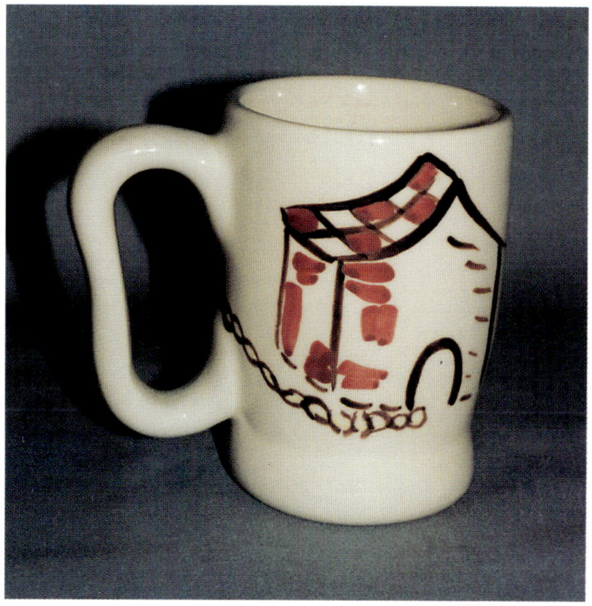

Unusual dog house decoration added to the back of a child's dog mug.

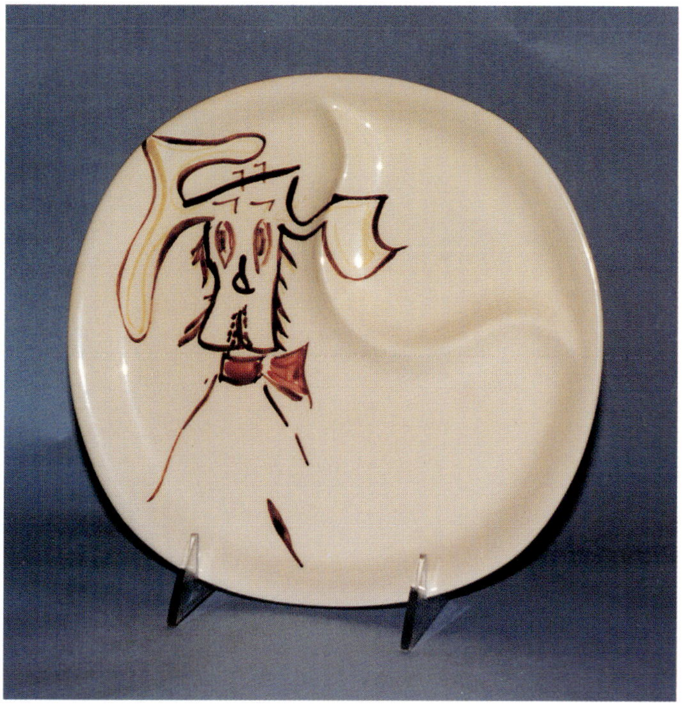

Dog tea and toast plate. $250.

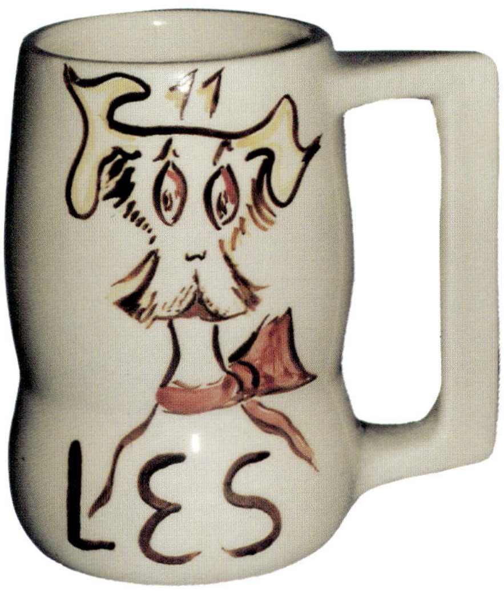

Beer mug mold with child's dog decoration, personalized "Les". $300

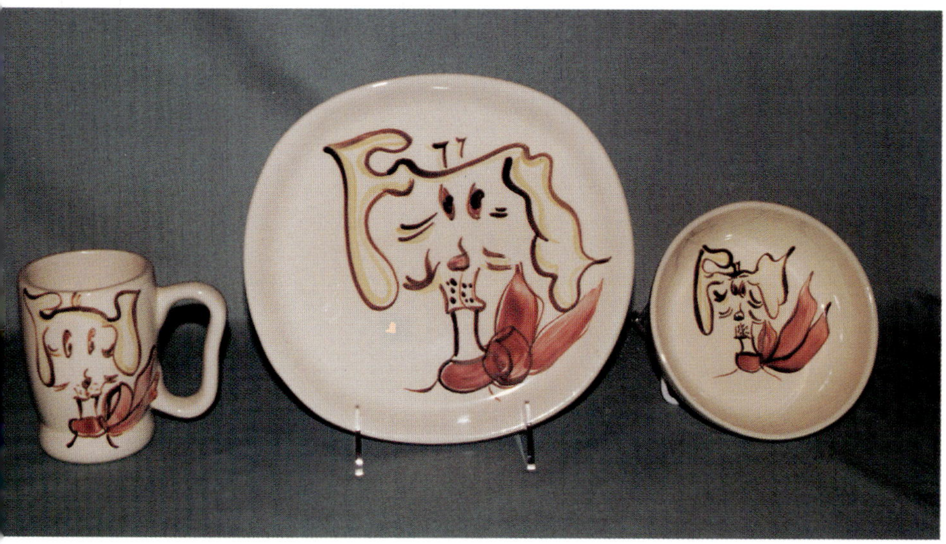

Dog mug. $150. Dog plate. $200. Dog bowl. $150.

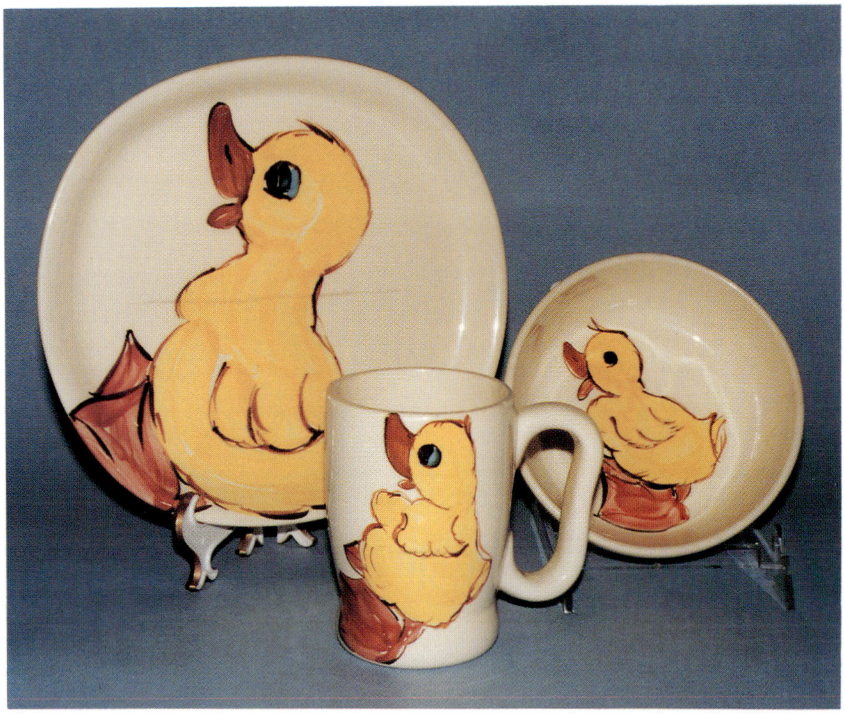

Duck plate. $200. Duck mug. $200. Duck bowl. $150.

Duck plate. $200.

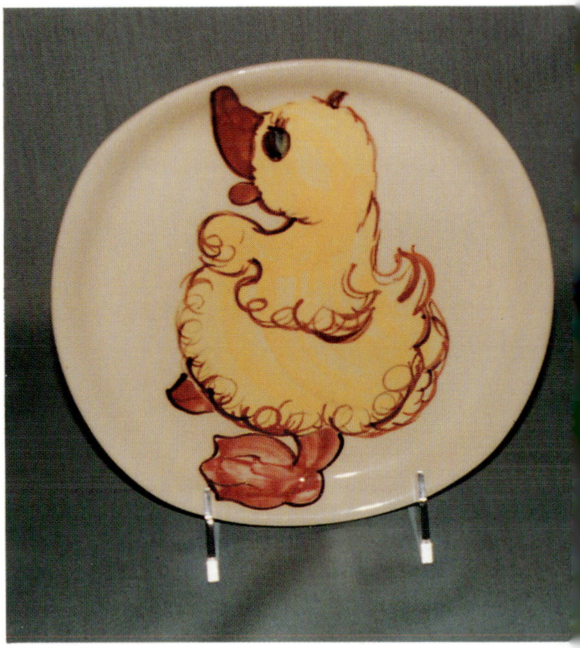

Cat bowl. $200.

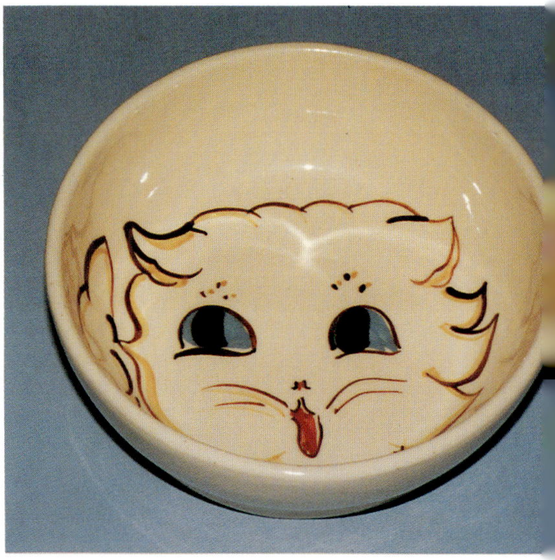

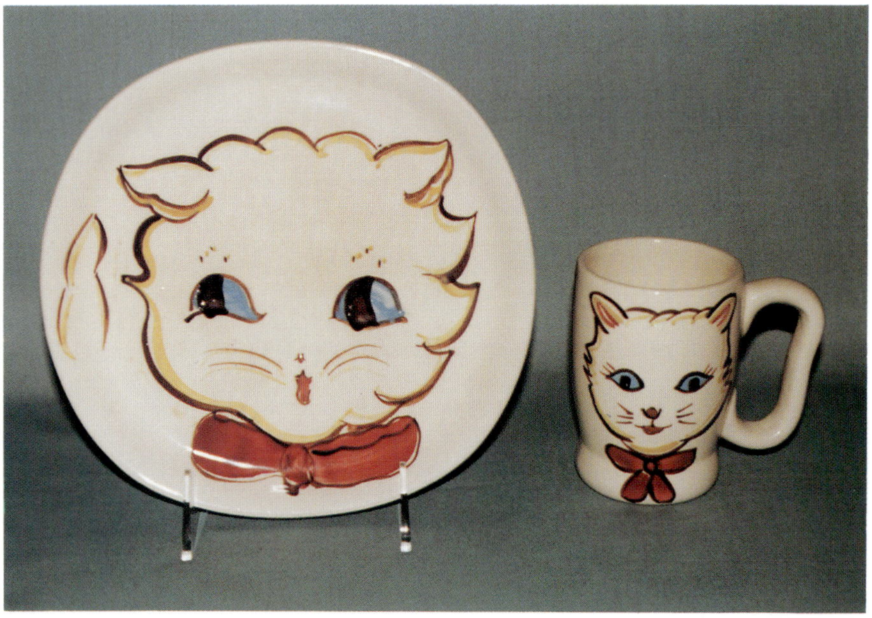

Cat plate. $200. Cat mug. $200.

Personalized child's mug with the Easter bunny. $250.

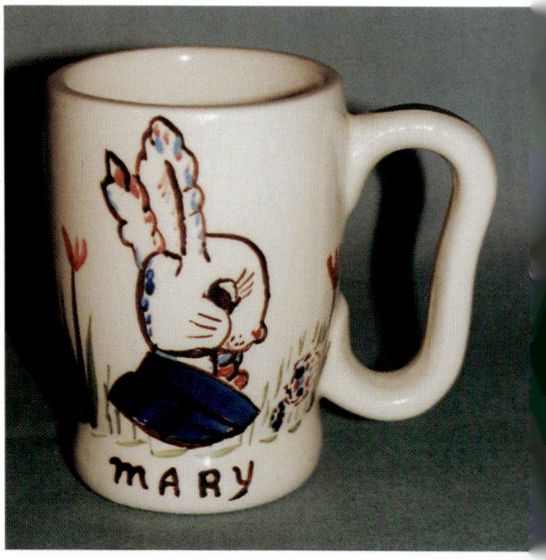

Juice mug personalized Carl with yellow flowers. $100.

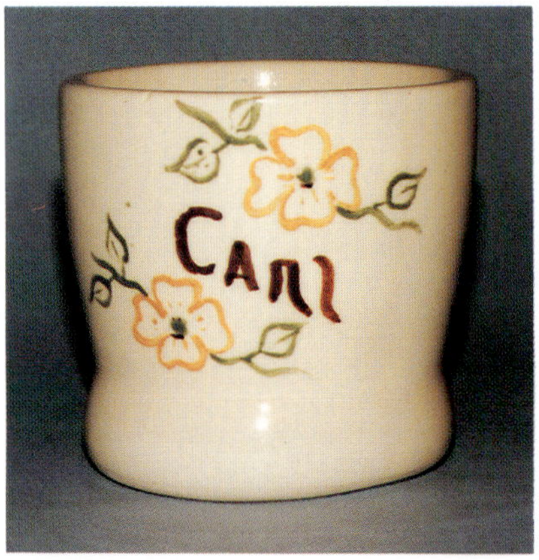

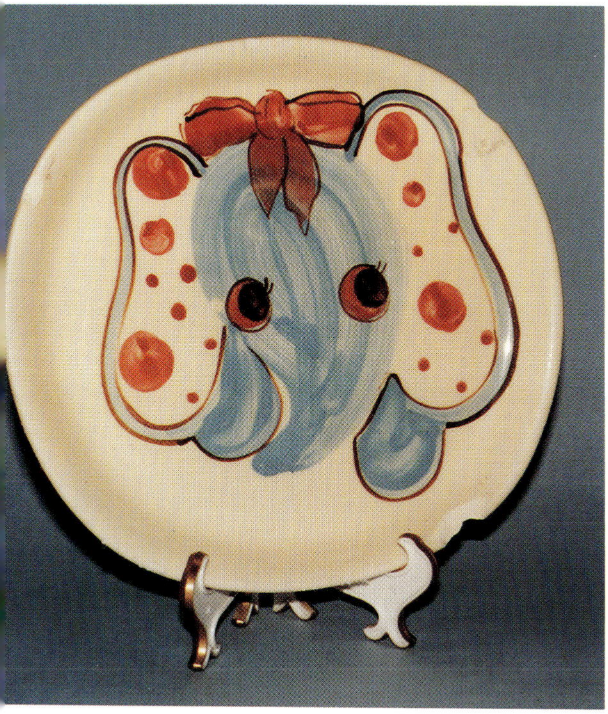

Elephant plate. $200.

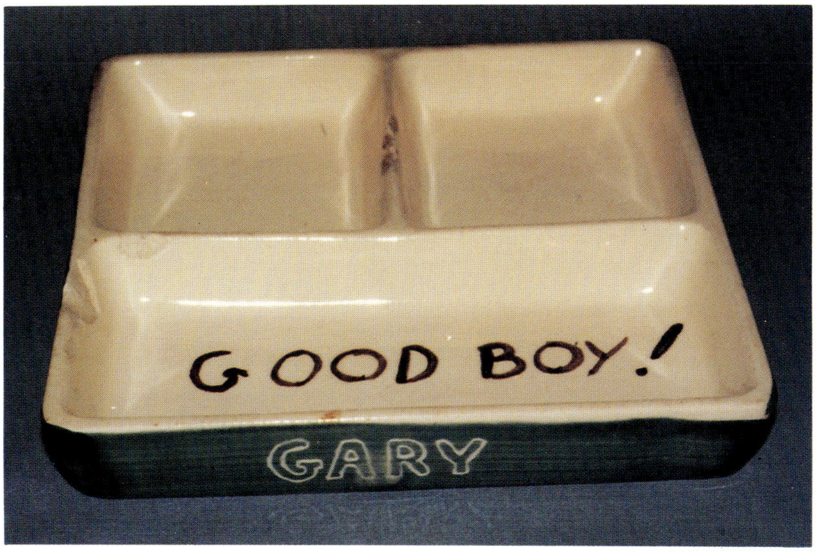

Turquoise Intaglio three part dish made for Gary Purinton, grandson of Bernard and Dorothy. $100.

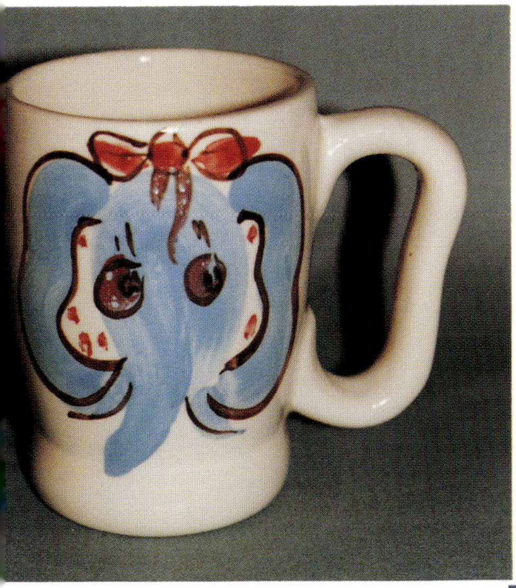

Elephant mug. $200.

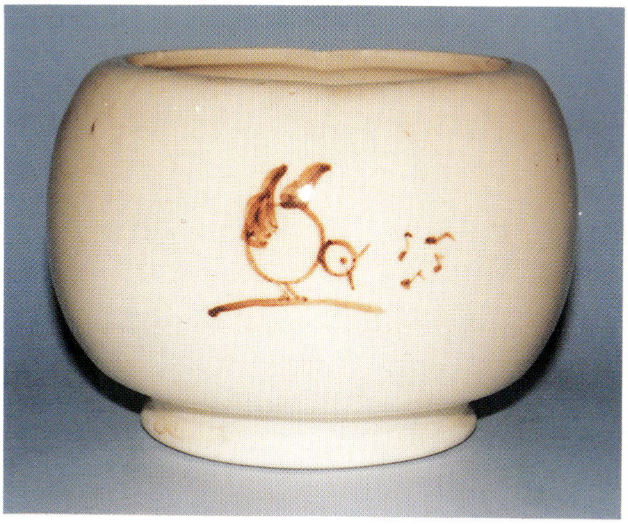

Cereal bowl with singing bird decoration. This is part of a stacking storage unit, but the former employee who owned this piece said that her child used it every day as a cereal bowl. $75.

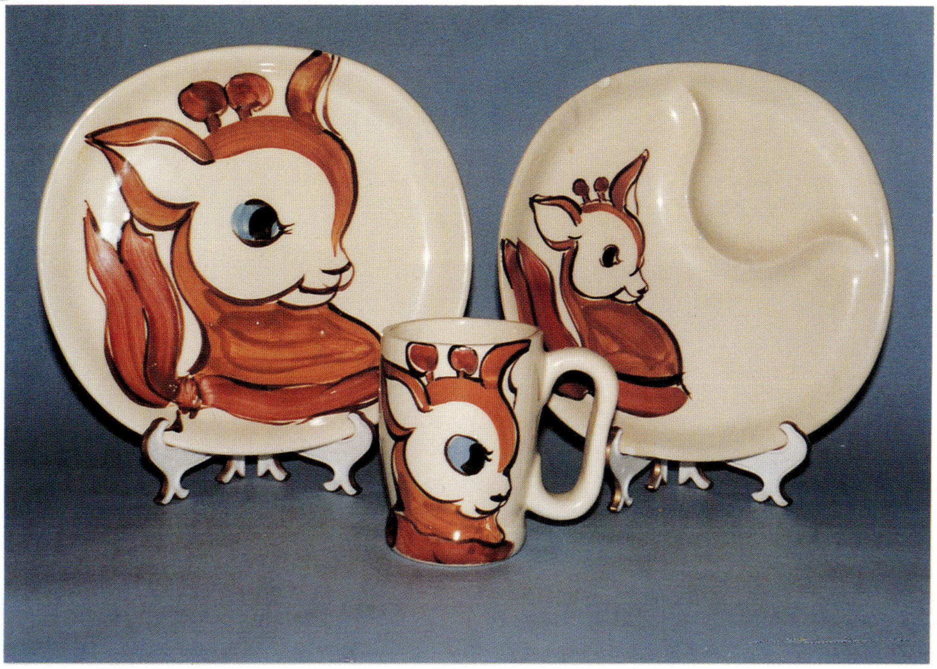

Reindeer plate. $250. Reindeer mug. $250.
Reindeer tea and toast plate. $250.

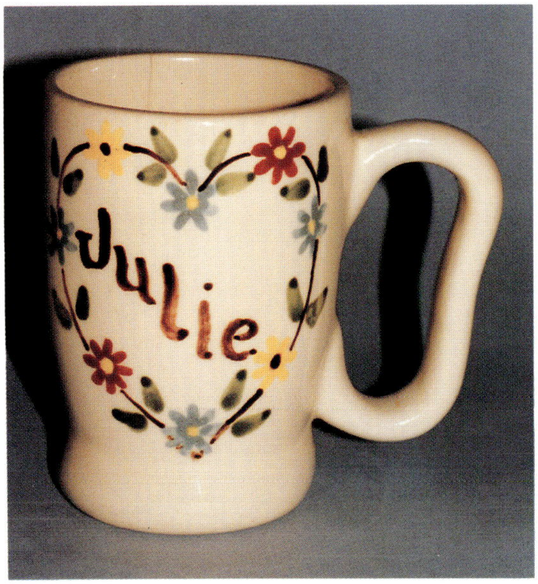

Mug personalized Julie for Bill Bower's daughter. $125.

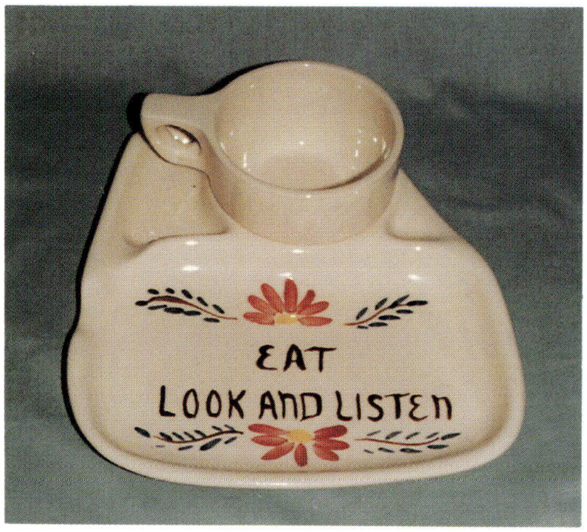

Rubel mold soup and sandwich plate personalized with "eat, look and listen". $200.

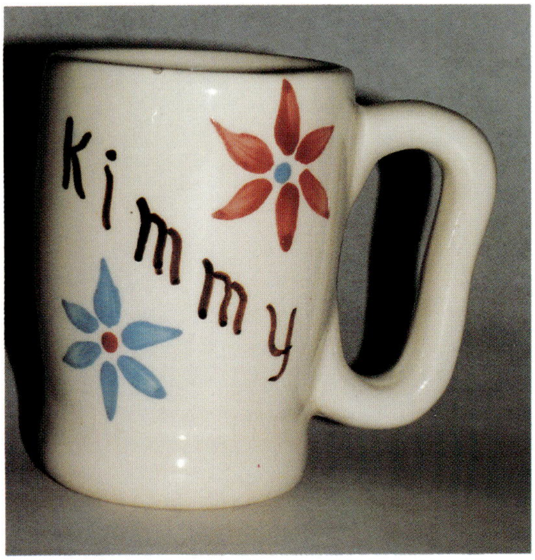

Mug with Starflower decoration, personalized Kimmy. $125.

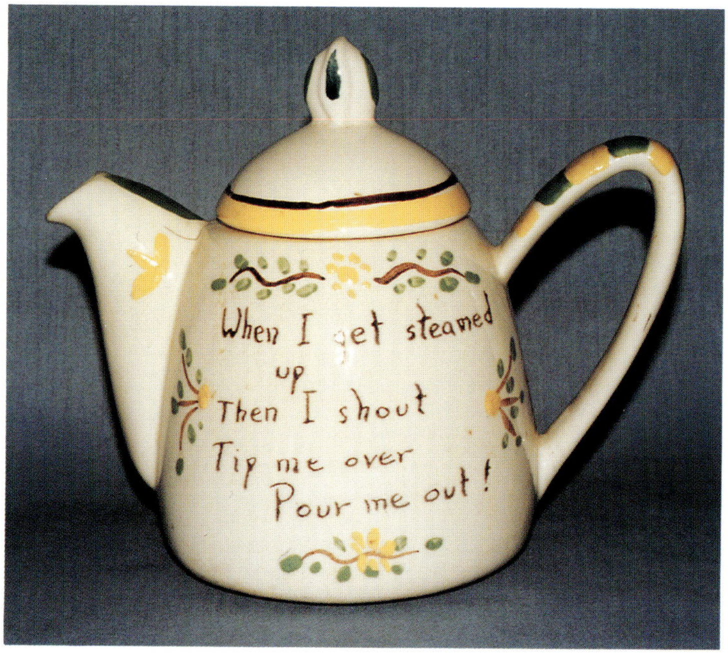

Reverse side of teapot with "I'm a little teapot" rhyme.

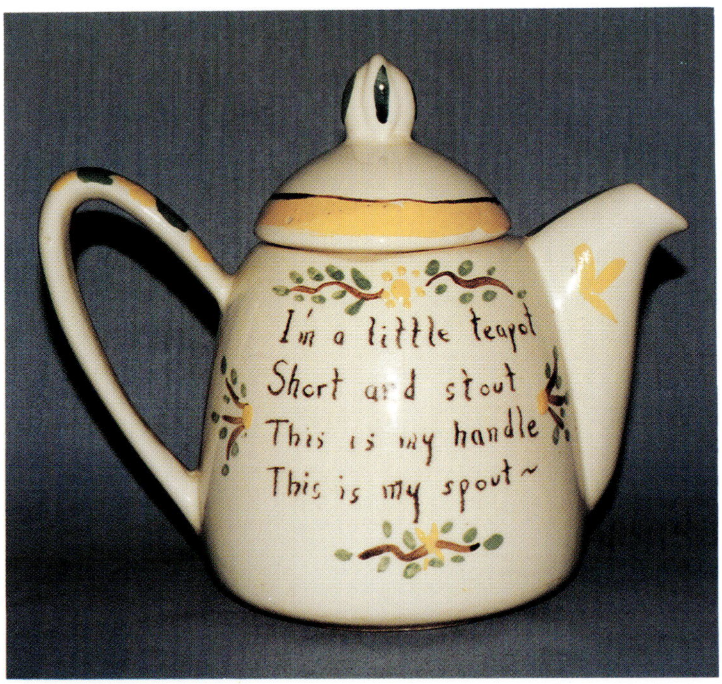

Six cup domed lid teapot with the "I'm a little teapot" rhyme. This item had the words etched into the body of the teapot. The pot was painted with brown slip. When the brown slip was wiped off, the letters remained colored. This handy work was executed by Blair Purinton, son of Bernard and Dorothy.

Christmas Items

Purinton made a variety of Christmas items. Although it was not a major part of their business, we felt this aspect of the company's production was significant enough to highlight the Christmas pieces in their own chapter. Most items were decorated with a Holly pattern. The Holly punch set is decorated on a Rubel mold punch bowl and is seen with cups or juice mugs. They also made a piece that is cone shaped with a tree painted on it and which has holes punched throughout as lights. The item is placed over a candle or an electric light. Some specialty plates were also made and demand a high price. Prices reflect a demand for the item and the limited supply.

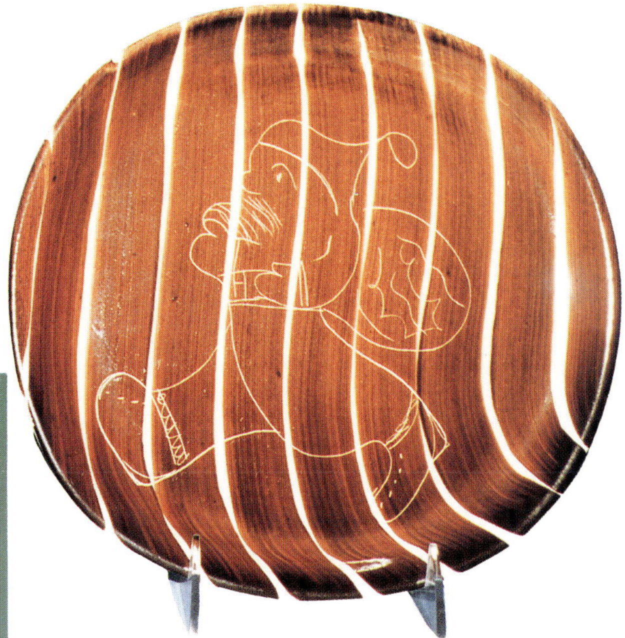

Dinner plate, Brown Intaglio with Santa Claus etch. $250.

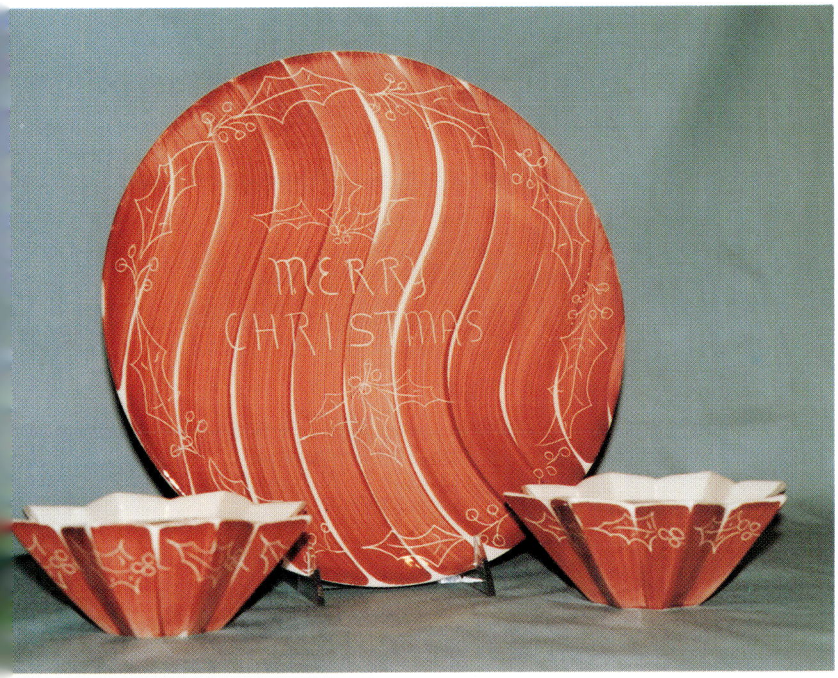

Chop plate, incised "Merry Christmas" along with a Holly pattern on Coral Intaglio. Signed Dorothy Purinton. $1000+. Star candle holders with inserts. Holly pattern incised on Coral Intaglio. One candle holder initialed DP, 1953. $400+ set.

Reverse side of the Merry Christmas chop plate.

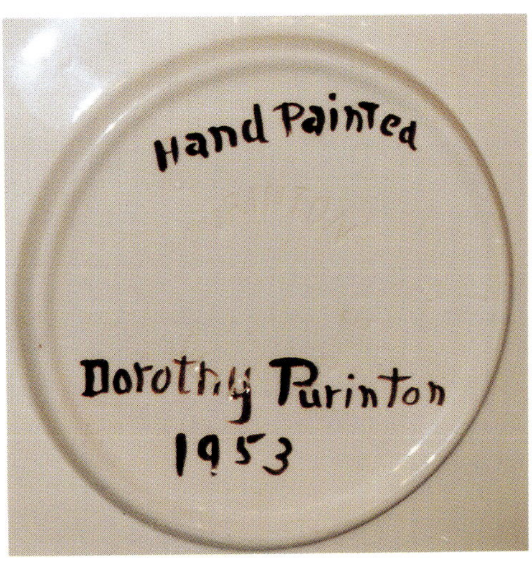

Dinner plate with Merry Christmas message, signed Dorothy Purinton. $500+. Coffee mug decorated with a burning candle and holly sprigs. $200.

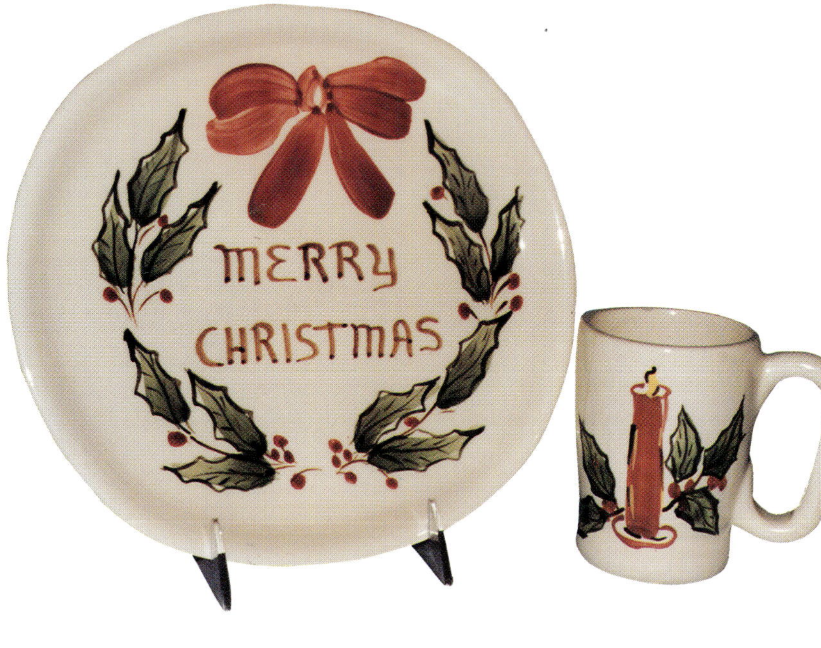

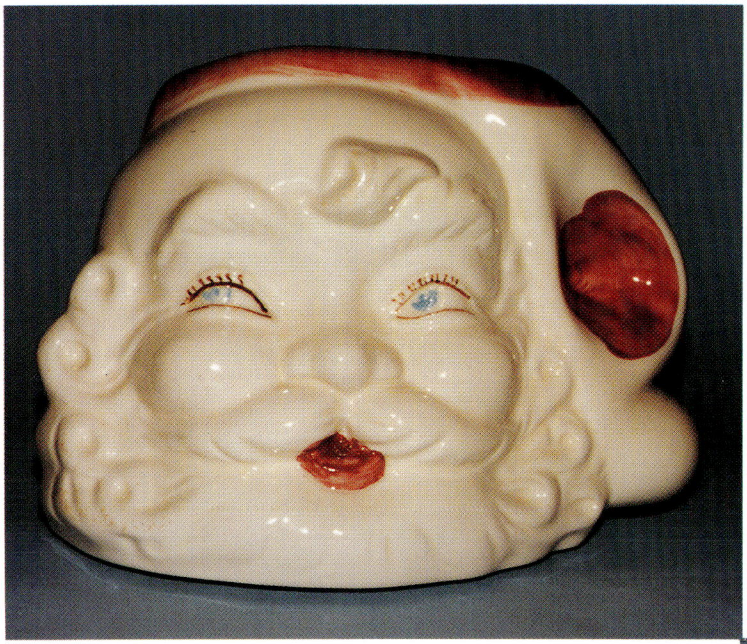

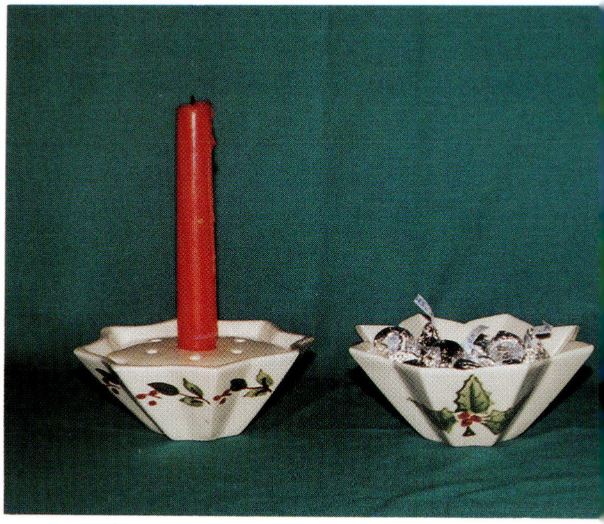

Berry star candle holders with inserts. $200 pair.
Holly star candy dish. $100.

Santa Claus planter, NAPCO mold. $50.

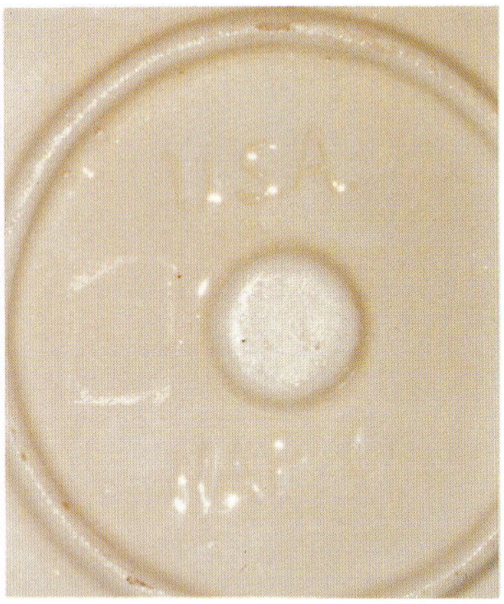

Bottom of the NAPCO Santa Claus. Note the circular configuration and NAPCO incised mark. Several companies made a similar Santa planter.

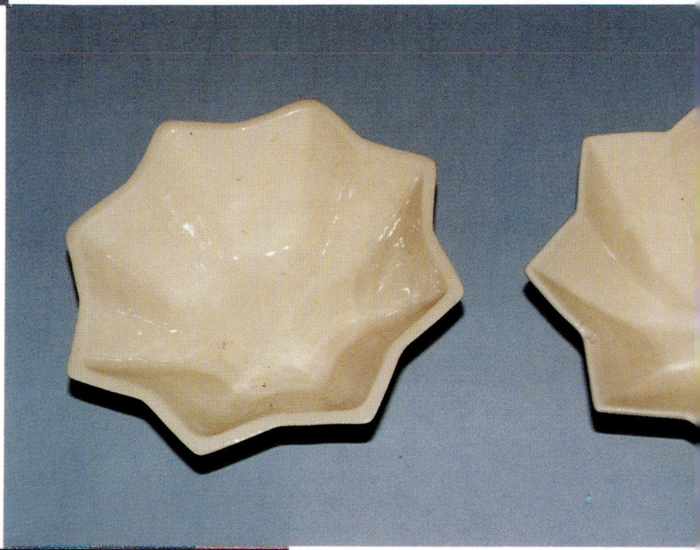

Photo to illustrate the difference between a star candle holder (on left) and a star candy dish. The candle holder is flat on the inside bottom to accommodate the star candle holder insert. The candy dish has a star shape inside.

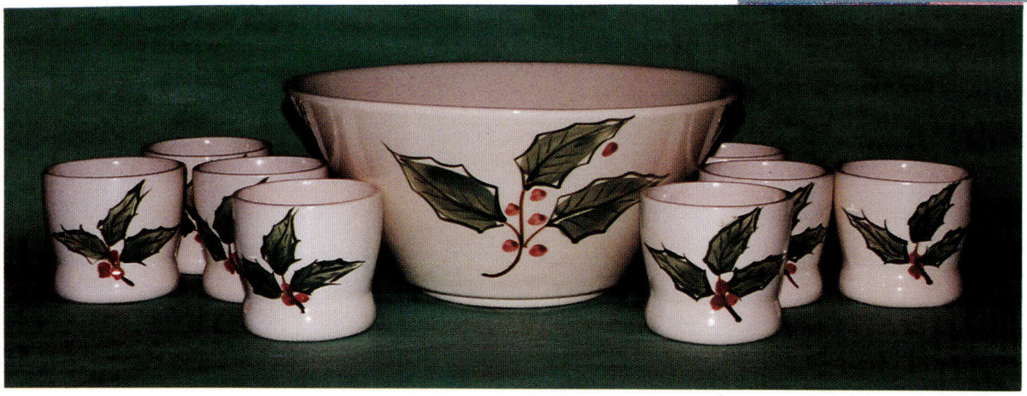

Holly juice mugs. $50 each. Holly punch bowl, Rubel mold. $200.

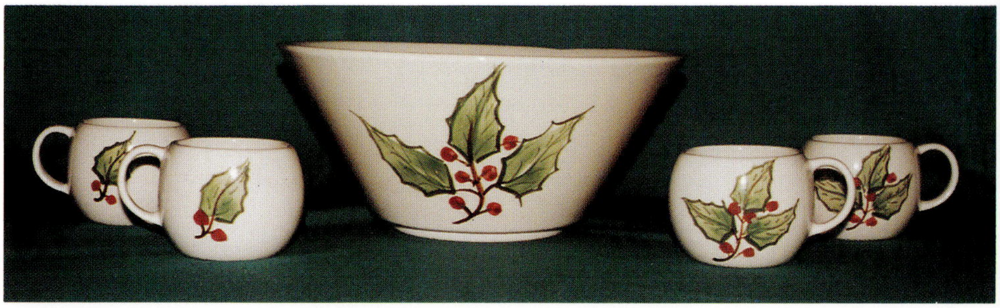

Holly cups. $40 each. Holly punch bowl, Rubel mold. $200.

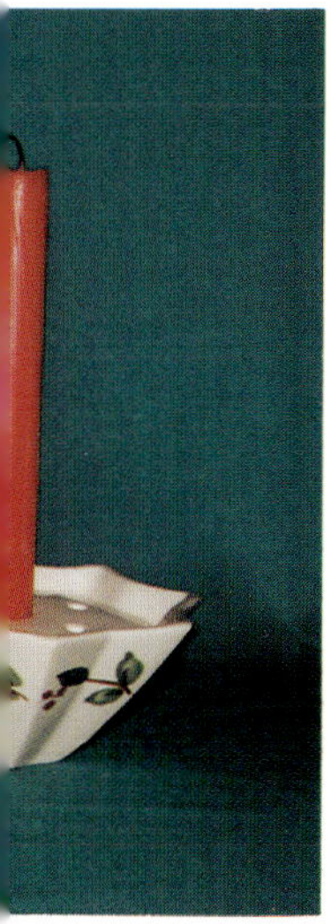

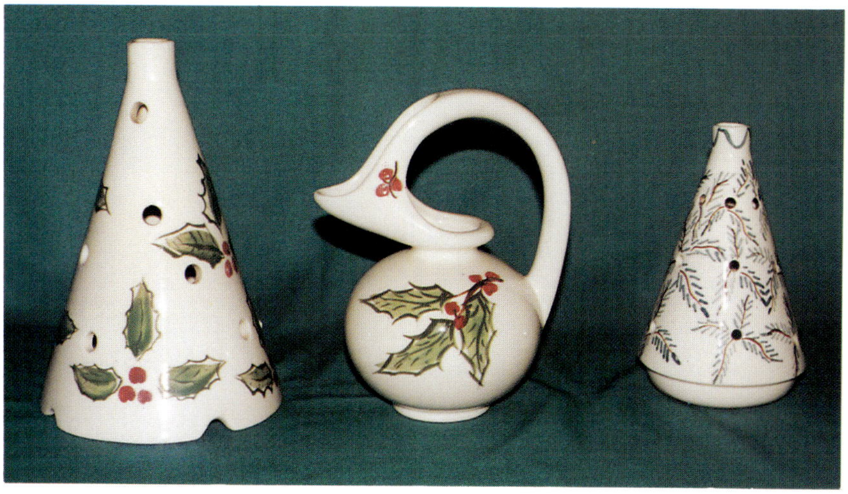

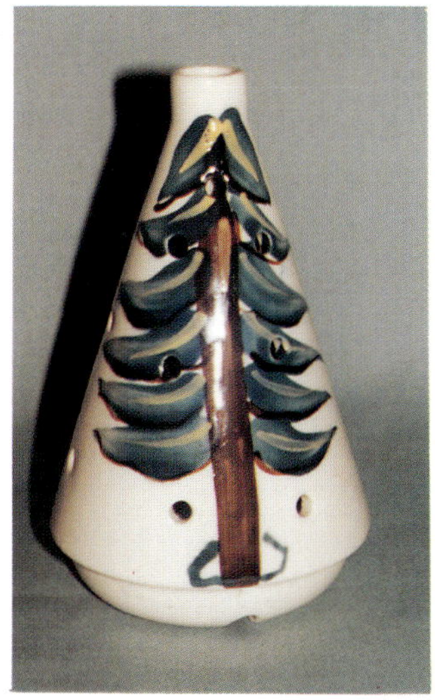

Christmas tree with Holly decoration (it can be placed over a lit candle or a light bulb — note the cut-out for electric cord). $150. Honey jug. $300. Christmas tree with Needles decoration. $150.

Christmas tree. $150.

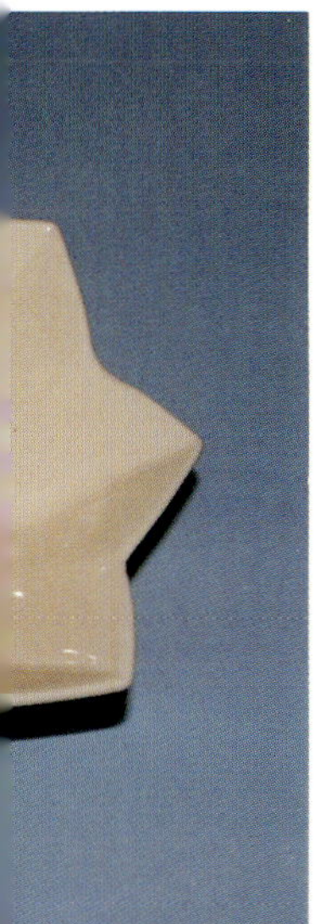

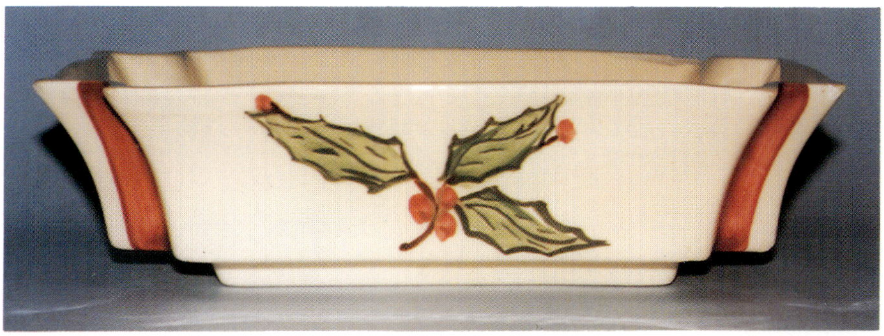

Holly candy dish, NAPCO mold, 9.5" long. $150.

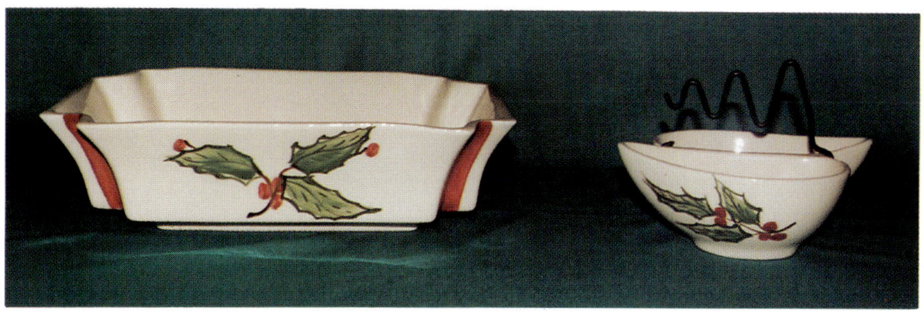

Holly candy dish, NAPCO mold, 6" long. $150. Holly ashtray. $150.

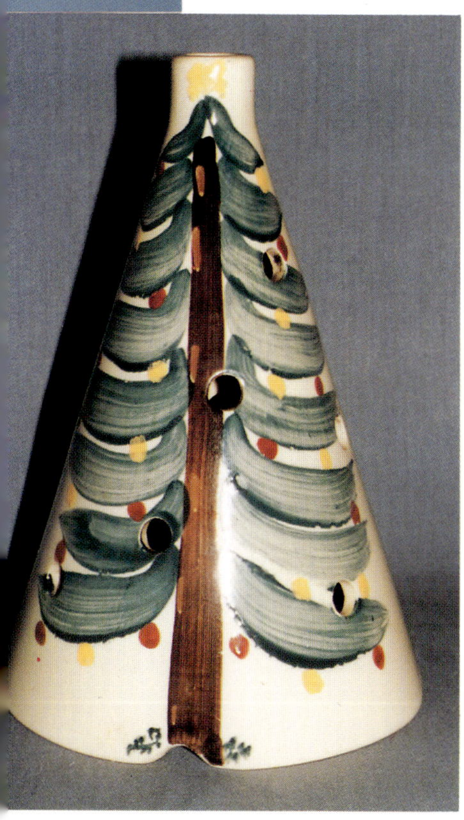

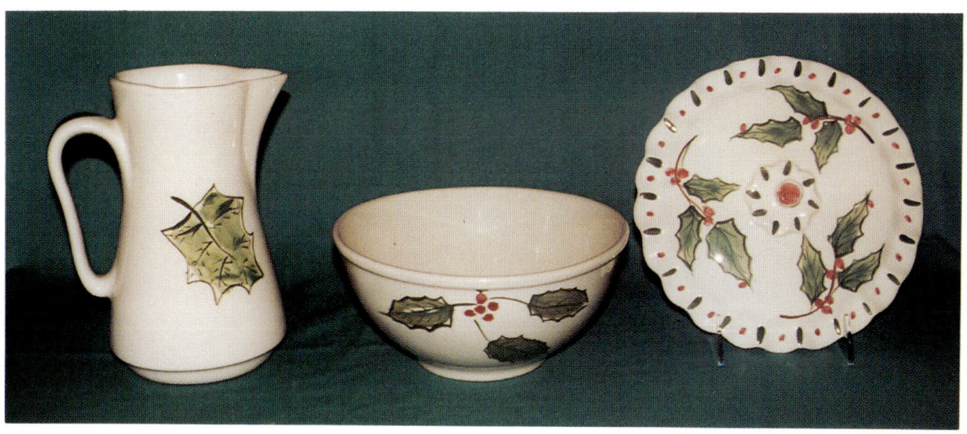

Christmas tree. $150.

Pitcher, Rubel mold with Holly leaf. $150. Holly bowl. $150. Holly lazy susan lid. $150.

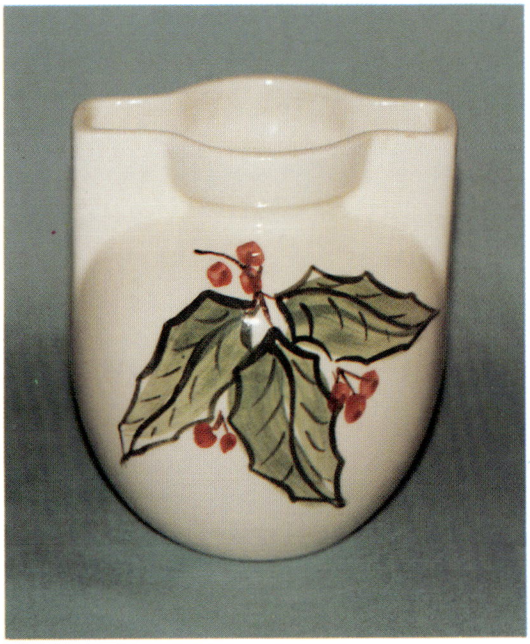

Holly winged vase. $150.

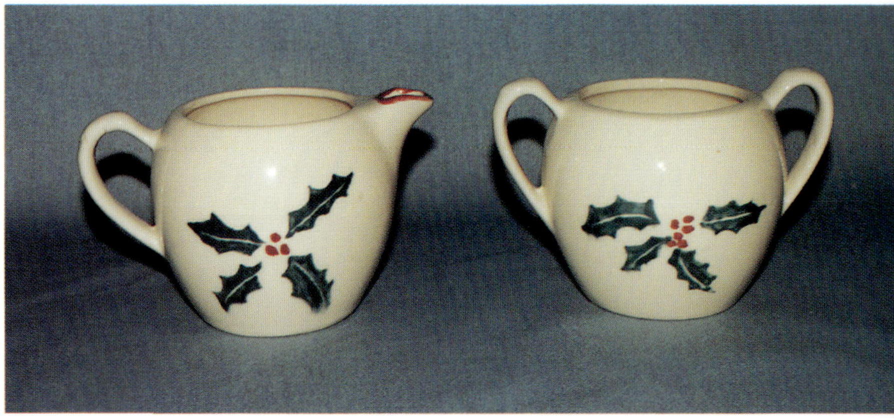

Holly round creamer and sugar (lid missing in photo). $150.

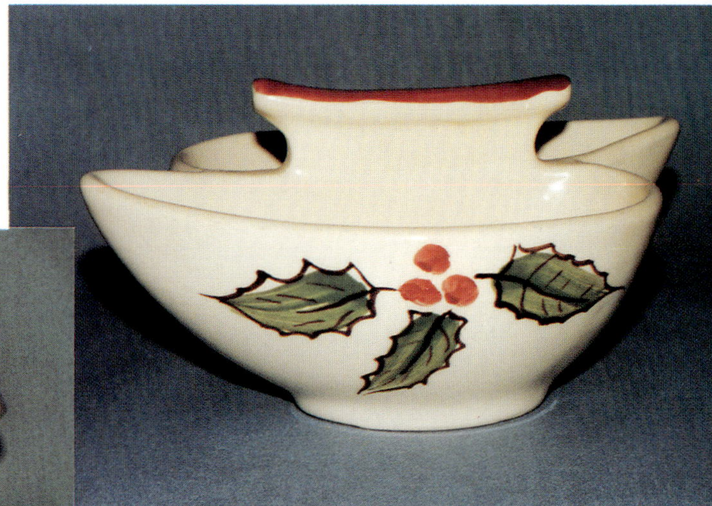

Holly jam and jelly. $200.

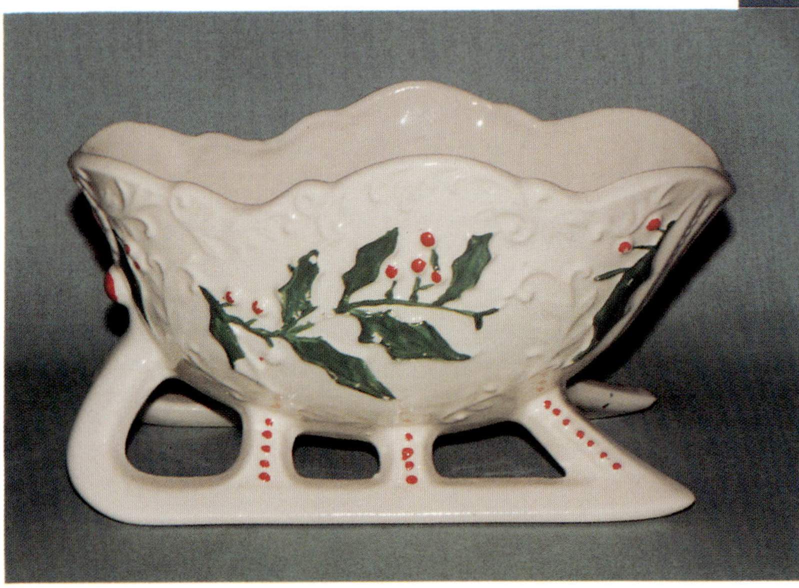

Sled. This item was made by a variety of companies. Purinton produced this sled in limited numbers at the Tionesta plant. $40.

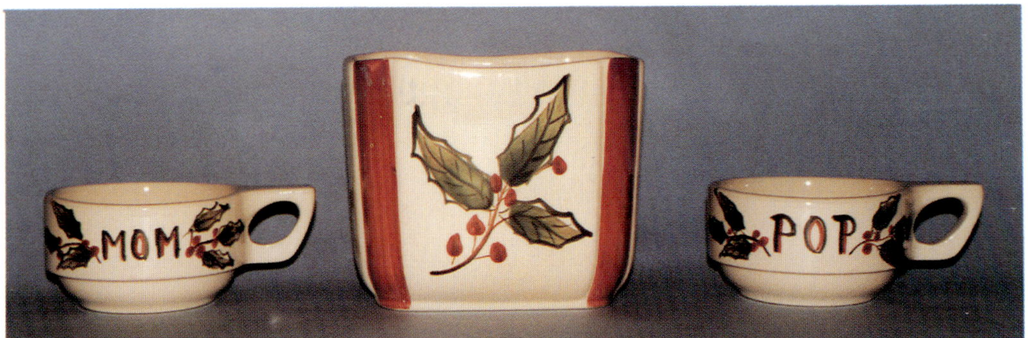

Holly soup cup, Rubel mold, personalized MOM and POP. $150 each. Vase, NAPCO mold. $200.

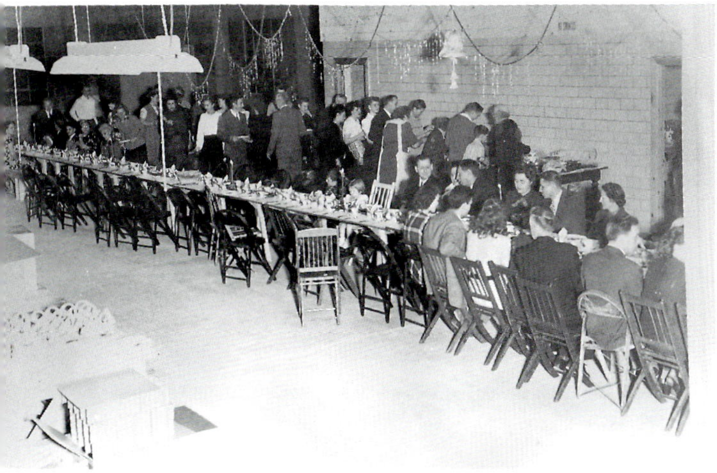

A 1950 or 1951 Christmas party with the Tionesta employees. Everyone is eating off of Apple pattern dinnerware.

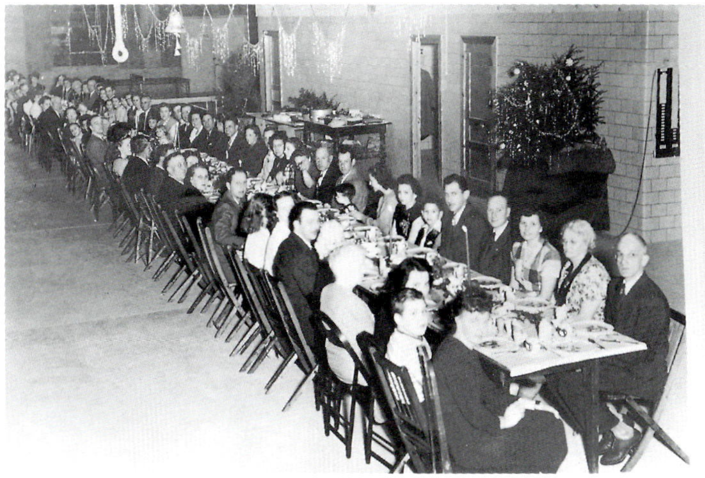

A 1950 or 1951 Christmas party with the Tionesta employees.

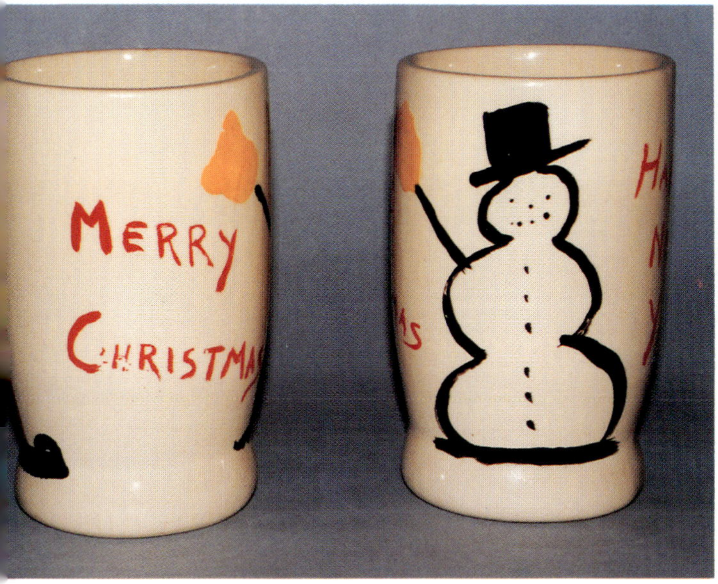

Tumblers personalized for Bill Bower's children, marked "Merry Christmas" and "Happy New Year" with a snowman decoration. $100 each.

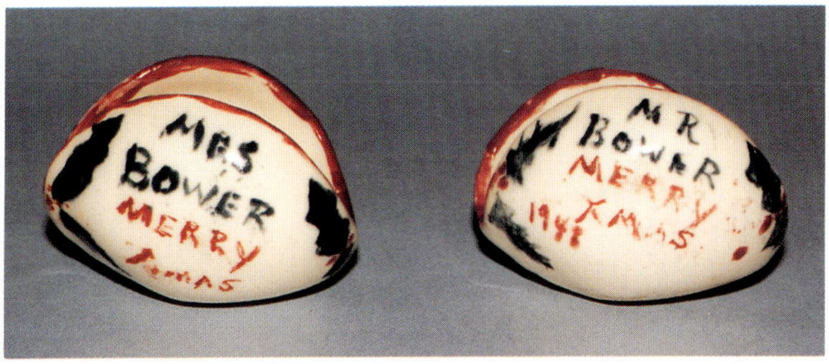

Napkin rings used at the 1948 employee Christmas party. Personalized with Mr. Bower and Mrs. Bower. Mr. Bill Bower was the secretary/treasurer of Purinton Pottery.

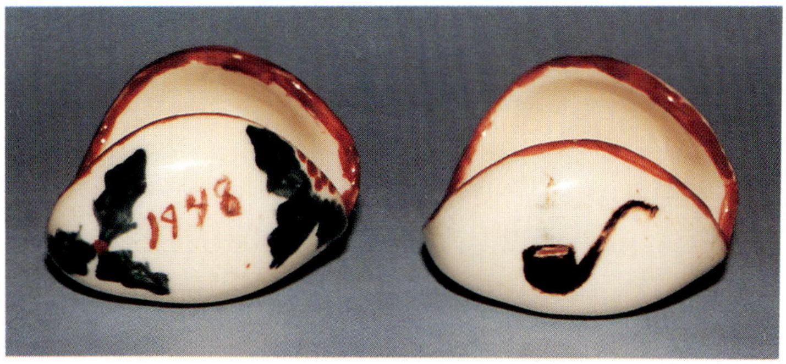

Reverse side of the napkin rings for Mr. and Mrs. Bower.

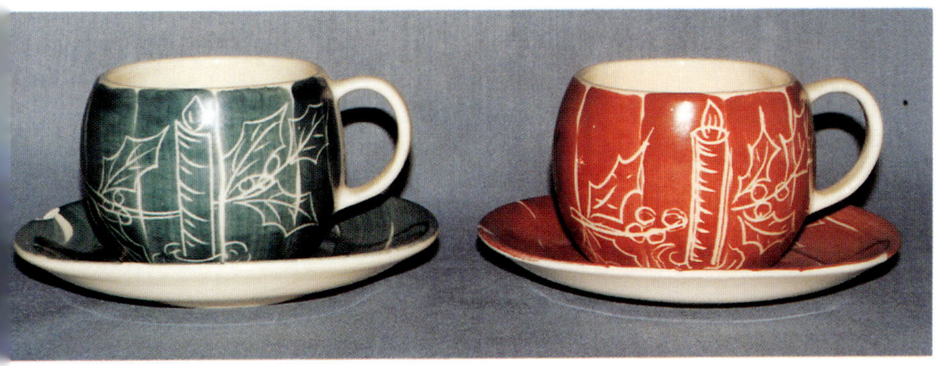

Cups and saucers in Turquoise and Coral Intaglio with incised candle and holly decoration. $150 each.

Figural Items

Purinton produced a variety of figural items. Most of them were made for other companies. Taylor Smith Taylor contracted Purinton to make a Howdy Dowdy cookies jar and bank. Purinton utilized the air brushing technology of the Tionesta plant to paint them. Taylor Smith Taylor also contracted for squirrels and cats. These were made to be hung from a tree or placed on the back of your couch. The Howdy Dowdy bank is much more difficult to find than the cookies jar.

Purinton produced three of their own figural cookies jars: a chicken, Humpty Dumpty, and a pig. The pig is the most difficult to locate. They also made an owl, Uncle Sam, and a small pig bank. These were either decorated with a solid glaze or a few flowers.

Purinton made a variety of animal figures. Not much is known about what is Purinton and what was made by other companies. Identification of the animals in this book has been based on employees' recollections of certain figures being made. A picture in a *Crockery and Glass Journal* edition featured a few of the figures. Demand for the figures is low, yet these characters are some of the more entertaining items to collect.

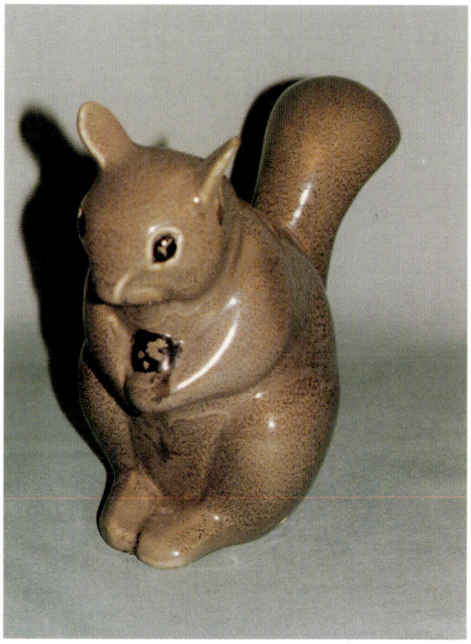

Squirrel made for Taylor Smith Taylor, 7" high. $100.

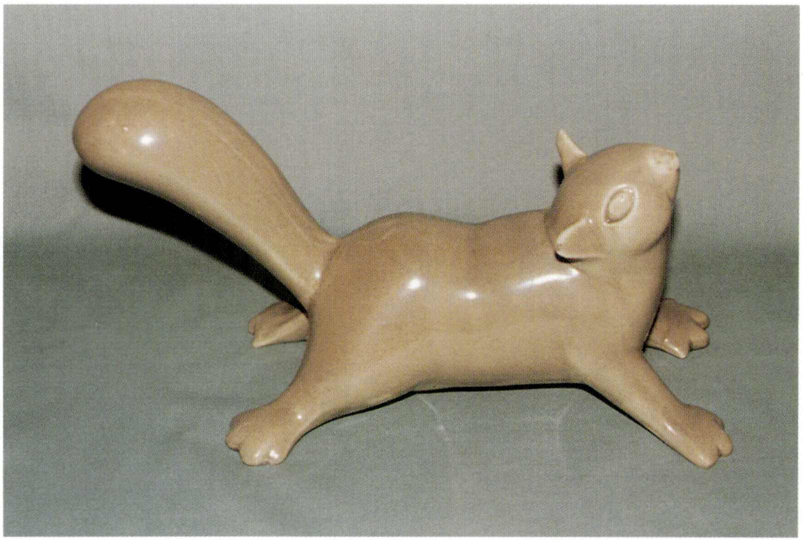

Squirrel made for Taylor Smith Taylor, 11" long. Made to hang on a tree. $100.

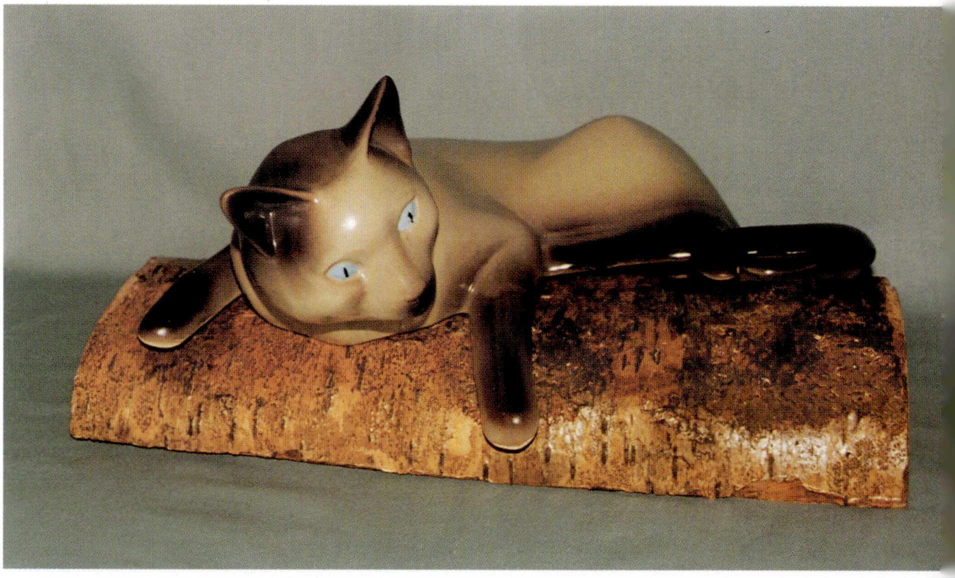

Siamese cat made for Taylor Smith Taylor, 14" long. Used on the back of the couch or hung in a tree. $100.

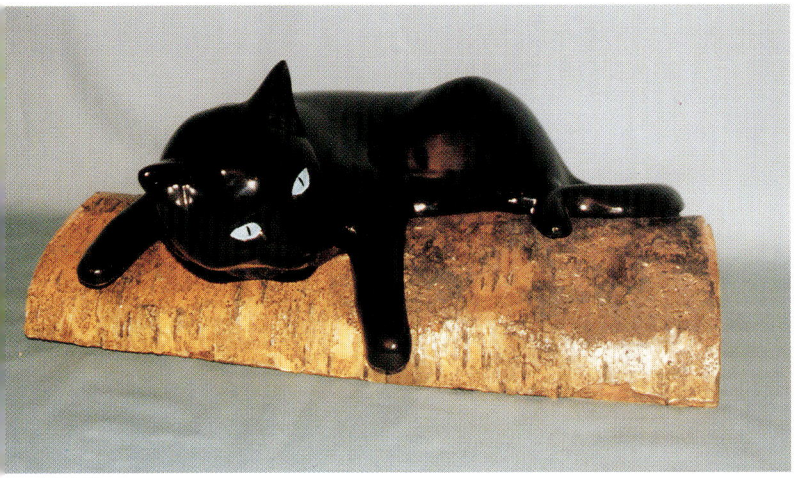

Black cat made for Taylor Smith Taylor. Used on the back of the couch or hung in a tree. $100.

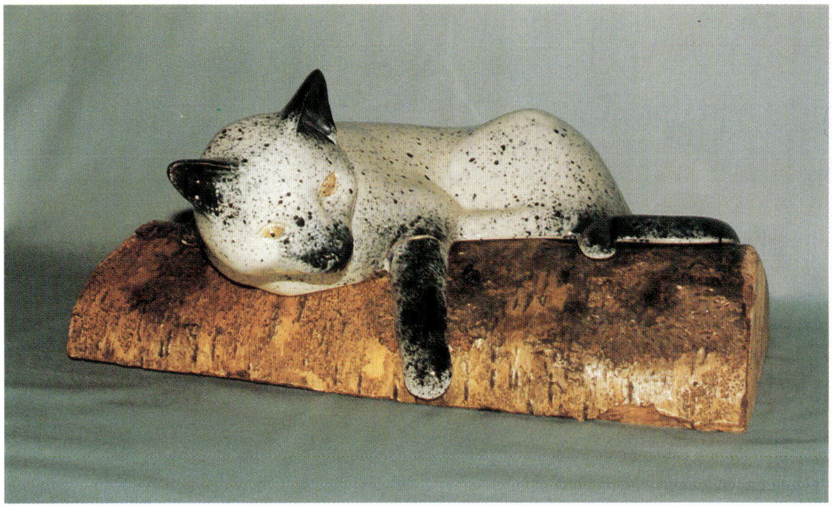

Spotted cat made for Taylor Smith Taylor. Used on the back of a couch or hung on a tree. $100.

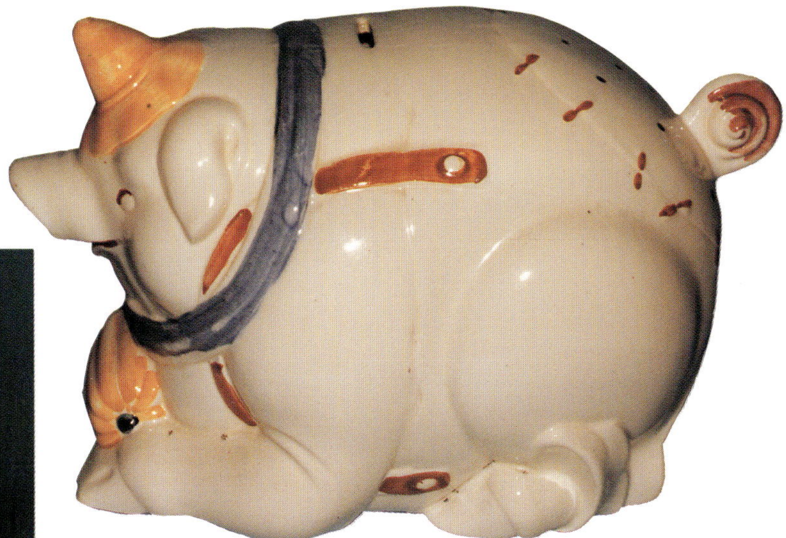

Whimsy bank made from the pig cookies jar.

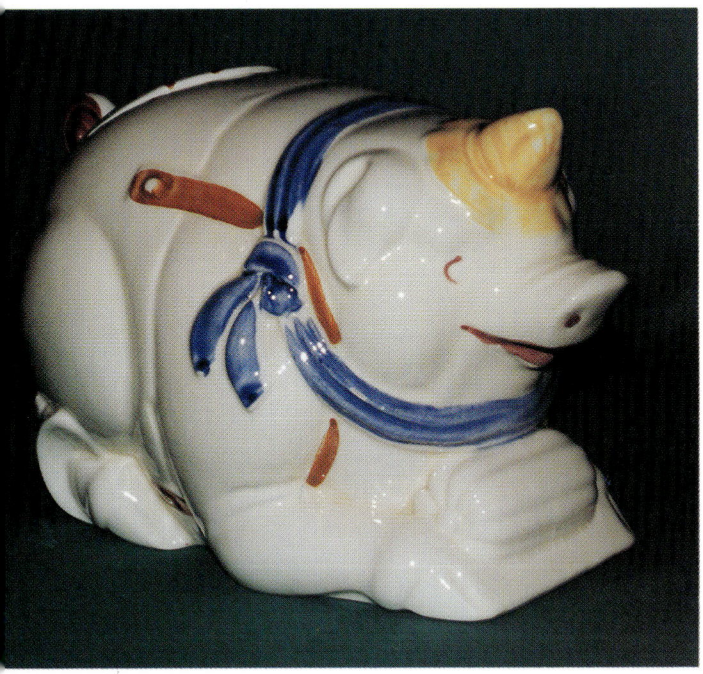

Pig cookies jar. This is a Purinton mold. $500+.

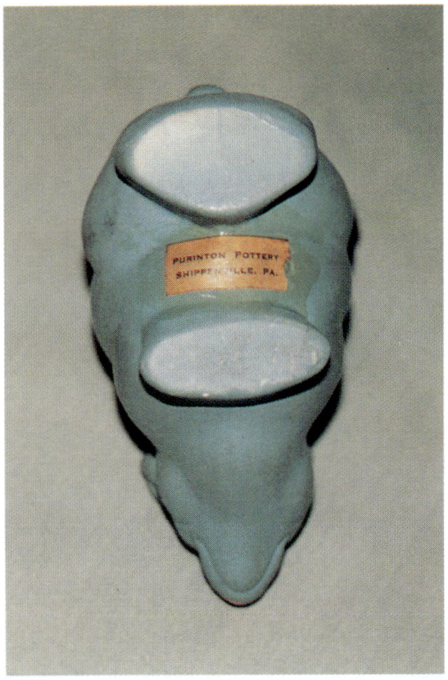

Pig bank in turquoise glaze with an original sticker on the bottom. Purinton Pottery, Shippenville, PA. $35.

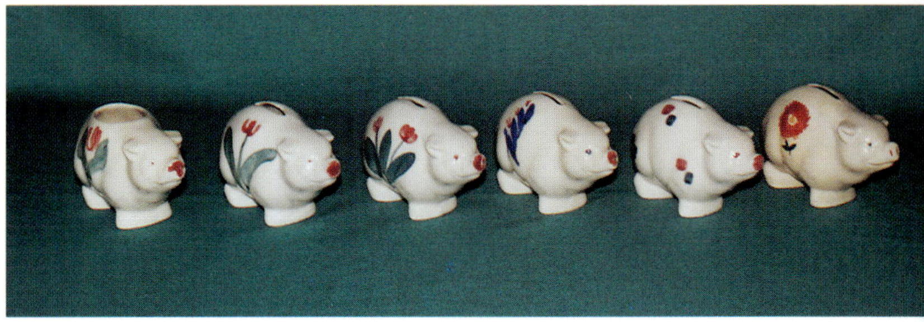

Pig banks with a variety of decorations. $30 each. The first pig on the left is a pig planter. $30.

Giraffe, whimsy piece made by a pottery employee. $20.

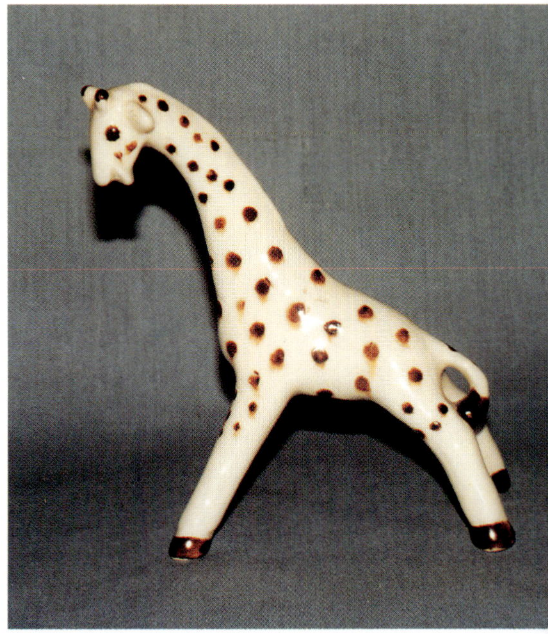

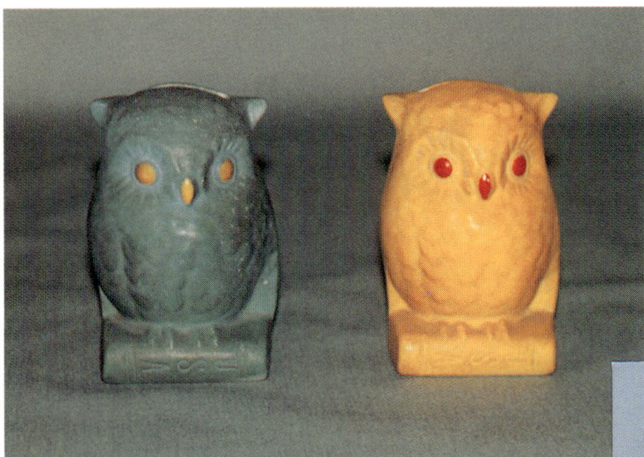

Owl banks with turquoise and yellow solid color glaze. $30 each.

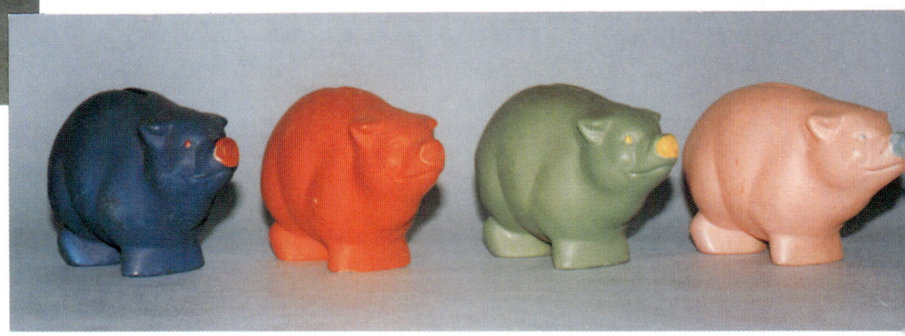

Pig banks in blue, red, green, and pink solid color glazes. $25 each.

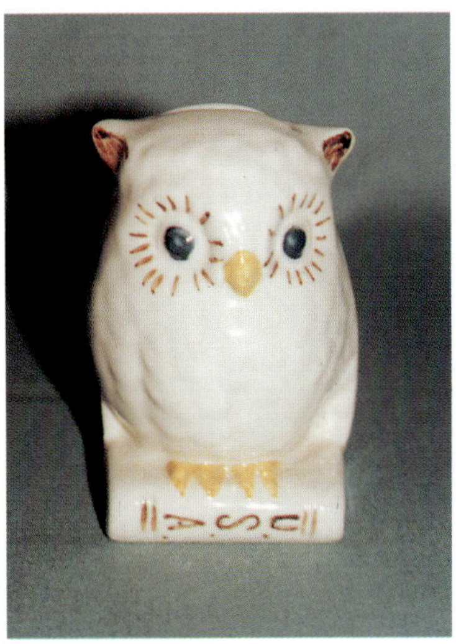

Owl bank. $40.

Owl banks. $25 each. Fish, may be used as toothpick holders. $25 each.

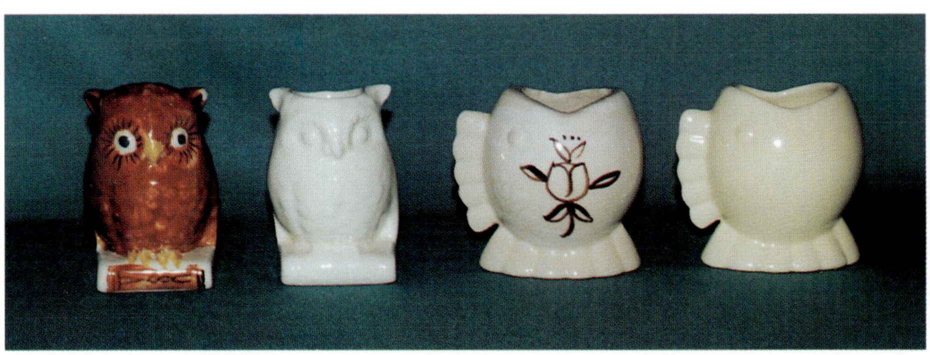

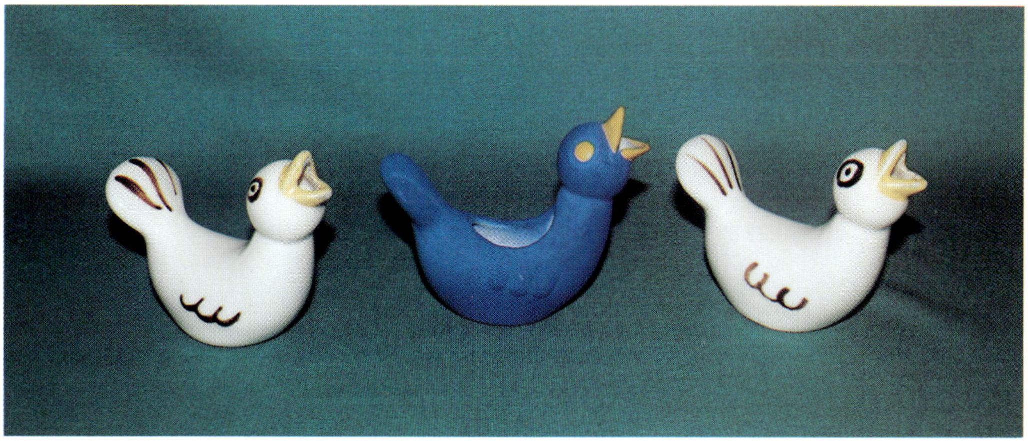

Birds. $20 each.

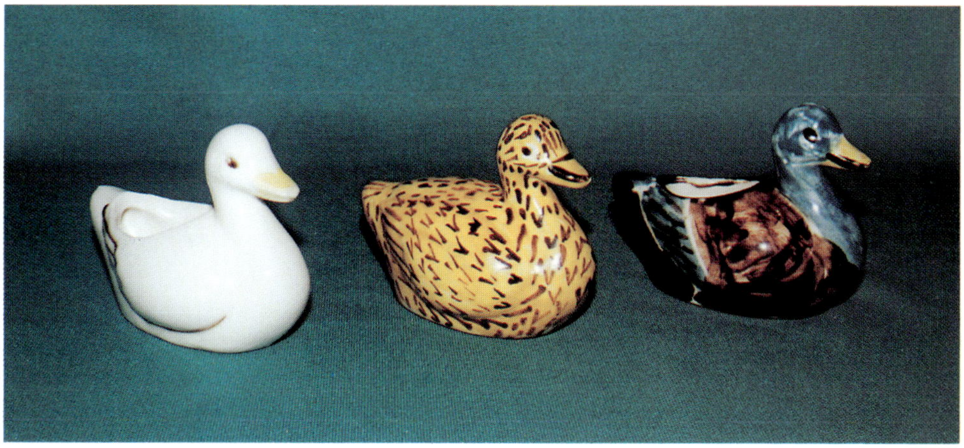

Ducks. The center duck is solid, the outer ducks are miniature planters. $20 each.

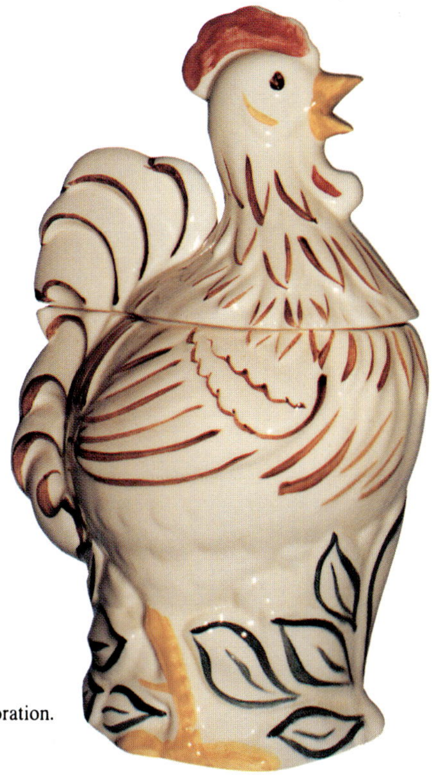

Chicken cookies jar with detailed decoration. $200.

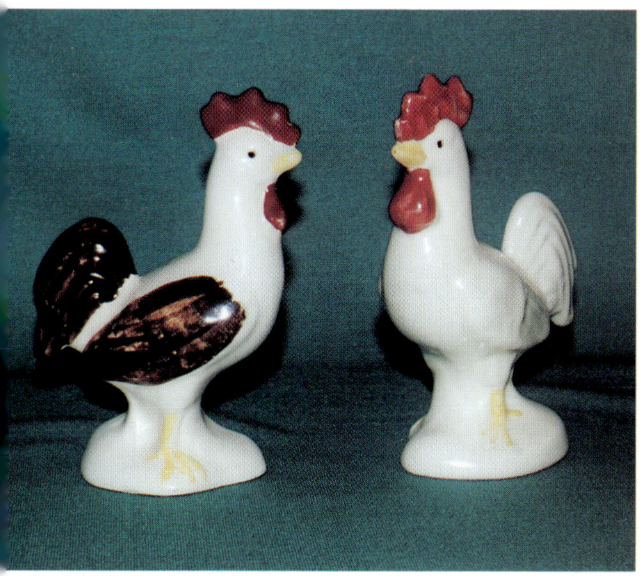

Roosters, 5.75" high. $25 each.

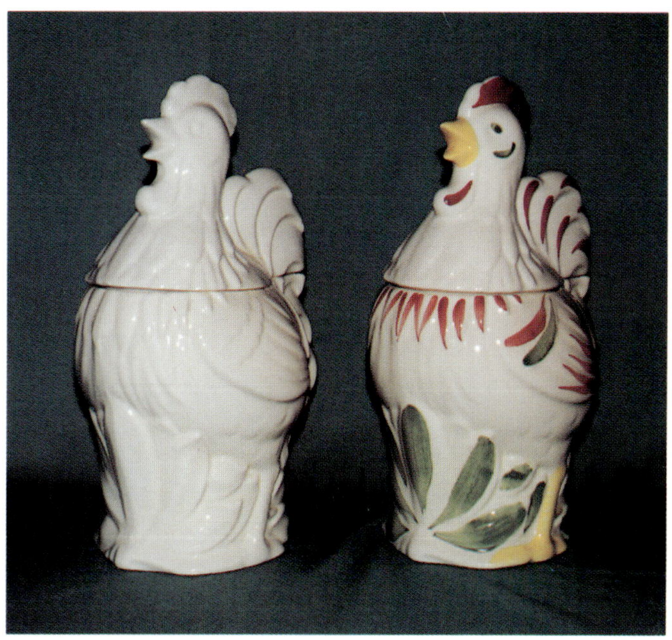

Chicken cookies jars. No decoration. $100. Decorated. $150. This is a Purinton mold.

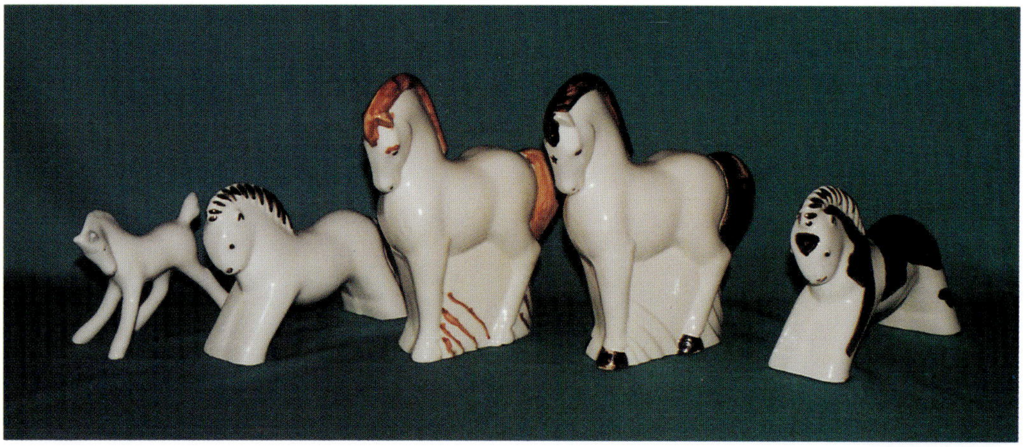

Purinton produced a variety of horses. $20 each.

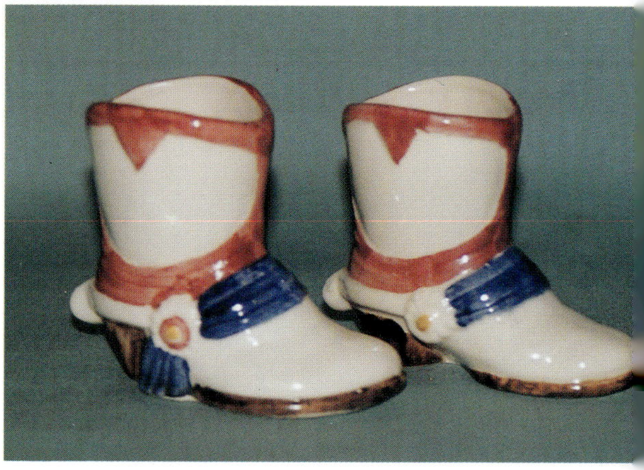

Boot toothpick holders. $40 set.

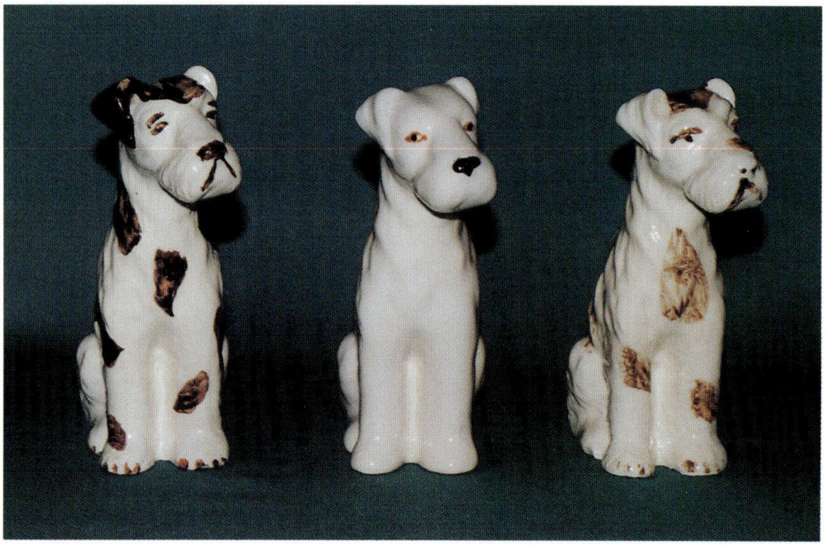

Dogs. $20 each.

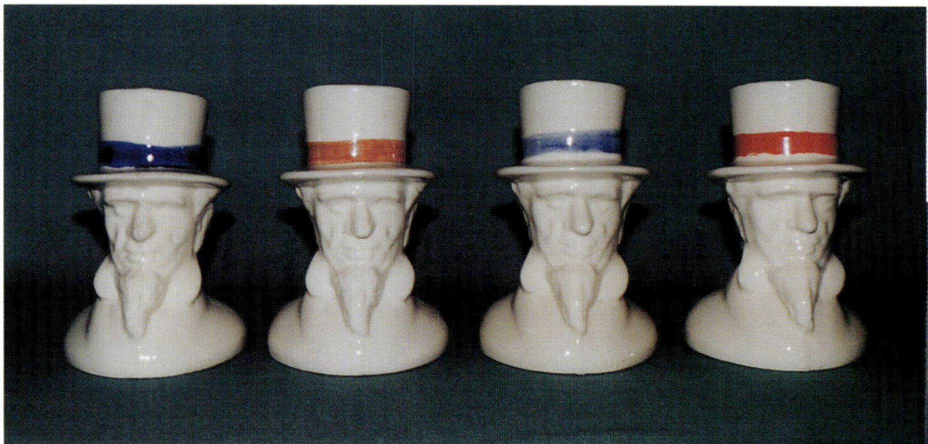

Uncle Sam banks. $40.

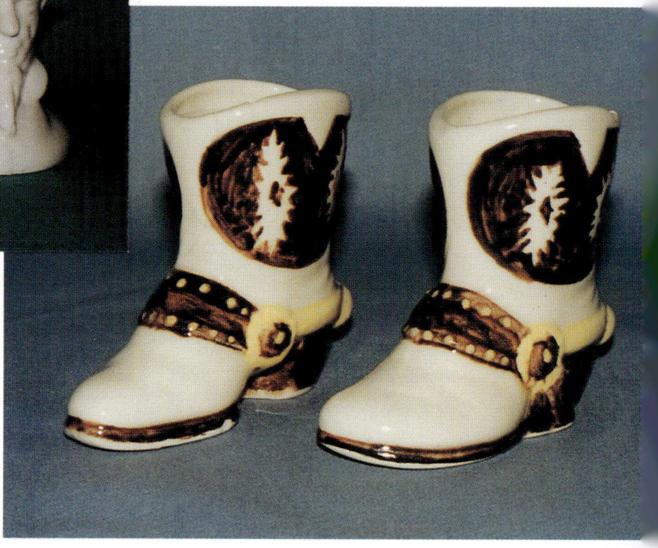

Boot toothpick holders. $40 set.

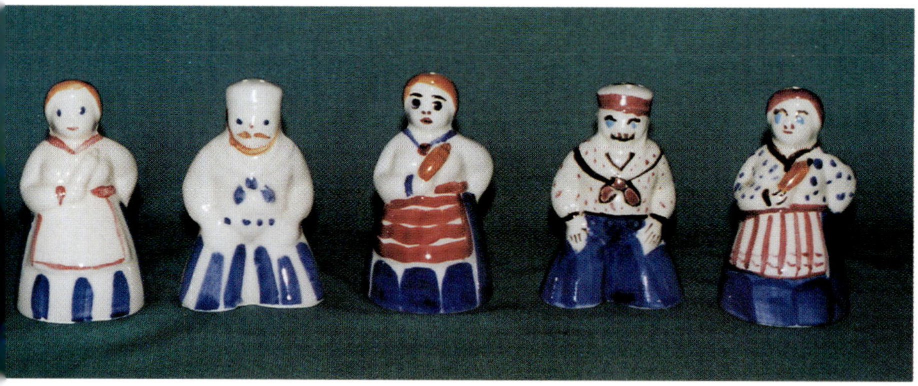

Old salt and wife pepper, shakers. Variety of decorations. $100 pair.

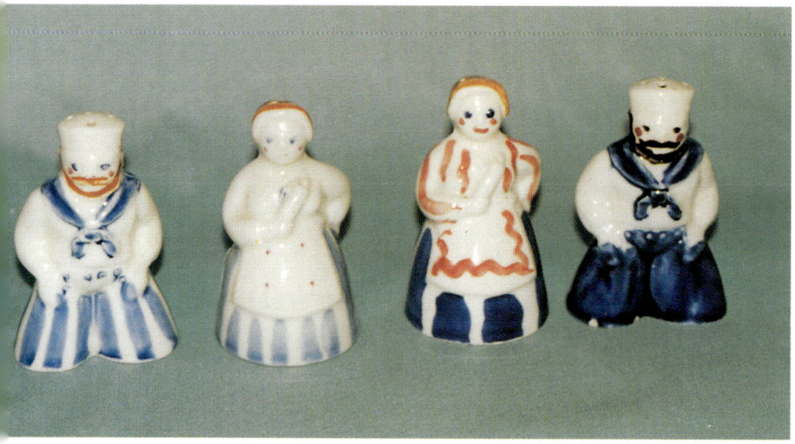

Old salt and wife pepper, shakers. Variety of decorations. $100 pair.

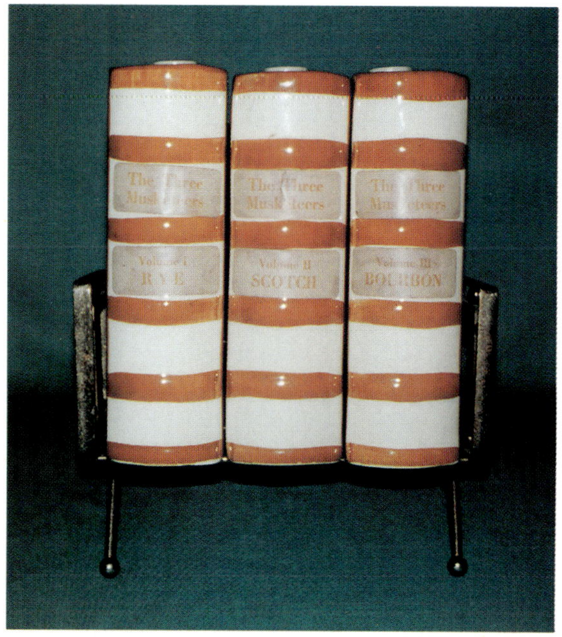

Book decanters in a metal rack. $100 set.

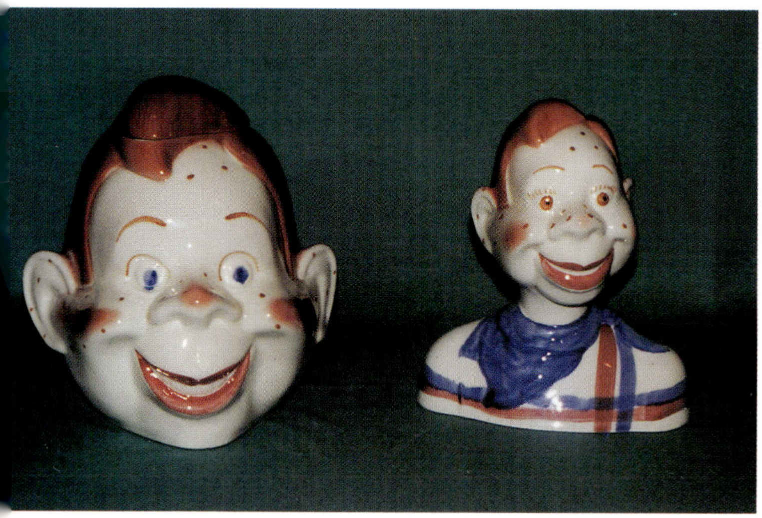

Howdy Doody cookies jar made for Taylor Smith Taylor. $350. Howdy Doody bank made for Taylor Smith Taylor. $600.

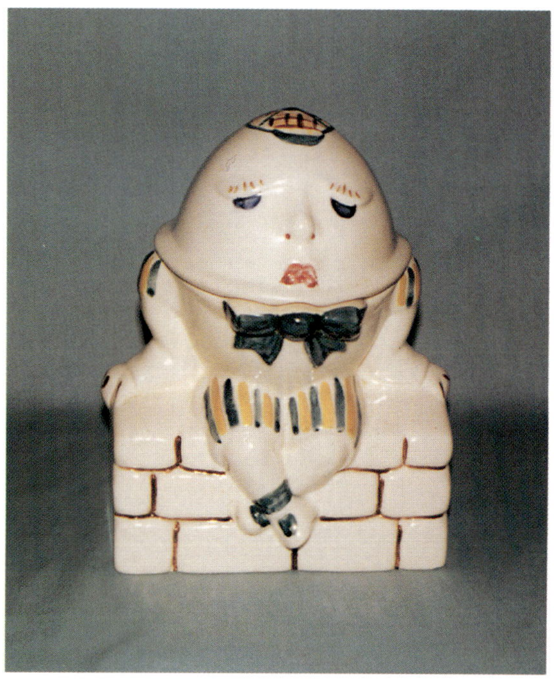

Humpty Dumpty cookies jar. This is a Purinton mold. $250.

Experimental Pottery

One wonderful thing about collecting Purinton Pottery is that there are always experimental pieces waiting to be discovered. A few of the employees made whimsy or personalized items and were allowed to take them home. A large table in the decorating area held numerous items with a variety of decorations. Some of these pieces were the works of Dorothy Purinton as she attempted to develop new designs. Others were the decorated wares of the employees who also contributed their artistic talents.

Some experimental and whimsy pieces have been identified in other chapters if they had a similar decoration. These items may have been sold from the Corner Cupboard or from the plant. We know some visitors to the plant were allowed to decorate their own item. It is exciting to see the variation in some production items.

Prices for these pieces reflect a demand for diverse items. A few items are not too attractive while others are quite beautiful when displayed.

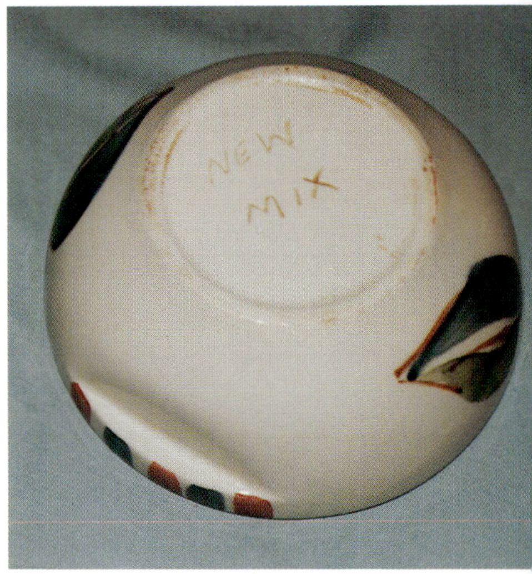

"New Mix" inscribed on the bottom of an Apple cereal bowl.

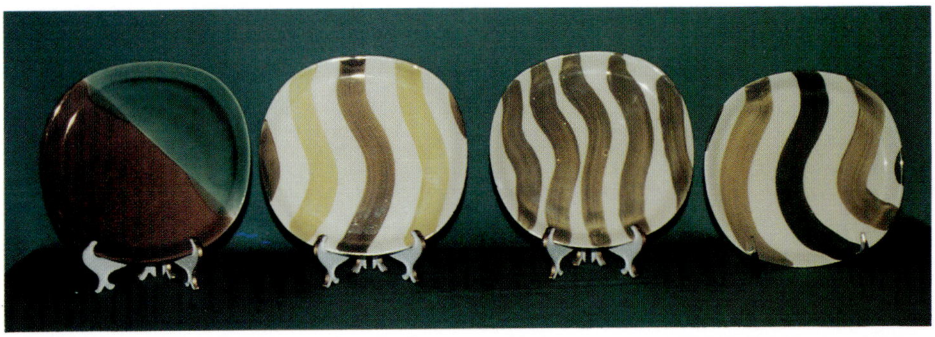

Salad plates with experimental slip colorings.

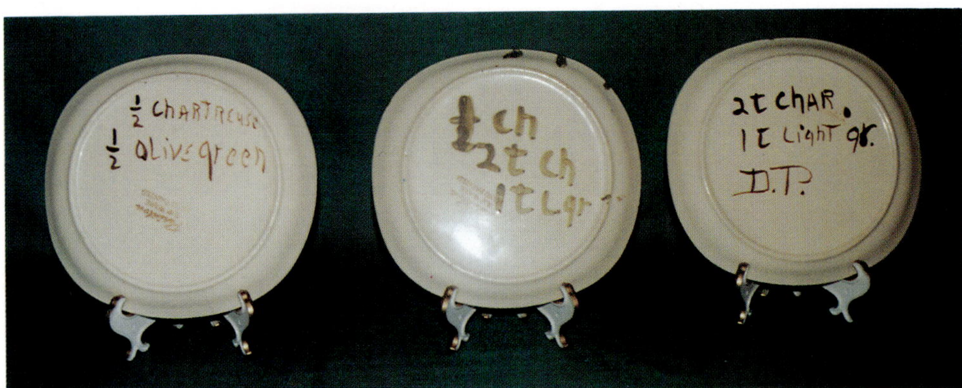

Reverse sides of the previous salad plates with recipes for their slip mixture colors. Note the far right example is initialed DP.

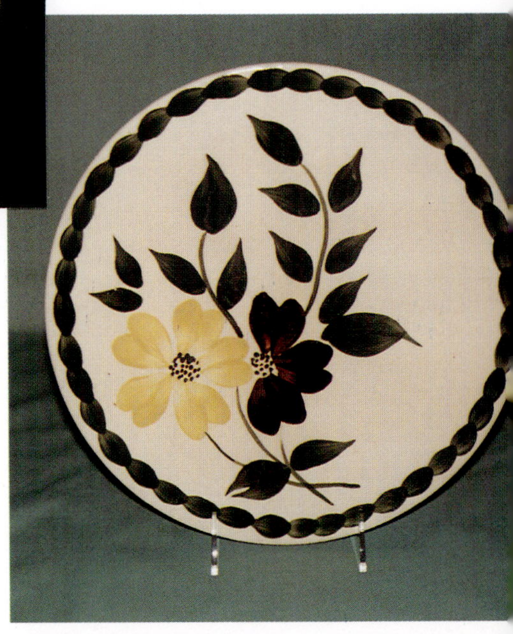

Chop plate, Blue Ridge Green Briar pattern decoration. $100.

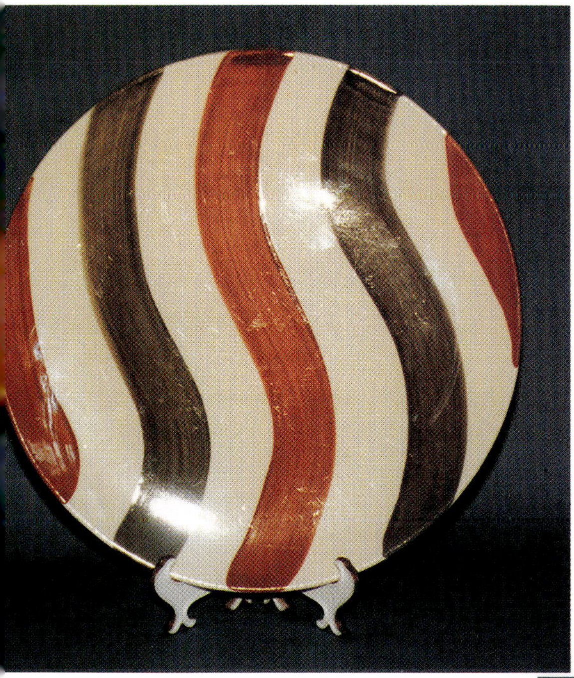

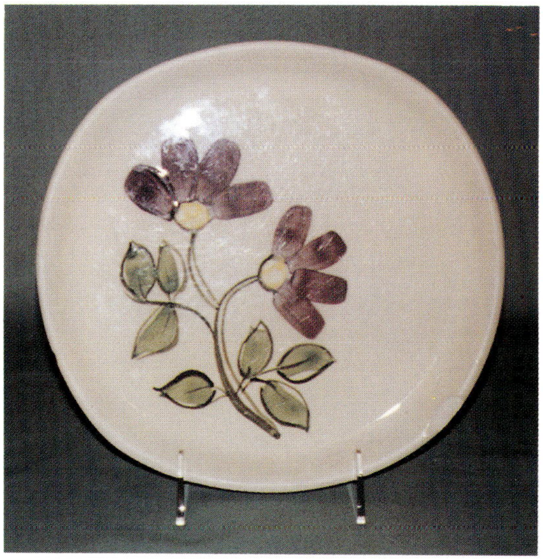

Dinner plate, purple half-flower. $75.

Chop plate, golden brown and green stripes. $75.

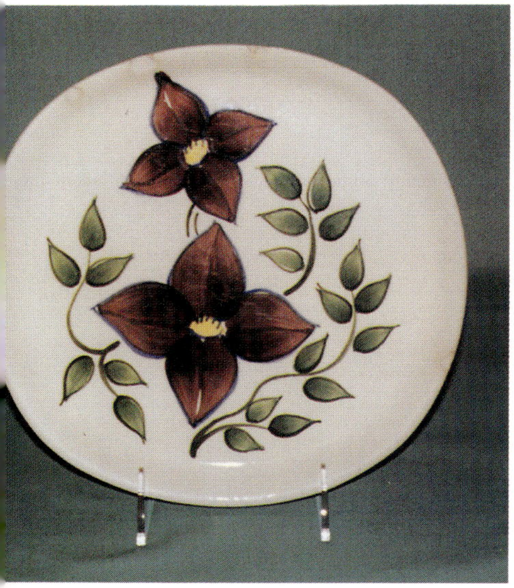

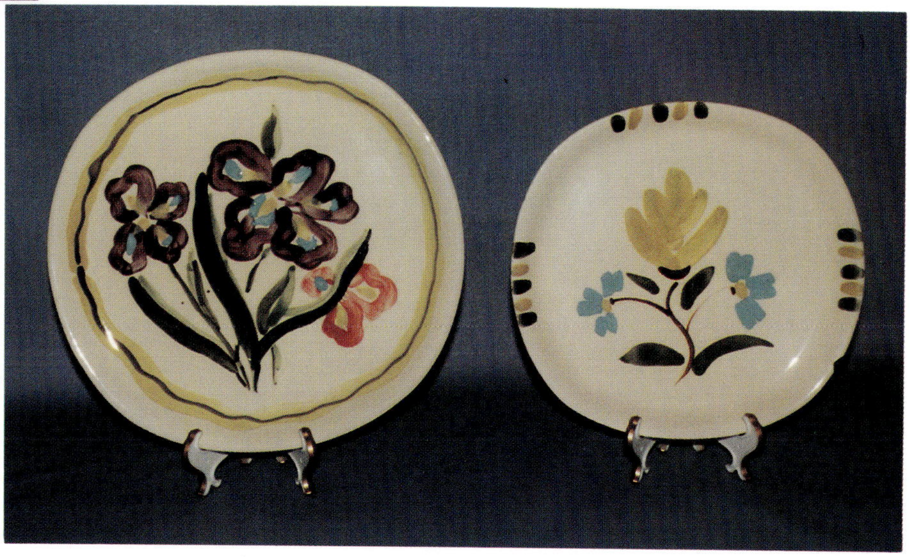

Dinner plate, purple flower. $75. Breakfast plate, chartreuse flower. $75.

Dinner plate, violets. $75.

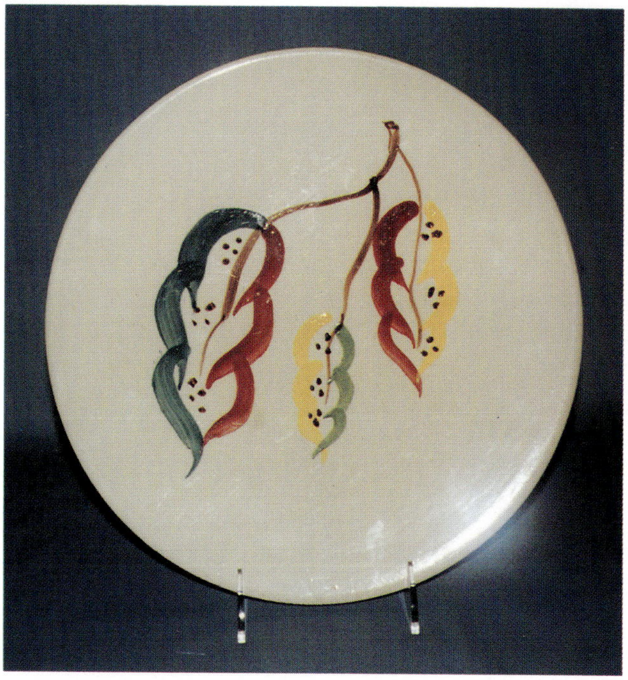

Chop plate, multi-colored leaves. $150+.

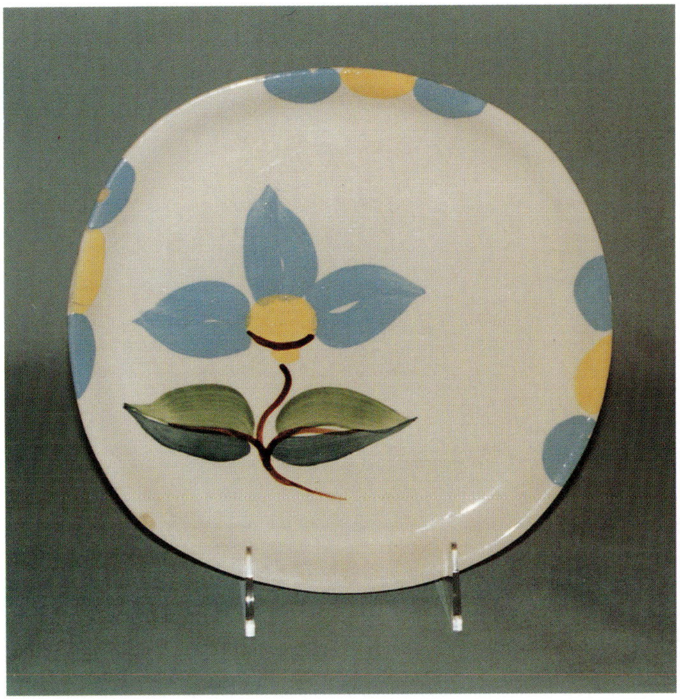

Dinner plate light blue half blossom flower. $75.

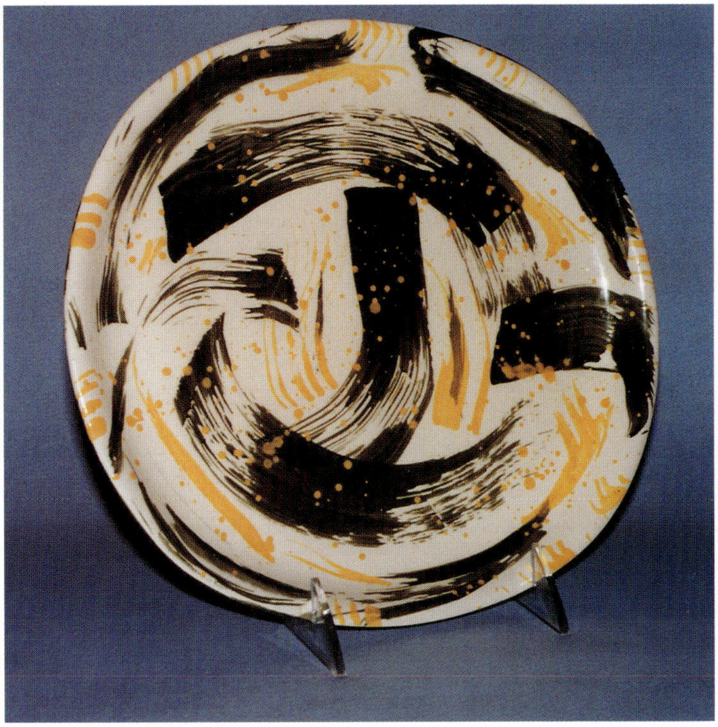

Dinner plate, yellow and green abstract decoration. $75.

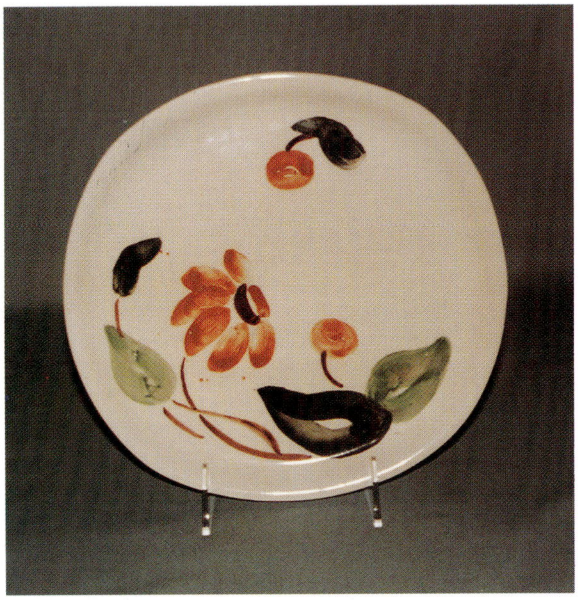

Dinner plate, orange flower. $50.

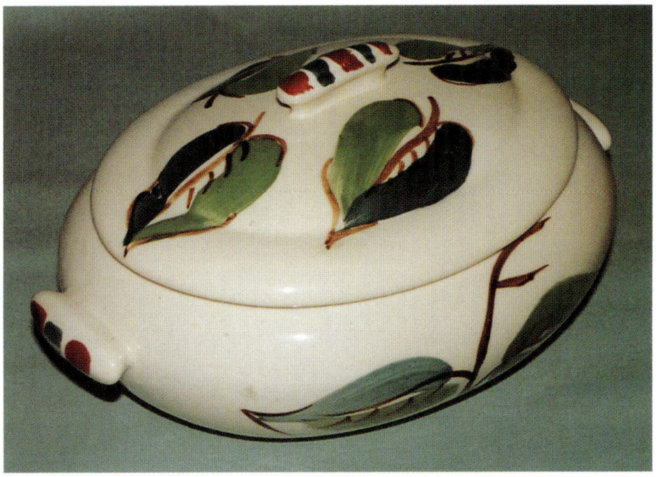

Covered vegetable with Apple pattern leaves as the only decoration. $75.

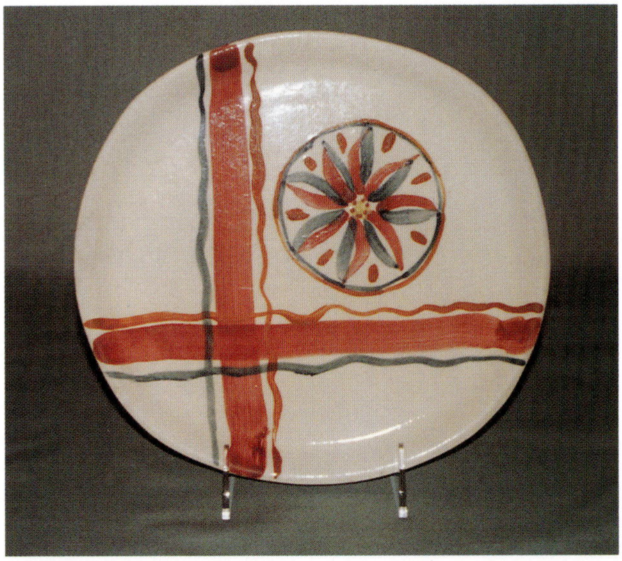

Dinner plate, Normandy Plaid with hex sign flower. $75.

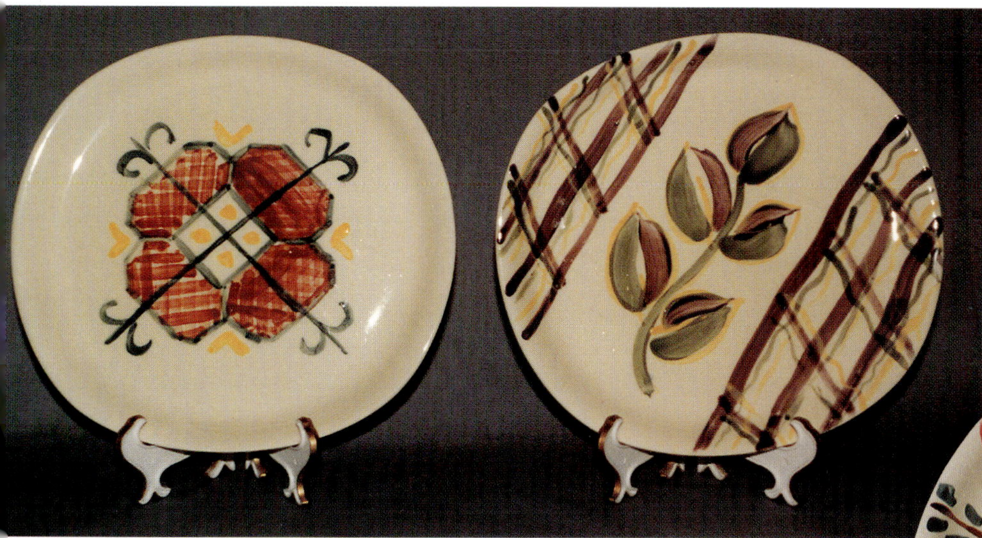

Dinner plate, red coat-of-arms. $75. Dinner plate, purple and green leaves with purple plaid. $75.

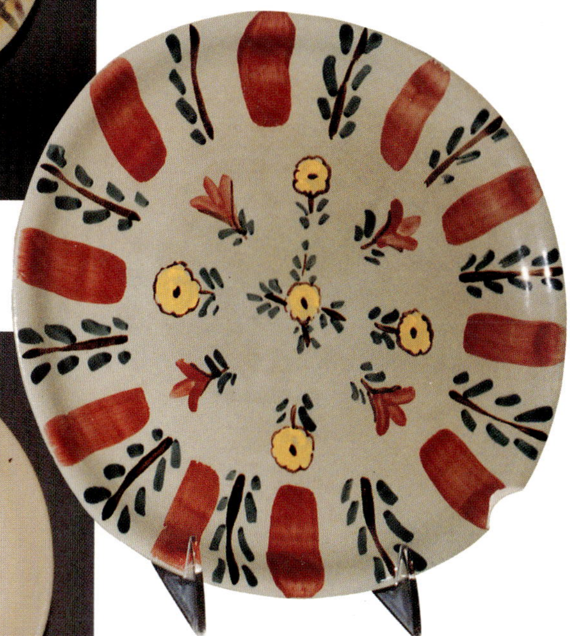

Dinner plate, Peasant Garden pattern on a Maywood slip plate. $75.

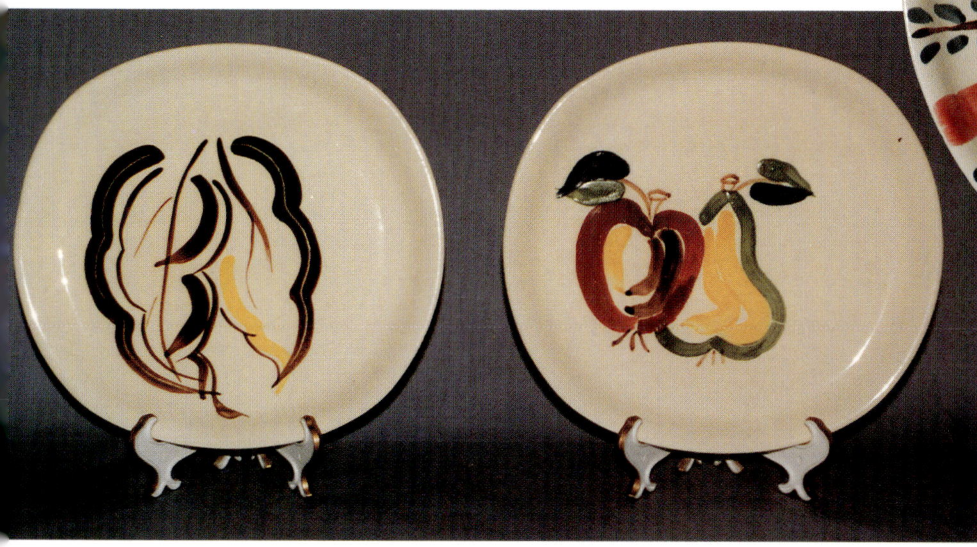

Dinner plate, brown and yellow leaves. $75. Dinner plate, open apple and open green pear. Seen on covered casserole lids. $100.

Dinner plate, rooster. $100. Dinner plate, stylized rooster. $100.

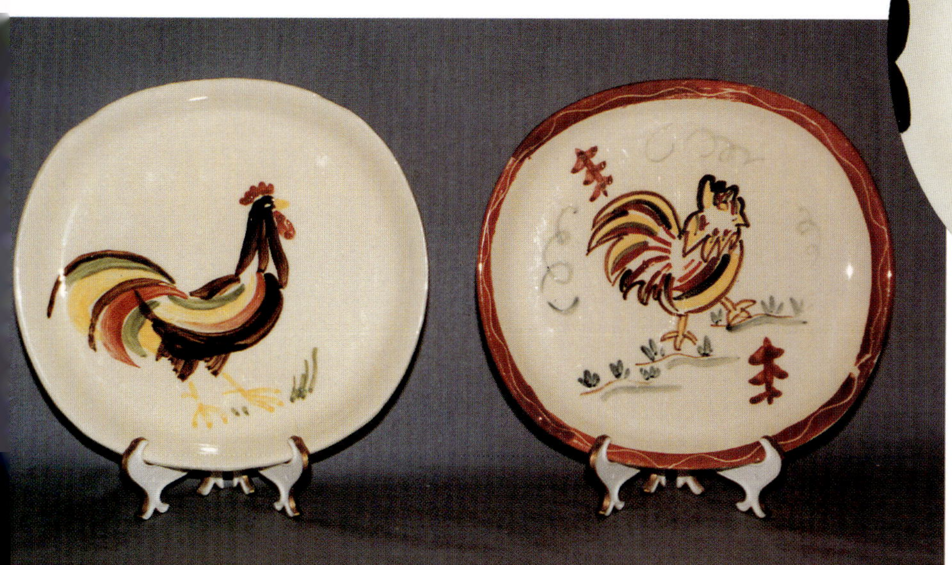

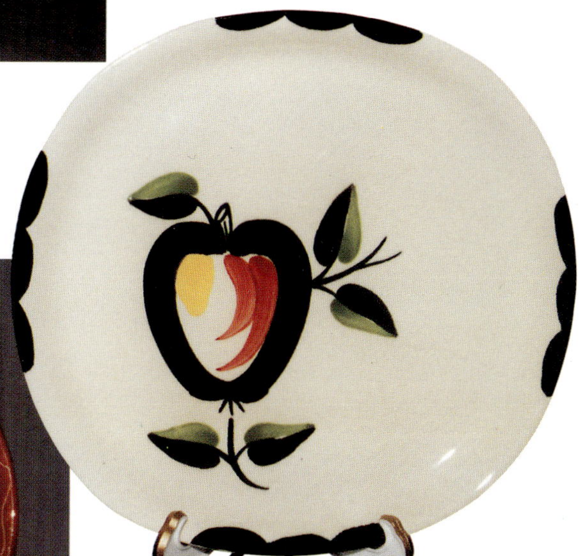

Dinner plate with Apple pattern utilizing a black colored slip. $150.

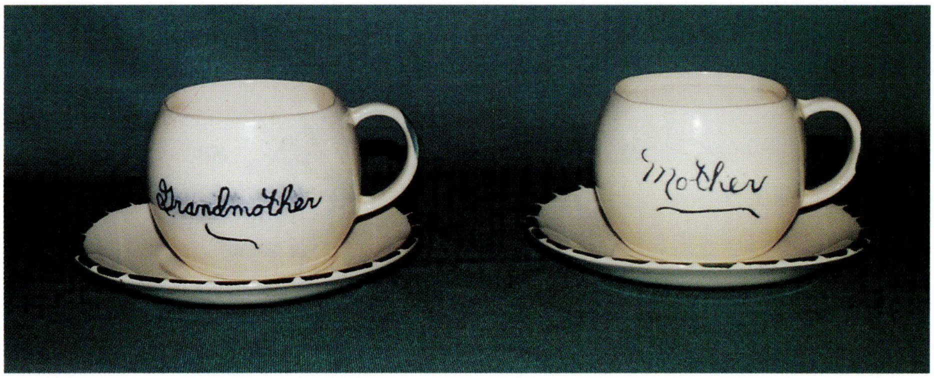

Cups and saucers marked Grandmother and Mother. $50 each set.

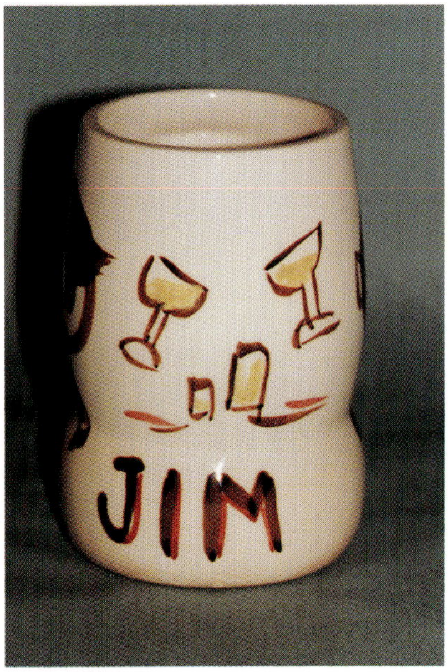

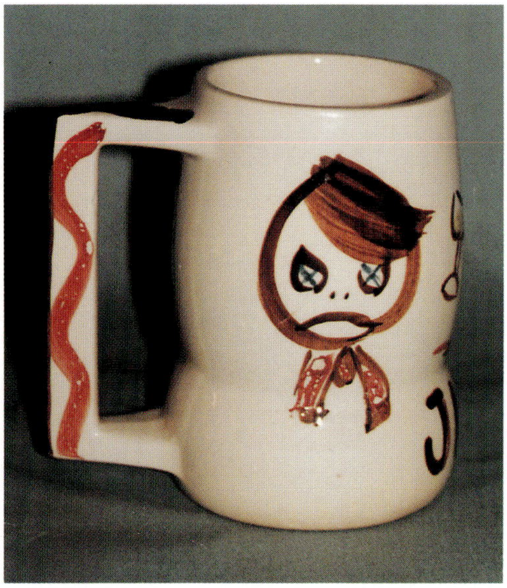

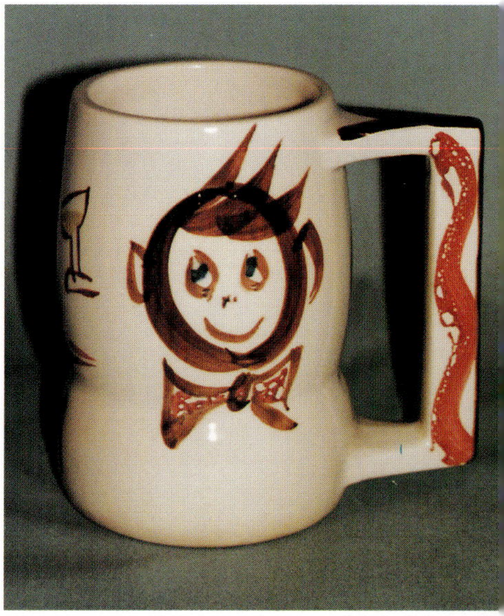

Three views of a beer mug personalized with the name Jim. $150.

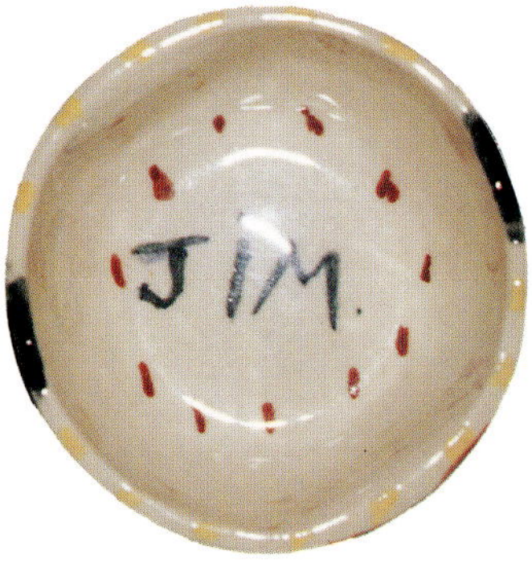

Whimsy ashtray made from a dessert bowl and personalized Jim. $30.

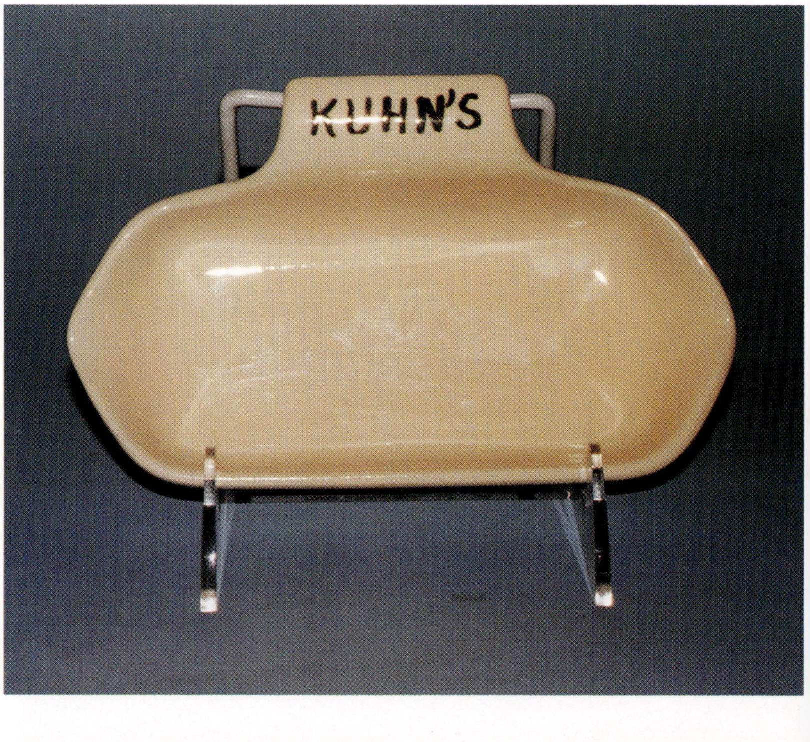

Butter dish personalized Kuhn's. Kuhn's is thought to be a grocery store in the Pittsburgh area. This item was given as a premium. $80.

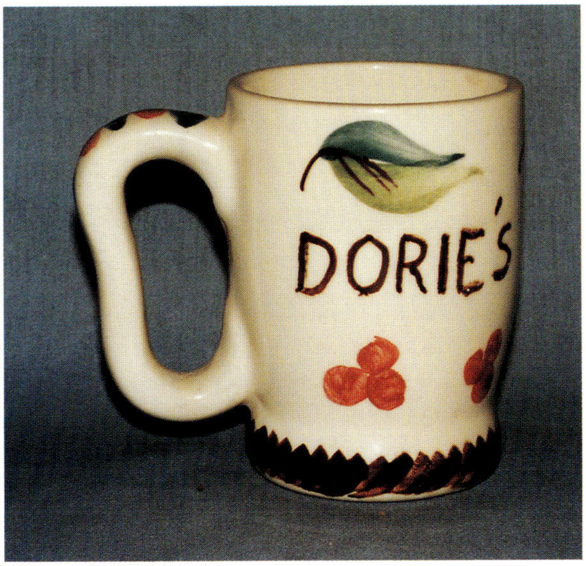

Coffee mug personalized for Dorie Purinton, Blair's wife. $75.

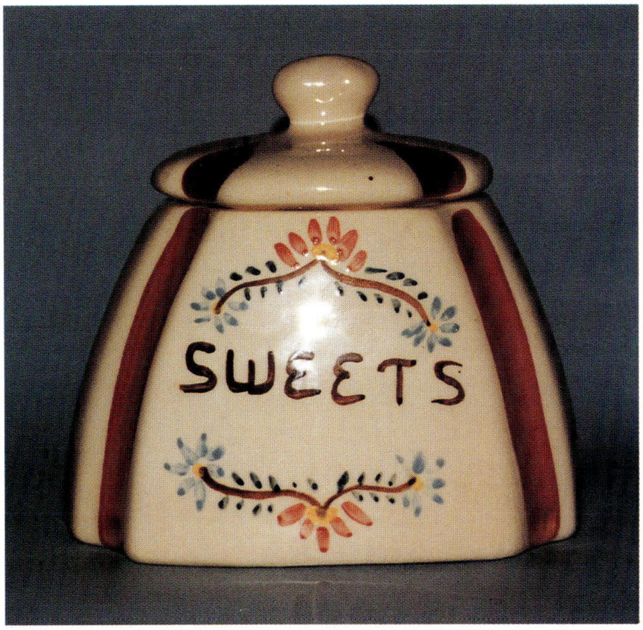

Covered range grease jar personalized Sweets. $150.

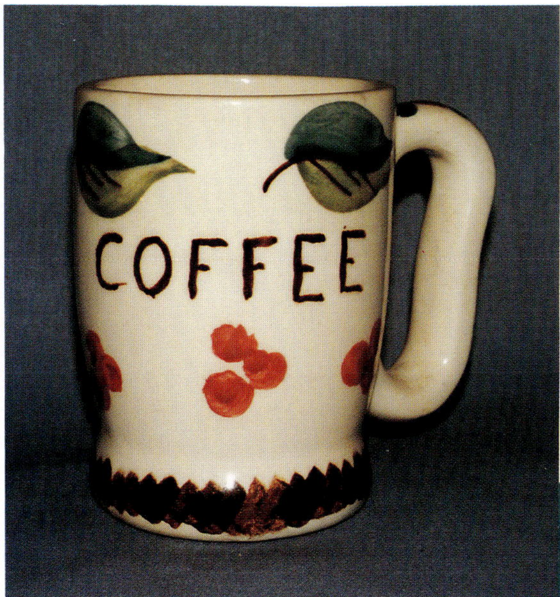

Reverse side of Dorie's mug (she doesn't even drink coffee).

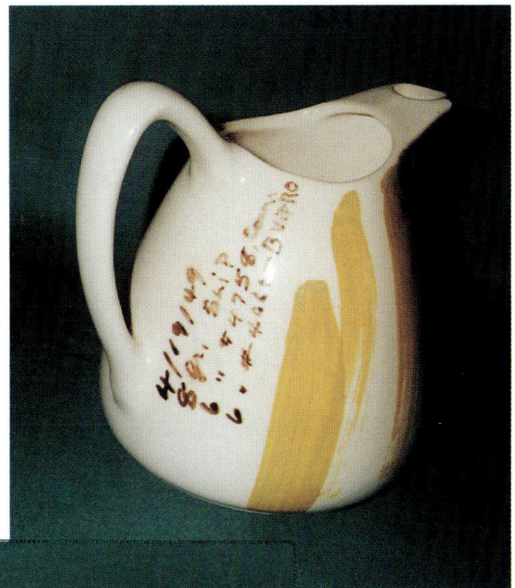

Beverage pitcher. Used as a test for coloring. Dated 4/19/49 with the following recipe for slip mixture coloring: 8 gr. slip, 6 gr. #4758 com, 6 gr. # 4062 burro.

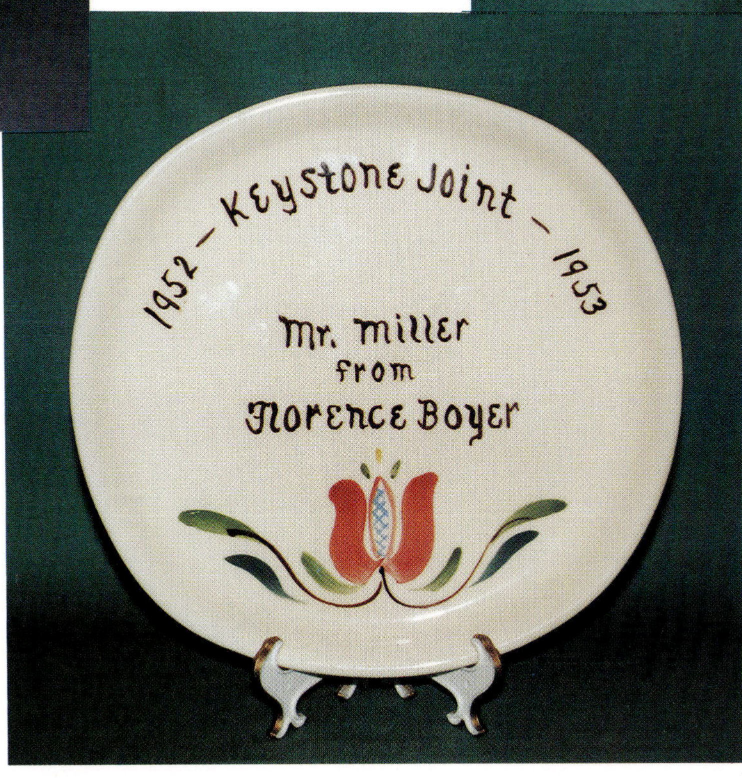

Dinner plate with Pennsylvania Dutch decoration given to Mr. Miller who was probably a teacher at Keystone High School, the school district for Shippenville. $200.

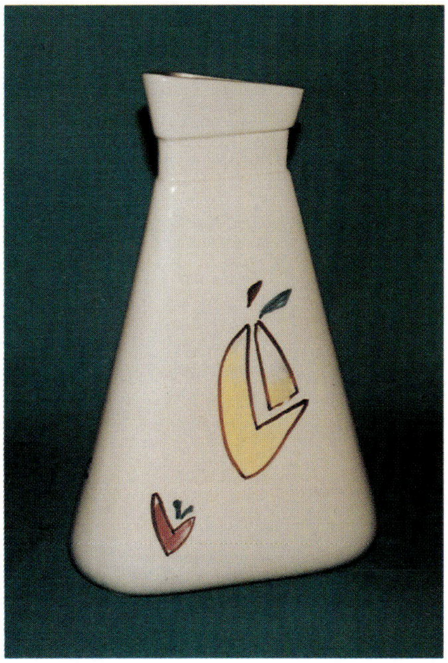

Triangular pitcher, 10.5" high, with abstract decoration. $75.

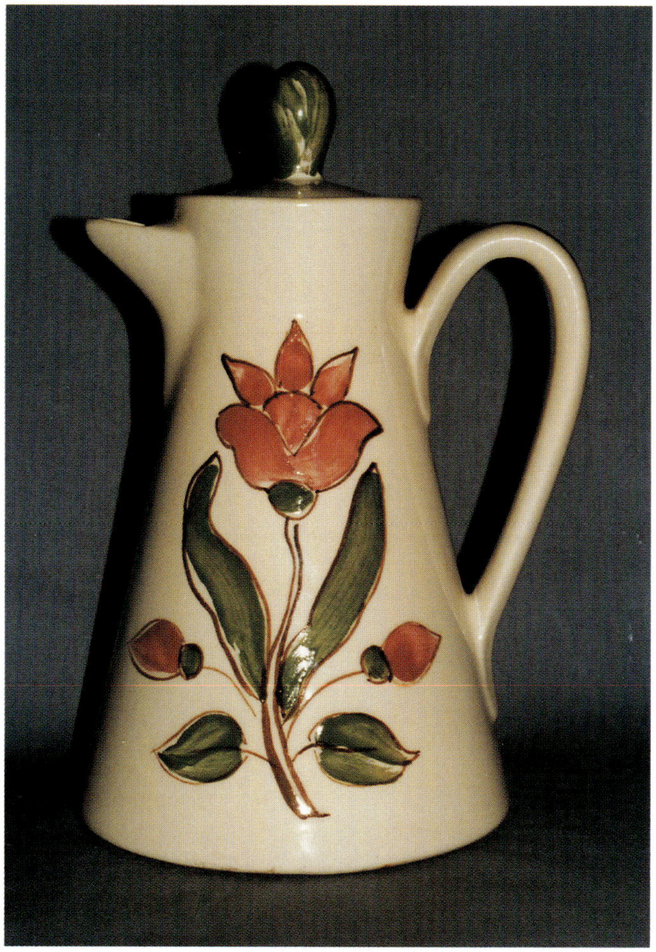

Coffee server, Taylor Smith Taylor mold, 10.5" high, with a pink flower. $125.

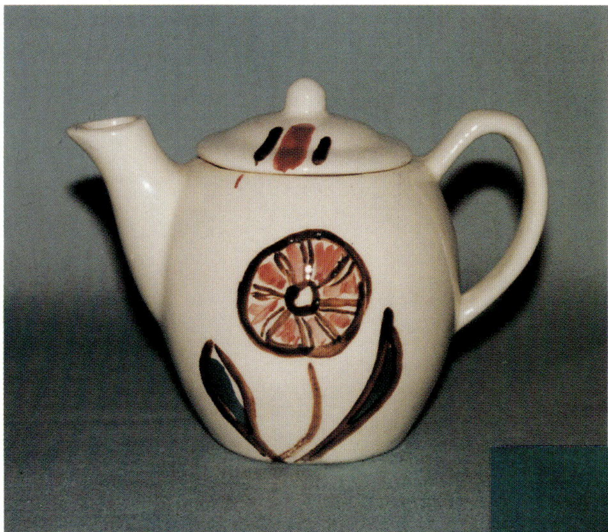

Two cup teapot with pink and brown flower. $75.

Four cup teapot, Wellsville style, with Red Wavy Line decoration. $75.

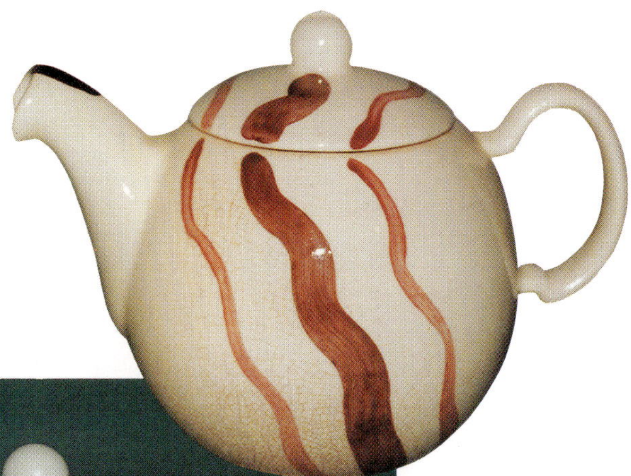

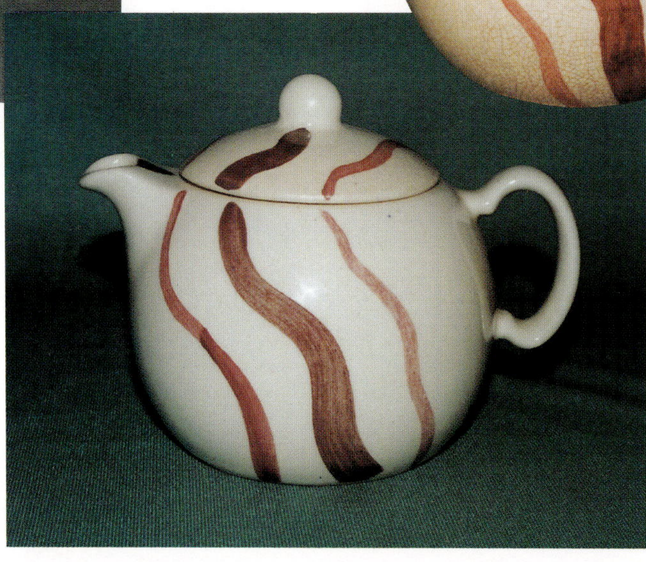

Covered creamer with Red Wavy Line decoration. $60.

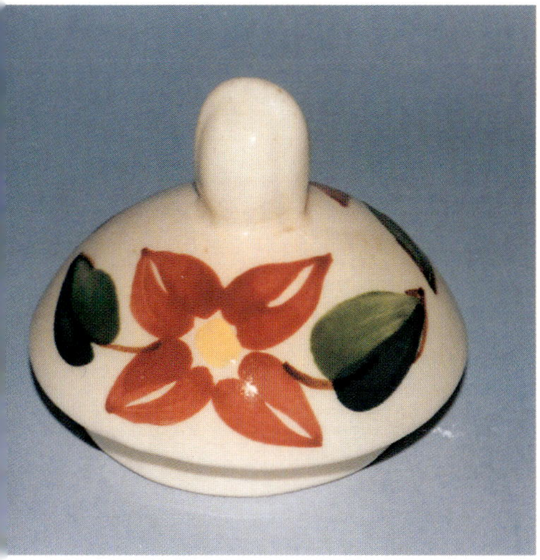

Lid to a six cup domed lid teapot with a red flower. $10.

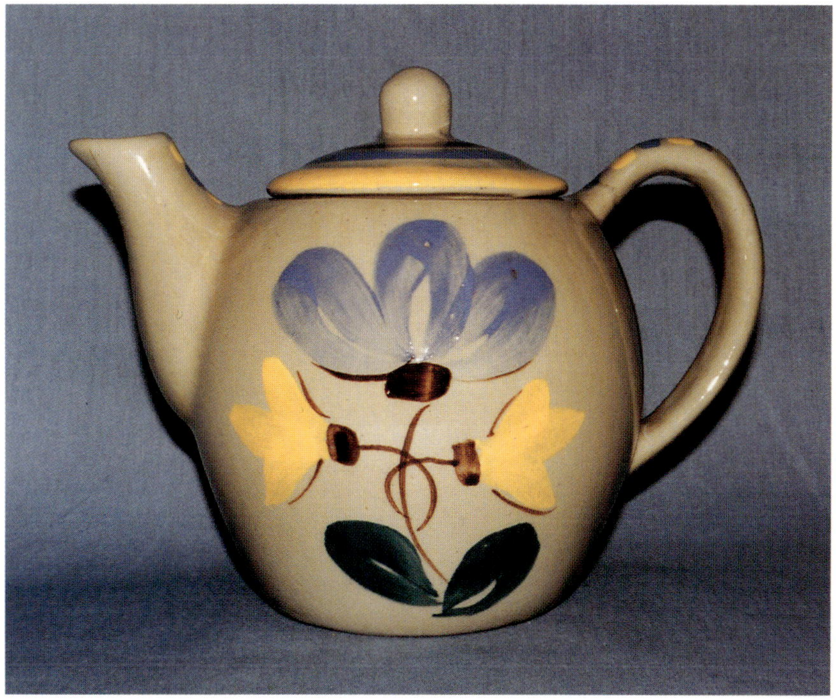

Six cup teapot in Maywood slip with purple and yellow flowers. $75.

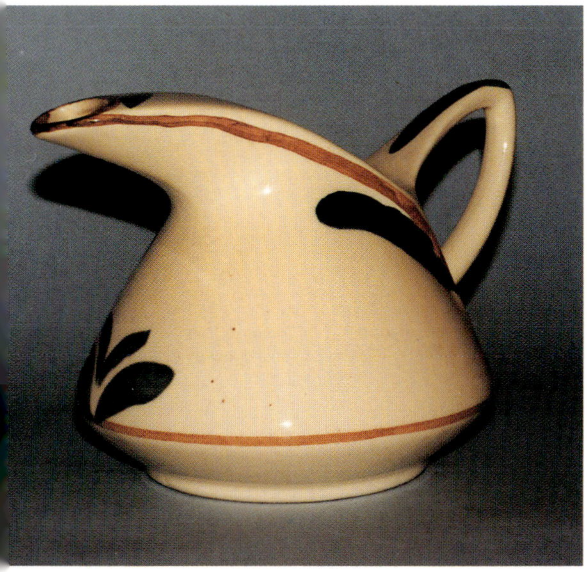

Two pint dutch jug with very plain decoration. $30.

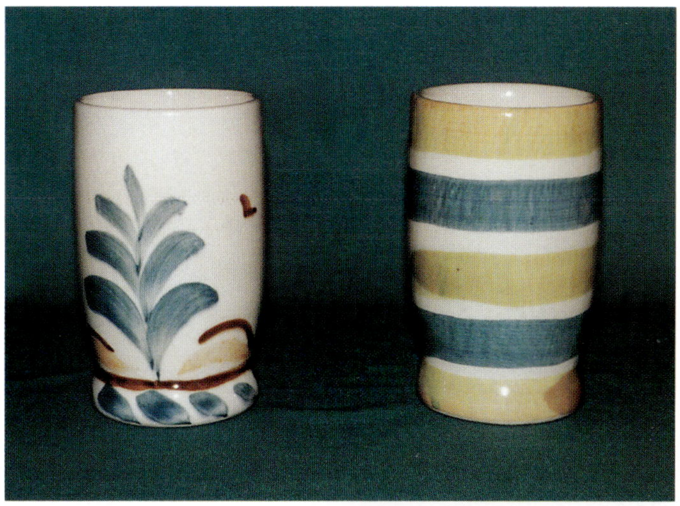

Tumblers. $50 each.

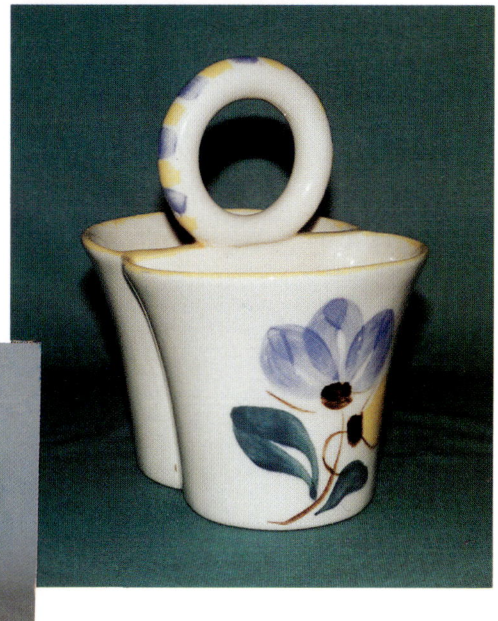

Candy basket with purple and yellow flowers. $90.

Maywood design with Ming Tree orange coloring, cups $50 each. Covered sugar and creamer. $100 set.

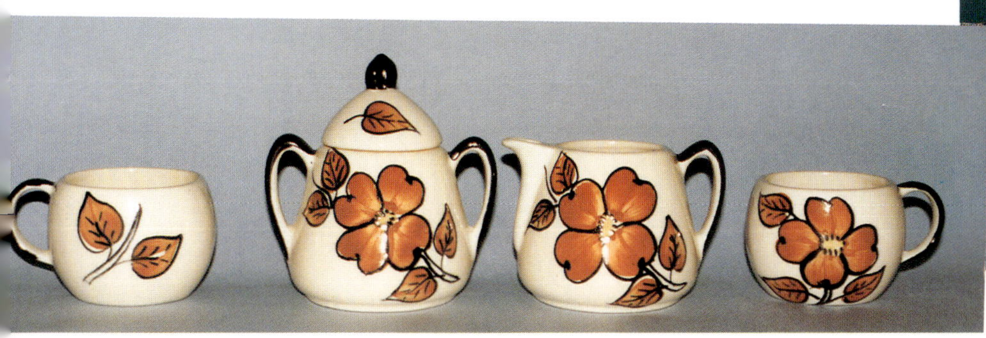

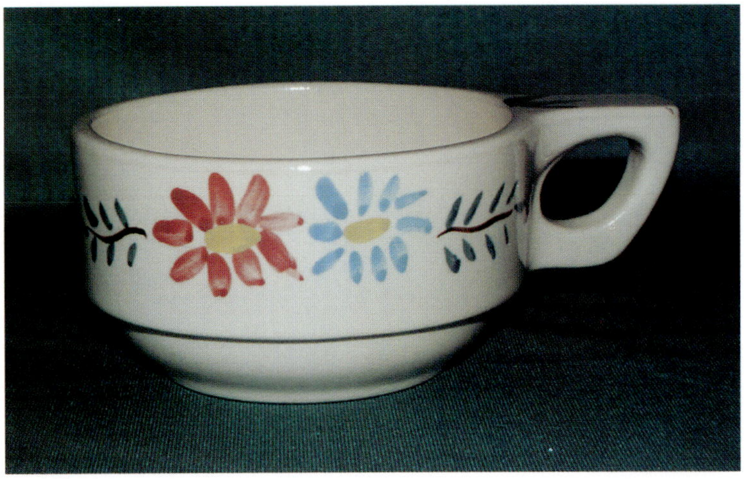

Soup cup, Rubel mold, Daisy decoration. $40.

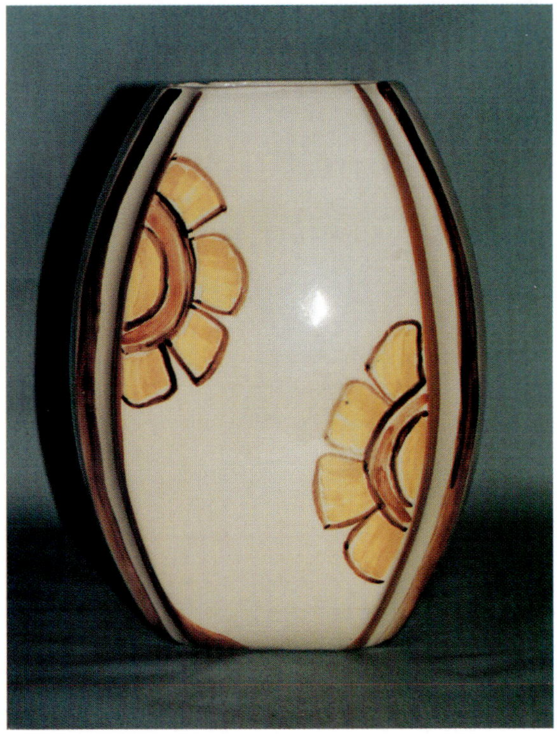

Half sunflower tall oval canister vase, 7.5" high. $60.

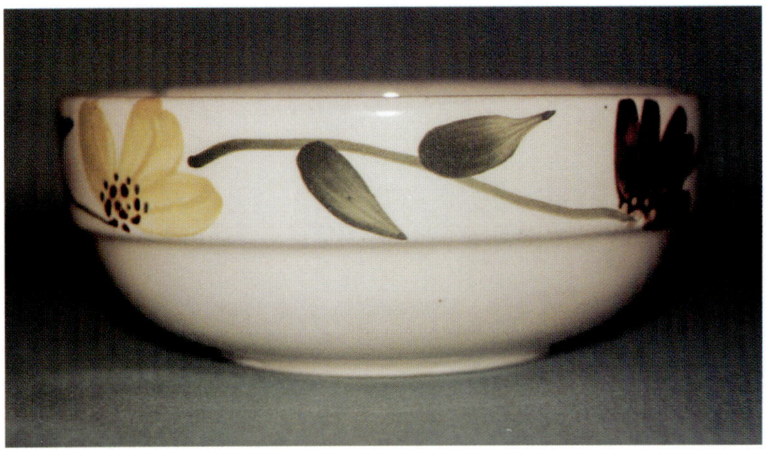

Individual salad bowl, Rubel mold with green and brown flower decoration, 5.5" diameter. $20.

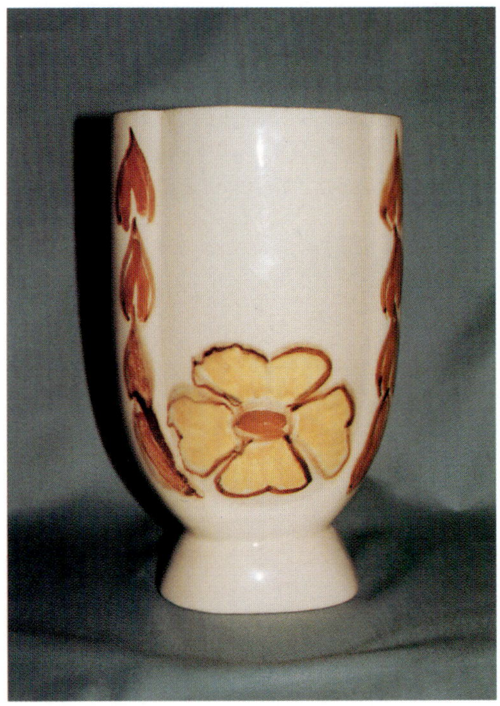

A 9" high vase with a yellow flower. $75.

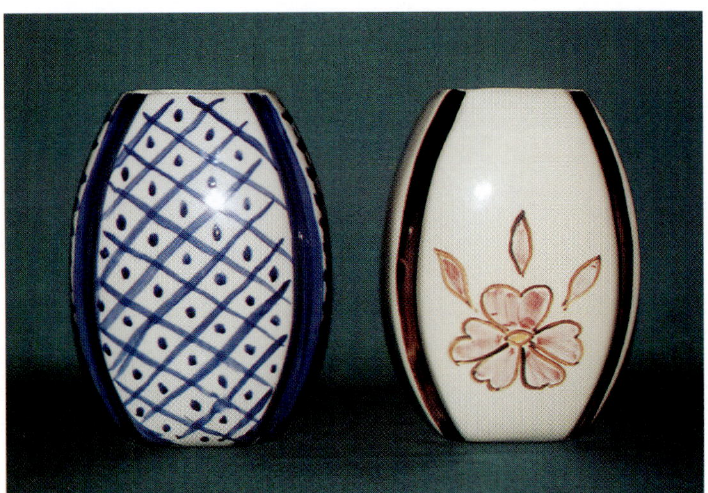

Tall oval canister vases, 7.5" high. $60 each.

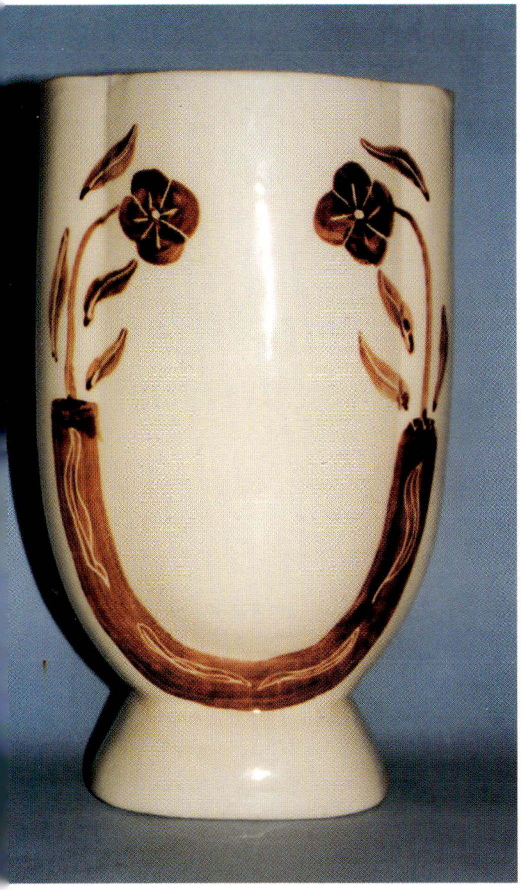

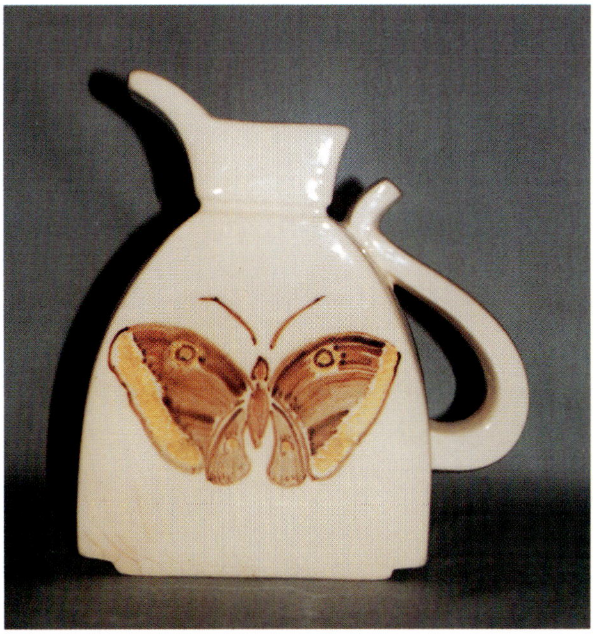

Bell shaped pitcher with butterfly decoration, 8" high. $75.

A 9" high vase with brown flowers that looks a bit like a smile. $75.

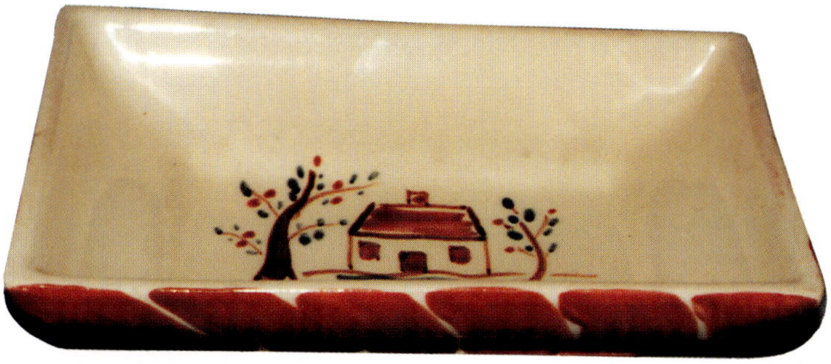

NAPCO planter, Coral Intaglio with a house painted inside. $50.

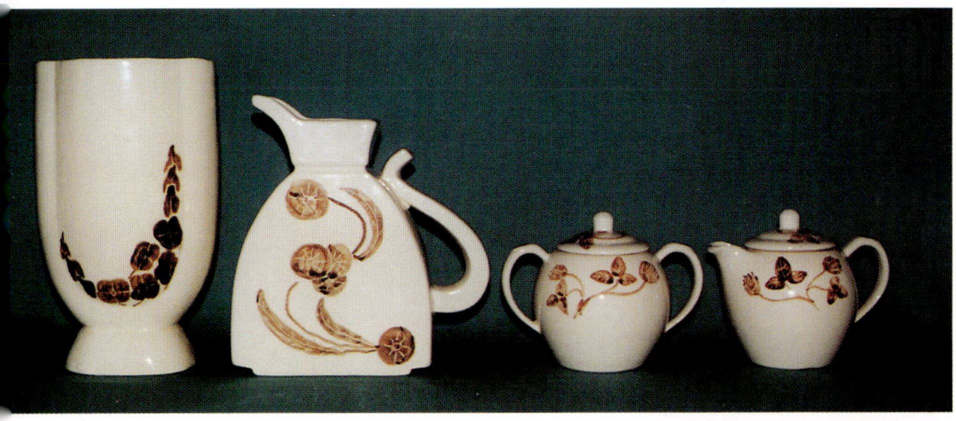

Tall vase with brown flowers, 9" high. $60. Bell shaped pitcher, 8" high with brown flower. $50. Covered sugar and covered creamer with brown clover. $50 set.

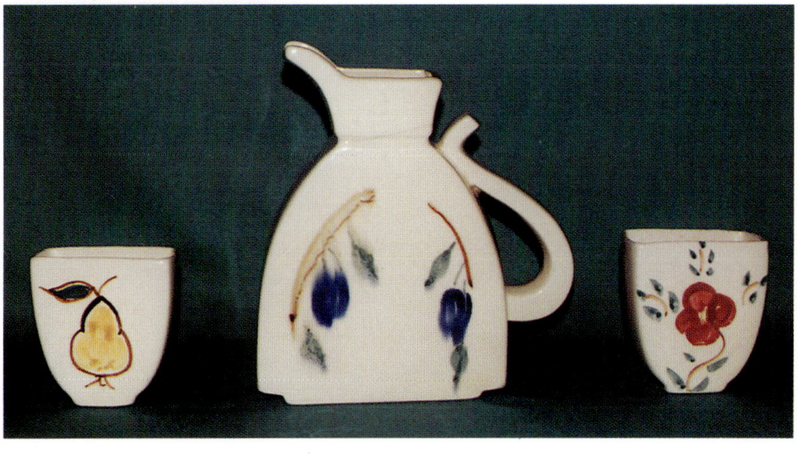

Bell shaped pitcher with blue flowers, 8" high. $50. Rectangular top tumblers with Pear and Mt. Rose decoration, 3.5" high. $30 each. A Mr. Hoenburg from Germany was hired as a designer. This was his most well-known work. It is a spouted pitcher that fits into the rectangular tumbler's top. There was no spilling, but you could not drink from the tumbler.

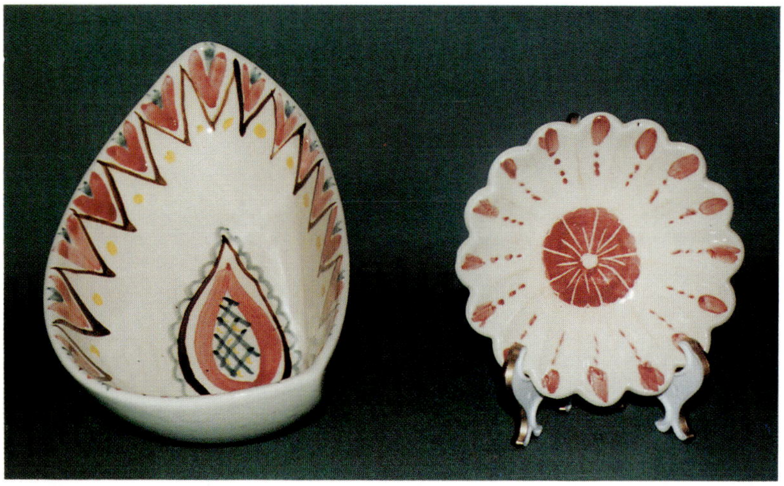

Teardrop shaped bowl, Rubel mold, pink decoration. $40. Ruffled dish, pink decoration, unknown mold. $35.

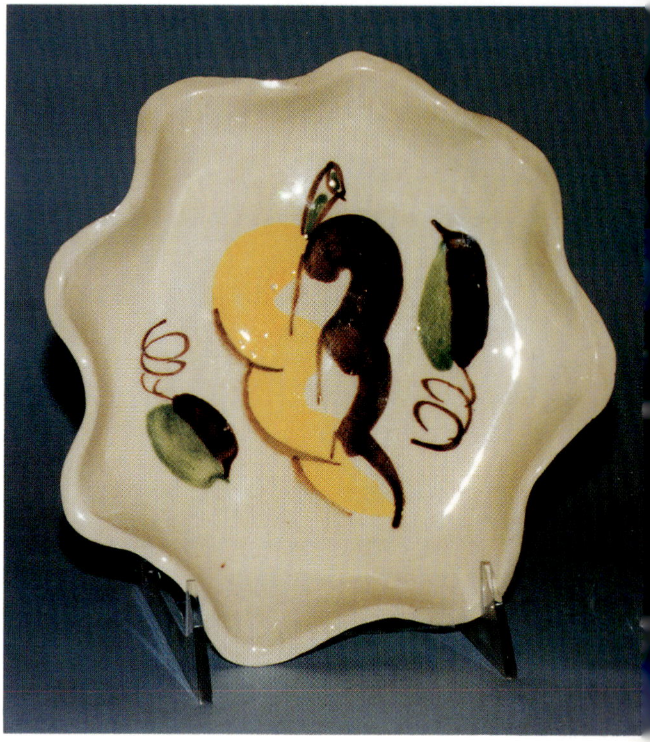

Ruffled bowl, yellow and brown leaf decoration. $40.

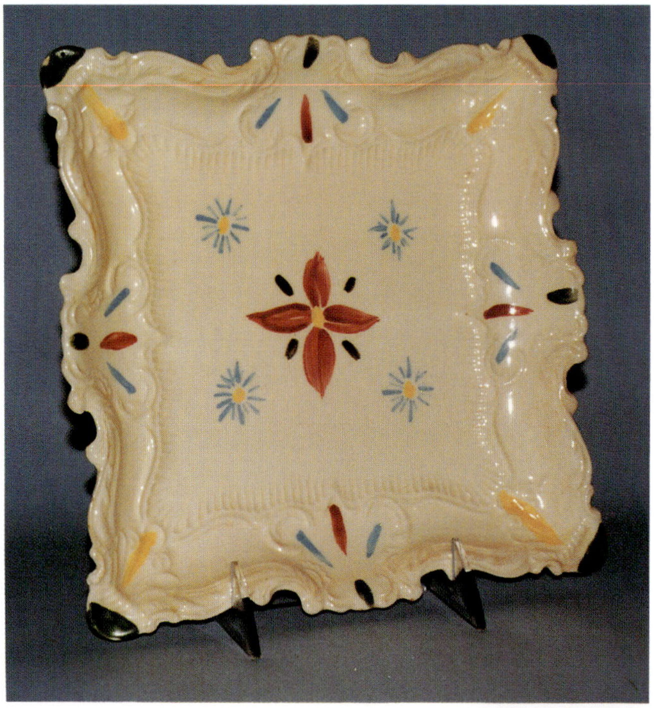

Square shaped bowl, 8.75" diameter. Thought to have been decorated in Wellsville. $50.

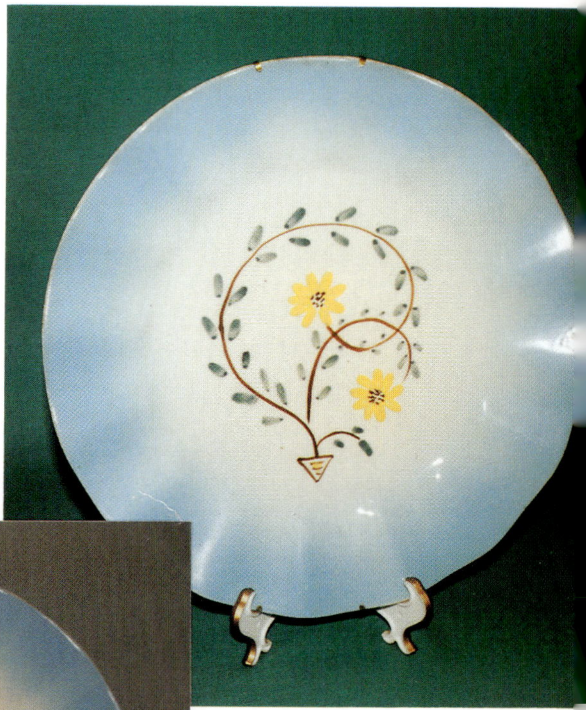

Dinner plate, Seaform style, yellow starflowers with light blue trim. $100.

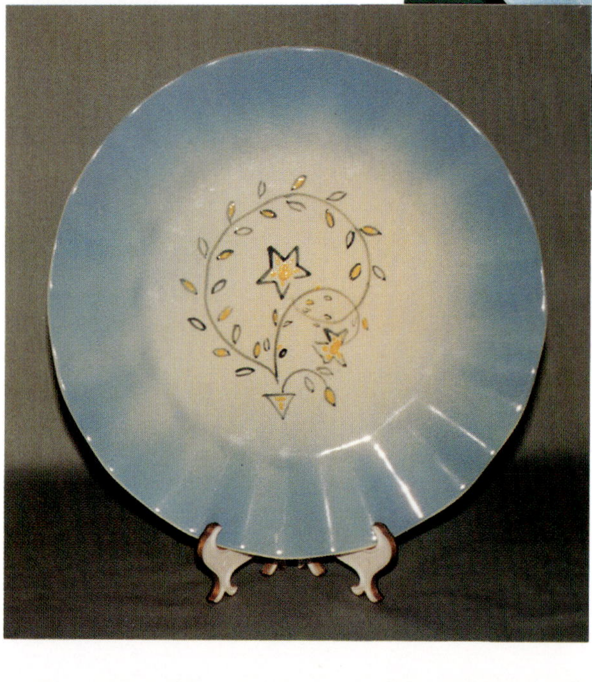

Dinner plate, Seaform style, yellow daisies with light blue trim. $100.

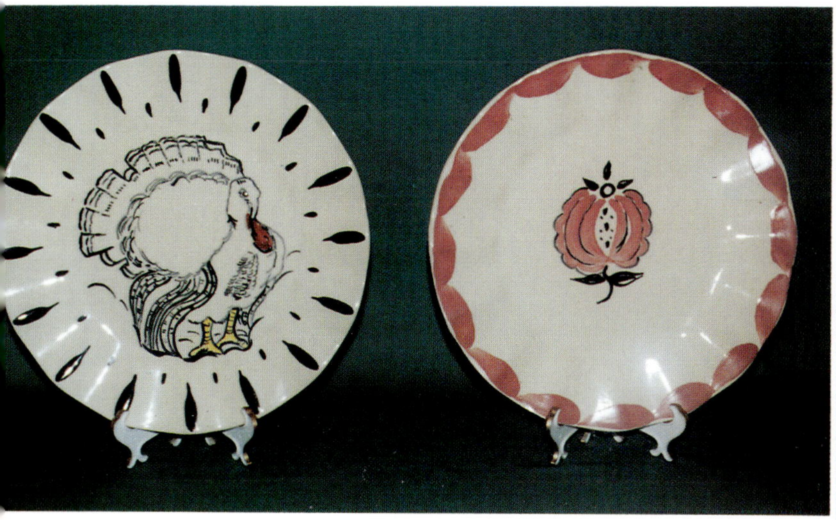

Dinner plate, Seaform style, turkey decoration. $150. Dinner plate, Seaform style, pink flower. $100.

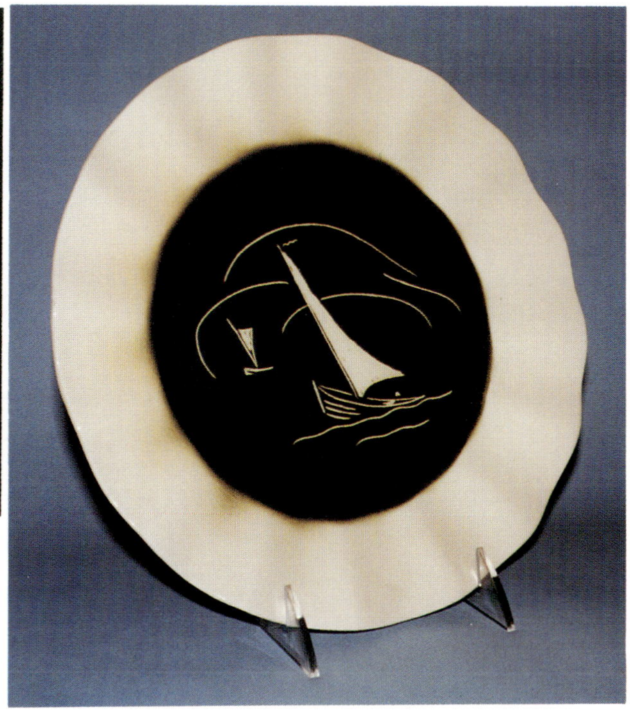

Dinner plate, Seaform style, sailboat incised on green background. $150.

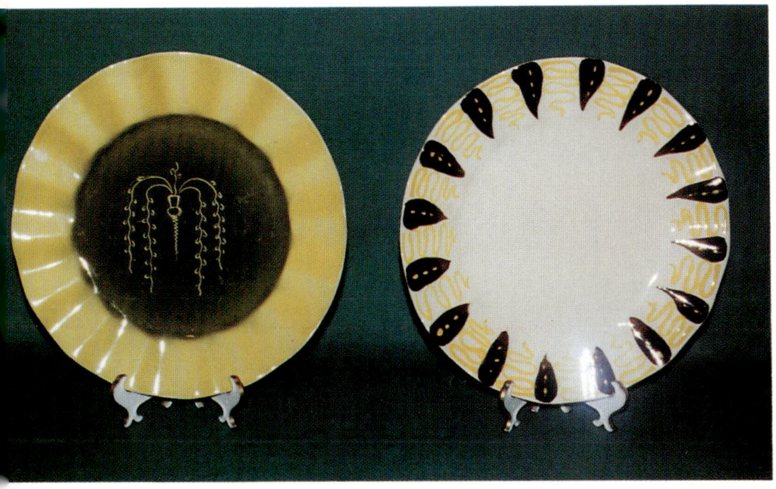

Dinner plate, Seaform style, chartreuse and green. $100. Dinner plate, Seaform style, brown and yellow trim. $100.

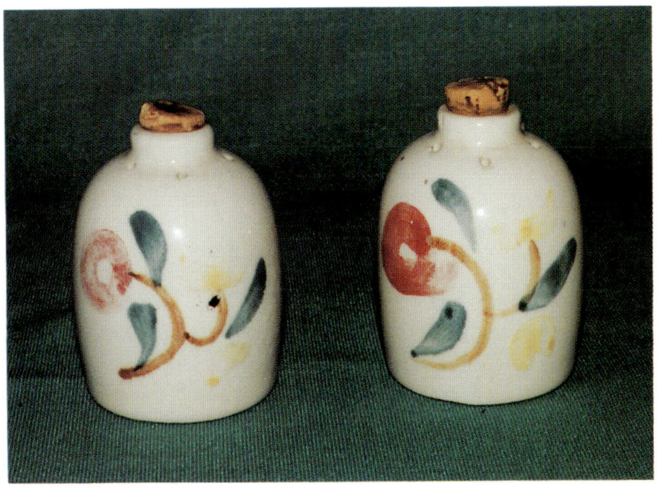

Jug salt and pepper shakers, red flower decoration. $40 set.

Jug salt and pepper shakers, Bittersweet decoration. $75 set.

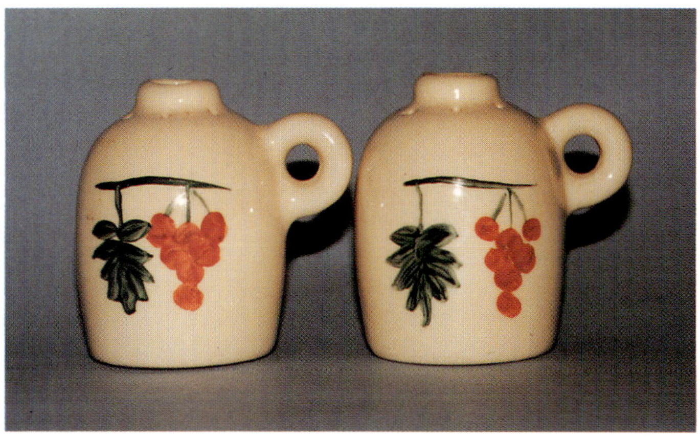

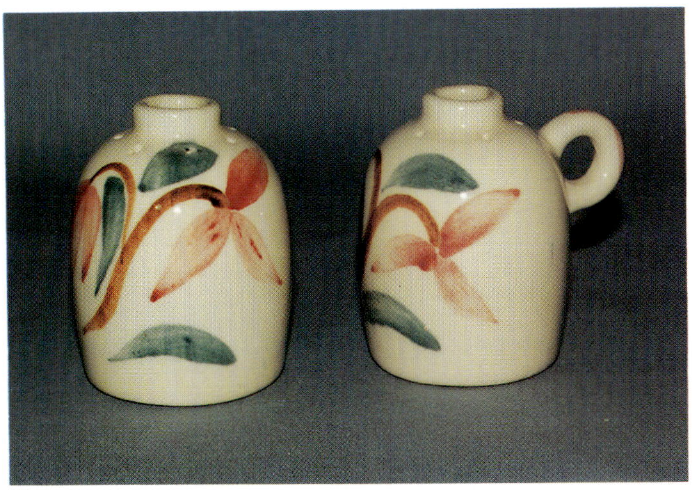

Jug salt and pepper shakers, Windflower decoration. $50 set.

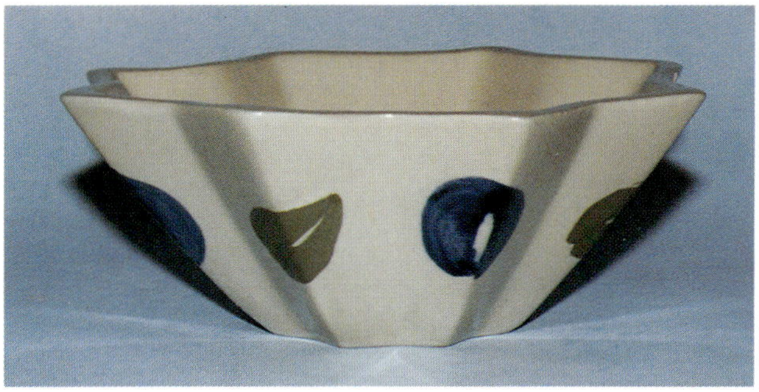

Star candle holder, Maywood slip with cobalt blue and green leaves. $30.

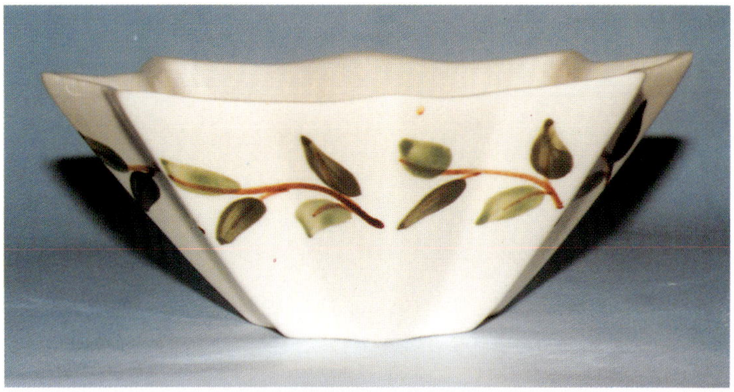

Star candle holder with Leaf and Vine decoration. $30.

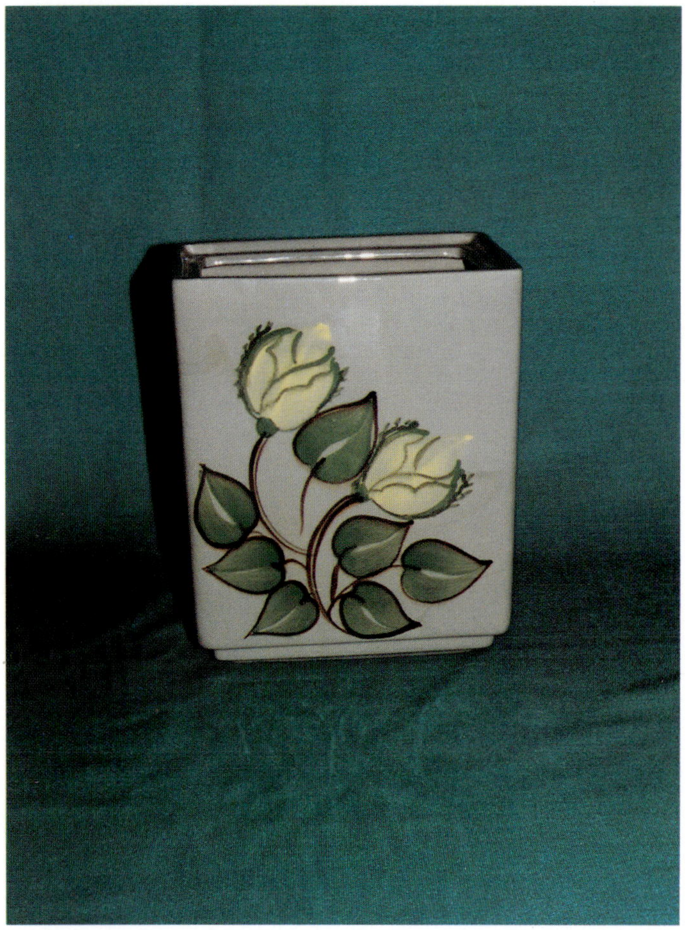

Pillow vase, tall, NAPCO mold, Yellow Tea Rose on Maywood slip. $75.

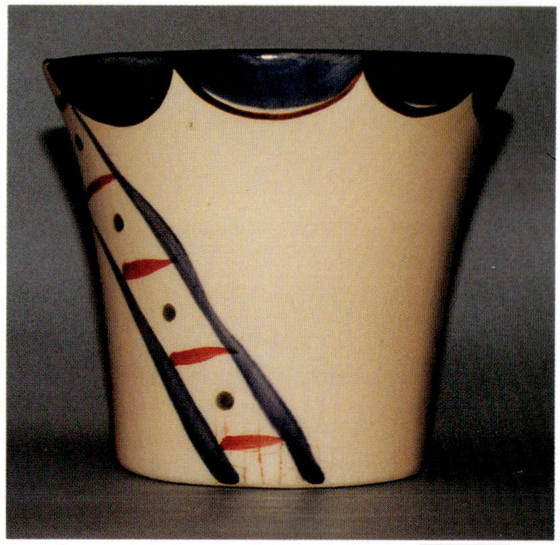

Wall pocket, Ladder decoration. $75.

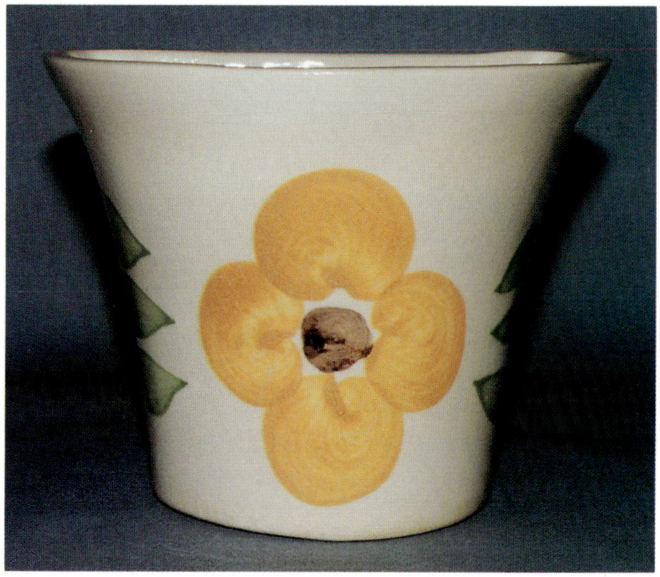

Wall pocket, Yellow Pansy. $75.

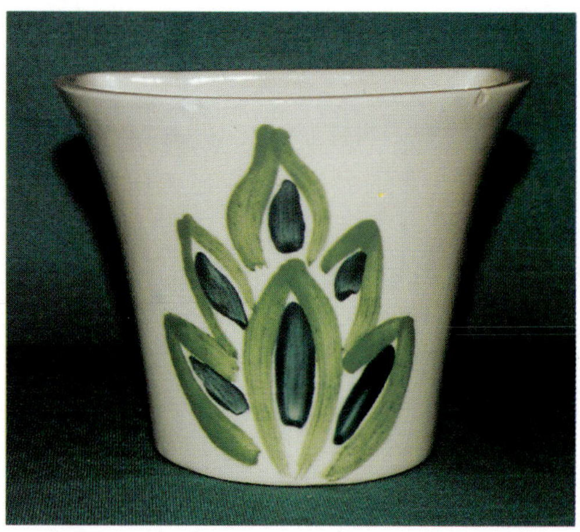

Wall pocket with Fern decoration. $75.

Appendix.

Table of Measurements

These are the shapes produced by Purinton Pottery accompanied by their standard measurements. Please refer to the pictures to identify specific items.

ashtray	5.5" long
baker	7" long
basket planter	6.25" high
bean pot, individual	3.25" high
beans pot	5.75" high
beer mug	4.75" high
beverage pitcher	6.25" high
biscuit jar	8" high
bowl, cereal	5.25" diameter
bowl, child's	5.25" diameter
bowl, dessert	4" diameter
butter dish	6.5" long
candle holder, round	5" diameter, 2.5" high
candle holder, star	6" diameter, 2" high
candy dish	6.25" high
canister, bulbous	7" high
canister, half-oval	5.5" high
canister, four piece long set	19" long
canister, pie-shaped wedge	7" high
canister, round with wooden lid, large	8" high
canister, round with wooden lid, small	7.5" high
canister, square, apartment, large	7.5" high
canister, square, apartment, small	5.5" high
canister, square with wooden lid, large	9.5" high
canister, square with wooden lid, small	5.5" high
canister, tall oval	9" high
chop plate	12" diameter
coaster	3.5" diameter
coffee mug	4" high
coffee carafe, Wellsville	7.5" high
coffee pot, eight cup	8" high
coffee server, seaform style	9" high
coffee server, Taylor Smith Taylor	10.5" high
console bowl, NAPCO mold	11" long
cookies jar, slant top, wooden lid	7" high, 7" wide
cookies jar, square with ceramic lid	9.5" high
cookies jar, square with wooden lid	9.5" high
cookies jar, tall oval canister	9" high
cookies jar, wide oval	9.5" high
creamer and sugar:	
creamer	3.5" high
sugar with lid	5" high
creamer and sugar, individual	2" high
creamer and sugar:	
round creamer	3.5" high
sugar with lid	4.5" high
creamer and sugar (on tray), seaform style	5" high
creamer and sugar, Wellsville mold:	
creamer	2.75" high
sugar with lid	3.5" high
cup	2.5" high
cup, Rubel for soup and sandwich plate	2.25" high, 4" diameter
decanter, miniature jug	2.5" high
drip filter, eight cup coffee pot	4" high
drip filter, six cup teapot	2.75" high
dutch jug, two pint	5.75" high
dutch jug, five pint	8" high
ewer, short	4" high
ewer, tall	9" high
fruit bowl	12" diameter
gravy boat, Taylor Smith Taylor	3.75" high
grease jar, covered, range	5.5" high
grease jar, covered, winged	6" high
honey jug	6.25" high
jam and jelly	5.5" long
jigger jug	2.25" high
juice mug	2.5" high
kent jug	4.5" high
kent jug, oversized	6.25" high
lazy susan	17" diameter
marmalade jar	4.5" high
marmalade jar, Wellsville	4" high
mug, child's	4" high
mug jug	4.75" high
night bottle	7.5" high
nut dish	5.5" long
oasis cookie jug	8.5" high
oasis jug	9.5" high
oil and vinegar, jug shaped	5" high
oil and vinegar, square	5" high
oil and vinegar, tall	9.5" high
pickle dish	6" long
pitcher, miniature	2.5" high
pitcher, Rubel mold	5" high
planter, NAPCO	6" long
plate, breakfast	8.5" diameter
plate, child's	8.5" diameter
plate, dinner	9.75" diameter
plate, dinner, oversized	11" diameter
plate, salad	6.75" diameter
plate, soup and sandwich, Rubel	11" diameter
plate, tea and toast	8.5" diameter
platter, grill	12" long
platter, large	12" long
platter, small	11" long
pour and shake shaker	4.25" high
rebecca jug	7.5" high
relish, three part, ceramic, metal, or no handle	10" diameter
relish, three part, rectangular	6.75" long, 4.75" wide
roll tray	11" long

rum jug planter	6.5" high
salad bowl	11" diameter
salt/pepper shaker, cone shape	3.25" high
salt/pepper shaker, jug style	2.5" high
salt/ pepper shaker, range	4" high
salt/pepper shaker, round, Wellsville	2.75" high
salt/pepper shaker, seaform style	3" high
salt/pepper shaker, stacking, Rubel	2.25" high
sandwich plate (chop plate with center handle)	12" diameter
saucer	5.25" diameter
seahorse cocktail	11.75" long
spaghetti bowl	14.5" diameter
spoon rest (butter dish)	6.5" long
sprinkler (watering can)	5.5" high
stacking storage jar	5.5" high
tea server, seaform style	7" high
teapot, two cup	4" high
teapot, four cup	5" high
teapot, six cup	6" high
teapot, six cup, domed lid	6.5" high
teapot, angle handled	5.75" high
tumbler	5" high
vase, cornucopia	6" high
vase, NAPCO	5" high
vase, pillow, short	4.5" high
vase, pillow, tall	6.5" high
vase, winged	5" high
vegetable, covered	9" long
vegetable, divided	10.5" long
vegetable, open	8.5" long
wall pocket	3.5" high

Other References

Clarion Republican, The. (February, 1941).
Clarion Republican, The. (April, 1941).
Clarion Republican, The. (November, 1941).
Forest (Tionesta, Pennsylvania) Republican. (October, 1948).
Hinterleiter, Lori and Jim Schulte. *Purinton Pastimes*

A newsletter about Purinton Pottery is published in January, April, July, and October and is available for a minimal yearly subscription rate. Please contact: Purinton Pastimes, P.O. Box 9394, Arlington, VA 22219.

Bibliography

Crockery and Glass Journal, The. East Stroudsburg, PA: Haire Publishing Co., 1948- 1955.

Dole, Pat. *Purinton Pottery Book II.* Denton, NC: Denton Publishing Co., 1990.

Morris, Susan. *Purinton Pottery, An Identification and Value Guide.* Paducah, KY: Collector Books, 1994.